The Pilot's Manual

Flight School

The Pilot's Manual

Flight School

Master the flight maneuvers required for private, commercial, and instructor certification

Sixth Edition

Foreword by Barry Schiff

AVIATION SUPPLIES & ACADEMICS, INC.
NEWCASTLE, WASHINGTON

The Pilot's Manual: Flight School
Master the flight maneuvers required for private, commercial, and instructor certification
Sixth Edition

Aviation Supplies & Academics, Inc.
7005 132nd Place SE
Newcastle, Washington 98059
asa@asa2fly.com | 425-235-1500 | asa2fly.com

Sixth edition published 2021 by Aviation Supplies & Academics, Inc.
Originally published 1990–1998 by Center for Aviation Theory.

ASA-PM-1D
ISBN 978-1-64425-140-9

Additional formats available:
eBook EPUB ISBN 978-1-64425-142-3
eBook PDF ISBN 978-1-64425-143-0
eBundle ISBN 978-1-64425-141-6

Printed in the United States of America
2025 2024 2023 2022 2021 10 9 8 7 6 5 4 3 2 1

Acknowledgements:
Original illustrations: Rob Loriente
Photographs: FM Photographics, Aviation Theory Centre, Cessna, Cirrus, and Lightwing
Page 450: Maria Dryfhout/Shutterstock.com
Front cover: Photo by Mark Jordan on Unsplash
Back cover: iStock.com/NNehring

Library of Congress Cataloging-in-Publication Data:
Title: Flight school : master the flight manuevers required for private, commercial, and instructor certification / foreword by Barry Schiff.
Other titles: Pilot's manual. Flight school : master the flight manuevers required for private, commercial, and instructor certification
Description: Sixth edition. | Newcastle, Washington : Aviation Supplies & Academics, Inc., 2021. | Series: The Pilot's manual ; 1 | Includes index.
Identifiers: LCCN 2021013309 (print) | LCCN 2021013310 (ebook) | ISBN 9781644251409 (hardback) | ISBN 9781644251423 (epub) | ISBN 9781644251430 (pdf) | ISBN 9781644251416
Subjects: LCSH: Airplanes—Piloting—Handbooks, manuals, etc. | Air pilots—Licenses—United States. | Flight training—Handbooks, manuals, etc. | Aeronautics—Study and teaching—Handbooks, manuals, etc. | LCGFT: Handbooks and manuals.
Classification: LCC TL710 .F55 2021 (print) | LCC TL710 (ebook) | DDC 629.132/52—dc23
LC record available at https://lccn.loc.gov/2021013309
LC ebook record available at https://lccn.loc.gov/2021013310

Contents

Personal Progress Table

Foreword

When it was time to take my private pilot written examination in 1955, my flight instructor handed me a pocket-size booklet. It was published by the Civil Aeronautics Administration (FAA's predecessor) and contained 200 true/false questions (including answers).

"Study these well," he cautioned with a wink, "because the test consists of 50 of these." As I flipped through the dozen or so pages, my anxiety about the pending examination dissolved into relief. Nothing could be easier, I thought. One question, for example, stated: "True or False: It is dangerous to fly through a thunderstorm." Really. (I passed the test with flying colors—but so did everyone else in those days.)

The modern pilot, however, must know a great deal more to hurdle today's more challenging examinations. This has resulted in a crop of books developed specifically to help pilots pass tests. Unfortunately, some do little else, and the student's education remains incomplete.

An exciting exception is *The Pilot's Manual* series. These voluminous manuals provide far in excess of that needed to pass examinations. They are chock-full of practical advice and techniques that are as useful to experienced pilots as they are to students.

The Pilot's Manuals are a refreshingly creative and clever approach that simplifies and adds spice to what often are regarded as academically dry subjects. Reading these books is like sitting with an experienced flight instructor who senses when you might be having difficulty with a subject and patiently continues teaching until confident that you understand.

Barry Schiff
Los Angeles

Barry Schiff has over 27,000 hours in more than 300 types of aircraft. He is retired from Trans World Airlines, where he flew everything from the Lockheed Constellation to the Boeing 747 and was a check captain on the Boeing 767. He has earned every available FAA category and class rating (except airship) and every possible instructor's rating. He also received numerous honors for his contributions to aviation. An award-winning journalist and author, he is well known to flying audiences for his many articles published in some 90 aviation periodicals, notably AOPA Pilot, of which he is a contributing editor. ASA publishes several Barry Schiff titles.

About the Editorial Team

David Robson

David Robson is a career aviator having been nurtured on balsa wood, dope (the legal kind) and tissue paper. He made his first solo flight shortly after his seventeenth birthday, having made his first parachute jump just after his sixteenth. His first job was as a junior draftsman (they weren't persons in those days) at the Commonwealth Aircraft Corporation in Melbourne, Australia. At that time he was also learning to fly de Havilland Chipmunks with the Royal Victorian Aero Club.

He joined the Royal Australian Air Force in 1965 and served for twenty-one years as a fighter pilot and test pilot. He flew over 1,000 hours on Mirages and 500 on Sabres (F-86). He completed the Empire Test Pilots' course in England in 1972, flying everything from gliders to Lightning fighters and Argosy transport aircraft. He completed a tour in Vietnam as a forward air controller flying the USAF 0-2A (Oscar Deuce). In 1972 he was a member of the Mirage formation aerobatic team, the Deltas, which celebrated the RAAF's 50th anniversary.

After retiring from the Air Force he became a civilian instructor and lecturer and spent over ten years with the Australian Aviation College, a specialized international school for airline cadet pilots. During 1986–88 he was the editor of the national safety magazine, the *Aviation Safety Digest*, which won the Flight Safety Foundation's international award. He was recently awarded the Australian Aviation Safety Foundation's Certificate of Air Safety.

David holds an ATP license and instructor's rating. His particular ambition is to see the standard of flight and ground instruction improved and for aviation instruction to be recognized as a career and be adequately rewarded.

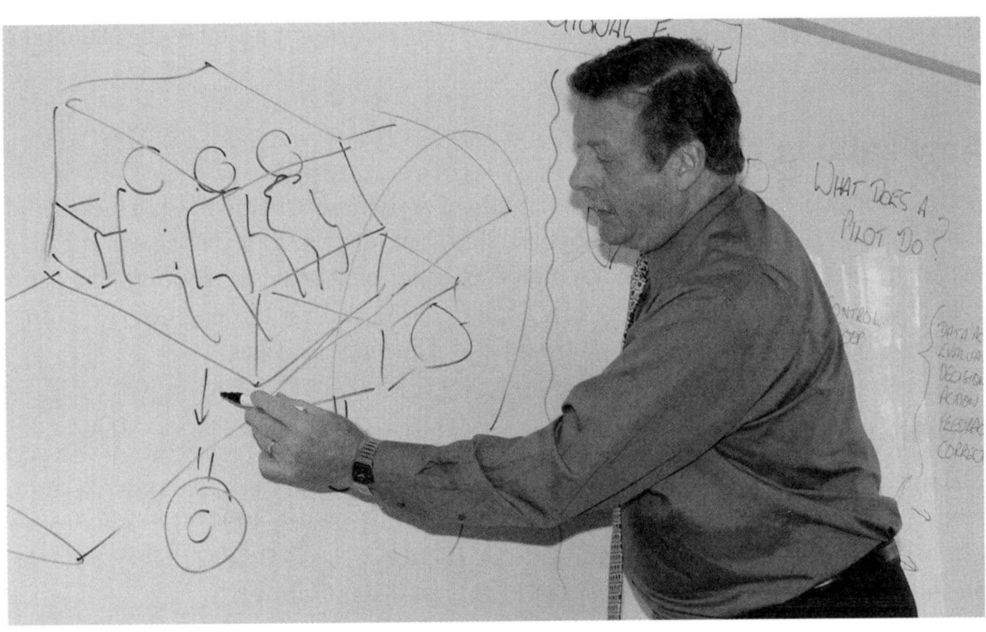

Jackie Spanitz

As ASA General Manager, Jackie Spanitz oversees maintenance and development of more than 1,000 titles and pilot supplies in the ASA product line. Ms. Spanitz has worked with airman training and testing for more than 25 years, including participation in the Airman Certification Standards (ACS) development committees. Jackie holds a B.S. in Aviation Technology from Western Michigan University, an M.S. from Embry-Riddle Aeronautical University, and Instructor and Commercial Pilot certificates. She is the author of *Guide to the Flight Review*, and the technical editor for ASA's Test Prep and FAR/AIM series.

James Johnson

James Johnson is the Director of Aviation Training for ASA. He has accumulated many years of aviation industry experience, from flight and ground instruction to working within corporate flight departments. James received a B.S. in Aeronautics with minors in Aviation Safety and Airport Management from Embry-Riddle Aeronautical University. He holds certificates for Commercial Pilot, Advanced Ground and Instrument Instructor, and Remote Pilot sUAS.

Madeline Mimi Tompkins

Madeline Tompkins is an experienced flight instructor, current Boeing 737-300/400 airline captain and crew resource management facilitator. She is well known for her part as copilot in an airliner emergency in Hawaii, about which a TV movie was made. She has received many honors, including the AOPA Air Safety Foundation's Distinguished Pilot award. A former FAA designated flight examiner, she is currently an FAA accident prevention counselor, designated knowledge test examiner, and she also teaches CFI refresher courses.

Martin E. Weaver

Martin Weaver is an experienced flight and ground instructor in airplanes, helicopters, and gliders. He is a former chief flight instructor and designated pilot examiner, who has been closely involved with standardization procedures for over 14 years. He holds a B.S. from the University of Southern Mississippi. He is currently a pilot in the Oklahoma Army National Guard.

Amy Laboda

Amy Laboda is a freelance writer, editor, and active flight instructor. She is a member of the American Flyers Judith Resnik Scholarship committee and former editor at *Flying* magazine. She has recently been appointed as editor of *Women in Aviation*. She has a rotorcraft category, a gyroplane rating, a glider rating and a multi-engine ATP rating. She also holds a B.A. in Liberal Arts from Sarah Lawrence College.

Melanie Waddell

Melanie began flying in 1994 and was awarded a Bachelor of Technology in Aviation studies from Swinburne University, Melbourne, Australia in 1997. She is a current commercial, multi-engine and instrument-rated pilot as well as a Grade I flight instructor. She hopes to captain a wide-body jet in the not-too-distant future.

Introduction

BECOMING A PILOT

Good habits must be developed right from the start with balanced and reinforced learning.

Every pilot begins as a student. If we learn by listening, observing, practicing and reading, we can make better use of our flight time. Learning is reinforced by reliving our flight lessons and by anticipating the next. To gain the maximum benefit from each hour in the air, you need to be well prepared. This is the purpose of this book. It will answer many questions, and it may promote you to ask more questions of your instructor. All of this dialogue is valuable.

Learning to fly does not take long: within the first 20 hours of flight time you will have learned the basic skills and you will have flown solo, which is a great achievement. Since the training period is so short, good habits must be developed right from the start. Habit patterns, attitudes and disciplines that are formed in the first few hours will stay with you throughout your flying life. Learn them well.

A commercial pilot must demonstrate greater accuracy and a higher level of knowledge than a private pilot. However, the basic skills for visual flight are common. The commercial pilot may have the advantage of flying regularly. It is important to reinforce your flight training after you gain your pilot's certificate. All skills and knowledge fade with time unless exercised. This manual will assist you in recalling the structure and content of each of the flight tasks.

Planning your Training Schedule

Fly frequently for the most efficient training progress.

Try to fly regularly and fairly often. If you can have flights on consecutive days, especially as you approach first solo, then the retention of learning from one flight to the next is improved, and there will be little need for repetition. As you fly you will gain confidence and skill. At the beginning you may feel some sensitivity to motion and some anxiety. This is normal. The flight environment is a new experience and therefore unknown. It is natural to be apprehensive until you become acclimated to the environment.

HOW AN AIRPLANE FLIES

The basic training airplane is simple in design and straightforward to operate. It has:

- a control wheel (or control column) to raise or lower the nose and to bank the wings;
- a rudder to keep the airplane coordinated so the tail follows the nose and the airplane does not fly sideways; and
- a throttle to control engine power.

The largest and fastest airliners have the same basic controls as your training airplane.

How the Pilot Controls the Airplane

The pilot uses the control wheel or column, rudder and throttle to set the attitude and power and control the speed and flight path of the airplane.

The pilot controls the airplane by setting the attitude (the position of the nose), the configuration (flaps and landing gear) and the power. It's that simple. A certain combination of these settings produces a certain flight path and speed. It is a matter of learning these settings for your airplane. Once these are learned the pilot can achieve the *four basic maneuvers*:

- straight and level flight;
- turns;
- climbs; and
- descents.

The flight profile then is a combination of these basic maneuvers.

The flight limits (speeds and altitudes) are defined by what is called the flight envelope for the airplane. A jet airplane has a much greater flight envelope than a small trainer.

Maximum and Minimum Speed

The aircraft's maximum speed when flying level is limited by power. However, an airplane can dive, and for this reason, there is a published never-exceed speed to avoid airframe damage. The minimum speed is called the *stalling speed.* It is determined by the maximum angle of the wing, beyond which the lift reduces and the aircraft sinks-not unlike the minimum speed of a bicycle when it can no longer remain upright.

Maximum Altitude

The maximum altitude is limited by the power of the engine and the ability of the pilot to breathe the thinner air. Larger airplanes are pressurized to maintain a lower cabin altitude.

IS FLYING SAFE?

Very. All airplanes are serviced to a strict schedule. Their engines are very reliable and the systems are well proven. Your instructor will show you the maintenance routine for the airplane. The most common cause of accidents is the pilot. Therefore you are in charge of your own destiny. Learn the craft well and apply the rules of safe practice and you will have a very enjoyable and rewarding hobby or career.

YOUR FLYING LESSONS

The cockpit is not an easy place to learn, so always be prepared for your flight lessons. Also visit the hangar.

Because of noise, workload and distractions, the cockpit can be a difficult place in which to learn, so thorough preflight preparation is essential. For each training flight you should have a clear objective and be mentally prepared to achieve it. Ideally, the actual training flight should be an illustration of principles that you already understand, rather than a series of unexpected events. Anything taught in the air should have been previously explained and discussed on the ground. Your objective is, with the guidance of your flight instructor, to achieve a standard where you:

- show good judgment, self-discipline and airmanship (common sense and sound procedure);
- apply your aeronautical knowledge;
- operate the airplane safely and within its limits; and
- demonstrate control of the airplane by confidently performing each maneuver or procedure smoothly, consistently and accurately.

The flight instructor wants to see you making decisions and correcting any deviations without prompting. You are expected to take command of the airplane. Then he or she knows you can fly safely alone.

Airmanship is a term that embraces many things: skill in flying the airplane, thorough knowledge, common sense, caution, courtesy, quick reactions and alertness. It comes with the right attitude, training and experience. It is the ultimate measure of a pilot.

Becoming a Better Pilot

An average person can learn to be a pilot. An average person can also choose to be a better-than-average pilot. An advanced, formal education is not a requirement to become a pilot. Clear English language is required for radio calls, and basic mathematics (proportions and fractions) are used. Beyond that, no special academic skills are required. The most important attribute that the student can bring and develop is their attitude to flight. This means how thorough, accurate, consistent and professional they are determined to be. This determination makes the difference between an average pilot and a better pilot.

THE STRUCTURE OF THIS BOOK

This volume is structured in the form of flight tasks. You will not necessarily learn the tasks in the order they are presented. Students learn at different rates and the flight instructor will tailor your training to suit your ability and rate of progress. Having the book separated into tasks allows the instructor to assemble the flight lessons to suit your individual needs.

How to Use This Manual

For each stage of your training, this manual sets out:

- clear objectives;
- the principles involved;
- how to fly the maneuver;
- the actual task, summarized graphically;
- any further points relevant to the exercise; and
- review questions, to self-test and reinforce the main points.

This will prepare you well and help to minimize your training hours (and your expense). As your training progresses, the manual can also be used for revision. Earlier maneuvers can be revised simply by referring to the task pages (which act as a summary), and working through the review questions again.

The review questions should be answered mentally and confidently. For this reason, they are phrased as direct questions and are intended to be posed and answered orally. If there is doubt about a review question, check the answer in the back of the book and refer to the text for the explanation.

In Appendix 1, entitled "Your Specific Airplane Type," there are questions that will help you to better understand your airplane. You can apply this information not only to your basic training airplane, but to any other type you may fly later on. It is essential information for all airplanes that you fly.

An Important Note to Pilots Regarding Flight Training

Our manual will help you prepare for each flight lesson. This will make your training more efficient (better understanding and better retention) and therefore less costly. However, the ultimate responsibility for your training rests with your own flight instructor, so his or her words have authority. Ask many questions and discuss any aspects about which you are unsure. A clear understanding on the ground enables a much better opportunity for success in the air.

We welcome written comments and suggestions for improvement of this manual. Send your feedback to:

Aviation Supplies and Academics, Inc.
7005 132nd Place SE
Newcastle, Washington 98059-3153
Phone: (425) 235-1500
E-mail: asa@asa2fly.com
Website: asa2fly.com

A Note to the Flight Instructor

First impressions are very important. Students remember best what they learn first. Our manual has been designed so correct understanding is possible the first time around. It is not just one book, but a collection of 61 tasks, each one standing alone and presenting everything that needs to be known for a specific element of flight. You will choose the content of each flight according to the progress and ability of your student. It is simply a matter of forewarning the student of the content of the next flight lesson, so he or she can study the appropriate task.

We aim to make the learning interesting, colorful and meaningful so a student will be motivated, assimilate it easily, and understand it well enough to be able to explain the main ideas in his or her own words.

New material is presented carefully, building on knowledge and experience already gained—a building block approach to learning. The main points in each chapter are expressed in different ways and repeated periodically throughout the text to reinforce the knowledge. Active participation by the student in the learning process is encouraged with the review questions in each chapter.

The flight instructor, especially the very first flight instructor, plays a vital role in the life of a pilot. What the student learns first will stick. Remember the student will learn by your example. They will do what you do, not what you say. If you are thorough, professional and careful, they will take on those same attributes, modified by their own personality. You are under continuous close scrutiny. The best you can do is to show your student how to be a good pilot by being one yourself. We wish you well with your students.

An Introduction to Flight

1 The Training Airplane

OBJECTIVES

To name and describe:

- the main components of a basic training airplane; and
- the systems, controls and instruments used by the pilot.

Figure 1-1 A Cessna trainer.

CONSIDERATIONS

The Airframe

The structure of the airplane is called the *airframe*. It consists of a *fuselage* to which the *wings*, the *empennage*, the *landing gear* and the engine are attached. A propeller converts engine *torque* to generate *thrust* to propel the airplane through the air. Forward speed causes the airflow over the wings to generate an aerodynamic force, known as *lift*, that is capable of overcoming the force of gravity (*weight*) and that supports the airplane in flight. The airplane can even fly temporarily without thrust if it is placed in a *glide*—its forward momentum assisted by gravity keeps it moving through the air, and this allows the wings to produce lift. However, the path is inevitably downward. In the absence of vertical air currents, thrust is essential to allow level, turning and climbing flight.

Lift is the means by which flight is attained.
Thrust is the means by which flight is sustained.

The tail assembly of the aircraft is situated some distance to the rear of the main load-carrying sections of the fuselage and provides a balancing, or *stabilizing*, force much like the tail feathers on an arrow or a dart. The tail section consists of a *vertical stabilizer* (or *fin*) and a *horizontal stabilizer* (or *tailplane*), both of which are shaped to produce stabilizing forces. The pilot and passengers are housed in the cockpit, usually in side-by-side seating—the pilot (or *pilot in command* in a two-pilot aircraft) sits on the left side.

Figure 1-2 Tobago aircraft.

Controls and instruments are placed in the cockpit to enable the safe and efficient operation of the airplane and its systems, and for navigation and communication.

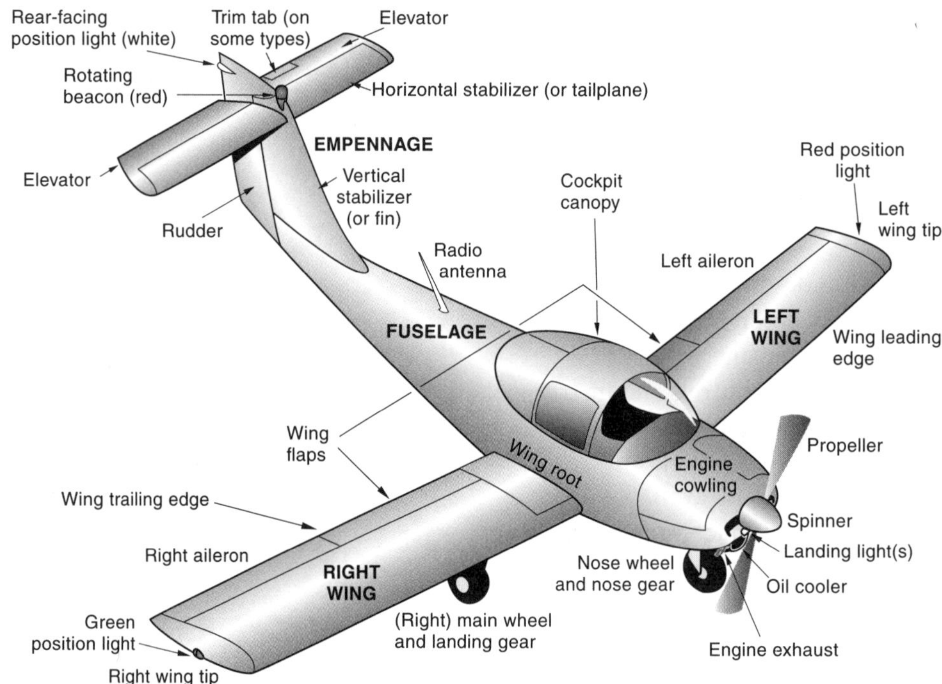

Figure 1-3 Parts of an airplane.

Aircraft Types

Light aircraft were traditionally classified under Title 14 of the Code of Federal Regulations (14 CFR) Part 23 which described structural and performance standards. These represented the fleet of General Aviation (GA) aircraft up to a certain weight limit.

More recently, the FAA has introduced a new category—the *Light Sport Aircraft* (LSA) category which offers relaxed construction, performance and licensing standards for pleasure flying and for training.

Figure 1-4 Vans Aircraft RV-6A light-sport airplane.

The LSA category allows a wide range of designs that are placed between the ultralights and the GA categories. It allows adventurous designs and fun flying at lower cost, using less energy and with less of the burden of regulations and testing.

Many pilots are now introduced to aviation via the LSA category and traditional, well respected manufacturers such as Cessna are now testing new designs that will be placed within this category.

This manual describes flight techniques which are equally applicable to all GA and LSA airplanes although there will be unique characteristics shown by some more radical designs and configurations. The techniques remain a vital foundation for a trainee pilot.

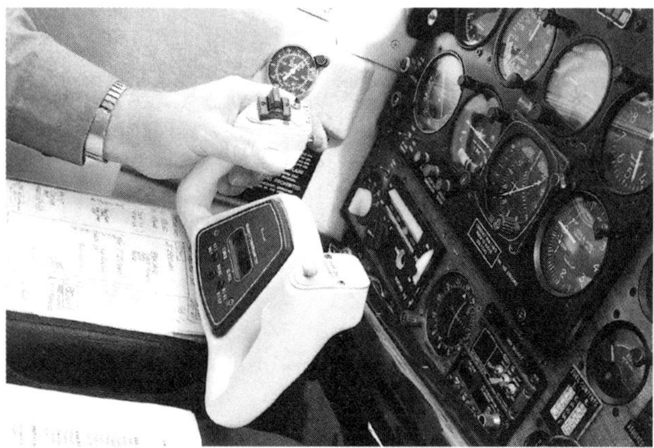

Figure 1-5 Traditional control wheel or yoke.

Primary Controls

Flight Controls

The most common primary flight control has been the wheel or *yoke*. This is still prevalent although there are more diverse options available now. The yoke came about because of high control forces and the need to be able to use both hands for control inputs. It also allowed relief so that the pilot could change hands. Also, the yoke provided a convenient place for transmit buttons, trim switches and some autopilot functions. It is retained in many larger aircraft even though the control forces have now been overcome by hydraulic actuators.

Figure 1-6 Traditional joystick—Lancair.

With the widespread use of ultralights and homebuilt aircraft there was a reappearance of the central control column or *joystick*. Many feature the transmit button on the top and some even have electric trim switches. The stick is better for highly maneuverable aircraft—for aerobatics, display flying and crop dusting—as it provides greater leverage and instantaneous control deflection. (It can also be held between the knees when cruising).

As more advanced types have been introduced into the GA fleet the *side-stick* as used in modern complex transport airplanes, has appeared. The control forces and response have been refined to the point where only a small mechanical advantage is needed. The magnificent Cirrus and Sky Arrow aircraft both used side sticks—as does the Australian Lightwing Speed.

Figure 1-7 Side stick control—Cirrus.

Aircraft Attitude

The attitude of the aircraft together with thrust from the propeller allows the aircraft to sustain a particular flight path. This is the essence of aircraft control. Thus the pilot's task is to set an attitude and power, check the response from the instruments and make a correction if necessary. This is the process of piloting the aircraft.

The *attitude* is simply the position of the nose of the aircraft in relation to the horizon: high, low, tilted left or right, and by how much. It is a matter of a visual judgment that is easy to learn.

Figure 1-8 Visual attitudes—nose-up and right bank.

The attitude, or position in flight, of the airplane is controlled using the flight controls. These are surfaces that, when deflected, alter the pattern of the airflow around the wings and tail, causing changes in the aerodynamic forces they generate.

Control Surfaces

The movable parts of the aircraft's structure are called *control surfaces*:

- The *elevators* (hinged to the trailing edge of the horizontal stabilizer) control pitching of the nose up or down and are operated from the cockpit with backward and forward movements of the control column.
- The *ailerons* (hinged to the outer trailing edge of each wing) control rolling of the airplane and are operated by left and right movement of the control column.
- The *rudder* is the movable surface controlled by the rudder pedals on the floor of the cockpit (hinged to the trailing edge of the fin or vertical stabilizer). The rudder is used to steer the aircraft on the ground and to balance the aircraft in the air.
- The *flaps* are surfaces that move down only, operated by a manual lever or dedicated switch. They are attached to the inner rear section, known as the *inboard section*, of each wing and move together. They provide additional lift and better forward and downward view for flight at low speeds. They are used mainly for the approach and landing.

The primary controls include the elevators, ailerons and rudder.

Figure 1-9 Left aileron (left); vertical stabilizer and rudder (right).

- The elevator has a smaller hinged surface, to balance the elevator control force, called a *trim tab*. It is usually operated by a trim wheel or handle beside the pilot or above in the cabin ceiling. Some aircraft also have trim tabs on the rudder and ailerons.

The secondary controls include flaps and trim tabs.

Figure 1-10 Flaps (left); elevator and trim tab (right).

Even though the aerodynamic components of various airplane types serve the same basic functions, their actual location on the structure and their shape can vary. For example, the wings may be attached to the fuselage in a high-, low- or mid-wing position; the horizontal stabilizer is sometimes positioned high on the fin (known as a *T-tail*); and the combined horizontal stabilizer and elevator is sometimes replaced by a *stabilator* (or *all-flying tailplane*). The stabilator is also fitted with a tab.

Figure 1-11 Stabilator with tab.

Engine/Propeller Controls

The throttle, which is operated by the pilot's right hand, controls the power (thrust) supplied by the engine-propeller combination. *Opening* the throttle by pushing it forward increases the fuel-air supply to the engine, resulting in increased revolutions and greater power. Retarding the throttle, or *closing* it, reduces the power to idle RPM but does not stop the engine, being just the same as the accelerator in your car.

Push the throttle forward for a greater power and pull it back for reduced power.

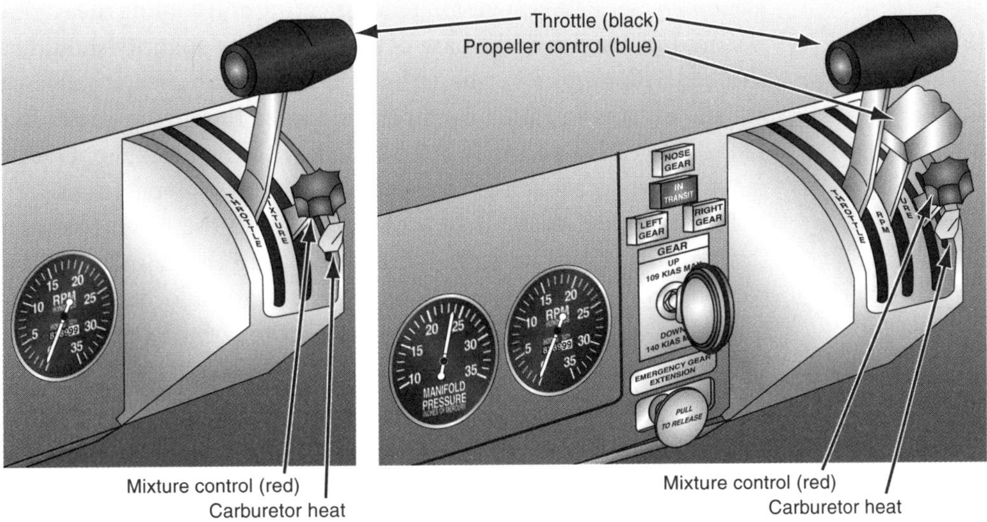

Figure 1-12 Engine controls—fixed-pitch propeller (left) and constant-speed propeller (right).

Some airplanes have the engine controls in the form of push/pull knobs. Push/pull controls are direct mechanical plungers which are pushed forwards (in) for greater power or propeller RPM. Some have a vernier (rotational) facility for fine adjustment once the broad setting has been made.

The engine rotates the propeller and together, they produce the thrust to propel the aircraft. The power of the engine is controlled by the throttle, which determines the amount of fuel to the engine. The propeller is driven directly by the engine and may have fixed blades or variable-pitch blades. In the case of variable-pitch blades, there is an additional propeller lever next to the throttle and an additional instrument, called the *manifold pressure gauge*, next to the RPM indicator or tachometer.

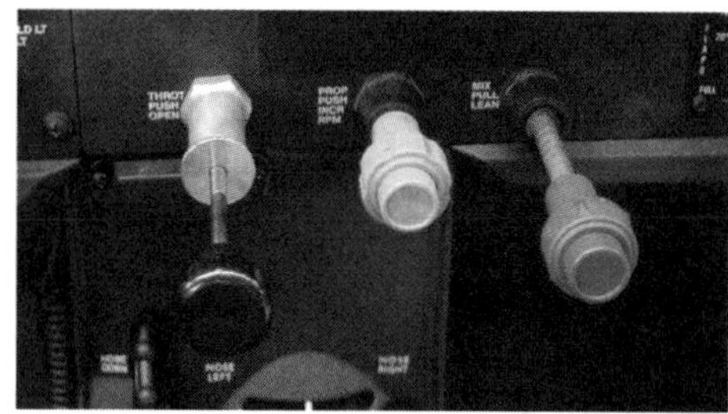

Figure 1-13 Push/pull knobs for throttle, propeller and mixture controls (Cessna aircraft).

Figure 1-14 Manifold pressure gauge and tachometer.

Landing Gear

Most modern training airplanes have a tricycle landing gear (or undercarriage) that consists of two main wheels and a nose wheel to provide support on the ground. Other aircraft have a tail wheel instead of a nose wheel. The nose wheel on most aircraft types is connected to the rudder pedals so that movement of the pedals will turn it, assisting in directional control on the ground. Most aircraft have brakes on the main wheels. Brakes are operated individually or together by pressing the top of the rudder pedals; thus, they can be used to assist steering as well as braking. There is also a parking brake knob or lever.

Figure 1-15 Tricycle landing gear.

Aircraft Systems

Engine and Propeller

The typical training airplane has a piston engine that uses aviation gasoline (AVGAS). The engine revolutions per minute (RPM) are controlled by the throttle. This is indicated in the cockpit on the *tachometer*, or RPM gauge. Oil for lubricating and cooling the engine is stored in a sump at the base of the engine. Its quantity should be checked with a *dipstick* prior to flight. There are two cockpit gauges to register oil pressure and oil temperature when the engine is running. These gauges are normally color-coded, with the normal operating range shown as a green arc or by upper and lower green marks.

Fuel is mixed with air in a *carburetor*, and the mixture passes through the induction system (*manifold*) into the cylinders where combustion occurs. The carburetor heat control, located near the throttle, is used to supply hot air to protect the carburetor from icing.

Figure 1-16 Tail wheel landing gear.

Fuel System

The fuel is usually stored in wing tanks. High-wing airplanes usually rely on gravity to supply fuel to the engine-driven pump, whereas low-wing airplanes have an additional electric fuel pump (*boost pump*). There are fuel gauges in the cockpit to indicate the quantity, but

Figure 1-17 The oil quantity should be checked during the preflight inspection prior to every flight.

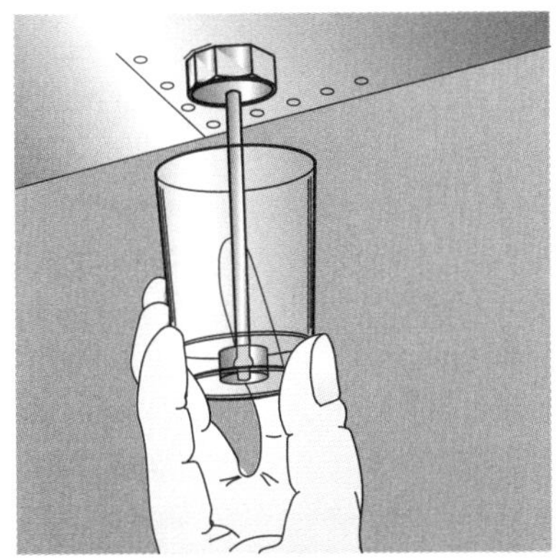

Transparent container to check quality and type of fuel sample

Figure 1-18 A typical method of checking the fuel.

they are not always totally reliable. Therefore, it is a requirement to check the contents of the tanks, either visually or by using a dipstick, prior to each flight. It is also essential to confirm both that the fuel is of the correct grade (which is identified by its color) and that it is not contaminated, the most likely contaminant being water. Water is more dense than AVGAS and gathers at the lowest points in the fuel system. The check is performed by inspecting a small sample taken from the fuel drain valve beneath each fuel tank and from the fuel strainer or filter.

Fuel management is a high priority—the fuel tanks should be checked visually prior to each flight.

A fuel tank selector in the cockpit allows fuel to be supplied from each tank as desired or, in some cases, from both tanks simultaneously. The fuel selector can also be used to prevent the supply of fuel to the engine compartment in the event of a fire.

A mixture control adjusts the richness of the fuel-air mixture provided to the engine and is suited for flight at higher altitudes, generally above 5,000 feet. When pulled fully out, the mixture control has the function of cutting the fuel supply to the engine altogether. It is used to shut down the engine to ensure the fuel lines are evacuated.

Ignition System

The engine has dual ignition systems that provide sparks to ignite the fuel-air mixture in the cylinders. The electrical current for the sparks is generated by two *magnetos* geared to the engine. The dual ignition systems provide more efficient combustion and greater safety in the event of one system failing. They function with the rotation of the engine and do not require an electrical current. Battery power is only required for starting the engine.

Figure 1-19 The combined ignition/start switch.

An ignition switch in the cockpit is normally used to select both magnetos, although it can select the left or right magneto individually to check for correct functioning of each. It also has an off position to prevent inadvertent starting of the engine if the propeller is turned.

The ignition switch is not generally used to stop the engine. The fuel mixture control has a *cutoff* position. Most ignition switches have a further position, *start*, that connects the battery to an electric starter. Once the engine starts, the ignition switch returns to *both*—it springs back to this position when released—and the engine runs without electrical supply from the battery.

Electrical System

The battery is used to start the engine. The alternator (or generator) is used to power the electrical system once the engine is running.

The battery is a source of electrical power to start the engine. The battery also provides an emergency electrical backup supply for lights and radios if the engine-driven alternator (or generator) fails. There is a master switch to turn the battery circuit on and off.

The electrical system supplies various aircraft services, such as some flight instruments, the radios, cabin lights, landing lights and navigation lights. In some aircraft, it also supplies the flap motor, the pitot heater and the stall warning system. Airplanes equipped with an alternator need a serviceable battery so that the alternator has an exciter current. The electrical system incorporates an ammeter and/or warning light to verify the electrical current is flowing. There may be a separate switch for the alternator circuit. Each electrical circuit is protected from excessive current by a fuse or a circuit breaker. Note that the two magneto systems providing the ignition sparks to the engine are totally separate from the electrical system (alternator/generator, battery, circuit breakers and fuses).

Radios

The radios have an on/off switch and volume control (usually combined in the one knob), a *squelch* control to eliminate unwanted background noise, a microphone for transmitting, and speakers or headphones for receiving messages. There may be an avionics master switch for all radios and navigation aids. There will be a separate control panel for the *intercom* (internal communications system).

Figure 1-20 Radio control panels.

Instruments and Units of Measurements

Instruments

The panel in front of the pilot contains instruments that provide important information. The main groups of instruments are the *flight instruments* (which are directly in front of the pilot) and the *engine instruments* (which are generally situated near the throttle).

Figure 1-21 Typical instrument panel (Cessna).

Figure 1-22 Typical instrument panel (Piper).

The flight instruments include an *airspeed indicator* (ASI), an *attitude indicator* (AI) to depict the airplane's attitude relative to the horizon, an *altimeter* (ALT) to indicate height above a selected reference, a *vertical speed indicator* (VSI) to show climb or descent, a *heading indicator* (HI) (sometimes called a *directional gyro* (DG)) to show direction, and either a *turn coordinator* or *turn indicator* with an associated *balance ball.*

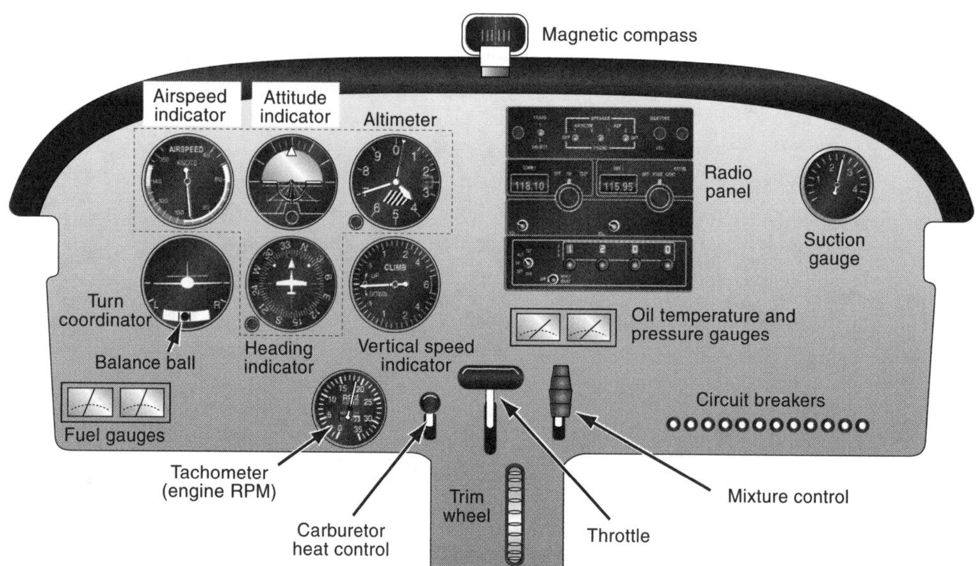

Figure 1-23 A typical instrument panel.

There are two types of flight instruments:

- *control* instruments (to set attitude and power); and
- *performance* instruments (to confirm that the flight path and airspeed are as desired).

The instruments related to airspeed and altitude are sensitive to static and dynamic (moving) air pressure obtained from the pitot-static pressure system. Those instruments related to attitude, direction and turning are operated by internal spinning gyroscopes (with the exception of the magnetic compass). The gyroscope rotors may be spun electrically or by a stream of air induced by suction from the vacuum system. The magnetic compass is usually located well away from the magnetic influences of the instrument panel and radio.

The engine instruments include the *tachometer* (engine RPM), and in the case of an aircraft with a constant-speed propeller, there is also a *manifold pressure gauge* (MP gauge). In this instance, the pilot sets both controls to a preset value to obtain a desired power output. There are oil pressure and oil temperature gauges, and there may be a fuel pressure gauge. Some aircraft also have a *cylinder head temperature* (CHT) or *exhaust gas temperature* (EGT) gauge. Other instruments may include an *ammeter*, to monitor the electrical system, a *suction gauge* for the vacuum system and a *carburetor inlet temperature gauge* to warn of possible icing.

Units of Measurement

In aviation, there is a multiplicity of units and variance in their use. Although some metric units are used, the international aviation community has retained some traditional units of measurement for very valid operational reasons. In particular, the United States is yet to transfer to international units and many aircraft are manufactured in this country. Be extra careful and check with your instructor for the units displayed in your aircraft.

Figure 1-24 Airspeed indicator (ASI).

Speed and Distance

The standard unit for airspeed is the *knot*, which is derived from nautical traditions. A knot is one nautical mile per hour. The knot is retained in aviation because it is a division of the system of measuring position and distance over the surface of the earth—*latitude* and *longitude*.

A distance of one nautical mile equates to one sixtieth of a degree of latitude at the equator. A *nautical mile* is 6,076 feet, 1.1508 statute miles or 1.852 kilometers. A knot is one nautical mile per hour. Thus 60 knots is close to 70 mph. Don't try to convert this: you will become familiar with knots and learn what flying at 100 knots feels like.

Some aircraft still use miles per hour, but such aircraft must also have knots shown on the airspeed indicator. Some European aircraft use kilometers per hour (kph), but this is not the standard. Wind speed is also given in knots for airports and for flight forecasts. Takeoff and landing performance charts outside the United States use units of meters for distance instead of feet. A foot is approximately 30 centimeters. A meter is 39.37 inches.

Figure 1-25 Pitot head.

Airspeed

Airspeed is measured in knots (nautical miles per hour). The ASI is provided with ram air pressure through the pitot head.

Figure 1-26 Altimeter.

Altitude

The unit for altitude is *feet* in hundreds or thousands. All aeronautical charts have the height of terrain in feet above mean sea level (MSL), and weather forecasts show the height of cloud in thousands of feet. The altimeter has three pointers for hundreds, thousands, and tens of thousands of feet. It is read cumulatively, in the same way as the traditional clock face of hours *plus* minutes—here thousands plus hundreds of feet.

Direction

Direction is indicated in degrees relative to magnetic north, since the compass aligns to this reference. North is both 000° and 360° (i.e. there are 360° in a full circle); however, it is always referred as 360°. East is 090°, south is 180° and west is 270°.

Runway direction is indicated to the nearest ten-degree increment, i.e. plus or minus 5°. Runway 27 points west (it is within plus or minus 5° of west or 270°) and Runway 4 points to the north east. The opposite direction on the same runway (called the *reciprocal*) is 180° about. Runway 27 and 09 are the same runway but in two opposite directions, as are 4 and 22.

A direct-reading magnetic compass (see figure 1-28 on the next page) is also part of a standard cockpit.

Figure 1-27 Heading indicator.

Figure 1-28 Magnetic compass.

Figure 1-29 Attitude indicator.

Figure 1-30 Tachometer.

Figure 1-31 Manifold pressure gauge.

Attitude

The vertical direction in which the nose of the aircraft is pointing relative to the horizon is described in degrees of *pitch* (how far above or below the horizon). *Bank* is the degree of tilt, left or right. Turns are described by the *angle of bank*, e.g. a 30°, or 45°, banked turn, or bank. Attitude is a combination of pitch and bank and is set by reference to the visual horizon or the attitude indicator (AI).

On all instruments, except the HI and the AI, the needles move. On the HI, the card rotates to show heading at the top. In the AI, the horizon moves to remain aligned with the earth's horizon.

Weight/Mass

United States aircraft have performance charts and load sheets with units of pounds (lb), whereas other parts of the world use the kilogram for weight. A kilo is approximately 2.2 pounds.

Fuel

United States aircraft have fuel tanks, gauges and charts calibrated in U.S. gallons (USG) and gallons per hour. Many other countries use metric units and so the volume of fuel is measured in liters, and consumption of fuel is measured in liters per hour. One USG is approximately four liters.

Pressure

Tire and fuel pressure is indicated in *pounds per square inch* (psi), and manifold pressure (in the engine intake) is indicated in *inches of mercury* (in. Hg), which is a very traditional unit of atmospheric pressure. This is also used for atmospheric pressure but metric is again common outside the United States where millibars (mb) or hectopascals (hPa) are used.

The altimeter's pressure setting is adjusted for surface pressure. The standard setting is 29.92 in. Hg. This setting varies with changing weather patterns, and the altimeter is adjusted for the day and the time of the flight.

Propeller Speed

The speed of rotation of the propeller is indicated in *revolutions per minute* (RPM) on the tachometer. The typical range is from 800 RPM as the engine idles to about 2,700 at full power.

Manifold Pressure

Your first aircraft may have a constant-speed propeller, in which case, the power is a combination of RPM and manifold pressure (MP). Units for MP are *inches of mercury* or *simply inches*. A typical cruise power setting might be 23 inches and 2,300 RPM.

Cockpit Design

The modern GA or LSA aircraft has made great advances in design. At last the private pilot can have features and comfort that was previously only available to high performance and expensive airplanes—military or civilian.

The structures are more efficient with beautiful aerodynamic shaping, well balanced and responsive control and electronic displays (glass cockpits) with powerful computing power and data processing for flight planning, weather reporting, navigation and flight management.

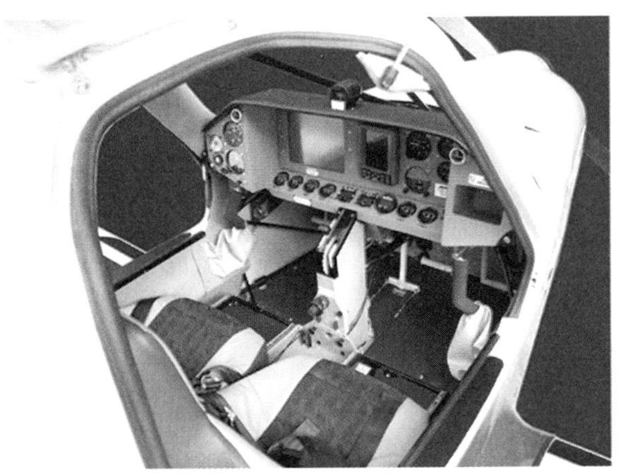

Figure 1-32 Cockpit of Lightwing aircraft.

Electronic Instruments

While the data required by a pilot remains the same, many modern aircraft display this information in novel ways.

If we take a closer look at the primary flight display (PFD) you can see the essential data.

Figure 1-33 Cirrus instrument panel showing the primary flight display (PFD) and multi function display (MFD).

Other Equipment

A fire extinguisher may be provided in the cockpit. The fire extinguisher should be checked for serviceability and that it is security-fitted. Light aircraft fire extinguishers may be toxic in a confined space, and ventilation must be provided as soon as possible after use. *Control locks* may be carried. These are fitted internally to lock the control column and externally on the actual flight controls. The purpose of control locks is to prevent control-surface

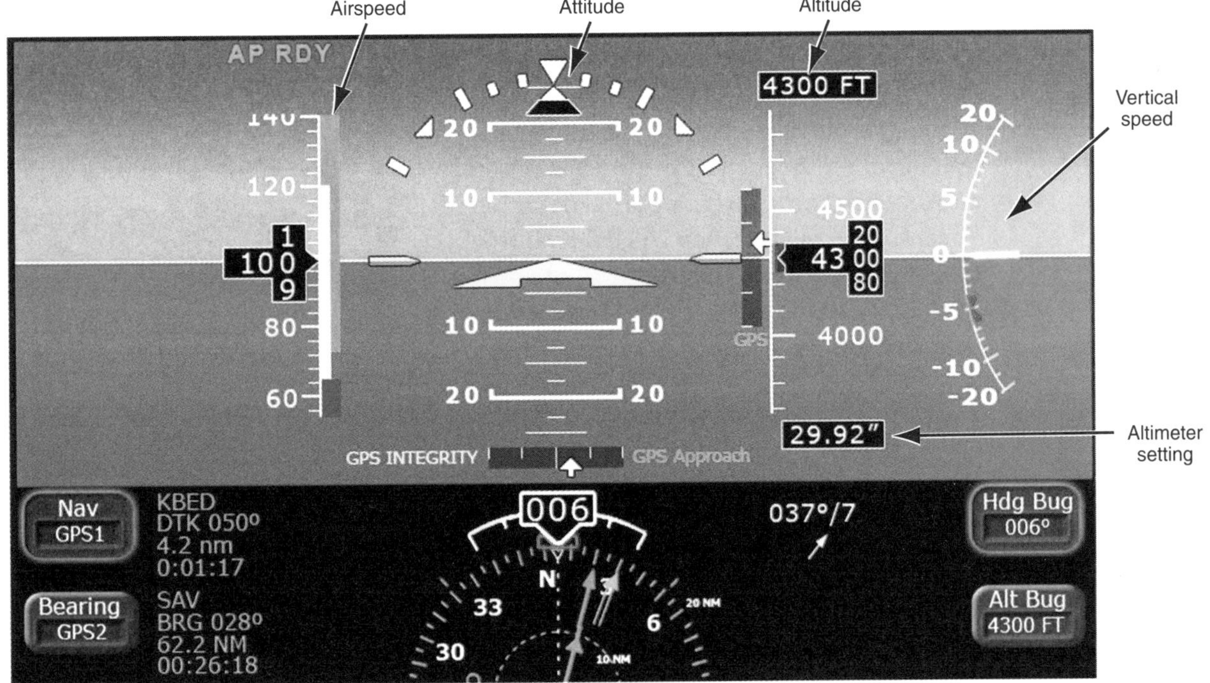

Figure 1-34 Close-up of Avidyne PFD.

movement and damage from the wind when the airplane is parked. It is vital that you remember to remove control locks prior to flight.

A *pitot cover* may be carried to protect the pitot head from blockage by insects and water while the airplane is parked. The pitot cover must be removed prior to flight if the airspeed indicator is to read correctly. Wheel chocks may be carried to place ahead of and behind the wheels as a precaution against movement when the airplane is parked. There may also be a tie-down kit of ropes, pegs and mallet to secure the airplane to the ground and prevent strong winds lifting the wings or tail. A first-aid kit may be carried.

Figure 1-35 Pitot cover and tie-down rope.

Additional Design Features

While most student pilots will commence their training in a conventional Cessna, Piper or similar airplane, many will start on an airplane with additional features. This section will briefly introduce these various systems and features, but you must learn in detail the features and idiosyncrasies of your aircraft.

Figure 1-36
Socata TB 20 Trinidad.

Constant-Speed Propeller

Many pilots learn to fly in an aircraft with a variable-pitch (constant-speed) propeller. In this system the propeller blade angle can be adjusted in flight within a governed range to provide the optimum power versus fuel economy.

This propeller acts in much the same way as the automatic transmission in your car with best acceleration when required (fine pitch) and best economy when cruising (coarse pitch). The mechanism is powered by oil pressure, and if the oil is lost, the propeller goes automatically to fine pitch for maximum thrust at low speed. The mechanism, called the *constant-speed unit* (CSU), is contained within the spinner.

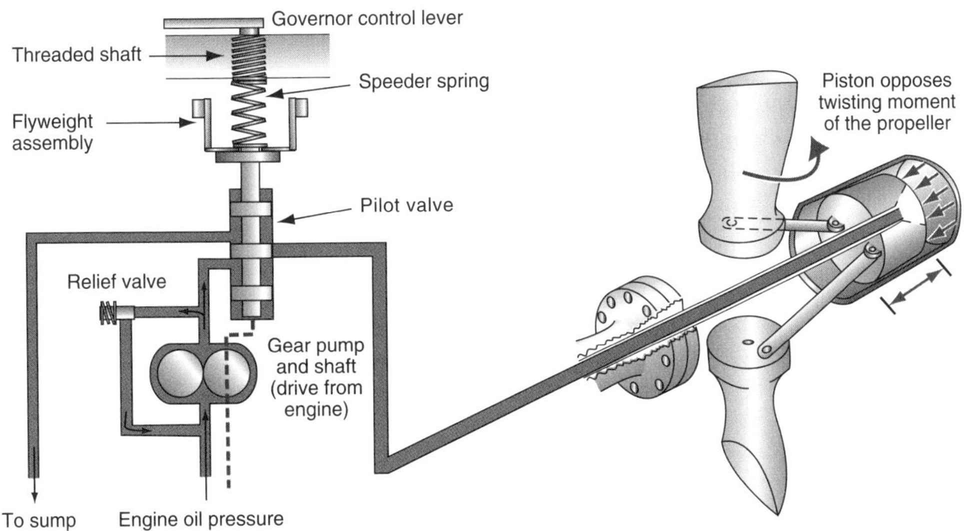

Figure 1-37 Constant-speed mechanism.

Why Complicate Things? The fixed-pitch propeller is a one-piece unit made from wood, kevlar or aluminum. The CSU adds weight and complexity. However, in return, it optimizes the angle of the propeller blades to produce maximum thrust at a particular forward speed and RPM.

How to Operate the CSU. The pilot now has two controls, one for engine power and one for propeller blade angle (together they generate thrust):

- the throttle controls manifold pressure (the pressure and amount of fuel-air mixture inducted to the engine); and
- the propeller lever (sometimes called the pitch lever) to set blade angle.

The throttle lever is topped by a smooth black knob and the propeller lever by a blue ribbed disc so they can be felt as well as seen. (The mixture lever is capped by a red indented knob.) With the propeller lever fully forward, the throttle changes the engine speed and manifold pressure just like a fixed-pitch propeller. A governor limits the maximum RPM (provided the throttle is used smoothly and slowly).

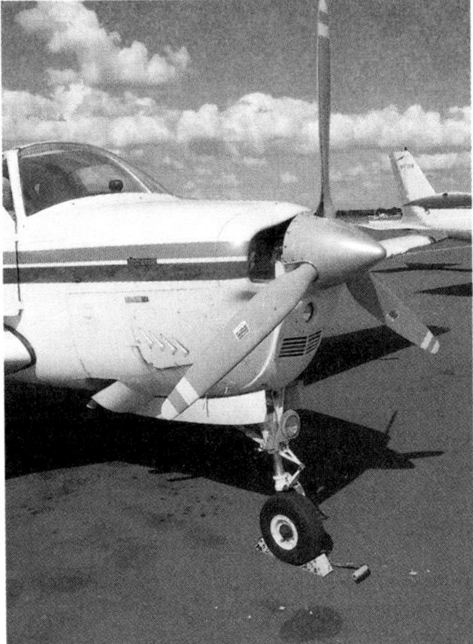

Figure 1-38
Constant speed propeller (Beechcraft Bonanza A36).

When the airplane is climbing or cruising, the pilot can set the optimum RPM by retarding the propeller lever and adjust the manifold pressure by retarding the throttle to achieve optimum engine conditions and fuel economy. Full power is used for takeoff and usually reduced to around 25 inches or 2,500 RPM for climb and maximum continuous power and around 23 inches or 2,300 RPM for cruise, but check the settings for your airplane.

Figure 1-39
Engine instruments—CSU.

When increasing power, advance the propeller lever first. When reducing power, reduce the throttle first.

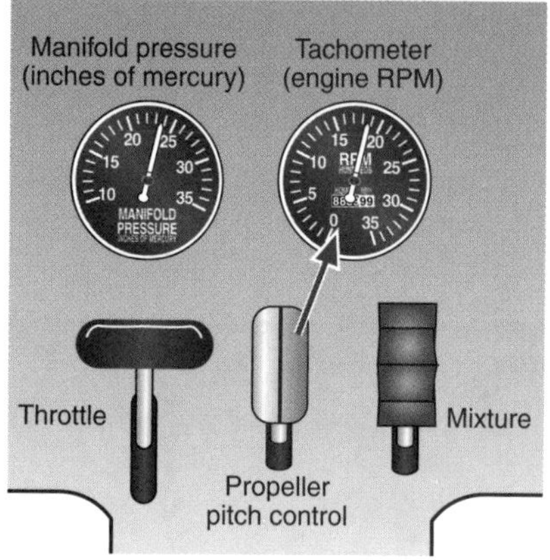

Figure 1-40
Engine controls—CSU.

Figure 1-41
Two-stroke engine.

For changes in airspeed and small changes in throttle setting, the governor maintains the set RPM. As the aircraft climbs, the manifold pressure will drop (no turbocharger) and so the throttle must be advanced to maintain 25 inches. For all engines, make the throttle and RPM changes smoothly and not too quickly. About two full seconds from idle to full power is normal. For the propeller RPM, a similar time is needed from cruise settings to full power.

The main principles to recall are:

- when operating at low power (start, taxi, run-up etc.) always have the propeller in fine pitch (high RPM, lever fully forward);
- for engine start and shutdown have the propeller lever fully forward;
- when increasing power always advance the propeller lever before the throttle;
- when reducing power always retard the throttle before the propeller RPM;
- when reducing power to idle always set the propeller to high RPM for a power increase when you may need it;
- for takeoff the propeller must be in high RPM and there may be a time limit (5 minutes or so) on maximum RPM;
- in the climb, adjust the throttle to maintain manifold pressure;
- on base leg or final approach, always put the propeller to high RPM in case you need to go around;
- before critical exercises, such as stalling and unusual attitude recoveries, place the propeller in high RPM for instant power for recovery (also full rich mixture is usual); and
- for a practice forced landing, have the propeller in high RPM for the go-around but, for an actual forced landing, the propeller generates less drag in the low RPM (full coarse) position.

Fuel Injection

A fuel-injected engine has the fuel injected directly into the engine cylinders in metered amounts. Most systems are electronically controlled and are more efficient than the traditional carburetor.

However, some are prone to fuel vaporization and overfuelling on start, and they may be difficult to start when hot. If your engine is designated, say, IO 360 or IO 540, it is the injected version of the engine. Learn and practice the hot-start procedure with your instructor.

Two-Stroke Engine

Many light or ultralight aircraft have two-stroke engines, which are lightweight, powerful, have a high RPM and may be air-cooled or liquid-cooled. Because the two-stroke engine works best at very high RPM, the propeller may be driven via a gearbox or belts to reduce propeller RPM and noise. (Airplanes usually have a direct drive to the propeller, even with a CSU.)

Low-Inertia Airplanes

Many pilots learn on ultralight airplanes that have relatively high drag and low momentum. They are often called *low-inertia* airplanes. These require greater and quicker pilot reaction in the event of engine failure and also when operating near the ground. They are more vulnerable to wind, vertical gusts and turbulence. Some have limited control and performance. However, they are great fun to fly if treated with respect.

Figure 1-42
Low-inertia tailwheel airplane.

Tail Wheel

A tail wheel airplane requires particular consideration. If you are learning to fly in a tail wheel airplane, which is very valuable training, consider the ASA publication in the Focus series entitled *Conventional Gear: Flying A Taildragger* (Newcastle, Washington: ASA, 2001) by David P. Robson.

Figure 1-43
Leading-edge slats.

High-Lift Devices

Some training airplanes have high-lift devices in addition to conventional trailing-edge flaps. These may include less common drooped ailerons (which act like additional flaps) and leading-edge slats. Slats are small airfoil sections (miniature wings) attached ahead of the leading edge of the main wing. Slats may extend along the complete span of the wings. They considerably increase the maximum lift that can be generated by a wing and so minimize speeds and distances for takeoff and landing. They also allow a much slower but steeper climb and approach path. The slats may be fixed open or may be retractable to reduce drag when cruising.

These devices retain attachment of the airflow over the upper surface of the wing at high angles of attack (the angle the wing presents to the air) and thus increase the lift coefficient (the lifting capacity of the wing). The higher lift allows the aircraft to fly at lower speeds—sometimes very slow speeds. Airplanes with full-span slats need very long landing gear legs because their attitude on landing is so high.

Figure 1-44
Washout.

Features for Safer Stall Characteristics

Most airplanes have devices to reduce the symptoms of the stall and in some cases prevent the full stall altogether. Features include:

- limited elevator deflection;
- slots;
- stall strips;
- vortex generators;
- tapered wing planform;
- wing twist (called *washout*); and
- different airfoil section of the outer part of the wing to encourage the inner area to stall first.

All of these affect the symptoms and behavior of the aircraft at the stall and you should know about any that are fitted to your airplane. Don't forget the other factors such as CG position that also affect stall behavior.

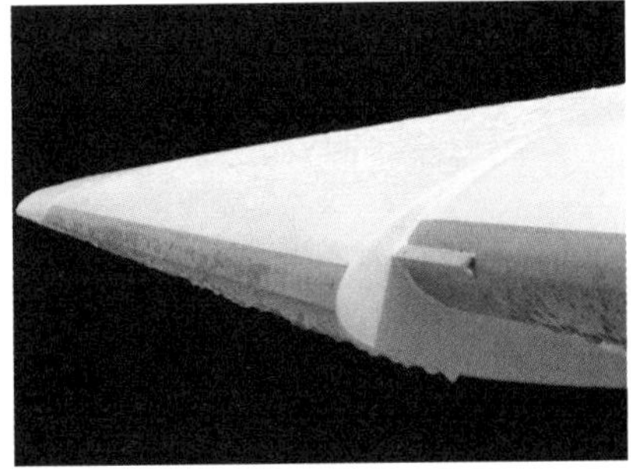

Figure 1-45
Modified leading edge.

Figure 1-46 Electric flaps.

Figure 1-47 Retractable gear.

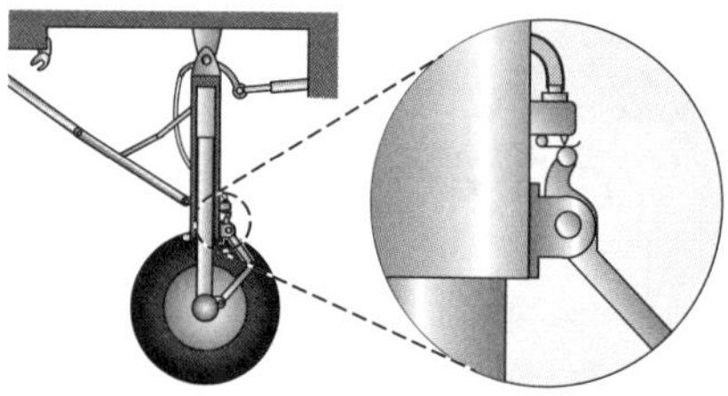

Figure 1-48 Squat switch.

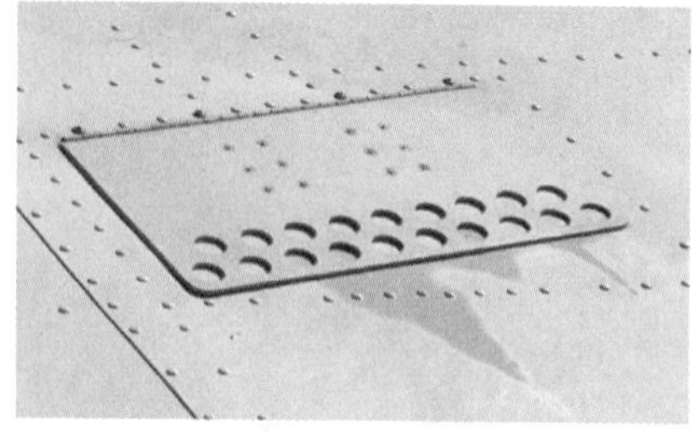

Figure 1-49 Speed brake.

Electric Flaps

Your airplane may have mechanically actuated flaps (operated by a handle as with the parking brake) or electrically operated by a switch. These may have two to three predetermined settings or may be infinitely variable over the range of travel. In the event of electrical failure, there may be a need to conduct a no-flap landing, hence it is taught in emergency procedures.

Retractable Gear

The retractable landing gear is usually electrically operated by a direct-drive motor or hydraulically by an electrical hydraulic pump. Both have specific techniques for emergency (manual) extension of the gear in the event of electrical or hydraulic system malfunctions.

The direct-drive version has to be cranked down; the hydraulic version may have a hand pump, emergency pressure accumulators or simply use gravity by unlocking the gear legs and allowing them to fall into the down and locked position. The emergency extension for your airplane must be learned but also practiced in clear conditions— for example, one aircraft requires 50 cranks of a handle that is located behind the front seats, and this requires some skill to operate and fly at the same time.

All airplanes have a maximum airspeed for gear extension and perhaps a higher speed for flight with the gear down and locked. The gear can be damaged above these speeds. Some aircraft with very high gear-down speeds can make use of this added drag for emergency descents as the drag of the gear allows a much steeper and quicker descent.

Retractable gear airplanes have a warning horn that sounds if the throttle is closed with the gear retracted. There is also a micro-switch (squat switch) that prevents retraction on the ground if there is weight on the landing gear.

Speed Brakes/Air Brakes

Some very low drag airplanes have speed brakes to increase drag for slowing to approach speeds and to contain speed during cruise descents.

Aileron/Rudder Interconnect

You will learn about a negative feature, called *adverse aileron yaw*, where the drag of the aileron causes yaw in the opposite direction to the commanded roll. Thus it is adverse because it resists the roll.

One method to counter this effect is to have the rudder automatically deflect in the same direction as the applied aileron, thus yawing the airplane in the same direction as the roll. This is a mechanical interconnect and as well as the positive counter to adverse yaw has some limitations.

When taxiing, the yoke rotates as the rudder is applied as there is a tendency to try to steer the airplane with the yoke, which is less effective than the rudder. So, in a crosswind landing, where the pilot needs to apply aileron and rudder in opposite direction, there is some resistance due to the interconnect. Discuss these features with your flight instructor.

Supercharger/Turbocharger

It is unlikely you will have a boosted engine in your training airplane. If you do there are strict conditions on power increases and reductions to allow the temperatures to stabilize before descent, glides and engine shutdown. Some turbos have manual controls; other are completely automatic and produce power on demand.

The primary purpose of the turbocharger in an airplane is to compensate for the reduction in power as the airplane climbs. The turbocharger maintains sea-level full power until a certain altitude, called *full throttle height*.

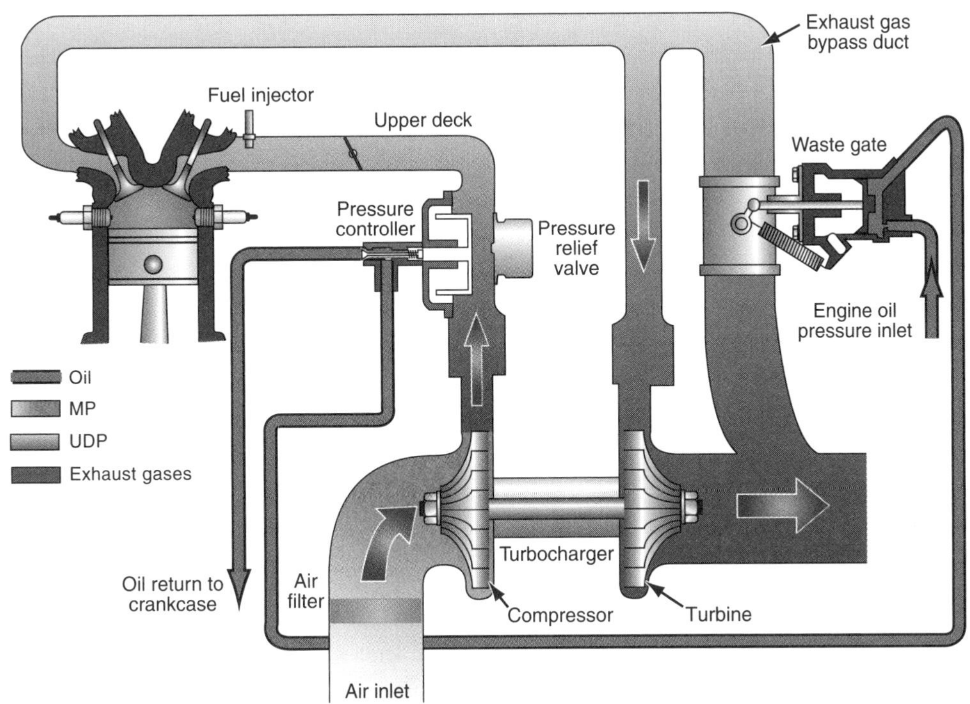

Figure 1-50 Turbocharger.

Tip Tanks

Some airplanes have additional fuel carried in tanks mounted on the wing tips. These tip tanks also provide structural and aerodynamic advantages. Check how to fill these tanks and how to access all the aircraft's fuel in the correct sequence and the tank selections needed.

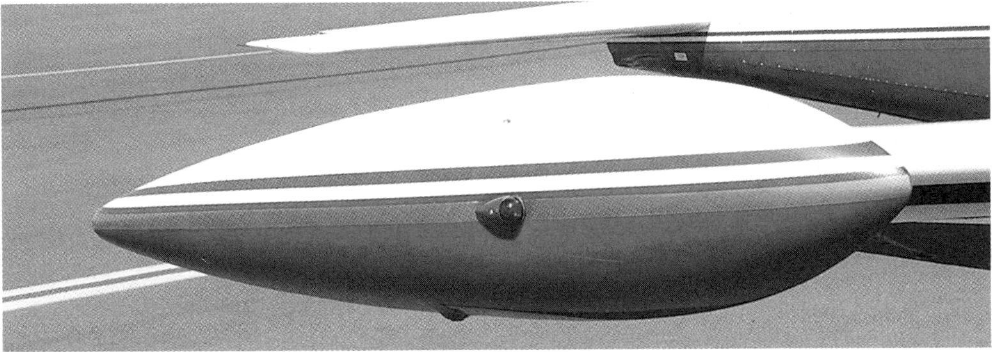

Figure 1-51 Tip tank.

Oxygen

The use of supplemental oxygen is recommended above cabin altitudes of 10,000 feet MSL.

An airplane that can climb and cruise above 10,000 feet (probably turbocharged) will also require crew oxygen or cabin pressurization. In the latter case emergency oxygen and quick-donning masks are also essential elements. You should not only learn to operate the system but practice using it. Be careful to use only *aviator's grade* oxygen in certified delivery systems.

While the use of supplemental oxygen is *recommended* above cabin altitudes of 10,000 feet MSL, it is *required* by the Federal Aviation Regulations for:

- all time in excess of 30 minutes above 12,500 feet MSL cabin altitude; and
- all time above 14,000 feet MSL cabin altitude.

The term cabin altitude is used to describe the air in the cockpit that a pilot is breathing. A pressurized airplane flying at 31,000 feet may have the cabin pressurized to 8,000 feet, which means the pilots have the same amount of oxygen to breathe as in an unpressurized airplane at 8,000 feet MSL. In this case, there is no need to use the oxygen masks. If, however, there was a sudden depressurization and the cabin air escaped, the pilots would require oxygen immediately.

Pressurization and Air Conditioning

A training airplane has insufficient excess power to be able to power pressurization turbines and air-conditioner compressors. It is the higher-performance turbocharged airplane that carries these systems and their use will be part of your type rating. You need to learn about the particular system in your airplane. Also check the maximum cabin pressure differential your aircraft can accept as this will impose maximum altitude limits.

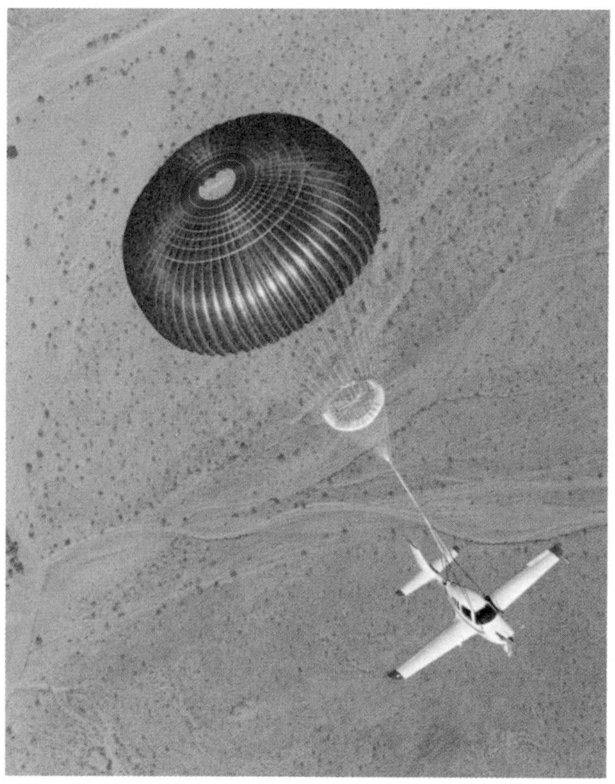

Figure 1-52 Cirrus CAPS system.

Cirrus Airframe Parachute System

Some designs even feature a unique safety measure—a parachute system that will lower the complete aircraft and its passengers safely to earth. One is called the *Cirrus Airframe Parachute System* (CAPS). This feature offers a safe escape in the event of engine failure at night or over harsh terrain, if control is lost in marginal weather, or safe recovery by a passenger in the event of pilot incapacitation.

REVIEW 1

The Training Airplane

1. Locate the following on the diagram below:
   - fuselage;
   - right wing;
   - left wing;
   - empennage;
   - nose wheel;
   - oil cooler;
   - wing trailing edge;
   - vertical stabilizer;
   - elevator;
   - propeller;
   - rudder;
   - left and right wing tips;
   - wing root;
   - flaps;
   - spinner;
   - wing leading edge;
   - radio antenna;
   - (right) main landing gear;
   - cockpit canopy;
   - rotating beacon (red);
   - red position light;
   - right aileron;
   - elevator trim tab
   - green position light;
   - engine cowling;
   - rear-facing position light (white);
   - landing light(s);
   - left aileron; and
   - horizontal stabilizer.

2. Will easing the control column rearward in normal flight raise or lower the nose of the airplane?
3. Rotating the control column to the right will cause the airplane to roll in which direction?
4. How is the rudder operated?
5. Will moving the throttle forward increase or decrease engine power?
6. On the ground, wheel brakes can be operated by pressing the top of which pedals?
7. Where are the fuel tanks located?

8. What fluid is used to lubricate and cool the engine?
9. Identify the following on the diagram below:
   - the flight instruments;
   - the engine gauges and controls;
   - the radio panel;
   - the magnetic compass.

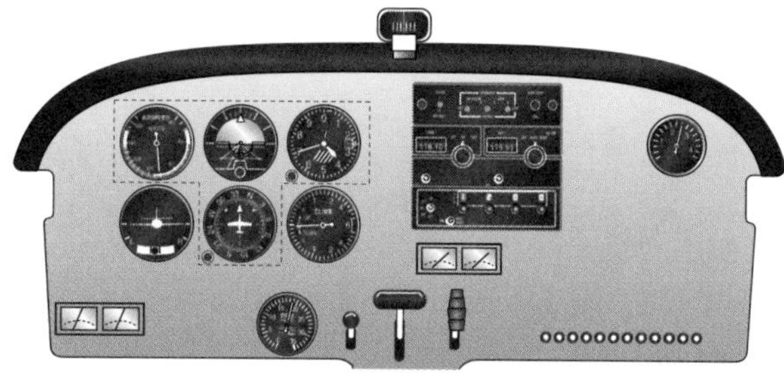

10. Which control adjusts the fuel-air mixture?
11. Which components generate the spark that ignites the fuel-air mixture? In what way do dual ignition systems affect the efficiency of the combustion in each cylinder? Do dual ignition systems provide more safety in the case of failure to one system?
12. What is the source of the electrical power needed to start the engine?
13. Radios and other electrical services can be powered by the battery when the engine is not running. When the engine is running, how are the radios and other services powered and the battery recharged?
14. Which switch is pictured below?

15. Identify the item of equipment pictured below. What does the SQ label stand for? What is removed when this control is activated?

16. Where on an instrument panel are the following instruments located: attitude indicator, heading indicator, airspeed indicator, turn coordinator, altimeter and vertical speed indicator? Where is the balance ball located?

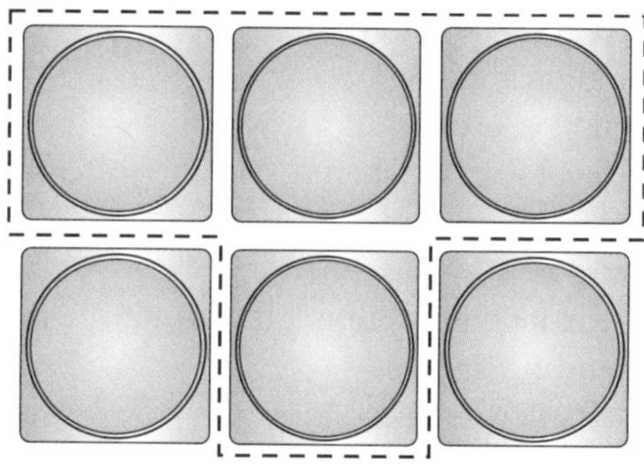

Answers are given on page 575.

2

Flight Preparation

OBJECTIVES

To consider, discuss and describe:

- the preparation of the aircraft for flight;
- the necessary documentation;
- an objective self-examination; and
- precautions for carrying passengers.

CONSIDERATIONS

The success of a flight depends largely on thorough preparation. In the course of your training, a pattern of regular preflight actions should be developed to ensure that this is the case. This includes planning the flight, and checking the airplane. These preflight actions must be based on the checks found in the *pilot's operating handbook* (POH), *manufacturer's information manual* or the FAA-approved *airplane flight manual* (AFM) for your airplane.

Information Manual

The typical information manual contains the following numbered sections:

1. General" has diagrams and a description of the airplane, symbols, abbreviations and terminology.
2. "Limitations" details airspeed limitations, engine limitations, weight and balance limitations.
3. "Emergency Procedures" contains emergency operations for engine failure, forced landings, fires, icing, flat tires, electrical malfunctions.
4. "Normal Procedures" contains procedures and checklists for normal operations.
5. "Performance" has charts and/or tables for takeoff and landing distances, range and endurance, and so on.
6. "Weight and Balance/Equipment List" contains loading data, plus a list of available equipment.
7. "Airplane and Systems Descriptions."
8. "Airplane Handling, Service and Maintenance" has procedures for ground handling, servicing and maintenance.
9. "Supplements" is usually quite a large section describing optional systems and operating procedures.

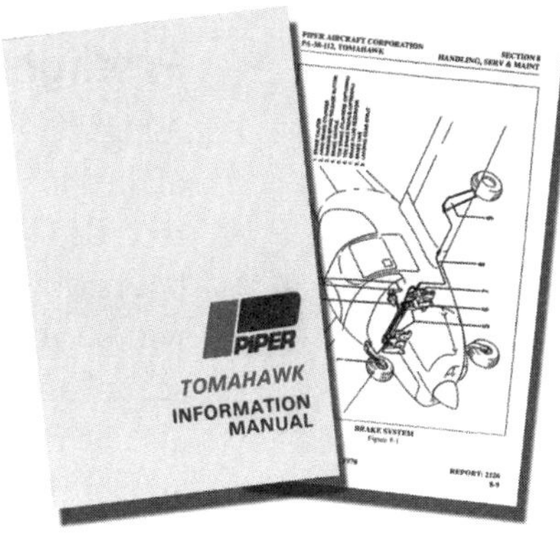

Figure 2-1 Typical information manuals.

Pilot Responsibilities

The pilot in command is the person designated as such before or during flight and has final authority and responsibility for the operation and safety of the flight.

The pilot in command is responsible for determining that the airplane is airworthy prior to every flight. Use of authorized checklists facilitates this. Prior to each flight you, as pilot in command, are required to familiarize yourself with all the available information concerning the flight. Preparation for a flight commences well before you actually enter the airplane and consists of:

- assessing your personal health and well-being;
- personal preparation;
- weather and NOTAM check;
- satisfying the preflight documentation requirements;
- confirming that the runway lengths available are adequate for the proposed takeoffs and landings, including those at possible alternate airports;
- the preflight inspection of the airplane; and
- the checks associated with start-up and taxiing and the before-takeoff check.

Personal Preparation for Flight

The pilot is the key person on any flight and must be properly prepared. If you are planning a flight, calm, unhurried and thorough long-term preparation a day or two ahead of time might be useful. Preparing the charts for a cross-country flight, for instance, or reading up on an imminent flight lesson will greatly contribute to the outcome of the flight. *Short-term preparation* involves such things as being properly equipped, arriving early enough at the airport for any briefing or flight preparation to proceed in an unhurried manner, and carrying out the required preflight checks of the airplane calmly and thoroughly. A typical list of items to check before even leaving home should include:

- Am I fit to fly—physically and mentally?
- Have I consumed alcohol in the last 8 hours, or is there any alcohol in my bloodstream?
- Am I using pills, medication, drugs, and so on, that could impair my abilities?
- Do I have a cold, blocked nose, blocked ears or any other upper respiratory complaint?
- Do I have the required equipment for this particular flight?
- Am I suitably clothed? Natural fibers and materials are generally best, such as a cotton shirt, wool slacks and leather shoes, as these allow the body to breathe as well as being somewhat fire-resistant.
- Do I have my current medical and pilot certificates with me?
- Am I aware of the expiration date of my medical certificate, and the privileges and limitations of my pilot certificate?

Preflight Documentation

A high level of flight safety is maintained partly because of the thorough documentation required. Items that are recorded include the history of the airplane in terms of hours flown and maintenance carried out. Each flight will be authorized by your flight instructor or flight school and will be recorded on a schedule. There may also be a book containing local rules and regulations appropriate to your training and which you should check prior to flying.

Figure 2-2 Flight documentation.

Flight Plan, Weather and Fuel

A go/no-go decision is based on weather and other considerations and is an essential step in each and every proposed flight.

AC 91-92, "Pilots Guide to a Preflight Briefing," can be referenced for additional information on obtaining a proper preflight self-briefing.

It is not usual to compile a flight plan prior to a local training flight, but it is a consideration during your more advanced training when cross-country flights will be undertaken. Based on weather and other considerations, make a go/no-go decision.

Weather is a consideration for every flight, and you should obtain a weather briefing or discuss the weather with your flight instructor each time you go flying. For a cross-country flight, you should obtain, read and analyze the available weather information, and then make a competent go/no-go decision based on this. *Notices to Airmen* (NOTAMs) should be checked, to ensure that you are aware of items that may affect your flight, such as runway closures, unserviceability of airport equipment, unmanned aircraft operations, and so on.

Always plan to carry sufficient *fuel* for the flight, plus sufficient in reserve—at least 30 minutes by day at normal cruise rate, and 45 minutes by night. Once you have decided how much you require, contact the fuel agent early enough so there is time to fuel the airplane and not delay your departure. Specify the quantity and type of fuel, and be prepared to supervise the fueling if necessary. The following checks should be made:

- confirm correct grade and type of fuel;
- confirm fire extinguisher is handy;
- check that the airplane is grounded by a ground wire to equalize electrical potential (static electricity cannot be seen until it actually sparks and can ignite nearby fumes);
- check fuel quantity;
- check fuel purity; and
- check fuel caps are replaced firmly and ground wire is removed.

If the fuel is contaminated by water, all of the water should be drained away; if the fuel is contaminated by dirt or other solid contaminants, the whole fuel system may have to be drained. Do not fly with contaminated fuel!

Weight and Balance (Loading)

The airplane must always be within weight and balance limitations.

It is vital to the safety of every flight that no weight limit is exceeded, and that the load is arranged to keep the center of gravity within approved limits. The ability of the airplane to fly to meet performance standards and remain controllable depends upon this. Generally, heavy articles are best loaded forward. Remember that an article weighing 100 pounds will, during a 2g maneuver such as a 60°-banked turn, exert a force on the airplane structure equal to double its weight to 200 pounds force. Cargo and loose equipment must be secured. Weight and balance documents, usually in the form of charts or tables, must always be available on board.

Most training airplanes are satisfactorily loaded with one or two persons on board, and so there may be no need to actually do a weight and balance calculation prior to every training flight (depending on runway length). All the same, you should develop the habit of considering weight and balance and performance before each flight.

Airworthiness Documents

It is a pilot's responsibility to check certain documents prior to flight to ensure the airplane is airworthy. You should know the significance of each document, and know where to locate them in the cockpit or at the flight school. The documents important to the individual pilot are:

- maintenance records (check every flight);
- the pilot's operating handbook (POH) with aircraft limitations and placards (should always be in the airplane);

- aircraft weight and balance data, and equipment list (check the POH or flight manual);
- the Certificate of Airworthiness (must always be in the airplane), which shows that the airplane has met certain FAA safety requirements, and remains in effect if required inspections and maintenance has been performed; and
- the Certificate of Registration (must always be in the airplane), containing airplane and owner information—a new owner requires a new Certificate of Registration.

An easy way to remember the required documents is with the mnemonic MAROW:

M Maintenance records.

A Airworthiness certificate.

R Registration certificate.

O Operating limitations (shown in the pilot's operating handbook, color-coding on instruments, and cockpit decals).

W Weight and balance. This is included in the POH or FAA-approved AFM, and sometimes found folded and stapled in the glove box or a seat pocket; weight and balance paperwork needs to be available on board the aircraft, but on many flights need not be filled in. An equipment list should always be on board, and this is often found with the weight and balance information.

The maintenance records should be checked prior to each flight, and any maintenance that you think is required should be specified after flight. Sometimes there will be no formal written maintenance release; however, do not accept responsibility for the airplane if it has defects that may make it unacceptable for flight.

If in any doubt, discuss the matter with your flight instructor or with an aircraft mechanic. There are some simple maintenance actions that may be performed by a qualified pilot, such as topping up the oil, but certainly not anything that might affect the airworthiness of the airplane, such as the flight controls. Aircraft and engine logbooks should be available, but it is not required that they be on board.

Minimum Equipment List (MEL)

It is permissible to operate an airplane with temporary inoperative instruments or equipment. *14 CFR §91.213: Inoperative Instruments and Equipment* explains what is acceptable.

Takeoff and Landing Distances

Check performance data applicable to your planned operations. You should confirm that the runway lengths available at the airports of intended use are adequate for your takeoff and landing requirements. This performance check is vital at unfamiliar airports, especially if the runways are short or have obstacles in the takeoff or landing path, if the airport is high, or if the temperature is high.

APPLICATION

Preparing the Airplane

Written checklists are a valuable back-up.

The information manual for your airplane will contain a list of items that must be checked during:

- the preflight inspection (external and internal);
- the preflight cockpit checks;

- the engine power check; and
- the before-takeoff check.

At first, these checks may seem long and complicated, but as you repeat them thoroughly prior to each flight, a pattern will soon form. It is vital that the checks are carried out thoroughly, systematically and strictly in accordance with the manufacturer's recommended procedure. Use of *written checklists*, if performed correctly, will ensure that no vital item has been missed, but some pilots prefer to memorize checks. The comments that follow are only general comments that will apply to most airplanes.

The External Inspection

Always perform a thorough external inspection. This can begin as you walk up to the airplane and should include:

- the position of the airplane being safe for start-up and taxi (note also the wind direction and the likely path to the takeoff point); and
- the availability of fire extinguishers and emergency equipment in case of fire on start-up (a rare event, but it does happen).

Figure 2-3 Area inspection.

Some of the vital items are:

- all switches off (master switch for electronics, magneto switch for engine) as a protection against the engine inadvertently starting when the propeller is moved;
- fuel check for quantity and quality (drain into a clear cup);
- oil check; and
- structural check.

A list of typical walkaround items is shown below. Each item must be inspected individually, but do not neglect a general overview of the airplane. Be vigilant for things such as buckling of the fuselage skin or popped rivets since these could indicate internal structural damage from a previous flight. Leaking oil, fuel forming puddles on the ground, or hydraulic fluid leaks from around the brake lines also deserve further investigation. With experience, you will develop a feel for what looks right and what does not. The walkaround inspection starts at the cockpit door and follows the pattern specified in the checklist provided by the aircraft manufacturer.

Cabin

- Parking brake on.
- Magneto switches off.
- Landing gear lever (if retractable) locked down.
- Control locks removed.
- Master switch on (to supply electrical power).
- Fuel quantity gauges checked for sufficient fuel for the planned flight.
- Fuel selector valves on.
- Flaps checked for operation; leave them extended for external inspection.
- Stall warning (if electrical) checked for proper operation.
- Rotating beacon (and other lights) checked, then off.
- Master switch off.
- Primary flight controls checked for proper operation.

Figure 2-4 Check the cockpit before walk around.

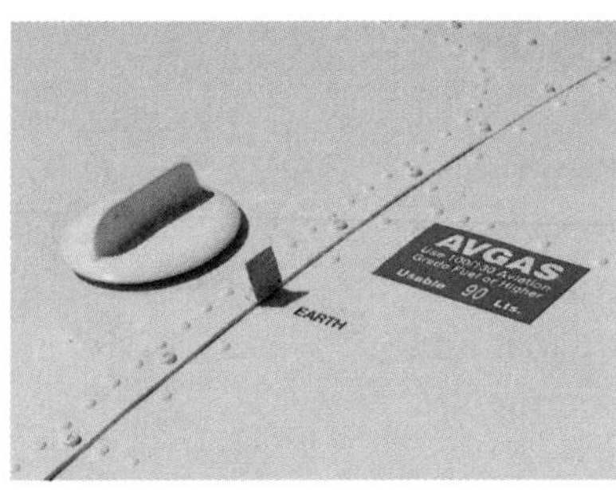

Figure 2-5 Fuel caps.

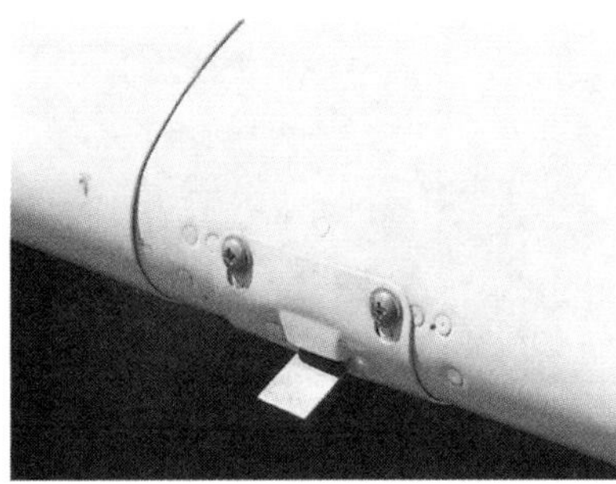
Figure 2-6 Stall warning vane.

- Required documents on board: MAROW plus airman certificate and medical certificate for the pilot. (Note: under some circumstances a medical certificate may not be required.)
- Cabin door securely attached, and latches working correctly.
- Windshield clean (use correct cloth and cleanser).

Wing

- All surfaces, the wing tip, leading and trailing edge checked for no damage or contamination; remove any frost, snow, ice or insects (on upper leading edge especially, since contamination here can significantly reduce lift, even to the point where the airplane may not become airborne).
- Wing tip position light checked for no damage.
- Flaps firmly in position and actuating mechanism firmly connected and safety-wired.
- Aileron locks removed, hinges checked, correct movement (one up, the other down) and linkages safety-wired, mass balance weight secure.
- Pitot tube cover removed and no damage or obstructions to tube (otherwise airspeed indicator will not respond).
- Fuel contents checked in tanks and matching fuel quantity gauge indications; fuel caps replaced firmly and with a good seal (to avoid fuel siphoning away in flight into the low-pressure area above the wing).

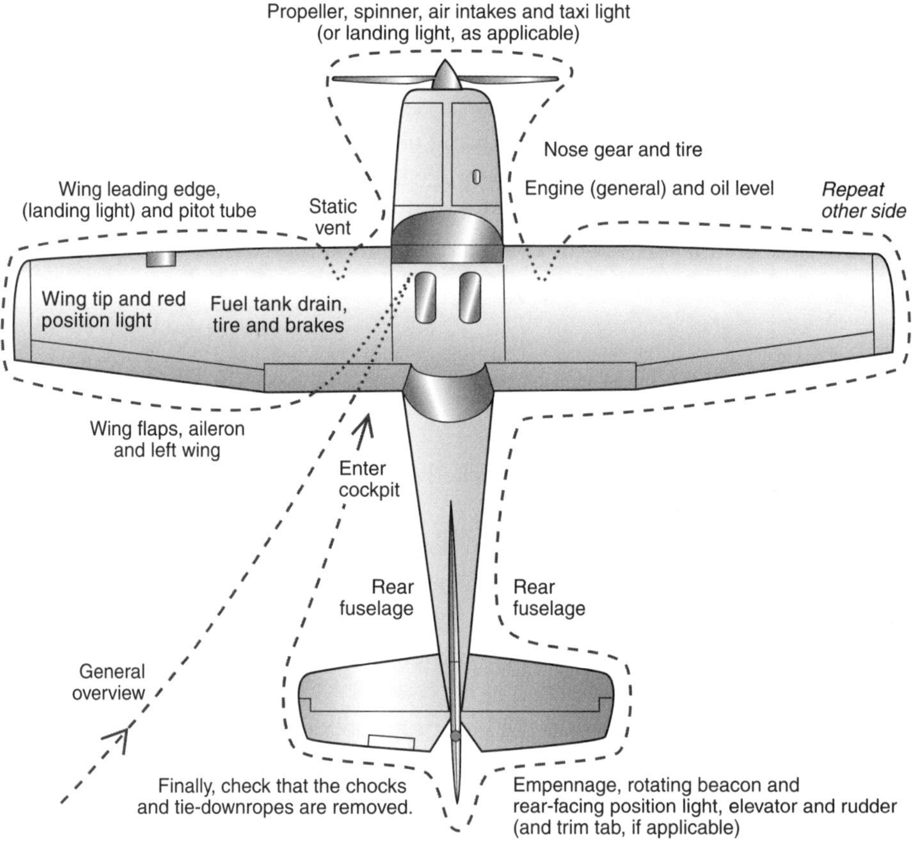

Figure 2-7 A typical walkaround pattern for the external check.

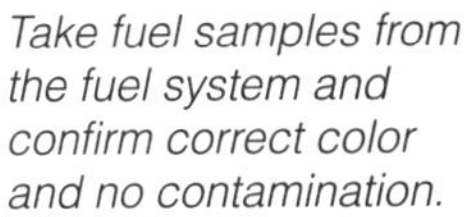
Take fuel samples from the fuel system and confirm correct color and no contamination.

- Fuel sample drained from wing tanks and from fuel strainer into a clear container. Check for correct color (blue for 100LL, green for 100-octane), correct fuel grade, correct smell (aviation gasoline and not jet fuel or kerosene), no water (being denser, water sinks to bottom), sediment, dirt or other contaminant (condensation may occur in the tanks overnight causing water to collect in the bottom of the tanks, or the fuel taken on board may be contaminated).
- Fuel port, or fuel vent (which may be separate or incorporated into the fuel cap) clear (to allow pressure equalization inside and outside the tanks when fuel is used or altitude is changed, otherwise the fuel tanks could collapse or fuel supply to the engine could stop as fuel is used).
- Stall warning checked (if possible).
- Inspection plates in place.
- Wing strut checked secure at both ends.

Fuselage

- All surfaces, including underneath checked for skin damage, corrosion, buckling or other damage (corrosion appears as surface pitting and etching, often with a gray powdery deposit); advise a mechanic if you suspect any of these.
- No fuel, oil or hydraulic fluid leaking onto the ground beneath the aircraft.
- Inspection plates in place.
- Static ports (also called static vents)—no obstructions (needed for correct operation of airspeed indicator, altimeter and vertical speed indicator).
- Antennas checked for security and no loose wires.
- Baggage lockers—check baggage, cargo and equipment secure, and baggage compartments locked.

Figure 2-8 Stabilator linkage.

Main Landing Gear

- Tires checked for wear, cuts, condition of tread, proper inflation, and security of wheel and brake disk.
- Wheel oleo strut checked for damage, proper inflation, and cleanliness.
- Hydraulic lines to brakes checked for damage, leaks and attachment.
- Gear attachment to the fuselage—check attachment, and be sure there is no damage to the fuselage (buckling of skin, popped rivets).

Nose Section

- Fuselage checked for skin buckling or popped rivets.
- Windshield clean.
- Propeller checked for damage, especially nicks along its leading edge, cracks and security (and for leaks in the hub area if it is a constant-speed propeller).
- Propeller spinner checked for damage, cracks and security.
- Engine air intake and filter checked for damage and cleanliness (no bird nests or oily rags).
- Nose wheel tire checked for wear, cuts, condition of tread, proper inflation, and security of nose wheel.

Figure 2-9 Nose wheel strut.

Figure 2-10 Oil check.

- Nose wheel oleo strut checked for damage, proper inflation (four to six inches is typical), security of shimmy damper and other mechanisms.
- Open engine inspection panel; check engine mounts, engine, and exhaust manifold for cracks and security (to ensure that no lethal carbon monoxide in the exhaust gases can enter the cockpit—exhaust leaks may be indicated by white stains near the cylinder head, the exhaust shroud or exhaust pipes).
- Check battery, wiring and electrical cables for security (firmly attached at both ends).
- Check the oil level; top up if necessary (know the correct type and grade of oil to order); ensure that the dipstick is replaced properly and the oil cap is firmly closed to avoid loss of oil in flight.
- Close the inspection panel and check its security.

Other Side of Airplane

Repeat as appropriate.

Empennage

- Remove control locks if fitted.
- All surfaces checked for skin damage (vertical stabilizer and rudder, horizontal stabilizer, elevator and trim tab); remove any contamination such as ice, frost or snow.
- Control surface hinges checked for cracks, firmness of attachment, safety-wiring and correct movement.

Chocks and Tiedown Ropes

Chocks and tiedowns removed and stowed (after checking the parking brake is on).

Overall View

Stand back and check the overall appearance of the airplane. It cannot be emphasized too greatly just how important this preflight inspection by the pilot is. Even if you have no experience in mechanical things, you must train yourself to look at the airplane and notice things that do not seem right. Bring any items that you are unsure of to the attention of your flight instructor or a mechanic. At this stage, you are now ready to seat yourself in the airplane and begin the *internal cockpit inspection.*

The Cockpit Inspection

Always perform a thorough cockpit inspection. The cockpit inspection involves preparing the cockpit and your personal equipment for flight. It should include:

- Parking brake set (on).
- Required documents on board (MAROW items).
- Flight equipment organized and arranged in an efficient manner so they are readily available in flight (flight bag, charts prefolded to show your route, computer, pencils, flashlight, and so on).
- Fuel on.

- Seat position and harness comfortable and secure, with the seat definitely locked in position and rudder pedals (if adjustable) adjusted and locked into position so that full movement is possible.
- Ignition switch (magnetos) off (so that the engine is not live).
- Master switch on (for electrical services such as fuel gauges).
- Flight controls checked for full and free movement (elevator, ailerons, rudder and trim wheel or handle). Trim set to takeoff position.
- Engine controls checked for full and free movement (throttle, mixture control and carburetor heat).
- Scan the instruments systematically from one side of the panel to the other for serviceability and correct readings.
- No circuit breakers should be popped nor fuses blown (for electrical services to operate).
- Microphone and/or headsets plugged in (if you are to use the radio) and test intercom if used.
- Safety equipment (fire extinguisher, first aid kit, supplemental oxygen if planning to fly high, flotation equipment for overwater flights) on board and securely stowed.
- Loose articles stowed.
- Checklists on board and available.
- Read the preflight checklist, if appropriate.

Checklists

Normal checklists are found in Section 4 of the typical pilot's operating handbook, and emergency checklists are found in Section 3. Written checklists are used to confirm that appropriate procedures have been carried out, for example, the before-takeoff checklist or the engine fire checklist. In earlier days, when airplanes were simpler, checks were usually memorized. Nowadays, in more complex airplanes and in a much busier operating environment, many checks are performed with the use of standard written checklists for that airplane. Checklists are usually compiled in a concise and abbreviated form as *item* and *condition* (for example, fuel—*on*), where the item to be checked is listed, followed by a statement of its desired condition. Explanations for actions are usually not included in the concise checklist, but may generally be found in the pilot's operating handbook if required.

Figure 2-11 Checklists must be carried in the cockpit.

Vital checklists are best committed to memory so that they may be done quickly and efficiently, followed by confirmation using the printed checklist if required.

Emergency checklists, such as the engine fire checklist, often have some items that should be memorized, since they may have to be actioned immediately, before there is time to locate the appropriate checklist and read it. These items are often referred to as memory items or phase-one items, and are often distinguished on checklists by bold type or by being surrounded with a box. The method of using checklists may be one of:

- carrying out the items as the checklist is read; or
- carrying out the items in full, followed by confirmation using the checklist.

The procedures for your training will be made quite clear by your flight instructor.

REVIEW 2

Flight Preparation

1. Which personal documents should a pilot carry in flight?
2. Which aircraft documents should be on board?
3. Is it good airmanship to check relevant weather information prior to flight?
4. Is it good airmanship to check performance aspects prior to flight, such as whether the runways are long enough for takeoff and landing in the current weather conditions?
5. Should you cancel a flight if you feel the weather conditions or some other aspect of the flight is beyond your capabilities? What sort of decision is this known as?
6. Must an airplane remain within weight and center-of-gravity limitations throughout a flight?
7. Should current maintenance status of an airplane be checked prior to flight?
8. Should a thorough and systematic external check be made prior to each flight?
9. Should cargo and equipment be secured?
10. When is material and equipment to be used in flight best prepared and organized so that they are readily available in flight?
11. When should seat and rudder pedals be adjusted and locked?
12. Should the use of seat belts and safety harnesses be briefed?
13. Rehearse the preflight inspection.

Figure 2-12 Preparing to fly.

Answers are given on page 575.

3 Communications

OBJECTIVES

To describe:

- the process of connecting, selecting and adjusting the headset, intercom and radio;
- the phonetic alphabet and pronunciation of call signs;
- the information that must be read back;
- the standard calls and when they must be made; and
- the content of emergency calls.

Figure 3-1 Microphone position.

CONSIDERATIONS

The most important element of in-flight instruction is having a clear communications channel with the instructor. A training aircraft usually has an electronic intercommunications system (intercom), but the quality varies considerably. If you cannot hear clearly, you cannot learn, so ask for a different headset or aircraft. Good communications are equally important outside the aircraft and can be a major obstacle to learning if they are not well rehearsed. There are set sequences of calls and standard patterns of speech for use in aircraft. Many instructions have to be read back. If you learn these well before flying, then the instruction will proceed much more easily.

Aviate, navigate, communicate.

You will probably hear the expression "aviate, navigate, communicate." It is a guide for the priorities that a pilot establishes to ensure that the important things are addressed before the less important ones. You must certainly retain control of the aircraft and maintain situational awareness, but having said that, you must not downgrade the importance of communications. In most training operations, you are on a *see-and-be-seen* basis. Much of what you are trying to avoid cannot be easily seen early enough to avoid conflict, so you have to forewarn your senses. This you do by forming a mental picture of where the traffic is and where it will be in relation to yourself as you proceed. The mental plot is a significant part of your ability to detect and avoid other traffic, and it relies totally on you ability to communicate. You must provide your own separation.

Communications are that important. Moreover, you do not merely communicate: you also annunciate and articulate. You must be clearly understood, and it must be clearly understood that you clearly understood what was said to you. Now you are communicating!

ICAO: International Civil Aviation Organization.

With the introduction of ICAO radio procedures, there has been an increased requirement to read back clearances and instructions. This makes sense as it confirms that what was instructed was correctly received and understood. However, in more congested airspace, the need for the transmissions to be clear, concise and correct the first time has become essential.

There is another significant factor. Most of the time you are out of sight. So your professionalism is measured by the quality of your radio transmissions—both the technical quality of the radio and the clarity and content of the message. Whether you are flying a Boeing 747 or a Cessna 150, the rest of the world only hears the radio calls. On that, you are judged, and on that alone. A trainee pilot can be just as professional as the Jumbo captain, and his/her radio can be equally well maintained. It is a matter of professional pride—as it should be.

And money is no excuse. We can practice aloud in the shower at no cost:

Hot Shower, this is November Four Five Kilo, request a straight-in approach?

November Four Five Kilo, you are cleared to land. The surface wind is light and variable. The temperature is two three. There is significant precipitation over the runway!

The VHF COM provides good line-of-sight voice communications.

This may sound a little childish, but it works. It is the same as an actor learning lines. It is not only the words themselves, but hearing yourself say them and how you say them that is important—with what clarity, what intonation, what ease of understanding. Pilots are no different to actors: it is just that our role has an immediate real-world effect, and how we play the role directly affects others in the same theater of operations. We have a responsibility to play our part well, and not to forget our lines.

VHF Radio

Many airplanes are equipped with at least one VHF radio, usually called VHF COM. This radio is for voice communication and is both a transmitter and receiver. Sometimes a second set is installed so the radios are called COM 1 and COM 2. Most airplanes also have a VHF navigation radio that is a receiver only and is called VHF NAV. This radio is used to receive signals from ground-based radio transmitters.

Figure 3-2 Radio/navaid stack.

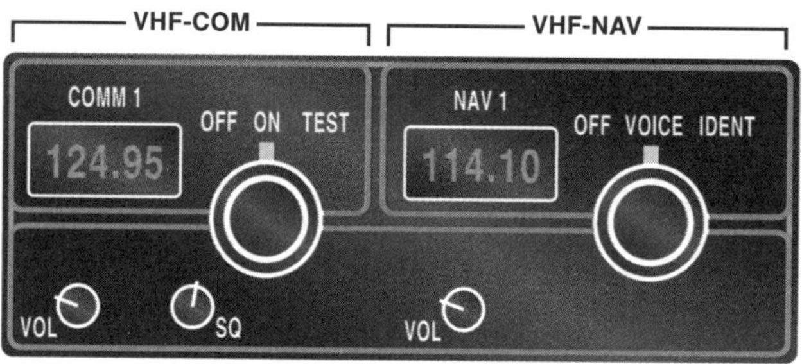

Figure 3-3 Combined VHF NAV/COM receiver.

Because VHF transmissions are line-of-sight (like TV), their effectiveness depends upon the distance to the other station and whether or not there are obstructions between the two stations. The following is a guide to the approximate coverage of VHF radio between an airplane and a ground station. The higher you go above the ground, the further you can receive radio signals.

- below 5,000 feet, the signal can be received up to 60 nautical miles; and
- from 5,000 to 10,000 feet, the coverage is 90 nautical miles.

Local conditions, such as mountainous terrain, may reduce VHF range. In recent years, automatic relay equipment located on the ground and in satellites has enabled long-range, high-quality communications using VHF (line-of-sight) frequencies.

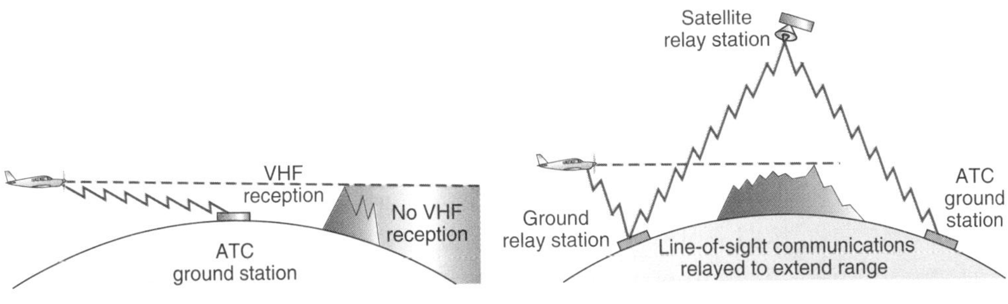

Figure 3-4 Satellite relay.

Radio Installation in the Cockpit

Avionics is an abbreviated term for aviation electronics.

Connected to the radios are:

- a transmit button (or press-to-talk switch) on the horn of the control column;
- a hand-held microphone;
- headset;
- speaker;
- intercom (for internal cockpit communications);
- an audio selector panel (in radio stack);
- the battery master switch; and
- possibly an avionics master switch.

When the airplane's engine is running, the electrical power to the radio is supplied by the alternator. When the engine is not running, the electrical power is supplied by the battery. Power is supplied to the radios via the on/off switch and, in some cases, the avionics master switch.

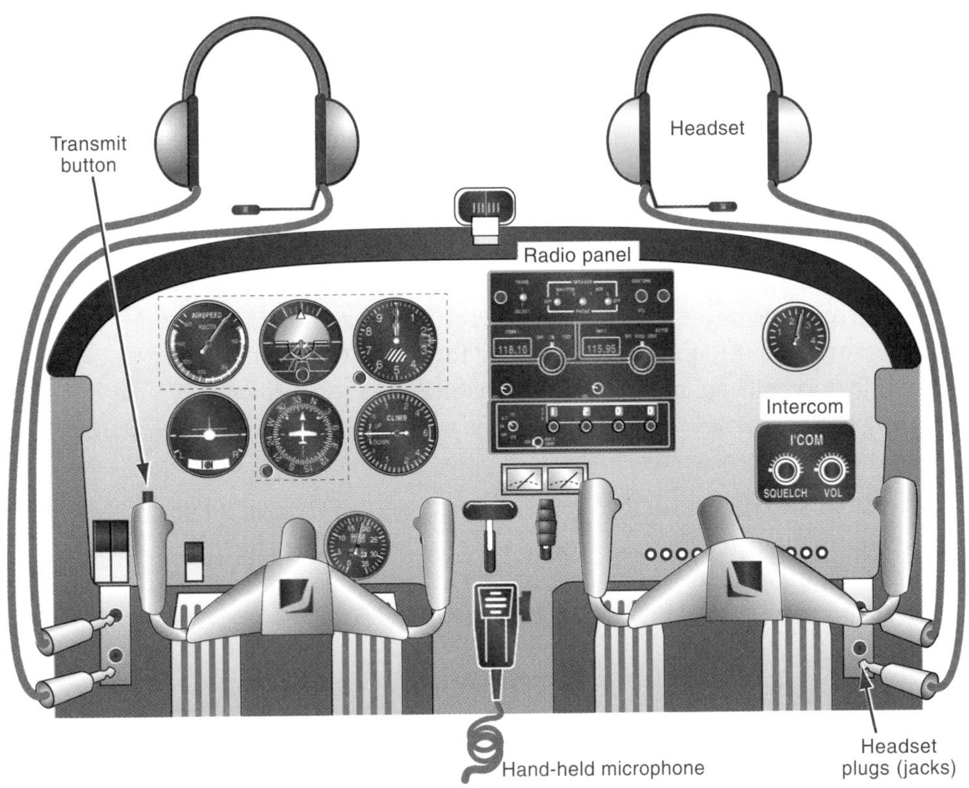

Figure 3-5 Communications system components.

Headset and Intercom

The headset has two plugs that are connected to a socket on the instrument panel or the center console. Training airplanes usually have headsets and an electronic intercom for communications within the aircraft. There will be a small intercom control panel with two knobs: one for volume and one for squelch. The squelch controls the sensitivity of the microphones. If the squelch is turned down, the background noise is removed, but the first word you speak may be clipped as it is used to trigger the sensitivity from a passive (quiescent) mode to active. Too much squelch and the background noise will keep the intercom active, but this may be distracting. It is a matter of finding the right balance.

Figure 3-6 Hand-held microphone.

Some headsets also have individual volume controls on the ear piece, so if everything is quiet, it may have been turned down on one or both sides. Touring aircraft may dispense with the headset and instead use a hand-held microphone and a loudspeaker in the roof of the cabin. This is not a good arrangement as there is no internal communications other than shouting, and the pilot's hand is occupied with the microphone instead of controlling the aircraft.

APPLICATION

Using the Headset

When the headset is comfortably fitted, check the earphone volumes are up and connect the two plugs. As soon as the battery master switch is turned on, the intercom will be active and can be set. However, it is better to set the levels of squelch and volume after the engine is started. After engine start, when the radio or avionics master switch is turned on, the main selector panel will be active and the radios themselves can be tuned and set.

The intercom works purely in a voice-activation mode. It is triggered when you speak, and the sensitivity is controlled by the squelch. Transmissions outside the aircraft are initiated by pressing the transmit button on the control column or on the side of the hand-held microphone (figure 3-6). Set the boom mike or hold the hand-held mike directly in front of your mouth so that your lips touch if puckered as for a kiss. Speak normally but avoid the tendency to rush the call or to shout. Speak positively and concisely, just as if you were giving directions rather than chatting.

While you are transmitting, no one else can.

The microphone is like a telephone with the important distinctions that:

- the transmit button must be depressed for you to transmit;
- while transmitting, most radio sets are unable to receive; and
- only one transmission from one station within range can occur on the frequency in use without interference.

Your COM set will continue to transmit as long as the transmit button is depressed. Even if you are not speaking, the carrier wave will continue to be transmitted, blocking out other stations that are trying to call on that particular frequency. So at the end of your transmission, ensure that the mike button is released.

Use of the VHF COM

Switching on the Radio

- Check that the master switch is on (and avionics power switch if applicable).
- Switch the radio on.
- Select the desired frequency. (It is digital and there is no need to tune.)
- On the audio panel, select the appropriate radio switches to speaker or phones as desired.
- Adjust volume to desired level and adjust squelch control (if installed) to cut out undesired background noise.
- Select transmitter to desired radio, i.e. COM 1 or COM 2.

Squelch Control

Eliminate the unwanted noise with the squelch control.

The function of squelch is to eliminate unwanted weak signals that cause background noise (*static* or *hash*). Noise makes it difficult to hear the desired stronger signals. Some squelch controls are automatic and others are manual.

To adjust the manual squelch control:

- turn the squelch up high (i.e. clockwise) until strong background noise or static is heard; then
- rotate the squelch knob counterclockwise until the noise just disappears (or is at least at an acceptably low level).

This means that unwanted noise from weak signals is electronically suppressed, allowing only the strong signals to be heard. (Squelch is like a net, or filter, that only allows strong signals to pass through to the receiver, making life easier for the busy pilot.) Turning the squelch down too far may also cut out the signal that we want to hear as well as the unwanted noise. Many radios have concentric knobs for frequency selection, and some have a combined volume and squelch control knob that has to be pulled out for squelch setting.

What If the Radio Does Not Work?

- If there is no noise in headset, even your own, check earphone volumes and plug connections. Check that the intercom is on, volume and squelch is up.
- If you are hearing the instructor okay but not yourself, check the microphone plug is fully in.
- If having to puff to trigger voice, the intercom squelch is set too low.
- If the intercom is okay but there is no radio reception, set the audio selector panel to phones and correct radio. Check that the radio is on, avionics master is on, radio on the correct frequency, and radio squelch is set. If still no reception, check the second radio on same frequency.
- If the reception is weak, check the squelch and volume or try other radio.
- If there is no reply to your transmissions, note whether there is a sidetone, i.e. a change in the nature of your voice and a slight hiss as you talk with the transmit button depressed. If no sidetone and the intercom is normal, try the second radio. If you can only receive the intercom, then use the hand-held mike to talk to the tower.

Transmitting

You can identify yourself as a student pilot so the controller can assist you with the procedures if necessary.

Before transmitting, there are some basic rules that you must always follow:

- Listen on the frequency to be used and avoid interference with other transmissions. If another station, be it another aircraft or an air traffic control (ATC) unit,is transmitting and if a response to its call is awaited, *do not interrupt.* Be particularly aware of this in the rare situation of hearing a distress (mayday) call, or an urgency (pan-pan) call. Of course, if you wish to transmit a distress or urgency call, then you are entitled to interrupt any transmissions of lower priority.
- Decide what you want to say. For most communications, use a standard radio phraseology, which is easily learned. This simplifies things for both parties: the person transmitting and the person receiving. Avoid long silences and hesitation sounds (*ah*, *um*, *er*, etc.) during your transmission. Having the wording of your intended transmission clearly in your mind (or even written down) prior to pressing the transmit button will help you to avoid hesitation.

Figure 3-7
Plan what you are going to say.

When using a microphone:

- Actuate the press-to-transmit or press-to-talk switch (PTT) before commencing to talk, and do not release it until after your message is completed.
- Speak with the microphone close to or just touching your upper lip.
- Do not significantly vary the distance between your lips and the microphone.
- Speak directly into the microphone.
- Speak a little slower than normal, but at normal volume; do not raise your voice or shout, and do not speak in a whisper.
- Pronounce each word clearly and ensure that you clearly annunciate the end of the word. Running words together, or slurring them, may make reception difficult.
- Pause briefly before and after the transmission of numbers.

Standard Words and Phraseology

The most important thing in radio communication is that the message gets across efficiently and the frequency is not blocked unnecessarily. In aviation, English is the internationally accepted language for radio communications, and whenever possible, standard phraseology should be used.

Pronunciation of Letters and Numbers

In transmitting individual letters, the following standard words should be used. Stress the syllables that are printed in capital letters. Thus, in the word *November*, the second syllable *vem* is emphasized so that it is pronounced *no-VEM-ber.*

If you are transmitting single digits, then you should use the following words, stressing the syllables in capitals.

It is especially important to differentiate between five (pronounced *FIFE*) and nine (pronounced *NIN-er*) because, when spoken normally, they are often confused. If there is a decimal point in the number, then it is indicated by the word *DAY-SEE-MAL* or *POINT*. For example, an instruction to N8147B to change frequency to 118.3 MHz would be transmitted as:

Four Seven BRAH-VOH,
contact Scottsdale Tower on WUN WUN AIT DAY-SEE-MAL THREE.

The phonetic alphabet may also be used whenever it is thought necessary to spell a word to ensure correct understanding of a message (such as the names of towns in position reports) if radio reception is poor or if there is any confusion.

The phonetic alphabet is a way for all pilots and air traffic controllers to understand each other.

Letter	Word	Transmitted as	Letter	Word	Transmitted as
A	Alfa	AL fah	N	November	no VEM ber
B	Bravo	BRAH VOH	O	Oscar	OSS car
C	Charlie	CHAR lee	P	Papa	pa PAH
D	Delta	DELL tah	Q	Quebec	key BECK
E	Echo	ECK oh	R	Romeo	ROW me oh
F	Foxtrot	FOKS trot	S	Sierra	see AIR rah
G	Golf	golf	T	Tango	TANG go
H	Hotel	hoh TELL	U	Uniform	YOU nee form
I	India	IN dee ah	V	Victor	VICK tor
J	Juliette	JEW lee ETT	W	Whiskey	WISS key
K	Kilo	KEY loh	X	X-ray	ECKS ray
L	Lima	LEE mah	Y	Yankee	YANG key
M	Mike	mike	Z	Zulu	ZOO loo

Number/Numeral Element	Pronunciation
0	ZE-RO
1	WUN
2	TOO
3	THREE (or TREE)
4	FOW-er
5	FIFE
6	SIX
7	SEV-en
8	AIT
9	NIN-er
decimal	DAY-SEE-MAL
hundred	HUN-dred
thousand	TOU-SAND (or THOUSAND)

An easy way to learn the phonetic alphabet is, as you drive your car, to practice it aloud using the registration numbers of passing cars. ETV 309 would be pronounced:

ECK-oh TAN-go VICK-tor THREE ZE-RO NIN-er.

Call Signs of Aircraft

The most common use of the phonetic alphabet is for aircraft call signs. US civil aircraft have an identification number that consists of the prefix letter N followed by a group of numbers and letters. While operating locally, it is usual to use only the last three numbers or letters of the registration following the initial call-up. For example, *N8147B* would become *Four Seven Bravo.*

Registration Call Sign	Transmitted as:
N8147B	November 8147 Bravo
N8PB	November 8 Papa Bravo

For the initial call, the aircraft type and full call sign is included, for example, Cessna 8147 Bravo.

Transmission of Numbers

All numbers shall be transmitted by pronouncing each digit separately (e.g. 10 is *WUN ZE-RO*, 236 is *TOO THREE SIX*), except for:

- whole hundreds (e.g. 500 is *FIFE HUN-dred*);
- whole thousands (e.g. 7,000 is *SEV-en TOU-SAND*); and
- combinations of thousands and whole hundreds (e.g. 7,500 is *SEV-en TOU-SAND FIFE HUN-dred*).

The meteorological way of expressing cloud cover is in eighths of the sky covered. Eighths in radio transmissions is expressed as *oktas*. A little over half the sky covered, say, five eights, would be expressed as *FIFE OKTAS*.

Headings

Compass and radar headings are read as other numbers:

- 120° is one two zero;
- 185° is one eight five; and
- 300° is said as three hundred.

Runway Direction

Runway direction (the numbers on the threshold) is to the nearest ten degrees:

- 27 (270° ±5°) is runway two seven; and
- 05 (050° ±5°) is runway five.

Transmission of Time

Because airplanes are continually moving from one time zone to another, it is standard practice in aviation to use a specific time reference known as *zulu* (Z). Zulu time is the equivalent of Greenwich meantime (GMT) and coordinated universal time (UTC).

In aviation we use the 24-hour clock, the day beginning at 0000 and ending 24 hours later at 2400 (which is of course 0000 for the next day). For example:

- 8:30 in the morning is 0830.
- Midday (12 noon) is 1200.
- One hour later, 1 pm, is 1300 (i.e. 1200 plus 1 hour).
- 4:30 in the afternoon is 1630 (i.e. 1200 plus 4:30).
- 8 pm is 2000 (i.e. 1200 plus 8:00).
- 8:17 pm is 2017.

When transmitting time it is usual only to say the minutes of the hour. For example:

- 0815 is transmitted as WUN FIFE (or ZE-RO AIT WUN FIFE);
- 1720 is transmitted as TOO ZE-RO (or WUN SEV-en TOO ZE-RO);
- 2300 is transmitted as TOO THREE ZE-RO ZE-RO; and
- 0400 is transmitted as ZE-RO FOW-er ZE-RO ZE-RO or four hundred hours.

However, if there is any possibility of a misunderstanding or if your estimated time of arrival (ETA) is after the next o'clock, then the hour in zulu time should also be included.

Relationship of Standard Times to UTC

To convert local standard time to coordinated universal time:

- West Coast (Pacific)—add 8 hours, e.g. 0800 becomes 1600;
- Mountain—add 7 hours;
- Central—add 6 hours; and
- East Coast—add 5 hours.

Note: Do not forget variations due to daylight saving.

Standard Procedural Words and Phrases

The most important result in communication is for your message to be clearly understood. For this reason, you should use plain language and simple phrases. To make radio communications uniform, some standard words and phrases have been devised. Their meanings are clear. They are brief and so occupy less air time. Whenever possible, you should use this standard phraseology.

The air traffic controllers are your partners in the use of radio and will use standard phraseology whenever they can. If you cannot recall the appropriate standard phraseology for your particular situation, or if there is no standard phrase for the information that you wish to convey, then just go ahead and use plain, concise English.

Word/Phrase	Meaning
Acknowledge	Let me know that you have received and understood this message.
Affirm	Yes.
Approved	Permission for proposed action granted.
Break	I hereby indicate the separation between portions of the message (to be used where there is no clear distinction between the text and other portions of the message).
Break break	I hereby indicate separation between parts of a message directed to different stations in a very busy environment.
Cancel	Annul the previously transmitted clearance.

Continued on next page

Continued from previous page

Check	Examine a system or procedure (no answer is normally expected).
Cleared	Authorized to proceed under the conditions specified.
Confirm	Have I correctly received the following...? *or* Did you correctly receive this message?
Contact	Establish radio contact with...
Correct	That is correct.
Correction	An error has been made in this transmission (or message indicated) the correct version to...
Disregard	Consider that transmission as not sent.
Go ahead	Proceed with your message.
How do you read?	What is the strength and readability of my transmission? The readability scale is: 1. Unreadable. 2. Readable now and then. 3. Readable but with difficulty. 4. Readable. 5. Perfectly readable. The strength is also from 1 (very weak) to 5 (strong)—5 by 5 is perfect.
I say again	I repeat for clarity or emphasis.
Monitor	Listen out on (frequency).
Negative	No *or* Permission is not granted *or* That is not correct.
Over	My transmission is ended and I expect a response from you (not normally used in VHF communication).
Out	My transmission is ended and I expect no response from you (not normally used in VHF communication).
Readback	Repeat all or the specified part of this message back to me exactly as received.
Re-cleared	A change has been made to your last clearance and this new clearance supersedes your previous clearance or part thereof.
Report	Pass me the following information.
Request	I should like to know or I wish to obtain.
Roger	I have received all of your last transmission (under NO circumstances to be used in reply to a question requiring READBACK or a direct answer in the affirmative or negative).
Say again	Repeat all or the following part of your last transmission.
Speak slower	Reduce your rate of speech.
Standby	Wait and I will call you.
Verify	Check and confirm with originator.
Wilco	I understand your message and will comply with it.
Words twice	This is used rarely: as a request—"Communication is difficult. Please send every word or group of words twice"; or as information—"Since communication is difficult, every word or group of words in this message will be sent twice."

Radar

Primary Radar

A primary radar is a device that transmits an energy pulse (at radio frequency) and relies on part of that energy to be reflected back to a receiver that converts the time and angle information into bearing and distance. This type of system is used for weather radars. The return signal is called an *echo* or *skin paint.*

Secondary Radar

While major airports have primary radars, most rely on *secondary surveillance radar* (SSR) for positive traffic information as the strength and clarity of the return allows it to be used to greater distances, and the signal can also be encoded for aircraft altitude and identification. An SSR system requires an interrogator station (which is also a ground radar and which triggers a response) and an airborne responder for it to determine an aircraft position and identification. The aircraft equipment is known as a *transponder.* It is literally a transmitting responder. The transponder has several operating modes:

OFF	Power is off.
SBY	Standby power on, ready to operate.
ON	Will transmit the window code if interrogated.
ALT	Will transmit the window code and the aircraft altitude if interrogated.
TST	Test function, transmits code once.

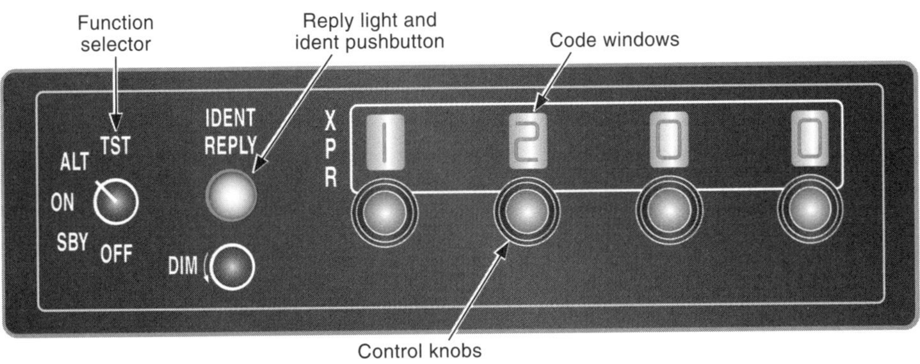

Figure 3-8 Transponder control panels

Codes

Air traffic control will assign you a discrete transponder code when required. The code for VFR aircraft not participating in radar information services is 1200. Other than the 1200 code, at this stage you need only remember two other codes:

- 7600, which will indicate to the ATC that you have a radio failure (and why you are not talking to them); and
- 7700, which indicates a serious emergency (mayday).

These codes trigger alarms on the ground.

When making routine transponder code changes, select standby and avoid inadvertent selection of codes 7500, 7600, or 7700.

Transponder Response

The transponder is normally operated in the ALT mode. This means that when it is interrogated, its transmitted response is the code that is set together with the aircraft's altitude (in relation to the datum that is set). The air traffic controller will see the code and altitude on a screen that is then marked with your call sign. This gives the controller a complete three-dimensional picture of the aircraft's distance, bearing, flight path, speed and altitude from the radar site.

Activate the ident feature (button) only upon request of the ATC controller.

If the controller is not receiving a correct response from your aircraft, you might be requested to *reselect code, recycle transponder* or *squawk ident*. To transmit (squawk) without being interrogated, simply select TST momentarily on the mode switch.

TCAD/TCAS

Many small aircraft are now equipped with a traffic alert and collision avoidance device (TCAD). The TCAD can provide:

- audio alert;
- distance from other aircraft; and
- altitude difference from other aircraft.

TCAD relies on the air traffic control radar illuminating both aircraft and triggering the transponders so it will work near major airports but not in remote areas. Large aircraft are equipped with a traffic alert and collision-avoidance system (TCAS). The TCAS does not rely on air traffic radar illumination because the system is coupled with its own interrogator/transmitter to trigger other aircraft transponders. All require the target transponder to be turned on.

Summary

When changing codes, always select SBY first and then reselect ALT after a new code is set.

It is vital that, if a transponder is installed in your aircraft, you turn it on for all operations as follows:

- In the pattern, leave it set on 1200 and SBY.
- In the training area and outside controlled airspace (in Class G), set 1200 and ALT.
- In controlled airspace, set ALT and the code nominated in the airways clearance.

Automatic Dependent Surveillance–Broadcast (ADS-B)

FAA Next Generation Air Transportation System (NextGen) ADS-B technology is replacing conventional SSR to identify aircraft operating within the National Airspace System (NAS). ADS-B consist of two different services, *ADS-B Out* and *ADS-B In*. As of January 1, 2020, all airspace requiring the use of a transponder will now require all aircraft to be equipped with an FAA approved ADS-B Out system. Aircraft equipped with ADS-B Out must be operating in transmit mode at all times. The transponder itself will still operate and function similarly to SSR from within the cockpit, but the main difference is how the signal is transmitted and received. Instead of radar, ADS-B technology uses GPS satellites and ground-based transceivers to decode the information and relay it to ATC facilities as seen in figure 3-9. This technology provides a quicker and more precise way to track an aircraft's three-dimensional position and velocity.

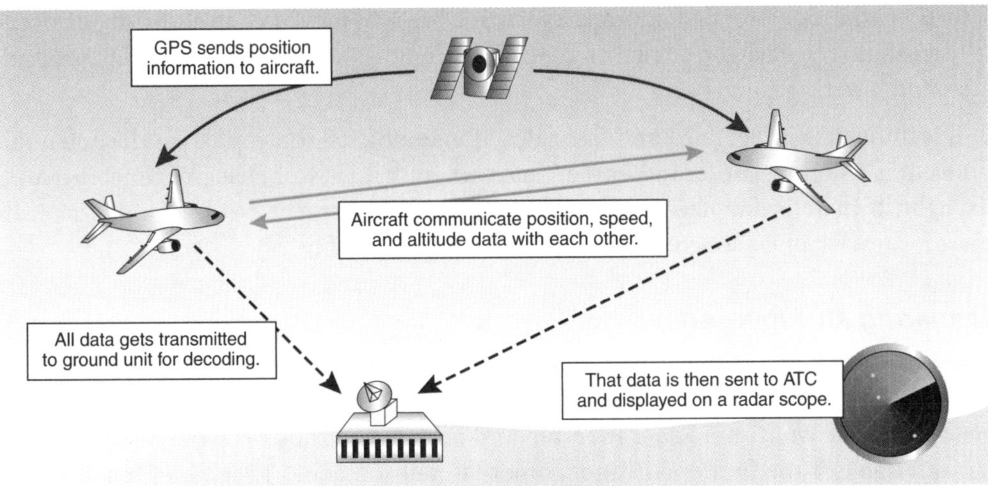

Figure 3-9 ADS-B network

Traffic Information Service–Broadcast (TIS-B)

ADS-B In is an optional capability that provides pilots with traffic information via TIS-B delivered directly to the cockpit, enhancing both situational awareness and safety. Aircraft properly equipped with this added capability can receive traffic position reports of other aircraft operating within a specified coverage area below FL240. From within the cockpit, the pilot will have the capability to see air-to-air targets and radar targets sent from ground-based transceivers on instrument displays.

Emergency Radio Procedures

Request assistance whenever you have any serious doubt regarding the safety of a flight. Transmission should be slow and distinct, with each word pronounced clearly so that there is no need for repetition. This of course should apply to all radio transmissions, but it is more important in emergency situations. If you do find yourself in real difficulty, waste no time in requesting assistance from ATC or on the appropriate CTAF or UNICOM frequency. Timely action may avoid an even more serious emergency.

What is Considered to be an Emergency?

The pilot has the ultimate responsibility for the safety of the aircraft.

It is impossible to cover all the possibilities here. The declaration of an emergency by the pilot in command is an area for your operational judgment. Emergencies can be classified according to the urgency and to the degree of seriousness of the consequences.

As the pilot, you decide, but always err on the safe side. Some categories might be:

- no urgency of time but need assistance, such as being uncertain of position and unable to confirm direction to proceed but with plenty of fuel and remaining daylight;
- some urgency of time, such as uncertain of position with fuel reserves or remaining daylight less than an hour or so;
- some urgency and potential for serious consequences, such as loss of oil pressure, rough-running engine or fuel depletion that may leave insufficient fuel to reach an airfield;
- potential seriousness but not yet developed, such as some doubt about the serviceability of the aircraft or systems, or the medical condition of the pilot;
- potential seriousness but no urgency, such as loss of primary attitude indicator with eight oktas of cloud but plenty of fuel and daylight; and

- potential catastrophe and urgency, such as risk of loss of control due to reduced visibility or daylight or risk of controlled flight into terrain due to rising ground and lowering cloud base.

It is impossible to set hard-and-fast rules. If in doubt, tell someone what the potential problem is and do it earlier rather than later, when there is still plenty of time, fuel and daylight. If there is any urgency, formally declare an emergency, at least a *pan-pan*. If there is any risk of loss of control or injury, declare a *mayday*.

Declaring an Emergency

Radio can play a vital role when assistance is required; however, in an emergency, remember always the first priority is to control and position the aircraft.

If an emergency arises, it is your responsibility as pilot in command to assess just how serious the emergency is (or could be) and to take appropriate safety action. Many emergencies require your immediate attention and occupy you fully for some moments, but it is advisable at the first opportune moment to tell someone. There are three degrees of emergency and, as pilot in command, you should preface your radio call with either:

- *mayday* (repeated three times) for a distress call;
- *pan-pan* (repeated three times) for an urgency call; and
- *security* (repeated three times) for a safety call.

Distress Message (or Mayday Call)

Mayday example:
Pilot:
Mayday, mayday, mayday, This is Cessna N8147D, two zero miles west of Scottsdale at this time, altitude four thousand, engine failure, forced landing in open country, two persons on board.

Distress is the absolute top priority call. It has priority over all others, and the word *mayday* should force everyone else into immediate radio silence. Mayday is the anglicized spelling of the French phrase *m'aidez*! which means *help me*! When you require immediate assistance and are being threatened by grave and immediate danger, the following applies:

- the mayday distress message should be transmitted over the air-ground frequency you are presently using;
- if you are currently using a UNICOM or tower frequency and receive no response to your distress call, and if you have time, repeat the call on the area frequency as shown on the sectional chart;
- if still no response, and if time permits, change frequency to 121.5 MHz (the international emergency frequency usually monitored by airliners and some ground stations) and repeat your distress call; and
- if your aircraft is transponder-equipped, squawk code 7700 (the emergency and urgency transponder code) which, if you are in a radar environment, causes a special symbol to appear around your aircraft on the ATC radar screen and rings an alarm bell immediately alerting the ATC radar controllers.

Urgency Message (or Pan-Pan Call)

Pan-pan example:
Pilot:
Pan-pan, pan-pan, pan-pan, Seattle, this is Cessna N8147D, two zero miles south of Vancouver at three zero, heading two five zero, airspeed nine zero knots, three thousand feet, experiencing severely reduced visibility in fog, descending to land in a clearing.

The urgency or pan-pan message is made over the frequency in use when an emergency exists that does not require immediate assistance. Typical situations when a pan-pan message is appropriate include the following:

- experiencing navigational difficulties that require the assistance of ATC or flight service;
- carrying a passenger on board that has become seriously ill and requires urgent attention;
- seeing another airplane or a ship whose safety is threatened and urgent action is perhaps needed; and
- making an emergency change of level in controlled airspace that may conflict with traffic below.

Loss of Radio Contact

In the event of a total radio failure, there is a standard system of light signals used for communications to and from the control tower.

Light Signals to Aircraft		
Light Signal	**Meaning in Flight**	**Meaning on the Ground**
Steady green	Authorized to land if pilot satisfied no collision risk exists.	Authorized to takeoff if pilot satisfied no collision risk exists.
Steady red	Give way to other aircraft and continue circling.	Stop.
Green flashes	Return for landing.	Authorized to taxi if pilot satisfied that no collision risk exists.
Red flashes	Airfield unsafe. Do not land.	Taxi clear of landing area in use.
White flashes	No significance.	Return to starting point on airfield.
Alternating red and green	Exercise extreme caution.	Exercise extreme caution.

Emergency Locator Transmitter

If you have never seen an *emergency locator transmitter* (ELT) before, ask your flying instructor to show you one and if possible have your instructor go through the procedures for its activation. This will certainly make this section a little more meaningful to you. The emergency locator transmitter is also known by other names:

- VHF survival beacon (VSB); and
- emergency locator beacon (ELB).

We will refer to the beacon as the emergency locator transmitter or ELT. The ELT is a VHF radio transmitter capable of sending a signal simultaneously on the international distress frequencies: 121.5 and 243 MHz. Each unit has its own power source (battery), so before setting out on a flight where the carriage of an ELT is required, *check that the battery recharge date (stamped on the ELT) has not expired.* When activated, emergency locator transmitters transmit on the international standard emergency frequencies of 121.5 MHz and 243 MHz. Since 121.5 MHz lies within the frequency band receivable by VHF COM radios, it is recommended that pilots listen to this frequency once or twice on each long flight and report any signals heard. This will ensure that an early report of an ELT activation is received by a rescue coordination center, allowing earlier detection of a possible emergency situation.

Figure 3-10
ELT antenna (nearest).

ELTs can easily be activated unintentionally, possibly causing unnecessary rescue action to be commenced and putting other people at risk. For this reason, you should ensure that your ELT is not inadvertently activated. As a check, it is a good idea to monitor the VHF COM radio briefly on 121.5 MHz prior to leaving the taxiing area at the commencement of a flight and also when taxiing back to the parking area at the completion of the flight. If an ELT signal is detected, check the status of your own ELT and, if the signal is from another ELT, report reception of the signal to the nearest air traffic controller.

REVIEW 3

Communications

1. What is the phonetic alphabet used for? What is each letter transmitted as? Say HAPPY in phonetics.
2. What is MHz?
3. What is amplitude?
4. Should the squelch be set at minimum or maximum or somewhere in between?
5. Why have a transmit button on the control column?
6. Is the transmit button the same as the PTT?
7. What significance does the word mayday have?
8. What transponder mode is set for pattern operations?
9. If the radio fails completely in the traffic pattern, what would you do?
10. What do the letters ELT stand for?
11. What is the significance of VHF COM versus VHF NAV?
12. About how far can you expect to receive VHF transmissions from an altitude below 5,000 feet?
13. What are the pros and cons of a hand-held microphone versus a headset?
14. If another aircraft says "how do you read me" and the transmission is faint and the clarity is blurred, what numbers, in regard to readability, would you choose?
15. True or false? ADS-B Out is required for operations in controlled airspace unless otherwise authorized.
16. If the oil pressure drops slowly, would you declare an emergency, and if so, what call would you make?
17. If the radio fails completely in the training area, what would you do?
18. In the event of no noise whatsoever in your headset, what actions and checks would you undertake?
19. What is the international VHF distress frequency?
20. What do you do if you are on the final approach and see a red light from the control tower?

Answers are given on page 575

4
Your First Flight

OBJECTIVES

To experience and recall:

- the local operating environment;
- the airplane you will learn to fly; and
- the concepts of *attitude* and *situational awareness.*

Figure 4-1
Discussion dispels uncertainty.

CONSIDERATIONS

The first flight is called the *trial instructional flight, air experience flight* or *trial lesson.* Unlike a scenic flight, you will be seated in the pilot's seat and will have the opportunity to feel the controls. On the morning of your first flight, have a light breakfast—cereal or toast. It is important to have something to eat, but avoid the traditional bacon and eggs. Call the flight school to check the weather or, better still, leave your contact number when you book the flight and the instructor will call you if there are any difficulties or delays. Similarly, if you can't make it for any reason, call and cancel so another appointment can be made. It is completely normal to feel a mixture of excitement and slight nervousness before your first flight. This is a normal reaction to an unknown situation, and it will soon disappear when you get started.

Arrival

The flight school will welcome you and perhaps give you some general information on the school, the airport and the aircraft you are to fly.

Your introductory flight lesson will be your first opportunity to test out the pilot's seat—make yourself comfortable and relax.

Briefing

Your instructor will talk to you about the flight and will be able to answer your questions. He or she will give a *briefing*, which is a description of where you will be going and what you will be doing. Tell the instructor you are reading this book and ask for the call sign of your aircraft. It helps to show you are keen!

Figure 4-2
My call sign is …

Walkaround

Ask to accompany the instructor on the preflight inspection, or *walkaround* as some call it. This is primarily a check of important items such as the following:

- fuel and oil quantities are physically checked;
- a sample of fuel is taken to ensure it contains no water;
- the flight controls are checked to ensure that all function correctly and locks have been removed;
- the exterior is inspected for external damage to make sure no bird-strikes or other damage was sustained from the previous flight;
- the windows are checked to be clean;
- the engine compartment is examined for leaks; and
- all covers, flags, and plugs are removed.

How valuable it would be to do a similar predrive check of your car! With an aircraft, you have to. You can't stop in the air.

Entry

You will be shown how to enter, strap yourself in with the seatbelt and shoulder harness and adjust the seat as well as plug in your headset. The instructor will show you the control column and how to raise and lower the nose and to bank the aircraft left or right. You will be shown the throttle and how to increase or reduce power. You will also be shown the two instruments of importance on this flight: the airspeed indicator (calibrated in knots) and the altimeter (calibrated in feet).

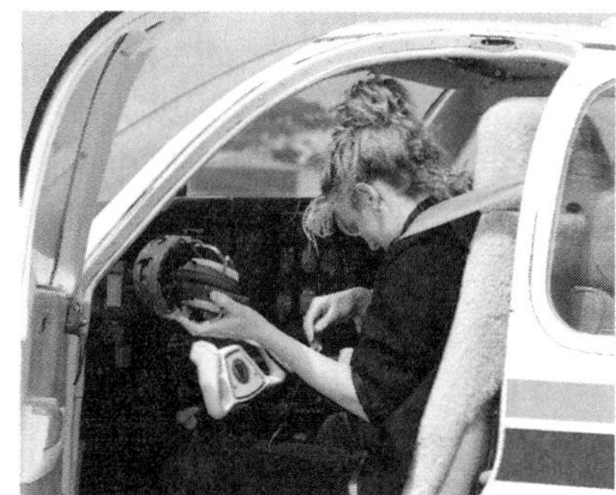

Figure 4-3 Strapping in.

Starting the Engine

The instructor will start the engine, which is a similar process to starting your car although the engine is *primed* with fuel before start. The instructor will call out "clear prop!" before start to warn people near the aircraft that the propeller is about to turn. When the engine is started, the instructor will appear to be very busy for a while as the oil pressure is checked, lights and radios are turned on and the control tower is listened to. The instructor will increase power, check the brakes are working correctly and away you will go.

Taxiing

Taxiing most light aircraft is easy. You adjust the speed with the throttle (or brakes if necessary) and steer with the rudder pedals. To steer, you slide each foot backward and forward: you push the left foot forward to turn to the left and the right foot forward to turn to the right. To brake, you depress the top of the pedals. Think of sliding your heels forward and back to steer and pressing your toes down to brake, independently or together.

Figure 4-4 Taxiing.

The instructor will probably taxi the aircraft on this first flight but may give you a try. If so, you will find that the brakes are firm but not very powerful—nothing like your car. An aircraft has more momentum and less braking and it is important to anticipate and allow plenty of stopping distance. Taxi speed should be no faster than a normal walking pace. It is difficult at first to brake in a straight line as your feet will press the brakes and forget to steer the nose wheel. But you will soon get the hang of it. The throttle should be set to produce the desired speed without having to brake to prevent the aircraft accelerating.

Takeoff

The instructor will be a little busy with radio calls but, hopefully, will describe the takeoff. The takeoff is simply a process of aligning the aircraft with the runway, increasing the power and keeping the aircraft straight until flying speed is reached. The instructor will then apply back pressure to the control column and raise the nose to a position that he or she knows will cause the aircraft to lift off at the correct speed. The instructor will then maintain this attitude until the aircraft is climbing positively and is clear of the ground. Please do not talk to the instructor during the takeoff.

Climb

The instructor will then climb the aircraft and turn toward the training area.

Cruise

When the aircraft has reached an altitude of about 2,000 feet, the instructor will show you the altimeter and the airspeed indicator and some of the local terrain features—perhaps your home. The instructor will then show you the most important aspect of flying you will ever learn: *attitude.*

Figure 4-5 Cruising.

APPLICATION

Controls

The airplane flies straight and level by default—the pilot is there to change the flight path.

The instructor has already shown you the control surfaces during the preflight inspection and the cockpit controls before engine start. In flight, the instructor will show you how forward and backward pressure on the control column lowers and raises the nose respectively, and how left and right movement of the controls causes a left and right rolling of the aircraft. Don't be afraid of the controls. The aircraft is naturally stable and resists any change. You are there to modify its flight path rather than struggle to keep it straight and level. An aircraft basically flies itself. It is like a bicycle. You just tilt and point it where you want to go.

To hold the control column correctly, simply place your left hand around the grip on the stick (or on the left horn of the yoke). Hold the control gently but firmly. It is just like holding a child's hand when you are crossing the street: you hold firmly enough so the child can't slip out of your hand but gently enough not to hurt them. Some people advocate holding the control with the thumb and forefinger only, as a means to teach you not to squeeze the control like a tube of toothpaste. Holding with two fingers actually causes you to hold more tightly as you have less grip. It is much better to have your whole hand gently in contact with the control column. Remember also to hold the control with your left hand only. It is not held with both hands like the steering wheel of a car. The right hand should be free for setting the engine controls, radios and the trim wheel.

Positive exchange of flight controls between instructor and student is a critical aspect of flight training.

When the instructor wants you to fly, he or she will say, "You have control." You then say, "I have control." Simply maintain the attitude, especially keep the wings level (parallel) with the horizon. You may notice the instructor reaching down and winding a small wheel backward or forward. This is the *trim* wheel, and it is used to balance changes in speed, power or weight that occur during the flight. The trim wheel is a form of fine-tuning and relieves the force that the pilot needs to apply to maintain the attitude of the aircraft. The instructor will operate the engine controls for this flight.

Attitude

The pilot controls the flight path of the aircraft by setting the attitude and the power and then checking the response of the aircraft by reading the instruments. Attitude is the most important piece of information that the pilot uses to control an aircraft, no matter whether it is your little trainer or a Jumbo jet. Remember attitude is simply the position of the nose of the aircraft in relation to the horizon. It is the "picture" that you see through the windshield. How accurately a pilot discerns and maintains the attitude determines how accurately and how easily the pilot flies the aircraft.

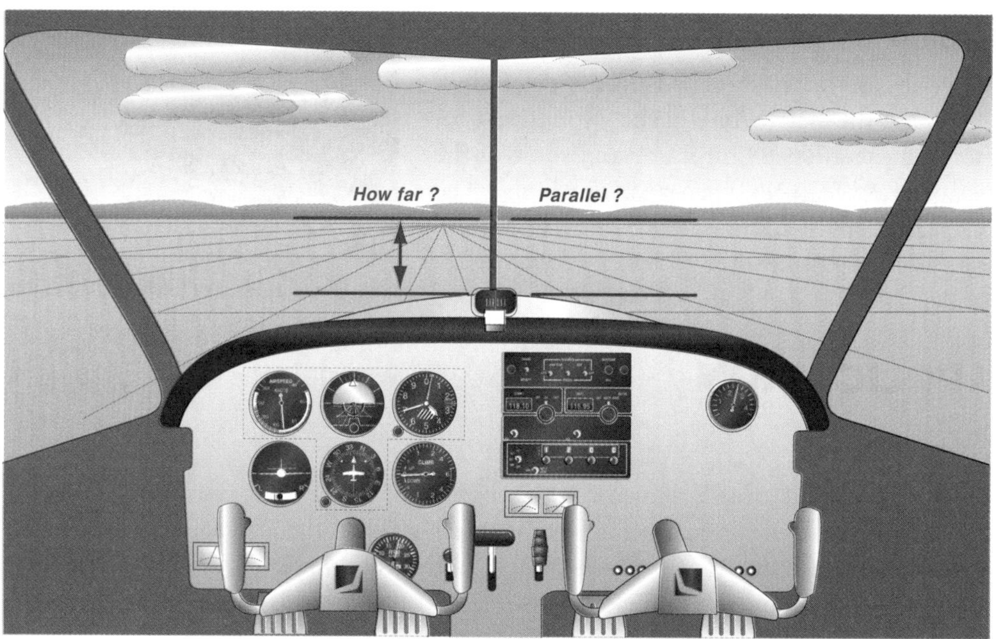

Figure 4-6 Pitch (how far above or below the horizon) and bank (whether parallel to the horizon or tilted, and by how many degrees).

Descent

For return to the airport, the instructor will reduce the power, lower the nose attitude and then trim the aircraft for this new attitude and power. As you relax and return to the airport, you may find that you will feel a little queasy. This is normal as you relax from the slight inner tension you may have had up to this point. Keep looking outside, especially at the horizon, and keep talking to the instructor.

Approach and Landing

The approach can be a busy time. If the traffic is not too busy, the instructor may describe what is happening. But don't worry. If you remember the operation of the controls and the importance of attitude, you will be well placed for your next flight—if, by now, you have been bitten by the aviation bug! Look around and note some of the major geographical features in you area. They will help you to locate and identify your airport for future flights.

Figure 4-7 Approach to land.

Debriefing

Ask your instructor to spend a little time explaining what you did, and he or she will record the flight in a pilot log book for you. You may have missed or forgotten much of it, and a brief discussion is most useful. When you get home sit down and relive the flight, in detail, in your mind. This reinforcement is of enormous benefit in cementing the information that was gained in an all-too-brief, intense flight.

Figure 4-8 Way to go!

Now you have been flying not just as a passenger but as a student pilot. You have operated the controls, and you now know some of the mysteries of the wonderful world of flight. Read as much as you can and ask lots of questions. Talk to other pilots, especially those with experience. It is time now to focus on some serious study of this hobby, sport and amazing profession. This study will form the foundation for all of your future training. It is that important.

Figure 4-9 Ask lots of questions.

REVIEW 4

Your First Flight

1. What was your call sign?
2. What type of aircraft did you fly?
3. Did the airplane have a high or low wing?
4. What was the HP of the engine?
5. Was the gear fixed or retractable?
6. Did the airplane have a fixed-pitch or constant-speed propeller?
7. What units does the airspeed indicator display?
8. What units does the altimeter display?
9. At what altitude and speed did you cruise?
10. What is the correct taxi speed?
11. What are the two measures of attitude?
12. What was the most enjoyable aspect of this flight for you?

Answers are given on page 576.

Aircraft Control on the Ground

5 Engine Starting

OBJECTIVES

To describe:

- the correct procedures for safely starting, running and shutting down the engine;
- the technique modified for starting a hot or cold engine; and
- the response to an engine fire on start.

Figure 5-1
Check all clear.

CONSIDERATIONS

The engine of a light aircraft may be started by turning it over using:

- the starter motor powered by the onboard battery (usual method);
- the starter motor powered by an external electrical power source; or
- by turning the engine over by rotating the propeller manually, known as *hand cranking* or *hand propping*.

The usual method uses the starter motor and onboard battery, and this is the method we discuss first. The other two are non-standard procedures.

Prior to starting the engine, check that the surrounding area is suitable for start-up. The airplane should be on a surface suitable for taxiing, preferably in a clear area well away from any buildings, fuel storage areas and public areas. It should be parked facing in a direction that will not cause loose stones or gravel to be blasted back over other aircraft or into open hangars when the engine is running. There should also be no fuel spills in the vicinity, as this creates a fire risk. The airplane should be manually moved to face into a strong wind prior to starting the engine.

The *parking brake* should be on prior to start to prevent any airplane movement during and after the start-up. The engine then needs to be properly prepared for the start-up. In extremely cold weather, this may include preheating the engine. The correct procedure for this is found in your pilot's operating handbook. Use the specified *checklist*, and do not miss any items. Ensure that no person is near the propeller by checking visually and by calling out "stand clear" loudly a few seconds before you engage the starter. It is important immediately the engine is started that you set the proper RPM and check the engine gauges for the desired indications, especially oil pressure to ensure that the engine is being lubricated and cooled adequately.

Entry/Egress

Traditionally, cockpit entry was via a single door (Piper, Beechcraft) or dual (Cessna) side doors.

Many sport aircraft have clear canopies which are hinged or slide for entry and may be jettisoned for emergency egress.

A very easy entry is provided by gull wing doors such as those fitted to the Tobago, Cirrus and Lightwing airplanes.

Figure 5-2
Traditional door entry (Cessna).

Figure 5-3
Side hinged canopy on the Sky Arrow.

Figure 5-4
Angled doors on Cirrus.

Engine Starting

The procedure for starting an engine varies for avgas and diesel, piston and turbine, two-stroke or four-stroke. It is vital to learn the correct procedures for starting your airplane in normal, very hot, and very cold conditions.

The descriptions here apply to the air-cooled, four-stroke gasoline piston engine fitted to most traditional general aviation aircraft.

Prestart and Starting Check

The prestart and starting checklist will include such items as:

- Seat locked into position and secure.
- Doors closed and locked with no harness strap outside that could flap about in the airstream.
- Brakes on.
- Unnecessary electrical equipment off—for example, radios.
- Master switch on (for electrical power).
- Fuel on, and suitable tank selected (some aircraft may also have an auxiliary electrical fuel pump to augment or boost the engine-driven fuel pump).
- Cowl flaps (if fitted) open.
- Carburetor heat control cold.
- Mixture rich.
- Throttle closed (or cracked one-quarter inch open).
- Fuel primer locked (one to three priming strokes to pump some fuel directly into the cylinders, if applicable; the priming pump may be manual or electrical).
- Rotating beacon on (as a warning to other people).
- Read the preflight checklist if applicable.

- Clear the area around the airplane, especially near the propeller. The pilot is responsible for people around the airplane, so loudly call clear to warn anyone that may be approaching the airplane.
- Starter engaged to crank the engine; then, when the engine has started, release the starter.
- Ensure that the airplane does not move (if it does, use the brakes); set the recommended RPM, and check normal indications on the engine gauges. Avoid using excessive engine RPM or creating an excessive engine temperature.

After starting, various items to be checked may include:

- Ensure airplane remains stationary.
- Oil pressure gauge shows sufficient pressure within 30 seconds of start-up (slightly longer in very cold weather—60 seconds maximum).
- Set the recommended RPM with the throttle—usually 1,000 to 1,200 RPM—to ensure adequate cooling.
- Ammeter indicating charging of the battery following the drain on it during start-up.
- Suction gauge checked for sufficient suction to operate the gyro instruments.
- Gyroscopic flight instruments erecting; when they have erected, align the heading indicator (HI) with the magnetic compass.
- Magnetos—check left and right magnetos individually, as well as with the ignition switch in the usual *both* position; the RPM should decrease slightly on each individual magneto and return to the previous value when the switch is returned to *both*, but if the engine stops, then a problem exists.
- Radios on, correct frequency selected, volume and squelch set; it is a good idea to select the emergency frequency 121.5 MHz on the VHF COM and check for inadvertent emergency locator beacon activation, before reselecting the local communications frequency.
- Lights—rotating beacon on, position lights and taxi light set as required.
- Electrical fuel pump (if fitted) off, to check operation of the engine-driven fuel pump.
- Complete the after-start checklist, if applicable.

Possible Problems During Start-Up

Most engine starts are uneventful if correct procedures are followed, but occasionally, a problem may occur. Refer to your pilot's operating handbook that may contain checks similar to those following.

Use of the Accelerator Pump

Many aircraft engines are fitted with a carburetor that has an accelerator pump operated automatically by the throttle. Any rapid inward movement of the throttle will send an additional burst of fuel into the carburetor to provide a rapid and smooth acceleration of the engine. If an engine is a little reluctant to start, a couple of quick pumps on the throttle will send extra fuel into the carburetor. This will richen the fuel-air mixture, and may assist the start-up.

The throttle-pumping technique slightly increases the risk of a fire since the extra fuel goes to the carburetor, whereas the primer sends fuel directly to the cylinders, bypassing the carburetor.

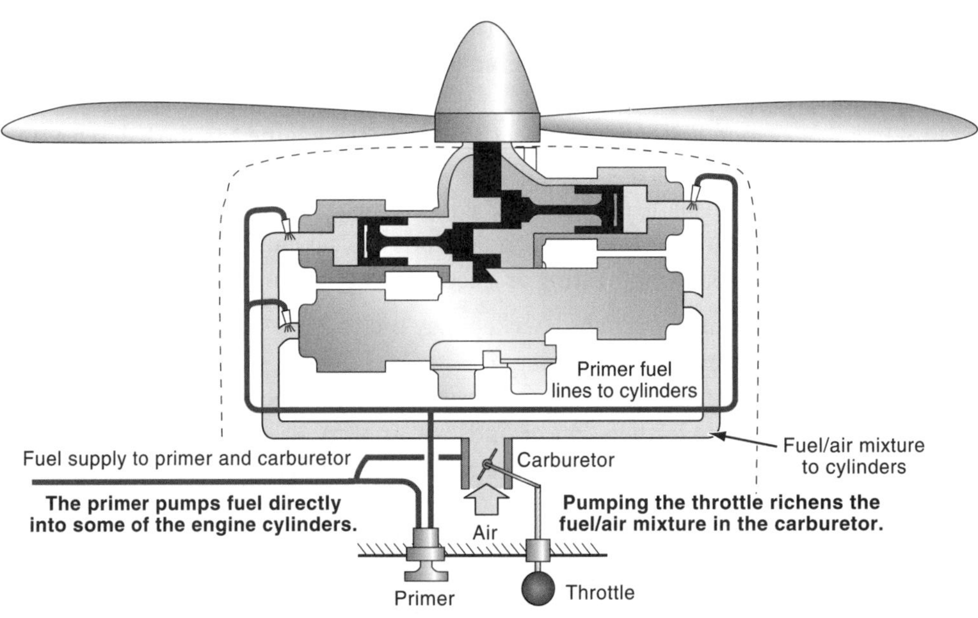

Figure 5-5 Pumping the throttle to activate the accelerator pump.

Electric Fuel Pump

All aircraft engines have an engine-driven fuel pump that operates when the engine is rotating to ensure a continuous supply of fuel to the engine. Some aircraft also have an electric fuel pump fitted as a backup in case of failure of the engine-driven fuel pump or to provide a boosted fuel pressure.

You can check the function of the electric fuel pump, prior to starting the engine, by switching the pump on and:

- watching the fuel pressure rise on the gauge; and
- possibly hearing it operate.

After start-up, it is good technique to switch the electric fuel pump off to ensure that the engine-driven fuel pump is delivering fuel to the engine satisfactorily (better to find this out on the ground than in flight!), but then switch it back on for takeoff and landing.

Starting a Hot Engine

Hot engines can become flooded with excess fuel.

Starting an engine that has just been shut down, especially on a hot day, may require a special technique. A hot engine often becomes flooded with excess fuel, with the resulting fuel-air mixture in the cylinders being too rich for a good start. The cylinders should be cleared of this excess fuel prior to start-up by either:

- cranking the engine through several revolutions using the starter motor; or
- by pulling the propeller through several times by hand, with the usual precautions for hand propping having been taken.

No *priming* should be necessary. A normal start should now be possible.

Advanced Techniques

If you commence a start that you expect to be normal, but then realize that the engine is flooded with excess fuel, you can continue the start by moving the throttle halfway to increase the airflow and so help clear out the excess fuel. This should bring the over-rich mixture back into the normal range and allow the engine to start. Immediately after the engine starts, close the throttle to avoid excessively high RPM, along with unwanted thrust and noise. If you are about to start an obviously flooded engine, use the technique described below.

A Flooded Engine

It is possible to flood an engine with too much fuel, making a start difficult and placing a strain on the battery. Sometimes the excess fuel can drain away naturally in about five minutes. If flooding is suspected *prior* to start-up, adopt the following procedure.

- Ignition switches off.
- Throttle fully open (so that maximum airflow through the carburetor will help clear the excess fuel out of the cylinders).
- Fuel on with suitable tank selected, but electric fuel pump off (to avoid pumping in unwanted additional fuel).
- Mixture control set to idle cutoff (no fuel is now being supplied to the engine).
- Crank the engine through several revolutions with the starter—this should clear the intake passages of excess fuel—or pull the propeller through several times by hand (taking suitable precautions).

Now repeat the starting procedure without priming the engine.

Starting in Very Cold Weather

Cold engines can be difficult to start.

The oil in an engine that has been very cold for some time becomes thick and will not flow easily. This means it cannot properly perform its functions of:

- lubricating, cooling and cleaning the engine; and
- forming a seal between the piston rings and the cylinder wall to gain maximum power from the combustion.

Airplanes operating continually from cold airports often use a lighter grade of oil in winter than in summer—for instance, the thinner SAE 30 in winter, and the thicker SAE 50 in summer—or a multi-grade oil. If the oil is suspected of being too cold and too thick, then the engine may be *preheated*, typically using an electric heater to blow hot air over the engine. Another technique is to turn the engine over by hand by pulling the propeller through. This will loosen the oil and get it moving. Be sure to read the following paragraphs on hand propping before you try this technique, to ensure that you do not accidentally start the engine (chocks in place, brakes on, throttle closed, set mixture to idle cutoff, magnetos off). The technique used to start a very cold engine is:

- first create a rich mixture by priming the engine (using the manual or electric priming pump to send fuel directly into the cylinders), and consider pulling the propeller through a few times to loosen the oil and get it moving;
- follow the normal starting procedures and checklist, but be prepared to continue priming the engine, sending fuel directly into the cylinders, until the engine has warmed up, then lock the primer, otherwise the mixture in the cylinders could be too rich causing the engine to run roughly or even stop;
- immediately apply carburetor heat after start-up to assist in warming the engine; and
- allow the engine to idle for a few minutes, if necessary, until it warms up and the oil is at normal operating temperature and able to circulate normally through the engine and perform its functions.

Engine Fire on Start-Up

Engine fires are a rare event these days, but they can still occur, possibly as a result of over-priming the engine with fuel. In such a case:

If the engine starts:

- throttle—set about 1,700 RPM for a few minutes (to suck the fire through); and
- engine—shut down and inspect for damage.

When the fuel has been eliminated, the fire should stop. Release the starter.

If the engine fails to start:

- if still engaged, continue cranking the starter (to suck flames and accumulated fuel through the carburetor and into the engine);
- mixture control to idle cutoff (to stop fuel supply to the engine);
- fuel selector off; and
- throttle open (to allow maximum airflow through to purge the induction system and engine of fuel).

If the fire continues:

- ignition switch off;
- master switch off;
- fuel shutoff valve off or closed;
- brakes on; and
- evacuate, taking the fire extinguisher with you.

Figure 5-6
External power supply.

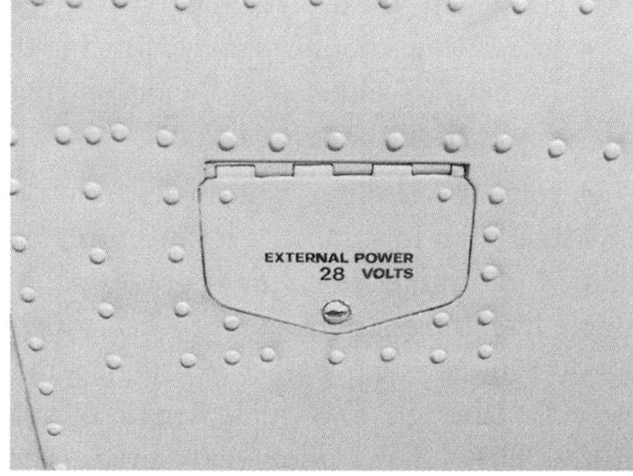

Figure 5-7
External power receptacle.

Supplementary Starting Methods

External Power Source

Some aircraft have a ground service plug receptacle that permits the use of an external electrical power source for the following purposes:

- engine start, especially in very cold weather when difficult starts can drain the battery; and
- providing electrical power during periods when lengthy maintenance work is being carried out on electrical and avionics equipment.

The external power source should be suitable for your aircraft and should be plugged in to the ground service plug receptacle using correct positive/negative polarity. This normally disconnects the onboard aircraft battery from the aircraft circuitry. Using an external power source will preserve the charge of the aircraft battery. Information regarding the use of an external power source will be found in the pilot's operating handbook, Section 9 on supplements. You should refer to your POH before using any external power source, since procedures and checklists to use before and after an external-power start-up vary between aircraft types. Ensure that the external power source is removed and placed clear of the aircraft before taxiing away.

Hand Cranking

If not performed correctly, hand cranking (or hand propping) can be dangerous, either from the engine starting unexpectedly because of a loose or broken magneto groundwire, or by compression in the cylinders causing the propeller to kick back. Training from a flight instructor or mechanic on how to hand crank a propeller is absolutely essential. Always have a pilot or mechanic in the cockpit and at the controls, and have a briefing of the required actions and call outs before starting the procedure.

Hand cranking (propping) means turning the engine over by manually rotating the propeller, rather than using the electric starter motor.

Do not consider hand propping an airplane unless you have received expert instruction in the procedure.

Ensure that the parking brake is on and that the wheels are chocked, to prevent the airplane moving forward when the engine starts. Never hand crank an aircraft without a person in the cockpit. The propeller is usually hand cranked from the front but another technique is to stand behind the right side of the propeller (as seen from the cockpit), so that the airflow pushes you away from the propeller.

In-Flight Restart

If the engine stops providing power in flight (possibly from fuel starvation caused by an empty tank or an iced-up carburetor, or by a faulty ignition system), it may be possible to restart it if you can rectify the cause of the stoppage.

- *If the propeller has stopped rotating,* you can use the starter motor to turn the engine over.
- *If the propeller is windmilling in the airstream,* there is no need to use the starter motor at all—just introduce fuel and ignition, and the engine should start.

AIRMANSHIP

Always perform each check thoroughly and read the appropriate checklist carefully. Do not just respond to a checklist item automatically, but actually check that the item has been accomplished or the switch position is correct before answering the checklist challenge. Reading checklist challenges and responses aloud is a good technique, especially when two pilots are in the cockpit. Always be aware of any person standing near the propeller or moving toward it, even when the engine is stopped. Always treat the propeller, even when stationary, as a lethal weapon, and set a good example by never leaning against it. Never board or deplane passengers while the propeller is turning.

REVIEW 5

Engine Starting

1. Are loose stones a potential hazard for engine start-up?
2. Is a clear area preferable to a crowded area as one in which to start the engine?
3. Name three ways to start an engine on the ground.
4. How should the parking brake be set for start-up?
5. For an engine start, should you systematically follow the approved before-starting and starting procedures, and read the appropriate checklists?
6. Before starting the engine, should you check outside for other people? Do you need to loudly call out "stand clear?"
7. Immediately after the engine starts, do you need to check that the airplane is not moving forward?
8. Should you check the engine gauges as soon as the engine starts? If so, which one in particular?
9. Does oil pressure take longer to rise in hot weather?
10. For a normal start, how should the throttle be set?
11. Does using the priming pump send fuel into the carburetor or cylinders?
12. Pumping the throttle actuates which pump? Where does this send a burst of fuel?
13. What position should the mixture control be in when clearing a flooded engine of excess fuel by turning it over using the starter motor? What position should the throttle be set?
14. Information on using an external electrical power source for engine starts can usually be found in which section of the pilot's operating handbook? What is the title of this section?
15. Should you hand crank an airplane if you have not received expert instruction?
16. Is it safe to deplane passengers while the propeller is still turning?
17. Is it essential that all checklists, both normal and emergency, be followed precisely?
18. Is the electric starter motor required for an in-flight restart of an engine that has stopped providing power but the propeller is still wind-milling?

Answers are given on page 576.

6

Taxiing and Pretakeoff Checks

OBJECTIVES

To describe:

- the procedures and techniques for taxiing an aircraft;
- the right of way for surface movement; and
- the run-up and pretakeoff checks.

CONSIDERATIONS

Taxiing—Control on the Ground

Speed

Control of forward speed of an airplane on the ground is via individual wheel brakes. These are most commonly operated by the pilot depressing the upper part of the rudder pedal. However, some types have heel operated pedals (Piper Cub) or hand levers (Jabiru and Sky Arrow).

Direction

The direction of the airplane on the ground is controlled by one of the following options:

- steerable nosewheel or tailwheel—connected to the rudder pedals where fore and aft movement is used to steer and still depression of the pedals applies the wheel brakes.
- differential braking—by applying brake pressure to one side the aircraft changes in direction. The nosewheel casters (follows the changing direction). The Cirrus, Grumman and many Light Sport Aircraft (LSA), including the Cessna 162, are steered by differential braking.

  Note: Aircraft with nosewheel steering have some provision for further displacement of the nosewheel if the turn is tightened by use of differential braking.

Figure 6-1 Australian lightwing has a castering nosewheel.

Clearances and Radio Calls

Your local airport will have specific procedures to be followed before taxiing. Some require a clearance from the ground controller, some an advisory radio call, and for others no call is required. Check with your instructor.

ATIS

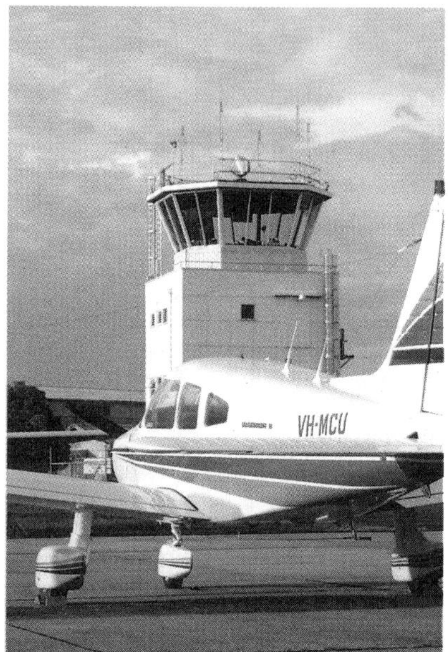

Figure 6-2 Listen to the ATIS.

Always listen to the automatic terminal information service (ATIS) if available. It will not only advise the runways in use but also any unserviceable areas, obstructions and, if crosswind circuits are in progress, which runway crossings require a specific clearance.

Plan Your Taxi Path

Engine power is required to start the airplane moving; directional control is achieved using the rudder pedals, with the occasional assistance of differential braking if necessary; stopping is achieved by frictional drag on the wheels, assisted by brakes when necessary.

Aircraft wheels are usually chocked when the airplane is parked for long periods. The chocks must be removed prior to taxiing. Most aircraft have a parking brake that can hold them stationary without the use of chocks.

To taxi an airplane means to move it about on the ground under its own power.

A reasonable taxiing speed is a *fast walking pace*, provided you are on a clear taxiway. In a confined space, such as an apron congested with parked aircraft, the taxiing speed should be much less.

To determine the active runway (also known as the runway in use), you can:

- listen to the automatic terminal information service (ATIS), or otherwise call UNICOM or the flight service station; or
- look at the wind direction indicator.

It is good airmanship to know where you are going to taxi before you actually start moving.

At simple, single-runway airports, the best taxi path will be easy to determine. At more complicated airports, you may have to study an airport chart showing the taxiway and runway layout to determine the best route to take.

Runways are numbered by their magnetic direction, rounded off to the nearest 10°. For instance, a runway aligned with 264 degrees magnetic (°M) would be called Runway 26; in the opposite direction, 084°M, the runway would be known as Runway 8 or Runway 08.

If two runways are parallel, they will be designated right and left, as seen from the approach and takeoff direction—for example, 19L and 19R. At major airports there may even be a center runway—for example, Runways 3C and 21C at Detroit Metropolitan.

Study the airport chart prior to taxiing at an unfamiliar airport so that your taxi route from the parking area to the takeoff holding point follows the shortest and most expeditious route. The same applies when taxiing back to the parking area after landing. Some airports have a simple layout (for example, Santa Ynez, California); others are more complicated (for example, Las Vegas, Nevada, with the various taxiways designated by letters, such as *taxiway Bravo* and *taxiway Delta*, parallel runways, and the need for clearances to taxi and to cross runways).

You many also seek assistance from ground control by asking for a *progressive taxi* where you will be given advice on how to reach your desired location.

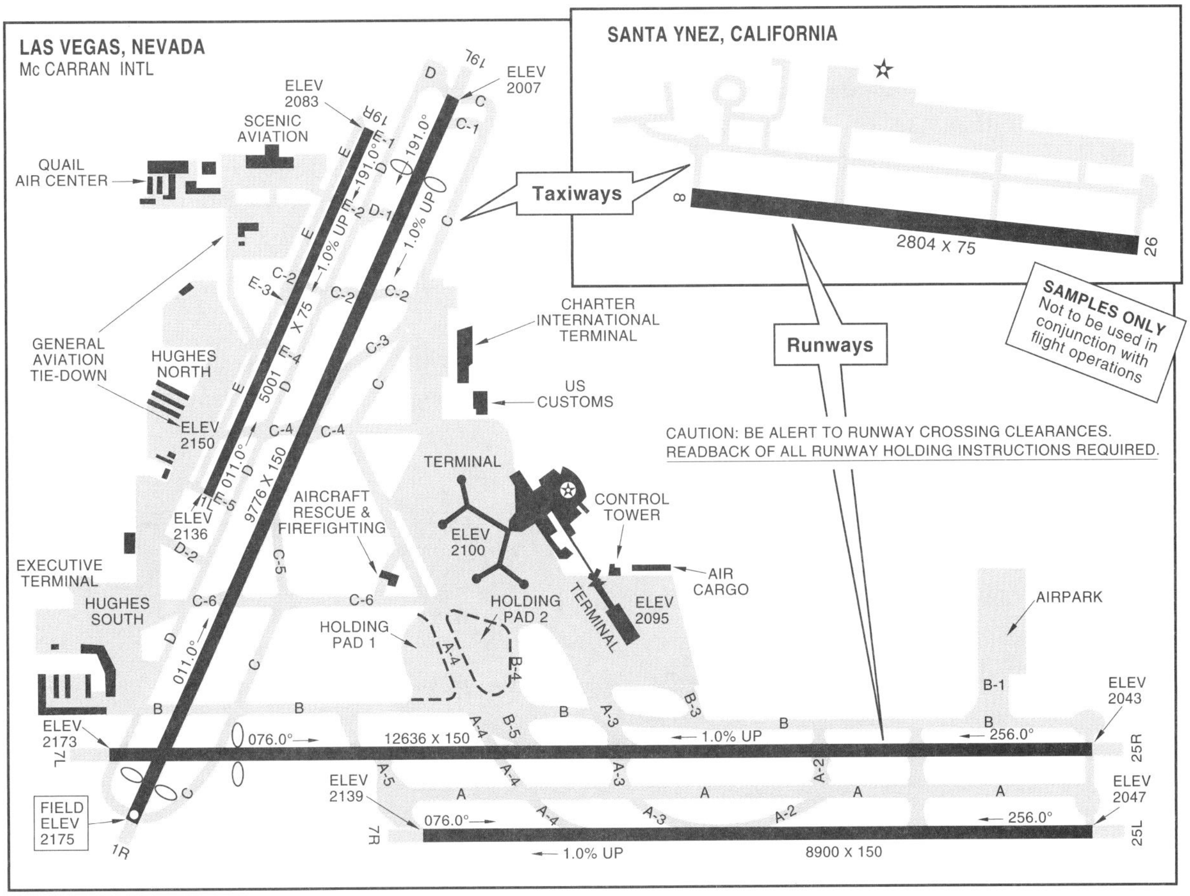

Figure 6-3 Taxiway and runway layout for Santa Ynez, CA and Las Vegas, NV.

Look Out

You must maintain a good lookout ahead and to the sides when you are taxiing; adequate wing tip clearance from objects such as buildings and other aircraft is essential.

Keep a good look out when taxiing—especially in confined areas.

Figure 6-4 The view from the cockpit when taxiing.

The shadows that your wings throw onto the ground sometimes help. On a crowded tarmac area, have an experienced person marshal you or provide wing tip guidance. In a very tight situation, you can even shut down the engine, complete the shut down checklist, then hand-maneuver the airplane.

Taxi vision is usually good in a nose wheel aircraft, but it may be obstructed by the nose of a tail wheel aircraft. In this case, you may have to zig-zag along the taxiway to give yourself a clear view of the area ahead by looking out the sides of the cockpit.

Taxiway Markings

Taxiway markings are yellow. The taxiway centerline may be marked with a continuous yellow line, and the edges of the taxiway may be marked by two continuous yellow lines six inches apart.

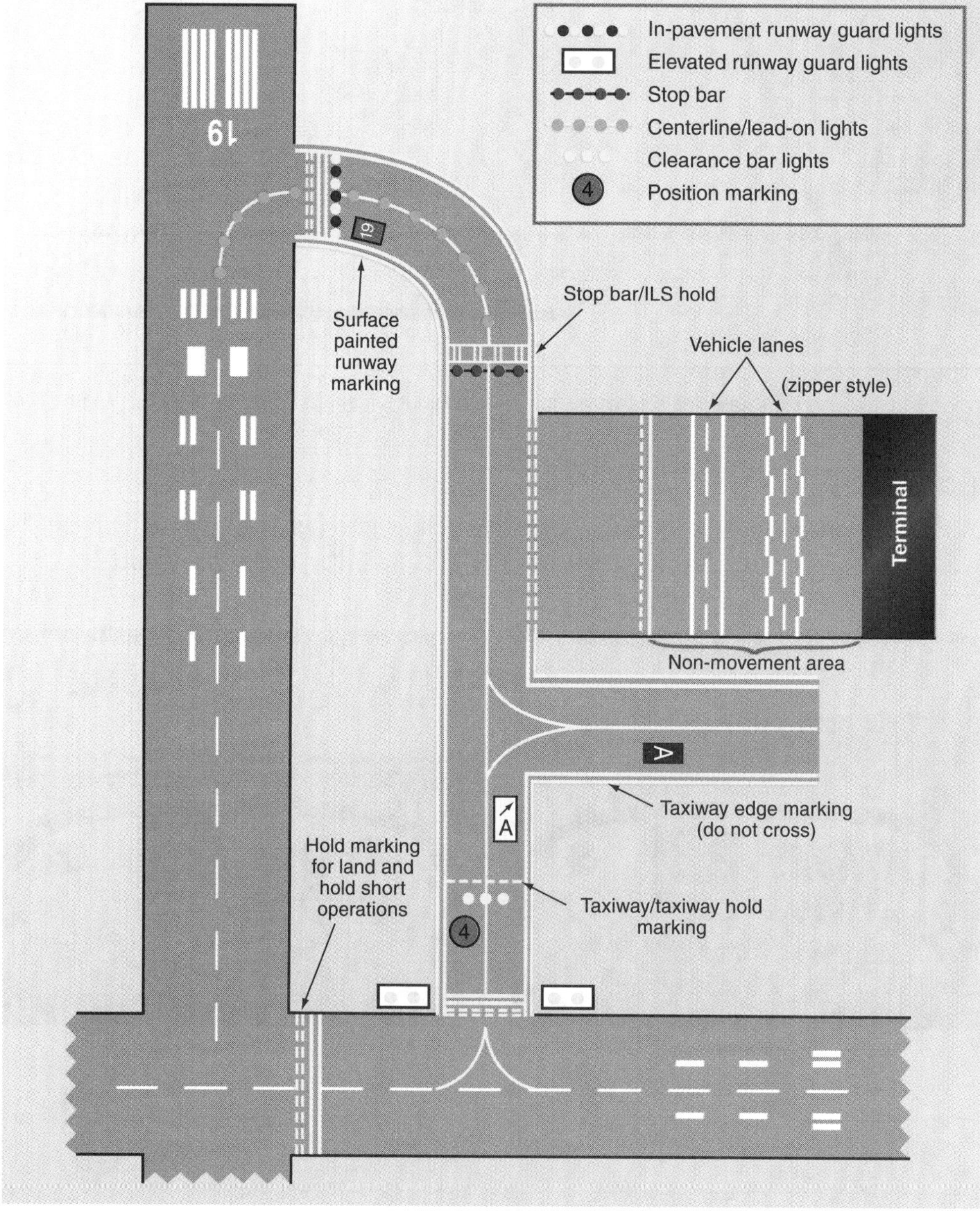

Figure 6-5 Taxiway markings.

Taxiway *holding lines* across the width of the taxiway consist of two continuous and two dashed yellow lines, spaced six inches between dashes. The two continuous lines are on the side from which an aircraft will approach a runway when taxiing, and if instructed to hold short of the runway or if not cleared onto the runway, then you should stop with no part of the aircraft extending beyond the holding line. There may be *holding signs* at the edge of the taxiway, with white characters on a red sign face. An aircraft exiting the runway after landing is not considered clear of the runway until all parts of the aircraft have crossed the holding line.

Taxi Clearances

At airports with an operating control tower, you should obtain a clearance to taxi to the takeoff runway. Your request for a taxi clearance should include:

Listen to ATIS prior to calling for your taxi clearance.

- the station called;
- your call sign;
- your location on the airport;
- a request for taxi instructions;
- type of operation planned (VFR or IFR); and
- destination or direction of flight.

If you have a radio communications failure while taxiing at a tower-controlled airport, light signals from the tower mean the following:

- steady red—STOP;
- flashing red—taxi clear of the runway in use;
- flashing green—cleared for taxi (i.e. to taxi back in and have the radio fixed);
- steady green—cleared for takeoff;
- flashing white—return to starting point on airport; and
- alternating red and green—exercise extreme caution.

For example:

Pilot: *Hagerstown Ground Control,*
Beechcraft three eight seven four Alpha,
at city ramp, ready to taxi,
departing VFR northwest bound.

Tower: *Beechcraft seven four Alpha,*
Hagerstown Ground Control,
wind calm, altimeter two nine point nine five,
taxi Runway Two,
contact tower one two zero point three when ready for departure.

Some typical taxi clearances provided by ATC at other airports with operating control towers include:

Tower: *Runway One Eight, taxi via Taxiway Echo.*

This clearance permits you to taxi along the designated taxi route to the assigned runway. You may cross other runways that intersect the taxi route, but you may not cross or enter the assigned runway.

Tower: *Runway One Eight, taxi via Taxiway Echo, hold short of Runway Two Seven.*

This clears you to taxi along the designated taxi route toward the assigned takeoff runway (Runway 18), but only as far as the holding point prior to Runway 27. A further taxi clearance is required to proceed. It may take the form of something like: "Cross

Runway Two Seven without delay." Leave your radios tuned to the ground frequency until ready to enter the runway for takeoff. Read back any "hold short of runway" instructions issued by ATC.

Taxi Intentions

At airports without an operating control tower (where a clearance to taxi is not required), you should advise your taxi intentions on the appropriate common traffic advisory frequency (CTAF).

Pilot: *Vero Beach Radio,*
Cessna five one three six Delta,
ready to taxi, VFR,
departing to the southeast,
request airport advisory.

Runway Incursions

Entry to a runway without clearance presents a major hazard to yourself and to other aircraft, perhaps even large aircraft that cannot maneuver to avoid you. Do not enter or cross any runway unless you are certain that you have a clearance, that you are on or entering the correct taxiway and that there is no chance of conflicting traffic. Otherwise, stop, wait and call.

Right of Way on the Ground

Taxiing frequently occurs on crowded tarmacs and taxiways. Five guidelines, understood and followed by all pilots when taxiing, make life easier for everybody.

- Regardless of any ATC clearance, it is the duty of the pilot to do all possible to avoid collision with other aircraft or vehicles.
- Aircraft on the ground must give way to airplanes landing or taking off, and to any vehicle towing an aircraft.

If in any doubt, STOP!

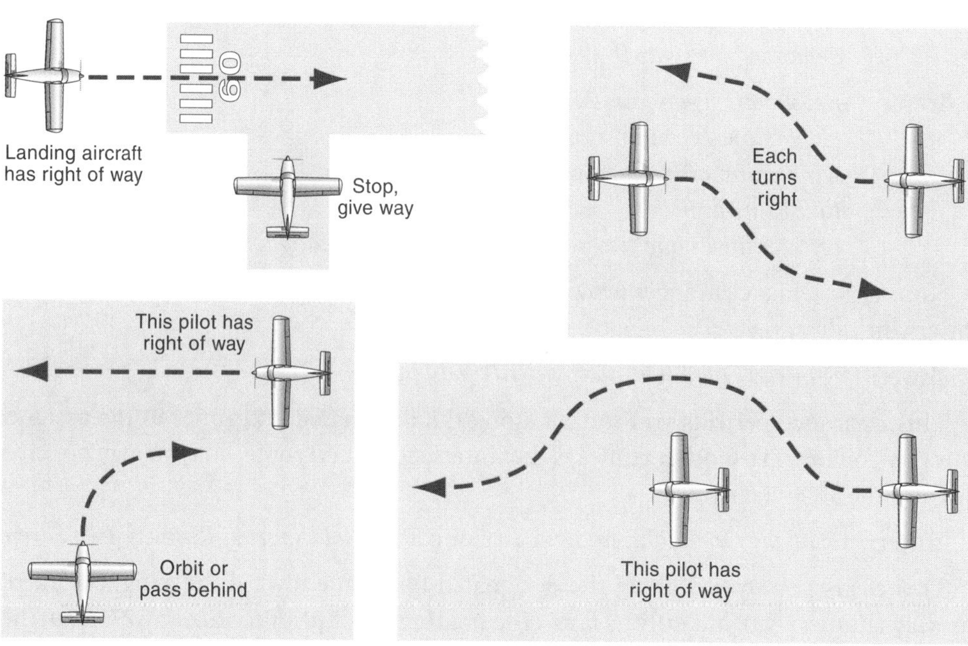

Figure 6-6 Right-of-way guidelines for taxiing.

- Two aircraft taxiing and approaching head on or nearly so should each turn right.
- When two aircraft are taxiing on converging courses, then the one that has the other on its right should give way and avoid crossing ahead of the other aircraft unless passing well clear.
- An aircraft that is being overtaken by another should be given right of way, and the overtaking aircraft should keep well clear of the other aircraft.

APPLICATION

Marshaling

Although the pilot is ultimately responsible for the safety of the airplane on the ground, taxiing guidance on a tarmac area may be given by a marshaler. Some of the basic signals are illustrated, but you should only follow them if you consider it safe to do so. On a crowded tarmac or in very strong winds, it may be preferable to have wing tip assistance from experienced personnel, or to shut down the engine and move the airplane by hand or with a tow bar.

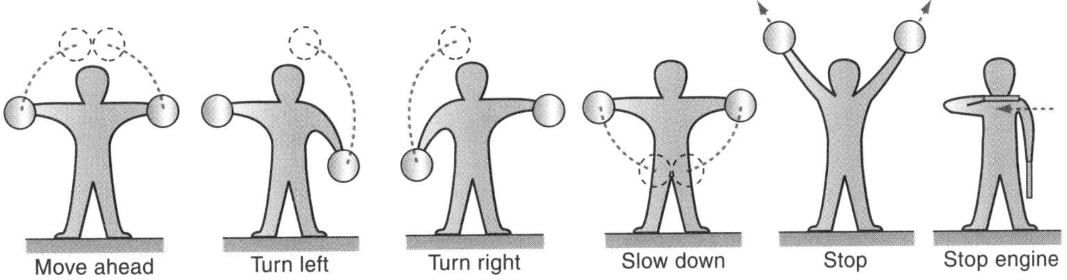

Figure 6-7 Some useful marshaling signals.

Taxiing Speed

Power is used to commence taxiing an airplane. The effects of wheel friction and the brakes are used to stop it. Like all objects, an airplane has inertia and is resistant to change, so it requires more power to start moving than to keep moving. Once the airplane is rolling at taxiing speed, the power can be reduced simply to balance the frictional forces and any air resistance so that a steady speed is maintained. On a straight and smooth taxiway with no obstructions, a fast walking pace is a safe taxiing speed, and this can be judged by looking ahead and to the left of the airplane. In a confined area, the ideal speed is somewhat less.

Figure 6-8
Use minimum power and taxi slowly.

The amount of power required to maintain taxiing speed depends on the ground surface and its slope, a rough, upward-sloping, grassy surface requiring much more power than a flat, sealed taxiway. High power may also be required to turn the airplane, especially at low speeds.

Use power and brakes to control speed.

To slow the airplane down, the power should be reduced. Friction may cause the airplane to decelerate sufficiently, otherwise the brakes can be used gently, but firmly. Generally speaking, power should not be used against brakes; that is, if you wish to slow down, first close the throttle. It is a waste of energy to have excess power and be slowing the aircraft with braking. It will lead to overheated brakes and increased brake wear, and if you need maximum braking to abort a takeoff, it will not be available.

Some aircraft have engines with a high idle RPM, and occasional braking may be required to avoid excessive taxi speed. Also, some aircraft have a castering nose wheel and therefore the aircraft is steered by brakes. In this instance, it is almost inevitable to have some power applied while trying to brake and steer. There is a natural tendency to steer with the control column and, of course, nothing happens. In this case, taxi for a while with your hands on your lap. It is usual to hold the control column while taxiing but only to protect the control surfaces from being damaged by wind gusts or to prevent the wind lifting the tail or wing.

TECHNIQUE

Moving Forward

Before commencing to taxi, plan the path that you will follow, taking note of the surface and the position of other aircraft. Ensure that tie-down ropes and chocks have been removed before releasing the parking brake. Check that the tires are correctly inflated and the tread is acceptable. Soft tires increase friction, reduce steering and braking effectiveness. Worn tires will skid on wet surfaces and may deflate when heated.

Figure 6-9 Taxi at a walking pace.

As soon as the aircraft starts to roll, retard the throttle and check the brakes. If there is any softening of the resistance in the pedals, then do not taxi. Stop and shut down the engine. Maintain a normal walking pace, and avoid using power against brake (unless a high idling speed is required for better engine cooling). Cross ridges and small ditches at an angle, avoiding long grass and rough ground, and have an escape route in mind in case of brake failure. Hold the control column to prevent wind gusts from deflecting the control surfaces, and hold the control column rearward when crossing bumps or soft surfaces.

On the taxiway, check the rudder and flight instruments (gyros) for correct operation. Whenever the airplane is stopped, the parking brake should be applied and the engine set to fast idling speed. Usually the engine will idle at 600–800 RPM, but this may be too slow to warm the engine and charge the battery. It is usual to set 1,000–1,200 RPM for this purpose.

Braking and Steering Technique

Steer with your feet when taxiing.

Brake cylinders are situated on top of each rudder pedal. They are individually applied using the ball of each foot. Normally, taxi with your heels on the floor and the balls of your feet on the rudder pedals, thereby avoiding inadvertent application of the toe brakes. When braking is needed, slide your feet up and, with the ball of each foot, apply the toe brakes as required. To brake the airplane while taxiing in a straight line, both brakes should be applied evenly, but you may have to steer with the rudder pedals at the same time. There is a tendency to freeze the rudder movement while applying the brakes. It is simply a matter of practice.

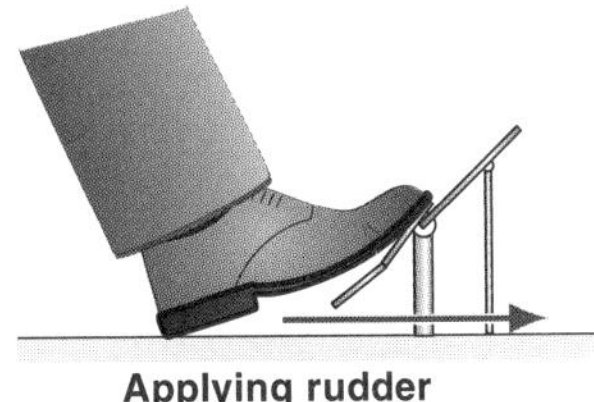

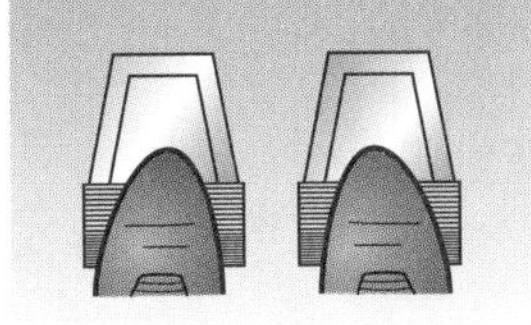

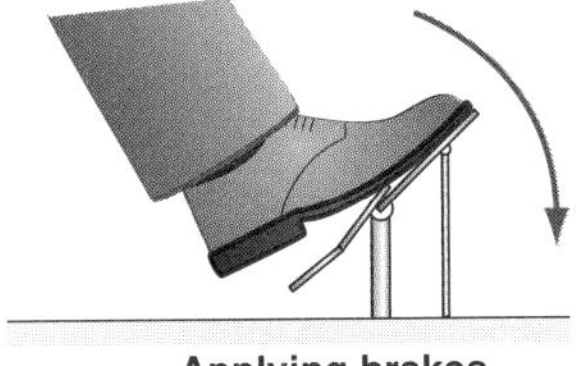

Figure 6-10 Using rudder and toe brakes.

Power should not be used against brakes.

Brakes should be used gently so that the airplane responds smoothly; harsh braking being avoided except in an emergency. For a normal stop, a good technique is to relax the braking pressure (or perhaps even release it) just as the airplane comes to a halt. The resulting stop will be smooth. Differential braking is available by pressing each toe brake individually. This is useful both for turning sharply and for maintaining directional control when taxiing in a strong crosswind.

Test the brakes early. During extended taxiing, the brakes should be tested occasionally, and they should certainly be tested just prior to entering a congested tarmac area. Pay due attention to the ground surface, especially in wet weather when taxiways and tarmacs can become slippery. Always have an escape route in mind to avoid collisions in case the brakes fail to stop the airplane.

Allow for the fact that the wings of an airplane are wide and the tail-section is well behind the main wheels. Maintain a good lookout ahead and to the sides. If the taxi path is obscured by the nose, then turning slightly left and right will permit a better view. Should you unfortunately run into something while taxiing, stop the airplane, shut down the engine, set the brakes to park, turn the master switch off and investigate.

Brake Failure

If the brakes fail:

- close the throttle; and
- steer away from other aircraft and obstacles toward a high-friction surface if possible (e.g. grass).

If a collision is imminent:

- retard the mixture control to idle cutoff;
- turn off the fuel;
- switch off the ignition; and
- turn off the master switch.

Ground Surface Condition

Ensure that propeller clearance will be adequate when taxiing in long grass or over rough ground, especially if there are small ditches or holes. Striking grass or the ground can seriously damage the propeller and the engine.

When taxiing on loose surfaces, minimize the use of high power.

Loose stones or gravel picked up and blown back in the slipstream can also damage both the propeller and the airframe. Damage may even be caused to other airplanes or persons quite some distance behind. So when taxiing on loose surfaces, avoid the use of high power as much as possible. Small ridges or ditches should be crossed at an angle so that the wheels pass across the obstruction one at a time. This will minimize stress on the landing gear and avoid the nose pitching up and down excessively, which not only stresses the nose wheel but also puts the propeller at risk.

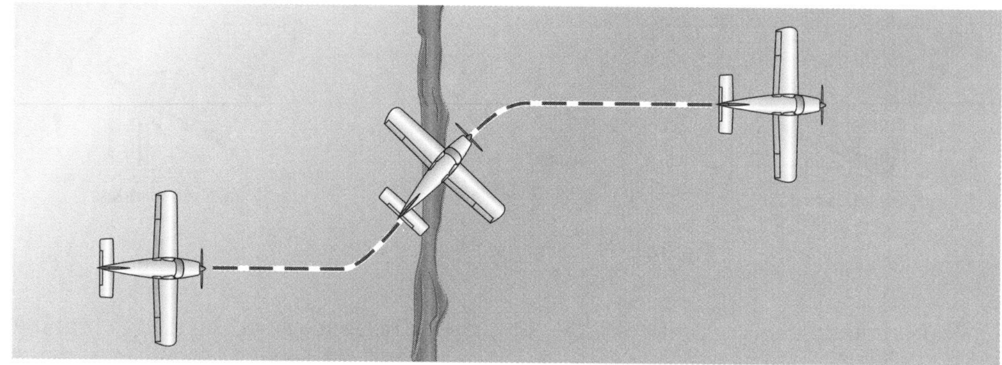

Figure 6-11 Cross small ridges and ditches at an angle—slowly.

However, be careful not to straddle a hump and risk a prop-strike. Hold the control column fully rearward, and the propeller slipstream will reduce the weight on the nose wheel, maximize propeller clearance and help the aircraft negotiate humps and bumps. This also applies to patches of wet or soft ground. Whenever you need to increase power, say, to negotiate uneven surface conditions, pull back on the control column. Large ditches or ridges should be avoided altogether. It is no disgrace to park the airplane, shut down the engine and walk the ground before proceeding.

Wind Effect

The flight controls should be held in a position to avoid either the tail or a wing being lifted by a strong wind.

Head Wind. When taxiing into a strong head wind, hold the control column either neutral or back. This holds the elevator neutral or up, and the tail down, and takes the load off the nose wheel.

Tail Wind. When taxiing with a strong tail wind, hold the control column forward to move the elevator down. This stops the wind lifting the horizontal stabilizer from behind.

Figure 6-12 Think wind.

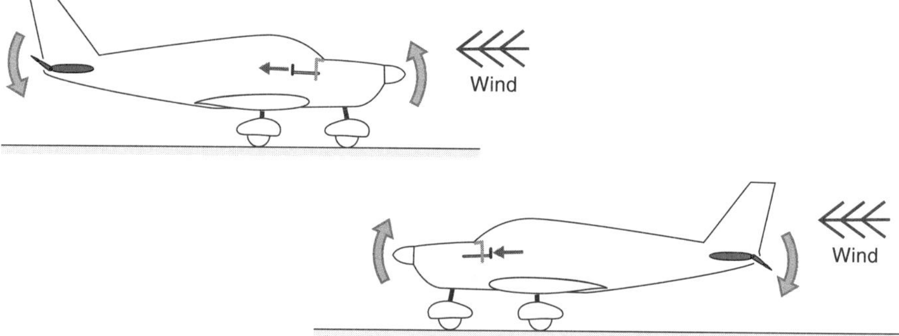

Figure 6-13 Taxi into-wind with the control column neutral or back, and taxi downwind with the control column forward.

Crosswind. A crosswind will try to weathervane the airplane into the wind because of the large keel surfaces behind the main wheels. Using the rudder pedals, especially if nose wheel steering is fitted, should provide adequate directional control, but, if not, then use differential braking. To avoid a crosswind from ahead lifting the upwind wing, raise its aileron by moving the control column into the wind.

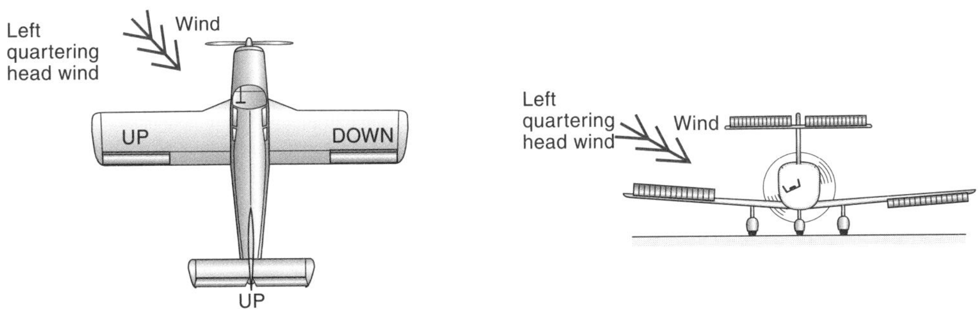

Figure 6-14 Taxiing with a left quartering head wind.

To avoid a crosswind from behind lifting the upwind wing, lower its aileron so that the wind cannot get under it, by moving the control column out of wind.

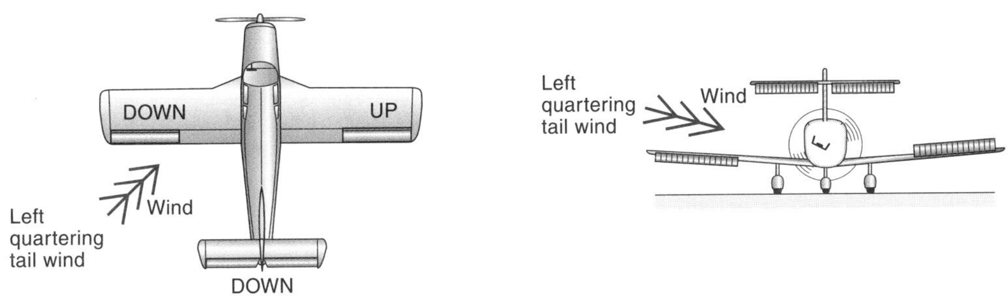

Figure 6-15 Taxiing with a left quartering tail wind.

The propwash or jet blast of another airplane will produce the same affect as a wind, so always be cautious if you have to taxi close behind other aircraft, especially at an angle.

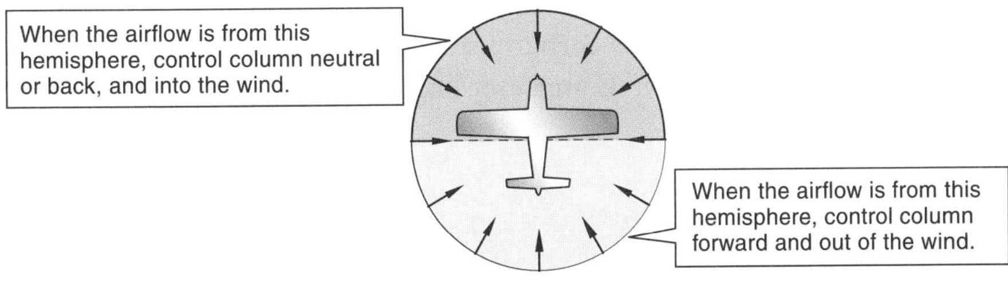

Figure 6-16 Summary of the use of controls when taxiing in windy conditions.

Checks While Taxiing

Several items are checked once the aircraft is clear of the tarmac area and moving along on a straight taxiway. The rudder should be checked for full and free movement, and directional flight instruments should be checked for correct operation:

- Turning left:
  - the compass and heading indicator should decrease in heading;
  - the turn coordinator or turn indicator should indicate a left turn;
  - the balance ball should show a skid to the right (turning left, skidding right); and
  - the attitude indicator should stay level.
- Turning right:
  - the compass and heading indicator should increase in heading;
  - the turn coordinator or turn indicator should indicate a right turn;
  - the balance ball should show a skid to the left (turning right, skidding left); and
  - the attitude indicator should stay level.

Turning left, skidding right, wings level, compass decreasing

Turning right, skidding left, wings level compass increasing

Figure 6-17 Instrument indications when taxiing.

Run-Up Check

After the airplane has been taxied to the run-up bay, or holding point, prior to entering the runway, it is brought to a halt and the brakes parked while the *run-up checks* and *pretakeoff vital* actions are performed. One of these actions is a check of the engine.

The aircraft is stopped and the parking brake applied. The aircraft should be facing into the wind. After the engine temperatures and pressures are *in the green*, the engine is run at 1,800–2,000 RPM and the carburetor heat, propeller pitch and magnetos are checked. The pretakeoff vital actions are described later.

REVIEW 6

Taxiing and Pretakeoff Checks

1. To assist in directional orientation, should you align the heading indicator with the magnetic compass before starting to taxi?
2. Which controls turn the nose wheel, steering the airplane on the ground?
3. In most aircraft, which part of the rudder pedals is used to operate differential braking?
4. Should the brakes be gently tested immediately after the airplane begins to move?
5. When should you use the brakes when taxiing? Should you use power against brakes?
6. After the aircraft has started to move, will it probably require more or less power to keep moving?
7. How should you control the taxiing speed?
8. What is a reasonable taxiing speed?
9. In order to turn left when taxiing, the bottom of which rudder pedal do you move forward? In order to turn right, the bottom of which side rudder pedal do you move forward?
10. Should you avoid taxiing over loose stones or through long grass?
11. How do the power requirements differ when taxiing over a soft surface as opposed to the usual hard, smooth surface?
12. Are wet surfaces usually more slippery than dry surfaces?
13. When taxiing with the wind from ahead, in what position do you hold the control column?
14. When taxiing with the wind coming from behind, in what position do you hold the control column?
15. In relation to the wind, what direction will a crosswind tend to weathervane the nose of a taxiing airplane?
16. What can be used to counteract the effect of crosswind on a taxiing airplane?
17. Usually, what color are taxiway markings?
18. Should you comply with clearances and markings when taxiing?
19. Following a radio communications failure, you first of all receive a red light signal from the tower, followed some time later by a flashing green light signal. What do these mean?
20. Will you require a taxi clearance at a tower-controlled airport?
21. At an airport without an operating control tower, should you advise your taxiing intentions on the CTAF? What does CTAF stand for?
22. When taxiing, the general right of way procedure is to give way to which side?
23. Which has right of way: an airplane taking off or landing, or one that is taxiing?
24. Does a taxiing aircraft have right of way over a vehicle towing an aircraft?
25. If two taxiing aircraft are approaching head-on, in which direction should each turn?
26. Does the ultimate responsibility for avoiding collisions between taxiing aircraft rest with air traffic control or the pilots?
27. When taxiing at a tower-controlled airport, do you need to read back any "hold short of runway" instructions issued by ATC?
28. When taxiing, even with a marshaler, who carries the onus?
29. How is vision of the runway when taxiing different in a tail wheel airplane compared to a nose wheel airplane?
30. How are small ridges or small ditches best crossed? Should large ridges or large ditches be crossed?
31. Should you taxi behind a large aircraft with its engines operating?
32. If you must taxi over a gravel surface or a surface with loose stones, what level of power (high or low) should you try to use?
33. When turning left during taxiing, what change in heading should be indicated on the compass and heading indicator? Which way should the turn coordinator indicate the turn? To which side should the balance ball move?
34. What are the marshaling instructions for the following: turn left, turn right, move ahead, slow down, stop, and stop engine?

Answers are given on page 576.

TASK

Taxiing

Aim: To maneuver the aircraft safely on the ground.

1. *Commencing Taxiing*

Look out:

Observe the surrounding area for obstructions and other airplanes. Consider the taxiing surface.

If taxi clearance is required at your airfield, obtain this prior to taxiing.

Reduce the power to idle (perhaps loosen the throttle friction nut).

Release the parking brake.

Moving off:

Apply sufficient power to get the airplane moving forward.

Reduce the power to idle and gently test the brakes.

Apply sufficient power to recommence taxiing.

Reduce power as necessary to maintain a safe taxiing speed (a fast walking pace).

2. *Taxiing the airplane*

Note: Steering is not possible until the airplane is rolling forward.

Control direction with the rudder pedals and, if necessary, differential braking. An increased slipstream over the rudder also helps.

Remember to allow ample clearance for the wing tips and tail.

Position the control column suitably to counteract any wind effect from the side or behind.

Cross rough surfaces slowly and at an angle.

Monitor engine temperature gauges for adequate cooling.

3. *Stopping the airplane*

(a) To stop the airplane:

Anticipate.

Close the throttle.

Allow the airplane to roll to a stop with the nose wheel straight.

If necessary, gently apply the brakes, releasing them just as the airplane stops.

(b) When completely stopped:

Set the brakes to PARK and set the engine to fast idle, usually 1,000 to 1,200 RPM (to keep the alternator charging).

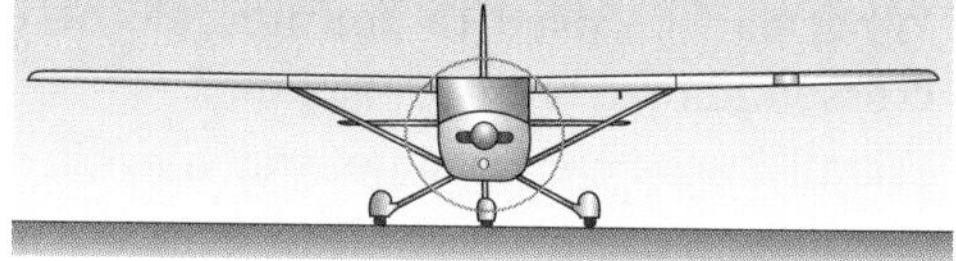

7

Postflight Actions and Refueling

OBJECTIVES

To describe:

- the procedure for shutting down the engine; and
- securing the airplane.

CONSIDERATIONS

Shutting Down the Engine

There will be a shutdown procedure specified in the pilot's operating handbook for your aircraft that will include such items as:

- set the parking brake with the airplane (ideally) pointing into any strong wind;
- ensure the engine is cool (having taxied or set 1,000 to 1,200 RPM for a minute or two should be sufficient); and
- both magnetos should be checked individually—there should be a slight RPM drop as you go from both to an individual magneto, and a return to the set RPM when the switch is returned to both.

  Note: Sometimes a *dead-cut* check is made by moving the ignition switch very quickly from *both* to *off* and back to *both* to check that the engine will actually cut. This checks that the off position does indeed break the circuit to each magneto by grounding them. If this were not the case, the engine and propeller would be live even with the magneto switched to off. An innocent movement of the propeller could start the engine unexpectedly—a dangerous situation! Some engine manufacturers advise against this check as it may damage the engine, especially if the switch is held too long in the off position. Seek your instructor's advice.

Do not simply turn the key to shut down the engine.

- Turn all individual electrical services off (radio, lights, etc.).
- Switch the avionics master off.
- Set the mixture control to idle cutoff (fully out) to starve the engine of fuel and stop it running.
- After the engine stops, switch the ignition off and remove the key.
- Turn the alternator and battery master switch off.

Postflight Inspection

An airplane has a life of its own in the sense that it passes continually from the command of one pilot to the command of another—the postflight check of one being followed by the preflight check of the next. To a certain extent, each pilot relies on the fact that previous pilots have performed their duties, even though we must all accept individual responsibility.

Figure 7-1 Use the towbar.

Figure 7-2 Refueling.

Figure 7-3 Ground the airplane.

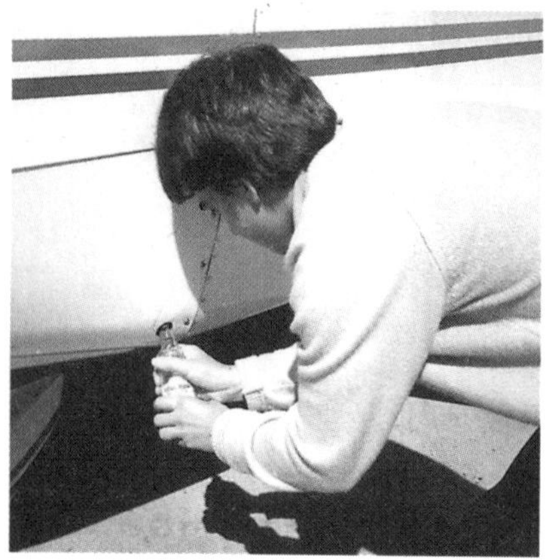

Figure 7-4 Check for water.

Positioning the Airplane

Sometimes it is necessary to reposition the airplane for refueling, for parking or for taking the airplane into or out of a hangar. Always use an approved tug or towbar and be careful of the propeller (double-check the switches are off).

Check with your instructor for correct positioning of the towbar. Some airplanes can be scratched or damaged by mishandling of the towbar.

Refueling

One task that you may be required to perform is refueling the airplane. There are three aspects to ensure:

- the quantity of fuel you have added and the total you now have on board;
- the quality of the fuel; and
- the minimization if risk of fire during refueling and subsequent engine start.

Precautions

When refueling observe the following:

- ensure there is a safe distance from buildings and other aircraft;
- have the aircraft completely shut down with no engine systems, radios or electronics on;
- have no one on board;
- permit no smoking;
- allow no radio transmissions;
- have the parking brake off so the airplane can be pushed clear of the fuel tank or pump;
- ground the airplane to the fuel truck or pump and the nozzle to the airplane before opening fuel caps;
- avoid banging the nozzle against the aircraft skin;
- check the fuel type (octane rating and color) before accepting fuel;
- check the quantity added by the fuel tank and the fuel gauges;
- dip the tanks to physically check the total quality on board;
- if the airplane is wet, or it is raining, prevent water entering the tanks when you remove the caps;
- tighten the caps positively after refueling;
- if the aircraft is on uneven ground (not level) you may need to rock the wings to settle the fuel and fill to capacity; and
- drain fuel samples from all tanks and the strainer to check for water and contamination.

If the fuel is from drums check the date and filter the fuel through a chamois cloth.

Securing the Airplane

The airplane should not be left unattended unless it is adequately secured against movement and possible damage.

- Ensure that the parking brake is on (if required) and that the wheel chocks are in place, in front of and behind the wheels.
- Fit the pitot covers, control locks and tie-down ropes if required.
- Secure the seat belts.
- Lock the door and return the key.
- Replace all covers.

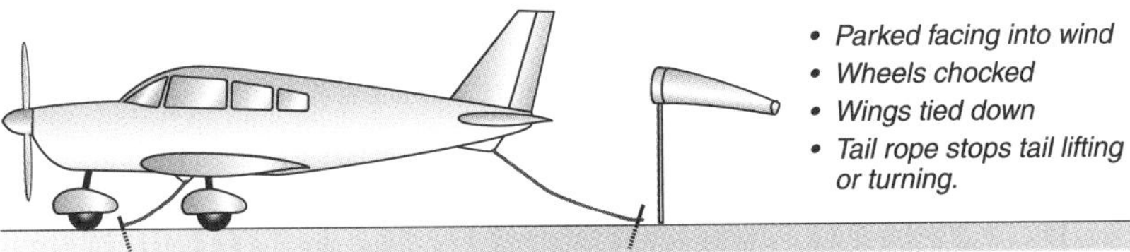

• Parked facing into wind
• Wheels chocked
• Wings tied down
• Tail rope stops tail lifting or turning.

Figure 7-5 Securing the airplane.

Figure 7-6 Lock the controls.

Figure 7-7 Cover the cockpit.

Figure 7-8 Secure the airplane.

Postflight Documentation

Part of the postflight actions also includes documenting the flight:

- record the engine time (or Hobb's gauge time) in the log;
- report any airplane defects (squawks) to your flight instructor or to a mechanic and, when appropriate, note them on the maintenance log to ensure that necessary maintenance will be attended to and that the following pilot will have a serviceable airplane; and
- complete your personal logbook.

During your training, a debriefing by your flight instructor will probably occur following the completion of your postflight duties. You can also reread the appropriate chapters of this manual to consolidate what you have learned in the particular flight lesson and briefing.

REVIEW 7

Postflight Actions

1. In what direction should the airplane face when parked?
2. Does the shutdown checklist need to be completed before deplaning any passengers?
3. Should any defect noted during or after the flight be made known to the flight instructor or mechanic?
4. When you tie the airplane down, how tight should the rope tension be?

Answers are given on page 577.

Aircraft Control in the Air

8
Primary Controls

OBJECTIVES

To describe:
- the direct and indirect effect of the primary controls;
- the effect of airspeed and slipstream on the response of the primary controls;
- the effect of power changes; and
- the handover and takeover of aircraft control between the instructor and student pilot.

Figure 8-1
The controls link the pilot to the airplane.

CONSIDERATIONS

Your training airplane is flown in exactly the same way as a Jumbo or an F-15. Attitude, thrust and configuration produce a flight path and speed. Balance, trim and fuel controls make it more efficient.

Classification of Controls

Each control input the pilot makes has a direct or immediate effect and an indirect, delayed or induced effect. The accelerator pedal in your car can be used to increase speed or to maintain speed up a hill. An aircraft is the same. If you increase power the aircraft will go up (climb or increase altitude) or, alternatively, the pilot can use the increased power to accelerate (increase speed) at the same altitude. The "hills" are invisible to the aircraft, but the principle is the same. Control of the flight path and speed (together called *performance*) is made by the pilot setting an attitude and a power; that is, setting a direction (left or right, up or down) where the aircraft is pointing and setting the power to sustain that selected direction. The controls themselves are classified as primary, secondary or ancillary.

The *primary* controls are used to set attitude, power, balance and trim. They are:
- elevators and ailerons, which are actuated by the control column;
- the rudder, which is actuated by the rudder pedals;
- the throttle, for constant-speed propellers, and pitch control; and
- the trim.

The *secondary* controls change the configuration of the airplane and manage the fuel/air supply to the engine. They are:
- flaps;
- mixture and carburetor heat; and
- boost pump and fuel selectors.

Some aircraft have a retractable landing gear. The position of the landing gear and flaps is called the *configuration* of the aircraft. Setting the configuration is the third element of the pilot's control of the aircraft (together with attitude and power).

The ancillary controls are specific to your airplane and are those associated with operation of the systems and aids such as:

- wheel brakes;
- lights;
- electronics;
- hydraulics; and
- radios.

Types of Effect

Because the aircraft is suspended in space, any change, in one sense, also inevitably affects other conditions. The controls have an immediate, direct and obvious effect, but they also have an indirect, less immediate, and more subtle effect. For example, if you go up, you also slow down and, if you go down, you also speed up. We'll discuss the obvious ones first.

Airplane Motion

An airplane moves in three dimensions (plus time).

Like all objects, the aircraft is balanced at a point called the *center of gravity* (CG). To describe an airplane's position or movement in space, three mutually perpendicular reference *axes* (like the axle of a wheel, which is the center or neutral line of the rotation) are used. Any change in airplane's attitude can be expressed in terms of motion about one or more of these three axes. (It is three because we move in three dimensions. Time is the fourth dimension and describes the speed or rate of rotation or movement.) The motions are:

- motion about the lateral axis called *pitching* (nose going up or down);
- motion about the longitudinal axis called *rolling* (wings tilting left or right); and
- motion about the vertical axis called *yawing* (nose moving left or right).

We refer to the axis of yaw as the vertical axis, because it is perpendicular to both the longitudinal axis and the lateral axis. It may be confusing as it may not necessarily be vertical to the earth. It is only truly vertical when the airplane is in straight and level flight. Whenever the airplane is banked, or the nose is pitched up or down, the vertical axis is not vertical to the earth but is vertical to the other two axes. The single

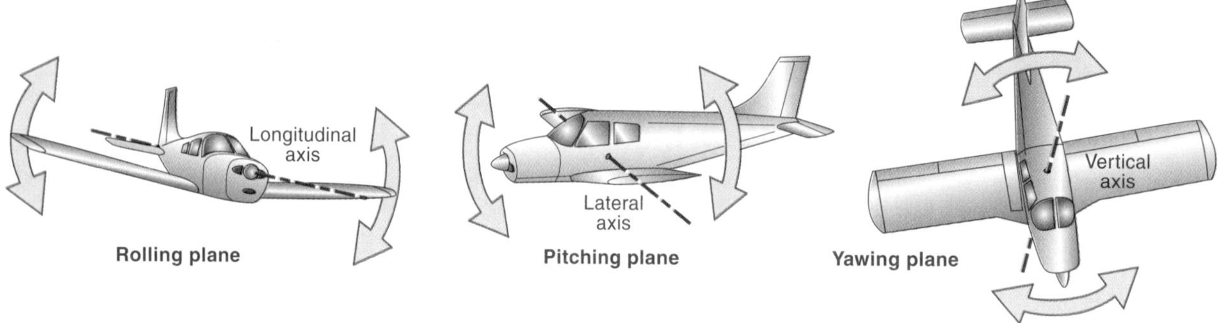

Figure 8-2 Angular motion is described in three planes.

dimension in which the angular movement occurs is called the *plane* of rotation. Thus we have pitching, rolling and yawing planes purely for descriptive purposes. A turn is a combination of rolling and yawing.

Stability of the Aircraft

Stability is the natural tendency for the aircraft to remain in its flight condition (its airspeed and angle of attack), or to return to it following some disturbance (such as a wind gust) without any action being taken by the pilot. Most training airplanes are reasonably stable in the pitching plane. If correctly trimmed, they will maintain steady flight with the pilot flying *hands-off.* In other words, the nose position relative to the horizon will remain reasonably steady without too much attention from the pilot. The stability of most airplanes in the rolling and yawing planes, however, is usually not as great as in the pitching plane. If the wings are disturbed from their level position (say by a gust), the airplane will eventually enter a gentle, descending, tightening spiral turn until the pilot actively corrects it, in this case, by leveling the wings and raising the nose.

Flight Path and Speed

An aircraft's flight path and speed is controlled by the pilot setting the configuration (flaps), an attitude (the nose position in relation to the horizon) and thrust (power) with the throttle and/or propeller lever. To maintain the set flight path, the pilot may then apply trim and rudder to balance the aircraft and to relieve control pressures. The mixture and carburetor heat may also be adjusted for engine efficiency.

The change of aircraft attitude is described as a motion around a particular axis:

- the elevator is moved by forward and backward pressure on the control column and causes the aircraft to pitch about the lateral axis (thus it causes a change in the angle of attack of the wing and the pitch attitude of the aircraft);
- the ailerons are displaced by left or right movement of the control column and cause rolling motion about the longitudinal axis;
- the rudder, controlled by fore and aft movement of the rudder bar or pedals, causes a yawing motion about the vertical axis (vertical to the aircraft not necessarily the earth); and
- the power levers, which may be a single lever (throttle) or two levers (throttle and propeller RPM), vary the power to maintain or reduce speed, to climb or to descend.

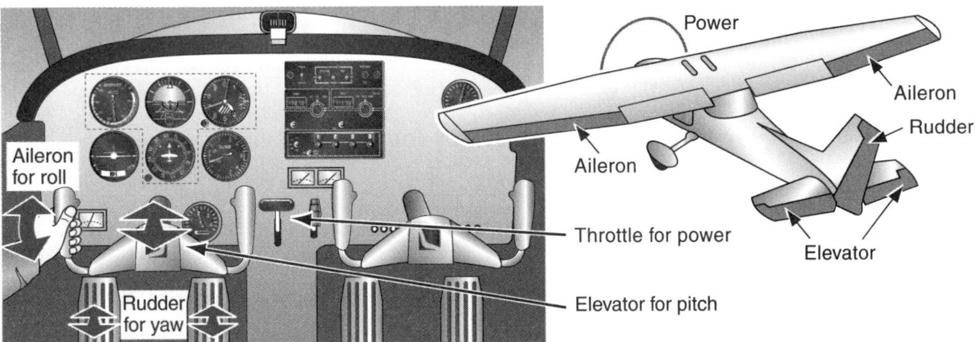

Figure 8-3 The primary controls: elevator, ailerons, rudder and power.

Attitude Control

Each of the three primary aerodynamic controls operates in the same sense relative to the airplane, regardless of its attitude in pitch or bank. For example, moving the control column forward will move the nose in a direction away from the pilot, even if (taking an extreme case) the airplane is inverted.

Direct Effect of the Elevators

The elevators controls pitch.

The elevators control pitching and are operated by fore and aft movements of the control column. The conventional elevator is one control surface (or two halves bolted together) hinged to the rear of the *horizontal stabilizer* (also known as the *tailplane*). Some aircraft have a *stabilator* (or *all-flying tail*), which is a single, moving surface acting as both the horizontal stabilizer and the elevator. Either type has the same effect on the airplane when the control column is moved. They directly change the pitch attitude of the aircraft (even when it is banked). Changing the pitch attitude of the aircraft also changes the angle of attack of the wing and therefore the lift and drag. This is the significant source of control that the pilot has over the flight path of the aircraft. Power is adjusted to sustain the desired path and airspeed.

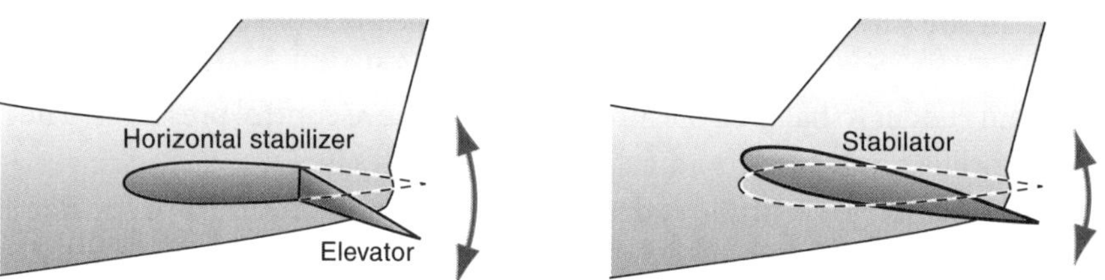

Figure 8-4 Fixed horizontal stabilizer with moving elevator and the stabilator.

Deflecting the elevator with the control column alters the airflow around the horizontal stabilizer and changes the aerodynamic force generated by it. This force pivots the aircraft around the center of gravity causing a change in attitude and angle of attack.

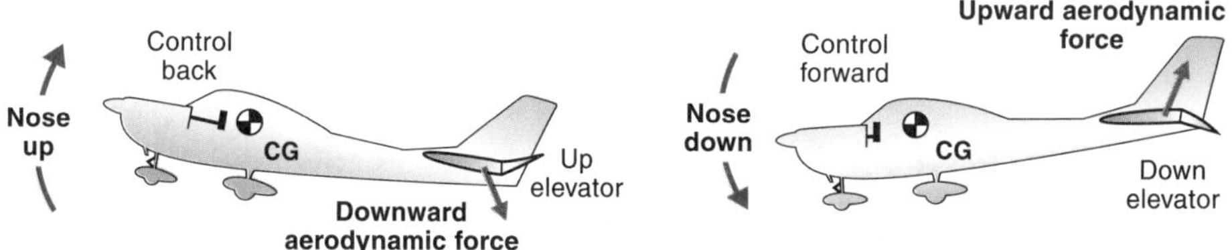

Figure 8-5 The elevator controls pitching and pitch attitude.

The rate of pitching of the airplane increases with larger elevator deflections. At normal flight speeds, the movement of the control column can be quite small and may feel more like pressure changes than actual movements. Higher speeds give greater effect from the elevator but also greater resistance to change due to the stability of the aircraft. At higher power settings, slipstream from the propeller can also increase the power of the elevator while the aircraft's stability is still low.

Fore and aft movement of the control column is used to place the nose in the desired position relative to the horizon (i.e. to set the *pitch attitude*). This, together with the power setting, determines the flight path that the aircraft can maintain.

The Stabilator and Anti-Balance Tab

Because of their combined function, stabilators have a much larger area than elevators and so produce more-powerful responses to control input—that is, small movements of the control column can produce large aerodynamic forces. To prevent a pilot from moving the stabilator too far and overcontrolling—especially at high airspeeds—a stabilator often incorporates an *anti-balance tab* (sometimes called an *anti-servo tab*).

An anti-balance tab moves in the same direction as the stabilator's trailing edge and generates an aerodynamic force that makes it increasingly harder to move the stabilator further, as well as providing *feel* for the pilot. Correct movement of the anti-balance tab can be checked during the preflight inspection by moving the trailing edge of the stabilator and noting that the tab moves in the *same* direction as the trailing edge but further.

Figure 8-6
Stabilator and anti-balance tab.

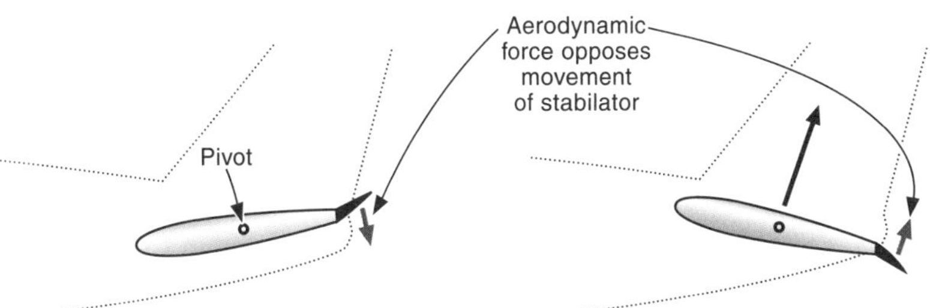

Figure 8-7 The anti-balance tab opposes further stabilator movement and increases control feel for the pilot.

Indirect Effect of the Elevators

Relationship Between Pitch Attitude and Airspeed

The indirect effect of the elevator is an airspeed and altitude change.

The primary effect of elevator is to change the pitch attitude. For example, by moving the control column back, the nose is raised. Following a pitch change, the momentum of the airplane (its resistance to any change) will cause it to follow the original flight path for a brief period. The airflow will then strike the wings at a greater angle of attack, and as a consequence, they will generate a different aerodynamic force. Lift will increase and the flight path will change to a climb. Drag will increase, causing the airplane to slow down. Thus, raising the nose with no power adjustment will lead to an increase in altitude and a decrease in airspeed. Conversely, by moving the control column forward, the nose is lowered and the airflow will strike the wings at a lesser angle of attack, less drag will be

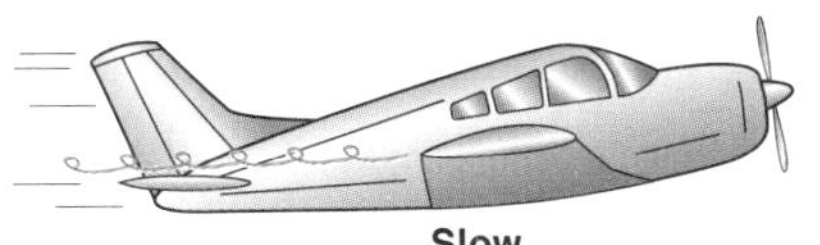

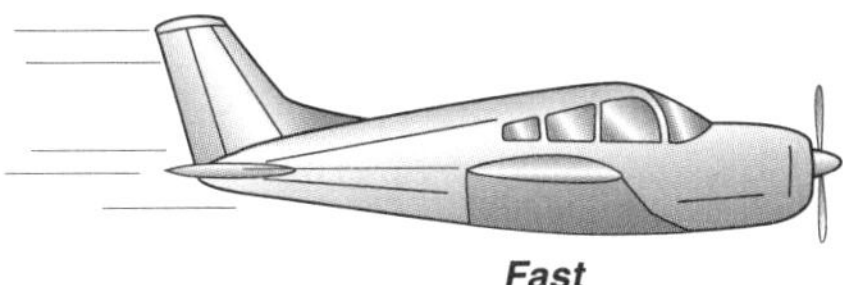

Figure 8-8 The indirect effect of elevator is a change of airspeed and altitude.

created and so the airspeed will increase. Thus, lowering the nose with the elevator will lead to an airspeed increase and a decrease in altitude.

When deflected by moving the control column, the elevator has:

- the primary effect of pitching the airplane, which changes the flight path; and
- the further effect of changing the airspeed and the altitude (because the flight path changes).

When the elevator changes the pitch attitude of the airplane, it will gradually settle at a new airspeed. This control of flight path and airspeed by use of the elevator is used whenever the power is set as it is in most flight conditions. Airspeed is used as the reference for attitude.

Direct Effect of the Ailerons

The ailerons control roll and bank.

The ailerons are controlled by lateral movement or rotation of the control column. When the control is displaced to the left, the left aileron is deflected upward and the right aileron is deflected downward. The raised aileron reduces the lift on its wing and the lowered aileron increases the lift generated by that section of that wing. The difference in lift between the two wings causes the airplane to roll: moving the control column to the left causes a roll to the left and moving it to the right causes a roll to the right.

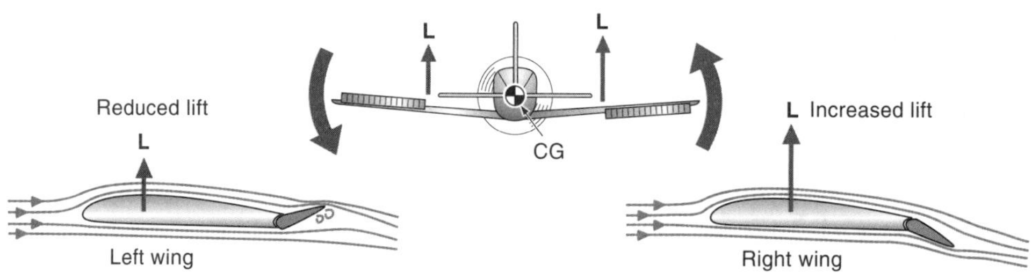

Figure 8-9 A roll to the left (control column left, left aileron up).

The roll rate is proportional to the amount of aileron deflection. Centering the control column places the ailerons in the neutral position and the roll will stop at that angle of bank. The aircraft will tend to roll into or out of the bank as a result of sideslipping.

Indirect Effect of the Ailerons

Yaw is the indirect effect of the ailerons.

There are two causes of yaw associated with rolling the aircraft:

- *adverse aileron yaw* caused by the difference in drag between the wings, one with aileron up and one with aileron down; and
- *yaw due to sideslip* caused by the bank angle.

Yaw Due to Aileron Deflection

Yaw due to aileron deflection is usually adverse, against the direction of roll. In a simple aircraft, the lowered aileron has more drag and so when the pilot wishes to roll to the left, the aircraft will tend to yaw to the right; that is, it is *adverse* to the pilot's wishes. It is pronounced in vintage aircraft, some gliders and many ultralights. It requires large amounts of rudder to correct it and, in these aircraft, rudder becomes an important control. If the effect is pronounced then it can cause a sideslip that can counter the aileron input. Therefore, it requires the use of rudder to be coordinated or even anticipated. Adverse aileron yaw is most pronounced at high angles of attack (i.e. low airspeed) and so, in the circuit, much active use of the rudder is required to keep the aircraft balanced.

Some airplanes have differential ailerons, Frise ailerons, or interconnected aileron and rudder to reduce adverse aileron yaw. However, the best method is for the pilot to actively apply rudder to balance the aircraft to counter adverse yaw and to prevent sideslip.

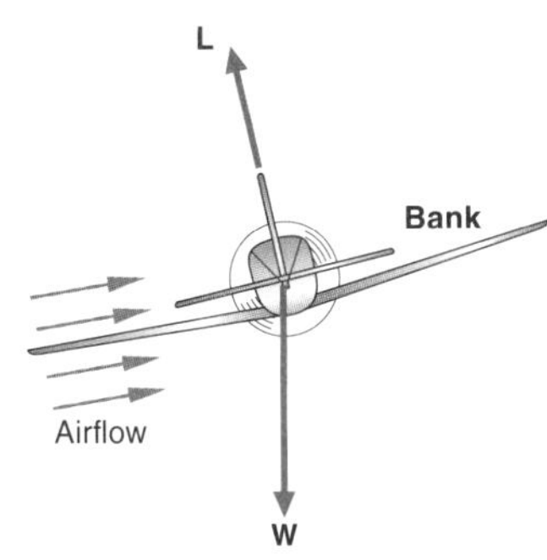

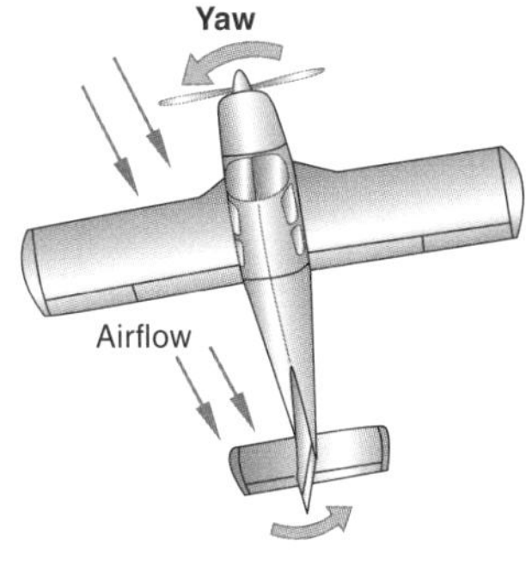

Figure 8-10 Bank causes sideslip followed by yaw.

Yaw Due to Sideslip

Banking the airplane tilts the lift force generated by the wings. A sideways component of the lift force now exists, causing the airplane to *sideslip* toward the lower wing. In this sideslip, the large *keel* surfaces behind the center of gravity (such as the fin and the fuselage) are struck by the airflow, which causes the airplane's nose to yaw in the direction of the sideslip. The nose will drop and a spiral descent will begin (unless prevented by the pilot leveling the wings). Yaw and roll due to sideslip can be marked in crosswind conditions, and for this reason, active coordinated use of rudder and ailerons is required.

Direct Effect of the Rudder

Moving the left rudder pedal forward deflects the rudder to the left (opposite to a go-cart where left foot forward turns it right). The airplane rotates about its vertical axis and so, with left rudder applied, the nose yaws left. Conversely, moving the right rudder pedal forward yaws the nose of the airplane to the right. The aircraft's stability resists this motion and so the aircraft will only yaw through a few degrees and then stop.

Yawing the airplane can be uncomfortable and is aerodynamically inefficient because it causes a sideslip that increases drag. This is not the way an aircraft is turned. A turn is made by banking, just like a motorcycle. Indeed, the rudder has a similar function to the handlebars: a balancing function. It is not used to steer the vehicle (although it is very useful at low speed to help to point the nose of the aircraft—or the motorcycle).

Although it can yaw the airplane, the main function of the rudder is to cancel any imbalances due to speed or power changes. This balance is indicated to the pilot by the balance ball, which is part of the turn coordinator, and also by *seat of the pants*. If the airplane is out of balance, the ball moves out to one side

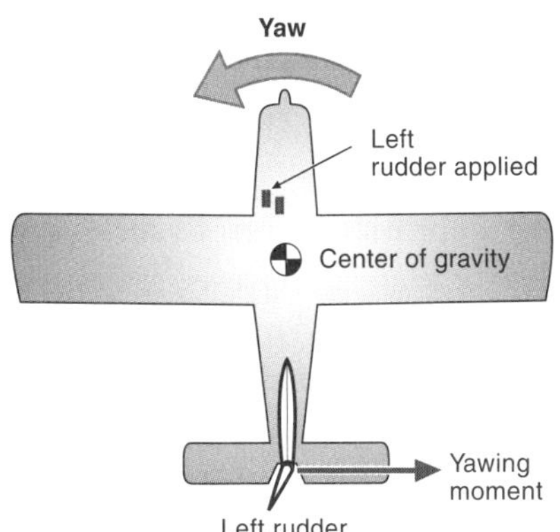

Figure 8-11 Left rudder pressure yaws the nose left.

Figure 8-12 Apply same-side rudder pressure to center the balance ball.

(the pilot, reacting in the same way as the ball, will feel pressed to the same side—like skidding in a car). You can, with practice, feel the imbalance. Balance is restored by applying *same-side* rudder pressure; that is, if the ball is out to the right, apply right rudder pressure. Remember the advice, "step on the ball."

Indirect Effect of the Rudder

Yaw Causes Roll

The rudder controls yaw and sideslip.

Applying rudder will yaw the nose of the airplane: a yaw to the left if left rudder pressure is applied, and a yaw to the right, if right rudder is applied. As a result of yaw, the outer wing is moving faster than the inner wing and so generates more lift, and the imbalance in lift causes a roll in the same direction as the yaw. The rudder effect will now cause the aircraft to sideslip.

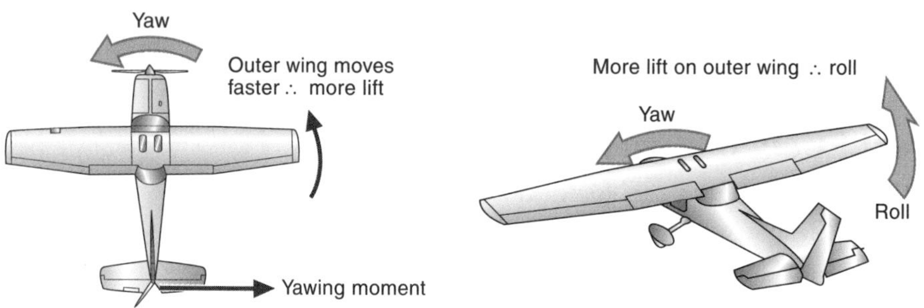

Figure 8-13 Rudder causes yaw followed by roll.

Yaw Causes Sideslip

Yaw causes roll—the indirect effect of the rudder.

Although it is yawed sideways, the airplane will continue to move in its original direction due to momentum. The inner wing will be partly shielded from the airflow by the fuselage, and therefore will produce less lift. The sideslip will cause a rolling moment in the direction of the rudder.

If the aircraft has dihedral (the wings are mounted in an upward tilt relative to the fuselage the airflow will meet the unshielded wing at a greater angle of attack again increasing lift and causing a rolling moment in the direction of the applied rudder. Rudder deflection, therefore, causes yaw followed by roll, a pause and then further roll. The roll causes further sideslip that yaws the aircraft into a steeper turn. This all happens very slowly, but unless the pilot takes corrective action (by preventing unwanted yaw with opposite rudder or by leveling the wings), a gently steepening, spiral descent will result.

Demonstrating the Controls

Normal flying requires the coordinated application of all primary controls, such as the need to correct the effects of a power change if we wish to accelerate. However, to illustrate the separate effects in this flight exercise, they will be demonstrated individually —like steering, braking and acceleration in a car—first one at a time, then all together.

The instructor will place the aircraft in steady flight and will demonstrate the effects of each control separately. This will entail negating or camouflaging some of the indirect effects by unusual control applications. Once you have seen, for yourself, the direct and indirect effects, then you will use the controls quite naturally and in a complete, coordinated way.

Effect of Airspeed and Slipstream on the Primary Flight Controls

Control Power

The power (response) of the primary flight controls, and the rate at which the airplane moves in all three planes (pitch, roll and yaw), depends on:

- the amount of control deflection; and
- the airflow over the control surface, which can be increased by:
  - higher airspeed; and/or
  - slipstream from the propeller.

Airspeed

All flight controls are more powerful at higher airspeeds.

The elevator, ailerons and rudder will all experience an increased airflow when the airplane is flying at a higher airspeed. Each control will feel firmer and only small movements will be required to produce an effective response. There is, however, greater stability and aerodynamic pressure and so greater resistance to control inputs. Conversely, at low airspeeds the airflow over each of the flight controls is less and their effectiveness is reduced. The elevator, ailerons and rudder will all feel *sloppy* and large movements may be required to produce the desired effect.

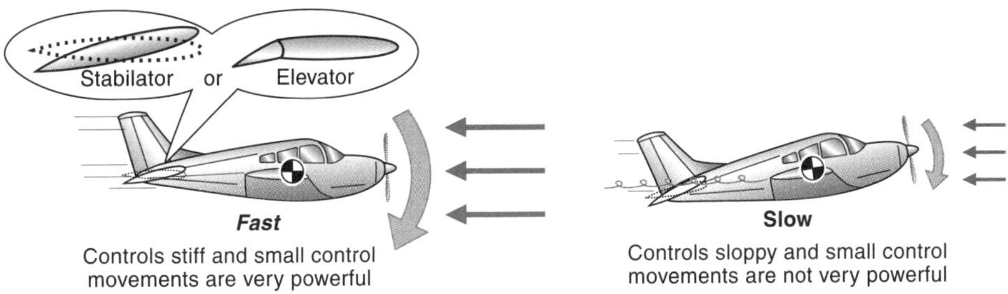
Stabilator
or
Elevator
Fast
Controls stiff and small control movements are very powerful
Slow
Controls sloppy and small control movements are not very powerful

Figure 8-14 All of the flight controls are more powerful at high airspeeds.

Propeller Slipstream

The slipstream from the propeller flows rearward around the airplane in a corkscrew fashion, which energizes and propels the airflow over the tail section, making the rudder and elevator more effective. The ailerons, being outside the slipstream airflow, are not affected by it and will remain *sloppy* at low airspeeds irrespective of the power set. The elevator on T-tail aircraft may also be somewhat out of the slipstream and therefore not affected by it.

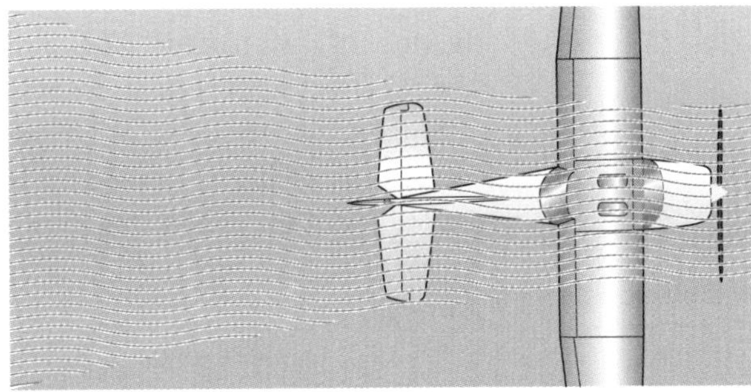

Figure 8-15 The slipstream increases elevator and rudder power.

Effects of Power Changes

Direct Effect of Power

The other primary control of the flight path and speed is the throttle. It is a primary control because no flight path can be sustained without it. Thus any prolonged flight path change must include both an attitude setting and a power setting. However, an aircraft is not like a car. If you press on the accelerator of a car, you go faster. In an aircraft, if you increase power, it does more than just accelerate.

Indirect Effect of Power

In a single-engine aircraft, the airflow from the propeller is not symmetrical, thus any change in this airflow caused by a change in speed or propeller RPM produces an imbalance (a yawing *moment* or tendency). There is also a change in the balance of the aircraft between the forces of thrust, drag, weight and lift (the pitching moment). The effect depends on the direction of rotation of the propeller, but for most airplanes, an increase in power causes a tendency for the nose of the aircraft to move up and left (a nose-up pitching moment and a yawing moment to the left), and conversely, a reduction in thrust causes a tendency for the nose to drop and to move to the right. Thus the immediate effect of the power lever is not a change in speed unless the pilot makes other corrections. If uncompensated, a power increase will result in a climb and a pitch up, and a reduction will result in a descent and a pitch down.

If you wish to accelerate in the same direction, you must counter these out-of-trim forces to maintain the flight path and then retrim. If you wish to climb rather than accelerate then you allow and assist the change of attitude associated with the power change. Some aircraft are equipped with rudder trim in addition to elevator trim that is used to trim off any steady pressure on the rudder pedals, e.g. on the climb.

Constant-Speed Propeller

There are considerations in the use of the throttle/propeller levers in an airplane with a constant-speed propeller. For this exercise, the propeller will be set to maximum continuous RPM and the throttle used in exactly the same way as in a fixed-pitch airplane. However, the instructor will also demonstrate the use of the power levers, the instrument indications and settings for climb and cruise.

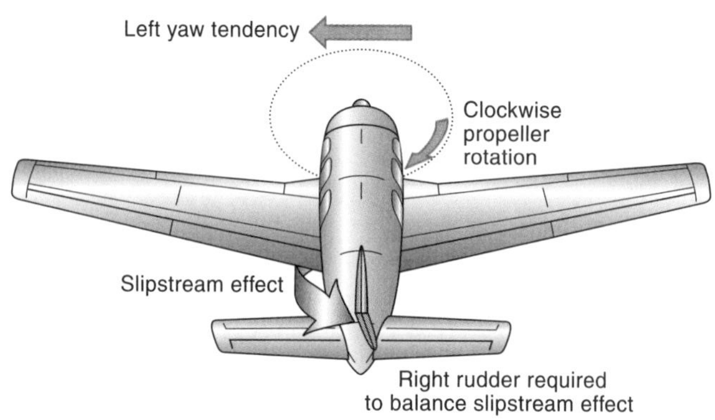

Figure 8-16 Slipstream tends to yaw the airplane.

Yawing Moment (Tendency)

The slipstream from the propeller flows back in a corkscrew fashion over the horizontal stabilizer, meeting the fin at an angle of attack. This generates a sideways aerodynamic force that tends to yaw the nose of the airplane. The pilot can balance this yawing effect with rudder pressure.

Slipstream effect is most pronounced under conditions of high power and low airspeed (e.g. during a climb), when the spiral path of the slipstream is tighter and its angle of approach to the fin is greater.

The direction of the yaw resulting from the slipstream effect depends on the direction of propeller rotation. If the propeller rotates clockwise when viewed from the cockpit (as is the case for many modern training aircraft), the slipstream passes under the fuselage and strikes the fin on its left-hand side. This causes a tendency for the nose to yaw left that can be balanced with right rudder. If the propeller rotates counterclockwise as seen from the cockpit (e.g. the Tiger Moth, Chipmunk), the slipstream passes under the fuselage and strikes the fin on the right-hand side. The nose will tend to yaw right and will require left rudder.

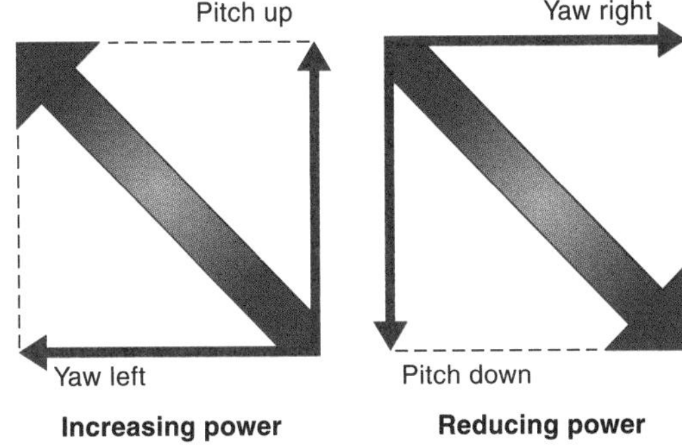

Figure 8-17 The effects of power changes (for a clockwise-rotating propeller—cockpit view).

Secondary Controls

Some books refer to the power levers as secondary controls; however, while they are not control *surfaces*, they are so fundamental to the control of the aircraft's flight path they have been discussed as *primary*. Conversely, the rudder may be called secondary as it is mostly used as a balancing device rather than a control device; however, it was included as a primary control since it is fundamental for control at low airspeed, in crosswinds and during taxiing.

Trim

All airplanes have an elevator trim that can relieve the pilot of steady fore and aft pressures on the control column. Some airplanes have a rudder trim to relieve steady pressures on the rudder pedals, and some also have aileron trim. The trim is used to relieve prolonged control pressures in steady conditions of flight, such as straight and level, climbing, and descending. The trim is not altered in transient maneuvers or when turning.

The elevator is used to hold or change the desired pitch attitude. If the new condition requires a steady pressure, then flying becomes quite tiring, making accurate flight difficult. Trim is used to relieve this steady pressure on the control column. Trim is never used to change the attitude of the airplane; it is only used to relieve steady control pressure after the change is made.

Elevator Trim

Elevator trim in most airplanes is achieved by a small trim tab located on the trailing edge of the elevator. The trim tab is operated by a trim wheel in the cockpit. In some aircraft the trim wheel applies a force via a spring tension that achieves the same effect.

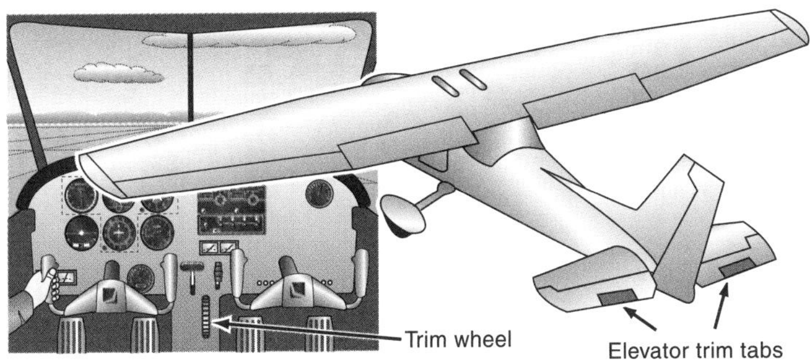

Figure 8-18 The elevator trim tabs and trim wheel.

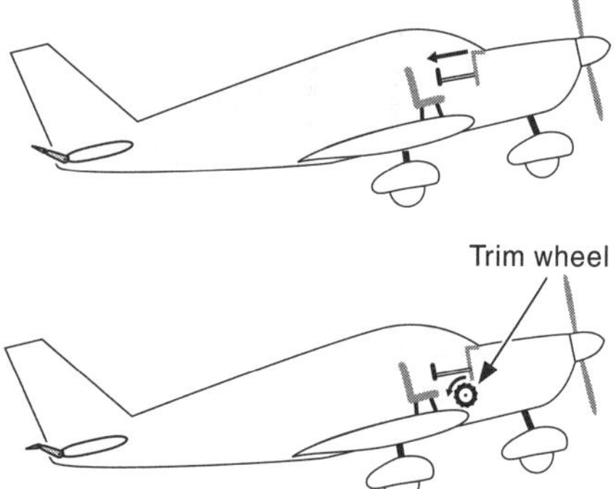

Figure 8-19 Using elevator trim to relieve constant pressures on the control column.

Trimming Technique

If the pilot has to hold a steady back pressure to maintain a constant attitude then this pressure is relieved by winding the trim wheel rearward until there is no residual pressure. The aircraft is now in trim and will hold that angle of attack. Conversely, if the aircraft had increased speed or power and the pilot was having to apply forward pressure to maintain a constant attitude, then the trim wheel would be wound forward until the force was removed. The aircraft's stability would then maintain that trimmed angle of attack. The essence of trimming is to hold the attitude constant with the hand that is flying and simultaneously remove the out-of-trim forces with the hand that is spare.

Retrimming

Retrimming will be necessary for the following reasons:

- after a new pitch attitude (angle of attack) is selected;
- whenever a new airspeed is stabilized;
- after a power and flight path change;
- after a configuration change (e.g. alteration of flap position or landing gear); and
- after a change in the position of the center of gravity (say as fuel burns off, passengers move, baggage is shifted or parachutists depart).

While you are trimming the airplane, the pitch attitude should be held constant.

Correct trimming is achieved by moving the trim wheel in a natural sense. If you are holding back pressure on the control column, then wind the trim wheel back, gradually releasing the pressure so that the pitch attitude does not change.

Conversely, if forward pressure is needed to maintain pitch attitude, then wind the trim wheel forward until there is no steady pressure required on the control column.

While you are trimming the aircraft, the pitch attitude should be held constant with the hand. If the aircraft is equipped with rudder trim, it is used in the same way to remove rudder pressure once the balance ball is centered. If the aircraft has aileron trim as well, first hold the attitude and balance constant, trim out the pitch force, do the same for the rudder while holding the wings level, and finally, trim out the aileron forces.

Change

Check, Hold, Adjust, Trim

Figure 8-20 Control sequence when trimming.

AIRMANSHIP

Airmanship is the practice of safe, courteous and professional flying. Part of this is being aware of other users of the training airspace and planning for eventualities. Looking out for other aircraft will be stressed and each exercise will include an introduction to some *emergency procedures* so that you can cope with non-standard aircraft responses and malfunctions. These situations are rare, but it is better to know how to cope.

Control Technique

Taxi with one hand on the control column to prevent the controls being blown around by the wind. Fly with one hand on the control column and keep the other free for trim, throttle, radios etc.

Control Pressures

The control of an aircraft is by the pilot applying pressure to the control column to overcome the resistance of the controls to move. This will become second nature. But there is no place for large, insensitive inputs as these are potentially damaging at high speed and potentially disconcerting at low speed. Fly the aircraft as if you were driving a sports car rather than a truck. Be firm in telling the aircraft where you want it to go. Set the attitude you want, overcome any resistance to maintain that attitude and then trim.

Engine Handling

Be gentle with the engine and it will always respond. Take 2–3 seconds to apply full power from idle and vice versa. Sudden power changes cause sudden temperature changes that are not beneficial.

Who Has Control?

Ensure a positive exchange of flight controls between instructor and student at all times.

Believe it or not, aircraft have taken off with neither pilot in control. Therefore, there is a formal process where the instructor and student take or pass control of the aircraft.

During your training, control will be passed from your instructor to you and then back again quite frequently. Your flying instructor will say, "You have control" (or words to that

1. You have control
2. I have control

Figure 8-21 Be clear at all times as to who has control.

effect) when you are to take control. On hearing this instruction, you should place your hands and feet on the controls lightly but firmly and, once you feel comfortable to take control, respond by saying, "I have control." Each change of control should be preceded by an initial statement followed by a response from the other pilot.

Look Out for Other Aircraft

During your early flights, you will be too busy to see anything but, nevertheless, it is useful to be looking out. Looking at a distant object orients you, which reduces any motion sickness and builds an awareness of other traffic. When you can, look outside and scan from left to right, and up and down, in a methodical way as if you were searching for a missing aircraft. Visual flying requires that the pilot maintains a high visual awareness of the environment outside the cockpit so as to adjust the attitude of the airplane to the natural horizon, look out for other aircraft, check passage over the ground and remain clear of cloud.

Used a series of short, regularly spaced eye movements to scan for other aircraft.

Figure 8-22 The view from the cockpit.

There is a blind spot under the nose of the airplane that the pilot cannot see, which you should periodically clear by making shallow turns that enable you to see this area out of the side window. Get to know the blind spots of your airplane, and periodically take action to clear the areas normally obscured.

The relative position of other airplanes is best described by using the clock code, based on a horizontal clock face aligned with the airplane's nose. An airplane ahead of you, but higher, would be described as *12 o'clock high*, while one slightly behind and below you on the left-hand side would be at *left 8 o'clock* low. Always say *left* or *right* before the clock number (e.g. *left eight o'clock low*). It will get the pilot looking in the right direction before you finish speaking and avoid confusion.

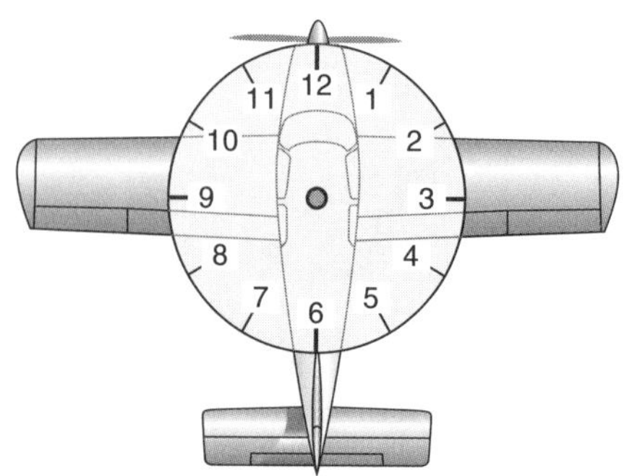

Figure 8-23 The clock code.

REVIEW 8

Primary Controls

1. What are the primary flight controls?
2. What is used to control pitch?
3. What are used to control roll and bank?
4. What is used to control yaw and balance?
5. How is the balance ball kept in the center?
6. Which motion occurs about which axis in the diagram below?

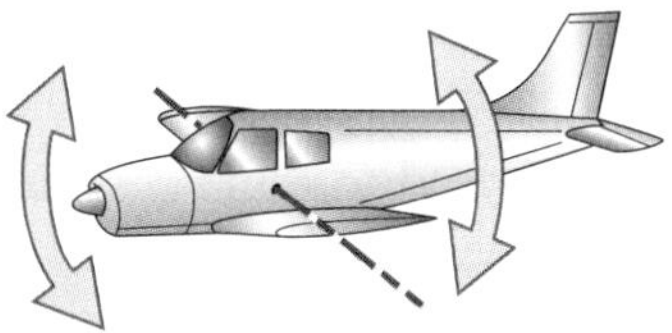

7. Which motion occurs about which axis in the diagram below?

8. Which motion occurs about which axis in the diagram below?

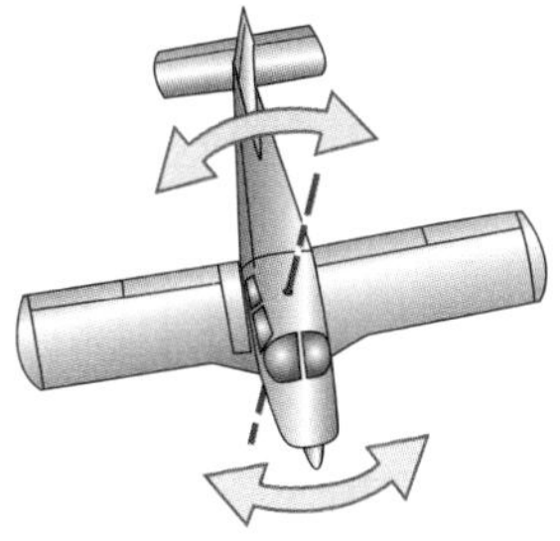

9. Moving the elevator causes motion in which plane and movement about which axis?
10. Moving the ailerons causes motion in which plane and movement about which axis?
11. Moving the rudder causes motion in which plane and movement about which axis?
12. Is the rudder generally used to yaw the airplane or prevent unwanted yaw or sideslip?
13. To which side will the nose yaw, and from which side will it be prevented yawing, if the right rudder pedal is moved forward?
14. To which side will the nose yaw if the left rudder pedal is moved forward?
15. To which side will the airplane roll if the control column is rotated to the left?
16. To which side will the airplane roll if the control column is rotated to the right?
17. Which way is the control column of the airplane below rotated? Which way will it roll?

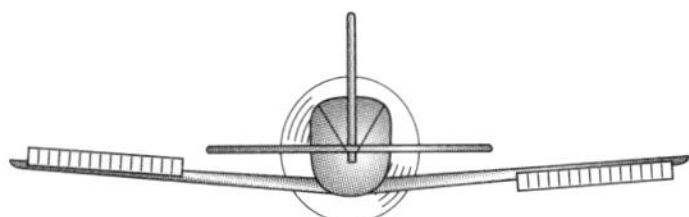

18. If the control column is rotated to the left, which way does the left aileron move? Which way does the right aileron move?
19. If the control column is rotated to the right, which way does the left aileron move? Which way does the right aileron move?
20. Which way will the elevator deflect if the control column is moved backward? How will the nose attitude change?
21. Which way will the elevator deflect if the control column is moved forward? How will the nose attitude change?
22. In which direction will the trailing edge of the rudder move if the left rudder pedal is moved forward?
23. In which direction will the trailing edge of the rudder move if the right rudder pedal is moved forward?
24. What is the natural ability of an airplane to remain in, or return to, its original attitude?

25. At normal flying speeds, how should movement of the control column feel when making control inputs?
26. To center the balance ball on the instrument pictured below, which side rudder pressure do you need to apply?

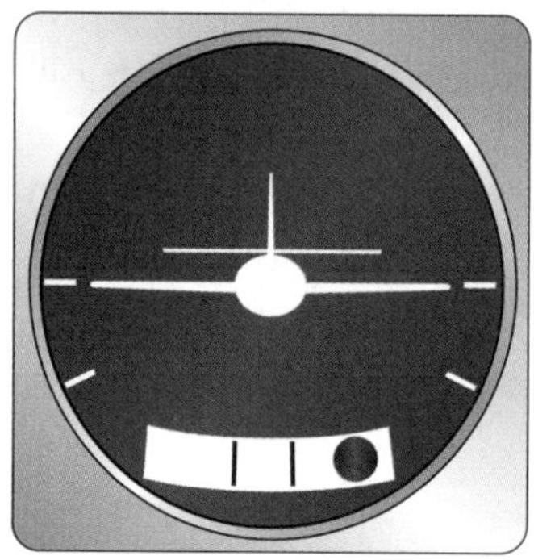

27. Moving each of the three primary flight controls causes a direct effect followed by what sort of effect?
28. How does rotating the control column to the left affect the left aileron? How is the right aileron affected? Which way will the airplane roll? To which side may there be a slight tendency to yaw? What is this yaw know as?
29. How does rotating the control column to the right affect the left aileron? How is the right aileron affected? Which way will the airplane roll? To which side will there be a slight tendency to yaw? What is this yaw know as?
30. What is deflected to cause adverse aileron yaw?
31. When the ailerons are neutralized, even when the airplane is banked, does the tendency for adverse aileron yaw cease?
32. In which direction will the airplane tend to yaw in a left turn with ailerons centered? How will the pitch attitude change?
33. Applying left rudder will yaw the nose to which side? This will cause the indirect effect of a slight roll to which side?
34. Applying right rudder will yaw the nose to which side? This will cause the indirect effect of a slight roll to which side?
35. How will the airspeed normally change when lowering the nose with elevator.
36. How will the airspeed normally change when raising the nose with elevator?
37. What can be used to keep the balance ball centered to counteract the adverse aileron yaw caused by deflected ailerons?
38. What can be used to remove steady unwanted pressures on the control column?
39. As well as the elevator trim, what other sort of trim are some airplanes also fitted with?
40. While you are trimming the airplane, should the pitch attitude be allowed to change?
41. Should elevator trim be used to alter pitch attitude?
42. Should the trim be altered in transient maneuvers such as turning?
43. To relieve yourself of steady back pressure on the control column, in which direction do you wind the trim wheel?
44. To relieve yourself of steady forward pressure on the control column, in which direction do you wind the trim wheel?
45. As the trim takes effect, what should happen to the steady pressure on the control column? Should you allow the nose attitude to change when trimming?
46. Your aircraft has a small trim tab on the back of the elevator. To trim nose up, in which direction should the trim tab move? What sort of force is used? In which direction will this hold the nose of the airplane? Which way do you wind the trim wheel to do so?
47. Is trimming necessary after a new pitch attitude has been selected with the control column?

48. Is trimming necessary after a power change?
49. Is trimming necessary after the flap position has been altered?
50. Is trimming necessary after a heavy brief case is passed back to be stored behind the rear seat?
51. Is back pressure usually required in a turn if a constant altitude is to be maintained? Is it usual to trim in a turn? What sort of maneuver is this?
52. How does the effect of moving a flight control surface change in relation to the magnitude of movement of the control?
53. How does the effect of moving a flight control surface change with the speed of the airflow over the surface? How does the speed of the airflow over the flight control surface change with the airspeed of the airplane?
54. With an increase in airspeed, which of the following flight controls feel firmer and are more effective: elevator, ailerons or rudder?
55. In terms of magnitude, how does increasing power change the amount of air propelled rearward by the propeller?
56. What is the air propelled rearward by the propeller called?
57. Over which part of the airplane structure does the propeller stream flow?
58. With an increase in power while the airspeed is low, say in a steep climb, which of the following flight controls feel firmer and are more effective: elevator, ailerons, rudder?
59. Is the elevator on a T-tail affected to the same extent as the rudder by the propeller slipstream? In what way?
60. What shape is the propeller slipstream?
61. In conventional aircraft, in which direction does the propeller rotate, as seen from the cockpit? Which side of the fin will the slipstream impinge? In which direction does this cause a tendency for the nose to yaw as power is increased?
62. A very important aspect of airmanship while flying maneuvers is to always maintain a good lookout for other aircraft. True or false?

Answers are given on page 577.

TASK

Direct Effect of Each Primary Control

Aim: To observe the direct (immediate effect of moving each primary control.

1. The Direct Effect of the Elevator is to Pitch the Airplane

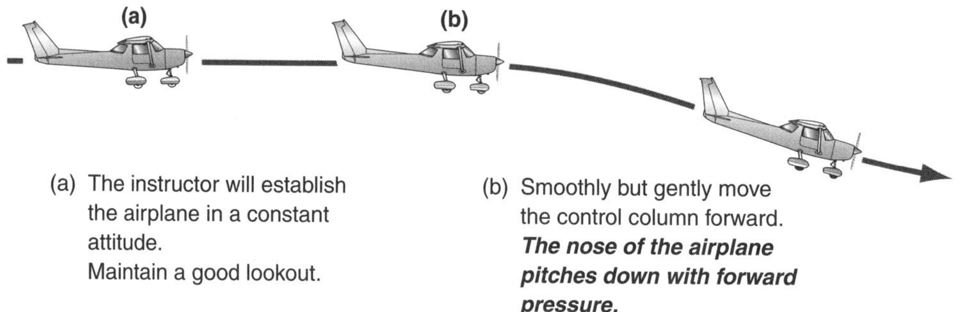

(a) The instructor will establish the airplane in a constant attitude.
Maintain a good lookout.

(b) Smoothly but gently move the control column forward.
The nose of the airplane pitches down with forward pressure.

2. The Direct Effect of the Ailerons is to Roll the Airplane

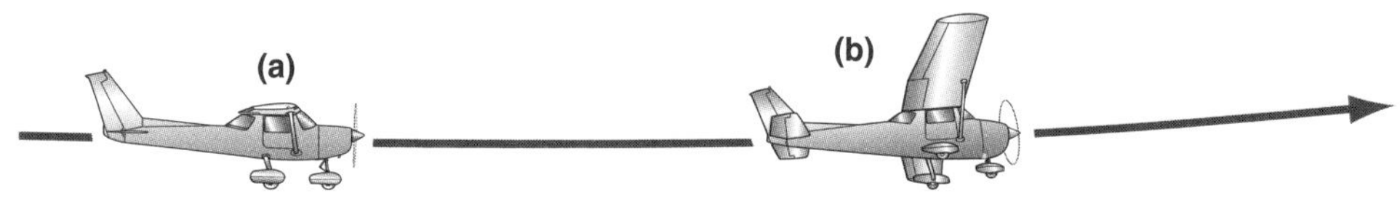

(a) Establish the airplane in a constant attitude.
Maintain a good lookout.

(b) Initially hold the wings level then smoothly rotate the control column to the left.
The airplane rolls to the left.

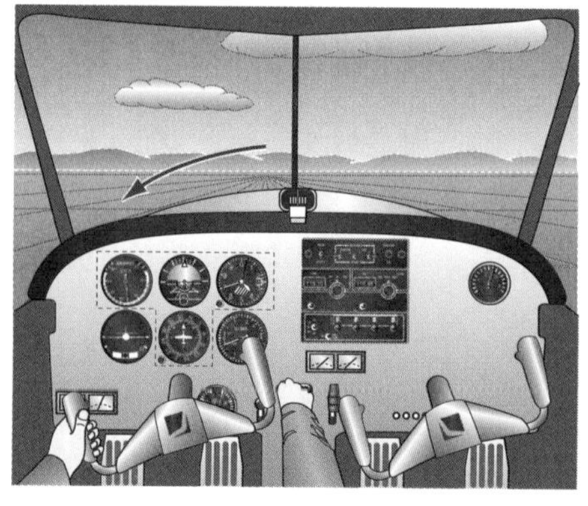

(c) Smoothly and gently move the control column rearward. ***The nose of the airplane pitches up.***

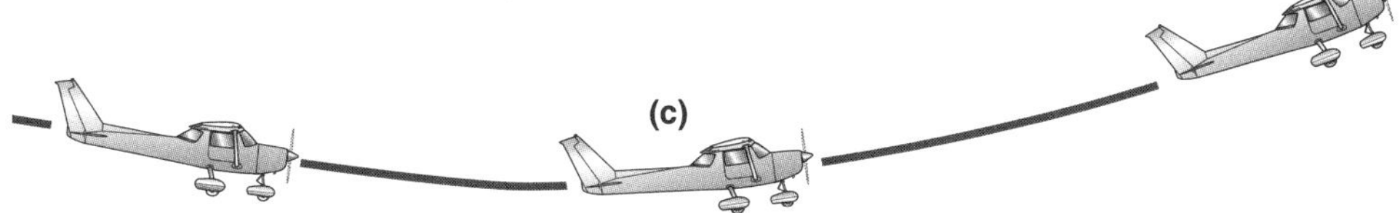

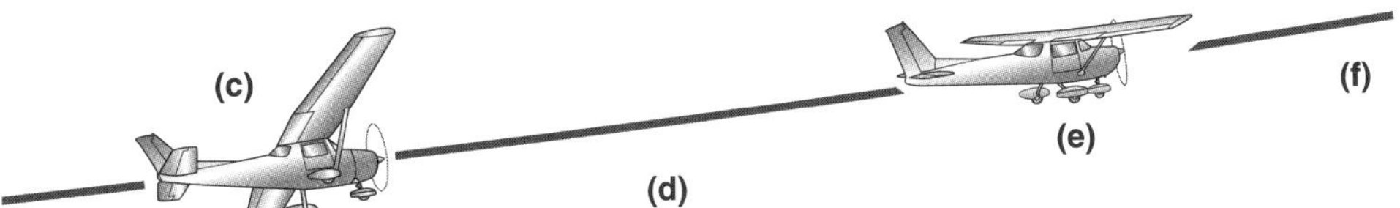

(c) Centralize the control column. ***Rolling ceases and a steady bank angle is maintained.***

(d) To roll to wings level, smoothly rotate control column to the right. ***The airplane rolls to the right***

(e) When the wings are level centralize the control column.

(f) Repeat this exercise for rolls to the right and left using different amounts of control movement.

3. The Direct Effect of the Rudder is to Yaw the Airplane

(a) Establish the airplane in a constant attitude. Maintain a good lookout.

(b) Select a reference point on the horizon.

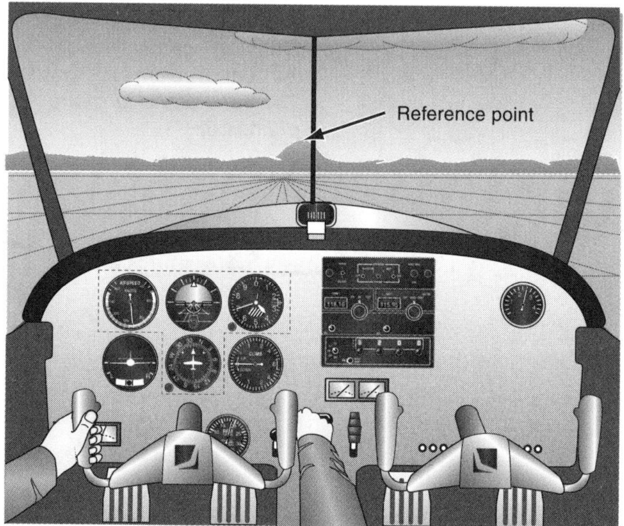

Steady, straight and level flight.

(c) Smoothly apply left rudder pressure.

The nose of the airplane yaws left (and the balance ball is thrown out to the right).

Left rudder—nose yaws left and balance ball thrown right.

(d) Centralize the rudder pedals (by removing left rudder pressure).

(e) Repeat using right rudder pressure and observe the reverse results.

4. The Controls Work in the Same Sense when the Airplane is Banked

(a) Establish the airplane in a constant attitude. Look out.

(b) Bank the airplane with the aileron control.

Forward pressure on the control column pitches the nose down and away from the pilot.

Rearward pressure on the control column pitches the nose up and toward the pilot.

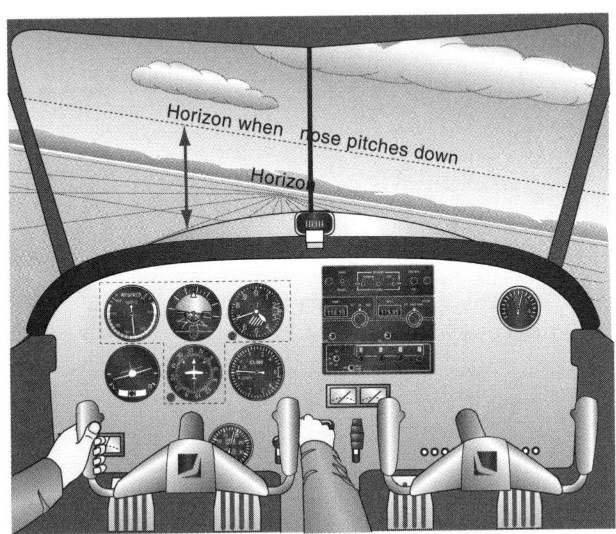

Airplane banked to the left—forward control column pressure still pitches the nose down

(c) Set the airplane with a high nose attitude.

Rotating the control column left causes the airplane to roll left.

Rotating the control column right causes the airplane to roll right.

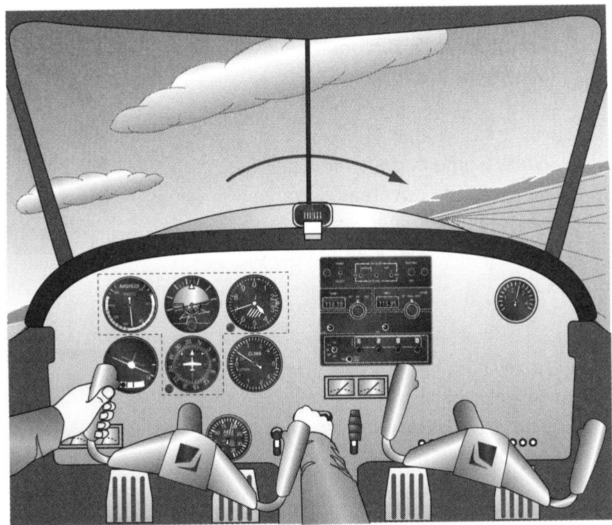

With a high nose attitude the airplane still responds to the aileron control—rolls right (and left)

(d) Bank the airplane with the ailerons.

Pushing the left rudder pedal causes the nose to yaw left relative to the pilot.

Pushing the right rudder pedal causes the nose to yaw right relative to the pilot.

TASK

Indirect Effect of Each Primary Control

Aim: To observe the indirect effect of moving each primary control.

1. Roll causes Yaw: the Indirect Effect of the Ailerons

(a) Establish a constant attitude, maintaining a good lookout.

(b) Remove your feet from the rudder pedals.

Left bank...

(c) Apply aileron by moving the control column.
The airplane banks and then, because of the resulting sideslip, yaws toward the lower wing and then rolls further, i.e. steepens the turn.

Note: Some aircraft will demonstrate adverse aileron yaw especially at low speed. Discuss this with your instructor.

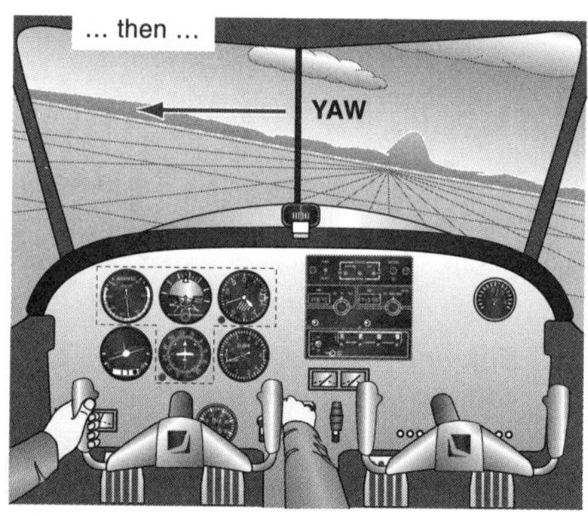

...causes a yaw to the left.

(d) At low airspeed apply a large aileron deflection.
The nose momentarily yaws in the opposite direction.

Adverse aileron yaw.

2. Yaw causes Roll: the Indirect Effect of the Rudder

(a) Establish straight and level flight, maintaining a good lookout.

(b) Take your hands off the control column.

(c) Apply trim rudder pressure.

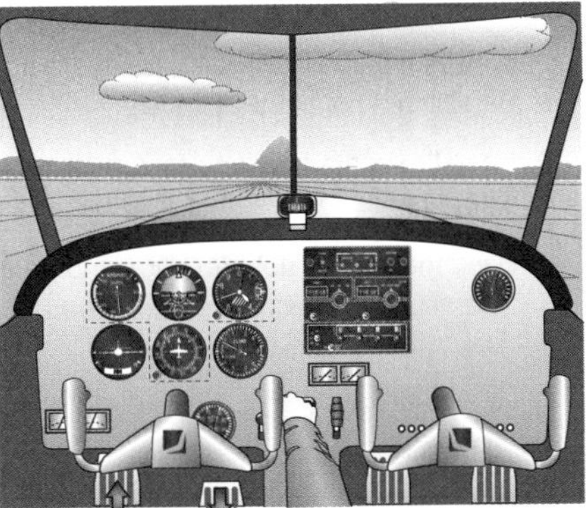

Left rudder applied

Left yaw...

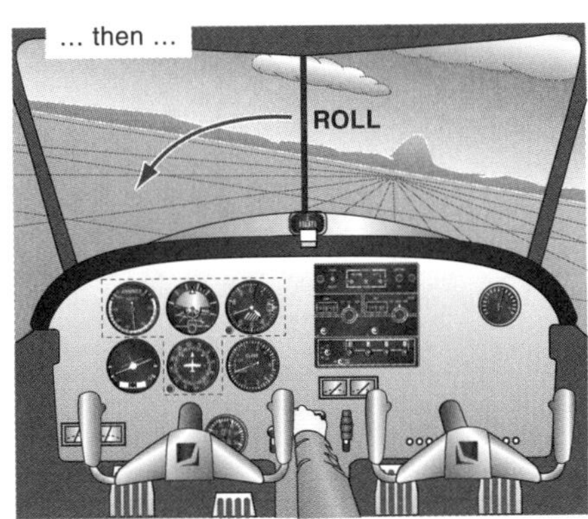

...causes a roll to the left.

The airplane yaws and then, because of the yaw, rolls in the same direction.

Note: The effects in step 1 and 2 will also be the same when the airplane is banked, climbing, or descending.

3. *The Indirect Effect of the Elevator Changing the Pitch Attitude Alters the Flightpath: (Airspeed and Altitude)*

(a) Establish a constant attitude.

(b) Ease the control column forward and hold the new attitude:
The airspeed increases and the aircraft descends.

(c) Ease the control column back and hold the new attitude:
The airspeed decreases and the aircraft climbs.

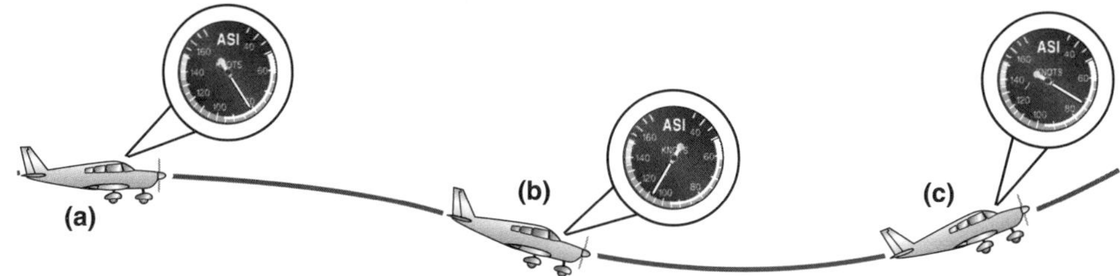

TASK

Effect of Airspeed and Slipstream

Aim: To observe the effect of increased airflow over each of the flight control surfaces as a result of airspeed and propeller slipstream.

1. The Effect of Airspeed

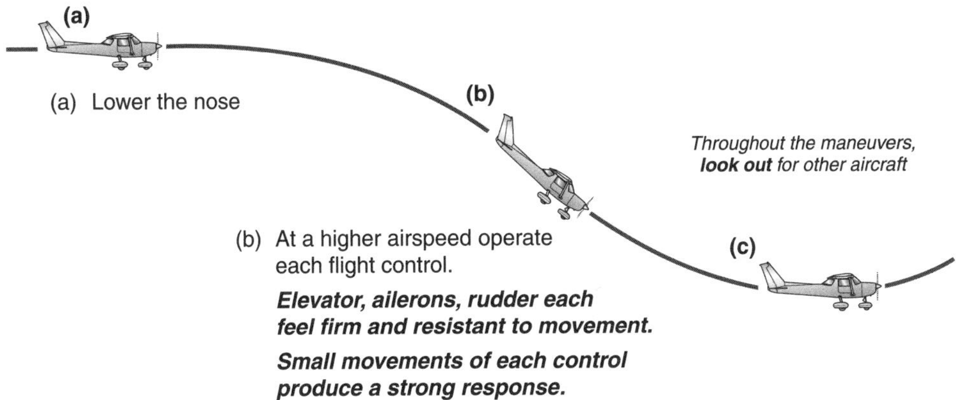
(a)
(b)
(c)
Throughout the maneuvers, **look out** for other aircraft

(a) Lower the nose

(b) At a higher airspeed operate each flight control.

Elevator, ailerons, rudder each feel firm and resistant to movement.

Small movements of each control produce a strong response.

(c) Raise the nose and hold attitude until a low airspeed.

Each of the primary controls feels sloppy.

Large control deflections are easy to make against little resistance.

The aircraft is less responsive to movements of the controls and large movements may be required.

2. The Effect of Slipstream

Continuing from the exercise above, with the airplane at low airspeed.

(d)

(d) Apply climb power and adjust pitch attitude to maintain same low airspeed.

Ailerons (outside slipstream) still feel sloppy. Large aileron control movements necessary to roll the airplane.

Elevator and rudder are firmer and more effective due to the energized airflow from the propeller slipstream.

The result of a low airspeed and high climb power (strong slipstream)—the airplane is responsive in pitch and yaw, but sluggish in roll.

TASK

Effects of Power Changes

Aim: To observe the effect of changing power.

The Effect of Changing Power

(a) Trim the airplane for constant attitude.

Remove your hands from the control column and your feet from the rudder pedals.

(b) Smoothly open the throttle to full power.

Nose pitches up and yaws left.

(c) Balance and trim

(d) Smoothly close the throttle

Nose pitches down and yaws right.

Straight and level, apply full power

Straight and level, throttle closed

Note: A good means of practicing this is to maintain the straight and level pitch attitude with the nose on a reference point on the horizon.

Smoothly move the throttle from idle to full power and back again, anticipating the changes and holding pitch attitude constant and balancing the unwanted yaw.

Aim: To counteract imbalances resulting from power changes.

The Correct Pilot Response When Changing Power

(a) When increasing power:

Hold attitude with elevator (forward pressure).

Balance with rudder.

Trim.

(b) When reducing power:

Hold attitude with elevator (back pressure).

Balance with rudder.

Trim.

Nose pitches up and yaws left (in most training aircraft)

Nose pitches down and yaws to right

Note: A good means of practicing this is to maintain the straight and level pitch attitude with the nose on a reference point on the horizon.

Smoothly move the throttle from idle to full power and back again, anticipating the changes and holding pitch attitude constant and balancing the unwanted yaw.

TASK

Trimming

Aim: To use the trim to relieve steady pressures on control column.

1. Trimming the Airplane Correctly

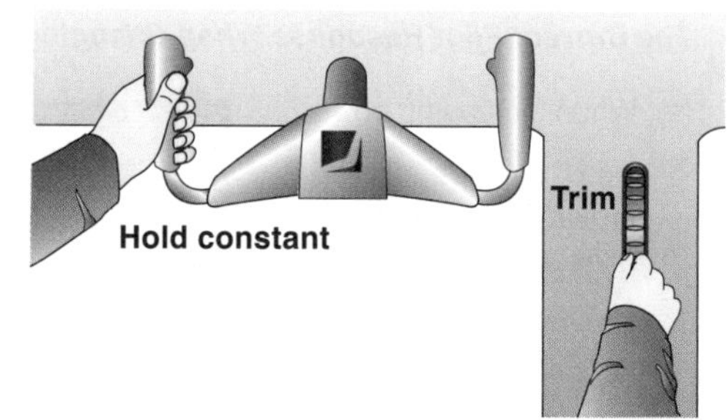

To trim the airplane correctly in pitch:

Hold the desired pitch attitude with pressure on the control column.

Then, without looking, place your hand on the trim wheel and trim (in a natural sense) to relieve pressures so that the desired attitude is held without exerting any pressure on the control column. If the load is high, trim quickly. As the load reduces, trim more finely. Gradually, the pressure on the control column can be relaxed.

2. Getting the Feel of Incorrect Trim

(a) To get the feel of incorrect trim, fly straight and level, holding the desired pitch attitude with elevator.

(b) Then, without letting the pitch attitude change, gradually wind the trim wheel forward.

You may need considerable back pressure on the control column to hold the nose up in the level flight attitude.

(c) Gradually wind the trim wheel back until the control column pressure is again reduced to zero.

(d) Repeat the procedure, winding the trim aft this time, noting the forward pressure required on the control column to maintain the level flight attitude.

Note: This is not a normal procedure. It is done to experience the effect of incorrect trim.

3. Common Situations Requiring Retrimming

Practice trim changes by holding a particular pitch attitude and then:

(i) adopt a new pitch attitude and flightpath;

(ii) change the power setting and airspeed; or

(iii) change the aircraft configuration (e.g. lower the flaps).

After each change, hold the pitch attitude constant for a short period (10 or 20 seconds) and allow the airplane to settle into the new flightpath and/or airspeed before retrimming.

If strong pressure is required on the control column, it is advisable to relieve most of it fairly quickly and then, after the airplane has settled down, trim more finely.

Note: For airplanes fitted with rudder trim these exercises can be repeated. The same technique applies—use rudder trim to relieve steady pressure on the rudder pedals.

9
Secondary Controls

OBJECTIVES

To describe the operation and effects of the secondary controls:

- configuration (flaps or slats, landing gear); and
- fuel-air supply to the engine (mixture, boost pump, carburetor heat, alternate air).

CONSIDERATIONS

Flaps

The flaps are the downward-deflecting, paired, movable surfaces attached to the inboard trailing edge of each wing. They are operated from the cockpit—in some airplanes, electrically by a switch and, in others, mechanically by a lever. They operate symmetrically and move only between a downward and a streamlined position.

Flaps move symmetrically.

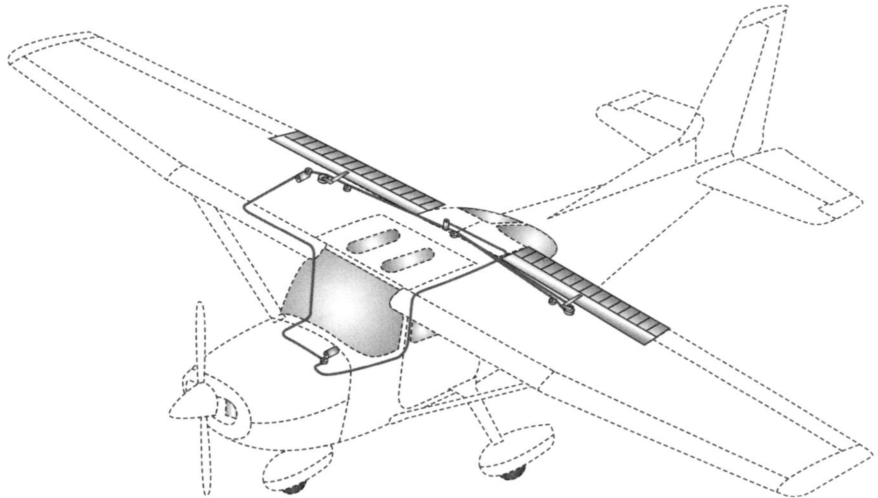

Figure 9-1 Flaps (these are electrically operated).

Flaps increase the lifting ability of the wings by changing its shape.

Flaps alter the curvature of the wings and change the airflow. This affects both the lift and drag. In a sense, flaps create new airfoils. They are used to:

- generate the required lift at a lower speed (which allows safer flight at low airspeeds as well as reducing takeoff and landing distances);
- increase drag to steepen the descent path and improve the pilot's field of view on approach to land; and
- allow the pilot, especially in jets, to set a higher thrust setting on the final approach thereby providing better engine response when required.

As the flaps are lowered the changes in lift and drag will also cause a pitching moment. This will result in the airplane *ballooning* unless counteracted with pressure on the control column.

Conversely, when the flaps are raised, there will be a pitching tendency in the opposite direction and a tendency to sink. Not all aircraft react in the same way as it depends on the position of the wings, the effect of the flaps and position of the horizontal stabilizer. You will need to ask your instructor how your aircraft behaves.

A lower pitch attitude is required as flaps are lowered.

Once attitude and power changes are complete and the airspeed has stabilized at the desired value, these pressures can be trimmed off. In general, a lower pitch attitude is required to achieve the same airspeed when flaps are lowered compared to when the wings are *clean*.

Figure 9-2 Flaps require a lower pitch attitude and provide a better forward view for the same flight path.

The initial stages of flap are sometimes called lift flaps because the lifting ability of the wing is increased considerably, but at the cost of extra drag. Flaps allow the required lift to be generated at lower speed. The larger flap settings are sometimes called *drag flaps* because they cause a marked increase in drag for little improvement in lifting ability. If airspeed is to be maintained, the increased drag must be balanced by either:

- additional power; or
- a greater component of the weight force acting along the flight path (achieved by descending or steepening the descent).

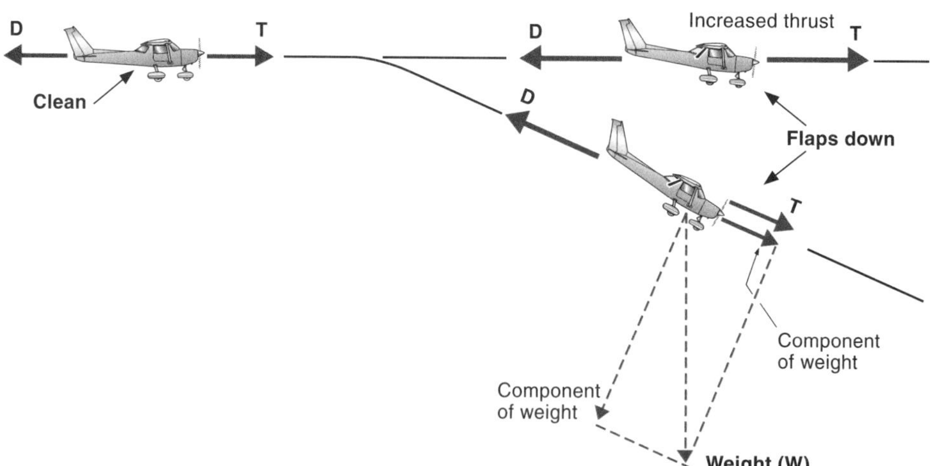

Figure 9-3 Flaps require increased power or a descending flight path if airspeed is to be maintained.

Flap Operating Speed Range

Move flaps in stages and retrim.

To avoid overstressing the structure, ensure that the airspeed is less than the maximum speed allowed with flaps extended (V_{FE}). This figure is stated in the pilot's operating handbook and is shown on the airspeed indicator as the high, speed end of the white arc.

Two straight and level stalling speeds (at maximum aircraft weight) are available on the airspeed indicator:

- with full flap (V_{S0}), the low-speed end of the white band; and
- with a clean wing (V_{S1}), the low-speed end of the green band.

They mark the approximate minimum flying speeds straight and level that the airplane can maintain in these configurations.

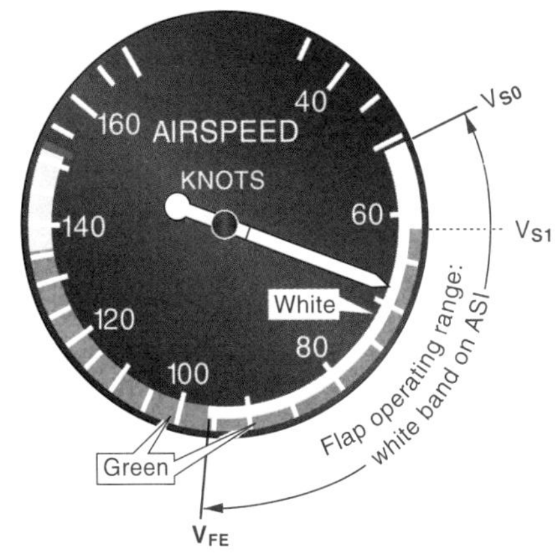

Figure 9-4 The flap operating range on the airspeed indicator.

Trim Change and Attitude Adjustment

Raising or lowering large amounts of flap may require large changes in pitch attitude and trim. For this reason, it is usual to operate the flaps in stages, retrimming after each selection. To operate the flaps:

- lower (or raise) one stage at a time;
- adjust and hold the desired pitch attitude and make necessary power change; and
- trim.

Retractable Landing Gear

If your airplane has retractable gear, the instructor will demonstrate the following:

- normal and abnormal operations and indications;
- the effect on drag and trim; and
- state the limiting speed.

Note the buffet and any trim and power change needed to maintain attitude and airspeed.

Fuel-Air Controls

Carburetor Heat

Carburetor heat is used to prevent or remove ice that can form in the carburetor under certain conditions.

Reduced static air pressure in the throat of the carburetor causes a drop in temperature. Further, vaporization of the fuel causes more cooling. These factors may reduce the temperature to below freezing. If the air is sufficiently moist, ice may form in the induction system, partially blocking the flow of fuel-air mixture to the cylinders. With high humidity, carburetor ice can occur at outside air temperatures of 100°F or more. It seriously affects maximum engine power adversely.

Noticeable effects of carburetor ice include:

- a drop in RPM;
- lack of throttle response;
- rough running; and
- possible engine stoppage.

How Carburetor Heat Works. The carburetor heat control, which is usually a knob or lever situated near the throttle, can be used to direct hot air into the carburetor to prevent ice forming or to melt any ice which has already formed. Being less dense that cold air, hot air lowers the mass of each fuel-air charge burned in the cylinders, reducing the maximum power available from the engine. Consequently, as carburetor heat is applied, the engine RPM will drop. If ice is present, the RPM will rise following the initial drop as the ice is melted by the warm air. As a precaution when operating at low RPM, it is usual to apply full hot carburetor heat, such as in a prolonged descent. The control is returned to full cold when higher power is required (and if protection from carburetor ice is not required).

In many airplanes, the hot air for carburetor heat is supplied from around the engine exhaust and is unfiltered (unlike the cold air that is filtered in the normal engine air intake). For this reason, it is usual to taxi with the carburetor heat control in the full cold position to avoid introducing dust and grit into the engine.

Alternate Air

If your airplane has a fuel-injected engine, there is no carburetor or carburetor heat. However, induction icing is still possible, and an alternate air control is provided.

Mixture Control

The mixture is normally leaned out on the cruise to improve fuel economy and optimize range.

The mixture control is usually a red serrated knob situated near the throttle. Its two functions are:

- to lean the mixture (reduce the ratio of fuel to air) for optimum engine performance and fuel economy; and
- to cut off the fuel supply to the carburetor and therefore stop the engine.

Using the mixture control is how the aircraft engine is normally stopped (unlike a car which is stopped by turning off the ignition). The reason is that, by cutting off the fuel, there will be no fuel left in the fuel lines and so the risk of fire is reduced.

The mixture control should be adjusted to maintain peak performance.

Because air density decreases with increase in height as an airplane climbs, there is a lower mass of air being mixed with the same mass of fuel in the carburetor. Thus, the fuel-air mixture becomes *richer* as height is gained and an increasing amount of fuel will remain unburned because of the reduced air available for the combustion process.

This fuel is not only wasted in the exhaust but eventually causes rough running and partial loss of power. Above 5,000 feet and when the power is less than 75% maximum continuous, the mixture is leaned by moving the mixture control partially out/backward. This reduces the weight of fuel mixing with the air being taken into the carburetor. As the fuel-air mixture is leaned and returns to its optimum ratio, the engine RPM will show a slight increase and the engine will run more smoothly. Leaning the mixture past the optimum ratio will cause the RPM to fall, at which point the mixture control should be moved back in slightly to the rich side of optimum.

Shut the engine down by moving the mixture control to idle cut off.

It is preferable to operate an engine slightly rich, rather than lean (when detonation may occur and damage the engine). Note that the maximum range figures published by the manufacturer assume cruising with the mixture correctly leaned. Moving the mixture control fully back to the idle cutoff position cuts off fuel to the carburetor completely.

Boost Pump and Fuel Selectors. A major part of the pilot's task is management of the systems and the progress of the flight. Fuel management is fundamental and a regular cycle of checking will be introduced into your training at an early stage.

Many aircraft have separate fuel tanks that must be selected during flight. The engine may also have an electrically driven fuel boost pump that is turned on when changing fuel selections and when needing high power from the engine for a go-around or a stall recovery.

AIRMANSHIP

Flap Selection

Do not exceed the maximum flap-extended speed (V_{FE}) and do not raise the flaps unless clearly above the clean stalling speed (say V_S plus at least 10 knots) above 200 feet AGL and positively climbing.

Carburetor Heat

Check your manufacturer's recommendations.

Mixture

Select full rich for normal operations but read the information manual for leaning procedures.

Figure 9-5 Not so complicated, is it?

REVIEW 9

Secondary Controls

1. Do wing flaps operate symmetrically? Is this like the ailerons?
2. Do flaps extend upward?
3. What effect does extending the flaps have on the lifting ability of the wing?
4. What effect does extending the flaps have on low-speed flight?
5. A small stage of flaps is often used for takeoff because it increases the lifting ability of the wing? What effect does extending the flaps have on drag?
6. How much drag does full flaps create? What effect does this have on the descent angle?
7. What change to the nose attitude of the airplane usually needs to be made to maintain airspeed when the flaps are extended? What effect does this have on forward view?
8. What effect does extending full flaps on approach to land have on the allowable airspeed? What effect does it have on forward vision? What effect does it have on the landing distance?
9. What color is the flap operating range shown on the airspeed indicator? Which end of the arc is it shown?
10. What is the stalling speed with full flaps extended called? On which color arc on the airspeed indicator is it shown?
11. What is the preferred technique for operating the flaps? Is it a good technique to trim unwanted control pressure off after each stage or only when full flaps are extended?
12. What are the initial stages of flaps often used for takeoff sometimes called?
13. What are the larger stages of flaps that are used for landing sometimes called?
14. Is it permitted to exceed the maximum flaps-extended speed, V_{FE}, with any flaps down?
15. Can you raise the flaps if the airspeed is above the clean stalling speed? At which speed end of which colored band on the airspeed indicator is this?
16. Airmanship means sometimes operating the airplane within its limitations. True or false?
17. To increase power, which way is the throttle moved? To reduce power, which way is the throttle moved?
18. How quickly should large throttle movements be?
19. What could be indicated by a loss of RPM on a warm, humid day in an airplane fitted with a fixed-pitch propeller?
20. What is fully applied to remove carburetor ice by introducing hot air into the carburetor?
21. As carburetor heat is applied, what will initially happen to the engine RPM? How does the density of the air in the carburetor heat system differ from that of the usual induction air? What happens to the engine RPM if carburetor ice was present and has been melted by carburetor heat?
22. When operating with low power, say during descent, is it good airmanship to apply full carburetor heat as a precaution against the formation of carburetor ice?
23. Is the hot air for carburetor heat filtered? Is it usual to taxi on dusty surfaces with carburetor heat hot?
24. Usually, what color is the knob for the mixture control? Where is it situated?
25. What are the two functions of the mixture control?
26. During climbs and descents, in which position should the mixture control normally be set?
27. Describe the technique for leaning the mixture at altitude?
28. To what position is the mixture control moved when shutting down the engine after parking the airplane?

Answers are given on page 578.

TASK

Carburetor Heat

Aim: To learn the correct use of carburetor heat.

1. ***If Carburetor Icing is Suspected (Rough Running and/or RPM Decay)***

   Apply full carburetor heat (by pulling the carburetor heat control knob fully out).

   Note drop in RPM (due to the less dense air now entering the engine cylinders).

   If carburetor icing was present and has been melted, a slight rise in RPM will occur following the initial drop.

   Push carburetor heat knob to full cold. Note RPM rise (denser air is now entering the cylinders).

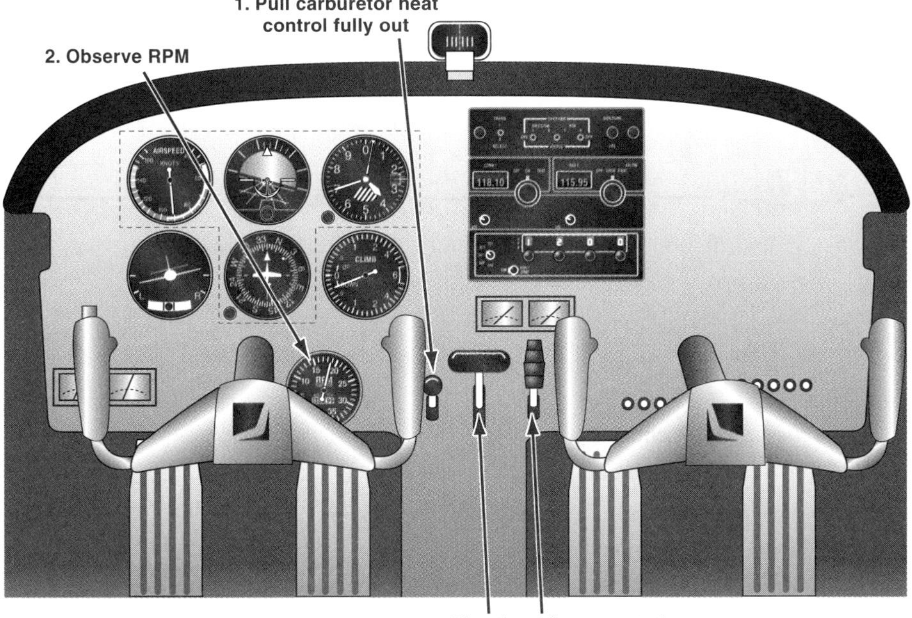

1. Pull carburetor heat control fully out
2. Observe RPM
Throttle
Mixture control

2. ***Using Carburetor Heat as a Precaution***

   (Normal procedure on descent and approach to land.)

   (a) When reducing power to idle:

   Select carburetor heat to full hot.

   Throttle closed.

   (b) When about to increase power:

   Carburetor heat to full cold (if hot air to carburetor no longer required).

   Apply power with the throttle, as required.

Your flight training organization's procedure for using carburetor heat as a precaution may differ from that given here, in which case you should follow it. (There may be variation in the order of operating the throttle and carburetor heat when both reducing and increasing power, perhaps due to manufacturer's recommendations.)

If in doubt as to the correct procedure to follow, consult your flight instructor.

TASK

Effect of Flap

Aim: (a) To observe the effect of altering flap position.
(b) To control the airplane smoothly during flap alteration.

1. Changing Flap Position Causes a Pitching Moment

(a) With the wing clean (i.e., flaps up), establish a constant attitude.

(b) The instructor will reduce the power. Maintain attitude and, when the airspeed is within the flap operating range (white arc on ASI), retrim. (Higher nose attitude is required to maintain height as airspeed is reduced.

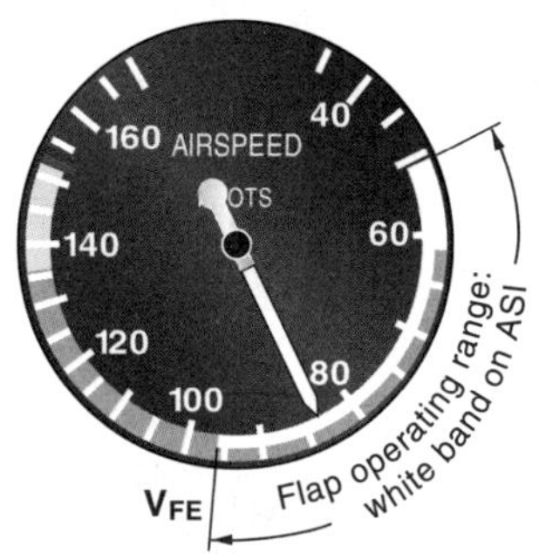

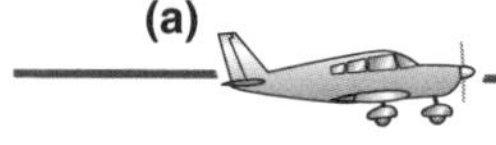

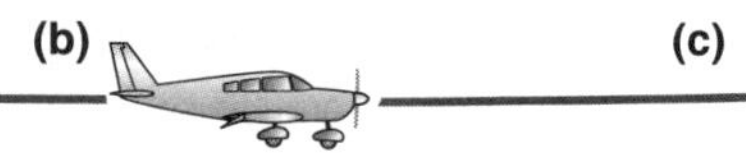

2. Flaps Increase Lift and Drag

(a) From a constant attitude.

Wings clean (flaps up).

Airspeed below V_{FE} (high speed end of white arc).

Leave the power constant throughout the operation.

(b) Lower the first stage of flap, holding pitch attitude constant.

The airplane gains some height (due to the increased lift) and slows down (due to the increased drag). (Check the airspeed.)

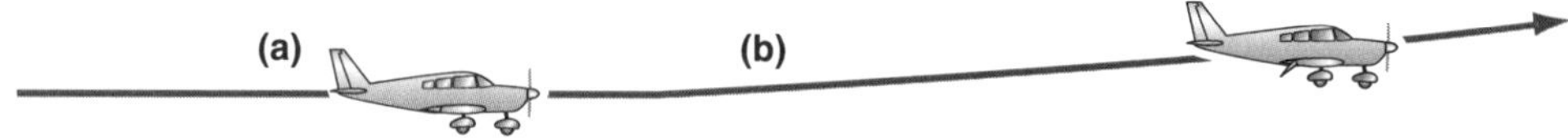

(c) To illustrate the pitching tendency when lowering the flaps, remove your hands from the control column (although normally you never do this).

Note the pitching moment.

Trim for the desired attitude.

Adjust the power.

(d) To illustrate the pitching tendency when raising the flaps, once again temporarily remove your hands from the control column.

Raise the flaps fully in one selection (an incorrect procedure not used in normal operations).

Note the effect. (There will most likely be a strong pitching tendency, accompanied by a height loss.)

Reestablish the attitude and retrim.

In normal flap operations, you will control any pitching moment when flap is changed with pressure on the control column.

(c) Lower the nose to maintain the height and retrim.

Notice the lower nose attitude, improved vision, and lower airspeed.

(d) Lower the remaining flaps in stages and maintain height by lowering the nose; retrim after each flap selection.

Notice the lower airspeed as the extra drag slows the airplane.

(e) Raise the flaps in stages and maintain height by raising the nose; retrim after each flap selection.

Notice the higher airspeed resulting from the reduced drag.

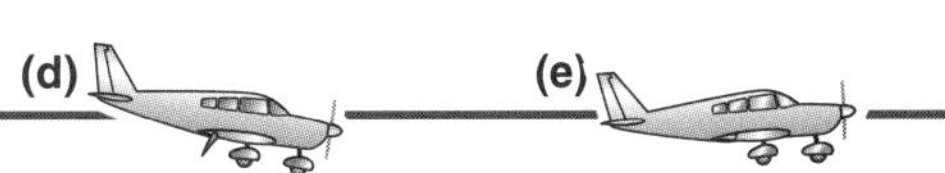

Straight and Level, Climbs, and Descents

10
Straight and Level Flight

OBJECTIVES

To describe:

- the forces that act on an aircraft in straight and level flight;
- the relationship between airspeed and angle of attack;
- the technique to establish, restore and maintain straight and level flight; and
- the configuration, power and attitude relationships and settings to achieve a desired level flight path and speed.

Figure 10-1
Straight and level is wings level and constant altitude.

CONSIDERATIONS

Flying *straight* means maintaining a *constant direction* (*heading*), and this is achieved by keeping the wings level by using the ailerons, and keeping the airplane balanced by using the rudder to prevent any yaw. The visual reference for direction may be a feature in the distance or a compass heading. The balance ball is used to indicate correct balance.

Flying *level* means maintaining a constant altitude, which is achieved by having the power set and the nose held in the correct attitude. Altitude is displayed in the cockpit on the altimeter. The aircraft is *trimmed* to maintain level flight, *force-free*, although the pilot never leaves the controls free. Precise, balanced, straight and level flight in trim is a measure of a good pilot.

Figure 10-2 Straight and level trimmed flight.

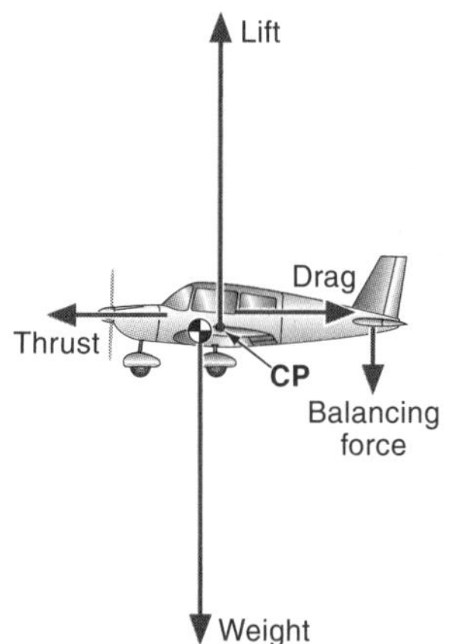

Figure 10-3
The main forces and moments in stabilized straight and level flight.

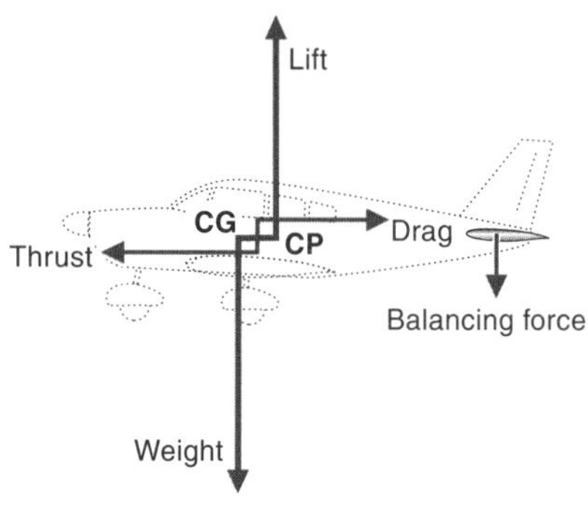

Figure 10-4
The horizontal stabilizer and elevator provides a final balancing moment.

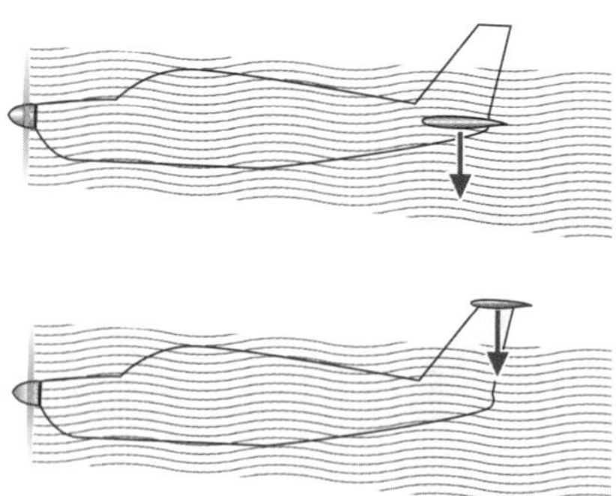

Figure 10-5
Reduction in propwash reduces downward force on the horizontal stabilizer (effect is less for T-tails).

Forces that Act on an Airplane

There are four resultant forces that act on an airplane in flight:

- weight;
- lift;
- thrust; and
- drag.

There are also balancing moments from the empennage.

In stabilized, straight and level flight, the airplane is in *equilibrium* with no tendency to accelerate or to change attitude or direction:

- lift balances weight;
- thrust balances drag; and
- the aircraft is in balance and trim.

It is unusual for the four main forces to counteract each other exactly without some residual *pitching* or *yawing moment* that tends to change the attitude or balance of the aircraft. Almost always, a balancing force, either up or down, is required from the horizontal stabilizer and elevator, and from the rudder. Most airplanes are designed so that the horizontal stabilizer creates a downward aerodynamic force. This balancing force is controlled by the pilot with the elevator and elevator trim. In normal flight, continual small adjustments with the control column are required.

Airplanes are usually designed and balanced so that, if there is a loss of power (or the pilot reduces power), the resultant forces will automatically tend to lower the nose to the gliding attitude, ensuring that a safe flying speed is maintained. (Some ultralight aircraft have insufficient momentum in these conditions and the pilot must positively and quickly lower the nose to the gliding attitude.)

Positive stability is achieved by having the center of pressure (through which the lift acts) located behind the center of gravity, so that the lift-weight couple has a nose-down effect. In normal flight, this is opposed by the thrust-drag, nose-up couple. (A couple is a pair of parallel opposing forces not acting through the same point, and therefore causing a tendency to rotate.) If thrust is lost, the nose-up couple is diminished, the lift-weight, nose-down couple predominates and the nose drops into the gliding attitude. The same effect occurs when the pilot intentionally reduces power, the nose dropping unless back pressure is exerted on the control column.

If power is also reduced and the slipstream over the horizontal stabilizer is reduced, then the downward aerodynamic force on the tail is less, and so the nose of the airplane will drop. (This effect does not apply to T-tail airplanes where the propeller slipstream passes beneath the horizontal stabilizer rather than flowing over and under its surfaces.)

Airplane Stability

Stability is the natural or built-in tendency for an airplane to return to its original attitude (angle of attack) following some disturbance (such as a gust) without the pilot taking any action. An inherently stable airplane will return to its original condition unassisted after being disturbed, and so requires less pilot effort to control than a neutral or unstable airplane.

Longitudinal Stability in Pitch

If, for instance, a gust causes the relative airflow to change and the angle of attack of the wing to increase, then the horizontal stabilizer is also presented to the airflow at a greater angle of attack. It will therefore generate a nose-down aerodynamic force (pitching moment). This will raise the tail and lower the nose.

The horizontal stabilizer provides longitudinal stability.

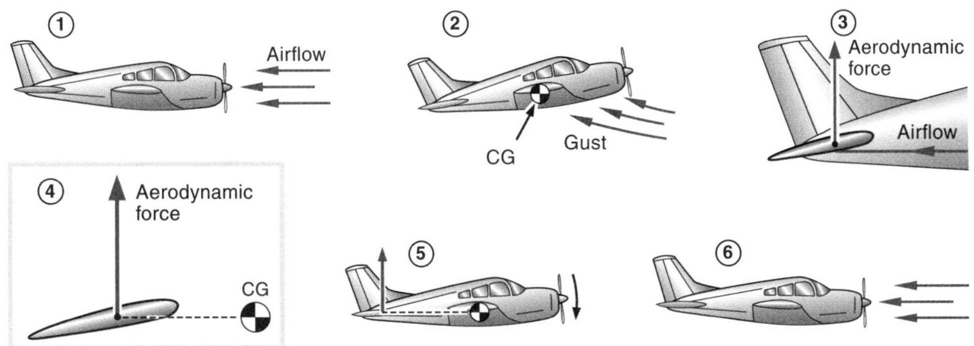

Figure 10-6 Longitudinal stability following a disturbance.

CG Position and Control in Pitch

A forward center of gravity (CG) makes the airplane more stable because of the greater restoring moment from the tail due to its greater moment arm. If the airplane is loaded so that the CG is too far forward:

- the excessive stability will require stronger controlling forces from the elevator, which may become tiring for the pilot when maneuvering; and
- during the landing, the elevator will be less powerful due to the low airspeed and, when the power is reduced, the nose-down moment may make it impossible to flare.

If the airplane is loaded with the CG too far rearward:

- the airplane will be less stable at all airspeeds, and constant attention will have to be given to maintaining the pitch attitude; and
- the tail-heavy moment requires down elevator to maintain balance and therefore there is less deflection available to recover from a stalled condition, making it perhaps impossible to recover from a spin once it stabilizes.

Stability and control considerations make it imperative that an airplane is flown only when the CG is within the approved range (as stated in the flight manual). It is the pilot's absolute responsibility to ensure that this is always the case.

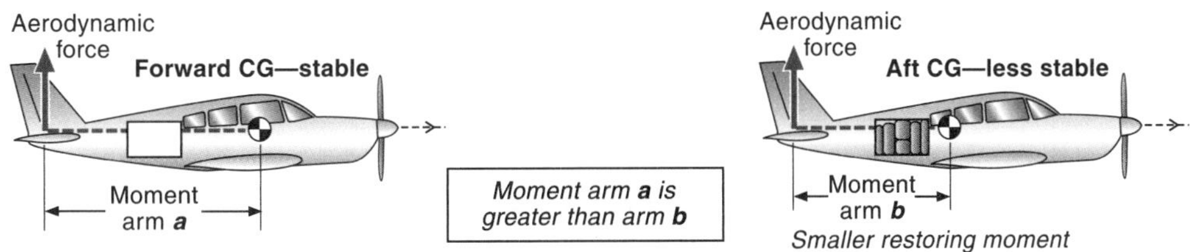

Figure 10-7 Loading affects longitudinal and directional stability and control.

Stability in Yaw and Roll

If the airplane is disturbed from a straight path (it is disturbed in yaw by turbulence), then the fin is presented to the airflow at a greater angle of attack and generates a sideways restoring aerodynamic force.

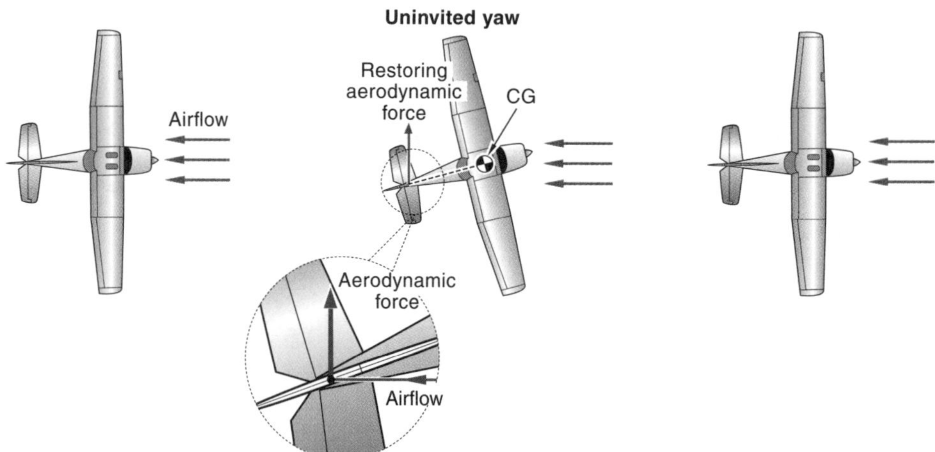

Figure 10-8 Directional stability following a disturbance.

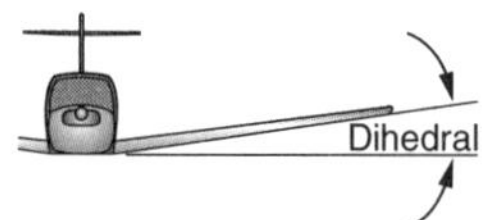

Figure 10-9 Dihedral is a design in which each wing is inclined upward toward the wing tips.

A disturbance in roll will cause one wing to drop and the other to rise. The lift force will be tilted, causing a slip sideways toward the lower wing. If the airplane has high keel surfaces, such as the fin and the side of the fuselage, then the airflow striking them in the slip will tend to restore a wings-level condition.

If the wings are mounted on the top of the fuselage or have *dihedral* (a design feature in which each wing is inclined upward toward the wing tips), the lower wing is presented to the airflow at a greater angle of attack in the sideslip, thereby generating a greater lift force that tends to restore a wings-level condition.

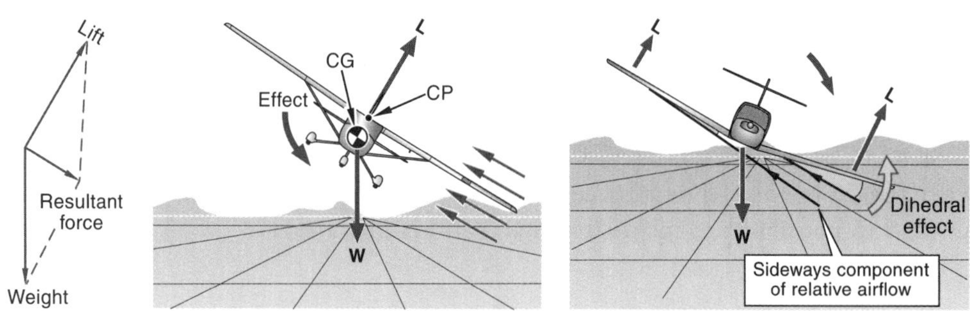

Figure 10-10 A high-wing aircraft acts like a pendulum. Also, high-keel surfaces, such as the fin (left) and dihedral (right), provide lateral stability.

Compared with stability in the pitching plane (longitudinal stability), the stability of the airplane in roll (lateral stability) is not as great. The stability in the yawing plane (directional stability) can be quite powerful. The interrelationship between roll and yaw is generally such that a disturbance in either roll or yaw will eventually lead to a spiral descent, because the yawing moment into the sideslip will dominate the rolling moment that is trying to level the wings. The pilot acts to cancel the sideslip by centering the balance ball and then leveling the wings. This is a continuous process in normal flight.

In general terms, however, the natural stability designed into the airplane will assist you in maintaining straight and level flight: provided you keep the wings close to level, the aircraft is balanced and in trim. You can let the airplane fly itself, with only small restorative corrections on the controls being required.

Lift

The wings are shaped so that the airflow speeds up over their upper surface, creating a reduced static pressure and, at the same time, a reduced airspeed under the wing increases the static pressure. The difference in static pressure between the lower and upper surfaces causes a force that acts mostly upward (perpendicular to the airflow) and slightly rearward (parallel to the airflow). The perpendicular element, or component, of this total force is known as *lift* and the component parallel to the flight path is called *induced drag* (because it is induced by the process of creating lift).

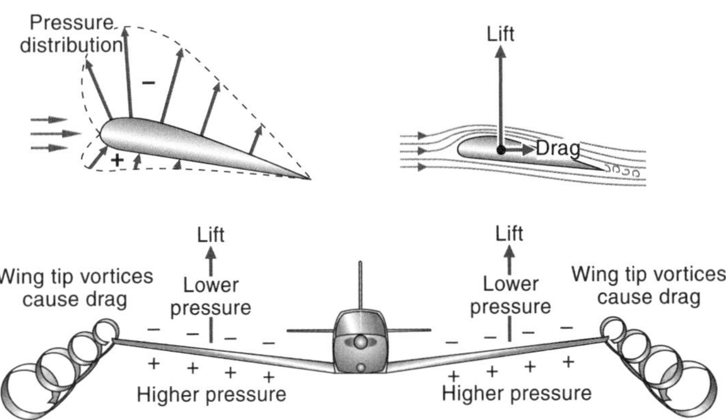

Figure 10-11 The wings produce lift and (consequently) drag.

The lifting ability of a particular wing, known as the *coefficient of lift* (C_L), depends on both the shape of the wing and its angle of attack (the angle at which the wing strikes the air, measured in relation to the chord line of the wing and the flight path of the aircraft, which is the same as the relative airflow).

To fly straight and level and obtain the required lift to balance the weight:

- at low speed, a high angle of attack is required; and
- at high speed, a low angle of attack is required.

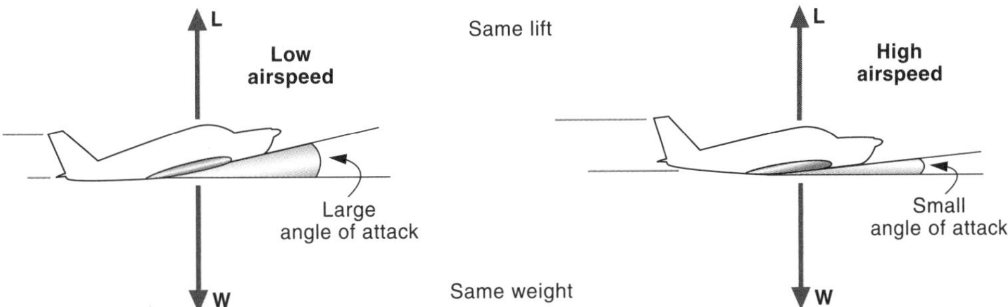

Figure 10-12 Lift is caused by a combination of angle of attack and airspeed.

The angle of attack, which is relative to the airflow, is not to be confused with the pitch attitude, which is relative to the horizon, although in level flight they are the same.

Angle of Attack

The pilot controls angle of attack with the elevator.

Backward movement of the control column raises the nose of the airplane. Because of the airplane's momentum (i.e. its momentary tendency to maintain its existing flight path), the airplane will continue in the same direction at the same airspeed for a brief period, but with an increased angle of attack. The wing will generate increased lift and the flight path will change to an upward direction, if the aircraft was previously straight and level.

Conversely, moving the control column forward lowers the nose and decreases the angle of attack. Since the airspeed has not had time to alter, the wings will generate less lift, and the airplane will descend.

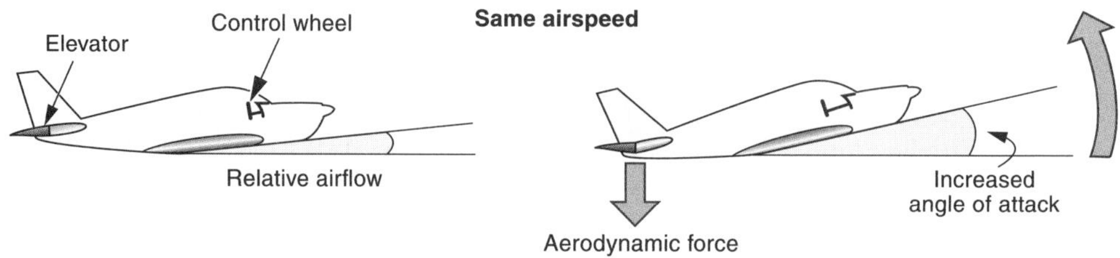

Figure 10-13 The elevator controls angle of attack.

Setting the power and pitch attitude produces a flight path and airspeed that give an indication of the angle of attack (small, medium, or large). However, as technology has advanced over the years so have the tools available to GA aircraft, like angle of attack (AOA) indicators. This system offers profound benefits to safe flying. The purpose of an AOA indicator is to provide a more reliable indication of airflow over the wings regardless of how the aircraft is configured (flaps, gear, etc.) and give a more precise indication of the angle of attack. These systems can also give visual, audible, or even physical indications (stick shakers) of an aircraft approaching its maximum angle of attack or an impending stall, when used in conjunction with existing stall warning systems.

Figure 10-14 An AOA indicator can be used in the cockpit to increase situational awareness.

Performance

Power plus attitude determines airplane performance.

Power plus attitude determines the performance of the airplane in terms of:

- flight path (up, level, down, turning); and
- speed (airspeed, rate of climb, rate of descent or rate of turn, which are, of course, constant or zero for straight and level flight).

Flying straight and level with constant power set, there will be a particular pitch attitude for straight and level flight. If the nose is too high, the airplane will climb; if the nose is too low, the airplane will descend. How do you know that you have set the correct pitch attitude? Because the airplane maintains altitude! You can observe this on the altimeter, with the vertical speed indicator (VSI) as a backup instrument indicating any tendency to deviate from the set altitude.

APPLICATION

Flying Straight

The essential elements in flying straight are to keep the wings level and to keep the airplane in balance with rudder pressure. The outside visual cue to the pilot that the wings are level is the natural horizon being level in the windshield or parallel to some part of the aircraft such as the instrument glareshield (coaming).

Keep the wings level.

Left wing down

Right aileron to correct

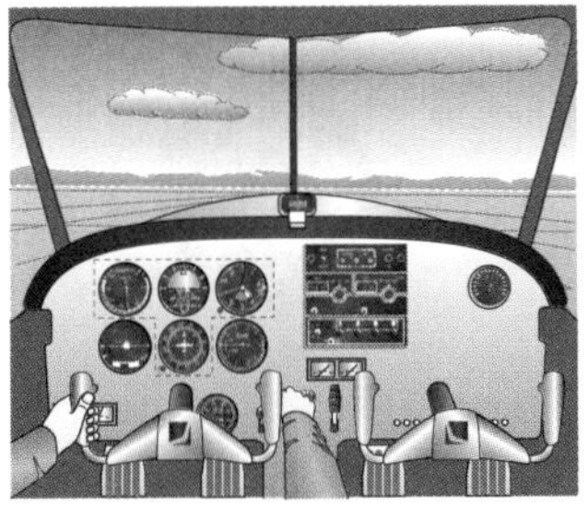

Wings level; controls neutral

Figure 10-15 Level the wings with the ailerons.

Balance

Balance is achieved by keeping the balance ball centered. If it is out to the left, more left rudder pressure is required; if it is out to the right, more right rudder pressure is required. In straight flight, a reference point ahead on the horizon will remain in the same position relative to the nose of the airplane. In the cockpit, straight flight is indicated by a steady heading on the heading indicator. If the airplane is deviating from straight flight, first of all, stop the deviation by leveling the wings and centering the balance ball. Later, you will learn how to make a gentle turn back onto the desired heading.

Keep the balance ball centered.

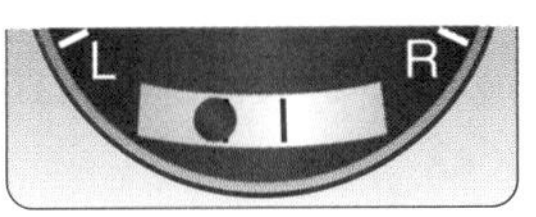

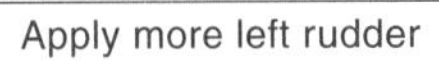

Apply more left rudder

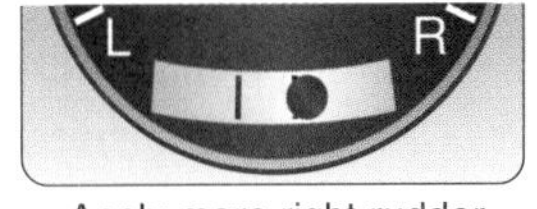

Apply more right rudder

Figure 10-16 Balance ball—indications and responses.

Flying Level

The essential element in maintaining a constant altitude is to establish the correct nose attitude for the power set. The external reference is the natural horizon, which should appear at a particular position in the windshield relative to the nose cowl or the top of the instrument panel. This position will vary for the aircraft concerned, your physical seating position in the cockpit, airspeed, configuration (flaps and landing gear position) and gross weight of the aircraft. Thus it cannot be nominated specifically, but you will come to recognize it for your personal situation.

Thus there is no single straight and level attitude. It is set approximately and then confirmation of the correct nose attitude is provided by the altimeter with some trend information being provided by the vertical speed indicator. (It reacts more quickly and indicates what the altimeter is about to do.) The pilot uses this information to tell if, when, and how much to change the attitude.

Confirm you are maintaining a constant altitude by referring to the altimeter and VSI.

Figure 10-17 Cruising flight.

Establish the correct nose attitude for the airspeed.

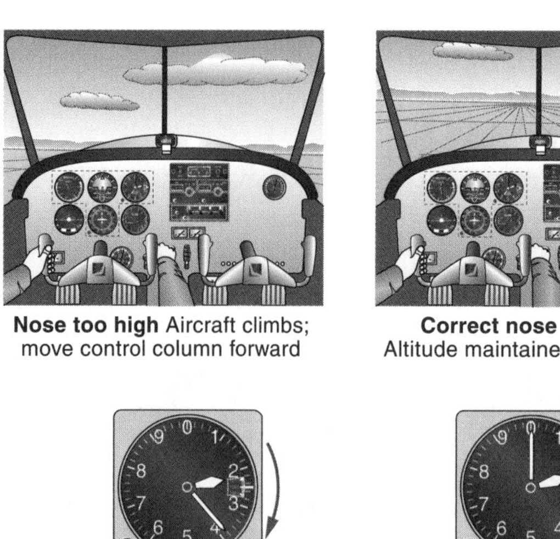

Nose too high Aircraft climbs; move control column forward
Correct nose attitude Altitude maintained accurately
Nose too low Aircraft descends; move control column back

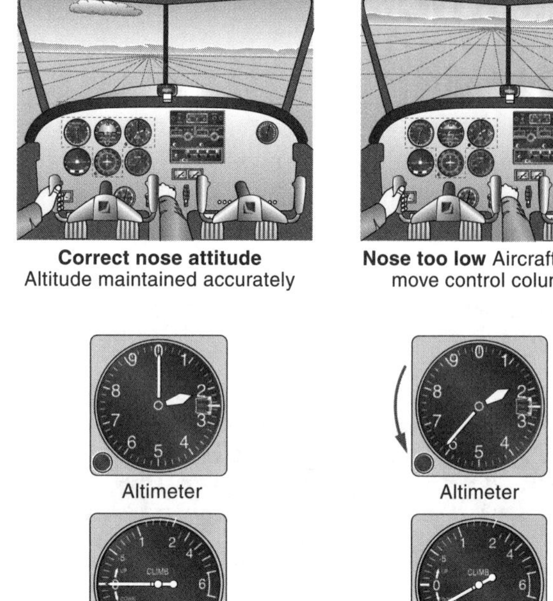

Figure 10-18 With cruise power set, maintain altitude by adjusting attitude.

The relationship between the horizon and the nose cowl will differ for different pilot eye heights in the cockpit. You should establish a comfortable consistent seating position and use it for every flight. This will make it easier to commit to memory the correct attitude for normal cruise. Then, with cruise power set at cruise speed, you can place the airplane in this attitude and be reasonably certain that level flight will result. This can be confirmed (fine-tuned) by the altimeter and vertical speed indicator.

- If the pitch attitude is too high and the airplane climbs, lower the nose slightly and regain the desired altitude.
- If the pitch attitude is too low and the airplane descends, raise the nose to regain the altitude.

Accuracy

Maintaining heading and altitude perfectly and indefinitely is almost impossible. There will inevitably be some deviations, but these can be corrected so that the airplane flies very close to the target heading and altitude. More comfortable flight results from continually making small corrections rather than occasionally making large ones.

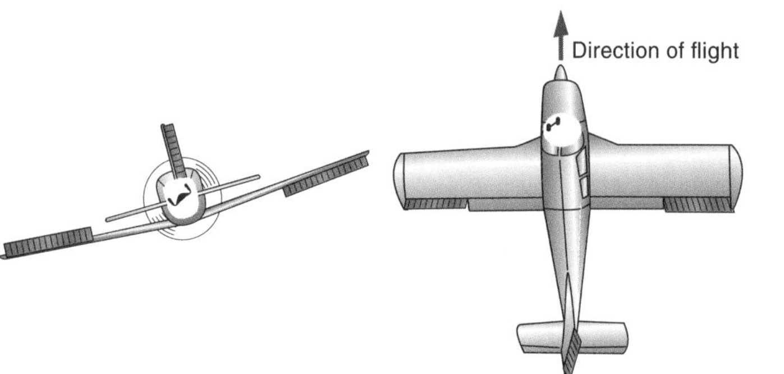

Figure 10-19 Crossed controls are inefficient (increased drag).

Balance

Do not fly with crossed controls. It is possible to fly straight and level with one wing down and the airplane out of balance. For example, if the left wing is down, right rudder can be applied to stop the airplane turning left. This is neither comfortable nor efficient and is known as a *sideslip* or *flying with crossed controls* (since the ailerons and rudder oppose each other). It degrades performance by increasing drag and results in a reduced airspeed and a higher fuel consumption. Crossed controls are corrected by leveling the wings with aileron and moving the balance ball back into the center with rudder pressure.

Trim

Keep the airplane in trim to make accurate level flight easier, the correct procedure being to hold the desired attitude and then trim off any steady control pressure. Any changes in power or attitude will cause a trim change. Set the power, hold the desired attitude, balance the ball and trim out any residual control pressures. Add power to increase airspeed or reduce power to decrease airspeed, while maintaining altitude by adjusting the attitude. Be prepared for the pitching and yawing moments that occur with power changes (nose-up pitch and left yaw as power is added, nose-down pitch and right yaw as power is reduced), counteracting it with control pressure.

To accelerate, the pilot increases power, balances the initial trim changes and then, as the airspeed builds, lowers the nose attitude incrementally to maintain altitude. The increasing airspeed causes a further nose-up trim change and so the aircraft wants to climb. Further forward pressure and trim is required to maintain level flight.

If a specific airspeed is required then, once it is attained, the power is adjusted to maintain it. Hold the attitude steady and then trim the airplane accurately. To reduce airspeed, the power is initially reduced and the initial trim change is countered. Then, as airspeed decays, the aircraft wants to lower its nose and to descend. This is its natural tendency to maintain flying speed. A significant rearward force and a pronounced nose-high attitude may be required at the lowest speed. Further, as the aircraft approaches its minimum level flight speed considerable power must be added to prevent further loss of speed and altitude. At very low airspeeds, where high power is required, close attention must be given to maintaining the speed using power. Frequent, and sometimes large, power adjustments may be required if the airspeed starts to decay or the aircraft begins to descend.

TECHNIQUE

Establishing Straight and Level Cruise Flight

You will come to know the attitude and power setting for your airplane at normal weight and CG position, and for your sitting height in the cockpit. Straight and level cruise flight is established by setting the power and the approximate attitude (the more accurate, the better), allowing the airplane to stabilize. Then adjust power, attitude and trim.

Regaining Straight and Level Following a Disturbance

If the airplane is banked, level the wings with the ailerons. If the nose is too high or too low, ease it back to the approximate visual attitude with the elevator, hold it steady and then check the altimeter and make a further correction. If speed is excessively high or low, or if large alterations of altitude are required, some adjustment of power may become necessary.

Straight and level flight can be maintained over a range of speeds, from a high-speed cruise, or maximum level speed, to low-speed flight just above the stalling speed. The principle is the same as before. The pilot sets the power, adjusts the attitude for the new

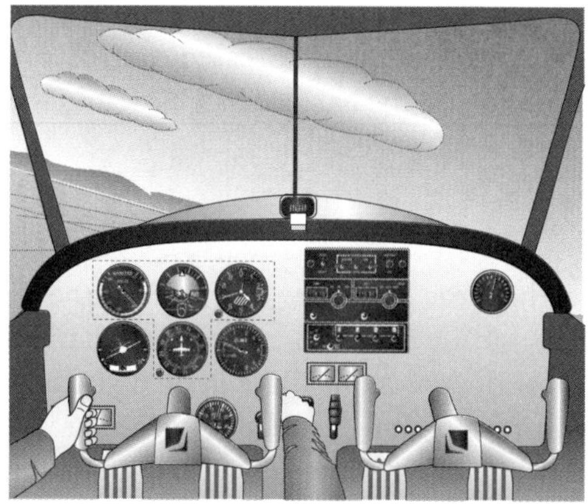

Figure 10-20 Nose high and turning left, lower nose and level wings. Nose low and turning left, level the wings and raise the nose.

speed, once it is stabilized, and then retrims. During the acceleration or deceleration the pilot is monitoring the altitude trend and adjusting the attitude by small increments to maintain level flight. It is quite difficult to fly a precise altitude with changing power and airspeed and, later, with flap changes.

With a fixed-pitch propeller, the RPM will increase with increasing airspeed and reduce with reducing airspeed, so the RPM is adjusted once the airspeed is stabilized.

Accelerating and Decelerating in Straight and Level Flight

In the cruise, thrust balances drag, the source of the thrust being engine power. If the desired airspeed is less than that being maintained then, by reducing power, the thrust will not balance the drag and consequently the airplane will slow down (i.e. decelerate). If, however, the desired airspeed is somewhat greater than that being maintained then, by increasing power, the thrust will exceed the drag and the airplane will accelerate.

Power

Once the airplane has accelerated or decelerated to the target airspeed, the power is adjusted to maintain it. Subsequent adjustments to the power may be required for the selected speed to be maintained accurately.

As the airspeed increases, the nose must be lowered to maintain altitude.

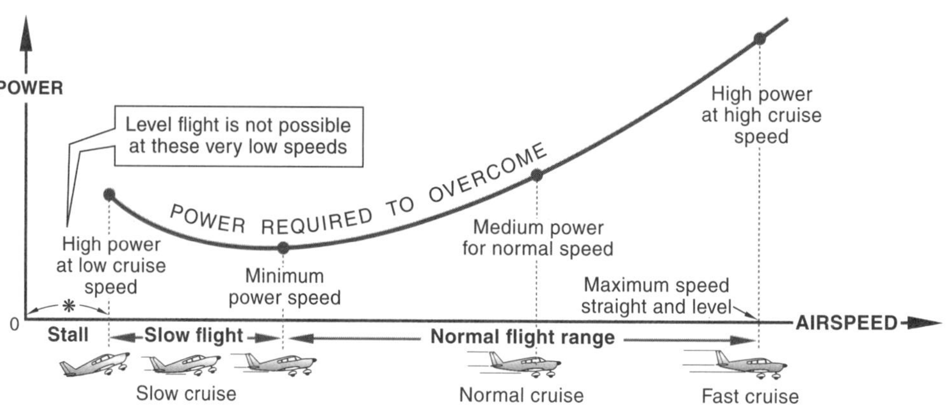

Figure 10-21 Vary the cruising airspeed by altering power and adjusting attitude.

Attitude

Since the lift generated by the wings depends on both the angle of attack and the airspeed, the lift will increase as the airspeed increases and, unless the nose is lowered, the airplane will start to climb. If the speed is decreasing, then the lift will decrease and the airplane will lose altitude unless the nose is raised.

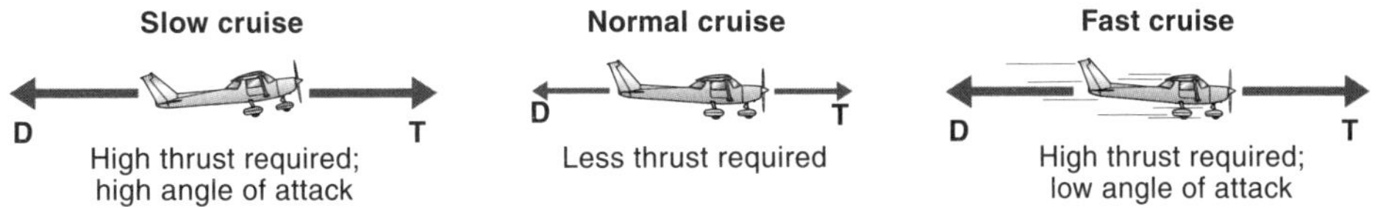

As the airspeed decreases, raise the nose to maintain altitude

Figure 10-22 Straight and level flight is maintained with a combination of power and attitude, which determine the stabilized speed.

Flying at Designated Airspeed (or Power)

The usual method of flying straight and level is to set the power (most economical, maximum continuous or somewhere in between) and to accept the resulting airspeed for the particular altitude and weight. In some cases, there are sound reasons for maintaining certain selected airspeeds, such as when either the maximum range or maximum endurance for a given quantity of fuel is desired.

Different airspeeds straight and level require different power settings. The thrust must balance the drag, which (like lift) depends on airspeed and angle of attack. At high airspeeds the drag is high; at medium speeds it is somewhat less. This is because the parasite drag decreases as airspeed decreases, the parasite drag being similar to the air resistance that you feel on a bicycle. What is different with an airplane, however, is that, unlike a bicycle (which is supported by the ground), an airplane in flight must generate its own support, i.e. lift. A byproduct of the production of lift by the wings is induced drag, and this is greatest at high angles of attack, i.e. at low airspeeds. As a result, the total drag is high when the airplane is flying slowly.

Parasite drag is caused by the friction between the air and the surface over which it is flowing, and increases as the velocity of the air increases.

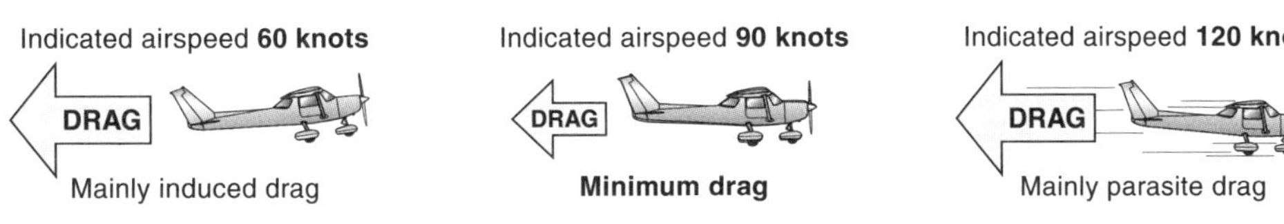

Total drag varies with airspeed.

Figure 10-23 Minimum drag occurs at an intermediate airspeed and drag increases either side from there.

A high power is required at both low and high airspeeds for the drag to be balanced. At intermediate speeds, the power requirement is less. The rate at which fuel is consumed depends on the power set, and an important aspect in operating an airplane efficiently is to obtain the maximum benefit from the fuel available.

Maximum-Endurance Speed

For minimum fuel consumption, fly at the *minimum-power* airspeed. This will achieve the maximum flight time for a given quantity of fuel. Since *holding* flight is sometimes required (for example, if holding near an airfield waiting for fog to clear or for the cattle to be chased from the runway), flying at the airspeed for maximum endurance provides the minimum fuel burn for a given flight time or, conversely, the maximum time in the air for the amount of fuel available. The maximum-endurance airspeed is found in the pilot's operating handbook. It is achieved at the minimum safe altitude.

Maximum-Range Airspeed

A more common requirement is to achieve the maximum distance for a given quantity of fuel: the maximum range. Since most flights are over a fixed distance, another way of expressing best range is the minimum fuel burned to cover a given distance. This occurs at the airspeed where the fuel-distance ratio is least, known as the *maximum-range airspeed.*

Correct leaning of the mixture is assumed in the manufacturer's range figures.

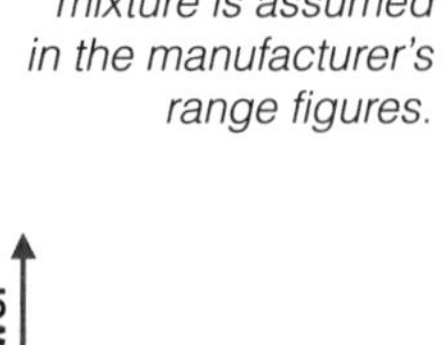

The maximum-range airspeed is in the pilot's operating handbook and is higher than that for maximum endurance. The range distances published by the manufacturer assume correct leaning of the mixture when cruising at power settings less than 75% maximum continuous power (usually occurring when cruising above 5,000 feet MSL).

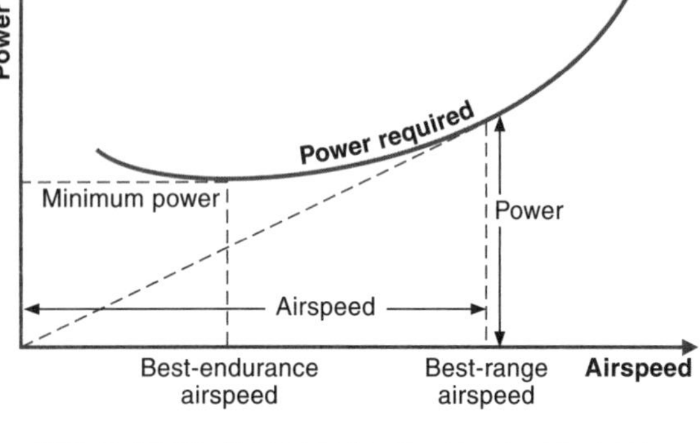

Figure 10-24 Airspeeds for maximum endurance and maximum range.

Referring to the maximum-range airspeed as shown on the graph (figure 10-24), the rate of fuel consumption depends on power. The rate of covering distance is the speed.

Therefore the ratio of fuel to distance will be the same as the ratio of power to speed, and so the minimum fuel consumption for a given distance (i.e. the best range) will occur at the airspeed where the power-speed ratio is least, as illustrated. The line from the origin to any other point on the graph has a steeper gradient; that is, the power-speed ratio is greater and so more fuel per mile will be burned.

Effect of Flaps

Cruising with partial flap extended is desirable when you wish to fly at a low speed as it offers better view and reduced stalling speed. It is used when inspecting a prospective landing field or when maneuvering in reduced visibility.

Lift is increased as the flaps are extended, so a reduced angle of attack and therefore a lower nose attitude will be required to maintain altitude. If the nose is not lowered as the flaps are extended, the airplane will *balloon.*

Avoid ballooning when lowering the flaps.

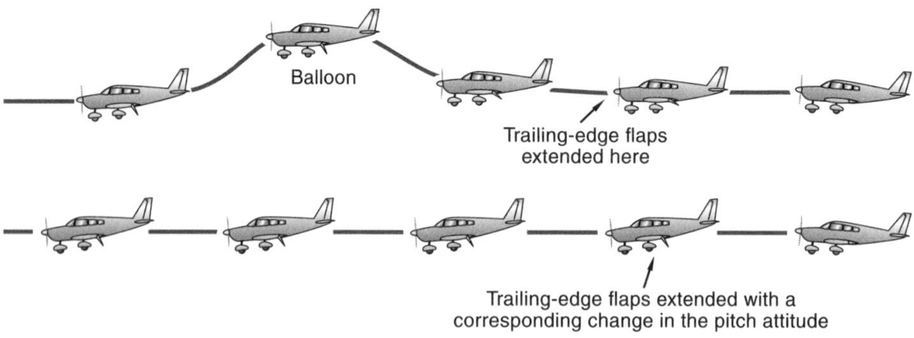

Figure 10-25 A balloon can be avoided by lowering the nose as flaps extend.

The flaps must not be operated at high speeds since this places stress on the linkages. The maximum flap-extended speed (V_{FE}) is the upper end of the white band on the airspeed indicator. A lower nose attitude improves the forward view from the cockpit,

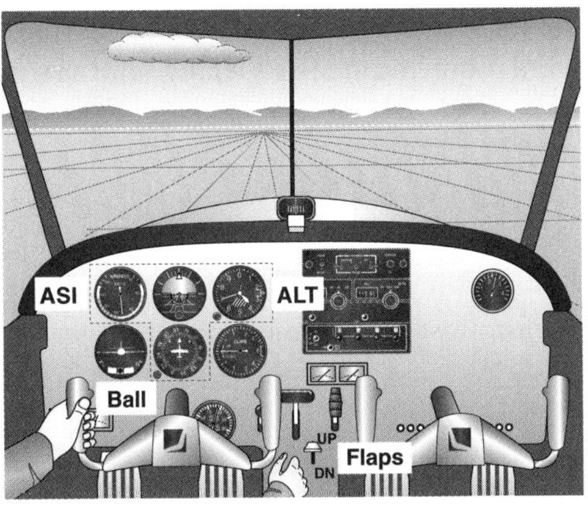

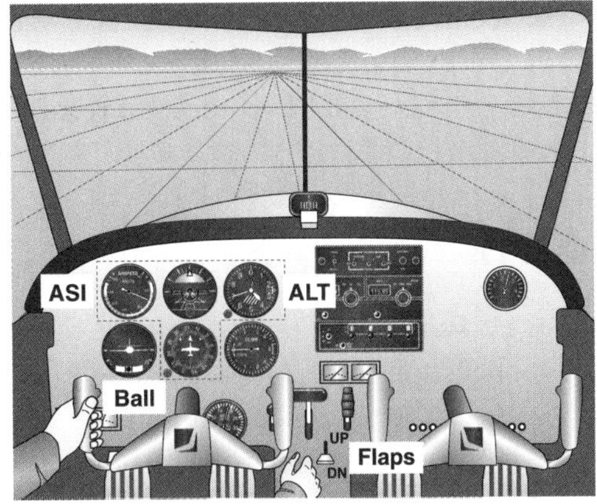

Figure 10-26 Flaps improve the forward view for the same flight path; they require a lower nose attitude and offer better control response due to higher power needed.

which is very useful along with the lower yet safe airspeed when you want to inspect a potential landing field.

Lower speeds are possible with the flaps extended because of the increased lifting ability of the wings and the reduced stalling speed. The stalling speed with the flaps extended for straight and level flight is the low-speed end of the white band on the airspeed indicator; the clean stalling speed, flaps retracted, is the low-speed end of the green band.

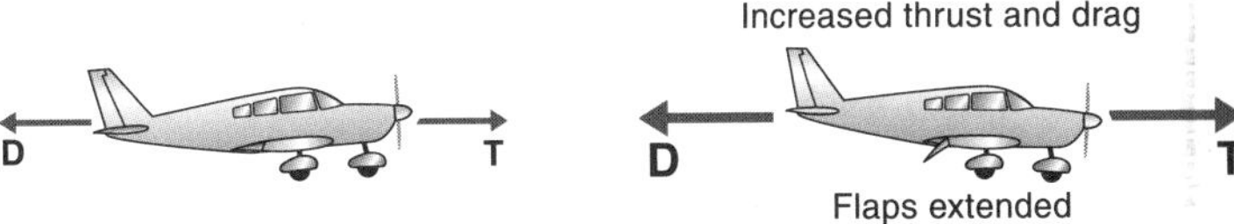

Figure 10-27 Flap increases drag.

Extending the Flaps

Only extend flaps when the airspeed is in the flap-operating range.

Extending the flaps also increases the drag, so thrust must be increased if airspeed is to be maintained in straight and level flight, even at the reduced airspeed. As the flap position is changed, be prepared to make any necessary adjustments to power and attitude to achieve the desired performance.

- Lowering the flaps will require a lower nose position to avoid *ballooning* and an increase in power to maintain airspeed. Once the adjustments are made, any steady control pressure should be trimmed off.
- Raising the flaps will require a higher nose position to avoid sinking and an adjustment to power to maintain airspeed. Trim off any steady control pressures.

Do not operate the flaps at too high a speed: V_{FE} is the limit. Do not raise the flaps unless 10 knots or more above the clean stalling speed.

Flying Straight and Level with Flaps Extended

Cruising with flaps extended requires more power and therefore more fuel.

The aircraft with flaps extended flies differently. The airspeed is lower and so the aileron control is less responsive. The view ahead is good because of the lower nose attitude. However, the power is relatively high and so is the drag. There is a tendency not to hold the attitude and to allow the aircraft to sink or to decelerate. It is better to make power changes too much rather than too little. Later you will learn to maneuver with flaps extended in the *precautionary search and landing*.

Retracting the Flaps

When retracting the flaps, increase the power and have the airspeed clearly above the clean stalling speed and increasing. The aircraft will want to sink as the lift is lost and what seems to be a large attitude change may be required to prevent a descending flight path. Once the aircraft is descending its downward momentum resists change and a large power increase will be required to regain altitude.

AIRMANSHIP

Your eyes should be looking outside the cockpit for most of the time to:

- check the correct nose attitude;
- check the reference point on the horizon; and
- look out for other aircraft above, below and to either side.

An occasional glance into the cockpit lasting only one or two seconds is sufficient to cross-check relevant instruments. Only look at the instruments from which you need information, then look about to make a correction to the attitude. Maintain firm, positive and smooth control over the airplane and keep it well trimmed. Pay particular attention to keeping the wings level. This will considerably reduce your workload as the heading will not wander and you only need to make attitude corrections to maintain altitude. Do not allow any deviations from the desired altitude, heading or airspeed to develop. Small and subtle movements of the controls made sufficiently early will avoid this, and these small movements are preferable to slower, later but larger corrections. Remember the basic rules of the air:

Figure 10-28 Don't be focused inside the cockpit—look out.

- Give way to airships, gliders, balloons and aircraft towing gliders or banners.
- Give way to aircraft to the right and avoid passing over, under or ahead of other aircraft, unless well clear.
- Turn right if there is any danger of a head-on collision.
- Remain well clear of cloud.
- Try to maintain an awareness of your geographic position and the training airspace boundaries.

REVIEW 10
Straight and Level Flight

1. In straight and level unaccelerated flight, what is lift equal to? What is thrust equal to?
2. What is a final balancing force in pitch provided by?
3. What are the 4 main forces and the small balancing force in the diagram at right?
4. What are angle of attack and pitch attitude controlled by?
5. Is flying accurately easier if the airplane is in trim or out of trim?

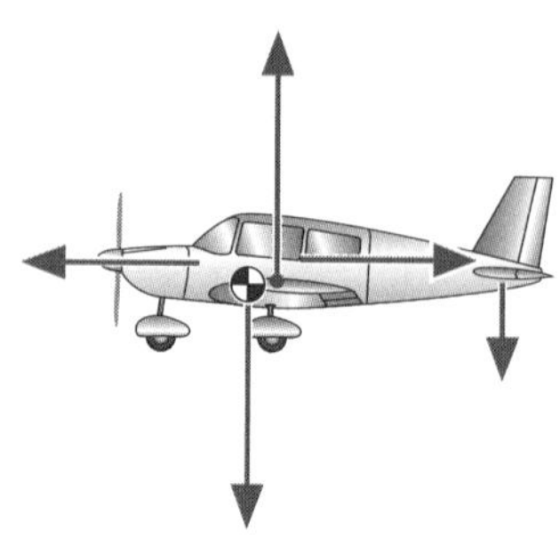

6. Is the correct trimming technique to hold the desired attitude with elevator and trim off any steady pressures, or to change the attitude using trim?
7. What are wings kept level with?
8. What is the balance ball kept centered with?
9. Which instrument is altitude indicated on? Within how many feet should you aim to hold the selected altitude accurately?
10. Which instrument is heading indicated on? With what other instrument should this instrument be periodically aligned? The accuracy required for a specified heading is plus or minus how many degrees?
11. If the airplane starts to climb, which instruments is this shown on? If your objective, however, is to fly straight and level, what change, if any, should be made to the nose attitude?
12. Any required corrections to heading are shown on which two instruments? How should these correction to heading be made?
13. The performance capability of an airplane refers to which two aspects?
14. What two aspects of capability are increased in a high-performance airplane, compared with a low-performance airplane?
15. What two aspects determine performance?
16. What is the built-in natural ability of an airplane to return to its original condition following a disturbance?
17. What sort of stabilizer provides longitudinal stability in pitch?
18. What sort of stabilizer provides directional stability in yaw?
19. How does wing dihedral and high keel surfaces affect lateral stability?
20. Will an airplane be more stable longitudinally if loaded with the center of gravity well forward than with the center of gravity well aft?
21. Will loading heavy baggage in the rear locker, compared with securing it on the rear seat, make an airplane less stable as it moves the CG aft?
22. The lift produced by a wing depends on which two aspects?
23. What angle of attack (high or low) do you need for slow flight at a constant altitude?
24. What angle of attack (high or low) do you need for high-speed flight at a constant altitude?
25. For accurate flying, do you need to keep the balance ball centered?
26. If the balance ball is out to the right, which side rudder pressure would you apply to center it?
27. Flying with left aileron and right rudder with the balance ball well out of the center is known as what?
28. Is flying with crossed controls efficient? Is it comfortable?
29. What is the effect of the couple formed by the lift force and the weight?
30. What is the effect of the couple formed by thrust and drag?
31. Does the effect of the lift-weight couple counteracted the effect of the thrust-drag couple?
32. In which direction does the small aerodynamic balancing force of the horizontal stabilizer and elevator usually act? What effect does this have in maintaining nose attitude?
33. If thrust is lost in flight, which couple will weaken? How will the nose attitude be effected?
34. If thrust is lost in flight, how is the propeller slipstream over the horizontal stabilizer and elevator affected? How is the small downward balancing force provided by the horizontal stabilizer and elevator affected? What does this do to the nose attitude?

Answers are given on page 578.

TASK

Straight and Level Cruise Flight

Aim: To fly straight and level at a constant power setting.

Look out.

Select a horizon reference point on which to keep straight.

Keep the wings level with the ailerons.

Maintain balance with rudder pressure.

+ Plus

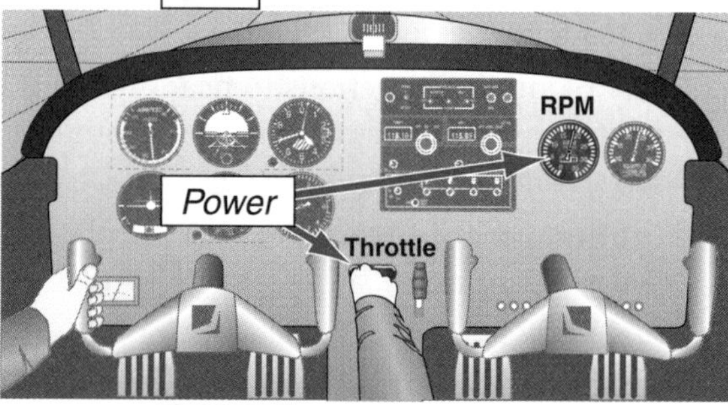

= Equals

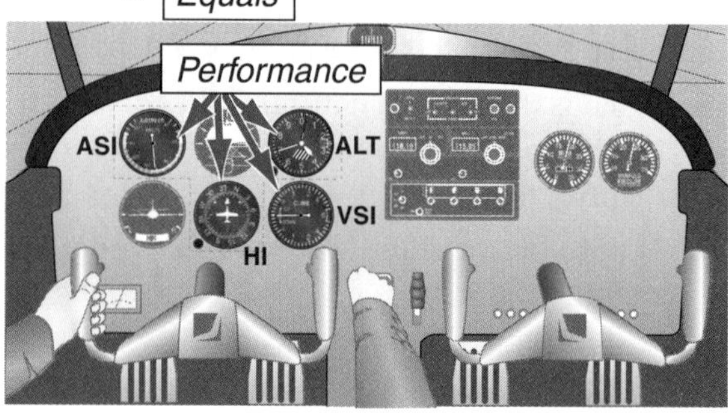

1. ***With Cruise Power Set and at Desired Altitude***

   Place the nose in the cruise attitude, and with constant power set:
   - cross-check the altimeter and vertical speed indicator;
   - make small attitude adjustments with elevator.

   Allow the airspeed to settle:
   - check the airspeed indicator for airspeed information;
   - cross-check the altimeter and vertical speed indicator for attitude information;
   - trim out elevator pressure, while holding the new pitch attitude constant.

2. ***The Correct Trimming Technique***

   Hold attitude constant with elevator pressure.

   Trim to relieve the control load.

   If rudder trim is fitted, trim off rudder pressure while keeping the wings level and keeping the balance ball centered.

If the Airplane Tends to Climb

Climb tendency

Regain desired attitude with gentle movement of elevator.

Regain altitude

Hold nose attitude slightly lower than previously with elevator pressure:
- allow airspeed to settle;
- check altimeter and vertical speed indicator.

Trim off elevator pressure for the new attitude.

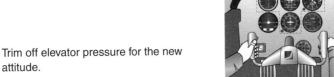

Slightly lower attitude, retrim

If the Airplane Tends to Descend

Descent tendency

Regain desired altitude with elevator (adding power if necessary).

Regain altitude

Hold nose attitude slightly higher than previously with elevator:
- allow airspeed to settle;
- check altimeter and vertical speed indicator.

Trim off elevator pressure.

Slightly higher attitude, retrim

Remember P-A-T: power–attitude–trim.

To Decrease Speed in Level Flight

Decrease power (balance with rudder pressure and control column).

Trim if desired.

Decrease power

Raise nose gradually to maintain level flight as airspeed decreases.

Adjust power to maintain desired airspeed.

Higher nose attitude

Trim out elevator pressure (nose-up).

Make minor adjustments to power, attitude and trim as required.

Adjust power and trim

TASK

Effect of Flap

Aim: To fly straight and level with flaps extended.

Reduce power.

Establish the airplane in straight and level flight clean (flaps fully retracted).

To Lower Flap, Maintaining Straight and Level Flight

Ensure airspeed is below maximum flap-extended speed (V_{FE}), i.e. in white ASI band.

Extend flaps in stages.

Place nose in lower attitude (to avoid ballooning and maintain altitude).

Adjust power to maintain desired airspeed.

Trim off elevator pressure for each stage of flap.

To Raise Flap

Check that the airspeed is suitable.

Raise the flaps in stages, holding the nose in a higher attitude to prevent sink and maintain altitude.

Adjust power to maintain desired speed.

Trim off elevator pressure.

11 Climbs

OBJECTIVES

To describe:

- the forces acting on an airplane in a climb;
- the relationship between power and rate of climb;
- the relationship between thrust and angle of climb;
- the factors affecting climb performance;
- the technique to enter, maintain and level from a climb; and
- the attitude-power combination for relevant climb in your airplane.

CONSIDERATIONS

Forces in a Climb

For an airplane to climb steadily (at a constant airspeed) the thrust must exceed the drag, otherwise the aircraft would slow down and the nose would have to be lowered to maintain airspeed. The thrust, in excess of that needed to balance the drag, is called the *excess thrust*. It is this spare capacity, or reserve, available to the pilot that allows the aircraft to climb—the more reserve available, the steeper the aircraft can climb. In a climb, the thrust balances the drag and supports a small component of the weight that acts along the flight path. The lift generated by the wings supports the component of the weight that is perpendicular to the flight path; hence the surprising result that, in a steady climb, the total lift is less than the total weight. In a vertical climb, if the aircraft had sufficient excess thrust, the thrust would balance all of the weight and no lift would be required from the wings.

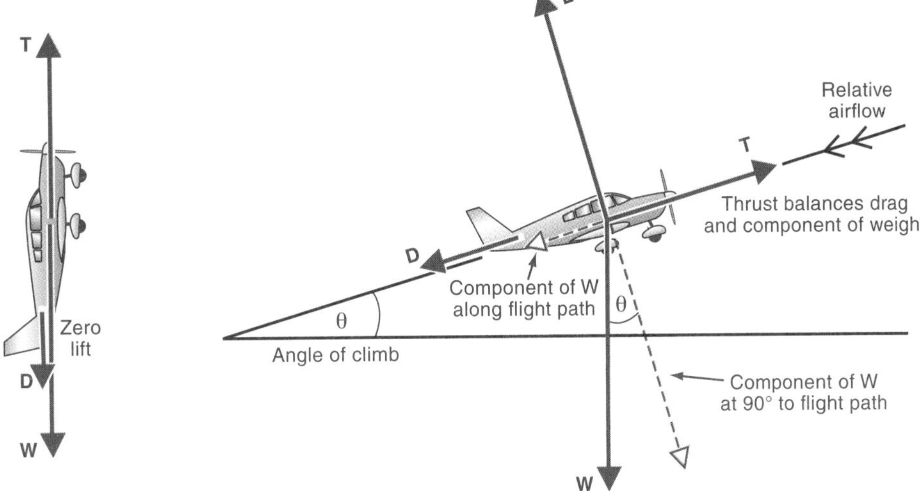

Figure 11-1 Vertical climb.

Figure 11-2 The four forces in a steady climb.

Climb Speeds

There are various climb speeds to achieve different types of climb.

Climb performance is a compromise between airspeed and rate of climb. The choice of airspeed in the climb depends on what the pilot wants to achieve. It may be either:

- a steep angle of climb to clear obstacles (best-angle climb, V_X);
- a rapid climb to gain altitude quickly (best-rate climb, V_Y); or
- a cruise climb (the most usual) which provides:
  - faster en route performance (distance traveled in the climb);
  - better airplane control due to greater airflow over the control surfaces;
  - improved engine cooling;
  - improved forward view; and
  - a more comfortable attitude (deck angle or body angle) for the passengers.

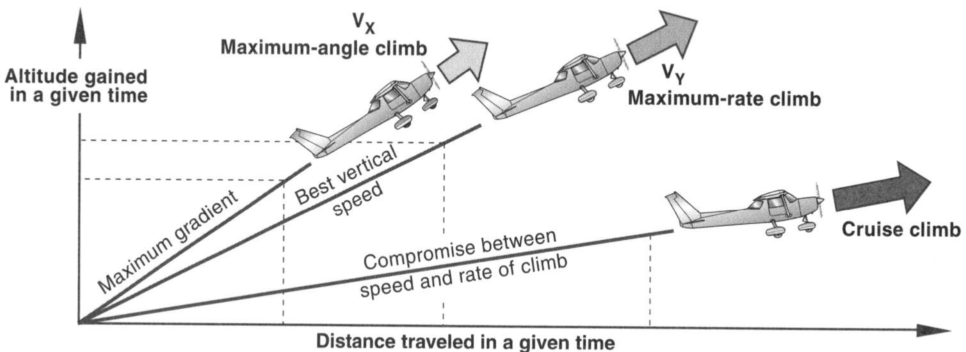

Figure 11-3 Different types of climb.

The airplane can be made to climb at any of the above speeds. Their values may be found in your pilot's operating handbook. With climb power set, simply set the appropriate attitude to achieve the indicated airspeed for the desired type of climb—the lower the nose attitude, the higher the climb airspeed. A normal climb may be a maximum-rate climb or a cruise climb.

Figure 11-4 Typical climb attitudes.

Forward View in a Climb

Periodically make small clearing turns in a climb.

Your forward view in a climb is restricted by the nose and other airplanes may be concealed. It is wise to bank 15° or so, left and right (or to lower the nose), every 500 feet or so, to look ahead and check the area is clear into which you are climbing. A reference point on the horizon will assist in returning to the original heading.

The attitude in a normal climb will provide better forward view and improved engine cooling than the higher nose attitudes required for best-angle and best-rate climb speeds.

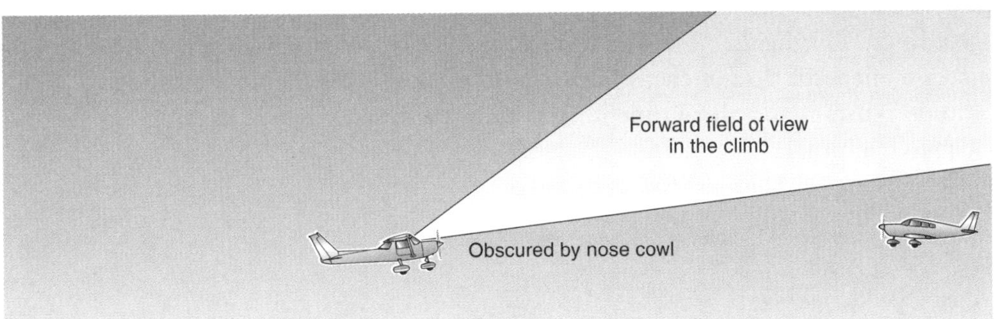

Figure 11-5 Periodically check the area obscured by the nose cowl.

Engine Considerations

Ensure that the engine is adequately cooled in the climb.

During a climb, using high power at low airspeed, the engine is producing more heat and there is less cooling airflow through the engine compartment. There is a risk of overheating and the pilot must ensure that sufficient cooling is taking place. The engine instruments should be monitored periodically in the climb and, if the engine temperature (oil temperature or cylinder head temperature) is too high, better cooling may be achieved by:

- increasing airspeed (by lowering the nose attitude);
- reducing power; and
- opening the cowl flaps (if available).

It is usual to climb with the mixture fully rich because excess fuel, as it vaporizes, has a cooling effect in the cylinders. However, above 5,000 feet, it may be necessary to lean the mixture.

APPLICATION

Performance

The power and the attitude that are set determine the climb performance in terms of:

- airspeed;
- rate of climb; and
- angle of climb.

Figure 11-6
Climb power plus climb attitude produces climb performance.

The power in a climb is greater than that used for the cruise and for many training airplanes is, in fact, full power. Because of the low airspeed and high power, the greater slipstream effect striking one side of the tail will cause a greater yawing moment. Counteract the yawing tendency with rudder.

In a climb, the usual balance rule applies. If the ball is out to the right, move it back into the center with right rudder pressure.

Most training airplanes have a propeller that rotates clockwise when viewed from the cockpit. This causes a yaw to the left with increased power. As climb power is applied, a coordinated increase in right rudder pressure will maintain the airplane in balance. Some airplanes have a rudder trim that may be used to relieve steady foot pressures in the climb (and at any other time).

With climb power set, pitch attitude determines the airspeed and whether the aircraft holds a constant speed. To establish the recommended speed, the attitude is adjusted accordingly. Raising the nose will decrease airspeed; conversely, lowering the nose will increase airspeed. Do not chase the airspeed after altering the nose attitude; hold the attitude constant and allow time for the airspeed to settle before making any further changes in attitude.

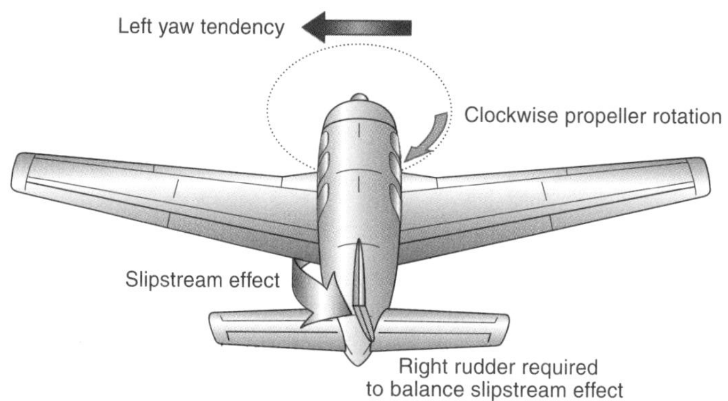

Figure 11-7 Balance the yawing moment from the slipstream with rudder pressure.

If the power and attitude are correct, then climb performance will be as desired and reference to the airspeed indicator need only be made for fine adjustments.

Figure 11-8 The climb attitude and power are higher than the normal cruise.

Once established in the climb, trim out any steady control pressures with the elevator trim, and the rudder trim (if available). An out-of-trim airplane is difficult to fly accurately. Climb performance is indicated on the flight instruments, in terms of:

- airspeed; and
- rate of climb.

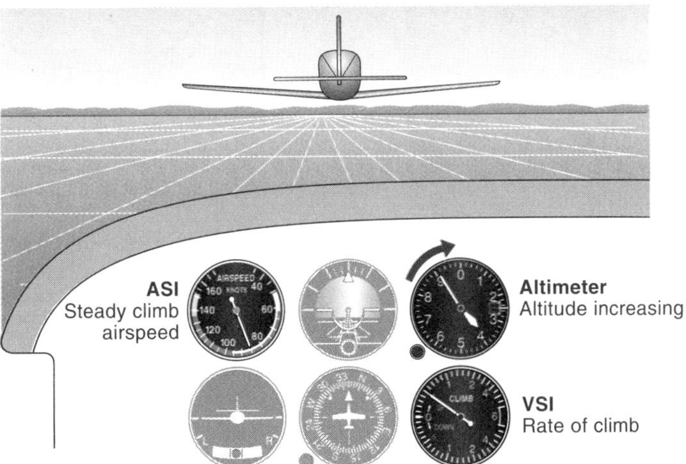

Figure 11-9 Monitor the climb performance regularly on the flight instruments.

Types of Climb

There are several different types of climb to achieve specific objectives:

- the *maximum-rate* (V_Y) climb achieves the greatest altitude in the shortest time;
- the *maximum-angle* (V_X) climb achieves the maximum altitude gain in the shortest horizontal distance regardless of how long it takes;
- the *normal* climb is usually to the maximum-rate climb but may be with a lower nose attitude and a higher airspeed for improved forward view and better engine cooling; and
- the *cruise* climb allows a lower attitude and further increase in airspeed for a shallower body angle (for passenger comfort) and to travel further along track while climbing, despite taking more time and fuel to reach cruise altitude.

For most aircraft, the climb is conducted with full power set, but in some circumstances, a maximum-continuous setting is used to reduce engine wear.

Factors Affecting Climb Performance

Power and Attitude

The flight path of the aircraft in a climb is determined, like straight and level, by the combination of power and attitude. The more power, the better the climb performance.

Airspeed

The curves below shows the power and the thrust that is required for a hypothetical airplane to maintain level flight at various airspeeds. If the engine can provide power greater than that needed (i.e. it has spare or excess power), then the airplane is capable of climbing. There is one speed where the amount of excess power is greatest. Power is

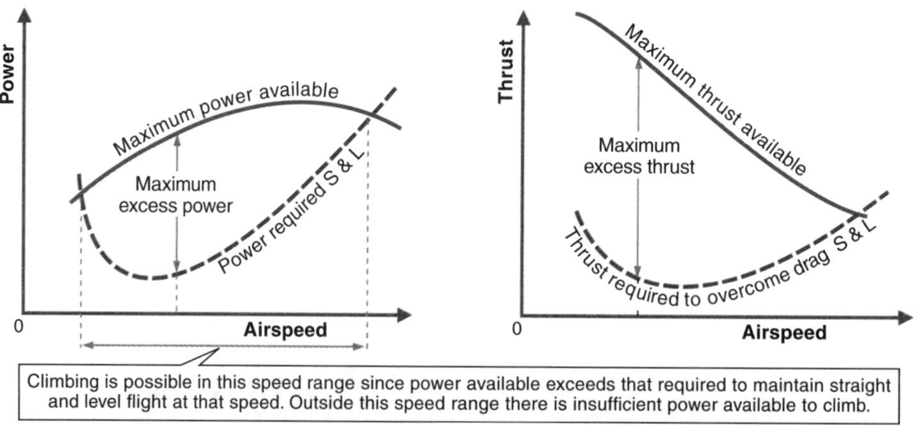

Figure 11-10 The power curve and the thrust curve (thrust curve is also known as the drag curve).

V_X is maximum-angle speed. V_Y is maximum-rate speed.

the rate of doing work, so the maximum rate of climb will be achieved at the airspeed for which maximum excess power is available. This speed is symbolized as V_Y.

The thrust available reduces with increasing speed as the propeller can no longer push the air. Power is the product of thrust and velocity so, as the velocity increases, the power curve flattens out. The best rate of climb speed is where there is the greatest margin between power available and power required, where there is the greatest gap between these two curves.

The angle of climb (steepness) depends on how much thrust (push) is available over and above the drag (i.e. the excess thrust), and so the steepest climb (i.e. the *best angle of climb*) is achieved with takeoff power set and at the airspeed where the *maximum excess thrust* occurs, which is at the lowest safe speed since thrust is greatest at low speed. Time is not considered in selecting the best angle of climb, only steepness. The best angle of climb speed is symbolized as V_X and is the lowest safe speed above the stall. It is slightly lower than the best-rate speed. The best-angle climb is only used to clear ground obstacles after takeoff or at low altitudes. Any error in airspeed above or below V_X or V_Y will adversely affect climb angle or rate respectively.

Wind

A head wind steepens the flight path over the ground.

Wind is air moving over the earth. The aircraft is climbing within the parcel of air so the climb performance within the parcel of air does not change. Hence the *time* to reach a given altitude does not change. However, because the aircraft is being blown along, the wind affects the distance traveled over the ground. For a normal climb, this affects the distance traveled along track before reaching cruise altitude as well as, after takeoff, the aircraft's ability to climb over obstacles; that is, the *angle* of climb is affected. It is steepened by climbing into the wind (a head wind) and made shallow by trying to climb with the wind from behind (tail wind). This is one reason why aircraft always take off into a head wind unless there are exceptional circumstances (such as runway slope or obstacles).

Weight

Climb performance decreases with increased weight and density altitude.

Because a climb is an attempt to travel upward, there is always an element of gravity resisting the climb. Weight is the force of gravity and thus, the greater the weight, the greater the force against the climb. An increased weight reduces both the angle and rate of climb.

Altitude and Temperature

As altitude or temperature is increased, the air becomes thinner and the engine produces less thrust and less power. Thus the angle of climb and the rate of climb are reduced. This is particularly significant at airports well above sea level in a hot climate. As an airplane climbs into less dense air, fewer molecules will be processed by the pitot-static system, and a lower IAS will be indicated, even though the actual true airspeed has changed little. If the nose is continually lowered to maintain a constant indicated airspeed, then the climb performance will deteriorate more than is necessary. To avoid this in climbs to high altitudes, maximum rate of climb tables will state the indicated airspeeds to use at various altitudes—the higher the altitude, the lower the recommended climbing IAS.

The higher the altitude, the lower the recommended climbing speed.

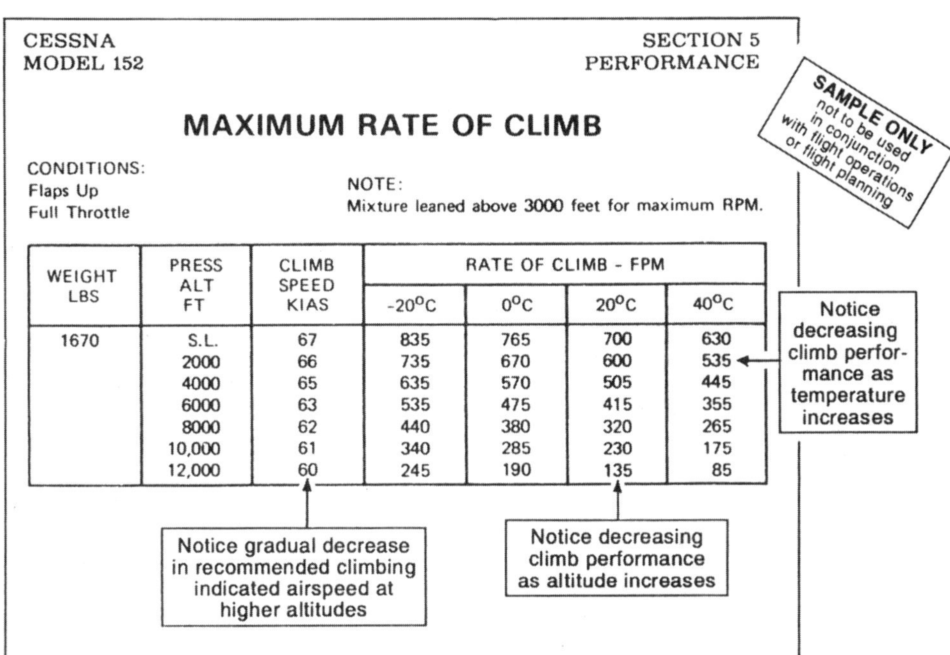

CESSNA
MODEL 152

SECTION 5
PERFORMANCE

MAXIMUM RATE OF CLIMB

CONDITIONS:
Flaps Up
Full Throttle

NOTE:
Mixture leaned above 3000 feet for maximum RPM.

WEIGHT LBS	PRESS ALT FT	CLIMB SPEED KIAS	RATE OF CLIMB - FPM			
			-20°C	0°C	20°C	40°C
1670	S.L.	67	835	765	700	630
	2000	66	735	670	600	535
	4000	65	635	570	505	445
	6000	63	535	475	415	355
	8000	62	440	380	320	265
	10,000	61	340	285	230	175
	12,000	60	245	190	135	85

Figure 11-11 A typical maximum rate of climb performance table.

Flaps

Flaps increase drag and so reduce the excess power and reduce the rate of climb. However, in some aircraft, a short-field takeoff (minimum ground run and steepest climb) is often made with a small amount of flap extended because it:

- allows the lift to be generated at a lower airspeed, shortening the takeoff distance;
- reduces the stalling speed, allowing safe flight at a lower airspeed, thereby reducing the takeoff speed and the best angle of climb airspeed which, in turn, gives greater excess thrust; and
- may enable a steeper angle of climb to be achieved (depending on the aircraft type) because of the lower airspeed and increased thrust.

Full flap causes a large drag increase and greatly reduces climb performance, so always ensure that only takeoff flap is set for takeoff. This is typically the first stage, or 10°–15°. For some airplanes, a normal takeoff is made with flaps retracted.

Normal climb without flap

Normal climb with takeoff flap extended

Figure 11-12 Nose attitude in the initial climb is lower with flap extended.

Take action to avoid sinking as you raise the flaps.

Raising the Flaps After Takeoff. When climbing after takeoff, it is usual to raise the flaps when well clear of the ground (say 200 feet above airport level) as there is a tendency to sink below the normal climb path as the flaps are retracted.

After clearing obstacles, accelerate to normal climb speed. To avoid the tendency for the airplane to sink as the flaps are raised:

- select the flaps up (in stages if there are more than one);
- keep looking out as you operate the lever or switch;
- at the same time, set and hold the nose attitude for a normal climb (there will be trim change, nose-up or nose-down, as the flaps come up);
- allow the airspeed to stabilize;
- adjust the power if necessary (from takeoff or full power to climb power or maximum continuous); and
- retrim.

TECHNIQUE

Before Entering the Climb

Select a reference point well ahead and look out to check the climb path is clear of other airplanes and obstacles ahead, above, below and to either side.

Entering the Climb

An easy way to remember the sequence of events when entering a climb is PAT: power-attitude-trim.

Increase power (first ensuring that the mixture is rich) by opening the throttle to climb power. (Increase RPM before throttle for constant-speed propellers. Remember *rev up and then throttle back* for the correct sequence.) Balance with rudder. Allow the nose to rise naturally to the correct climb attitude, and then maintain the climb attitude as the airspeed reduces. Retrim.

Maintaining the Climb

Flight path and speed are established by setting power and attitude. In a climb, the indication of whether the attitude is correct is the airspeed indicator. This is the measure of performance that the pilot uses to correct the attitude setting. The rate of climb is useful information as it tells approximately how long it will take to reach the desired altitude, but it is not a primary reference instrument. (It is only *approximate*, as the rate of climb reduces as the aircraft climbs and so is not constant.)

Maintain the desired airspeed with attitude—the higher the nose, the lower the airspeed. Set an attitude that your instructor will show you, hold it constant and trim. Then watch the airspeed and the trend. Make an attitude adjustment to correct any speed deviation, but don't focus on the airspeed indicator. Use it only as an indicator of the correct attitude. Maintain the wings level with aileron, and the balance ball centered with rudder pressure. The aircraft is at a lower airspeed and high power so the tendency to be out-of-balance is more powerful than usual. It is a characteristic of trainee pilots to relax their feet and to allow the aircraft to be out of balance in a climb.

Every 500 feet or so, either lower the nose or bank left and right to clear the area ahead. Periodically check engine temperatures and pressures, taking appropriate action if the engine is overheating, such as opening the cowl flaps (if available), increasing the airspeed or reducing the power. With a constant-speed propeller, the throttle must be advanced to maintain MAP in the climb.

Leveling Off from a Climb

Since cruise speed is higher than climb speed, it is usual to gradually lower the nose as the intended cruise level is approached, leaving climb power set. However, remember the attitude for low-speed flight. You were climbing at perhaps 90 knots and so your initial attitude must be the attitude for level flight at 90 knots. Only as the aircraft accelerates can you lower the nose further. There is a tendency to go straight to the cruise attitude at this reduced speed, meaning the aircraft will descend while it accelerates. Once level, allow the airplane to accelerate until cruise speed is attained, lowering the nose gradually to maintain altitude as airspeed increases.

Figure 11-13 Leveling off.

Anticipate reaching the cruise level by 20 feet or so and begin lowering the nose toward the cruise attitude before the cruise level is reached. This will make leveling off a smooth maneuver and avoid overshooting the cruise level. The greater the rate of climb, the more you should anticipate the leveling-off altitude employing, say, 10% of the rate of climb; for example, if climbing at 500 feet per minute, slowly begin lowering the nose 50 feet before reaching the desired altitude. As cruise speed is reached, reduce to cruise power, keeping the balance ball centered with rudder pressure. Trim. The sequence of events for leveling off is APPT: attitude-pause-power-trim.

AIRMANSHIP

Ensure that the engine is adequately cooled during the high-power, low-airspeed climb. The mixture should be set to full rich before power is increased but may be leaned during a prolonged climb above about 5,000 feet. Clear the area and maintain a continuous lookout. Clear the blind spot under the nose every 500 feet or so in the climb. Do not climb too close to clouds, and do not fly into clouds. Be aware of the nature of the airspace above you. For example, do not inadvertently climb into controlled airspace without a clearance to do so from ATC. Exert firm, positive, but smooth, control over the airplane.

REVIEW 11
Climbs

1. How does the amount of power usually required for a steady climb compare to that needed when cruising straight and level?
2. What is climb power for many training airplanes?
3. In entering a climb from straight and level flight, what power is set? What is the attitude to which the nose is raised?
4. When settled in the climb, should you trim off any steady control pressures?
5. What is climb performance is measured in terms of?
6. Which instruments are checked during a climb?
7. As you apply power to climb, which way will the nose pitch? Which way will the airplane yaw? To counteract these effects, in what direction is pressure applied to the control column? Which side rudder pressure is used?
8. In a climb with climb power set, how do you control airspeed?
9. If the climb airspeed is too low, what change in nose attitude should you make?
10. If the climb airspeed is too high, what change in nose attitude should you make?
11. Is it good airmanship to make small clearing turns in a prolonged climb so that you can clear the blindspot below the nose?
12. For the steepest climb-out with takeoff flaps extended, at what speed would you fly? To what tolerance should you fly this speed?
13. For the steepest climb-out with zero flaps, at what speed would you fly? To what tolerance should you fly this speed?
14. When clear of obstacles on a zero-flap takeoff, what change to the nose attitude is needed to achieve the best-rate climb speed V_Y? What accuracy should you fly this to?
15. What effect will a tail wind have on the climb gradient over the ground?
16. What effect will a head wind have on the climb gradient over the ground?
17. What setting should the mixture be for an en route climb?
18. An en route climb is flown with an airspeed within how many knots? Within how many degrees is the heading? Is the balance ball centered?
19. When leveling off from a climb, you should hold the specified altitude to an accuracy of how many feet?
20. What effect does warmer weather have on climb performance? How will climb performance change with altitude?
21. What effect does increased weight have on climb performance?
22. What will the engine temperature usually be in a climb compared with that in the cruise?
23. If the engine temperature is too high, what change in nose attitude and airspeed can be made to increase engine cooling?
24. For a climb from a sea-level airport, what position is the mixture control usually in?
25. What is looking after the engine in a climb and keeping a good lookout known as?
26. What is the altitude above which the airplane is unable to climb known as?
27. A pilot flies an airplane according to the IAS displayed on which instrument?
28. At high altitudes, how does the true airspeed compare with the indicated airspeed?
29. As the airplane climbs to higher altitudes, what is the effect on airplane performance, engine performance and human performance?

Answers are given on page 578.

TASK
Climbing

Aim: (a) To enter and maintain a constant airspeed climb on a constant heading.
(b) To level off at a particular altitude.

1. ***Prior to Entry***

   Note the appropriate climb speed.

   Look out—clear the area ahead, above, below and to either side.

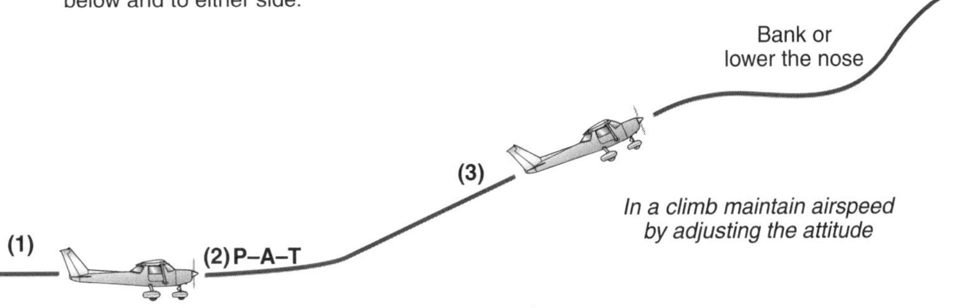

Bank or
lower the nose
(3)
In a climb maintain airspeed
by adjusting the attitude
(1)
(2) P–A–T

2. ***Entry to a Climb***

   Look out.

P – mixture rich;
– increase to climb **Power**;
– balance with rudder.

A – raise nose to climb **Attitude**;
– allow airspeed to reduce and settle;
– adjust attitude to achieve desired speed (check ASI).

T – **Trim.**

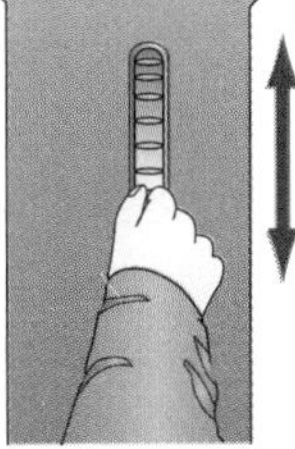

1. Set climb power.

2. Select climb attitude.

3. Trim.

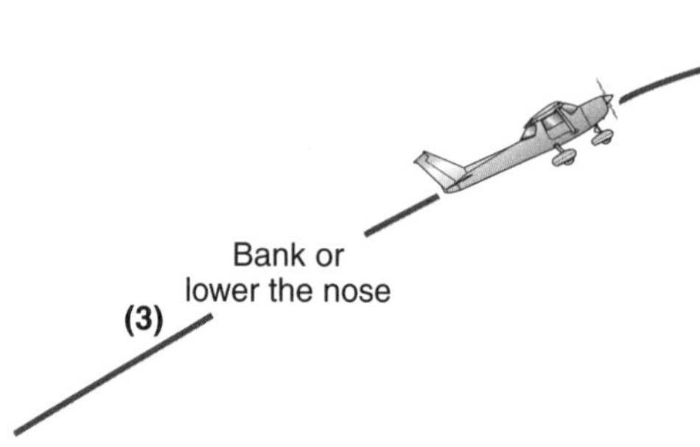

3. Maintaining a Climb

Look out.

Maintain:

Wings level with aileron.
Balance with rudder.
Airspeed with attitude.

Periodically check engine temperatures and pressures.

Look out for attitude reference and for other aircraft.
Lower nose or bank left and right every 500 feet or so, to clear area ahead.

ASI
Control airspeed with attitude

Altimeter
Increasing

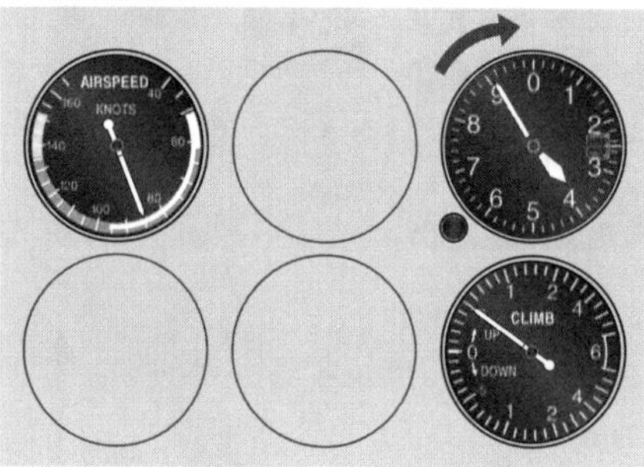

VSI
Rate of climb

Monitor climb performance

(4) A-P-P-T

4. Leveling off from a Climb

Look out.

A – gradually lower nose to <u>low-speed</u> cruise **Attitude** (monitor altimeter).

P – **Pause**, allow airspeed to increase to cruise speed (monitor ASI);

– adjust the attitude progressively.

P – at cruise speed, reduce to cruise **Power;**

– relax rudder pressure to balance.

T – **Trim.**

1. ***Set low speed level attitude.***
2. ***Allow aircraft to accelerate.***
3. ***Adjust power and attitude.***

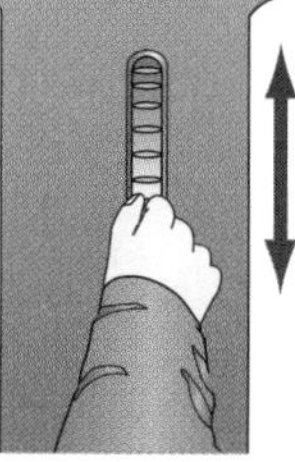

12

Normal (Powered) Descents

OBJECTIVES

To describe:

- the forces and moments acting on the aircraft in a powered descent;
- the relationship between attitude, airspeed, power and rate of descent;the technique to enter, maintain, adjust and level from a normal descent; and
- the attitude-power combination for the descent profiles for your airplane.

Figure 12-1 Free descent.

CONSIDERATIONS

Types of Descent

There are two primary descent modes:

- *free* descents, which are independent of geographic location; and
- *aimed* descents, which are used to reach a desired altitude at, or over, a ground feature.

Free Descents

A change of altitude during straight or turning flight that is independent of a ground position is a simple relationship between attitude, airspeed, power and rate of descent.

The prime reference is usually airspeed or rate of descent, e.g. to maintain cruise speed to reach a destination or to descend at 500 feet per minute (for passenger comfort). The pilot reduces power from the cruise setting by about 200 RPM or 2 in. Hg, and adjusts the attitude to maintain airspeed. A descent profile could also be at a reduced airspeed, e.g., perhaps 90 knots and 500 fpm. You need to note the attitude/power/performance references for your airplane.

Aimed Descents

A later task describes descent profiles in the cruise or approach configuration, which are designed to achieve a certain height over a specific geographic location, such as when passing a reporting point at a certain altitude, or achieving an aim point on the runway for landing.

Forces and Moments in a Powered Descent

The pitch altitude for a powered descent is not as low as for the glide.

When the power is reduced in level flight, there is a nose-down pitching moment and a yawing moment. The reduced thrust will result in a reducing airspeed, if the pilot maintains level flight. If the pilot allows the nose to drop, the airspeed can be maintained and altitude can be sacrificed. This is the principle of the powered descent. The more the power is reduced, the more the nose is lowered to maintain the airspeed, the steeper the descent, and the greater the rate of descent.

Conversely, if power is increased in a descent, the pilot can raise the nose to maintain airspeed and the descent will be shallower. Ultimately, if the power is increased sufficiently, and still the pilot adjusts the attitude, the aircraft will stop descending and return to level flight. A further power increase will result in a climb. This relationship has led to the expression that power controls rate of descent. It does in a way, if the pilot adjusts the attitude to maintain the same airspeed or allows the natural pitching moment to do the same.

Alternatively, the pilot can simply leave the power set and lower the nose attitude. The aircraft will descend but will also accelerate. In this instance, the pilot may use the higher speed to gain time but must be careful to avoid turbulence and not to exceed limiting airspeeds.

Performance

Power plus attitude equals performance. The performance achieved by an airplane depends both on the power selected and the attitude set. To alter the rate of descent and the flight path, while maintaining a constant airspeed, both power and attitude must be adjusted—power with the throttle and attitude with the control column. This is precisely what happens on a cruise descent and on a normal approach to land. The cruise descent is used to save time, say, at the end of a long cross-country flight, commencing descent to the destination airfield from the cruise level some miles out by reducing the power slightly and lowering the nose to maintain the cruise speed. It is a leisurely and comfortable descent.

Factors Affecting the Angle and Rate of Descent

Power and Attitude

Flight path is a combination of power and attitude. If power is increased, and the attitude is adjusted to maintain the same airspeed, the flight path must be shallower. Thus the rate and angle of descent are reduced. Indeed, this is a technique for flying a precision instrument approach. You will hear it expressed that *power controls the rate of descent and the attitude controls the airspeed*, but it is not quite that simple.

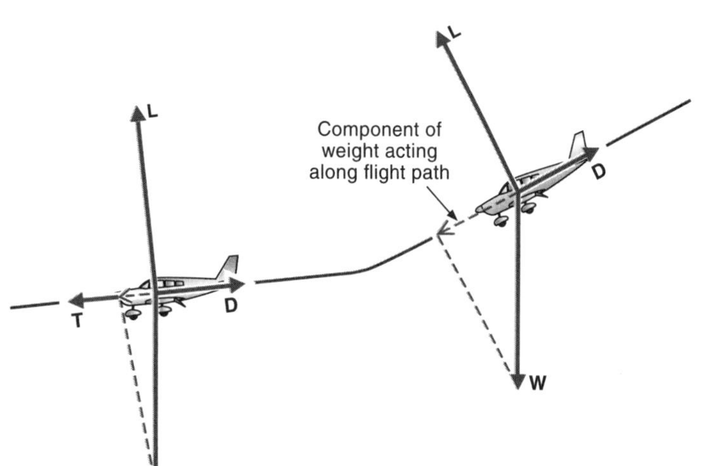

Figure 12-2 Increasing power shallows the descent and reduces the rate of descent.

Figure 12-3 Descent with flap.

Ultimately, a point is reached where the power is sufficient for level flight and the rate of descent will reach zero. You can continue to increase power and raise the nose to maintain airspeed and, eventually, the aircraft will be climbing.

Airspeed

For a constant power, attitude adjustments will change the airspeed and the flight path. A higher airspeed will mean a steeper path and higher rate of descent.

Weight

Weight has a component acting along the flight path. With a set power (or idle RPM) and a set attitude, the greater the weight, the higher the airspeed during the descent.

Wind

Wind has no effect on the path through the air and so the *rate of descent* will *not* change with wind. However, the path relative to a point on the ground will change because the air is moving. Descent into a head wind will have a steeper path, and that with a tail wind will have a shallower path.

Flaps and Landing Gear

Anything that increases drag will necessitate a steeper nose-down attitude to maintain airspeed so, for the same power, the descent will be steeper and the rate of descent higher.

APPLICATION

En Route or Cruise Descent

The en route descent is simply the means to reduce altitude when returning to your airfield. There is no particular airspeed or rate of descent to be followed, simply a descending path with controlled airspeed. There will be a cruise descent power setting for the aircraft.

Descent Point

A useful rule of thumb is to commence the descent at an approximate distance of five times your altitude; for example, from 3,000 feet, start descending 15 nautical miles from your airfield. During planned cross-country flights, you plan the descent point, but for now just use this approximation.

Alternatively, you can simply point at the place you want to go and adjust the power if the airspeed increases too much or if there is any turbulence. There are an infinite number of possible descent profiles.

TECHNIQUE

Entering the Descent

Power, attitude, trim.

The technique for entering the descent is to reduce power, adjust the attitude to maintain cruise airspeed, allow the aircraft to stabilize and then trim (PAT). The power setting will either be nominated for your aircraft, or as a rough guide you may use a reduction of 100 RPM, or 1 inch MP, for a rate of descent of 200 feet per minute.

As you reduce the power from its cruise setting, the nose will want to drop anyway so the aircraft's stability will assist you to enter the descent. A similar situation occurs when returning to level flight.

Figure 12-4 Power, attitude and configuration.

Maintaining the Descent

If the airspeed and the rate of descent are too high, the attitude is reduced. If the speed is correct but the rate is high, the attitude is reduced and the power increased a little. If the rate is too high and the airspeed is low the power is increased. There is an close link between the power, the attitude, and the resulting airspeed and rate of descent.

Like the climb, the airspeed indicator is the primary performance measure for the descent and the glide. Rate of descent, although useful information, is not used as a primary reference except during an instrument approach or a visual approach as a confirmation of other parameters. You can monitor the rate of descent on the vertical speed indicator.

To decrease the rate of descent and flatten the descent flight path:

- increase power;
- raise the nose attitude to maintain airspeed; and
- trim.

To increase the rate of descent and steepen the descent flight path:

- decrease power;
- lower the nose to maintain airspeed; and
- trim.

Returning to Level Flight

To level, simply increase power to the cruise value, allow the nose to rise while keeping straight with rudder, adjust the attitude for straight and level, and trim (PAT). To enter a climb directly from a descent, simply increase the power smoothly to climb power, again allowing the nose to rise to the climb attitude, balance and hold the attitude as the airspeed decays. Retrim. Retract the flaps, if necessary, readjust the attitude and retrim.

AIRMANSHIP

Take positive action to achieve the desired airspeed and approach path. Consider the engine. Warm it periodically on a prolonged descent and use the carburetor heat as required. Maintain a good lookout and bank to clear under the nose. Do not descend below 500 feet AGL.

REVIEW 12

Normal (Powered) Descents

1. Is the pitch attitude for a powered descent lower than that for a glide?
2. To increase the rate of descent and steepen the flight path, what power change do you make? How will this effect the nose attitude?
3. To reduce the rate of descent and flatten the flight path, what power change do you make? How will the effect the nose attitude?
4. If an airplane descends 100 feet in 15 seconds, what should the vertical speed indicator approximately read?
5. If an airplane descends 150 feet in 15 seconds, what should the vertical speed indicator approximately read?
6. If an airplane descends 150 feet in 20 seconds, what should the vertical speed indicator approximately read?
7. If the vertical speed indicator reads 300 fpm, how many seconds will it take for the airplane to descend 100 feet?
8. If the vertical speed indicator reads a rate of descent of 200 fpm, but you desire 250 fpm, what change in power should you make? What change to the nose attitude should you make?
9. If the vertical speed indicator reads a rate of descent of 250 fpm, how long will it take to descend 1,000 feet?
10. If the vertical speed indicator reads a rate of descent of 400 fpm, but you desire 300 fpm, what change in power should you make? What change to the nose attitude should you make?
11. What are the tolerances on a powered descent (include knots of chosen airspeed, degrees of heading, the fpm limitations of the descent rate and the target altitude)?
12. For a descent to an aim point, how does the pilot know he or she is on flight path?

Answers are given on page 579.

TASK

Normal (Powered) Descent

Aim: To enter, maintain and level from a constant airspeed descent with nominated power settings.

1. Prior to Descent

Recall the power setting.

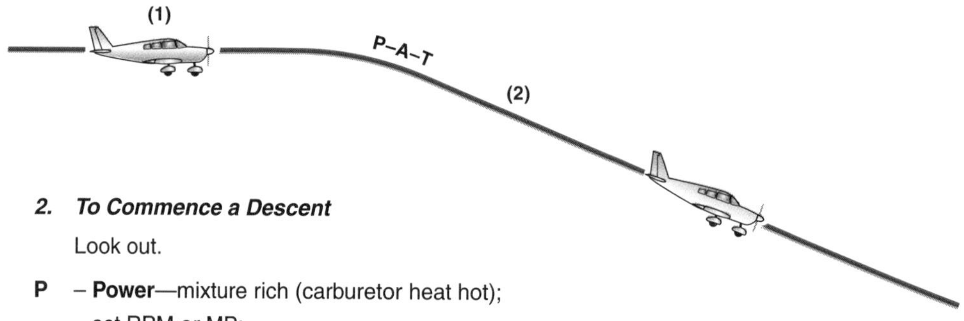

2. To Commence a Descent

Look out.

P – **Power**—mixture rich (carburetor heat hot);
– set RPM or MP;
– balance with rudder;
– maintain attitude until desired airspeed is attained.

A – **Attitude** set;
– adjust to maintain airspeed.

T – **Trim**.

1. Reduce power, maintain attitude
Balance

2. Select attitude.
3. Adjust, Trim.

3. *To Maintain the Descent*

Look out—bank or adjust attitude if necessary.

Maintain:

- wings level with ailerons;
- balance with rudder;
- airspeed with attitude;

Monitor engine instruments.

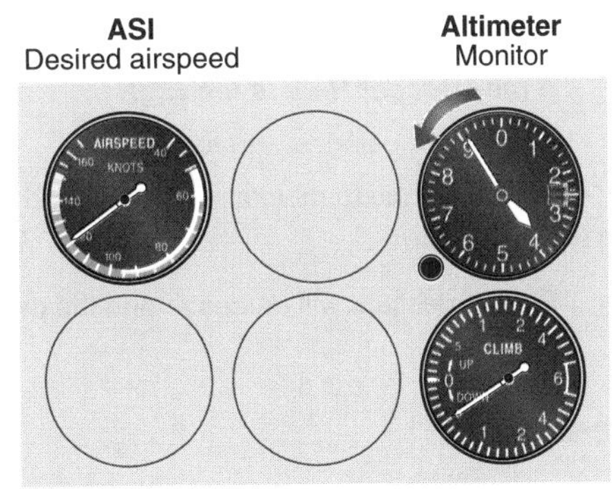

VSI
Accepted

Note the attitude and power for the descent profiles for your airplane

(3)

(4) P–A–T

4a. *To Level*

Anticipate by 10% of rate of descent.

P – **Power**—set for cruise (carburetor heat cold);
– balance with rudder.

A – **Attitude**—straight and level.

T – **Trim**.

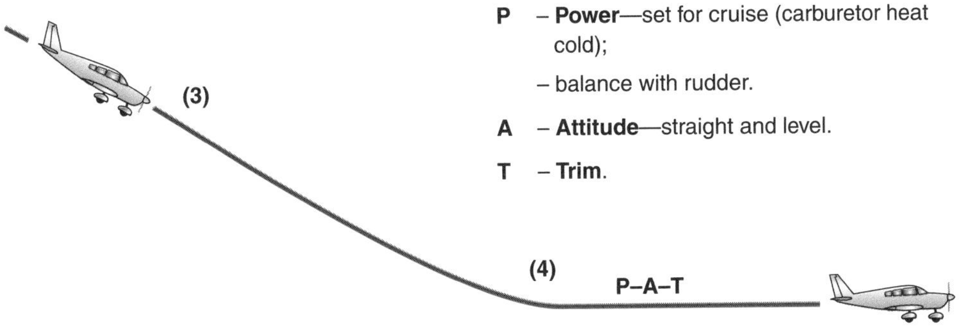

4b. *To Go Around*

P – **Power**—set climb power (carburetor heat cold);
– balance.

A – **Attitude**—set climb attitude.

T – **Trim**.

TASK

Controlling Rate of Descent

Aim: To control the flight path using attitude and power, while maintaining a desired rate of descent.

If the Descent Rate is too High

Add power; balance with rudder.

Adjust attitude to maintain airspeed (monitor airspeed indicator).

Trim.

Rate of descent will decrease and the descent flight path will be shallower.

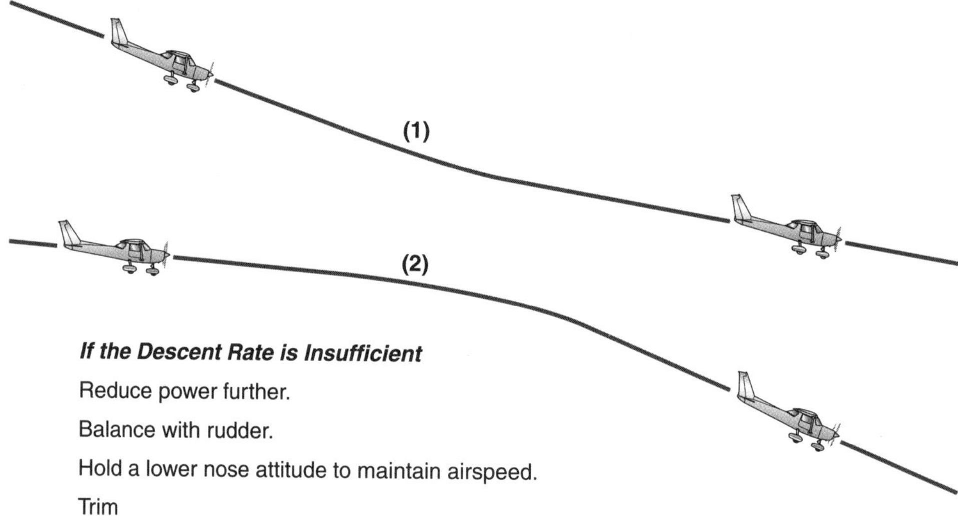

If the Descent Rate is Insufficient

Reduce power further.

Balance with rudder.

Hold a lower nose attitude to maintain airspeed.

Trim

The rate of descent will increase (monitor VSI and altimeter).

Descent attitude with higher power and lower rate of descent

Descent attitude with less power and higher rate of descent

13
Use of Flaps in the Descent

OBJECTIVES

To describe:

- the effect of extending the flaps on rate of descent, descent gradient and forward view in a powered descent or glide;
- the attitude-power combination for a powered descent or glide with flaps extended; and
- the technique for extending and retracting flaps in a descent or glide.

Figure 13-1 Flaps extended.

CONSIDERATIONS

Flaps, Drag, and Descent Angle

Extending the flaps causes a small increase in lift and a greater proportional increase in drag. If maintaining a constant airspeed in the descent, the flight path will be progressively steeper following the extension of each stage of flap.

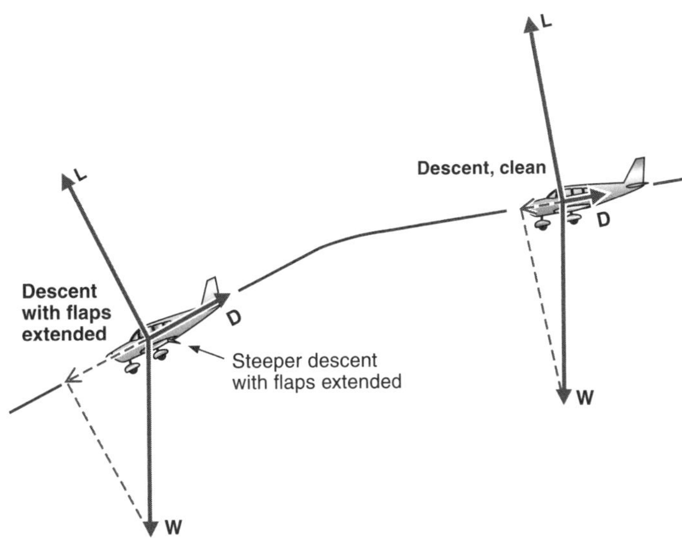

Figure 13-2 Flaps steepen the descent and glide.

Nose Attitude

The increased drag as the flaps extend requires a lower pitch attitude if airspeed is to be maintained. The lower nose attitude affords a better view through the windshield in a flapped descent. This is a significant advantage, especially on the approach to land. The greater the flap extension, the lower the nose attitude. The desired airspeed is maintained by adjusting the pitch attitude with elevator, trimming off any steady control column pressure.

With flaps extended, a lower nose attitude is required.

Clean

With flaps

Figure 13-3 A lower nose attitude is required to maintain speed with flaps extended so the aim point is closer.

Stalling Speed

Flaps lower the stalling speed.

Extending the flaps alters the shape of the wing and increases its lifting ability. The stalling speed is reduced and so safe flight at a (slightly) lower airspeed is possible, retaining an adequate safety margin above the stall.

APPLICATION

Flap Extension and Retraction

Operate the flaps at a suitable airspeed and be prepared for a pitching moment.

As flap is extended, the changing shape of the wing and the different aerodynamic forces produce extra stress on the airframe structure. For this reason, flap should only be extended when the airspeed does not exceed the maximum flap-extension speed (known as V_{FE}).

The flap operating speed range is shown on the airspeed indicator as a white band. V_{FE} is at the high-speed end of this white arc; stalling speed with full flap extended and wings level is at the low-speed end.

There may be a pitching tendency as the flaps are lowered due to the center of pressure (through which lift acts) moving fore or aft on the wing. There is also a changed airflow over the horizontal stabilizer. This can be counteracted with the control column and trim to hold the desired nose attitude.

TECHNIQUE

Extending the Flaps

Make sure your airspeed is within the white arc on the ASI before extending the flaps.

With the aircraft established in a normal descent, check that the airspeed is below V_{FE} (i.e. in the white band). Extend the flaps in stages as required, holding the desired pitch attitude for each stage of flap and controlling the airspeed with elevator trim.

The more flap that is extended, the lower the required nose attitude. Retrimming will be required after each stage of flap extension to relieve control column pressures. If the original airspeed is maintained, a higher rate of descent will occur. If the airspeed is reduced slightly (e.g. as on an approach to land), then the increase in the rate of descent will not be quite as much.

Raising the Flaps

As the flaps are raised, the loss of lift will cause the airplane to sink unless a higher nose attitude is set. Do not raise the flaps at speeds below the green band on the airspeed indicator; the lower end of the green arc is the stalling speed wings-level with a clean wing. To raise the flaps, retract them in stages, holding the desired nose attitude for each configuration and controlling the airspeed with elevator. Trim.

The flaps are generally used on the approach to land, so it is not a common procedure to raise the flaps in a continued descent having extended them for landing. It is, however, necessary to raise the landing flap in a go-around from a discontinued approach because the high drag would compromise the ability to climb. There is a strong pitch-up tendency as maximum power is applied to go around, and this has to be resisted with forward pressure on the control column. Full flap generates too much drag for a good climb-away and should be retracted in stages at a safe speed.

Figure 13-4 Raise the flaps at a safe speed and attitude.

AIRMANSHIP

- Do not exceed the maximum speed for flap extension (V_{FE}) and do not raise flap at airspeeds below the clean stalling speed.
- Fly the airplane smoothly as flap is extended or raised; hold the desired pitch attitude, changing it smoothly as required when the flap position is changed.
- Be aware of your airspeed.
- Correct for *ballooning* as flap is lowered, and avoid *sinking* as flap is raised.

Do not raise the flaps at speeds below the green band on the airspeed indicator.

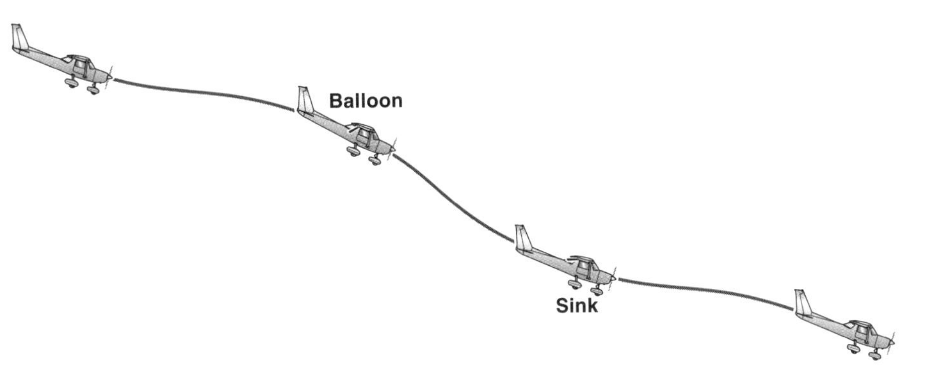

Figure 13-5 Balloon and sink.

REVIEW 13

Use of Flaps in the Descent

1. Can the flaps be used to steepen a descent path without any change in airspeed?
2. What effect does extending the flaps have on the nose attitude of an airplane on descent? What effect does this have on forward view?
3. Should the flaps be operated in stages or as one complete movement?
4. Does lowering the flaps increase stalling speed?
5. Will lowering the flaps cause a tendency for the airplane to balloon unless the nose is lowered?
6. After changing the flap setting, should you adjust the trim to remove any steady pressure?
7. What change to the flight path will occur if flaps are raised and no adjustment is made to nose attitude?

Answers are given on page 579.

TASK

Use of Flaps in the Descent

Aim: To steepen the descent using flaps.

To Lower the Flaps

(a) Check airspeed—speed **must** be below maximum flap-extension speed.

(b) Lower the flaps in stages.

(c) Set a lower nose attitude to maintain airspeed.

(d) Trim.

Note the increased rate of descent, steeper path and improved forward view, resulting from the flap extension in the descent.

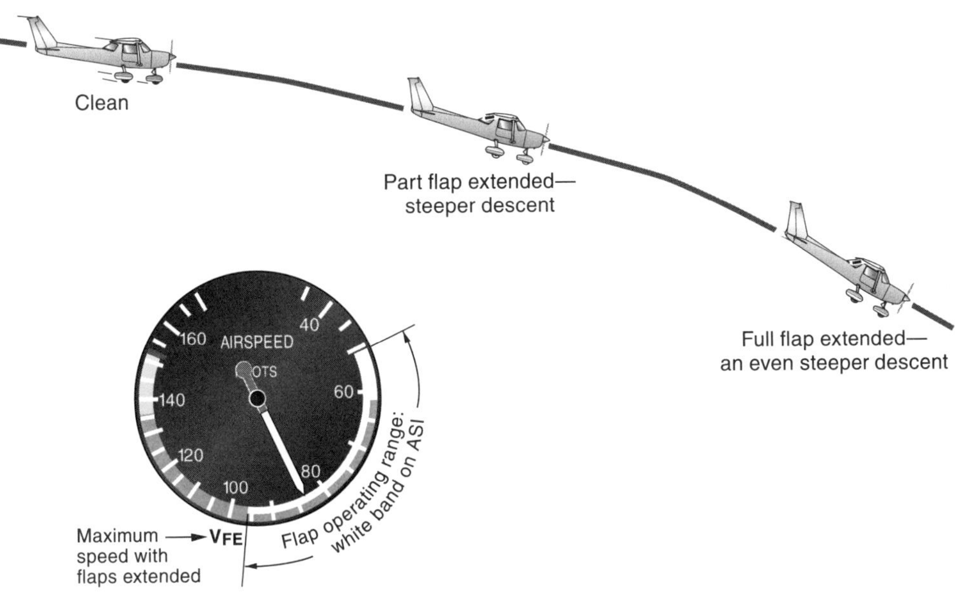

14

Descent to an Aim Point

OBJECTIVES

To describe:

- the technique to modify a normal (cruise) descent to arrive over a geographic location at a desired altitude; and
- the technique to achieve a desired approach path, centerline and airspeed to an aim point on the runway in the approach configuration.

Figure 14-1 Aimed descent.

CONSIDERATIONS

As soon as a ground reference is introduced, the pilot has the added complexity of accounting for wind and its vagaries.

Descent to a Geographic Feature

Commonly, the pilot plans the descent to arrive over a geographic location (the airfield or entry point) at a certain altitude. There are two techniques to achieve this. The first is to plan a set rate of descent and altitude change giving a time interval that then is used to establish a top of descent. For example 500 fpm with 3,500 feet to lose equals 7 minutes, which at a groundspeed of 2 nautical miles per minute gives a descent point of 14 nautical miles to go. This is then adjusted for wind gradient.

The second technique is, somewhere between 10–20 nautical miles from the reference point, to lower the nose to fly over the point at the arrival height. For example, to arrive over the airfield at 1,000 feet, aim about 3 nautical miles beyond the field—18:1 descent path). When the descent path is established, adjust the power to keep the airspeed below V_{NO} or V_A. If the descent is left too late, the power has to be further reduced and a higher rate of descent accepted or a less direct flight path has to be planned.

Controlled Descent to an Aim Point

Control the flight path with elevator and airspeed with power.

As a precursor to the visual approach to the runway, it is common to practice a controlled descent to a point or line on the ground before trying the maneuver to an active runway. The feature on the ground requires a straight line reference such as a road, fence or line of trees, plus a pinpoint feature on that line that may be used as an aim point. There are three stages to the technique:

- aligning the aircraft with and maintaining a straight path to the feature on an extended centerline (either as established from an extended centerline or a simulated base position);
- establishing a preferred angle of approach to an aim point on the ground while maintaining the centerline; and
- maintaining the above references while also controlling the airspeed within required tolerances.

Figure 14-2 Descent to an aim point.

This procedure also offers the opportunity to practice the go-around from final approach since the aircraft is established in a descent in the approach configuration. For the first exercises, the instructor will control the power; the student will be able to concentrate on positioning and aligning the aircraft in two dimensions.

Achieving Centerline

The imagined, projected centerline of the runway gives an instantaneous indication of alignment. If the centerline is vertical in the pilot's view (vertical to the horizon) regardless of where the nose of the aircraft is pointing, then the aircraft is, at that moment, on the centerline. If there is no wind, the aircraft will point at the runway. In a crosswind, it will have to be pointed offside.

Aim Point

The descending aircraft will ultimately hit a specific point on the ground. The pilot can tell where the aircraft will impact the ground as that particular ground feature or point remains stationary in the field of view and is a fixed point in the windshield if a constant nose attitude is maintained. It is the only point that stays constant. All other points radiate outward from the aim point.

Recognition of this radiating pattern is the most important aspect of judging the visual approach. Initially, the pilot may not be able to say what reference is being used but will just "know" where the aircraft is going to impact. It is subtle and not at all obvious.

The pilot's judgment is a continuous comparison of where the aircraft would impact versus where is the desired impact. The pilot's task is to make an appropriate correction whenever the path deviates. At the same time, the airspeed of the aircraft must be controlled.

The aim point is the primary reference during an approach to land, and adjusting the flight path and power to arrive at the chosen aim point on the runway at a particular airspeed is the most complex maneuver. It requires a series of continuous adjustments and a degree of anticipation that will come with experience. The basis for a good landing is a stabilized approach path on centerline with drift corrected, a set configuration and an accurate airspeed. That is why a good landing is the most rewarding experience and the measure of a pilot's skill and judgment.

During the descent, the aim point stays fixed in the windshield.

Figure 14-3 On the correct path, the aim point stays fixed in the pilot's view.

Achieving Glide Path

The aim point is where the aircraft would impact if there was no correction to its flight path. But this may be a one degree or a ten degree path relative to the ground. The optimum path for control of speed, terrain clearance and the ability to flare and land gently is three to four degrees. But how does the pilot differentiate?

The pilot uses a multiplicity of cues—whatever information is available. The start point is the base and final turn positions where the pilot establishes a certain altitude at a certain distance thereby establishing the basis for the approach angle. Once the angle is established, the pilot will use the shape and aspect of the runway or aspect ratio (the ratio of the width to the length at a given distance, such as on rollout onto final approach at 500 feet and just under two miles to run), the distance of the aim point below the horizon, the texture pattern of the ground, features on the ground versus the height above the threshold and TLAR (that looks about right). With experience a good approach just *feels* right. It becomes a trained/learned instinct. Runway width can distort the view, as you will see later.

Controlling Airspeed

The aircraft's flight manual will specify the approach speed for the weight. When the flight path is stabilized, the pilot looks to the airspeed indicator for two pieces of information:

- absolute (actual) airspeed; and
- the airspeed *trend* (e.g. steady, slowly reducing, quickly reducing, slowly increasing, or rapidly increasing).

The actual speed is compared to the desired speed and an adjustment is made to the thrust and the attitude. The change is modified by the trend. That is, if the aircraft is slow and the speed is decaying, the adjustment must be quick and significant. But if the speed is only slightly slow yet stable then the adjustment can be more moderate. Also, be sensitive to vertical acceleration. If you feel *lift* or *sink* then make a correction to attitude and thrust. Your butt will sense this acceleration before the flight path changes or the instruments respond.

Make an adjustment as soon as an error is seen, felt, or anticipated.

Again, it is a matter of experience. The most important aspect is to make an adjustment as soon as an error is seen, felt or is anticipated. Corrections, when anticipated, will be smaller and the aircraft will be better controlled. The landing will be more consistent. The pilot monitors the approach path by constantly referencing the desired aim point on the runway and estimating whether the flight path will take the airplane there. If not, corrections are made simultaneously to both power and attitude. If the aircraft is also fast or slow then the correction is more complex.

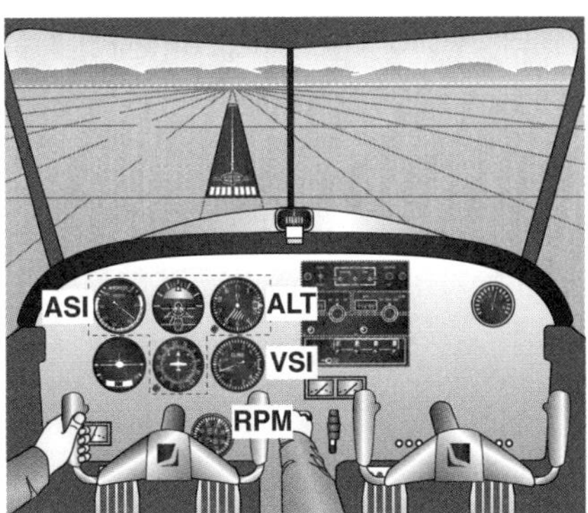

Figure 14-4 Control flight path with elevator, aileron and rudder and sustain airspeed with power.

AIRMANSHIP

Enter descents gently and warn your passengers—they may be alarmed. Anticipate the power/airspeed/descent profile. Lookout and check for traffic. Do not suddenly shock the engine with a large power reduction. Anticipate turbulence and control the airspeed.

REVIEW 14

Descents to an Aim Point

1. Your chosen aim point on the ground moves up the windshield during your descent. What does this indicate? What change in power in needed? What change to the nose attitude?
2. Your chosen aim point on the ground moves down the windshield during your descent. What does this indicate? What change in power in needed? What change to the nose attitude?
3. Your aim point in a powered descent is the approach end of the runway. In figure 14-5 below, what is the situation with the flight path? What power and nose position adjustments are needed to correct the situation?
4. Your aim point in a powered descent is the approach end of the runway. In figure 14-6 below, what is the situation with the flight path? What power and nose position adjustments are needed to correct the situation?

Figure 14-5 Question 3.

Figure 14-6 Question 4.

Answers are given on page 579.

15

Glide

OBJECTIVES

To describe:

- the balance of forces and moments in a glide;
- the relationship between lift-drag ratio and best glide ratio;
- the importance of airspeed to achieve best glide ratio;
- the factors affecting glide angle and rate of descent;
- the technique to enter, maintain and level (or go around) from a glide; and
- the attitude reference for a glide and the range of airspeeds for best glide in your airplane.

Figure 15-1 Glide, flaps up.

CONSIDERATIONS

A descent without power is called a glide.

An airplane may be descended in one of three ways:

- a powered descent, where power is set and attitude is adjusted to achieve a nominated airspeed or rate of descent;
- a cruise descent where the power is left at the cruise value, or very slightly reduced, the nose is lowered and the increase in airspeed is accepted; or
- a glide, where engine power is not used and the pilot sets the attitude to achieve a desired airspeed and accepts the resulting rate of descent.

Forces in a Glide

To maintain flying speed, the nose must be lowered when thrust is totally removed.

If power is reduced to idle when the airplane is in level flight, the drag will be unbalanced and, if altitude is maintained, the airplane will decelerate. Only three forces will act on the airplane when the power is totally removed: drag (no longer balanced by thrust), lift and weight.

To maintain flying speed when the thrust is removed, the nose must be lowered and a glide commenced. Drag (which by definition always acts in the direction opposite to the flight path) now has a component of the weight available to balance it. A steady gliding speed will be achieved when the three forces (L, W and D) are in equilibrium.

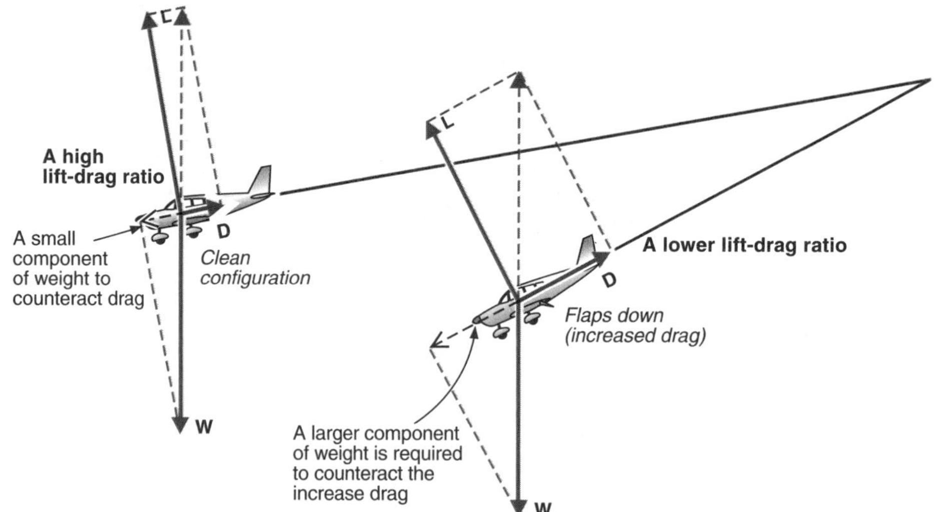

Figure 15-2 The forces in a glide.

Steepness of the Glide

If drag is increased more than lift (say by lowering flaps, sideslipping or flying at an incorrect airspeed), a greater component of the weight is required to balance it and maintain airspeed. A steeper flight path is the result. The gliding range through the air depends on the lift-drag ratio. For instance, if L/D is 6:1, the airplane will glide 6,000 feet (approximately 1 nautical mile) for each 1,000 feet lost in height; if L/D is 10:1, the airplane will glide 10,000 feet (1.7 nautical miles) for each 1,000 feet of altitude lost.

Figure 15-3
High aspect ratio and high L/D.

Gliding Range

Higher drag means a steeper descent.

Changing the angle of attack with the control column changes the flight path, the airspeed and hence the lift-drag ratio. This will have a significant effect on the glide path. A typical training airplane, flown at the best gliding speed, can achieve a lift-drag ratio of about 10:1 (2 nautical miles or 4 kilometers per 1,000 feet). Flown at another airspeed, the lift-drag ratio will be less efficient and, consequently, the glide path will be steeper. The pilot's

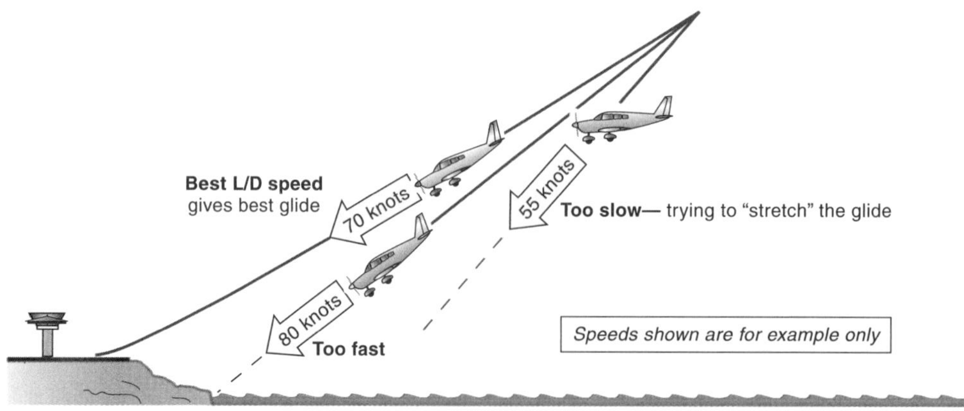

Figure 15-4 Glide at the recommended speed to obtain best still-air range.

operating handbook specifies the best gliding speed when the airplane is at maximum weight. At lower weights, the best gliding speed is less, but since training airplanes do not have significant variations in gross weight, the one speed is generally acceptable for the normal range of weights.

If the aircraft is at an airspeed below the optimum gliding speed, then, provided the airplane is still well above ground level, it will pay to lower the nose and gain airspeed. While the glide angle will initially steepen, the final glide angle will be flatter once the correct speed is achieved and maintained. The airplane will, in fact, glide further.

The maximum gliding range is achieved at the speed for best L/D. Low drag means a shallower glide.

Effect of Wind

Wind is moving air. If it is going in the direction you want to glide it will help by increasing your distance traveled over the ground; otherwise, it will hinder. A head wind will retard the airplane's passage over the ground and steepen the path; a tail wind will extend it and make the path more shallow relative to the ground.

Establish the optimum gliding speed by setting the correct pitch attitude.

In a tail wind, reducing the gliding airspeed slightly (perhaps 5–10 knots) below the recommended gliding speed may increase the range a little by reducing the rate of descent, allowing the airplane to remain airborne longer and be blown further by the wind. Conversely, the effect of a head wind can be reduced by gliding at a higher airspeed. The rate of descent will be increased, but the higher speed will allow the airplane to penetrate further into the wind and cover more ground. Increased speed could be a help on a marginal glide approach in a head wind. Any wind shear (reducing head wind) will also help as the aircraft gets closer to the ground and the aircraft has extra energy to convert into distance traveled.

A head wind steepens the descent over the ground; a tail wind flattens it.

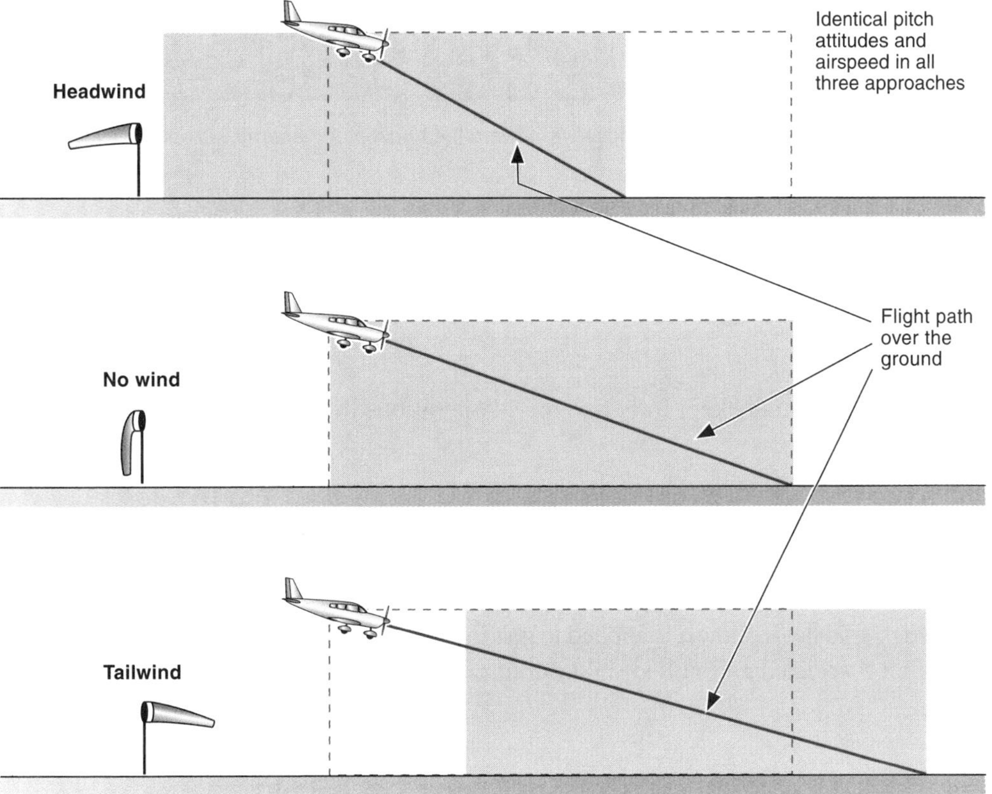

Figure 15-5 Compared to still air, more ground is covered when gliding with a tail wind and less with a head wind.

Estimating the Gliding Distance/Impact Point

The practical way to estimate how far the airplane could glide at a constant airspeed in a particular direction is to note the only feature on the ground that remains stationary in the windshield. It is the point where the aircraft would impact if that flight path was maintained.

The aircraft needs to be stabilized in speed and attitude, and it takes a little practice to visualize, but it is the only reliable way to see just where the aircraft would land. It is the same as judging a final approach but at a greater distance and approach angle. The cues are the same.

In the situation illustrated in figure 15-6, it appears that the glide will reach the field beyond the trees. The last picture shows that it will not be achieved because the tops of the trees have moved closer to the horizon. If they moved down, the aircraft (the pilot's eyes) would pass over them. Raising the nose in an attempt to reach the second field will have the opposite effect. If the speed falls significantly below the best gliding speed, the glide path will steepen and fall well short of even the first road. The only option now is to find a path between the trees.

Figure 15-6 Assessing the gliding distance—if object moves up toward the horizon, the aircraft will not clear it.

APPLICATION

Engine Handling

Mixture Control

The mixture is usually kept fully rich for all operations in the training area.

Carburetor Heat

Carburetor ice is more likely in a glide because of the low engine speed. Full power when needed may not be available. Consequently, before reducing power to idle, the carburetor heat should be set to hot to prevent the formation of carburetor ice. Carburetor heat is selected to cold before power is applied to go around. Confirm that it is the carburetor heat knob that is selected and pulled right out; it can be confused with the mixture control.

Power

Once the mixture and carburetor heat are set, the power can be reduced by smoothly pulling the throttle out/back. Full movement of the throttle should take about the same as a slow 1-2-3 count ("one potato, two potato, three potato"). The reduced slipstream effect will require rudder to prevent unwanted yaw. The tendency for the nose to drop too far will require back pressure on the control column once the glide attitude is reached. The tendency for the nose to drop as power is reduced is a safety feature that is designed to ensure that the aircraft will adopt a safe gliding attitude without any help from the pilot. However, this tendency can cause the nose to be too low, the speed to be too high, and the glide distance to be adversely affected.

Warm the Engine

Every 1,000 feet or so on a prolonged descent, the pilot should apply approximately 50% power for a few seconds to:

- keep the engine and oil warm;
- avoid carbon fouling on the spark plugs; and
- ensure that the carburetor heat is still supplying warm air.

Descent Rate

The rate of descent is a measure of how fast altitude is being lost (in feet per minute) and can be monitored on the vertical speed indicator. It gives an indication of how long before landing, if that is relevant.

Best-Endurance Glide

Generally, the aim in a glide is to achieve the maximum range (i.e. the greatest distance over the ground) and this is the situation addressed so far. Occasionally, but very rarely, time in flight (rather than distance covered) may be important, say, to maximize the time you have to transmit a mayday and have the passengers secured for a rough landing. The best-endurance glide is achieved at the speed that results in the *minimum rate of descent* as indicated on the vertical speed indicator. Typically, it is some 25% less than the more common gliding speed used for maximum range.

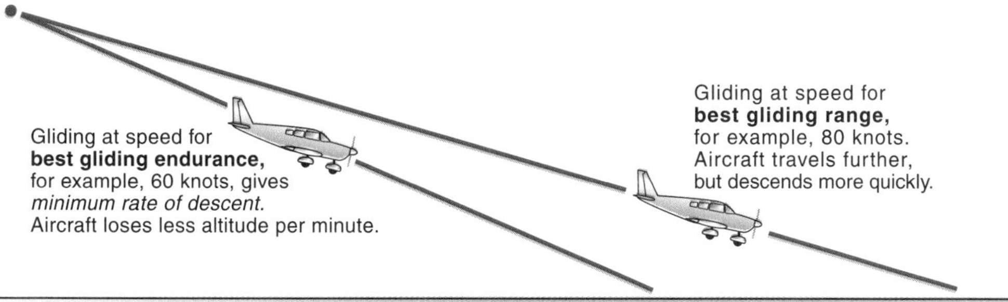

Figure 15-7 Select the best gliding speed for range or for endurance.

TECHNIQUE

Prior to commencing the descent, decide on an appropriate gliding speed, select a reference point well ahead and look out to check all clear of other airplanes and obstacles ahead, below and to either side. Lowering a wing to better view under the nose may be advisable.

Commencing the Glide

Select carburetor heat to hot before closing the throttle. Back pressure and rudder pressure will be required to counteract the pitch and yaw tendencies as the power is reduced. Hold the nose up and maintain altitude, allowing the airspeed to decrease. When at the desired gliding speed, lower the nose to the gliding attitude to maintain airspeed. An easy way to remember the sequence of events when beginning a descent is PAT (power-attitude-trim).

Maintaining the Glide

Maintain the wings level with ailerons and the balance ball centered with rudder pressure. Control airspeed with attitude: a higher nose attitude will be required for a lower speed and a lower nose attitude required for a higher speed.

Maintain a good lookout in the descent, possibly with clearing turns left and right every 500 feet to clear the area hidden by the nose.

To enable you to maintain the original direction, select a reference point on the horizon or use the heading indicator and/or the magnetic compass.

In a low-wing aircraft, there is still a blind spot under the wing and when you have learned turning, it is advisable not to descend in a straight line for very long. You will turn occasionally and have a look.

Warm the engine periodically (every 1,000 feet) by moving the throttle to full power and back to idle in about 5 seconds. Remain very aware of your altitude above the ground at all times and of the altitude still to be descended to your selected level. Ensure that the altimeter subscale is set correctly.

Leveling Off

When leveling off, anticipate by about 10% of the descent rate. For a descent rate of 400 feet/minute, for example, select carburetor heat off and apply power 40 feet above the desired level. Look ahead and gradually allow the nose to rise to the cruise attitude. The yawing and pitching effects of adding power (less pronounced than entering a climb) should be counteracted with rudder pressure and forward pressure on the control column to stop the nose rising too far. Once the cruise speed is achieved, retrim. This sequence is PAT (power-attitude-trim).

Climbing Away (Going Around)

Climbing away hardly differs from leveling off, except that you:

- select carburetor heat to full cold, smoothly apply full power (a silent "one potato, two potato, three potato" for correct rate of increase), and counteract the greater pitch/yaw tendency with pressures on the rudder and control column;
- go directly to the pitch attitude for the climb, and hold the nose up as the airspeed stabilizes (there will be little difference between the best-glide airspeed and the best rate of climb speed and little trim change except for the power effects);
- retract the flaps progressively, if extended;
- adjust the attitude (fine tune) to maintain the climb airspeed; and
- trim.

To climb away from a descent, such as in a go-around, P-A-T still applies.

AIRMANSHIP

Maintain a good lookout and clear the area under the nose, by banking left and right, every 500 feet or so, in the descent. If you are flying a low-wing airplane, look under the wings as well as the nose. Look over your shoulder also for faster aircraft descending into your area. Maintain a listening watch on the radio. Remain very conscious of your altitude above the ground when descending. Set the altimeter subscale correctly so that you can level off exactly at the desired altitude. Area pressure will normally be set so that altitude above mean sea level (MSL) is displayed, but be aware of the height of the terrain. Go around above 500 feet AGL.

Figure 15-8 Go around above 500 feet AGL.

REVIEW 15
Glide

1. Will a clean airplane glide further than an airplane in a high-drag configuration—for instance, with landing flaps extended?
2. Will an airplane flying slower than the best gliding speed glide further? Why?
3. Will an airplane flying faster than the best gliding speed glide further? Why?
4. How is the airspeed in a glide controlled?
5. In a glide, if the airspeed is too low, what change to the nose attitude should you make?
6. What effect does a tail wind have on the glide path over the ground? What effect does a tail wind have on the rate of descent?
7. What effect does a head wind have on the glide path over the ground? What effect does a head wind have on the rate of descent?
8. In a glide, how will a ground object that you will not reach move in the windshield?
9. What position should the mixture control and carburetor heat control be in for a glide?
10. Describe the accuracy of a glide in terms of the tolerances for airspeed, heading and target altitude.
11. As you reduce power for a glide, in which direction do you expect the nose to yaw? How will the nose pitch? How do you counteract this?
12. Is it good airmanship to periodically warm the engine in a prolonged descent? If so, how?
13. If the engine fails in flight when it is supplying cruise power, how will the nose attitude want to change?

Figure 15-9 Airspeed is crucial for best glide.

Answers are given on page 579.

TASK

Glide

Aim: To enter and maintain a glide at optimum airspeed on a constant heading, and to level off at a particular altitude, or establish a climb-out.

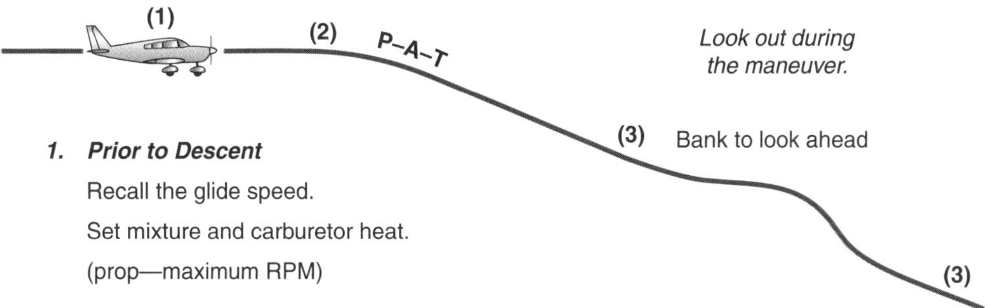

(1)
(2)
P–A–T
Look out during the maneuver.
(3)
Bank to look ahead
(3)

1. ***Prior to Descent***

   Recall the glide speed.

   Set mixture and carburetor heat.

   (prop—maximum RPM)

2. ***To Commence a Glide***

   Look out.

P – **Power**: throttle closed;

– balance with rudder;

– maintain attitude and allow speed to reduce to chosen gliding speed.

A – (when glide **Airspeed** is achieved) lower nose to glide **Attitude**;

– adjust attitude to maintain airspeed.

T – **Trim**.

1. ***Reduce power, maintain attitude.***

   Balance.

2. ***Select and hold the glide attitude.***
3. ***Trim.***

3. *To Maintain the Glide*

Look out—bank or adjust attitude if necessary.

Maintain:

– wings level with ailerons;

– balance with rudder pressure;

– airspeed with attitude.

Monitor engine instruments and warm engine periodically.

4a. *To Level Off*

Anticipate desired level-off altitude by 10% of rate of descent.

P – set cruise **Power** (carburetor heat cold);

– balance with rudder.

A – raise nose to low **Airspeed** straight and level **Attitude**.

T – **Trim**.

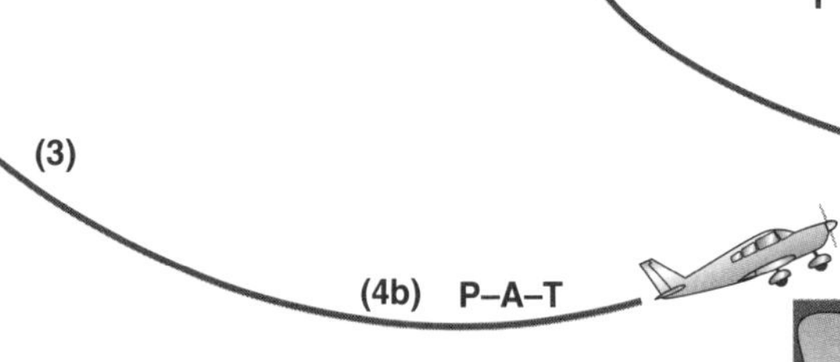

4b. *To Establish a Climb from the Glide*

P – apply climb **Power,** balance with rudder.

A – set climb **Attitude**.

T – **Trim**.

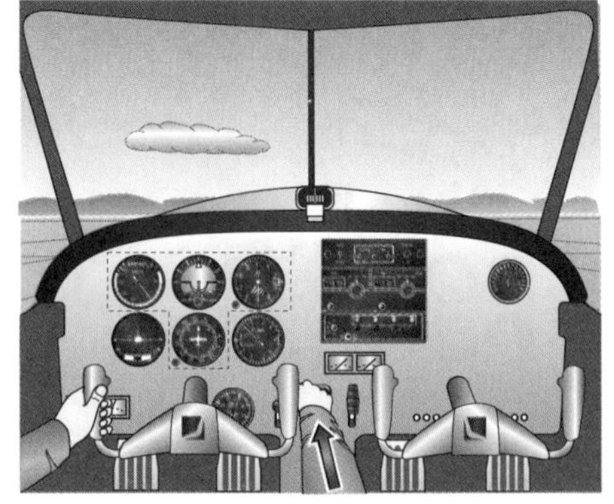

16 Slips

OBJECTIVES

To describe:

- the various forms of slips and their application;
- the limitations and precautions relating to slips in your airplane;
- the technique to enter, maintain and straighten from a forward slip, slipping turn and sideslip;
- the use of the forward slip and slipping turn in a forced landing;
- the use of a sideslip in a crosswind approach; and
- the attitude and airspeed references for safe slips in your airplane.

Figure 16-1 Sideslip in a crosswind approach.

CONSIDERATIONS

What Is a Slip?

The slip is an unbalanced flight condition with one wing lowered. It is uncoordinated because you use aileron and rudder in opposite senses—for example, left aileron to lower the left wing, with right rudder to stop the airplane turning left—and the balance ball will not be centered. The longitudinal axis of the airplane will be at an angle to the airplane's path through the air.

A slip is flown with crossed controls and the airplane is grossly unbalanced.

Even though the airplane is in an uncoordinated condition during a slip maneuver, you can still make it feel comfortable by applying the aileron and opposite rudder smoothly, and with no dramatic changes in the pitch attitude.

There are two main purposes in knowing how to slip an airplane:

- to steepen the descent during an approach to land, using a *forward slip* or *slipping turn*; and
- to counteract the wind drift during a crosswind landing, using a *sideslip*.

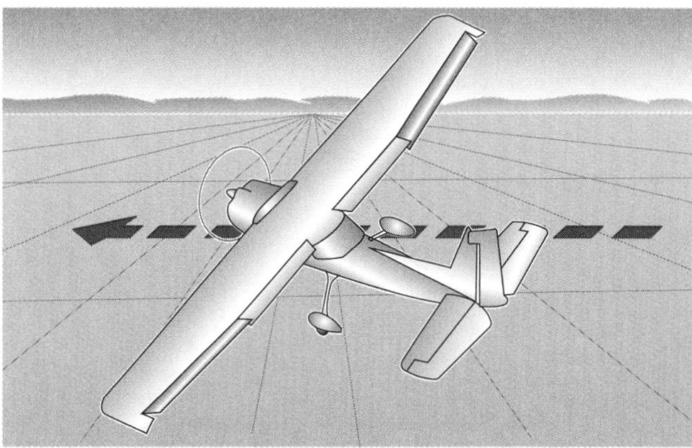

Figure 16-2 The forward slip.

Aileron Control and Yawing

The greater the bank angle, the greater the opposite rudder required.

When an airplane is banked using the ailerons alone, it will slip through the air toward the lower wing, and the nose will want to yaw toward the lowered wing. This natural yawing tendency can be opposed by applying opposite rudder (sometimes referred to as top rudder). If the bank is to the left, right rudder should be applied. The airplane will be uncoordinated, with the balance ball not centered but out to the low-wing side. You will have crossed controls—the control column one way and the rudder the other. This is a slip maneuver. The greater the bank angle and opposite rudder, the greater the slip, with the maximum slip possible usually being limited by the amount of rudder available. *The greater the bank angle, the greater the opposite rudder required.*

Figure 16-3 Typical control positions in a slip to the left (left aileron, right rudder).

Forward Slip

The forward slip is mainly used to steepen the glide without gaining airspeed, and is generally used in airplanes not fitted with flaps. The forward slip is an especially valuable maneuver when you find yourself too high on an approach to land, and flaps are not available to steepen the descent. If you tried to steepen the descent by diving, the airspeed might increase unacceptably—slipping avoids this by virtue of the greatly increased drag.

The forward slip steepens the descent by presenting the wing-down side of the airplane to the airflow, significantly increasing the drag. The lift-drag ratio is decreased, which causes the rate of descent to increase and the flight path to steepen. The greater the bank angle and amount of top rudder used, the greater the slip and the steeper the descent.

The power is usually at idle for a forward slip since the aim is to lose altitude quickly, and it would be contradictory to fly a forward slip maneuver using power at the same time. *Pitch attitude and airspeed control* in the forward slip can be maintained with pressure on the control column. Do not rely heavily on the airspeed indicator, since it may not give a reliable reading due to the disturbed airflow around the pitot tube and static ports in a slip.

With practice, and guidance from your flight instructor, you will soon be able to judge airspeed fairly accurately from the attitude of the airplane, the air noise and the feel of the flight controls.

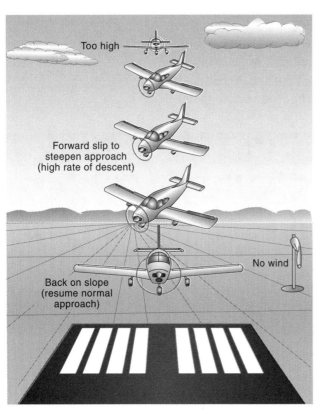

Figure 16-4 A forward slip to steepen the approach.

If there is any crosswind on the approach, it is more effective to slip into the wind, rather than away from it. For instance, if you are high on approach with a crosswind from the left, then use left aileron and right rudder (a forward slip to the left).

The importance of the forward slip maneuver in normal day-to-day flying has decreased because nearly all modern aircraft are fitted with flaps. However, it can still be a useful maneuver under certain circumstances, such as failure of the wing flap system, and so is still a worthwhile technique to practice and develop.

During the forward slip maneuver, the longitudinal axis of the airplane will have been yawed away from the original direction of flight. The direction of travel, however, should be the same as it was prior to you establishing the slip, the difference being that the airplane is now flying somewhat sideways. The steeper the slip, the greater the angle between the airplane's longitudinal axis and its flight path through the air.

If you are going to proceed with a landing, then the forward slip must be removed prior to the landing, both to align the longitudinal axis with the runway direction and to decrease the higher rate of descent. Some altitude is required to do this; your flight instructor will advise you on the altitude above the ground at which you should cease the forward slip.

A forward slip is useful when making an accurate approach to a short field (say during a forced landing) in an airplane without flaps. You can carry excess altitude early in the approach to ensure that you will definitely reach the field, and then slip off the extra altitude prior to the flare and touchdown.

The forward slip is used to steepen an approach to land.

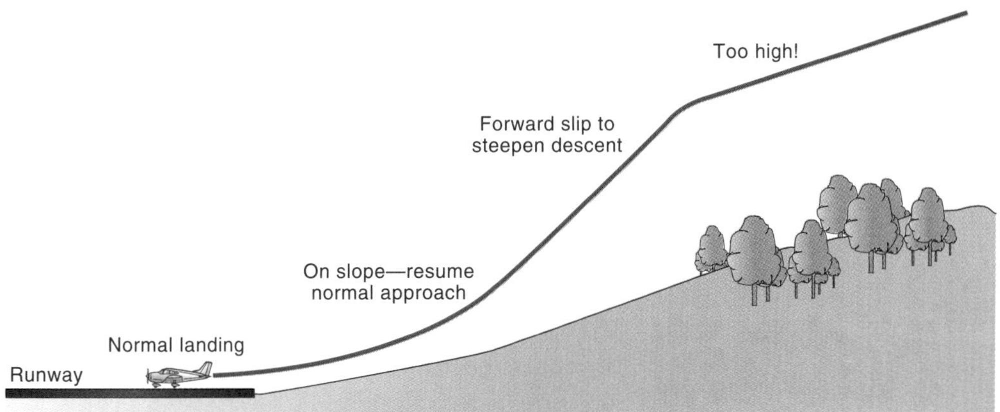

Figure 16-5 Profile view of a forward slip flight path.

The forward slip can also be used while turning, with more aileron than rudder being used to permit the airplane to turn. The slipping turn is considered in the next exercise.

Flaps and Forward Slips

The forward slipping maneuver is prohibited in some airplanes with flaps extended. This is to avoid excessively high rates of descent developing or situations where the elevator and rudder lose their effectiveness through blanketing of the airflow over them. If the fuel tanks are near-empty, a fuel port could be uncovered, causing an interruption of the fuel supply to the engine. The airplane flight manual or the pilot's operating handbook will specify this restriction if it applies. There may also be a placard in the airplane itself.

In some airplanes, forward slipping with flaps extended is not an approved procedure.

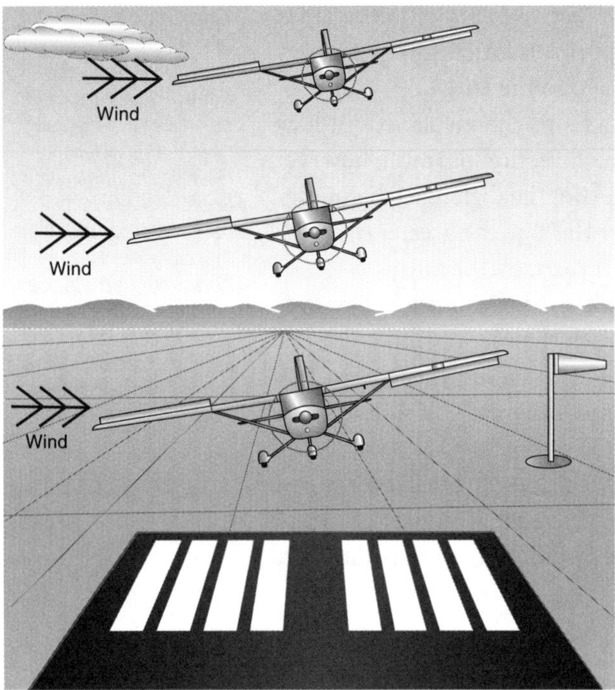

Figure 16-6 Using a sideslip to maintain centerline and align the airplane for a crosswind touchdown.

Figure 16-7 Wheel-down landing.

Slipping Turn

A slipping turn is a crossed-control turn that increases drag and steepens the approach path while continuing to turn. It is commonly used during the final turn to land in aircraft without flaps or with a restricted forward field of view.

Sideslipping and Crosswind

For a good landing, the airplane should approach directly along the centerline of the runway, and touch down with its wheels aligned with the centerline. Any sideways drift when the wheels touch will cause an uncomfortable landing and place an undesirable side load on the landing gear. In crosswind conditions, an airplane aligned with the runway centerline and flying with its wings level will drift sideways. You can prevent this wind drift by lowering the upwind wing into the wind, and using opposite rudder to keep the airplane pointed straight down the runway. The result is a slip into the wind and, with practice, you will be able to judge the amount of slip so that it exactly counteracts the wind drift. This is called a *sideslip* and will lead to a good touchdown in crosswind conditions. If you are drifting to the downwind side of the runway, increase the sideslip by applying more bank and an appropriate amount of rudder to keep straight; if you are drifting to the upwind side of the runway, the sideslip is too great, so reduce the bank with aileron and adjust the rudder pressure to keep straight.

Most pilots like to get the airplane into the side-slipping condition prior to commencing the landing flare—more of this later, in the chapter on landings. Note that, throughout the sideslip in a crosswind, the longitudinal axis of the airplane is aligned with the airplane's flight path over the ground, even though the airplane is slipping upwind. You will see airplanes of all sizes being landed in crosswinds using this technique, with the upwind wheel touching first, closely followed by the other main wheel and then the nosewheel. Any restrictions on forward slipping your airplane during approach should not apply to using the sideslip technique for crosswind landings.

TECHNIQUE

Forward Slip

To Enter a Forward Slip

Ensure you have adequate altitude to recover, since a high rate of descent can be achieved in a slip. Close the throttle, establish an in-trim glide, yaw the aircraft and bank the opposite way to track to the same aim point. Hold the desired nose attitude with elevator to maintain the required airspeed. Do not trim, since slipping is a transient maneuver.

To Maintain the Slip

Maintain the bank angle with aileron and control the heading with opposite rudder. The greater the bank angle and rudder used, the steeper the flight path. The airspeed is controlled with elevator, but bear in mind that the airspeed indicator may be inaccurate.

To Straighten From the Slip

Level the wings with aileron and centralize the balance ball by removing the excess rudder pressure. Resume a normal, coordinated descent at a suitable airspeed and rate of descent.

Slipping Turn

To Enter a Slipping Turn

During the final turn, the bank is increased and opposite rudder is applied.

Maintaining the Slipping Turn

Bank is then varied to complete the turn. Opposite rudder is used to control the steepness of the approach path.

Straightening From the Slipping Turn

To remove the sideslip, remove excess rudder and bank angle and rebalance.

The Sideslip

Sideslip to counteract wind drift in a crosswind landing.

Initially track along a line feature in a crosswind by *crabbing*—the usual method of maintaining a track over the ground and remaining in coordinated flight. The line feature on the ground could be a road, or it could be the runway centerline. The sideslip technique is normally used in a crosswind landing, but you can practice it while maintaining altitude using power. During this practice, fly at a suitable altitude above the surface, as determined by your flight instructor.

To Establish a Sideslip in a Crosswind

To establish a sideslip, simultaneously yaw the nose into alignment with the line feature on the ground using rudder, and apply opposite aileron to bank the airplane into wind before any drift develops.

Figure 16-8 Sideslip.

To Maintain the Sideslip

Keep the nose aligned with the line feature using rudder. If you are drifting downwind, increase the sideslip by increasing the bank angle and keeping straight with rudder; if you are drifting upwind, decrease the sideslip by reducing the bank angle, keeping straight with rudder. Control the airspeed with elevator, and the steepness of the descent path with power.

To Straighten the Sideslip

You may not want to remove the sideslip. If you are using the sideslip technique to counteract wind drift in a crosswind landing, then you will want to keep the sideslip going right through to the touchdown. If, however, you do want to remove the sideslip, then simultaneously level the wings and centralize the rudder.

AIRMANSHIP

Maintain a good visual awareness of other aircraft and your proximity to the ground, because of the high descent rates. Do not slip in nonapproved configurations, and do not slip with near-empty fuel tanks.

Be in a glide with the throttle closed before establishing a forward slip—the purpose of a forward slip is to lose altitude quickly, and using power would decrease its effectiveness. Maintain a safe airspeed.

REVIEW 16

Slips

1. In a slip, which side rudder is applied if the left aileron is used to lower the left wing? Is the balance ball in the center?
2. A slip is flown with what sort of controls?
3. Should you trim the airplane in a slip? What sort of maneuver is a slip?
4. What sort of slip is the airplane illustrated in the figure below performing?

5. Can a forward slip be used to steepen an approach?
6. Will the airspeed indicator be accurate during a slip?
7. Forward slips are generally used to steepen the approach and lose unwanted altitude during an approach with zero flaps. True or false?
8. Are forward slips with flaps extended a prohibited maneuver in some airplanes?
9. Do some airplanes have restrictions applied when slipping with wing flaps extended?
10. What sort of slip is the airplane illustrated in the figure below performing?

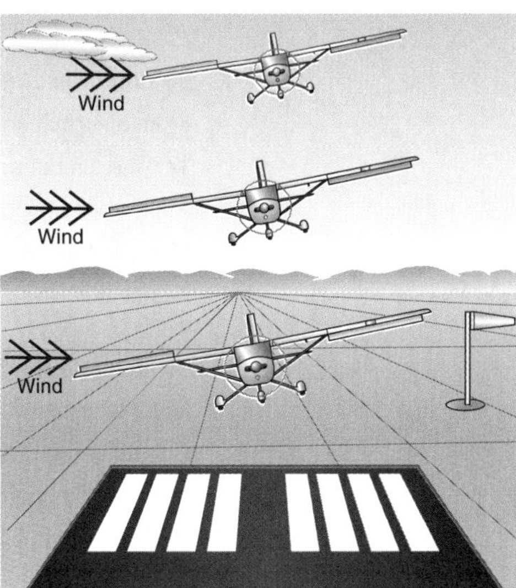

11. Are you permitted to use the sideslip technique during a crosswind landing with flaps extended?
12. During a forward slip when making a zero-flap approach, will the longitudinal axis of the airplane be aligned with the runway centerline?
13. Should the longitudinal axis of an airplane be aligned with the runway centerline on touchdown?
14. When using the sideslip technique in a crosswind landing, will the longitudinal axis of the airplane be aligned with the runway centerline during the final stages of the approach?
15. During a crosswind landing, the longitudinal axis of the airplane is aligned with the runway centerline before touchdown using what?
16. If the airplane is being carried downwind of the runway centerline by a crosswind just before touchdown, which wing is lowered to prevent the drift?

Answers are given on page 579.

TASK

Forward Slip

Aim: To increase rate of descent and steepen the descent flight path at a constant airspeed by sideslipping.

1. To Enter the Sideslip

From a normal descent:

Yaw the aircraft and hold the slip with rudder.

Apply opposite bank with ailerons.

Maintain track with bank and adjust rudder to suit.

Adjust attitude and maintain airspeed with elevator.

2. To Maintain the Sideslip

Maintain track with bank.

Control descent path.

Maintain airspeed with elevator.

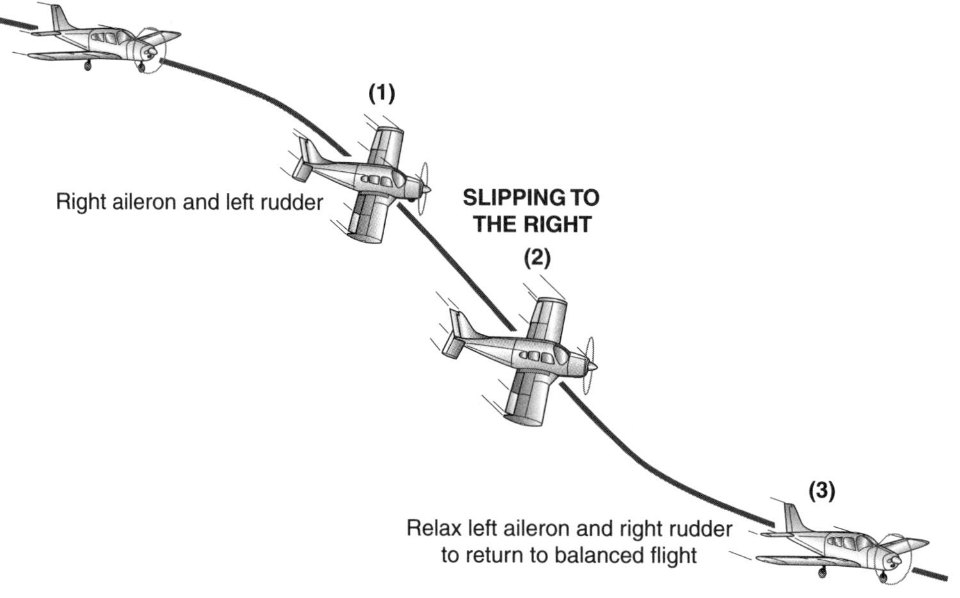
(1)
Right aileron and left rudder
SLIPPING TO THE RIGHT
(2)
(3)
Relax left aileron and right rudder to return to balanced flight

3. To Remove the Sideslip

Relax rudder.

Level wings with aileron.

Maintain desired airspeed with elevator.

TASK

Sideslip

Aim: To counteract wind drift in a landing by using the sideslipping technique.

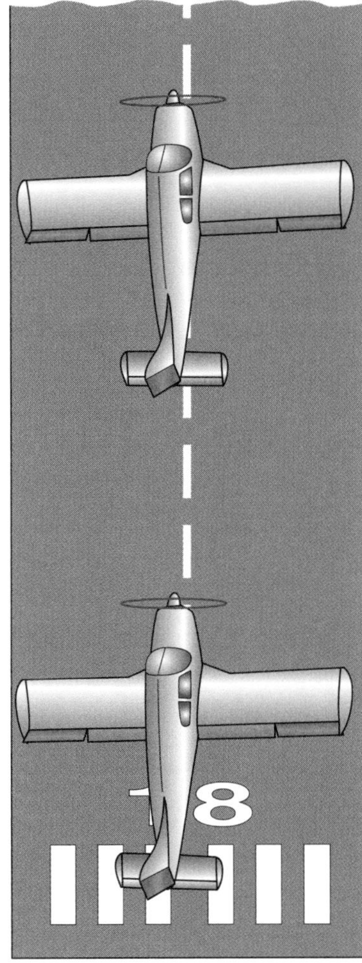

3. ***To Remove the Sideslip (say if not landing)***

   Simultaneously:

   Level the wings and centralize the rudder.

   Apply crab angle necessary for tracking.

2. ***To Maintain the Sideslip***

   If drifting across the runway (downwind):

   Apply more bank with aileron.

   Keep straight with rudder.

   Touch down on the upwind wheel.

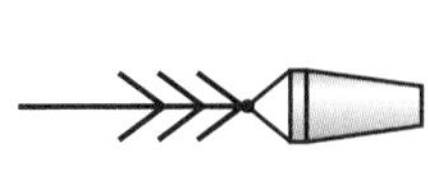

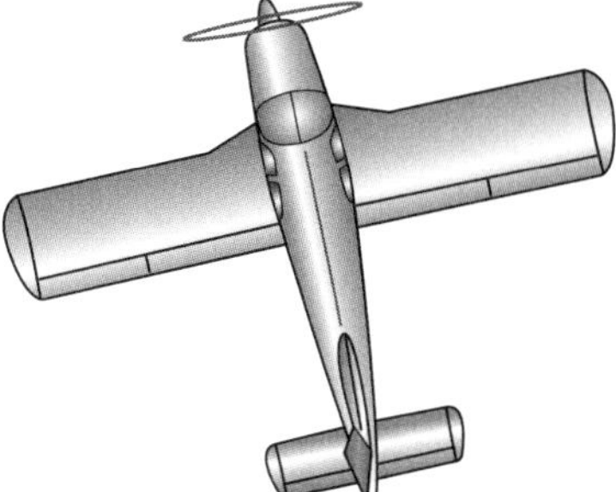

1. ***To Establish a Sideslip***

   On approach, simultaneously:

   Yaw the nose into alignment with the centerline using rudder.

   Apply opposite aileron to bank the airplane into wind before any downwind drift occurs.

TASK
Slipping Turn

Aim: To lose excess altitude in a gliding turn at a constant airspeed by sideslipping.

Note: Refer to the pilot's operating handbook to determine if sideslipping is an approved maneuver for your particular aircraft type. Some aircraft can only be sideslipped if the flaps are retracted.

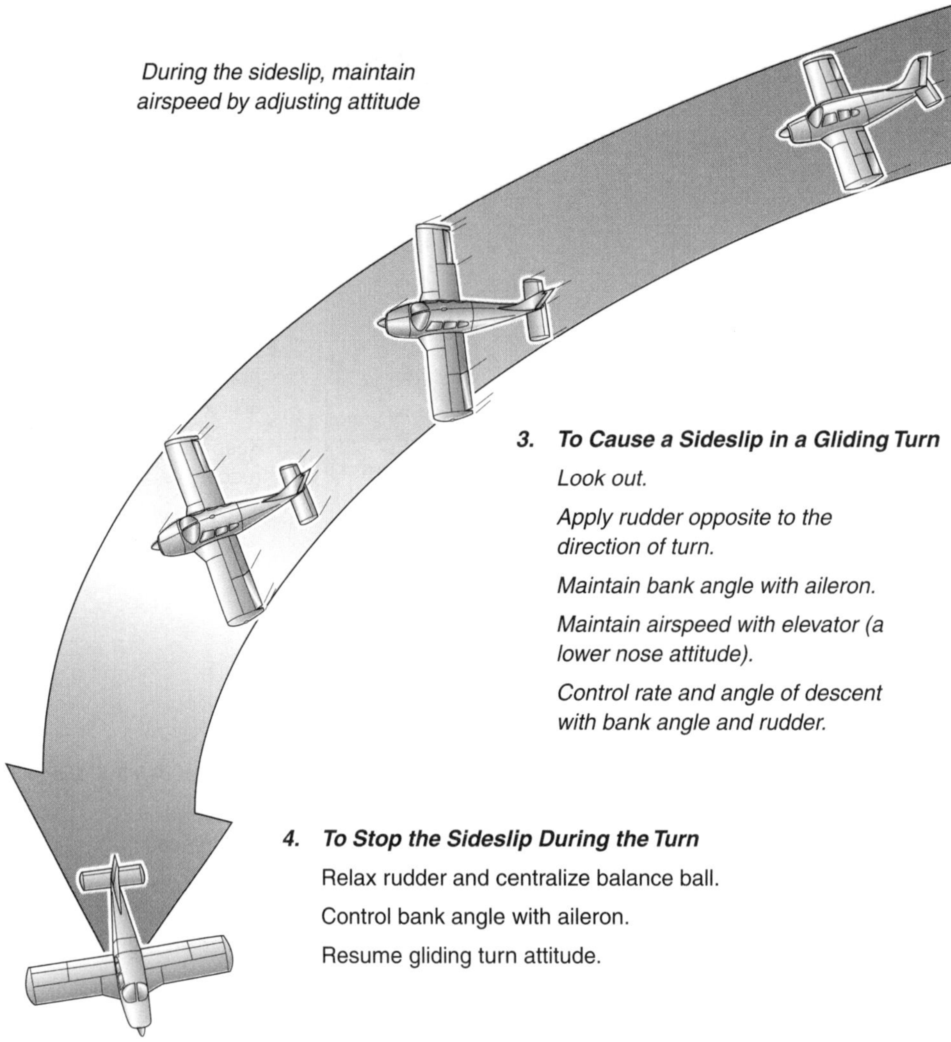

1 & 2. Enter a Gliding Turn
During the sideslip, maintain airspeed by adjusting attitude
3. To Cause a Sideslip in a Gliding Turn
Look out.
Apply rudder opposite to the direction of turn.
Maintain bank angle with aileron.
Maintain airspeed with elevator (a lower nose attitude).
Control rate and angle of descent with bank angle and rudder.
4. To Stop the Sideslip During the Turn
Relax rudder and centralize balance ball.
Control bank angle with aileron.
Resume gliding turn attitude.

Medium Turns

17 Medium Level Turn

OBJECTIVES

To describe:

- the balance of forces in a turn;
- how an aircraft is turned;
- the technique to enter, maintain and straighten from a medium level turn; and
- the attitude-power combination for left and right medium level turns in your airplane.

Figure 17-1 An airplane turns by banking.

CONSIDERATIONS

An airplane is turned like a motorcycle by banking or tilting. It has to because it has neither a road to grip nor an ability to drift sideways. It can only turn by tilting the wings and by pushing air sideways, like a slalom water-skier does with water.

What is a Medium Level Turn?

A turn is accomplished by banking the airplane.

A medium level turn is performed:

- at a constant altitude;
- with a medium angle of bank (30° or 20° is usual);
- at constant power (cruise power); and
- in balanced flight (balance ball centered).

Figure 17-2 A balanced turn.

Apart from the medium level turn, other turns that you will master in the course of your training are:

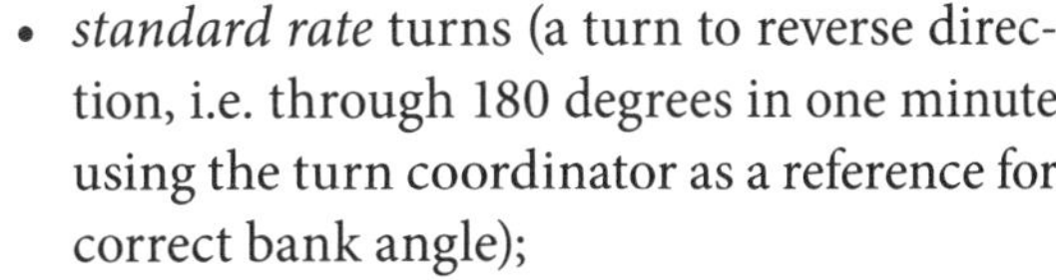

- *standard rate* turns (a turn to reverse direction, i.e. through 180 degrees in one minute using the turn coordinator as a reference for correct bank angle);
- climbing turns;
- descending turns; and, later
- steep turns (bank angle 45° or greater).

Forces in a Turn

Banking the airplane tilts the lift force producing a horizontal component that provides a turning force (known as the *centripetal* force) as well as the vertical component that is still needed to maintain altitude. Since there is no other horizontal force to counteract it,

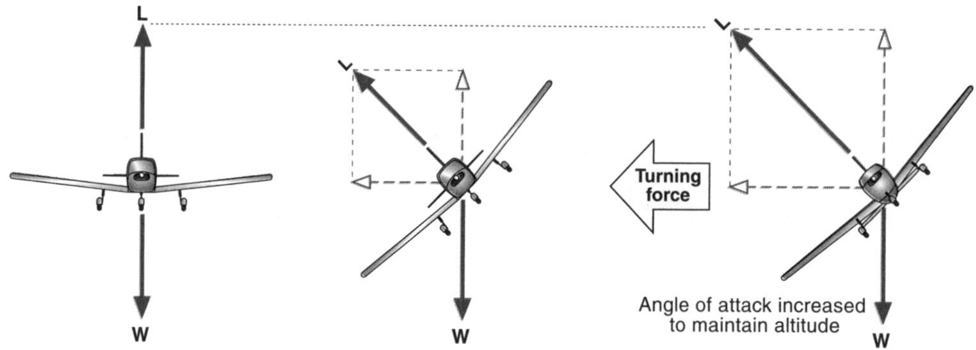

Figure 17-3 Banking an airplane creates a turning force.

the airplane is no longer in equilibrium and will be pushed into a turn. The greater the bank angle, the greater the angle of attack to maintain level flight, the greater the total force, the greater the turning force and the tighter/faster the turn.

Maintaining Altitude

To maintain in altitude in a level turn, you must apply back pressure to increase the lift.

Tilting the lift force reduces its vertical component that will result in a descent unless the pilot increases the total lift generated by the wings. By increasing back pressure on the control column, and increasing angle of attack, the vertical component of lift remains sufficient to balance weight and, at the same time, supplies the necessary centripetal force to turn.

Airspeed

Normally there is no requirement to increase power during a medium level turn.

Airspeed tends to decrease in a turn, due to an increase in induced drag, because of the increased angle of attack. As a consequence, the airplane will slow down, usually by 5–10 knots in a medium level turn. At normal flight speeds, this small airspeed loss is accepted.

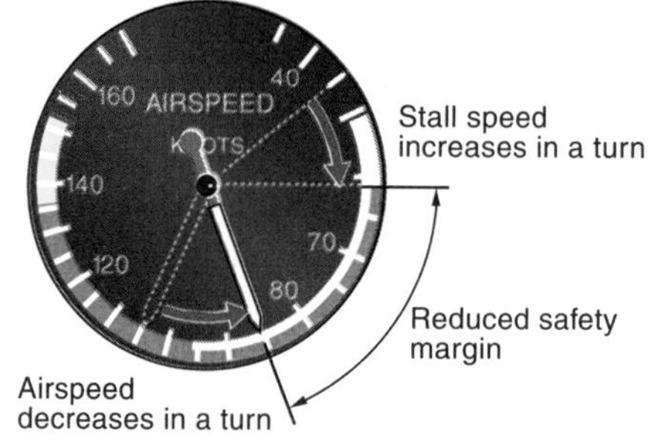

Figure 17-4 Airspeed decreases and stalling speed increases in a level turn.

Stalling Speed

Load factor increases in a turn.

Stalling speed increases in a turn. The wings are at a higher angle of attack in a turn than when flying straight at the same speed. They carry an extra load (i.e. they generate increased lift) and so experience a higher *load factor.* The stalling angle will therefore be reached at a higher speed in a turn than when straight and level. It is about 7% higher in a 30°-banked turn. For medium level turns at normal flight speeds, there is an adequate speed margin above the slightly increased stalling speed.

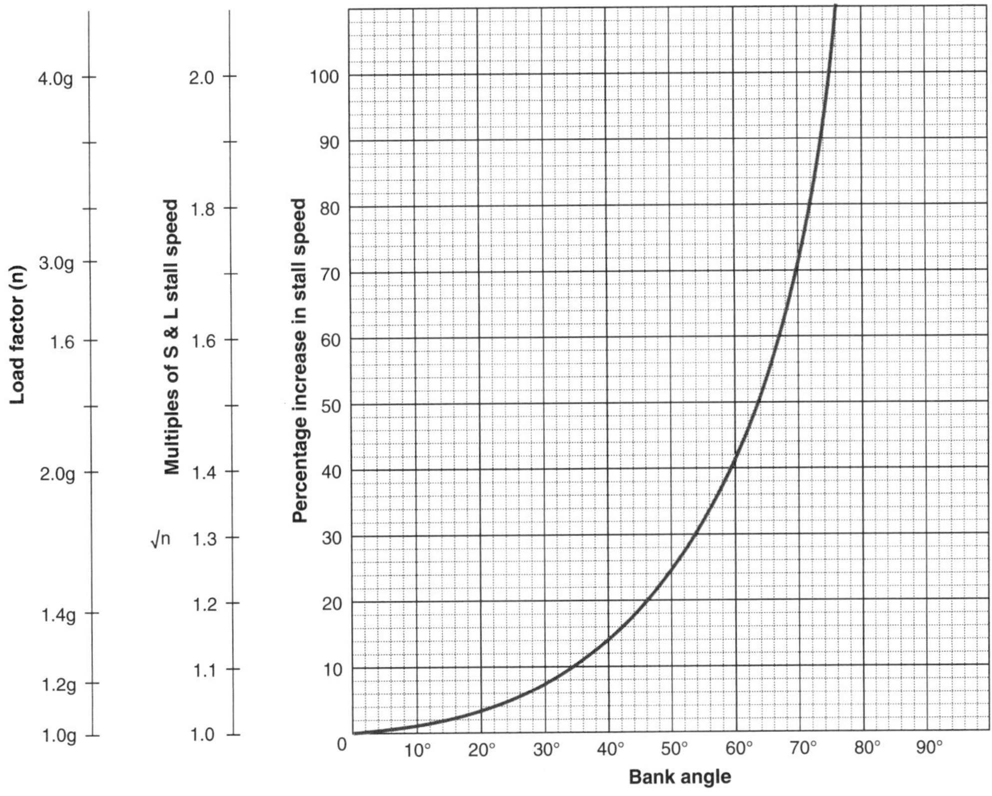

Figure 17-5 Increased stall speed in a turn.

APPLICATION

Bank Angle

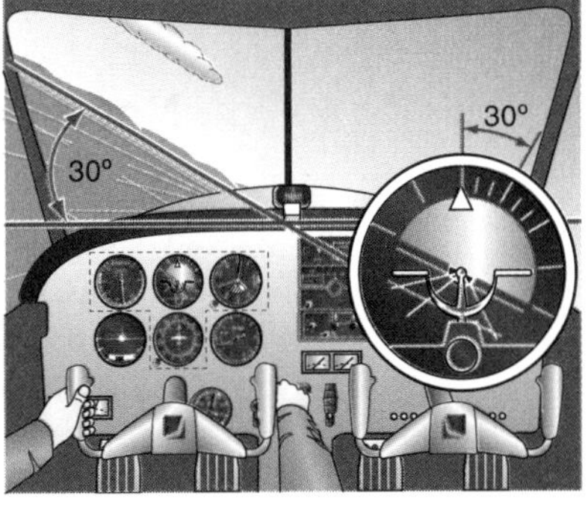

Figure 17-6 Estimate the bank angle then confirm with the AI.

The bank angle is set by reference to the natural horizon and confirmed or fine-tuned by reference to the attitude indicator, which has a bank pointer. A specific bank angle can be flown quite accurately by estimating the angle between the nose cowl of the airplane and the natural horizon. It can be verified in the cockpit on the attitude indicator using either the angle between the index airplane and the artificial horizon, or by using the bank pointer at the top of the instrument. However, a turn is like a descent: there is no specific parameter except when performing a standard rate turn as part of an instrument approach procedure and, for this, the turn coordinator is also used.

The pilot normally sets an attitude of pitch and bank for a medium turn by using some mark or feature on the engine cowl or windshield, and positions that feature relative to the horizon. The pitch attitude is then adjusted to maintain altitude, and bank is adjusted to keep the turn going (not too little) or to avoid the turn becoming too steep (not too much).

This technique is perfectly adequate for normal maneuvering in the training area. The turn is adjusted as it progresses and slackened or tightened to suit the situation. This is particularly so in the pattern when maneuvering relative to the ground as the pilot adjusts the bank to allow for the effect of wind. The important aspects are to retain control of altitude (by controlling attitude) and to prevent the bank angle becoming excessive, as it will gently, and subtly, try to do.

Overbanking

The higher speed of the outer wing in a level turn creates extra lift on that wing, which tends to increase the bank angle. There is no need for you to be particularly conscious of this: simply maintain the desired bank angle using the control column.

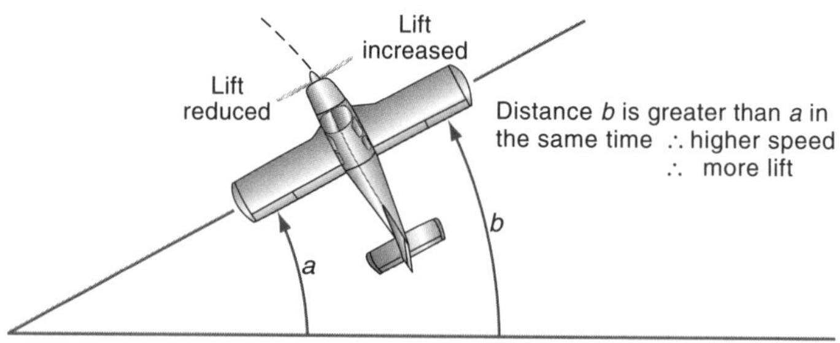

Figure 17-7 There is a tendency to overbank in a level turn due to increased speed of the outer wing.

Pitch Attitude

Pitch attitude is higher in a turn.

Lift is increased in a turn by applying back pressure on the control column to increase the angle of attack. For this reason, the nose attitude of the airplane will be higher in a level turn than when flying straight and level, even though it may not appear so when you are turning to the right and you are seated on the high side of the cockpit.

Estimating the correct pitch attitude against the natural horizon requires a little experience, especially if you are flying in a side-by-side cockpit, as is the case in most modern training airplanes. The pitch attitude for a given bank angle and airspeed will be correct if the airplane neither gains nor loses altitude. Once the instructor has demonstrated turns in each direction, take particular note of the position of some feature of the nose or windshield in relation to the horizon as viewed from your seating position. This will be your future reference for all medium level turns in this aircraft.

Nose Cowl and the Horizon

The nose-cowl/horizon relationship appears different in left and right turns.

The relationship of the nose cowl to the horizon appears different in left and right turns. These remarks apply to a side-by-side cockpit. In a left turn, the pilot in the left seat will be on the low side of the airplane's longitudinal axis and the position of the center of the nose cowl will appear to be higher relative to the natural horizon. Conversely, when turning right, the center of the nose cowl should appear lower against the horizon. After one or two turns left and right, you should have these attitudes fixed in your mind.

Figure 17-8 Different nose positions (attitudes) for left and right level turns.

Turning Performance

Figure 17-9 Turn performance varies with bank and airspeed.

The two aspects of turning performance are:

- the rate at which the heading changes; and
- the radius of the turn (its tightness).

Turning performance increases at steeper bank angles. The steeper the bank angle (for a constant airspeed), the better the turn rate with the rate of heading change increasing and the radius of turn decreasing as bank angle is increased. This assumes that the aircraft has sufficient airspeed to sustain the turn at that bank angle. It is like a bicycle. At very high speed, a turn is wide. As the speed decreases, the turn can be tighter, but at very low speed, the bicycle is struggling not to fall over.

Turning performance increases at steeper bank angles and lower airspeed—up to a point.

Turning performance increases at lower airspeeds. For the *same bank angle*, a lower airspeed will give a smaller radius of turn and a greater rate of change of heading (direction) but there is a limit to how much bank that can be applied at reduced speed (due to higher stalling speed).

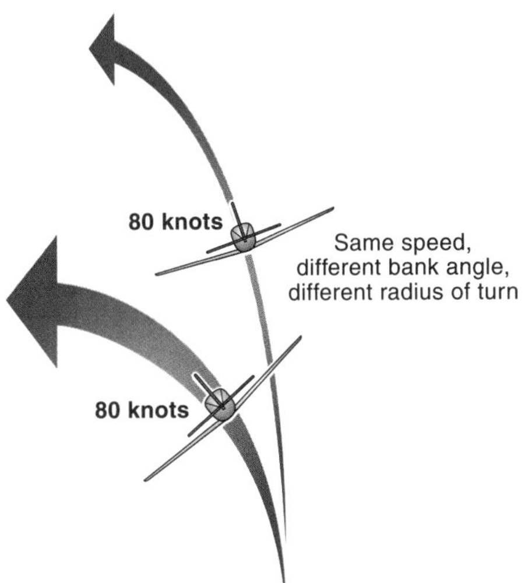

Figure 17-10
A steep bank angle increases turning performance at the same speed, but stalling speed increases with increased bank.

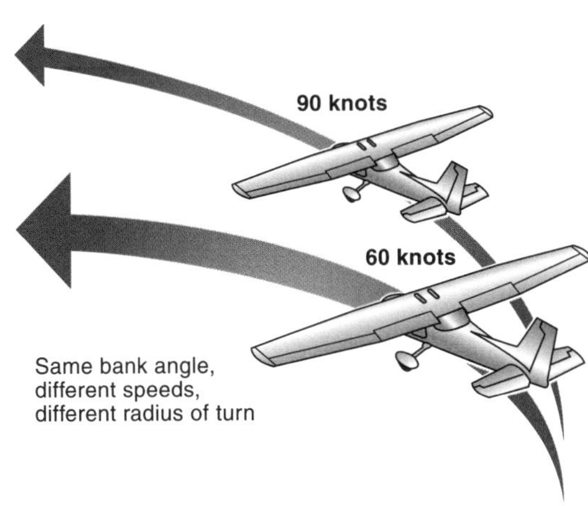

Figure 17-11
Turning performance increases at low airspeeds at the same bank angle, but stalling speed increases in the turn.

TECHNIQUE

Trim the Airplane Before the Turn

Unless an immediate turn is necessary, trimming the airplane properly for steady, straight and level flight makes it easier to maintain altitude before and after the turn. Do not trim during the turn since it is only a transient maneuver. Prior to applying bank, glance at the cockpit instruments and ensure that you are flying at the desired:

- indicated airspeed; and
- altitude (altimeter reading desired altitude and VSI on zero or fluctuating about zero, indicating no general tendency to climb or descend).

There is no need to trim in a turn.

Scanning for Traffic

Develop a thorough scanning technique from side to side and up and down before turning, remembering that airplanes move in three dimensions.

A good sky-scanning technique is:

- first look in the direction of turn, raising/lowering the wing to give you a view above and below;
- look in the direction opposite to the turn and as far behind as cockpit view allows; then
- commence a steady scan from that side of the windshield both up and down until you are again looking in the direction of turn.

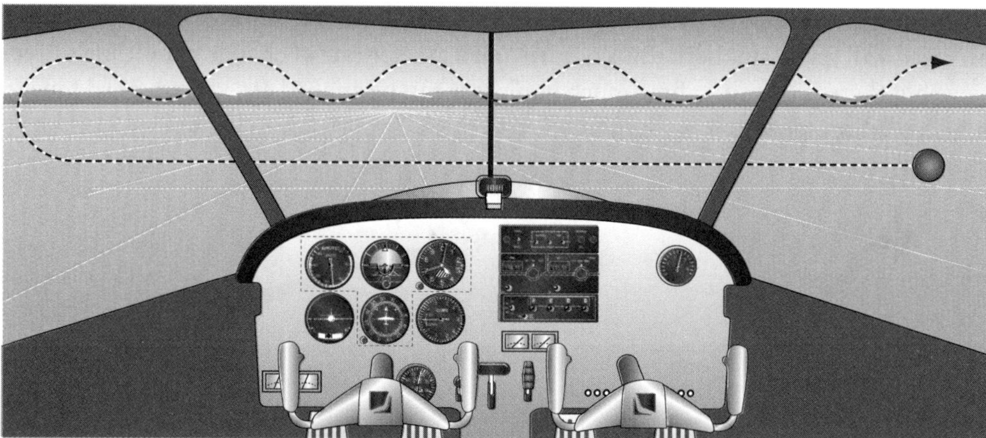

Figure 17-12 A suitable scan prior to a right turn.

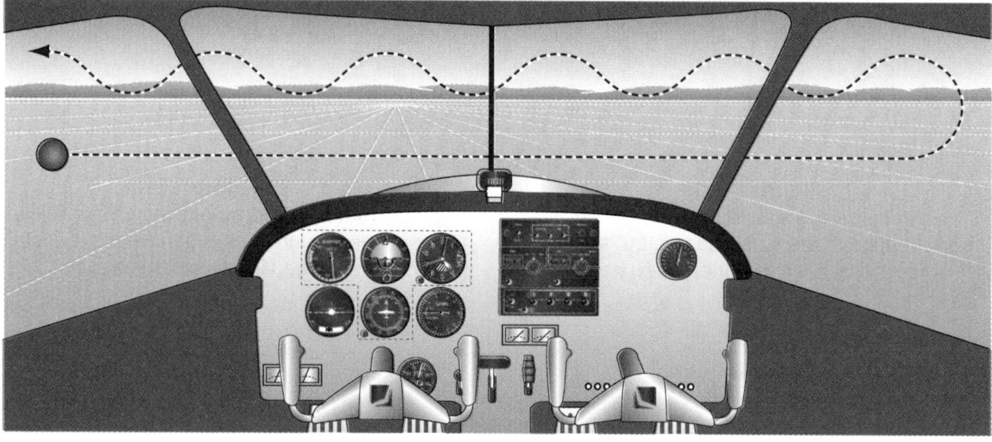

Figure 17-13 Scanning before a left turn.

Reference Point

Select a reference point on which to roll out.

While scanning for other aircraft, you can note visible landmarks helpful for orientation (i.e. knowing where you are). Select a landmark as a reference point on which to roll out following the turn. Anticipate the desired direction by commencing the roll-out about 10° prior to reaching it, since the airplane will continue turning (although at a decreasing rate) until the wings are level.

Entering the Turn

Check the area is clear and pick a point on the horizon, directly ahead, to use as a reference. Roll with ailerons and balance with same-side rudder pressure (keeping the nose of the aircraft pointing at the reference point by applying rudder pressure in the same direction as the aileron. When the bank angle approaches your reference visual attitude, center the aileron, apply a little back pressure and reduce the rudder pressure. Check the balance ball is centered and maintain with rudder. Back pressure on the control column will be needed to maintain altitude, which can be confirmed by the altimeter and VSI, but remember your primary reference is visual attitude. Estimate the bank angle against the horizon, cross checking the attitude indicator if desired.

Maintaining the Turn

To maintain the turn, control the bank angle with ailerons, balance with rudder and altitude with elevator. If gaining altitude, either the bank angle is too shallow or the back pressure is too great, so increase bank angle and/or lower the nose. If losing altitude, either the bank angle is too steep or the back pressure is insufficient, so decrease bank angle and/or raise the nose. Do not forget to look out for other aircraft.

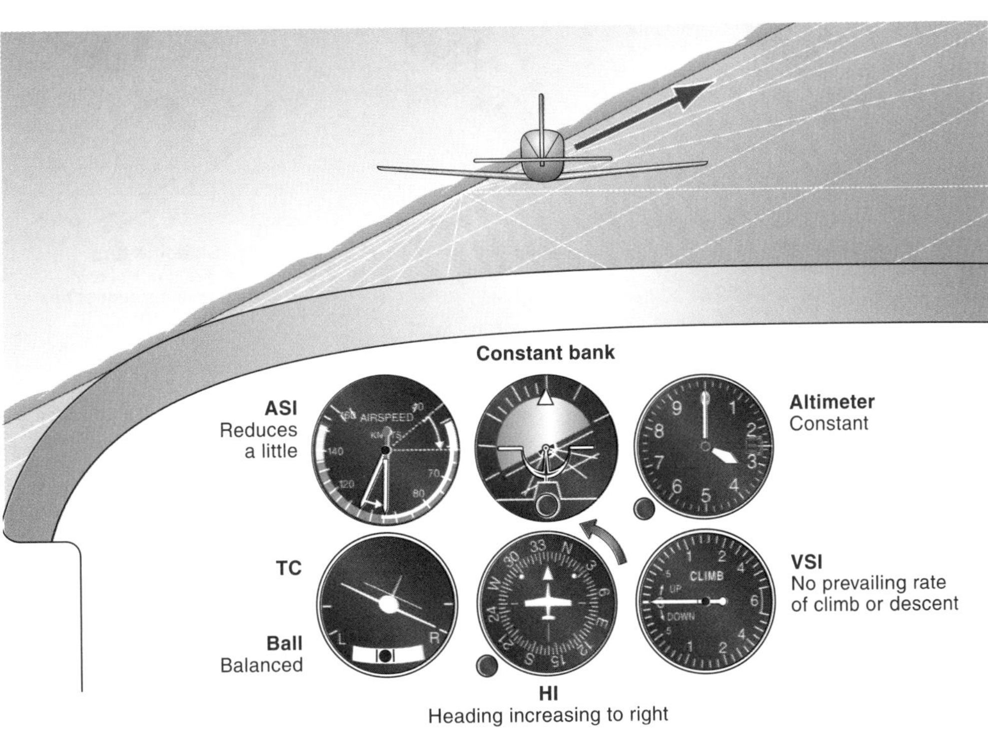

Figure 17-14 Flight instrument indications in a medium level turn to the right.

Rudder pressure is used to coordinate the turn.

Keep in balance using rudder pressure. Rolling right requires more right rudder pressure; rolling left requires more left rudder pressure. The balance ball indicates the precise balance of the airplane: if the ball is out to the right, more right rudder is needed; if the ball is out to the left, more left rudder is needed. Keep the balance ball centered throughout the turning maneuver. There is a correct amount of rudder for the angle of bank. If the rudder is insufficient, the aircraft slips; if there is too much rudder, the aircraft skids.

During the turn fly primarily by reference to the visual horizon and maintain a continuous scan cycle of lookout-attitude-performance.

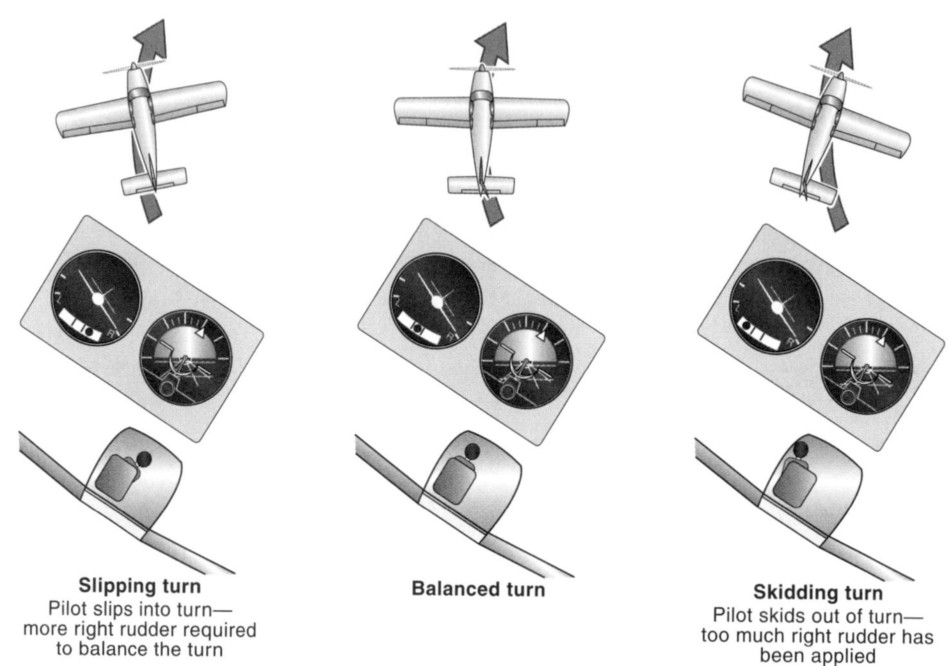

Slipping turn
Pilot slips into turn—
more right rudder required
to balance the turn
Balanced turn
Skidding turn
Pilot skids out of turn—
too much right rudder has
been applied

Figure 17-15 Keep the airplane in balance with rudder pressure.

Returning to Straight Flight

To roll out of a medium level turn, anticipate reaching the reference point by about 10° (⅓ of the bank angle) and start rolling to wings-level with aileron, balancing with same-side rudder pressure. Gradually release the back pressure as you roll and allow the nose attitude to return to the straight and level position. Fine-tune the heading and altitude as required.

AIRMANSHIP

Be aware of landmarks to keep yourself orientated with respect to the airfield. Your airplane will be changing direction in a turn and will fly through airspace that you were not able to see when the turn was commenced, so maintain a continuous lookout.

Since a constant power will be set, you can concentrate on placing the nose just exactly where you want it on the horizon. Become familiar with these attitudes for both left and right turns. Do not trim in the turn since it is only a transient maneuver.

Develop an awareness of balance and use rudder pressure to keep the ball in the center at all times. Aim for smoothly coordinated use of controls, being firm but gentle.

Look out and, in the case of a high wing airplane, you may need to raise the inner wing to check for traffic.

Figure 17-16
Look out while turning.

REVIEW 17

Medium Level Turn

1. Which force is tilted to turn an airplane?
2. Which controls are used to bank an airplane?
3. How is further banking stopped?
4. What size movements of the ailerons are used to maintain a desired bank angle precisely?
5. Does the horizontal or vertical component of the tilted lift force pull the airplane into a turn?
6. Which side rudder pressure will probably be required to keep the balance ball centered while the control column is rotated to the left?
7. Which side rudder pressure will probably be required to keep the balance ball centered while the control column is rotated to the right?
8. In a turn, to maintain a constant altitude, what change to the lift needs to be made? What effect will this have on drag? What effect will this have on airspeed?
9. How does the nose attitude in a level turn compare with that in straight and level flight?
10. How do you know that you have the right pitch attitude for a level turn?
11. What effect does aileron deflection have on roll rate?
12. What effect does the length of time that the ailerons are deflected have on the steepness of the bank angle in a turn?
13. Should you trim in a turn? What sort of maneuver is a turn?
14. What effect does the back angle have on the load that the wings have to supports in a turn?
15. How does stalling speed change in a turn?
16. What is the effect on the radius of the turn by an increase in bank angle? How does an increase in bank angle affect the rate of turn?
17. How does the radius of a 30°-banked turn at 60 knots compared with that of a 30°-banked turn at 100 knots? How does the time taken to turn through 360° compare?
18. Between what bank angles is a medium bank angle considered to be?
19. What are the accuracy tolerances in level turns in terms of altitude, nominated bank angle and nominated roll-out heading? During the maneuver, should the balance ball be centered?

Answers are given on page 579.

TASK

Medium Level Turn

Aim: To enter, maintain and roll out of a medium level turn, using constant power.

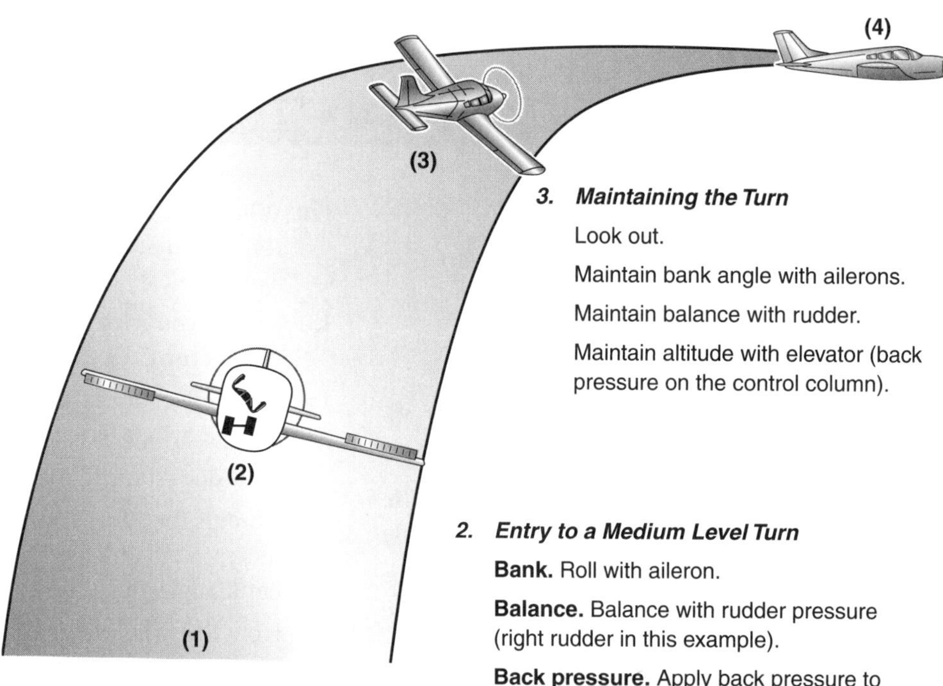

Maintain altitude with elevator and accept the slight loss of airspeed
(4)
(3)
(2)
(1)

*4. **Rolling Out of the Turn***

Look out.

Anticipate reference point (⅓ of bank).

Bank. Roll off bank.

Balance. Balance with rudder pressure.

Back pressure. Release back pressure.

*3. **Maintaining the Turn***

Look out.

Maintain bank angle with ailerons.

Maintain balance with rudder.

Maintain altitude with elevator (back pressure on the control column).

*2. **Entry to a Medium Level Turn***

Bank. Roll with aileron.

Balance. Balance with rudder pressure (right rudder in this example).

Back pressure. Apply back pressure to control column to maintain altitude.

START
HERE

*1. **Prior to Entry***

At desired altitude and airspeed.

In trim.

Select reference point for roll out.

Look out.

Note: Trim is not used during this transient maneuver.

18

Turning to Selected Headings

OBJECTIVES

To describe the technique to turn to a selected heading using:

- the heading indicator (directional gyro);
- the clock and the turn coordinator; or
- the magnetic compass.

Figure 18-1 Measured turn.

TECHNIQUE

Reference Point

Whenever possible, select a distant reference point to turn to. This acts as a backup to the instrument indications as well as aiding you in orientation.

Using the Heading Indicator

The heading indicator (HI) is easier to use and more accurate in a turn than a magnetic compass because it is a gyroscopic instrument and consequently does not suffer acceleration and turning errors. It must, however, be correctly aligned with the magnetic compass in steady flight. To turn to a specific heading using the HI:

- fly at a steady speed, straight and level;
- align the HI with the magnetic compass;
- decide the shorter way to turn (left or right) to reach the desired heading (e.g. from 090°M to 240°M, turn right 150°);
- look out and check that the area is clear;
- carry out a normal turn with occasional reference to the HI;
- commence the roll-out approximately 10° prior to reaching the desired heading; and
- make minor adjustments to maintain the desired heading.

Figure 18-2
The heading indicator.

Standard Rate Turns

Changing heading at 3° per second is known as a *standard rate turn* and is marked on the turn coordinator (or turn indicator). It is the standard rate of turn commonly used in instrument flying and will achieve a turn of 180° in one minute or 360° in two minutes (hence the label *2 MIN* shown on many turn coordinators).

Figure 18-3
Standard rate turn indications on the turn coordinator and turn indicator.

To achieve standard turning performance at different airspeeds, different bank angles will be required. These are easily estimated using a simple rule of thumb:

Divide the airspeed by 10, and add one-half the answer.

For example:

- At 80 knots for a standard rate turn, bank angle = 80 ÷ 10 (which is 8) + ½ of 8 (which is 4) = 8 + 4 = 12°.
- At 100 knots, bank angle = 10 + 5= 15°.
- At 120 knots, required bank angle is 12 + 6 = 18°.

You are not expected to set a bank angle so precisely, but the estimate gives you a target bank angle with which to achieve a standard rate turn that is verified and adjusted by reference to the turn coordinator (or turn indicator).

Using the Clock and the Turn Coordinator

The turn needle indicates correctly only if the aircraft is balanced.

The turn coordinator allows you to turn at a constant rate and the clock can be used to time the turn. A standard rate turn (3° per second) for 30 seconds will alter the heading by 90°.

To turn to a specific heading using a standard rate timed turn:

For example: A turn from 090°M to 240°M is 150°. 150° at standard rate (3°/sec) is 50 seconds.

- divide the change in heading by 3 to obtain the number of seconds (e.g. from 090°M to 240°M is 150° to the right, which at 3°/second will take 50 seconds);
- carry out a normal standard rate turn with reference to the turn coordinator (at, say, 120 knots, this will require an angle of bank of ¹⁄₁₀ of 120 plus half of 120 = 12 + 6 = 18°); and
- time the turn using the second hand on the clock (or by counting potatoes).

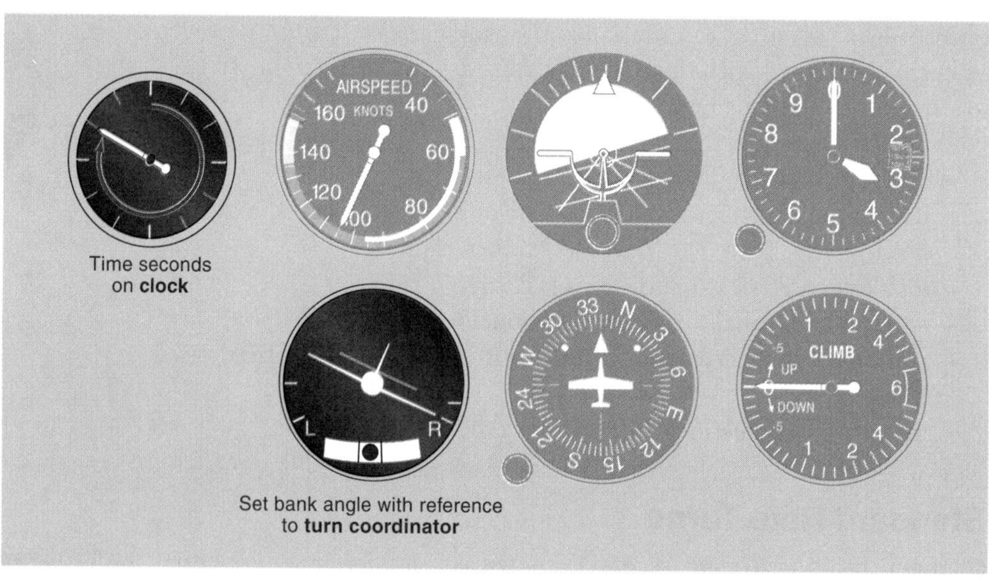

Figure 18-4 A timed turn using the clock and turn coordinator.

Using the Magnetic Compass

This is the least-preferred method since the magnetic compass suffers considerable indication errors in a turn. It can, however, be used to verify heading once the airplane has settled into steady wings-level flight and the compass oscillations have ceased.

The construction of a magnetic compass is such that, when an airplane is turning (especially through north or south), it will give false indications of magnetic heading. To allow for this in the northern hemisphere observe the following:

- when turning to northerly headings, roll out when the magnetic compass indicates approximately 30° before your desired heading; and
- when turning to southerly headings, roll out when the magnetic compass indicates approximately 30° after your desired heading.

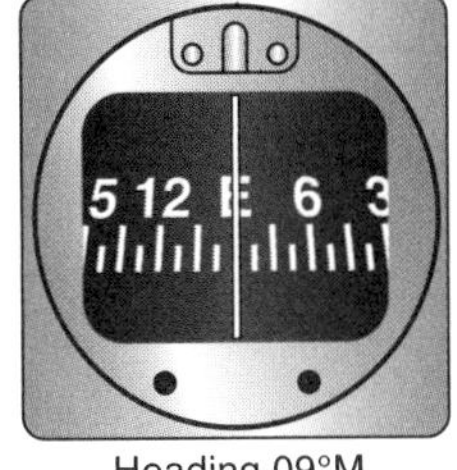

Heading 09°M

Figure 18-5
Magnetic compass.

When operating near the equator, the above allowances should be reduced:

- when turning with bank angles less than 30°; and
- when turning to headings well removed from north and south (in fact, when turning to due east or due west, no allowances need be made).

The allowances described above only apply to the magnetic compass because of the turning and acceleration errors associated with it. They do not apply to the heading indicator because it is a gyroscopic device that does not suffer from these errors and hence is easier to use.

If the airplane has an unserviceable heading indicator, perform a timed standard rate turn (using the turn coordinator and the clock) using the magnetic compass as a backup.

Figure 18-6 The magnetic compass reads in reverse. (In this case turn right to north.)

REVIEW 18

Turning to Selected Headings

1. When turning to selected headings, is it easier to use the heading indicator or the magnetic compass?
2. Does the heading indicator suffer turning and acceleration errors?
3. Under what flight conditions will the magnetic compass provide accurate indications?
4. Under what flight conditions should the heading indicator be periodically aligned with the magnetic compass?
5. To what accuracy should you aim to maintain the desired altitude when practicing turns to a selected heading? To what accuracy should you aim to roll out on the selected heading? How do you then achieve the desired heading perfectly?
6. To turn from MH 010 to MH 170 the shortest way, in which direction should you turn?
7. To turn from MH 010 to MH 340 the shortest way, in which direction should you turn?

8. To turn from MH 330 to MH 360 the shortest way, in which direction should you turn?
9. To turn from MH 033 to MH 030 the shortest way, in which direction should you turn?
10. To turn from MH 330 to MH 170 the shortest way, in which direction should you turn?
11. To turn from MH 190 to MH 030 the shortest way, in which direction should you turn?
12. To turn from MH 190 to MH 020 the shortest way, in which direction should you turn?
13. To turn from MH 200 to MH 090 the shortest way, in which direction should you turn?
14. To turn from MH 200 to MH 010 the shortest way, in which direction should you turn?
15. To turn from MH 200 to MH 020 the shortest way, in which direction should you turn?
16. To turn from heading 360°M to 120°M the shortest way, in which direction should you turn? How many seconds would this take for a standard-rate turn?
17. To turn from heading 360°M to 270°M the shortest way, in which direction should you turn? How many second would this take for a standard-rate turn?
18. To turn from heading 190°M to 010°M the shortest way, in which direction should you turn? How many second would this take for a standard-rate turn?
19. When turning to a northerly heading using the magnetic compass, when should you roll out of the turn? (You are in the northern hemisphere.)
20. When turning to a southerly heading using the magnetic compass, when should you roll out of the turn? (You are in the northern hemisphere.)
21. When turning to a easterly heading using the magnetic compass, when should you roll out of the turn? (You are in the northern hemisphere.)
22. When turning to a westerly heading using the magnetic compass, when should you roll out of the turn? (You are in the northern hemisphere.)
23. As in all turns, there is a tendency for the nose to rise when turning to a selected heading. True or false?
24. When turning and wanting to maintain a constant altitude, you can prevent the nose from dropping by using which control?
25. Should you trim in a turn? What sort of maneuver is a turn?
26. When turning to a selected heading at a constant altitude, what do you expect the airspeed to do if you retain constant power?
27. When turning to a selected heading in a descending turn, which of the following can you maintain airspeed with: elevator, aileron, rudder or power?
28. When turning to a selected heading in a descending turn, which of the following can you maintain a constant rate of descent using: elevator, aileron, rudder or power?
29. When turning to a selected heading in a climbing turn, which of the following can you maintain airspeed with: elevator, aileron, rudder or power?
30. In all turns, you should control the bank angle with which of the following: elevator, aileron, rudder or power?
31. A vital point of airmanship in all turns is to maintain what?

Answers are given on page 580.

19
Climbing Turn

OBJECTIVES

To describe:
- the balance of forces in a climbing turn;
- the need for small bank angles;
- the importance of airspeed;
- the technique to enter, maintain and straighten from a climbing turn; and
- the attitude-power combination for left and right climbing turns in your airplane.

Figure 19-1 Climbing turn.

CONSIDERATIONS

Climb Performance When Also Turning

The forces in a climbing turn are similar to those in a straight climb except that, because the lift is tilted to turn the airplane, its contribution to supporting the weight is reduced. The angle of attack must be increased slightly, and this increases the induced drag. The engine is already at climb power so, to maintain the optimum climb airspeed, the climb angle and rate are decreased. The nose is lowered slightly and then, when the bank is applied, the back pressure (angle of attack) is used to generate the turn.

The rate of climb decreases in a climbing turn.

The rate of climb relies on the amount of excess power. The increased drag in a climbing turn reduces the excess power available to climb. The result is a decreased rate of climb in a turn, as indicated on the vertical speed indicator and the altimeter. Similarly, angle of climb relies on excess thrust and the increased induced drag of the turn reduces the maximum angle of climb. It is a difficult situation when climbing to avoid obstacles if the aircraft also has to turn. The steeper the bank angle in a climbing turn, the poorer the rate and angle of climb. To retain a reasonable rate of climb, the bank angle in climbing turns should be limited to 15°. Turns should be avoided when climbing at maximum angle. (Remember that a maximum-angle climb is done at very low speed and that the stalling speed increases in a turn. The safety margin is therefore further reduced.)

Limit the bank angle in a climbing turn.

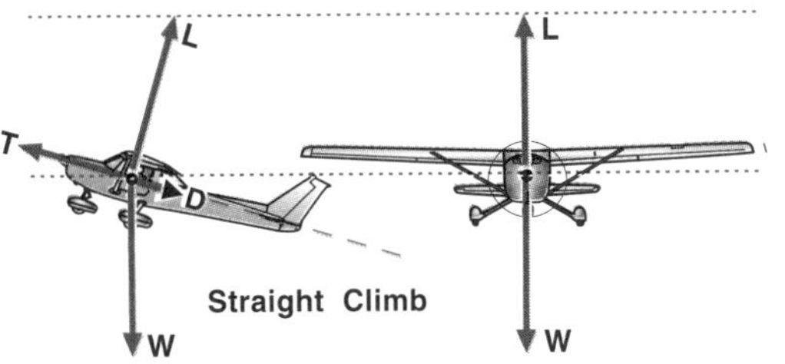

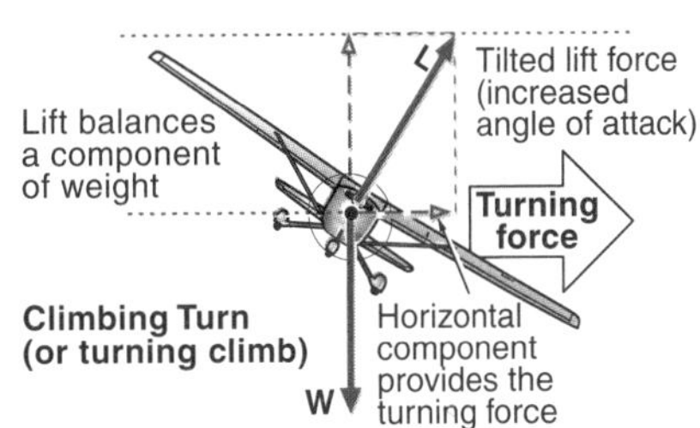

Figure 19-2 A straight climb and a climbing turn.

Figure 19-3 Maintain airspeed in a climbing turn by slightly lowering the nose attitude.

APPLICATION

Airspeed

Climb performance depends on the correct climb speed being flown with climb power set. For many training airplanes, climb power is maximum power, so the tendency to lose airspeed cannot be overcome by adding extra power (since there is no more). To maintain the correct climb speed in a turn, it is therefore necessary to lower the nose. There is a natural tendency for the nose to drop a little too far as bank is applied in a climbing turn, but this can be checked with slight back pressure on the control column. Hold the desired pitch attitude with elevator and monitor the airspeed with a regular scan of the airspeed indicator.

Slipstream Effect

Most airplanes are designed so that slipstream effect is balanced at cruise speed with cruise power set. Climbs are carried out with high power at an airspeed less than the cruise with the result that increased rudder pressure is usually required to balance the slipstream effect on the tail. The usual rules for maintaining balance apply, no matter what the maneuver involved. This is to say, capture the balance ball back into the center with same-side rudder pressure (step on the ball).

Overbanking

The higher speed and greater angle of attack of the outer wing in a climbing turn creates a slight tendency for the bank angle to increase. Bank may have to be held off in a climbing turn, but this will occur naturally as you monitor the bank angle against the horizon.

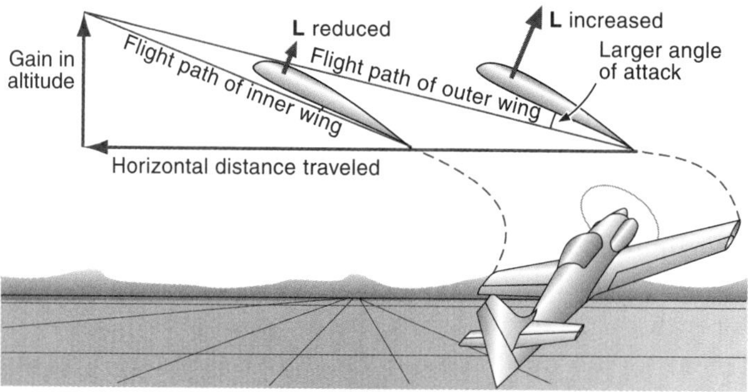

Figure 19-4 There is a slight overbanking tendency in a climbing turn.

TECHNIQUE

Entering a Climbing Turn

To enter a climbing turn, establish the airplane in a straight climb at the desired airspeed and in trim. Look out and select a reference point on which to roll out. Roll into the turn by applying bank in the direction of turn, using sufficient rudder to keep the ball in the center. Limit the turn to 15° bank angle and allow the nose to lower slightly. Apply slight back pressure to hold the new attitude and to control airspeed.

Maintaining a Climbing Turn

To maintain the climbing turn, control bank angle with ailerons, balance with rudder pressure and maintain the desired airspeed with nose attitude. Keep a constant airspeed throughout the climbing turn, even though the rate of climb will decrease. Maintain a lookout.

Straightening from a Climbing Turn

As the desired heading is approached, anticipate by one-third of the angle of bank, roll to wings level and slightly raise the nose to normal climb attitude.

AIRMANSHIP

Limit the bank to 15° maximum and maintain a constant airspeed with attitude. Exert firm, positive and smooth control over the airplane. Maintain a frequent lookout.

Keep climbing turns shallow.

REVIEW 19

Climbing Turn

1. How does the lift force in a climbing turn compare to the lift force in a straight climb?
2. In a turn, which component of the lift force provides the turning force?
3. Which component of the lift force in a turn counteracts the weight of the airplane?
4. How does the tilting of the lift force in a climbing turn affect its contribution to supporting the weight of the airplane?
5. What effect does turning in a climb have on climb performance?
6. Climb performance can be seen on two flight instruments. What are they?
7. If the rate of climb in a straight climb is 350 feet per minute, which of the following rates in feet per minute would the rate of climb be in a climbing turn: 200, 350 or 450?
8. To preserve some climb performance, what is bank angle limited to in a climbing turn?
9. How is the airspeed controlled in climbs and climbing turns?
10. As you roll from a straight climb into a climbing turn, which of vertical speed, airspeed or nose attitude is it important that you maintain?
11. To maintain the correct climb speed as you roll into a climbing turn, what change to nose attitude needs to be made?
12. In a climbing turn, you can maintain the desired bank angle using which of the following: elevator, aileron, rudder or power?
13. In a climbing turn, you can maintain the desired airspeed using which of the following: elevator, aileron, rudder or power?
14. How do you maintain balance in a climbing turn?
15. During a climbing turn to the left, where should the balance ball be?
16. If the balance ball is out to the left, which side rudder pressure should you apply? Which side should be applied if the balance ball is out to the right?
17. What is the desired accuracy in a climbing turn in terms of bank angle, climbing airspeed, balance ball position, and roll-out on the specified heading?

Answers are given on page 580.

TASK

Climbing Turn

Note that trim is not used during this transient maneuver.

Aim: To change heading while climbing at a constant airspeed.

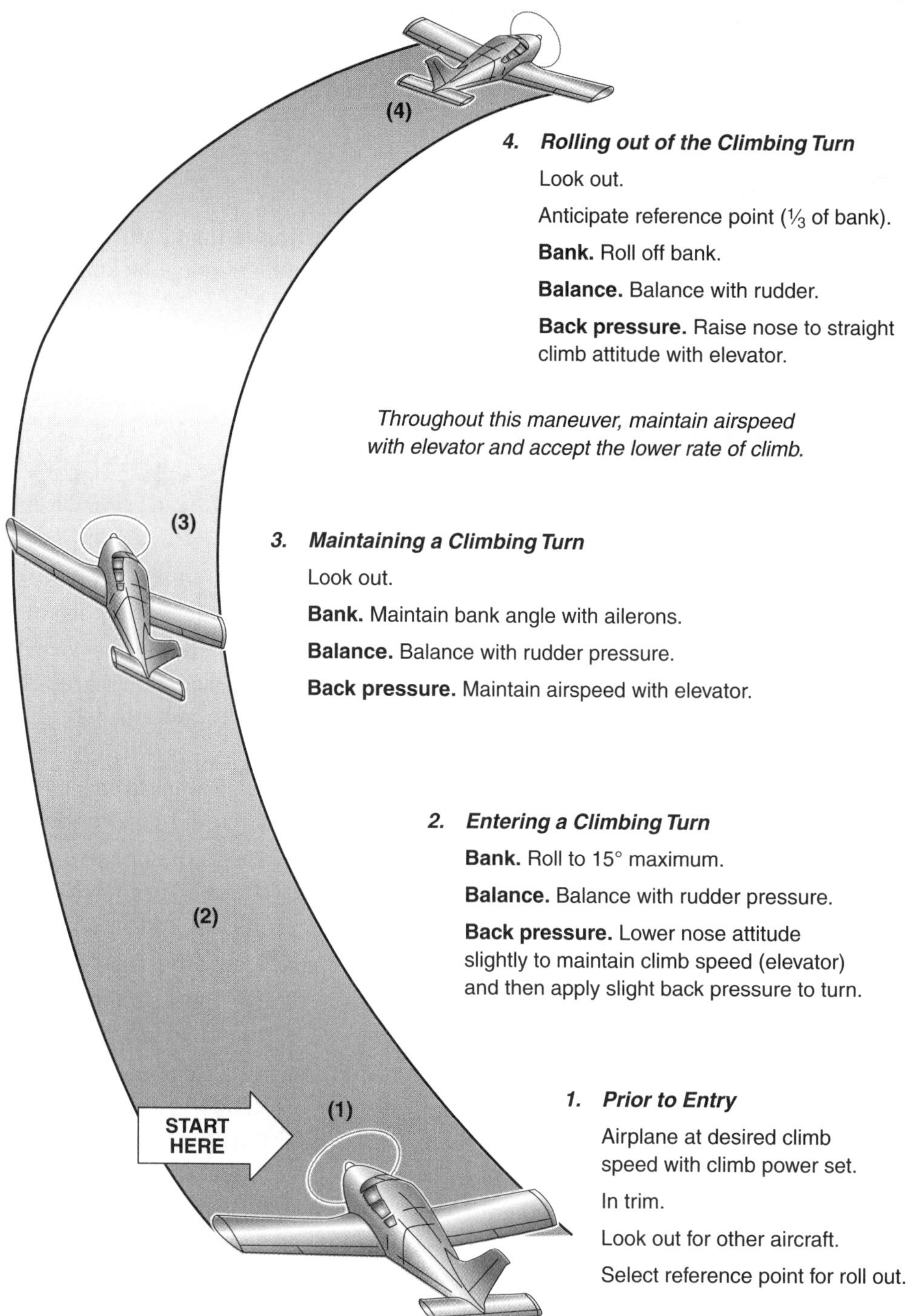

4. Rolling out of the Climbing Turn

Look out.

Anticipate reference point ($\frac{1}{3}$ of bank).

Bank. Roll off bank.

Balance. Balance with rudder.

Back pressure. Raise nose to straight climb attitude with elevator.

Throughout this maneuver, maintain airspeed with elevator and accept the lower rate of climb.

3. Maintaining a Climbing Turn

Look out.

Bank. Maintain bank angle with ailerons.

Balance. Balance with rudder pressure.

Back pressure. Maintain airspeed with elevator.

2. Entering a Climbing Turn

Bank. Roll to 15° maximum.

Balance. Balance with rudder pressure.

Back pressure. Lower nose attitude slightly to maintain climb speed (elevator) and then apply slight back pressure to turn.

1. Prior to Entry

Airplane at desired climb speed with climb power set.

In trim.

Look out for other aircraft.

Select reference point for roll out.

20

Descending Turn

OBJECTIVES

To describe:

- the balance of forces in a descending turn;
- the relationship between attitude and airspeed, power and rate of descent;
- the technique to enter, maintain and straighten from a descending turn;
- the attitude-power combinations for left and right descending turns in your airplane; and;
- the effect and technique for a descending turn with flaps extended.

Figure 20-1
Descending turn with flaps extended.

CONSIDERATIONS

Descent Performance

Descent performance (flight path and speed) is controlled by configuration, power and attitude: set the configuration, control airspeed with attitude and rate of descent with power.

Descending Turn With Flaps Extended

Turning with flaps extended is a very common maneuver when making an approach to land. Flying with flaps extended:

- allows the required lift to be generated at a lower airspeed;
- reduces the stalling speed, allowing lower landing speed; and
- requires a lower nose attitude for the same airspeed (better forward view).

Flaps increase lift and drag. The unnecessary increased lift is offset by reducing the angle of attack, which gives a much improved forward field of view. The increased drag is offset by a steeper descent path which provides an increased component of weight. At the same time, the angle of attack is slightly increased once bank is applied to generate the turning force. In some aircraft, flap extension produces a nose-down trim change and in others a nose-up pitching moment. This affects piloting technique, as the pilot maintains attitude and retrims.

APPLICATION

Descent With Flaps Up

Establish the aircraft in a powered descent at a steady airspeed and with a set power with the wings level, balanced and in trim. Enter the turn normally, lowering the nose attitude to maintain airspeed. Lower the attitude slightly for a 30°-banked turn. The steeper the bank angle in a descending turn, the greater the attitude change required to maintain airspeed and the greater the rate of descent (unless the power is increased).

To reduce the rate of descent and flatten the descent path:

- add power; and
- raise the nose to a slightly higher attitude to maintain airspeed.

To increase the rate of descent and steepen the flight path:

- reduce power; and
- lower the nose to a slightly lower attitude to maintain airspeed.

Rolling out of the turn, gradually reduce the power to maintain the desired descent rate and adjust the pitch attitude to maintain the airspeed.

Descent With Flaps Extended

Maintain airspeed in a descending turn with adjustments to pitch attitude.

The nose attitude is lower in a turn with flaps extended.

A descending turn with flaps extended is flown exactly the same as a clean descending turn with a lower nose position. Because such maneuvers are made during the approach to land it is important that suitable airspeeds and rates of descent are maintained. In general, do not exceed a 30° bank angle, and roll out of the turn above 500 feet AGL.

As in all turns:

- maintain the bank angle with ailerons;
- maintain balance with rudder pressure;
- maintain airspeed with elevator; and
- (if desired) control rate of descent with power.

Figure 20-2 With flaps extended, the nose attitude is lower, whether straight or turning.

TECHNIQUE

Entering a Descending Turn

From a stabilized powered descent, the aircraft is rolled to the desired angle of bank (usually 30°). Balance is maintained with rudder, the nose attitude is allowed to lower slightly as the aircraft rolls, and back pressure is then reapplied to generate the turn. For the same airspeed, the rate of descent will be greater but can be reduced by increasing power.

Maintaining the Turn

The turn is maintained by attitude, balance and set power.

The rate of descent increases in a turn but can be adjusted with power.

Straightening

Anticipate roll-out by one-third of the angle of bank, roll to wings level, balance, and slightly reduce the nose-down attitude. If also leveling, increase power and raise the nose to the level attitude.

Extending the Flaps Before Turning

Extend the flaps while adjusting the attitude to maintain airspeed. Retrim. Enter the turn while lowering the nose slightly. Apply back pressure to turn without raising the nose.

Extending the Flaps in the Turn

As the flaps are extending in the turn, the bank is maintained, but the back pressure is reduced to lower the nose attitude. Then the back pressure is reestablished. The task is adapted to allow for the trim change with flap extension in your airplane.

Retracting the Flaps

There should rarely be a need to raise the flaps until after landing. As the flaps are retracted, there will be an immediate tendency for the airspeed to increase unless the nose attitude is raised simultaneously.

AIRMANSHIP

Look out before, during and straightening from the turn. Do not let the nose lower during the turn. Treat the lowering of flaps as a commitment to land. Make the decision to land, then use flaps to modify the approach path and aim point.

During the turn, control any slight tendency for the bank to increase or the nose to lower.

REVIEW 20

Descending Turn

1. As you roll into a descending turn, to maintain a constant rate of descent at a constant airspeed, what power change needs to be made?
2. As you roll out of a descending turn, to maintain a constant rate of descent at a constant airspeed, what power change needs to be made?
3. In a descending turn, within how many knots should you aim to hold the desired airspeed?
4. Airspeed in a descent maintained with what?
5. What effect does having the flaps extended have on the attitude for a straight descent?
6. What effect does having the flaps extended have on the nose attitude for a descending turn?
7. What is the common situation when you fly a descending turn with flaps extended?
8. In a descending turn with flaps extended, where should the balance ball be?
9. During a descending turn to the left with flaps extended, what would you control airspeed with?

Figure 20-3 Maintain airspeed by adjusting attitude.

Answers are given on page 580.

TASK

Descending Turn

Aim: To alter heading in a powered descent at a constant airspeed and power.

1. ***Prior to Entry***

   At desired descent speed.

   In trim.

   Look out for other aircraft.

   Select reference point for roll out.

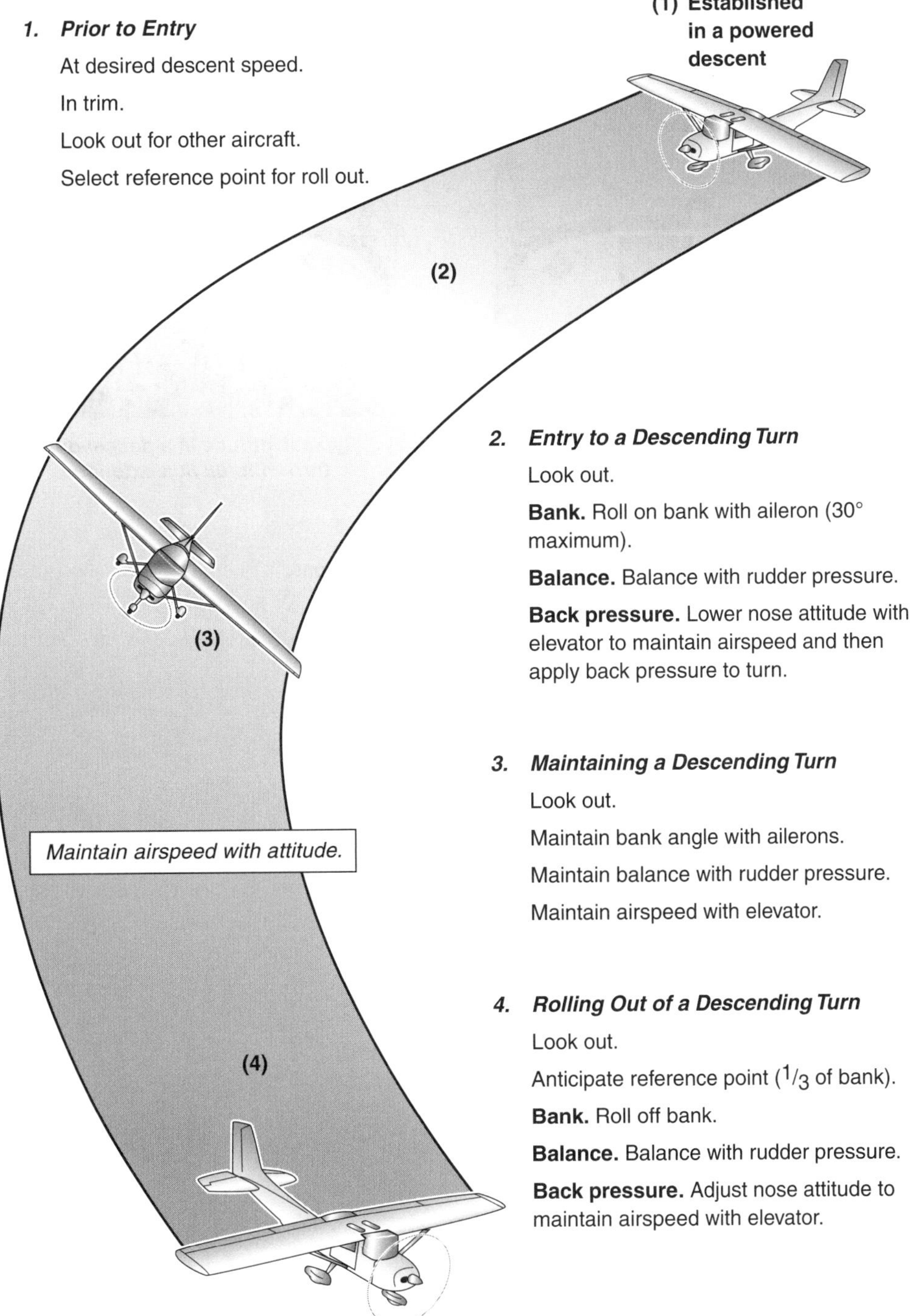

(1) Established in a powered descent
(2)
(3)
Maintain airspeed with attitude.
(4)

2. ***Entry to a Descending Turn***

   Look out.

   Bank. Roll on bank with aileron (30° maximum).

   Balance. Balance with rudder pressure.

   Back pressure. Lower nose attitude with elevator to maintain airspeed and then apply back pressure to turn.

3. ***Maintaining a Descending Turn***

   Look out.

   Maintain bank angle with ailerons.

   Maintain balance with rudder pressure.

   Maintain airspeed with elevator.

4. ***Rolling Out of a Descending Turn***

   Look out.

   Anticipate reference point ($^1/_3$ of bank).

   Bank. Roll off bank.

   Balance. Balance with rudder pressure.

   Back pressure. Adjust nose attitude to maintain airspeed with elevator.

TASK

Descending Turn with Flap Extended

Aim: To maintain a descending turn with extended flaps and adjusting attitude to maintain airspeed.

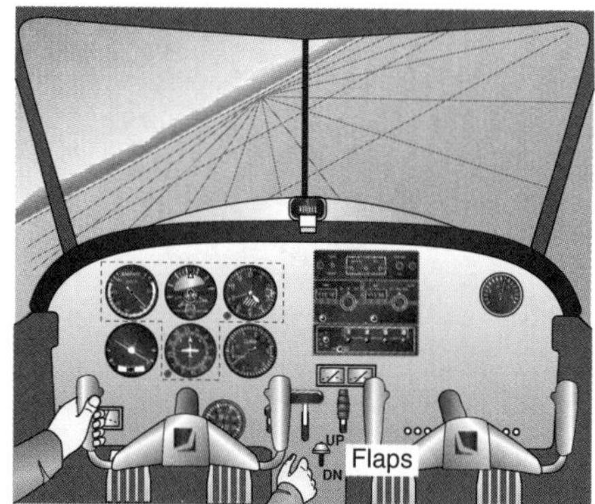

Typical attitude in a descending turn with wings clean (flaps up)

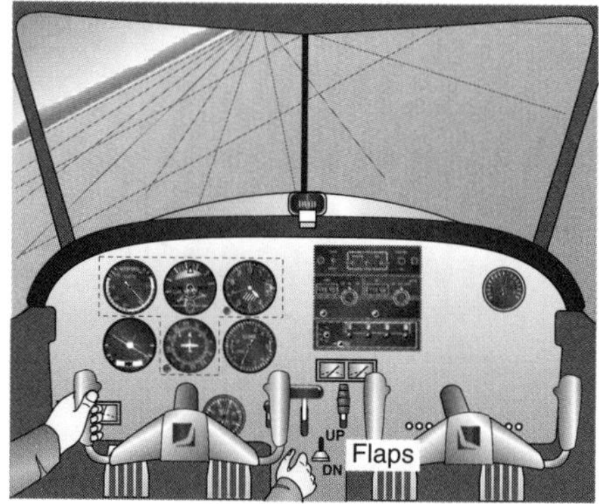

Typical attitude in a descending turn with full flap extended

Practice these turns in both directions.

21 Gliding Turn

OBJECTIVES

To describe:

- the forces acting in a gliding turn;
- the relationship between drag, airspeed and rate of descent;
- the technique to enter, maintain and straighten from a gliding turn; and
- the attitudes for left and right gliding turns in your airplane.

CONSIDERATIONS

Forces in a Gliding Turn

The forces acting on an airplane in a gliding turn are similar to those in a straight glide, except that the airplane is banked and the lift is tilted.

The angle of attack must be increased to supply the centripetal force to turn. This is achieved by applying back pressure that results in an increase in the induced drag. To maintain best-glide speed, while also turning, requires that the nose attitude be lowered so a greater component of weight is used to offset the increased drag. This is done by steepening the descent. Both the rate of descent and the angle of descent are increased.

Maintain airspeed in a gliding turn by lowering the nose.

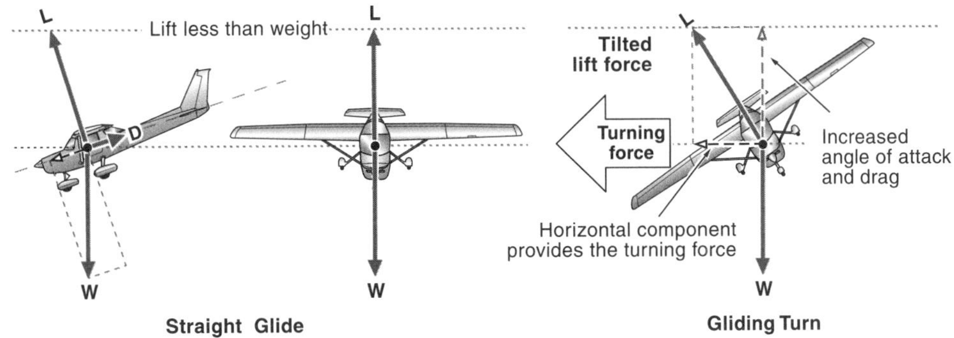

Figure 21-1 The forces in a straight glide and in a gliding turn.

APPLICATION

Airspeed

The increased drag in a turn will tend to decrease airspeed, so, to maintain the desired airspeed in a gliding turn, the nose must be lowered. As in all turns, there will be a tendency for the nose to drop, requiring back pressure to stop it dropping too far. Simply hold the attitude that gives the desired airspeed. For side-by-side cockpits, the position of the nose cowl relative to the horizon will differ for left and right turns.

Tilting of the lift in a gliding turn, and the lower nose position to maintain airspeed, results in an increased rate of descent and a steeper flight path. The more bank, the greater the effect, so be careful near the ground. Plan to roll out and go around (climb) by 500 feet AGL.

The rate of descent increases in a gliding turn.

Limit the rate of descent in a gliding turn by restricting the bank angle. In a glide approach, the turn onto final should be planned at 20° and not exceed 30°. If there is a need for greater bank then go-around and reposition for another approach.

Figure 21-2 Entering a gliding turn, let the nose lower to the new attitude to maintain airspeed.

Overbanking/Underbanking

Two effects tend to cancel each other out in descending turns, both when gliding and when using power. They are:

- an overbanking tendency due to the outer wing traveling faster; and
- an underbanking tendency due to the inner wing in a descending turn having a higher angle of attack.

There is less tendency to overbank in a descending turn.

There is no need to be conscious of this when flying: simply maintain the desired bank angle with aileron. Sideslip also causes a rolling and yawing tendency so it is also important to cancel any sideslip by keeping the balance ball centered by using rudder.

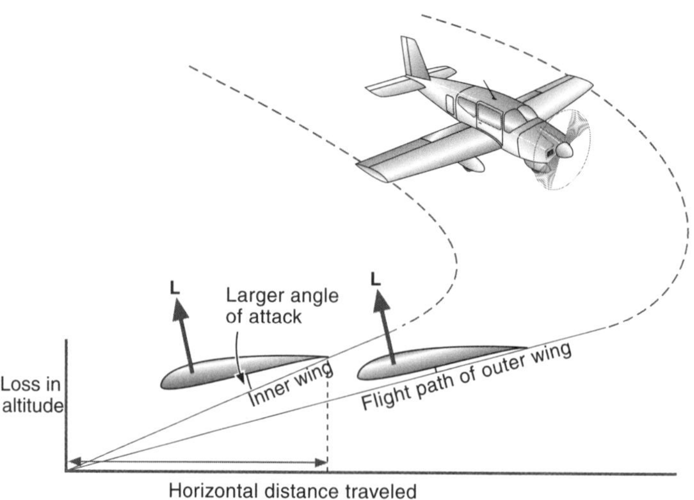

Figure 21-3 There is less tendency to overbank in a descending turn as the effects cancel.

Slipstream Effect

Most airplanes are rigged to be in balance (and require no rudder pressure) when cruising. In a glide at low power and airspeed (no slipstream effect), rudder pressure is required for balance. For an airplane equipped with a propeller that rotates clockwise as seen from the cockpit, left rudder pressure will be needed. If the airplane has a rudder trim, then make use of it to relieve this steady pressure. Normal balance rules apply. If the ball is out to the left, apply left rudder pressure. Left rudder pressure should then be increased when rolling left and decreased when rolling right.

Counteract the lack of slipstream effect in a glide with rudder pressure.

Engine Considerations

As in a normal straight glide, apply power from time to time (500–1,000 feet intervals). Advance the engine smoothly from idle to cruise power and back to idle. This will keep the engine and its oil supply warm and clear any spark plug fouling that may have built up. Use the mixture and carburetor heat as recommended by your airplane manufacturer.

Keep the engine warm in a prolonged glide. Control altitude and balance as the power is adjusted.

TECHNIQUE

Entering a Gliding Turn

To enter a gliding turn, establish the airplane in a straight glide at the desired attitude (confirmed by airspeed) and in trim. Look out for other aircraft and select a reference point on which to roll out. Roll into the turn with aileron and apply sufficient rudder pressure to keep the balance ball centered. Allow the nose to lower slightly to maintain airspeed and then back pressure may be required to stop it dropping too far and to increase the angle of attack. Do not exceed a bank angle of 30°.

Maintaining a Gliding Turn

To maintain the gliding turn, control bank angle with aileron, balance with rudder pressure and attitude with elevator (using airspeed as a reference). Note the higher rate of descent. Remember the cycle: attitude-instruments-attitude-lookout.

Straightening

To roll out of the gliding turn, anticipate reaching the reference point by 10° or so and commence removing bank with aileron, balancing with rudder pressure. Hold the nose in the straight glide attitude (slightly higher than in the turn). Level the wings and then make minor adjustments to maintain the desired heading and airspeed.

Gliding Turn with Flaps Extended

The principles and technique for a gliding turn with flaps extended are identical to the gliding turn without flap, except that the attitude and flight path are steeper still and the rate and angle of descent are further increased. This maneuver is only used for the final turn on a glide approach or a forced landing and only when the pilot is certain of being able to reach the planned aim point. Maintaining airspeed is the key safety factor.

AIRMANSHIP

It is especially important to maintain a good lookout in any turn. Be aware of your altitude since descent rates in descending turns can be high. Keep the aircraft balanced. There is no need to trim, since the turn is a transient maneuver.

REVIEW 21

Gliding Turn

1. How does the lift force in a gliding turn compare to the lift force in a straight glide?
2. In a glide, what effect does increasing the bank angle have on the rate of descent?
3. The increased rate of descent can be seen on two instruments. What are they?
4. What effect does the bank in a gliding turn have on drag? What effect does this have on the airspeed?
5. How does the tilting of the lift force in a gliding turn affect its contribution to supporting the weight of the airplane?
6. Which component of the tilted lift force causes the turn in a gliding turn?
7. During a gliding turn to the right, where should the balance ball be?
8. During a gliding turn to the left, where should the balance ball be?

Figure 21-4 Increased bank requires a lower nose attitude to maintain airspeed.

Answers are given on page 580.

TASK

Gliding Turn

Aim: To enter, maintain, and roll out of a gliding turn at a constant airspeed.

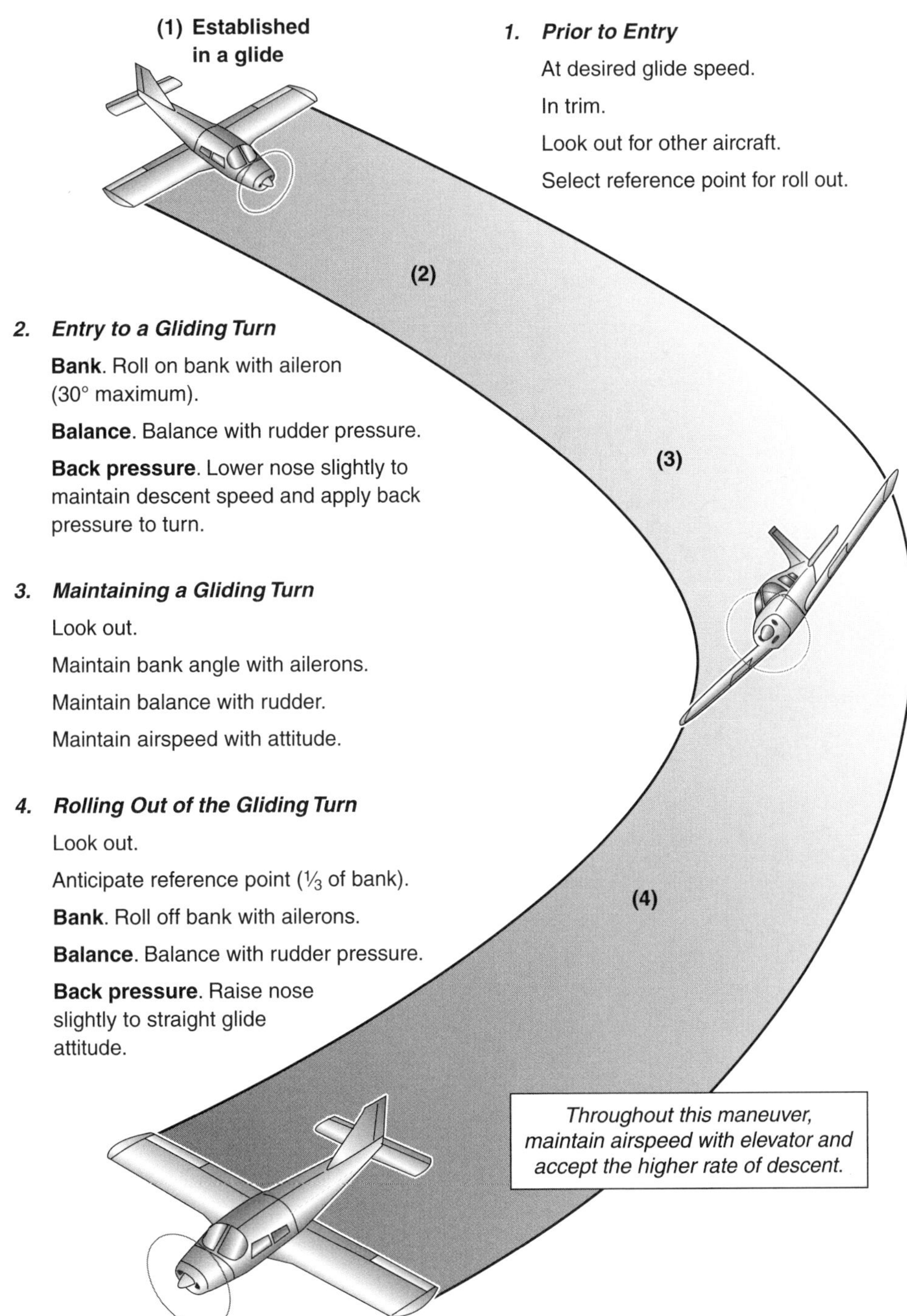

1. ***Prior to Entry***

   At desired glide speed.

   In trim.

   Look out for other aircraft.

   Select reference point for roll out.

2. ***Entry to a Gliding Turn***

   Bank. Roll on bank with aileron (30° maximum).

   Balance. Balance with rudder pressure.

   Back pressure. Lower nose slightly to maintain descent speed and apply back pressure to turn.

3. ***Maintaining a Gliding Turn***

   Look out.

   Maintain bank angle with ailerons.

   Maintain balance with rudder.

   Maintain airspeed with attitude.

4. ***Rolling Out of the Gliding Turn***

   Look out.

   Anticipate reference point (⅓ of bank).

   Bank. Roll off bank with ailerons.

   Balance. Balance with rudder pressure.

   Back pressure. Raise nose slightly to straight glide attitude.

Throughout this maneuver, maintain airspeed with elevator and accept the higher rate of descent.

Slow Flight and Stalling

22
Slow Flight and Stall Avoidance

OBJECTIVES

To describe:

- the difference in control response at low airspeed;
- the need for relatively gross attitude and power changes to achieve desired flight path and speed;
- the need for increased power to prevent airspeed decrease below minimum-drag speed;
- the symptoms of an approaching stall; and
- the technique to fly safely at low airspeed.

CONSIDERATIONS

Aircraft Behavior

Slow flying is an awareness exercise.

This exercise is designed to provide exposure to flight at low airspeeds so that the pilot can:

- experience the behavior and feel of the airplane at low airspeed;
- recognize the symptoms of an approaching stall; and
- take action to avoid the stall (sometimes called a recovery from an imminent or *incipient* stall).

The exercise also provides handling practice for those brief periods of low airspeed that do occur in normal flight, when the airplane is accelerating to climbing speed immediately after liftoff, and during the landing flare as the airspeed decreases prior to touchdown.

Adverse Aileron Yaw

When the ailerons are deflected to cause the aircraft to roll, they experience different amounts of drag. The downward deflected aileron experiences greater aerodynamic force, which tends to cause a yaw in the direction opposite to the commanded roll. This is called adverse aileron yaw. At lower airspeeds (and higher angles of attack), adverse aileron yaw is most pronounced. When entering, rolling out or reversing a turn at low airspeed, a significant amount of rudder needs to be applied with, and in the same direction as, the aileron. For example, for a turn right, use right aileron and right rudder, then center the aileron and reduce the rudder.

Power Required for Level Flight

Slow flight should be accomplished at an airspeed just above the stall warning.

To maintain a constant airspeed, there must be enough thrust from the propeller to balance the total drag. Higher power is required for steady flight at both high and low speeds, with minimum power occurring at a specific speed in between.

Minimum power will give minimum fuel consumption and consequently maximum endurance (maximum time in the air from the remaining fuel available). This speed is often listed as the endurance speed in the pilot's operating handbook. Flight below the best-endurance speed is considered to be slow flight.

APPLICATION

Power Management

At normal cruising speeds, higher speeds require higher power settings. Any minor speed variations due to gusts will automatically correct themselves in the normal flight range. For example, a slight increase in speed causes a drag increase that will slow the airplane down. Conversely, a slight decrease in speed reduces drag, allowing the airplane to regain speed. An airplane is *speed stable* (it tends to be self-correcting) in the normal flight range from minimum-drag speed up to the maximum flight speed.

In the slow flight range, the situation is reversed; that is, the lower the speed, the higher the power required. This is because at low speeds a high angle of attack is needed to produce the required lift, greatly increasing the induced drag. The increase in total drag will slow the airplane down unless power is applied. The lowest level flight speed that can be maintained by an airplane may be limited either by the maximum power that the engine-propeller can deliver, or by the stall.

The slower the steady speed you want to maintain, the more power you require.

In the slow-speed range, the airplane is not speed stable because an airspeed loss due to a gust will result in an increase in total drag that will slow the airplane down further (and continue to do so) unless the pilot takes corrective action by adding power or by descending. An airspeed gain, conversely, will reduce the total drag and the airplane will accelerate unless the pilot reduces power. Thus the pilot workload is increased since the control of airspeed deviations is a more active task within this regime. This is known as flying on *the back end of the power curve* (or in the case of jets, the back end of the *drag* curve).

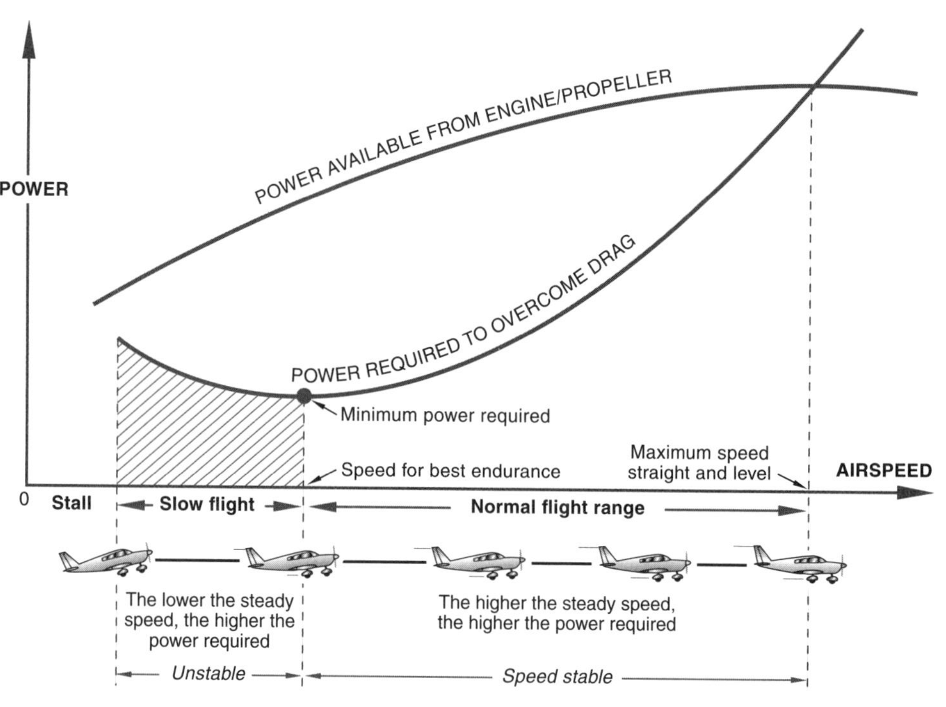

Figure 22-1 The power curve.

Control Response

At low airspeeds, the controls will feel sloppy and less effective. Large control movements (with reduced air loads) may be required to obtain the desired response, hence the expression *sloppy controls.*

At slow speeds, you need to be more active on the controls (make larger inputs earlier).

Since the elevator and rudder are in the propeller slipstream, they will be somewhat more responsive when high power is set. The ailerons will not be affected by the propeller slipstream, only by the aircraft airspeed.

The combination of high power and low airspeed will lead to a strong slipstream effect, which may require significant rudder deflection to balance the yawing moment. If the aircraft is not balanced there could be significant rolling moments due to the sideslip and this will require aileron input. The correct procedure is to keep the aircraft balanced and then only small amounts of aileron deflection will be required.

The *feel* of the airplane becomes very important in slow flight. The low speed, the less-responsive controls, the high nose attitude, the high power required and the large rudder deflection are all clues that the stalling angle is not far away.

Note how far the control column is back and if the aircraft was not retrimmed prior to slowing down how much pull force is required to hold the nose up. The natural stability of the aircraft is trying to return to the trimmed angle of attack and will naturally avoid a stall if the back pressure is released. The pilot has to force the aircraft to stall under these conditions—it won't happen otherwise.

At high power and low airspeed, some right rudder will be needed to keep the balance ball centered.

You will practice slow flight at 10 knots above the stall (and then possibly only 5 knots above). Stalling speeds for straight and level flight at maximum weight with power off are delineated on the airspeed indicator: V_{S1} at the lower end of the green band for a clean configuration, and V_{S0} at the lower end of the white band for full flap.

The airspeed needs to be monitored closely in slow flight. It should be controlled accurately with power and attitude changes due to the proximity of the stall. The tendency to lose speed in a turn should be anticipated with additional power.

Do not attempt steep turns at slow speeds near the stall: the stalling speed will increase to meet your actual airspeed! You can also feel through the seat of your pants when the aircraft is lifting or sinking. Use this cue to anticipate the need for power changes, in addition to the airspeed indicator.

TECHNIQUE

Establishing Slow Flight

To establish an airspeed 5–10 knots above the 1g stall speed:

- reduce power, progressively raise the nose to maintain altitude until the stall warning sounds, and note that airspeed;
- pitch down slightly to eliminate the stall warning;
- adjust power to maintain altitude and note airspeed required to perform slow flight maneuver (a few knots above stall warning speed);
- note the position of the control column and the force you must apply; and then,
- retrim and balance.

1g = 1 gravity; equals the weight of an object.

Once slow flight is established, the aircraft should be capable of maintaining controlled flight without activating the stall warning.

For example, if the stall warning is activated at 50 knots, an acceptable slow flight maneuvering speed could be 52 knots.

Maneuvering in Slow Flight

To maintain speed and attitude, be prepared to make relatively large throttle movements and readjust the attitude as necessary. There will be a continuing tendency for the nose to drop. The longer you leave corrections, the greater they will have to be. As always: power + attitude = flight path + speed (performance).

To correct speed variations:

- if speed increases, reduce power and hold the nose up; and
- if speed decreases, add power and then lower the nose a little.

To correct altitude variations:

- if the airplane climbs, reduce power a little and lower the nose a little; and
- if the airplane sinks, add power (more rather than less) and raise the nose slowly.

Slow flight is good practice for your coordination.

The use of elevator, power and rudder must be coordinated. Every time power is changed there will be pitching and yawing moments that must be countered. Slow flight is very good practice for your coordination.

To enter a climb:

- increase power;
- slowly increase attitude to maintain airspeed; and
- trim.

To level off from a low-speed climb:

- lower the nose a little;
- slowly reduce power but counter the trim change; and
- trim.

To commence a low-speed descent:

- reduce power;
- slightly lower the pitch attitude to maintain airspeed; and
- trim.

To level off from a low-speed descent:

- add power;
- gradually raise the nose to slow-cruise attitude to maintain airspeed; and
- trim.

To avoid high load factors, do not exceed a 30° bank angle—20° is preferred. Remember: in steep turns at a 60° bank angle, the load factor doubles to 2g and the stall speed increases by 40%.

To turn at a low airspeed:

- add power to maintain speed as bank angle is applied.

To make a maximum-performance climb away from a descent:

- open the throttle fully (and balance with rudder);
- allow the nose to rise and hold it in the climb attitude;
- adjust attitude to maintain airspeed; and
- trim.

To approach the stall:

- reduce the power;
- raise the nose to maintain altitude until a stall is imminent (stall warning horn);
- recover by applying full power, while holding the attitude constant and balancing with rudder; and
- ease the control column forward as the aircraft accelerates away from the stall.

These maneuvers should be practiced both clean and with flaps extended.

Avoiding a Stall

A stall occurs when the wing is forced to exceed its critical angle of attack—the wing won't stall if back pressure on the control column is removed.

The first symptom of an approaching stall could be any of the following:

- activated stall warning system;
- buffet;
- rearward position or high pull force on the control column; or
- loss of pitch response (especially during a turn).

At the first sign of any such symptom, remove back pressure, apply full power (balance pitching and yawing moments) and allow the aircraft to accelerate before entering a climb.

Figure 22-2 Prestall buffet.

REVIEW 22

Slow Flight and Stall Avoidance

1. Maintaining a steady airspeed that is slower than the minimum-power steady airspeed is known as flying on which side of the power curve?
2. How do the power requirements change for slow-speed flight?
3. If the airflow over a flight control surface is slow, how will the control feel? Will the control be more effective?
4. When flying at a low airspeed with a high power setting, what will the be speed of the airflow over those flight control surfaces not in the propeller slipstream? How will these controls feel? Which control will these be?
5. When flying at a low airspeed with a high power setting, what will the be speed of the airflow over those flight control surfaces that are in the propeller slipstream? How will these controls feel? Which control will these be?
6. With high power and low airspeed, which side rudder will be needed to keep the balance ball centered?
7. Which three flight instruments are particularly important when flying at a slow airspeed if accuracy is required and a stall is to be avoided?
8. What is the airspeed tolerance in relation to the 1g stall speed when establishing slow flight?
9. What is aircraft performance determined by?
10. If a slower airspeed is required, what change to nose attitude do you make?
11. If a higher airspeed is required, what change to nose attitude do you make?
12. Describe how to transition from a fast cruise speed to a slow airspeed, maintaining straight and level flight.
13. Describe how to accelerate from a slow airspeed to a fast cruising airspeed in straight and level flight.
14. Describe how to transition from a fast clean cruise to slow flight with flaps extended, maintaining straight and level flight.
15. Describe how to transition from slow flight with flaps extended to a normal fast clean cruise.
16. What action following any change in speed, power or configuration makes flying accurately easier?
17. What is the minimum altitude at which you can practice slow-speed flight? If the local terrain is 5,300 feet MSL, above what altitude must you practice?
18. What are the tolerances expected when you demonstrate flying at slow airspeeds? (Include altitude, airspeed, heading and bank angle, and give the tolerances for both private and commercial pilots.)
19. At low airspeed with high power, which side rudder pressure will be required to keep the balance ball centered? What are the two reasons for this?
20. The basic stalling speed clean is at which end of what colored arc on the airspeed indicator?
21. The basic stalling speed in the landing configuration is which end of which colored arc on the airspeed indicator?
22. At weights below the maximum weight, how does the actual stalling speed compare to the published stalling speed?
23. In maneuvers where g is pulled, how is the stalling speed affected?
24. In a 60°-banked turn, 2g is pulled. Will you feel your normal weight or twice as heavy? The stalling speed will have increased by what percentage? Should you use steep bank angles when flying at slow speeds?
25. In a 30°-banked turn, the stalling speed is increased by what percentage?
26. If a stall inadvertently occurs due to lack of attention by the pilot, describe the recovery.
27. In relation to the stall, when do stall warning devices usually activate?
28. If you inadvertently approach a stall when flying at a slow airspeed, when should you initiate a recovery?

Answers are given on page 581.

TASK

Slow Flight

Aim: To develop an awareness of the airplane's handling characteristics at very low airspeeds, and to return the airplane to a safe flying speed.

1. Establishing Slow Flight, Flaps Up

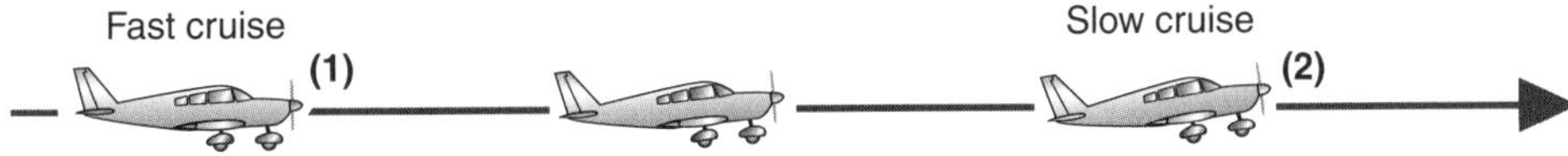

To adopt a slow cruise:

Reduce power.

Balance

Raise nose to reduce airspeed and maintain altitude.

To maintain a slow cruise:

Set power and attitude to maintain altitude and airspeed.

Note: The controls are less effective at low airspeed.

2. Recovering from Slow Flight

Increase power. Balance with rudder.

Lower pitch attitude to maintain altitude as the aircraft accelerates.

Adjust power as desired airspeed is approached.

Trim.

Repeat the above procedure with flaps extended.

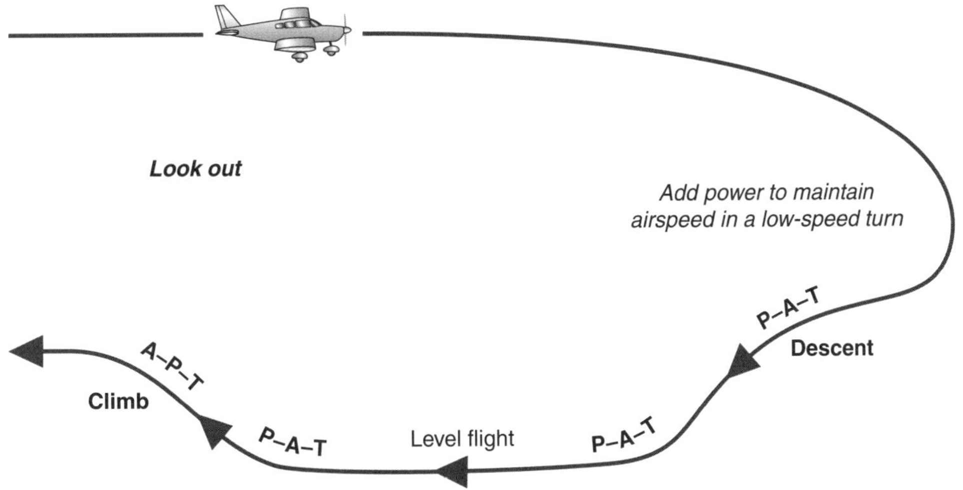

Practice gentle climbs, descents and turns at a constant airspeed.

TASK

Stall Avoidance

Aim: To recognize the approach of a stall (that is, imminent stall), and recover to normal flight before a full stall develops.

1. ***Prior to Stall Entry***

   Complete the HASELL check.

   Look out and clear the area.

   Maintain specific heading (±10°), or (if you want to practice in a banked turn) maintain a chosen bank angle (±10°) —suggested bank angle 20°.

2. ***Approach to the Stall***

   Power—off (carburetor heat—hot, throttle—closed).

   Maintain heading (±10°) or chosen bank angle (±10°).

   Continue bringing the control column back to maintain altitude (±100 ft).

3. ***Symptoms of an Approaching (Imminent) Stall***

   Decreasing airspeed and noise level.

   The controls are less firm and less effective.

   Stall warning (light, horn or buzzer).

   Initial shudder of airframe (on the edge of a stall, but not yet stalled).

4. ***Recovery from an Imminent Stall***

   Release the back pressure (and apply full power to maintain altitude).

   Roll wings-level if banked and lower the nose to the level flight attitude if power is used (otherwise lower the nose to a gliding attitude).

   Resume normal flight, and set carburetor heat to cold.

Practice this maneuver:

Straight and level.

In a banked turn.

With power off, then with power on.

Approaching a stall in a right bank

Symptoms of an imminent stall

Leveling the wings after recovery

23

Full Stall and Recovery

OBJECTIVES

To describe:

- the point of stall and the aircraft's behavior during a fully developed stall;
- the correct technique to recover from a stall with minimal loss of altitude; and
- the factors affecting stalling speed.

CONSIDERATIONS

What is Stalling?

Streamlined (laminar) airflow over the wings breaks down and separates over a major part of the upper surface of the wing when the critical (or stalling) angle of attack is exceeded, causing:

A stall occurs beyond the critical angle of attack.

- buffeting (shaking or shuddering) of the airframe that is felt through the controls and perhaps over the cockpit and through the seat;
- a marked drag increase;
- rearward movement of the center of pressure (through which the lift acts);
- a marked decrease in lift, resulting in loss of altitude despite every effort to hold the nose up (or loss of turn performance if the wing is stalled while maneuvering);
- possible yawing/rolling moments (wing drop) due to slipstream, torque, sideslip and variations in loss of lift between the left and right wings; and
- a descending flight path that changes the airflow over the horizontal stabilizer, resulting in the nose dropping (the severity of which depends very much on the individual aircraft and the CG position).

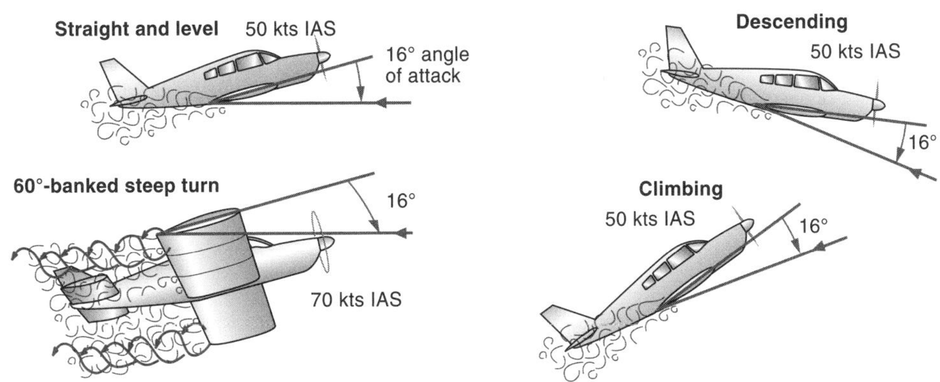

Figure 23-1 Stalling occurs at the critical angle of attack.

A stall will occur whenever the critical angle of attack is exceeded, regardless of the airspeed or attitude.

A stall will occur whenever the critical angle of attack is exceeded, regardless of airspeed and attitude. The only way to unstall the wing is to decrease the angle of attack (i.e. relax the back pressure or move the control column forward).

The pilot can increase the angle of attack (and reduce airspeed) by pulling the control column back. This happens in many maneuvers such as:

- establishing slow flight;
- turning (especially steep turns);
- pulling out of a dive; and
- landing.

A vertical gust of wind can also momentarily change the relative airflow over the wing and increase its angle of attack, perhaps beyond the critical angle.

What is Stalling Speed?

The published stalling speeds are only a guide, as they vary with weight, bank, power and flap position.

The basic stalling speed is considered to be the speed at which the airplane stalls when it is at maximum weight with the wings clean (that is, no flaps and, if appropriate, landing gear retracted) and flying straight and level with the power off. The stall is made to occur by the pilot progressively raising the nose as the aircraft slows.

The basic stalling speed is called V_{S1}. It is published in the pilot's operating handbook and shown on the airspeed indicator as the lower end of the green arc. V_{S1} for your airplane should be memorized as it is a valuable guide. The stalling speed with full flap extended (at maximum weight, straight and level, and idle power) is called V_{S0}. It is also found in the pilot's operating handbook and at the lower end of the white arc on the airspeed indicator. The V_{S0} speed should also be memorized.

The published stalling speeds are only a guide, since stalling always happens at the same angle of attack and not the same indicated airspeed. Turns, pulling out of dives and contaminated wing surfaces (e.g. frost or snow) will increase the stalling speed. High power and decreased weight will reduce it.

Stall warning devices activate before the stall occurs to allow stall avoidance.

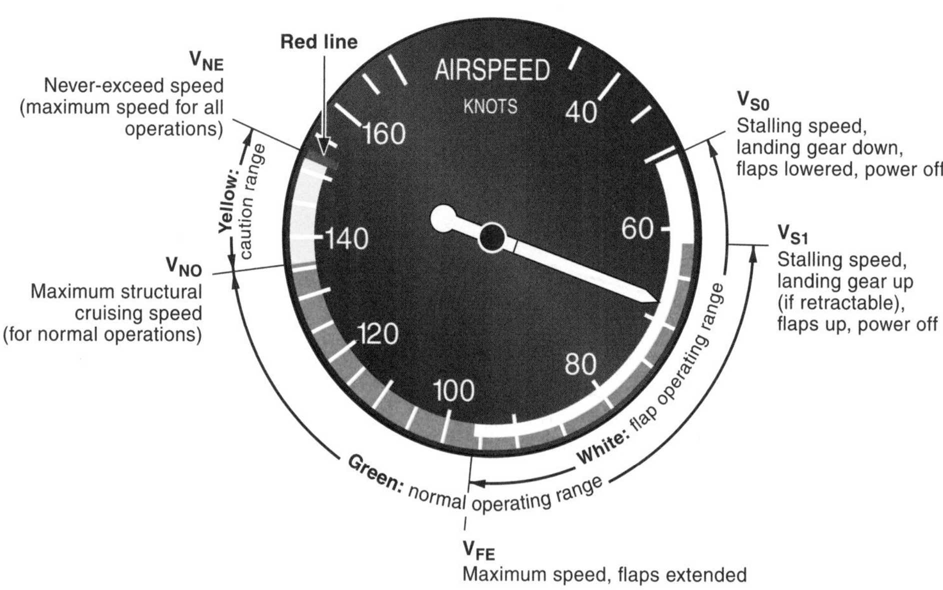

Figure 23-2 Color coding on the ASI.

Flight Controls in the Stall

A reduced airflow over the control surfaces will cause them to become less effective as speed reduces and the stall is approached. Control pressures will decrease and larger movements of the elevator and rudder will be required. It is the wing that stalls. The fin and the horizontal stabilizer remain unstalled (by design) so that during the stall the elevator and rudder remain effective. The ailerons may or may not remain effective during a stall, depending on the airplane type.

The flight controls are less effective near the stall.

Ailerons

A dropping wing can normally be picked up (returned to wings-level) by moving the control column in the opposite direction. This causes the aileron on the downgoing wing to be deflect downward, increasing the angle of attack and producing more lift on that wing.

If the wing is near the stalling angle, the aileron deflection could cause the critical angle to be exceeded on that wing and, instead of rising, the loss of lift would cause the wing to drop further. The additional drag on the wing with the aileron deflected downward may also cause a yawing moment in the same direction. As this wing stalls and drops further, there is a further increase in drag causing more yaw and more roll. This leads to a condition of rolling and yawing called *autorotation*. Autorotation, if uncorrected, can lead to a spin developing.

Thus the safest response to a wing drop is to prevent the roll and yaw with rudder (remember the indirect effect of yaw is a rolling moment). This will safely prevent the autorotation. Simply use rudder to stop the roll and yaw. Do not attempt to return the wings to level until the angle of attack is reduced and airspeed is increasing. Then the ailerons will have their normal function and response. The ailerons on more recently designed airplanes are effective right through the stall and their use, coordinated with rudder, may be acceptable, but it is not wise practice in general. This point should be discussed with your flight instructor.

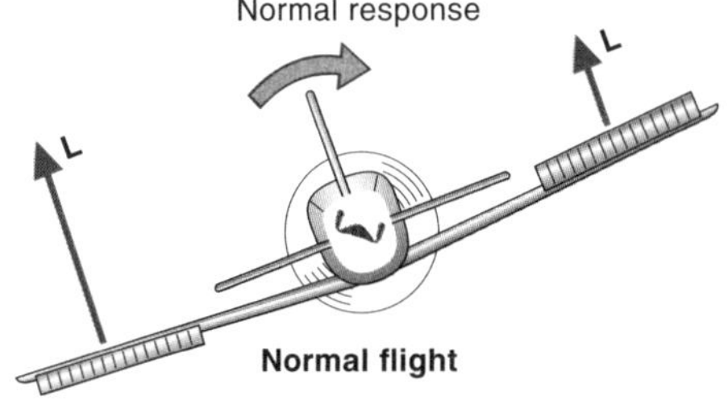

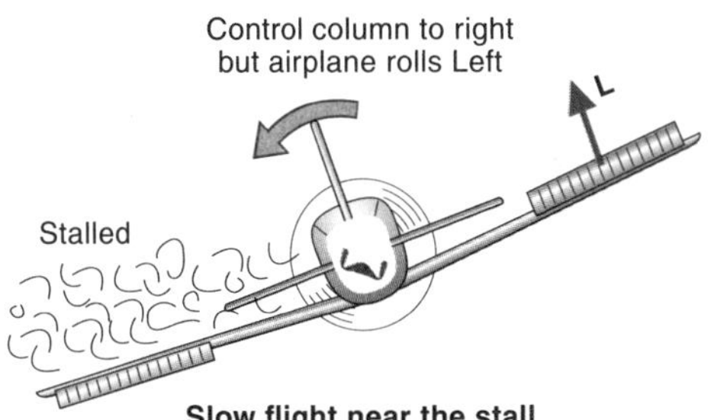

Figure 23-3
Near the stall, use of aileron may not level the wings.

Rudder

Near the stall, any tendency for a wing to drop or for the airplane to yaw should be prevented with opposite rudder (not aileron).

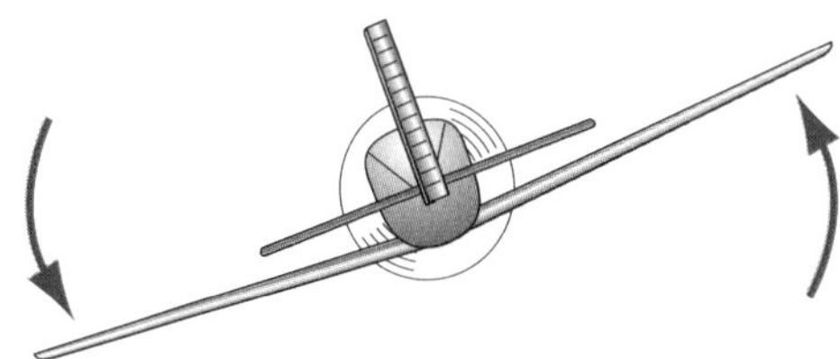

Figure 23-4
Near the stall, prevent wing drop and further yaw with opposite rudder.

Factors Affecting the Stall and Stalling Speed

Wing Surface

If ice, frost, insects or any other contaminant is on a wing or if the wing is damaged (especially its upper leading edge), the airflow could become turbulent at a lesser angle of attack than normal. Stalling will then occur sooner and at a higher airspeed. Always check the surface condition of the wings (especially the upper leading edges) in your preflight inspection.

Contaminated or damaged wings increase stalling speed.

Effect of Flaps

Extending flaps lowers the stalling speed and attitude and affects the stall characteristics of the airplane.

The stall with flaps extended will differ somewhat from the clean stall. Flaps increase the lifting capability of the wings, allowing the required lift to be generated at a lower speed. The stalling speed will be lower. The increased drag will cause the airplane to decelerate more rapidly when power is reduced and the lower speed may make the controls feel very sloppy. The uneven distribution of lift on the wings may also cause a greater tendency for a wing to drop.

With flaps extended, the nose attitude will be lower in each phase of flight, therefore stalling will occur at a lower pitch attitude than when flaps are retracted.

Stalling with flaps extended will occur at a lower pitch attitude than with flaps up (clean).

The recovery from a stall with flaps extended is standard. Altitude loss can be minimized by applying full power as the control column is moved centrally forward, but be prepared to hold forward pressure on the control column so that the nose does not rise too far with the strong pitch-up moment that full power produces. Do not use ailerons to roll the wings level until the wings are unstalled. If full flap is used, a climb-away may be restricted unless part flap is raised (once a safe speed is attained).

Effect of Bank Angle

Stalling speed in a level turn increases in a direct relationship with bank angle. In a turn, the load factor (g) increases. This has the same effect on the stalling speed as a change in weight. The change in V_{STALL} is shown as a ratio or percentage that applies to all aircraft in a level turn.

Bank angle (ϕ)	Load factor ($n = \sec \phi$)	Change in V_{STALL}	% increase in V_{STALL}
0°	1.01g	x 1.00	V_{STALL}
10°	1.02g	x 1.01	+1%
15°	1.04g	x 1.02	+2%
20°	1.07g	x 1.03	+3%
30°	1.15g	x 1.07	+7%
40°	1.30g	x 1.14	+14%
45°	1.41g	x 1.19	+19%
60°	2.01g	x 1.41	+41%
70°	3.01g	x 1.73	+73%
75°	4.01g	x 2.00	+100%

Effect of Power

Power creates a slipstream over the inner sections of the wings which may delay the stall. This will occur at a higher nose attitude. The slipstream makes the elevator and rudder more effective, but not the ailerons. The increased airflow may delay the stall on the inner sections of the wing; the stall occurring first on the outer sections, perhaps with a wing-drop tendency.

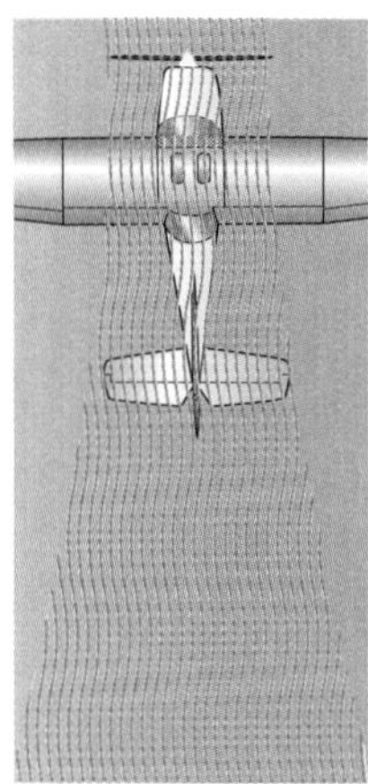

Figure 23-5 Power reduces stalling speed.

Effect of Weight

The lighter the airplane, the less lift the wings must generate for straight and level flight, and so the smaller the required angle of attack at a given speed. Therefore a light airplane can be flown at a slower airspeed before the stalling angle of attack is reached.

Stalling speed decreases as weight decreases.

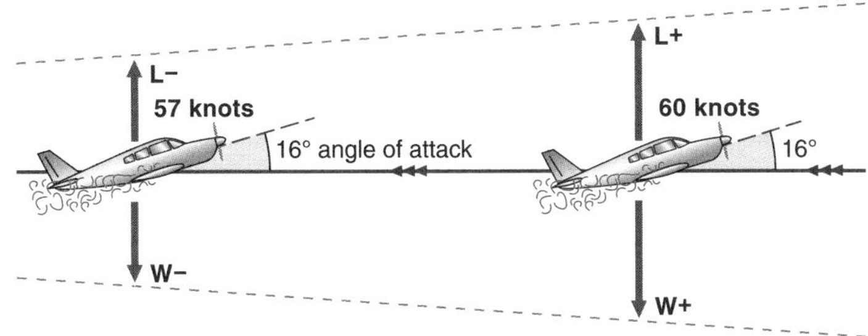

Figure 23-6 Stalling speed is less at lower weights (90% W = 95% V_S).

Effect of Center of Gravity Position

In many aircraft, the horizontal stabilizer generates a small downward force to balance the four main forces and prevent the airplane pitching. The lift from the wings in straight and level flight will therefore have to support both the weight and this downward aerodynamic force on the tail. The further forward the CG, the greater the downward horizontal-stabilizer force and so the greater is the lift required from the main wings. This requires a greater angle of attack at a given airspeed, therefore the stalling angle will be reached at a higher airspeed. This is another good reason why the airplane must be correctly loaded with the CG within approved limits.

A forward center of gravity (CG) increases the stalling speed.

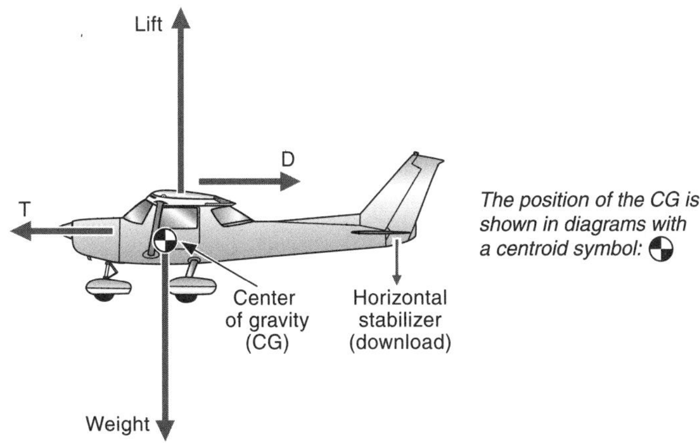

The position of the CG is shown in diagrams with a centroid symbol: ⊕

Figure 23-7 The forces in straight and level flight.

APPLICATION

Stalling from Straight and Level Flight

Stalling is first practiced from straight and level flight by reducing power and raising the nose to maintain altitude. The angle of attack must gradually increase as the speed reduces.

Warnings of an impending stall include:

- reduction of airspeed and air noise level;
- decrease of control effectiveness and a sloppy feel;
- operation of a prestall warning (such as a horn, buzzer or light);
- the onset of buffet, felt in the airframe and through the control column;
- high nose attitude for the maneuver being flown;
- rearward position of the control column; and
- high pull force on the control column (unless retrimmed).

The actual stall may be recognized by:

- rate of descent;
- inability to hold the nose attitude;
- the nose dropping or nodding; and
- possible yaw and wing drop.

TECHNIQUE

Stall Recovery

Stall recovery requires decreasing the angle of attack below the critical angle.

To recover from a stall, reduce the angle of attack by moving the control column centrally forward (releasing the back pressure may be sufficient) until the buffet or stall warning stops. Once the wings are unstalled, buffeting ceases, the airspeed increases, and the airplane can be eased out of the slight dive to level flight. The altitude loss will be of the order of 200–400 feet. Power can be added to regain or maintain altitude.

Altitude loss during the stall is minimized by use of power to quickly regain flying speed. This becomes the standard stall recovery action for all aircraft. Adding power is not required to recover from the stall; however, altitude loss will be minimized if full power is applied as back pressure is released and the nose is lowered. Recovery can be achieved with an altitude loss of less than 50 feet.

Standard Stall Recovery Technique

The standard stall recovery technique is as follows:

- reduce the angle of attack;
- simultaneously, but smoothly, apply full power;
- prevent any yaw or roll with opposite rudder;
- as the airspeed increases, level the wings and raise the nose; and
- raise the flaps, if they were extended.

Altitude loss is minimized by applying full power.

Stall

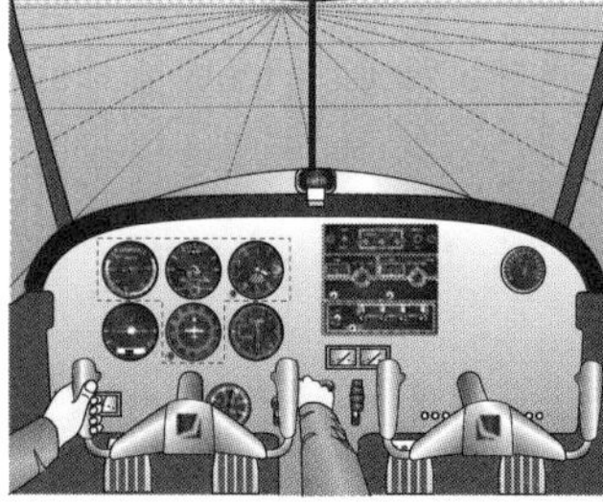

Recovery

Resume normal flight/power

Figure 23-8 Stall and recovery attitudes.

After Stalling

Following stall recovery, ease the airplane into normal flight by gently raising the nose and applying power as the nose passes through the horizon. The momentum of an airplane causes it to follow the original flight path for a brief time before the change in attitude and resulting change in forces move it into a new flight path. Pulling the nose up too sharply during the stall recovery may not give the airplane time enough to react and may merely increase the angle of attack beyond the stalling angle again. An accelerated stall will be induced, and a second recovery will be necessary. Fly gently. Feel your way.

Avoid entering a secondary or accelerated stall during stall recovery.

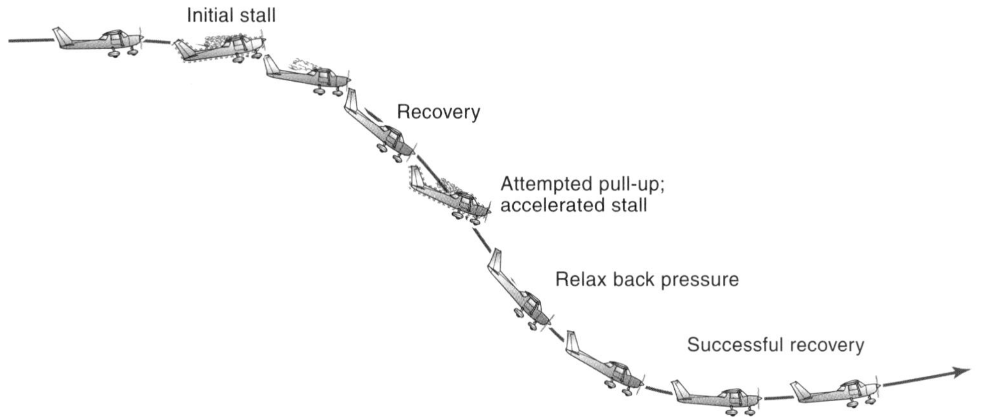

Figure 23-9 Raising the nose too sharply during recovery may induce an accelerated stall.

Stalling with Flaps Extended

When the trailing-edge flaps are lowered, the effective angle of attack of the wings is increased. This allows the airplane to fly at a slower speed with a lower nose attitude. The stall with flaps extended will occur with a much lower nose attitude and a lower airspeed than when the wings are clean. With full flaps extended on an approach to land, for instance, the stall could occur with the nose well below the horizon. Stall symptoms and aircraft behavior may also be affected.

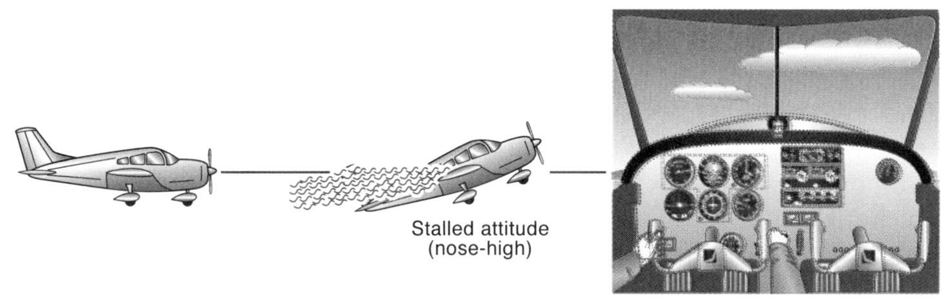

Figure 23-10 The clean stall.

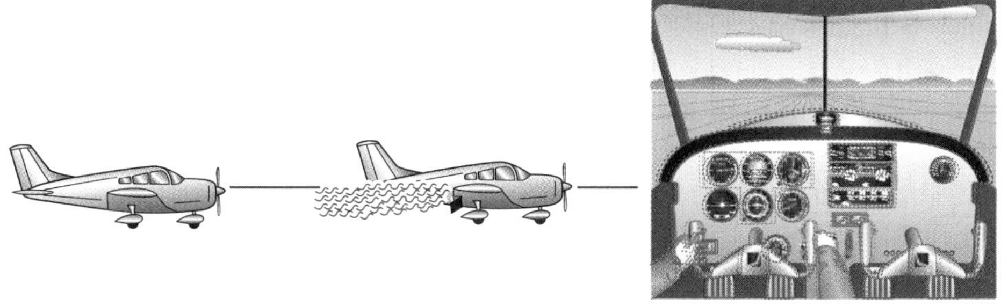

Figure 23-11 The pitch attitude in a flapped stall is much lower.

AIRMANSHIP

Unexpected stalls should never occur. Carry out the HASELL check prior to practicing stalls and stall recovery. Exert smooth but firm and positive control over the airplane. Be particularly conscious of your height above ground level and the area over which you are flying. Ensure that stalling is only practiced at a safe altitude. Note landmarks and the direction to the airport. Maintain a good lookout for other aircraft.

Prestall HASELL Checklist

Stalling is the first aerobatic-type maneuver that you will perform. Prior to doing any aerobatics, it is usual to carry out a series of checks to ensure safe operation. The pilot's operating handbook will contain a suitable check for items such as those in the HASELL check below. Realign the heading indicator with the magnetic compass once the maneuver is complete.

H	**Height**	Sufficient to recover by 3,000 feet above ground level (1,500 feet is the legal minimum).
A	**Airframe**	Flaps and landing gear as desired, brakes off, in trim.
S	**Security**	Hatches and harnesses secure. No loose articles in the cockpit (fire extinguishers, tie-down kits, etc.). Gyros caged (if necessary).
E	**Engine**	Normal engine operation. Fuel contents and selection checked (fullest tank selected, fuel pump on if appropriate). Mixture and carburetor heat as required.
L	**Location**	Away from controlled airspace, towns, active airfields and other aircraft, and in visual conditions.
L	**Look Out**	Make an inspection turn (of at least 180°, preferably 360°) to clear the area around and below you. Begin the maneuver immediately on completion of the clearing turn.

REVIEW 23
Full Stall and Recovery

1. A stall occurs when the streamline flow over a wing breaks down and becomes turbulent and separates. True or false?
2. The stall occurs at which angle?
3. Are published stalling speeds always exact for your flight situation? If not, why not?
4. For what flight situation and aircraft configuration does the published stalling speed apply?
5. How does the stalling speed for an airplane loaded at less than maximum weight compare with the stalling speed at maximum weight?
6. The stalling speed clean, straight and level at maximum weight is shown on the airspeed indicator as the lower end of which band?
7. State the checklist you will use prior to practicing stalls.
8. What is the minimum altitude by which you must complete the stall recovery when practicing stalls? If the local terrain is 2,300 feet MSL, what is the lowest altitude by which you must recover?
9. List four warnings of an impending stall.
10. How may the actual stall be recognized?
11. What is the primary objective in any stall recovery?
12. What is an imminent stall?
13. When do warning devices usually activate?

Answers are given on page 581.

TASK

Full Stall and Recovery

Aim: To fully stall the airplane and then recover with a minimum loss of altitude.

1. Prior to Entry

Prestall check:

H – Height sufficient to recover by 3,000 ft AGL (1500 ft is legal minimum).

A – Airframe (flaps as desired, in trim).

S – Security:
hatches and harnesses secure;
no loose articles.

E – Engine:
boost pump on
operating normally;
fuel contents and selection checked;
mixture & carburetor heat as required.

L – Location satisfactory.

L – Look out: clearing turn to check for any other aircraft.

Begin the maneuver as soon as the area is clear.

2. Stall Entry

Power off and throttle closed (carburetor heat hot).

Prevent yaw and maintain balance with rudder.

Maintain altitude with elevator.

Ailerons neutral.

Continue bringing control column fully back.

3. Symptoms of an Imminent Stall

Decreasing airspeed and noise level.

Controls less firm and less effective.

Prestall warning (light, horn or buzzer).

Shuddering airframe (buffet).

A relatively high nose-up attitude.

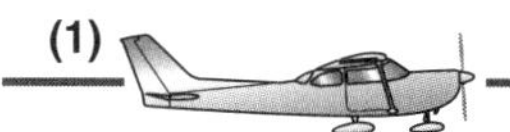

Look out *and clear the area.*

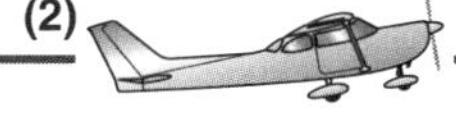

During the stall use rudder only to prevent further yaw or stall.

(3)

Practice stalls in various configurations:
Clean, power off
Clean, power on
Flapped, power off
Flapped, power on
Climbing, descending and turning

Recognize the actual stall:
sink (rate of descent)
buffet
nose drop (full back control)
possible wingdrop/yaw

4a. Stall Recovery without Power

Move the control column centrally forward to unstall the wings.

Prevent further yaw with rudder.

Level wings with aileron if necessary.

Attain safe flying speed.

Resume normal flight and regain altitude as required.

Note: Altitude loss 200 to 300 ft.

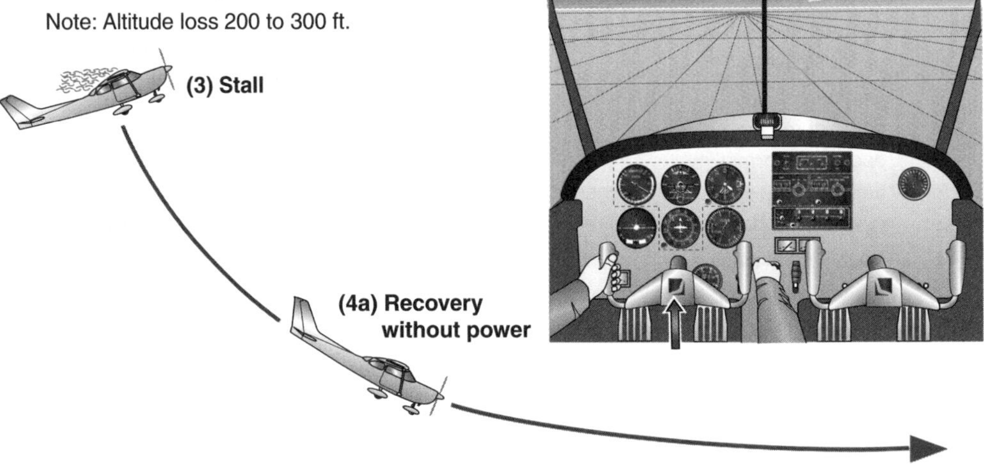

4b. Stall Recovery with Power (normal)

Simultaneously:

Move the control column centrally forward to unstall the wings.

Add full power—throttle smoothly fully open (carburetor heat cold).

Prevent further yaw with rudder.

Level wings with aileron if necessary.

Attain safe flying speed and regain altitude.

Should the wing not drop at the point of stall, keep straight on application of power with rudder.

Note: Altitude loss 50 to 100 ft.

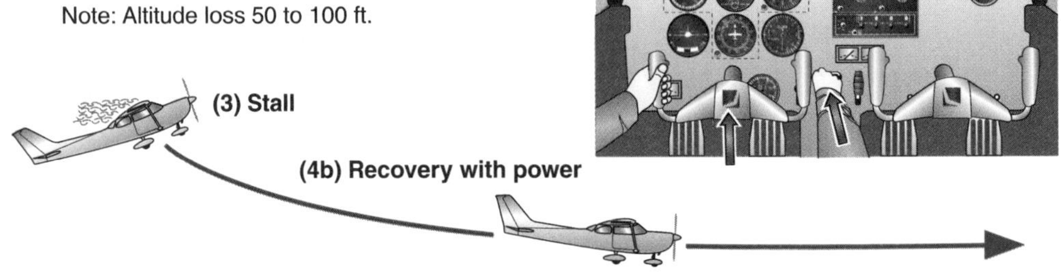

24

Variations on the Stall

OBJECTIVES

To experience stalls and recoveries:

- in the approach configuration;
- with power applied;
- while maneuvering; and
- with wing drop.

APPLICATION

Recovery from a Wing Drop

Stalling speed increases in maneuvers.

The recovery from a stall with a wing drop is really the same as for a developed stall with a wing drop. Simultaneously:

- ease the control column forward sufficiently to unstall the wings;
- apply sufficient rudder to prevent further yaw or roll (but don't try to raise the dropped wing);
- apply full power (use rudder to prevent yaw); and
- when the airspeed increases as the wings become unstalled, level the wings with coordinated use of rudder and ailerons, ease out of the descent and resume the desired flight path.

Stalls During Maneuvers

Accelerated stalls—at a higher stalling speed than straight and level—can occur with the higher g-loading in maneuvers such as turns.

To turn or pull out of a dive, the wings must produce more lift. This is achieved by the pilot using back pressure on the control column to increase the angle of attack. The relative airflow striking the wings at a greater angle causes the stalling angle to be reached at a

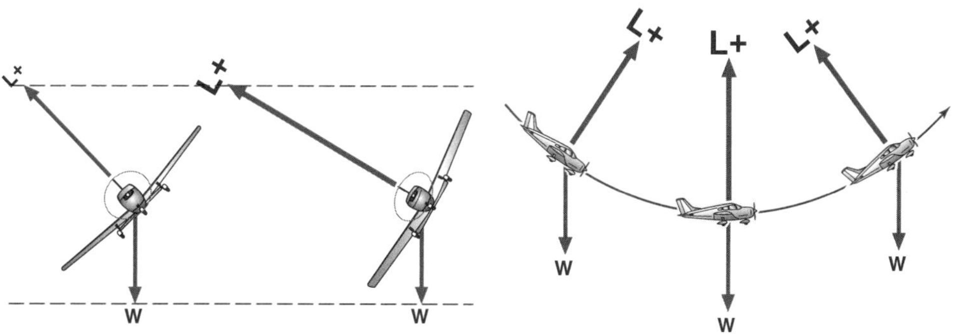

Figure 24-1 Increased wing loading (g) causes increased stalling speed.

Figure 24-2 Flying with crossed controls (left ailerons/right rudder).

higher indicated airspeed. For example, the stalling speed increases by 7% at 30° bank angle and by 40% when pulling 2g in a 60°-banked turn or dive recovery.

You can physically recognize an increased load factor by the increased g-loading, so any time your apparent weight is increased in maneuvers, the stalling speed is increased. When the airplane approaches a stall in maneuvers (say in a steep turn or pulling out of a dive), releasing back pressure is usually sufficient to prevent the stall occurring.

Stalls in a Turn

Back pressure on the control column increases the angle of attack and may cause a stall. Since the load factor is increased in a turn, the stall will occur at a higher speed than in straight and level flight—by how much depends on the g-loading. Stalls at a higher speed than normal are called *accelerated stalls*. Follow the standard recovery of moving the control column centrally forward (relaxing the back pressure may be sufficient) and, when the wings are unstalled, use coordinated rudder and ailerons to roll the wings level. Apply power and resume the desired flight path.

Stalls with Crossed Controls

Crossed controls means that the pilot is using aileron one way and rudder the other way. The balance ball will be well out of center, and you will feel yourself pushed against the same side of the airplane as the ball. Crossed controls are sometimes used intentionally (for example, during slips, and crosswind takeoffs and landings), but if used near the stalling angle, this condition can lead to a stall with a strong wing drop—an incipient spin.

The airplane will be flying somewhat sideways through the air, in this case slipping. If too much top rudder is used (in this case right rudder), the airplane will be flying even more sideways and the upper wing will be blanketed to a greater extent, possibly causing it to stall. This will be exacerbated if the control column is rotated further left, lowering the right aileron and bringing that wing closer to the stall.

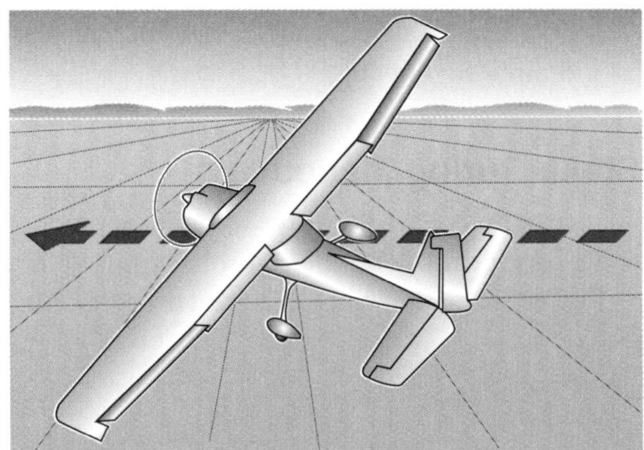

Figure 24-3 Slipping.

Top-Rudder Stall

A top-rudder stall can occur in poorly flown slips.

The result of too much top rudder could be a top-wing stall, with the airplane rolling toward the top-wing (or what was the top wing). This is known as top-rudder stall, and can occur in poorly flown slips.

Bottom-Rudder Stall

If too much bottom rudder is used, the outside wing speeds up, increasing its lift, and the lower wing slows down, reducing its lift. If a stall occurs, the lower wing will stall first, and the airplane will roll toward the lower wing. This is known as a bottom-rudder stall.

A bottom-rudder stall can occur when turning from base onto final approach.

This situation could occur when an inexperienced pilot is turning near the ground, say from base leg to final approach. The turn will be coordinated, with the ball in the center and probably not much aileron required when the turn is established.

The pilot appears to be overshooting the extended centerline of the runway, but is reluctant to increase the bank angle to increase the turn, and instead tries to skid the airplane around by applying bottom rudder. The upper wing speeds up and tries to rise because of the increased lift. To prevent this unwanted steepening of the bank angle, the pilot rotates the control wheel to the right, and now has left rudder and right aileron—crossed controls. The aileron on the inner, lower wing will now be down, bringing that wing closer to the stalling angle. If a stall occurs, the lower wing will stall first, and the airplane will roll toward it.

The correct technique when on base and turning final is to look out, but with quick glances in the cockpit to check the airspeed and that the balance ball is centered. Also feel the balance.

Do not allow a stall to occur near the ground.

Recover immediately at the first sign of an inadvertent stall.

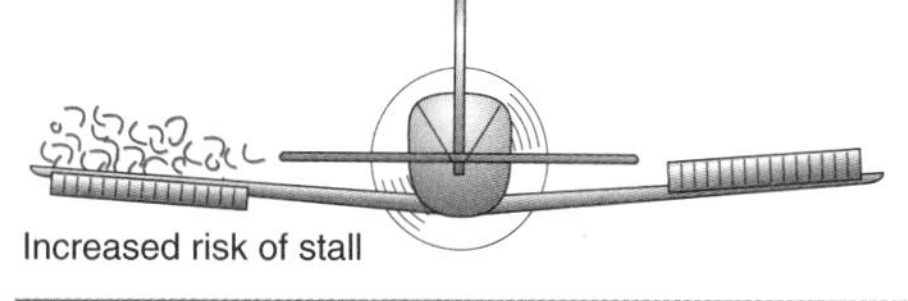

Nicely coordinated left turn (but about to overshoot centerline)

Left rudder to skid tail around, and right control wheel to stop bank increasing—crossed controls (left rudder/right aileron)

Figure 24-4 Skidding around to final approach—a poor technique since it increases the risk of the lower wing stalling.

If overshooting the turn to final approach, you should not try to skid around, but either:

- increase the bank angle (to a maximum of 30°) to tighten the turn; or
- fly through the extended runway centerline at the current bank angle, maintain the turn and re-intercept final from the other side.

Do not fly with crossed controls unless you really intend to—for example, in the last stages of a crosswind approach and landing.

Stalls with Power On

- The greater the applied power:
- the greater the imbalance of lift;
- the greater the yawing moment;
- the greater the elevator power; and
- the greater the masking of stall symptoms such as buffet, quietness and control position and force.

Thus with power on, the stall can be more sudden, more pronounced and have less warning symptoms.

Stalls in the Final Approach Configuration

Practice stalls in the approach configuration.

It is worthwhile practicing the developed stall in the approach configuration at altitude so as to familiarize yourself with it. This should ensure that you never allow a stall to occur near the ground.

A situation in which a stall might occur could be an approach that has got out of hand, for example, full flap extended and a tendency to undershoot, with the pilot raising the nose (instead of adding power). The airspeed will decrease and the undershoot will worsen. If the pilot continues to pull the control column back, a stall could occur. With full flap and possibly high power applied, the stall could be fairly sudden and with a wing drop.

Reduce flap in stages.

The standard recovery technique would be used. The control column may have to be moved well forward to unstall the wings, and care should be taken to avoid using ailerons until the wing is unstalled. The substantial drag from full flap may make a climb-away difficult; gain speed in level flight or a slight climb, reduce the flap in stages and then climb away as desired.

AIRMANSHIP

Be sure to realign the heading indicator with the magnetic compass following stalling practice.

Exert firm, positive and smooth control over the airplane, being prepared to make large and prompt power changes when required. Maintain airspeed in level turns at a low airspeed with the use of additional power. Coordinate the use of power, elevator and rudder. Monitor the engine instruments to confirm adequate cooling of the engine at the high power and low airspeed. Use carburetor heat as recommended. Maintain a safe height above ground level and obstacles if the slow flight is associated with low flying. Remember that a frequent lookout is important in all phases of visual flight.

REVIEW 24

Variations on the Stall

1. How does the nose attitude in a stall with power on compare to a stall without power? How will the airspeed for a power-on stall compare to that for a power-off stall? How will the angle of attack compare?
2. How will an airplane on final approach with flaps extended and a low airspeed usually be trimmed? If full power is applied for a go-around, in which direction will the nose pitch? To achieve the desired go-around attitude and avoid a stall, what pressure must be exerted on the control column? What sort of stall is this know as?
3. What effect does the high g-loadings that occur in maneuvers have on the stalling speed? What sort of stall is this know as?
4. What is a secondary stall?
5. List the accuracies required during stall entry for heading, altitude, bank angle climbing, and bank angle descending.
6. Which wing do you risk stalling if you are overshooting a turn onto final approach and try to skid the airplane around with rudder? What sort of stall is this known as?
7. If you are rough on the controls during a slipping maneuver and apply too much top rudder, which wing could you stall? What sort of stall is this known as?
8. An example of where flying intentionally with crossed controls is a correct procedure is during the final stages of what maneuver?
9. In a poorly flown slip, the airplane is likely to enter what sort of stall?

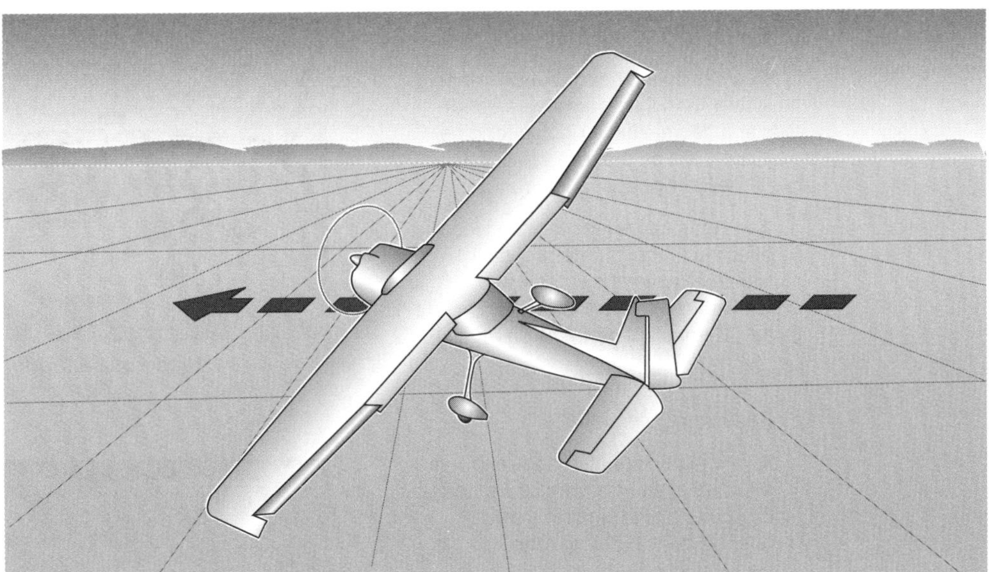

Figure 24-5 Be careful of stalling during a slip.

Answers are given on page 581.

TASK

Stall, Power On

Aim: To stall the airplane fully while power is applied, and then recover with a minimum loss of altitude.

1. *Prior to Entry*

Pre-aerobatic HASELL check.

Look out and clear the area.

Maintain a nominated heading (±10°), or maintain a selected bank angle—20° bank is adequate (±10°).

2. *Approach the Stall*

Leave the power applied.

Maintain heading (±10°), or bank angle (±10°).

Continue bringing the control column back to maintain altitude (±100 ft). The nose will be higher than in a power-off stall.

3. *Symptoms of the Stall*

Decreasing airspeed (but decreasing slower than if no power was used) and decreasing air noise (engine noise will be present, as well as propeller slipstream noise).

The controls are less firm and less effective (although the propeller slipstream over the rudder and elevator may keep them effective, but the ailerons will certainly be mushy).

Stall warning (light, horn or buzzer).

Shuddering airframe.

A very high nose attitude—followed by what could be a very sharp nose-drop with a high sink rate, and possibly a strong wing drop.

4. *Recovery from a Power-On Stall*

Release the back pressure and ensure that full power is applied (to minimize altitude loss).

Roll wings-level and lower the nose.

Resume normal flight.

Stall

High nose attitude

Recovery

TASK

Stall, Climbing Turn

Aim: To stall the airplane fully in a climbing turn with power applied, and then recover with a minimum loss of altitude.

1. ***Prior to Stall Entry***

   Complete the pre-aerobatic HASELL check.

   Look out and clear the area.

   Adopt the climb (or takeoff) attitude and airspeed, and then apply climb (or takeoff) power.

   Enter a climbing turn (15°–20° bank angle).

2. ***Stall Entry***

   Increase back pressure to try and achieve a steep climb (the climb will initially be steep, but keep the same shallow 15°–20° bank angle).

Climbing left turn, power on

3. ***Symptoms***

   Decreasing airspeed and air noise level.

   The controls are less firm and less effective (especially the ailerons).

   Stall warning (light, horn or buzzer).

   Shuddering airframe.

   A relative high nose attitude, followed by a nose drop, high sink rate, and perhaps a wing drop(especially if the balance ball was not centered).

Stall in a left turn

4. ***Stall Recovery***

   Release the back pressure (and apply full power, if not already applied, to minimize altitude loss).

   Roll wings-level with coordinated controls, and lower the nose.

   Resume normal flight.

Note: Practice at an altitude that allows recovery above 1,500 feet AGL. This maneuver is practice for an inadvertent stall on a poorly flown climbing turn after takeoff or on departure, which may be at a low altitude and which you should never allow to occur.

Release back pressure and apply full power

TASK

Stall, Power Off in a Turn

Aim: To stall the airplane in a banked turn, and recover with a minimum loss of altitude.

1. ***Prior to Entry***

   Complete the pre-aerobatic HASELL check.

   Look out and clear the area.

   Enter at a constant-altitude 20-banked turn at an airspeed about 20 KIAS above the normal straight and level stalling speed.

2. ***Stall Entry***

   Power off (carburetor heat hot, Throttle closed).

   Maintain the 20-banked turn (10).

   Continue bringing the control column back to maintain altitude (100 ft).

3. ***Symptoms of the Stall***

   Decreasing airspeed noise level.

   The controls are less firm and less effective.

   Stall warning (light, horn or buzzer).

   Shuddering airframe.

   A relative high noseup attitude, followed by a nose drop, high sink rate, and perhaps a left or right wing drop (which wing depends upon airplane type, and whether the airplane is balanced).

4. ***Stall Recovery***

   Release the back pressure (and apply full power if desired to minimize altitude loss).

   Roll wings-level with coordinated controls.

   Resume normal flight (and check carburetor heat cold).

Stall entry

Stall in a right turn

Use full power

TASK

Stall, Descending Turn in Landing Configuration

Aim: To stall the airplane fully in a gliding turn (power off), and then recover with a minimum loss of altitude.

1. ***Prior to Stall Entry***

   Complete the Pre-aerobatic HASELL check.

   Look out and clear the area.

   Reduce power (carburetor heat hot), establish the landing configuration with flaps extended, and establish a normal 30-banked gliding turn (10).

2. ***Stall Entry***

   Increase back pressure to raise the nose; try to achieve the landing attitude or higher.

Gliding right turn (power off)

3. ***Stall Symptoms***

   Decreasing airspeed and noise level.

   The controls are less firm and less effective.

   Stall warning (light, horn or buzzer).

   Shuddering airframe.

   A relative high nose attitude, followed by a nose drop, high sink rate, and perhaps a wing drop (especially if the balance ball was not centered).

Stall

4. ***Stall Recovery***

   Release the elevator back pressure and apply full power (carburetor heat cold).

   Roll wings-level with coordinated controls.

   Resume normal flight, and raise the flaps in stages if desired (check carburetor heat cold).

Note: Practice at an altitude that allows recovery above 1,500 feet AGL. This maneuver is practice for an inadvertent stall on a poorly flown climbing turn after takeoff or on departure, which may be at a low altitude and which you should never allow to occur.

Release back pressure and apply full power

Spins (Optional Task)

25

Incipient Spin

OBJECTIVES

To describe:

- the progression of the airplane from a stall through autorotation to an incipient (developing) spin; and
- the recovery from the incipient state before a spin fully develops.

CONSIDERATIONS

An incipient spin is the beginning of a spin.

Incipient spin means the beginning or onset of a spin. It is a recovery from a spin before the spin actually occurs, with a minimum loss of altitude. While spinning is not permitted in many training airplanes, the incipient spin is. Recovery should be initiated before the wings exceed a bank angle of 90°.

APPLICATION

Avoid unintentional spins by avoiding stalls.

An incipient spin can be deliberately induced from almost any flight conditions by flying slowly, continually bringing the control column back and then, when almost at the stalling angle (stalling speed for the weight and flight condition), applying full rudder to generate yaw and roll in the desired spin direction.

To recover from an incipient spin, simultaneously:

- move the control column centrally forward sufficient to unstall the wings;
- apply sufficient rudder to stop the yaw and roll (don't try to bring the wing up);
- as airspeed increases, level the wings with coordinated use of rudder and ailerons, ease out of the descent and resume desired flight path; and
- as the nose attitude reaches the level flight attitude, apply full power.

REVIEW 25

Incipient Spin

1. What sort of spin is an incipient spin?
2. A wing is most likely to drop in a stall under what conditions?
3. Flying with right aileron and left rudder, or vice versa, is known what?
4. What is the procedure to enter an incipient spin?
5. To avoid the risk of an incipient spin during turns onto final approach to land, what should you periodically glance into the cockpit and check?

Answers are given on page 582.

TASK

Incipient Spin

Aim: To recognize an incipient spin and to recover before a full spin develops.

1. To Induce an Incipient Spin

Fly slowly, bringing the control column progressively back, maintaining altitude as the speed reduces.

Just prior to the stall, apply full rudder in the desired spin direction and full back control column.

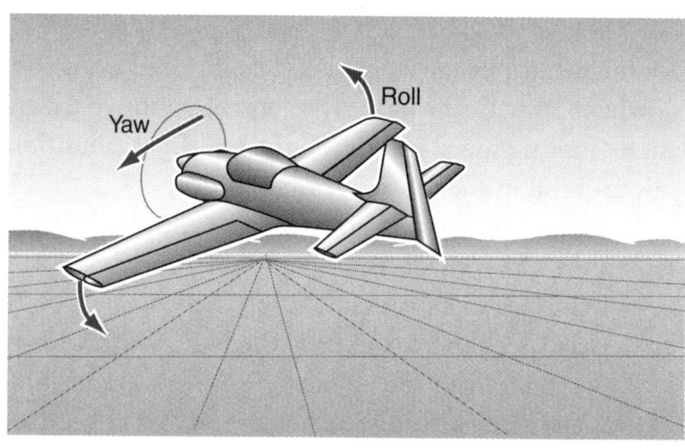

2. Recovery Procedure

As the rotation commences, simultaneously:

Move the control column centrally forward sufficiently to unstall the wings.

Apply rudder to prevent further yaw and roll.

As the airspeed increases when the wings are unstalled, level the wings with coordinated use of ailerons and rudder, ease out of the descent and resume desired flight path.

Apply power.

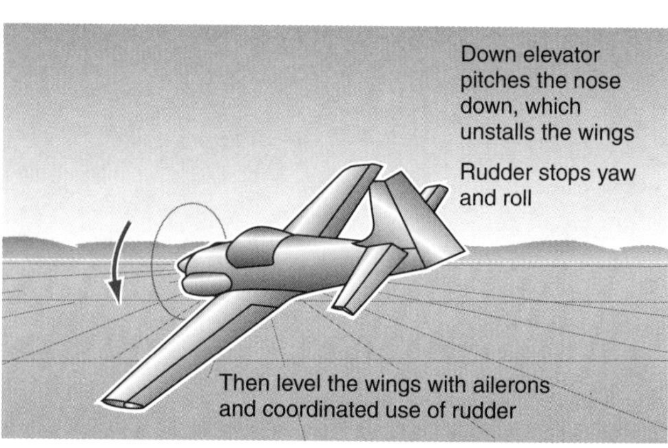

Down elevator pitches the nose down, which unstalls the wings
Rudder stops yaw and roll
Then level the wings with ailerons and coordinated use of rudder

26

Stabilized Spin

OBJECTIVES

To describe and experience:

- the departure of the aircraft from controlled flight through to a stabilized spin; and
- the identification and correct recovery technique for your airplane.

Spinning is an optional training exercise.

CONSIDERATIONS

What is a Spin?

A spin is a condition of stalled flight in which the airplane rotates in roll and yaw and to some extent also in pitch. It describes a tight and rapid spiral descent at low airspeed. As well as the airplane being in a stalled condition, one wing is producing more lift than the other (caused by yaw and roll) and this generates further yaw and roll. Greater drag from the stalled lower wing results in further yaw, further roll, etc. Pitching of the nose may also occur.

Eventually, the aerodynamic forces trying to push the nose down and accelerate out of the stall are balanced by the gyroscopic forces trying to flatten the attitude of the aircraft and therefore increase the angle of attack thus holding the aircraft in a spin. The aircraft has to be held in a spin by the pilot using the controls to overcome the natural tendency of the aircraft to recover.

The airplane is in motion about all three axes. In other words, much is happening! In a spin, the airplane is:

- stalled;
- rolling;
- yawing;
- pitching;
- sideslipping; and
- rapidly losing altitude, even though the airspeed is not increasing.

Characteristics of a stabilized spin include a low indicated airspeed (which does not increase until recovery action is initiated) and a high rate of descent.

Vital elements of the spin recovery are:

- use of the rudder to stop the yaw rate;
- movement of the control column centrally forward to reduce the angle of attack to unstall the wings;
- allowing the aircraft to build up flying speed; and then
- recovery from the dive.

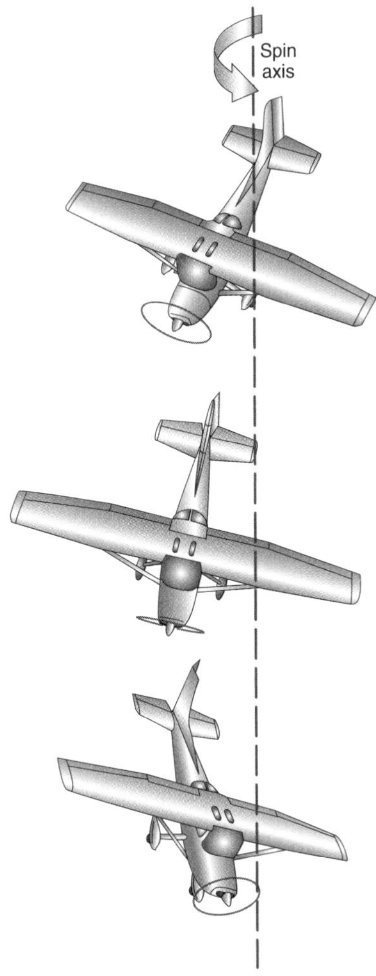

Figure 26-1 The spin.

Autorotation

A well-flown spin will not over stress a properly certificated airplane any more than a normal stall.

The spin is caused by the dropping wing being more stalled, producing less lift, and having higher drag. The two main features of the autorotation that occurs when a wing drops in stalled flight are:

- auto-roll, in which the more deeply stalled dropping wing will generate even less lift, and so will want to keep dropping, causing the airplane to continue rolling; and
- auto-yaw, in which the dropping wing will generate increased drag, and want to yaw the nose of the airplane in the same direction as the roll.

If a wing drops in flight—because of a gust or perhaps intentionally by the pilot's actions—the relative airflow will strike the wing more from below, and so its angle of attack will be greater. The rising wing, conversely, will have its angle of attack temporarily reduced.

In normal flight, at fairly low angles of attack well away from the stall, the increased angle of attack of the dropping wing will cause it to develop more lift. Conversely, the reduced angle of attack of the rising wing reduces its lift. The natural tendencies of the

The spin is caused by the dropping wing being more stalled, producing less lift, and having higher drag. This generates the roll and yaw.

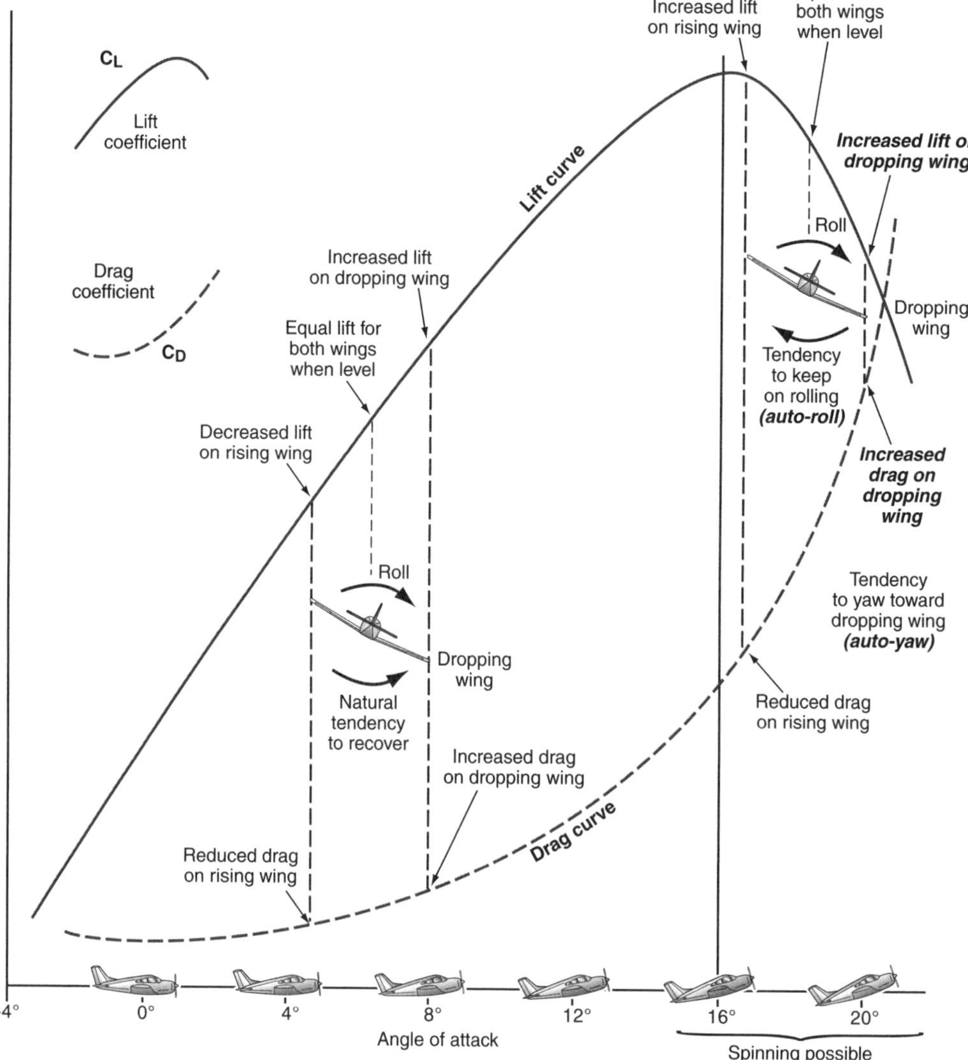

Figure 26-2 Lift and drag effects on a dropping wing.

airplane in normal flight will therefore be for the rolling motion to be damped, and for the wings to roll level.

In stalled flight, however, the increased angle of attack on the dropping wing will cause it to be even more stalled, and develop even less lift. The result is that the dropping wing in a stalled condition will continue to drop, and the rolling motion will tend to continue. This will occur without any movement of the ailerons, so this characteristic may be thought of as auto-roll. The auto-roll effect can be illustrated on the familiar lift curve, which shows lift increasing with angle of attack, but only up to the critical stalling angle of attack, beyond which the lift decreases.

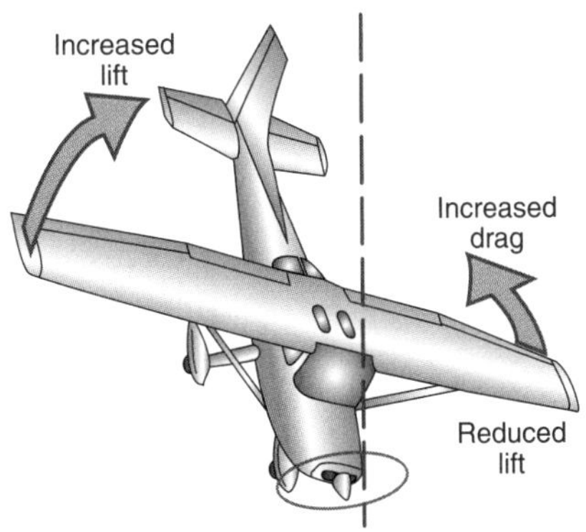

Figure 26-3 When stalled, reduced lift and increased drag on the dropping wing cause autorotation.

In normal flight, when the lift on a wing increases, so does the drag. In stalled flight, however, a dropping wing not only experiences reduced lift—causing it to continue rolling (auto-roll)—it also experiences increased drag, which tends to yaw it in the direction of roll (auto-yaw).

The yawing motion in the same direction as the roll will increase the rolling tendency, making the rolling-yawing cycle self-sustaining. This natural tendency to continue rolling and yawing in the same direction when stalled (because of the uneven lift and uneven drag on the left and right wings) is known as autorotation. Auto-rotation is the basis of the spin. A spin can occur with both wings stalled, as shown above; it can also occur with only one wing stalled (the dropping wing), with the rising wing unstalled and producing significant lift.

Rate of Rotation

If the airplane adopts a higher nose attitude and the spin flattens:

- the rate of rotation will decrease; and
- the rate of descent will reduce (due to increased drag from the higher angle of attack).

Spinning ice-skaters move their arms in and out from their body to alter the rate of rotation. The same effect occurs in an airplane. In a steep nose-down attitude, the mass of the airplane is close to the spin axis and the rate of rotation is high (more roll than yaw). If the spin flattens, some of the airplane's mass is distributed further from the spin axis and the rate of rotation decreases (more yaw than roll). If the nose pitches up and down in the spin, the rate of rotation will vary, becoming slower when the spin is flatter, and faster when the nose position is steeper. Since the nose is purposely lowered in the recovery from a spin, you can expect a temporary increase in the rate of rotation until the recovery is complete.

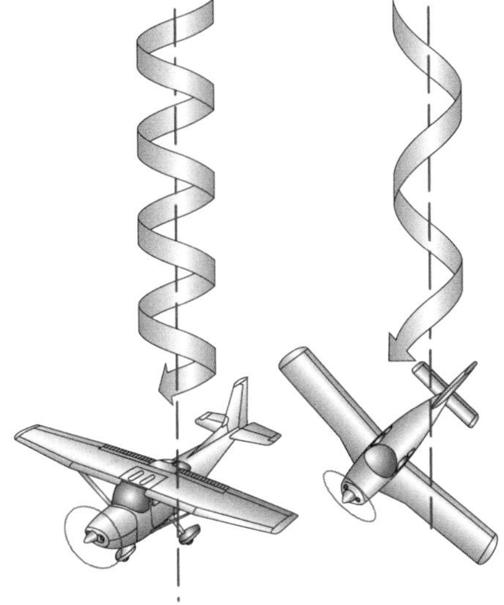

Figure 26-4 A flat spin and a steep spin.

A rearward CG will encourage a flatter spin and it will be more difficult to lower the nose in the recovery. This is one (very important) reason for ensuring that you never fly an airplane loaded outside its approved weight and balance limits. An airplane in the utility category that is approved for spinning must never be spun outside these limits. Conversely, a forward CG normally results in a steeper spin with a higher rate of descent and a higher rate of rotation. It may make recovery much easier and, in fact, may even prevent a spin occurring.

Spiral Dive

Do not confuse a spin (stalled) with a spiral dive (not stalled).

A maneuver that must not be confused with a spin is the spiral dive, which can be thought of as a steep turn that has gone wrong. In a spiral dive, the nose attitude is low, the wing is not stalled, the airspeed is high and rapidly increasing and the rate of descent and the g-forces are high. Because the wing is not stalled, the recovery from a spiral dive is very different from a spin recovery. The great danger in this case is overstressing the aircraft. The airspeed must be contained by closing the throttle and the recovery must be to gently roll the wings level and raise the nose to the horizon (the climb attitude). Once the airspeed is below V_{NO}, the power may be reapplied.

Three Stages in a Spin Maneuver

Your airplane must be certified for spinning and must be within weight and balance limits.

The spin maneuver can be considered in following three stages:

- the incipient spin (the beginning of the spin) is an unsteady maneuver in which the path of the airplane is combined with developing autorotation;
- the fully developed spin (or stable spin) forms as the airplane settles into a comparatively steady rate of rotation and steady rate of descent at low airspeed and high angle of attack; and
- the recovery from a spin is initiated by the pilot who:
  - opposes the yaw with rudder;
  - unstalls the wings with forward control column; and
  - eases out of the ensuing dive.

How a Spin Develops

A spin is a condition of stalled flight, so the first prerequisite is that the wings be at a high angle of attack. This is achieved by moving the control column progressively back, as in a normal stall entry.

Autorotation (wing drop) is essential for a spin to develop and this may occur by itself or (more likely) be induced by the pilot yawing the airplane with rudder or misusing the ailerons just prior to the airplane stalling. Autorotation will commence through the

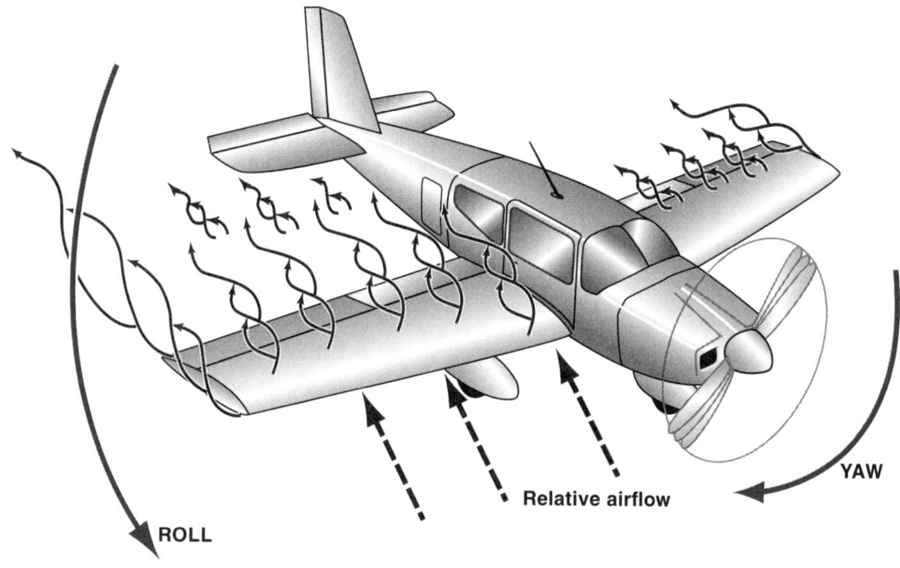

Figure 26-5 The airplane in a spin.

dropping wing becoming further stalled, with a consequent decrease in lift and increase in drag. The airplane will roll, sideslip will develop and the nose will drop. If no corrective action is taken, the rate of rotation will increase and a spin will develop.

The aircraft could seem to be temporarily inverted in a steep nose-down attitude. It may then seem to hesitate before the rotation builds up. It is an unsteady maneuver with the airplane appearing to be very nose-down. The rate of rotation may increase quite quickly and the pilot will experience a momentary change of g-loading due to the yaw and rolling motion. The load factor in the stable spin is not much higher than +1g.

An airplane will not usually go straight from the stall into a spin. There is usually a transition period that may vary from airplane to airplane, typically taking two or three turns in the unsteady and steep autorotation mode, before it settles into a developed spin.

Misuse of Ailerons

Misuse of ailerons can cause a spin.

Trying to raise a dropped wing with opposite aileron may have the reverse effect when the airplane is near the stall. If, as the aileron goes down, the stalling angle of attack is exceeded, instead of the wing rising it may drop quickly, resulting in a spin. This is the spin entry technique on some aircraft types.

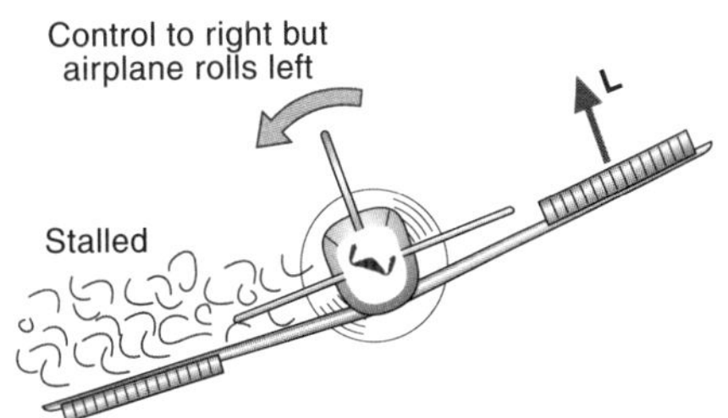

Figure 26-6
Inducing a spin with opposite aileron.

Use of Power

Power may destabilize an airplane before and during the spin.

At the incipient (early) stage of a stall, having power on may cause a greater tendency for a wing to drop, which could lead to a spin. Once the airplane is in a spin, power may destabilize it as the slipstream will tend to flow across the outer wing, increasing its lift and consequently increasing the rate of roll. If power is applied, the entire spin maneuver will be speeded up. It is essential, therefore, to remove power by closing the throttle either before or during the spin recovery.

Flaps

Flaps should be raised for spinning.

The flaps tend to decrease the control effectiveness of the elevator and rudder and so should be raised either before or during the spin recovery. For many aircraft, practicing spinning with flaps down is not permitted, since the aerodynamic loads on the flap structure may cause damage.

APPLICATION

Entering a Spin

It is usual to enter a deliberate spin by yawing with rudder just prior to the stall.

About 5 to 10 knots prior to the airplane stalling, with the control column being progressively moved back and the throttle closed, a smooth and firm deflection of the rudder will speed up one wing and cause it to generate more lift. The control column is now pulled fully back and held there. The airplane will yaw and roll and a spin will develop. The spin entry may require full rudder deflection. If left rudder is applied, the airplane will yaw and roll to the left and a spin to the left will develop. If right rudder is applied, the aircraft will yaw and roll to the right and a spin to the right will develop.

Maintaining the Spin

To cause a spin to develop and stabilize:

- hold the control column fully back;
- maintain full rudder; and
- keep ailerons neutral.

Practicing Spins

During your first spin, you will probably be a little overcome by the sensations and not really know exactly what is happening. After a few practice spins, however, you will become reasonably comfortable and the whole maneuver will seem to slow down enough for you to recognize the characteristics and count the turns.

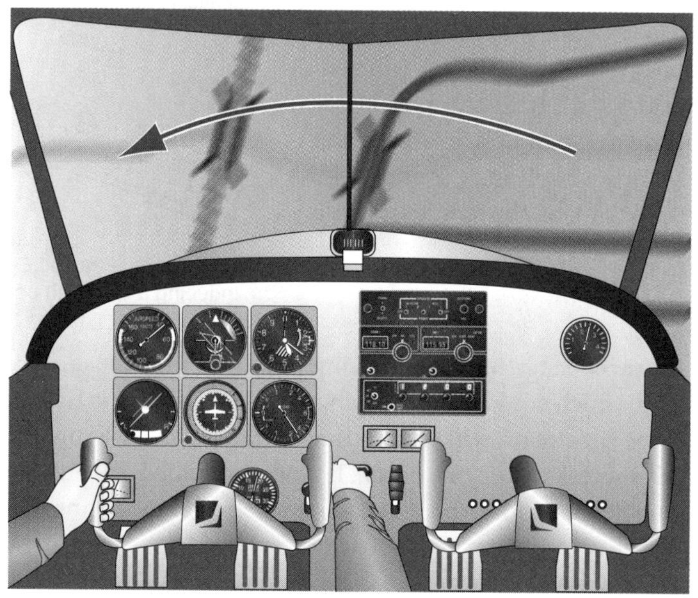

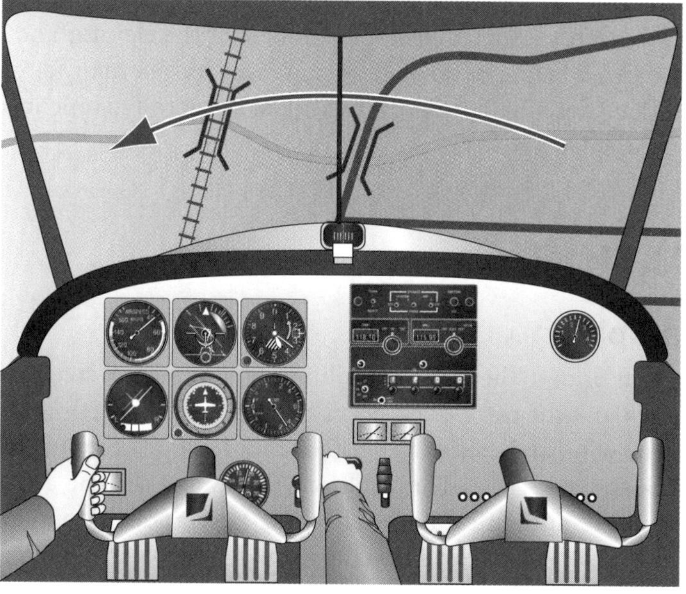

Figure 26-7 (Top) the spin as you first see it and (below) as you will see it.

Recognition of a Spin

You can recognize a spin by the following characteristics:

- a steep nose-down attitude;
- continuous, rapid rotation;
- buffeting (possibly);
- a low airspeed, perhaps oscillating; and
- a rapid loss of altitude.

The direction of the spin is determined by the direction of yaw on entry.

The gyros will topple in a spin, so information from the attitude indicator will be of no value.

The precise spin recovery depends on the spin direction. In practice, of course, you will know the direction of the spin that you have induced. In an inadvertent spin, however, the direction of spin may not be obvious. Remember you need to know the direction of yaw not of roll. Pay no attention to the balance ball in a spin. Your outside view of the ground may assist you, but the turn indicator is the best clue to spin direction (the turn coordinator responds to yaw and roll and so may not be correct).

Airspeed indicator
low airspeed

Attitude indicator
toppled and useless

Altimeter
altitude decreasing rapidly

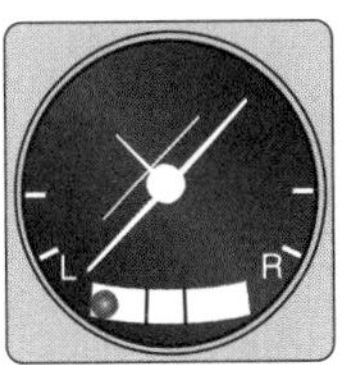

Turn coordinator
unreliable

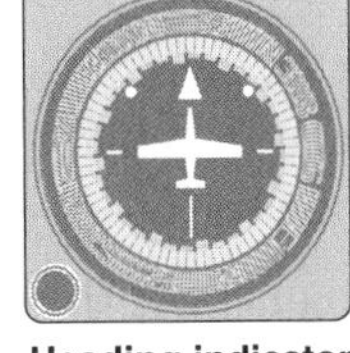

Heading indicator
toppled and useless

Vertical speed indicator
high rate of descent

Figure 26-8 The flight instruments in a spin.

Recovery from a Spin

The technique is:

- check throttle closed and flaps up;
- verify direction of spin visually or by the turn indicator;
- apply full opposite rudder;
- pause (to allow the rudder to become effective and stop the yaw);
- move the control column centrally forward (full forward if necessary);
- as soon as the rotation stops, centralize the rudder (it may take one, two or more complete turns for the rotation to stop);
- level the wings and ease out of the ensuing dive; and
- as the nose comes up through the horizon add power and climb to regain height.

In the process of unstalling the wings, the nose attitude will become steeper and the mass of the airplane will move closer to the spin axis. The result may be a noticeable increase in the rate of rotation just before recovery.

AIRMANSHIP

Ensure that your airplane is certified for spins and that weight and balance aspects are correct. Ensure that you know the correct spin recovery technique for your airplane type (found in the pilot's operating handbook).

Know how to recover from a spin, even though you may never have to do it.

The spin is an aerobatic maneuver and so the pre-aerobatic HASELL check must be performed prior to practicing. A thorough lookout is essential as a spin and recovery will consume a lot of height (possibly 500 feet per rotation).

Commence your practice at a height that will allow you to recover by 3,000 feet AGL. Exert firm control over the spin entry and recovery. You should fly the airplane, not vice versa. When climbing away after each spin recovery, reorientate yourself using familiar landmarks.

REVIEW 26

Stabilized Spin

1. Is the spin a condition of stalled flight?
2. In a spin, one wing is more stalled than the other. True or false?
3. The spin is caused by the dropping wing being more stalled and having more drag than the other wing. True or false?
4. What is the rotation called caused by the dropping wing being more stalled, producing less lift and more drag than the other wing?
5. How does the steepness of the spin of a airplane loaded with a rearward CG compared to that with a forward CG?
6. A spin is a maneuver with a high angle of attack and a high airspeed maneuver. True or false?
7. In a spin, how does the lift produced by the dropping wing compare to the lift produced by the rising wing? How does the drag experienced the dropping wing compare to that of the rising wing?
8. The spin maneuver can be considered in three stages. Name them.
9. Describe the conditions needed for a spin to begin.
10. On some older planes, misuse of which control surface near the stall can lead to a spin developing?
11. In a spin recovery, in which direction should full rudder be applied?
12. To avoid the rudder being blanketed by the elevator, should you pause before moving the control column forward to unstall the wings?
13. When the rotation stops, what change to the rudder, if any, should you make before leveling the wings and easing of the ensuing dive?
14. In a spin recovery, must the wings be unstalled by moving the control column forward?
15. Name two situations during flight near the ground where low speed and misuse of the rudder could lead to a dangerous inadvertent spin.
16. What is the minimum altitude by which a spin recovery must be completed when practicing spins? If the elevation of the terrain is 1,800 feet MSL, by what altitude should recover be completed?
17. Is spinning is a compulsory component of pilot training?
18. For stall training to be permitted, does an airplane need to be specifically approved for stalling?
19. For spin training to be permitted, does an airplane need to be specifically approved for spinning?
20. In term of the angle of attack, what sort of maneuver is the spiral dive? In terms of airspeed, what sort of maneuver is the airspeed? In a spiral dive, are the wings stalled? Is the spiral dive a spin?

Answers are given on page 582.

TASK

Fully Developed Spin

Aim: To enter, maintain and recover from a fully developed spin.

Note: Recovery from the spin should be completed by 3,000 ft AGL.

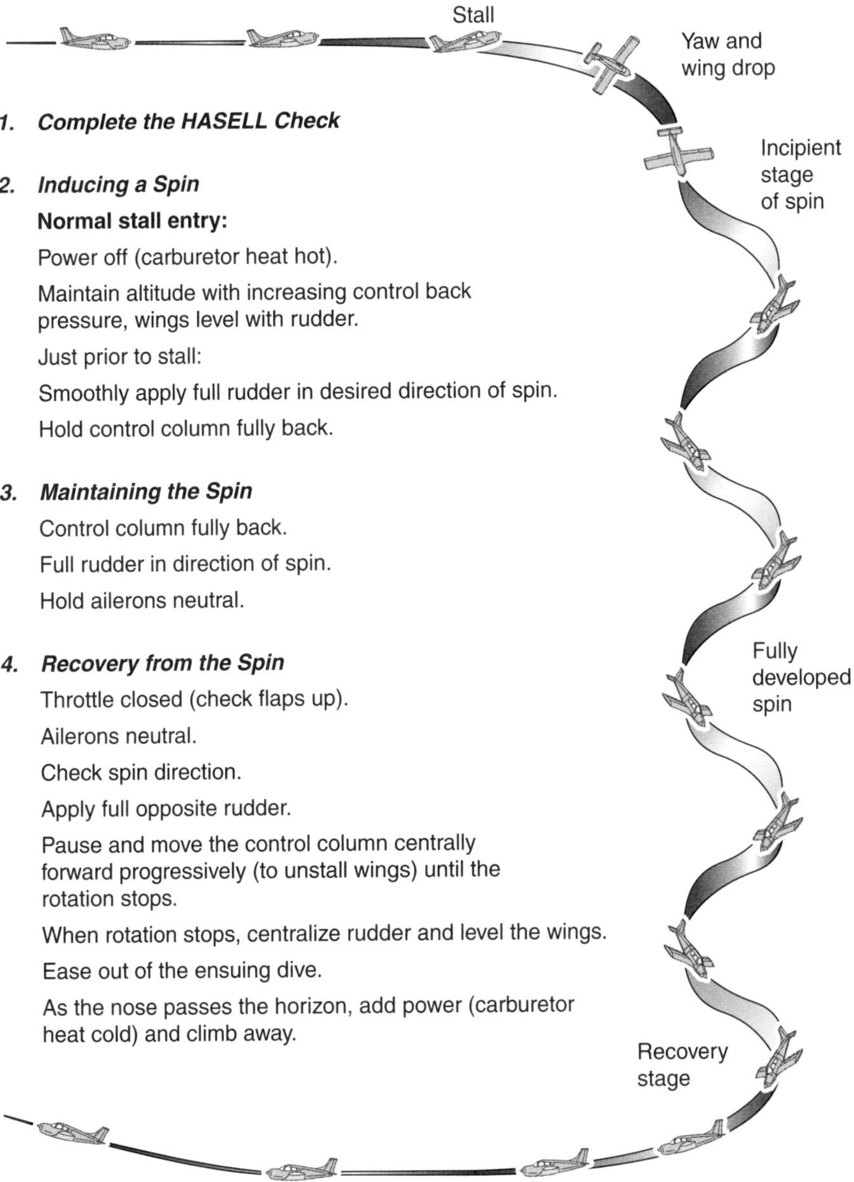

1. ***Complete the HASELL Check***
2. ***Inducing a Spin***

   Normal stall entry:

   Power off (carburetor heat hot).

   Maintain altitude with increasing control back pressure, wings level with rudder.

   Just prior to stall:

   Smoothly apply full rudder in desired direction of spin.

   Hold control column fully back.
3. ***Maintaining the Spin***

   Control column fully back.

   Full rudder in direction of spin.

   Hold ailerons neutral.
4. ***Recovery from the Spin***

   Throttle closed (check flaps up).

   Ailerons neutral.

   Check spin direction.

   Apply full opposite rudder.

   Pause and move the control column centrally forward progressively (to unstall wings) until the rotation stops.

   When rotation stops, centralize rudder and level the wings.

   Ease out of the ensuing dive.

   As the nose passes the horizon, add power (carburetor heat cold) and climb away.

Note: The spin entry and recovery technique in the pilot's operating handbook for your aircraft may differ slightly from this procedure. This is due to differences in control power, horizontal stabilizer configuration and mass distribution. Use the technique recommended for your airplane.

Normal Takeoff, Patterns, and Local Area Operations

27
Normal Takeoff

OBJECTIVES

To describe:

- checks prior to takeoff;
- factors affecting takeoff performance; and
- the technique to safely transition from ground to airborne.

Figure 27-1 Takeoff roll.

CONSIDERATIONS

This maneuver involves:

- preparing for takeoff and configuring the aircraft;
- accelerating to flying speed;
- flying the airplane off the ground and clearing any obstacles;
- establishing the initial climb attitude and flight path while the aircraft is reconfigured (flaps, power and boost pump);
- a normal climb with a turn to crosswind or the outbound track to the training area; and
- leveling and positioning the airplane for departure or onto the crosswind leg.

Run-Up Checks and Pretakeoff Vital Actions

The checks are completed in the run-up bay. As you taxi to the holding point check the wind direction and strength and anticipate the effect that it will have.

Takeoff Performance

Takeoff performance in terms of ground-run distance and distance to clear a 50-foot barrier will be shown in airplane information manuals, either in tabular or graphical form. Most of the factors, except humidity, is considered in performance charts. A head wind will decrease both ground-run and 50-foot distances (improved performance), and a tail wind will increase them (degraded performance). A correctly loaded airplane (at or below the maximum weight limit and with the center of gravity within limits) is absolutely essential.

> **Note:** The performance chart below is extracted from the pilot's operating handbook for the Piper Warrior, and is reproduced courtesy of Piper. We emphasize that is an example only and that you should use the proper performance charts for your particular airplane when involved in actual flight operations or flight planning.

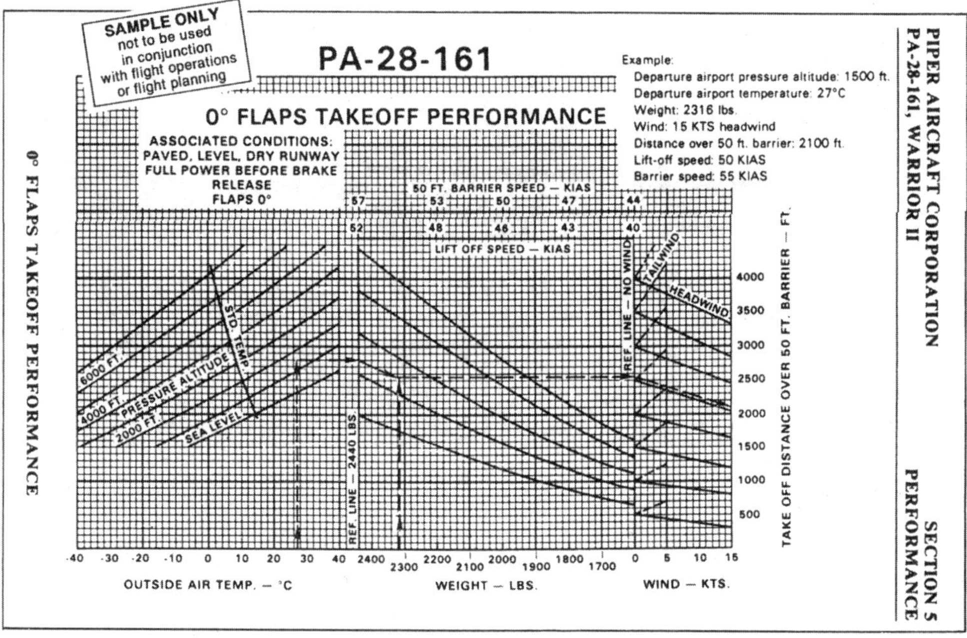

Figure 27-2 Piper Warrior Takeoff Performance chart—takeoff climb to 50 feet above the runway.

Wind Check

The takeoff will normally be into wind, since this benefits both takeoffs and landings. Knowing the wind, you can choose the most suitable runway and work out what the pattern will be. You can determine the wind direction:

- as you walk out to the airplane;
- from the wind direction indicator (i.e. the wind sock);
- from other clues such as smoke or dust; or
- from the ATIS or by asking air traffic control (ATC), who will advise you of the (magnetic) direction from which the wind is blowing and its strength, e.g. 360°/25 indicates a wind from the north at 25 knots (about 30 mph).

Lineup, ATC Clearance and Instrument Checks

Figure 27-3 Takeoff clearance.

It is now common to perform some final actions while holding short of the runway or upon entering the runway. These could include turning the landing light and/or strobes on, verifying the transponder is set to ALT mode, and setting the mixture control to the recommended takeoff setting. An easy way to remember this is "Lights, Camera, Action" (strobes, transponder, mixture). At a tower-controlled airport you will be given a clearance for takeoff, or possibly a clearance to simply taxi into position on the runway. A clearance to taxi into position is referred to by ATC as "line up and wait." A line up and wait clearance will allow you to enter the runway environment, line up your aircraft for departure, but then wait for further takeoff clearance. Often, this clearance is given to expedite traffic flow. Under ICAO regulations, takeoff and line up and wait clearances must be read back so ATC is sure that you understand the instructions.

Factors Affecting Takeoff Performance

Wind

A normal takeoff is made as closely as possible into the wind because it gives:

- the shortest ground run;
- the lowest ground speed for the required takeoff airspeed;
- the best directional control, especially at the start of the ground run, when there is not much airflow over the control surfaces;
- no side forces on the landing gear (as in a crosswind);
- the best obstacle clearance because of the shorter ground run and the steeper flight path over ground; and
- the best position in the climb-out from which to make an up-wind landing straight ahead (or slightly to one side) in the case of engine failure immediately after takeoff.

Be aware of the surface wind.

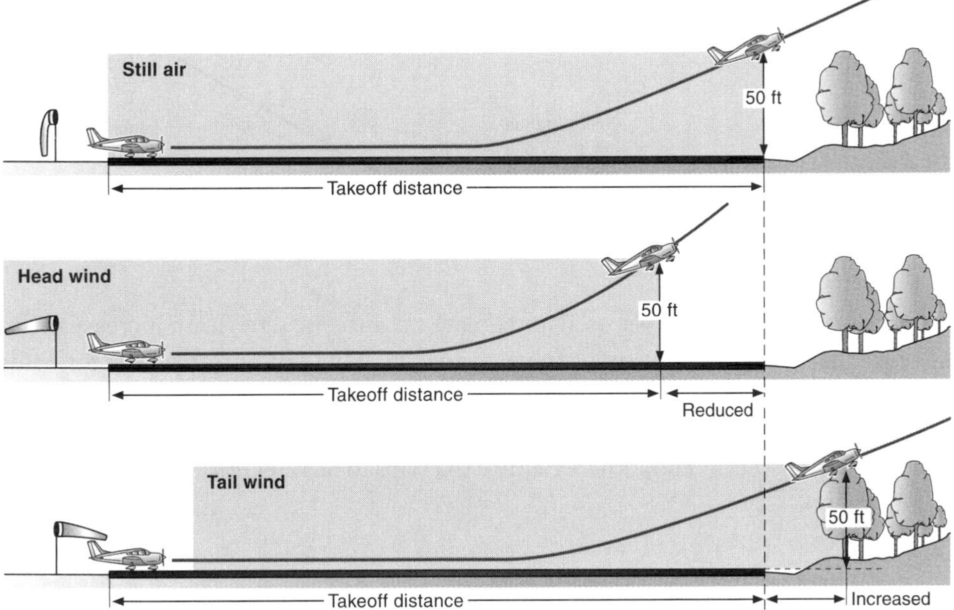

Figure 27-4 Effect of wind on takeoff.

Turbulence

Turbulence suggests some downdrafts and some disruption to accurate flying, both of which reduce the aircraft's best climb angle and rate.

Runway Length

Ensure the runway is of adequate length.

The takeoff performance chart should be consulted if you are not certain that the runway is adequate in all respects. High elevation and high temperatures will increase the runway distances required because of the decreased air density that degrades both engine and aerodynamic performance. Runway upslope and a tail wind component will also degrade the takeoff.

Runway Surface

Any element that increases friction on the wheels is adverse to takeoff performance. Water, long grass, mud, dust, potholes and uneven ground all extend the takeoff.

Runway Slope

Runway slope is very significant. If it more than a couple of degrees then it may be better to take off the other way even with a slight tail wind. Discuss the performance of your aircraft with your instructor.

Flaps

Use takeoff flaps to shorten the takeoff run if recommended for your airplane.

Some aircraft use a small amount of flap deflection for takeoff if it gives greater value in terms of lift than penalty due to increased drag. Your aircraft will have a specified configuration for normal takeoffs. Use of takeoff flap may shorten the takeoff run. Extending takeoff flaps increases the lifting ability of the wings, enabling the airplane to take off at a lower airspeed and with a shorter ground run. It is more appropriate for use on a shorter runway when it is important to lift off at the lowest possible speed.

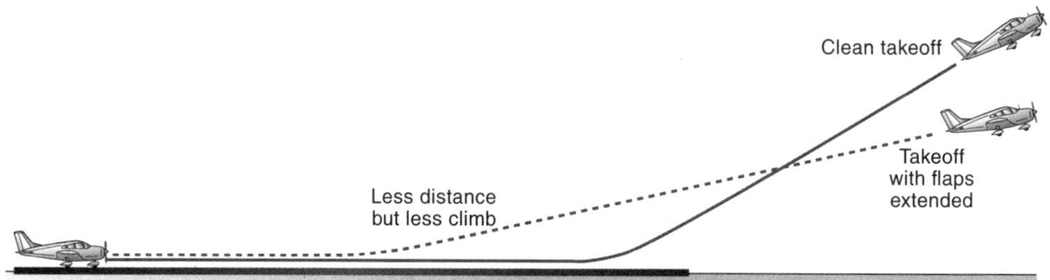

Figure 27-5 Flaps allow a shorter takeoff ground roll.

Landing (full) flaps are never used for takeoff, because the significant increase in drag will degrade the takeoff and climb-out performance. It is an important check for a stop-and-go landing that the landing flap is retracted and the trim is reset for takeoff. For a touch-and-go, follow your aircraft's procedures: some aircraft behave better if the flaps are left until after the takeoff; others require the flaps to be reset during the ground-roll.

Figure 27-6 Flaps for takeoff are less than those used for landing.

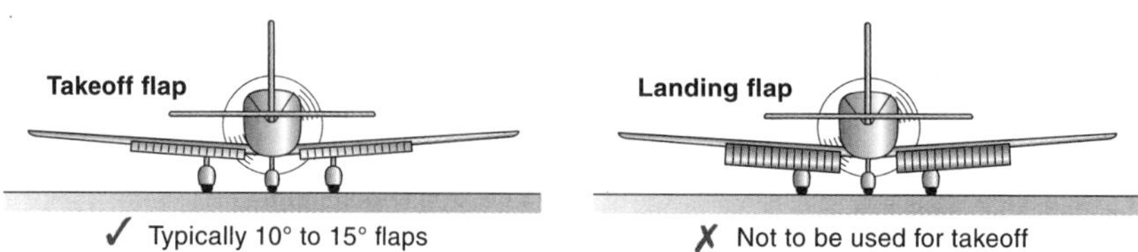

Takeoff Weight and CG Position

The greater the weight the less the acceleration and therefore the greater the takeoff distance. Increased weight means increased wheel friction. Increased weight also requires an increased liftoff speed again requiring greater distance. A forward CG position reduces the power of the elevators and, therefore, increases the force the pilot must apply to lift off. An aft CG position makes it easier. As long as the aircraft is loaded within prescribed limits there is no problem.

Aircraft Condition

An older aircraft will inevitably have some engine and propeller wear and tear and will not produce quite as much thrust as a new one. Propeller nicks though filed out still affect the shape and the aerodynamic efficiency of the propeller. The performance charts assume an aircraft in peak condition. Anything that adversely affects the aerodynamic shape of the wing or adds to the weight of the aircraft will have a similarly adverse effect on takeoff performance. The acceleration will be slower, liftoff speed will be higher and therefore the ground run and initial climb will be extended.

Any foreign matter attached to the wing such as mud and ice will not only spoil the shape of the wing but will add to the weight—both adverse factors. Always clean the aircraft of substantial mud or ice. Washing the aircraft will remove both but, on a very cold day, the water can refreeze before you are ready to takeoff.

The heavier the airplane, and the less dense the air, the poorer the takeoff performance.

Power and Density Altitude

Engine performance reduces with thinner air. This occurs at airports with higher elevations, high surface temperatures and high humidity. The effect is significant and should be checked in your aircraft's performance charts. Additionally, at higher density altitudes, the aircraft must accelerate to a higher TAS and ground speed to achieve the liftoff IAS, hence a longer takeoff run is needed.

Use maximum power for takeoff.

Pilot Technique

The aircraft takeoff distance and climb performance assumes a correct takeoff technique. Incorrect flap or propeller setting, slow power application (more than 2–3 seconds), early or late rotation to a takeoff attitude or holding the aircraft to a shallow initial climb all affect the planned takeoff distance and obstacle clearance. Late rotation also introduces the possibility of wheelbarrowing (reduced weight on the main wheels as the wings lift) and nose wheel damage.

APPLICATION

Pretakeoff

Taxi toward the runway and position the aircraft clear of the runway (or in a run-up bay if provided) to carry out your engine run-up and pretakeoff checks. Ensure that:

- the slipstream will not affect other aircraft;
- a brake failure will not cause you to run into other aircraft or obstacles; and
- loose stones will not damage the propeller or be blown rearward.

A suitable position is usually at 90° to the runway or taxiway, giving you a good view in either direction although, in other than very light winds, it is better to face into the wind.

Figure 27-7
Position the aircraft for pretakeoff check, facing into the wind.

The wind ensures adequate cooling of the engine and avoids spurious RPM fluctuations due to wind gusts during the run-up. The wind can also cause excessive side loads on the engine and propeller shaft.

Set the brakes to park and set 1,000 to 1,200 RPM. This allows the engine to warm up and the alternator to keep charging. Wait for the oil temperature to reach the green sector before increasing RPM for the magneto checks. Check that the aircraft is not creeping forward when you open the throttle. Look outside.

Vital Actions

Taxi to a suitable position for the pretakeoff checks.

The pretakeoff check contains vital actions (*vital* because they will literally keep you alive). Set the parking brake and complete the checklist. You are just about to take the airplane into the air. This is the last opportunity to check that everything is correct. *If there is any doubt, don't go.* Use the pretakeoff checklist for your aircraft. The mnemonic TMPFISCH covers the pretakeoff items well, but still use the checklist. It will typically include the points outlined below.

Typical TMPFISCH Checklist

T

- Trim: checked and set for takeoff.
- Throttle friction: sufficiently tight (to prevent the throttle slipping once it has been set), but not so tight that the throttle is difficult to move.

M

- Mixture: rich and carburetor heat to cold or off.

P

- Propeller: full fine or maximum RPM.

F

- Fuel: correct fuel tank selected and contents sufficient for flight.
- Fuel primer: off and locked.
- Fuel pump: on and fuel pressure adequate.
- Flaps: set for takeoff. Check visually.

I

- Instruments: follow a systematic scan around the instrument panel.
- Flight instruments:
  - Airspeed indicator: indicating zero.
  - Attitude indicator: erect. Set the miniature airplane against the artificial horizon.
  - Altimeter: pressure set and check that correct elevation is indicated.
  - Vertical speed indicator: showing zero.
  - Heading indicator: align with the magnetic compass.
  - Turn coordinator or indicator: previously checked with left and right turns during the taxi.
  - Balance ball: tested during the taxi with left and right turns.
  - Clock: wound up and check that the correct time is set.

- Engine and other instruments:
  - Tachometer: RPM remaining steady as set (typically 1,000 to 1,200 RPM).
  - Oil pressure: normal.
  - Oil temperature: normal.
  - Fuel pressure: already checked if a boost pump is fitted.
  - Ammeter or low-current warning light: charging with light out.
  - Suction gauge: checked during run-up.

S

- Switches:
  - Magnetos: confirm that there are no aircraft behind you and run the engine up (typically to 1,800–2,000 RPM).
  - While at high RPM, the carburetor heat can be tested at *hot*, which should cause the RPM to drop by about 100 RPM. This indicates that the system is working, the warm air entering the engine being less dense and causing a drop in the power produced. An RPM increase during the 10 seconds or so you leave the carburetor heat *hot* indicates that carburetor ice was present and has been melted. At the end of this test, return carburetor heat to *cold*. The magnetos can now be checked knowing that the carburetor is free of ice. If you think carburetor ice may form again prior to takeoff, take appropriate action (see later).
  - Switch from *both* to *left* and note an RPM drop, typically between 75 RPM and 175 RPM.
  - Switch from *both* to *right* and again note the RPM drop, typically between 75 RPM and 175 RPM and there may be a maximum differential allowed for your engine of perhaps 50 RPM between the left and right magnetos.
  - Reset to *both*, when the RPM should return to the original value.
  - Zero RPM drop, a total cut-out (i.e. the engine stops firing) or an imbalance in the two RPM drops (exceeding 50 RPM or so) indicates a problem. Don't accept the aircraft.
  - Sometimes the spark plugs may be oiled up from prolonged running at low RPM. In some cases you can run the engine at 2,000 RPM for a minute, lean the mixture to clear the oil and then repeat the magneto check. Ask your instructor before adopting this procedure.
  - If you inadvertently switch the magneto to *off* during the test, allow the engine to stop and then restart it normally.
  - Close the throttle completely (the engine won't stop) and check RPM (typically 600–800 RPM); then return to 1,000–1,200 RPM.
  - Other switches: check as required.

C

- Controls: full and free movement. Move the control column to full deflection in all directions and visually check the control surfaces move in the correct sense. Be sensitive to the friction and maximum control movement in the control system and be wary if there is any restriction, limit, rubbing or binding.
- Cowl flaps: set for takeoff.

H

- Hatches: doors secure (closed and locked), and no loose articles in the cockpit.
- Harnesses: secure, seat firmly locked in place on the floor, passengers briefed.

A Typical 10-Second Review

The 10-second review prior to takeoff sharpens your performance and improves the odds of a correct response to a takeoff emergency.

A typical 10-second review of the takeoff and departure made before lining up on the runway could sound something like this:

The wind is about 10 knots from straight ahead.

Liftoff speed for this takeoff is 50 knots, obstacle-clearance speed is 54 knots and, when the flaps are up, V_X *is 60 knots and* V_Y *is 76 knots.*

I expect the ground-run to be 1,000 feet, so we should lift off about half way down the runway, and be climbing through 50 feet at the 1,800-foot point, so we will be well above all obstacles.

I will climb straight ahead to 700 feet above the runway, which will be 1,400 feet on the altimeter, and then turn left onto the crosswind leg.

We will be remaining in the traffic pattern, so I expect to remain on tower frequency.

If I have an engine failure on the ground I will close the throttle, apply the brakes, and bring the airplane to a stop. I will set the brakes and carry out any emergency procedure and inform others by radio.

If I have an engine failure in flight, I will land on the remaining runway if sufficient remains, otherwise I will land approximately straight ahead with only slight turns if necessary. There is a large field slightly left of those trees ahead that is suitable.

Lineup

ATC and Radio Procedures

Line up and ensure the nose wheel is straight.

Consider air traffic control (ATC) and radio procedures before entering the runway. Readback the clearance you are given or make a broadcast. Check "clear left" and "clear right" along the runway and on final approach before you enter the runway. Aircraft already taking off or landing have right of way over a taxiing airplane.

Straighten the Nose Wheel

Line up, ensure that the nose wheel is straight and check the compass and heading indicator. Make full use of the runway length available (within reason). Scan the runway and pattern area for other aircraft that could conflict with you. Maintain an awareness of other pattern traffic, both visually and aurally (by listening to the radio). It is good habit to check the wind sock at this time, just before you roll. Also anticipate the effect of mechanical turbulence and wake turbulence.

TECHNIQUE

Takeoff Run

Release the Brakes and Open the Throttle Smoothly

Select a reference point, release the brakes and open the throttle smoothly.

Select a reference point at the far end of the runway (or beyond) on which to keep straight. In side-by-side cockpits, you should view this reference point straight ahead (parallel with the longitudinal axis of the airplane), and not over the propeller spinner.

Release the brakes and smoothly apply full power. A mental count of 1–2–3 will occupy the time required to advance the throttle to full power. Glance at the tachometer early in the takeoff run to confirm that the correct RPM has been achieved and check that the airspeed is increasing.

If the airspeed indicator is not increasing, close the throttle and stop the aircraft. It may mean that the pitot head is blocked or the cover has been left on. Place your heels on the floor with the balls of your feet on the rudder pedals to control steering (and not high enough to apply the toe brakes). Apply rudder by sliding your heel forward rather than by depressing the pedal.

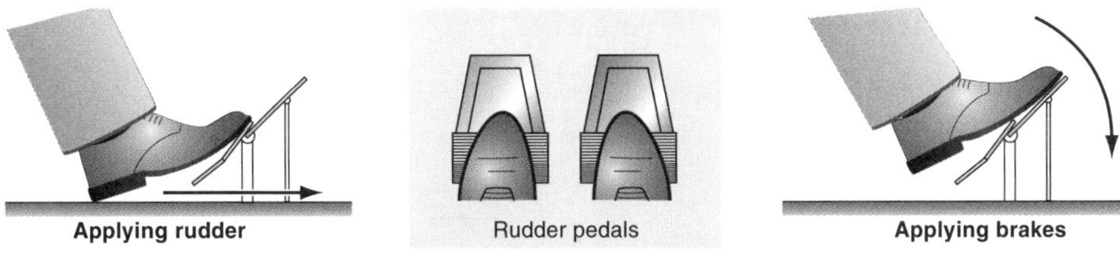

Figure 27-8 Heels on the floor (and no pressure on brakes).

Keep straight and accelerate smoothly in the first few seconds of the ground roll.

Use your reference point at or beyond the far end of the runway centerline to assist you in keeping straight. Even though you are focusing well ahead, the edges of the runway in your peripheral vision and the runway centerline disappearing under the nose provide supporting guidance.

With the application of power, there may be a tendency to yaw because of the:

- slipstream effect on the tail fin; and
- torque reaction pressing one wheel down.

For an airplane whose propeller rotates clockwise as seen from the cockpit, the tendency is to yaw left on takeoff.

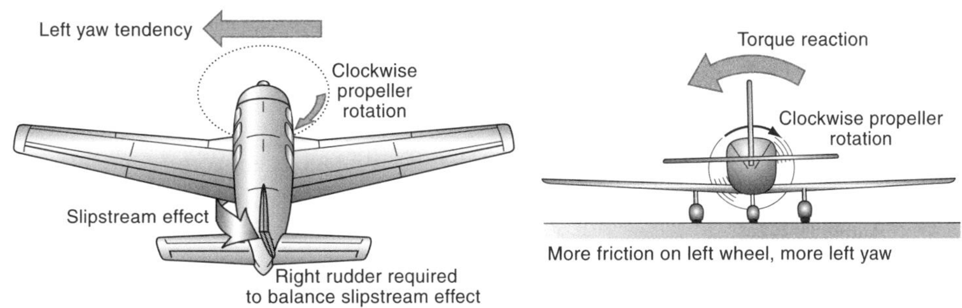

Figure 27-9 There is a tendency to yaw on the takeoff run.

Any yawing tendency should be counteracted with rudder. Large rudder movements may be required early in the takeoff run but, as the airflow over the rudder increases, smaller movements will be sufficient. Just look ahead and keep the airplane tracking straight down the centerline.

Crosswinds might need to be considered if an into-wind runway is not available. Any significant crosswind will tend to lift one wing. The wings can be kept level by holding the control column sufficiently into wind (by a large amount at the start of the takeoff run, reducing the amount as speed is gained and the ailerons become more effective).

Figure 27-10 Keep straight with the rudder pedals.

Protect the Nose Wheel

Protect the nose wheel by holding the weight off it.

On the ground, the nose wheel carries a fair load, especially if the takeoff surface is rough or soft. During the normal takeoff run of a tricycle-gear airplane, hold a little back pressure on the control column. This takes some of the weight off the nose wheel and protects it somewhat. Back pressure also prevents wheelbarrowing, a situation where the nose wheel is held on the ground after sufficient lift has been generated for flight. Wheelbarrowing is bad news for the nose wheel!

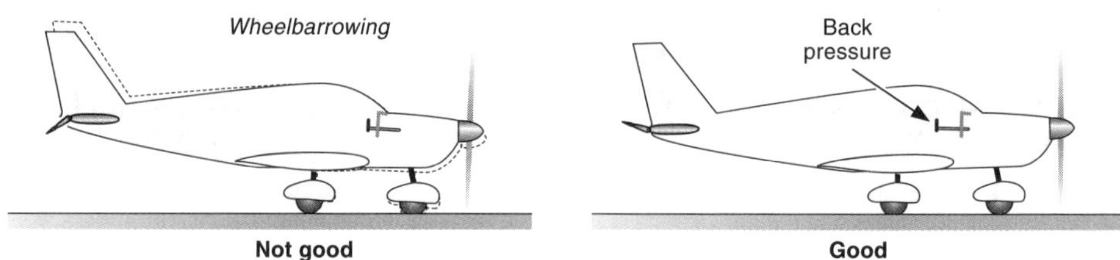

Figure 27-11 Protect the nose wheel by holding the weight off it.

Check the Power

After maximum power has been set and tracking down the runway centerline is under control, glance at the engine instruments to check that full power is being delivered. Engine RPM should be as expected. Oil pressure and temperature should both be within limits. This glance should take no more than one second.

Liftoff

Lift the airplane off the ground when you reach flying speed.

When flying speed is reached set the flight attitude. The airplane will become airborne when flying speed is reached.

If you lift off too soon, the airplane may not fly and will shudder and settle back onto the ground; if you lift off too late, the wheels and tires will have been subjected to extra stress, the airspeed will be excessive and the takeoff will have been unnecessarily lengthened. Obstacle clearance might also be a problem. Let the airplane fly when it is ready.

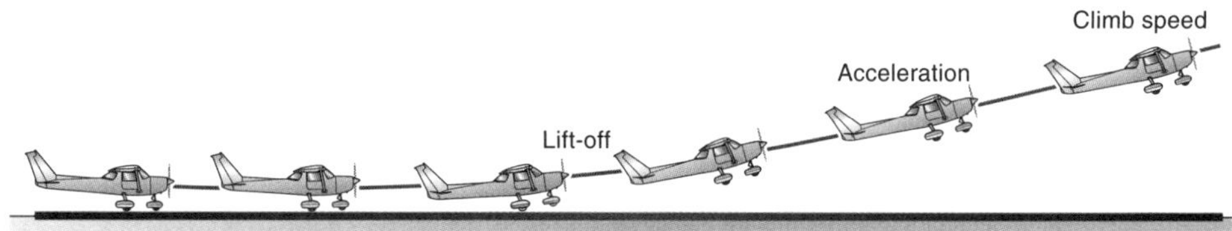

Figure 27-12
When flying speed is reached, the airplane will lift off smoothly.

Controls will feel firmer as airspeed increases.

Figure 27-13 Gradually assume the climb attitude and keep the wings level.

Ground Effect

Ground effect is the reaction of the airflow against the ground surface.

The cushioning of *ground effect* when the airplane is flying close to the ground allows flight at lower speeds than when the airplane is well clear of the ground. It is important that the airplane accelerates to the correct climbing speed soon after liftoff to avoid sink.

Birds know all about ground effect, and it is quite common to see large birds flying leisurely just above a water surface. They may not understand the physics of ground effect, but they certainly know how to use it! Ground effect is the interference of the airflow around the airplane by the ground surface. It cushions the air beneath the wings of an airplane when it is close to the ground, within an altitude equal to about one wingspan.

Ground effect enables an airplane to fly more easily. The runway surface restricts the upwash and the downwash of the airflow around the wings, causing more lift. It also restricts the formation of wing-tip and line vortices, thereby reducing drag.

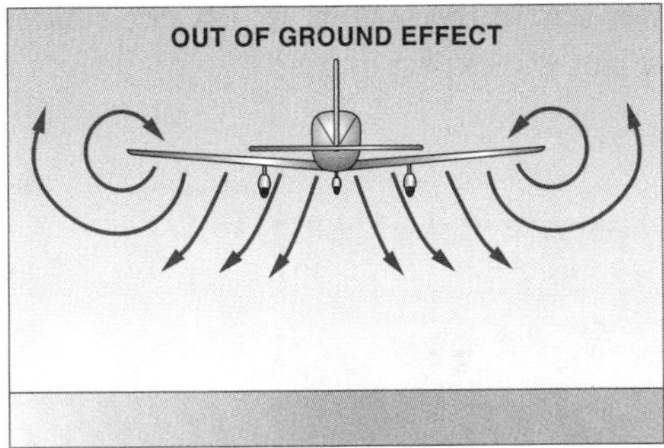

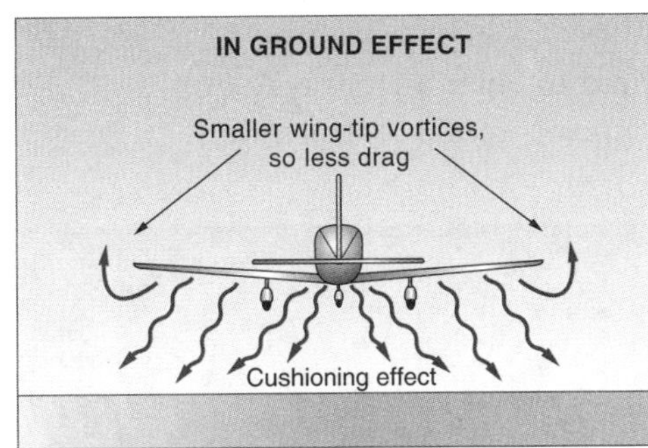

Figure 27-14 Ground effect occurs close to the surface.

When the airplane climbs out of ground effect, its performance decreases slightly—there is a decrease in lift and an increase in drag. In an extreme case, it is possible for a poorly performing airplane to fly in ground effect but be unable to climb out of it because of having insufficient power, insufficient airspeed or excessive weight or drag.

After Takeoff

Maintain the climb attitude, balance and concentrate on keeping the wings level. Do not retract the flaps, adjust the power or complete after-takeoff checks until above 200 feet AGL, at climb speed and positively climbing.

REVIEW 27
Normal Takeoff

1. What three items would you consider before using a runway for takeoff?
2. As a general rule, where on the runway should you take off from?
3. On takeoff, which wind direction will provide the shortest takeoff distance? Which wind direction will provide the best climb-out over obstacles?
4. What effect on the length of the ground run will using a small amount of flap on takeoff compared to using zero flap?
5. What is the power setting for a normal takeoff? What will be the mixture setting?
6. Does the before-takeoff checklist always need to be performed before lining up for takeoff?
7. Prior to takeoff, will a 10-second review covering your planned actions after takeoff sharpen your performance?
8. At a tower-controlled airport, is a clearance required from the tower to enter the active runway?
9. Is a clearance required to enter a runway at an airport where there is no operating control tower?
10. At a nontowered airport should you advise others of your movements on the CTAF? What does CTAF stand for?
11. Is it vital that you check the approach path before entering a runway?
12. Before lining up for takeoff, what items could you switch on to make yourself more visible, both visually and on a radar screen?
13. Should you be aligned with the runway centerline before applying full power? In what manner should full power be applied? How do you verify that full power is being developed?
14. What do you use to keep straight in the ground run? What do you use to keep the wings level?
15. What do we call raising the nose for liftoff?
16. During the ground run, what sort of pressure do you exert on the control column? Why is this done?
17. In which direction will the nose tend to yaw with full power set? In the takeoff, which side rudder pressure can you expect to use?

Figure 27-15 Normal takeoff.

Answers are given on page 582.

TASK

Normal Takeoff and Initial Climb

Aim: To take off into wind and climb in the pattern to downwind.

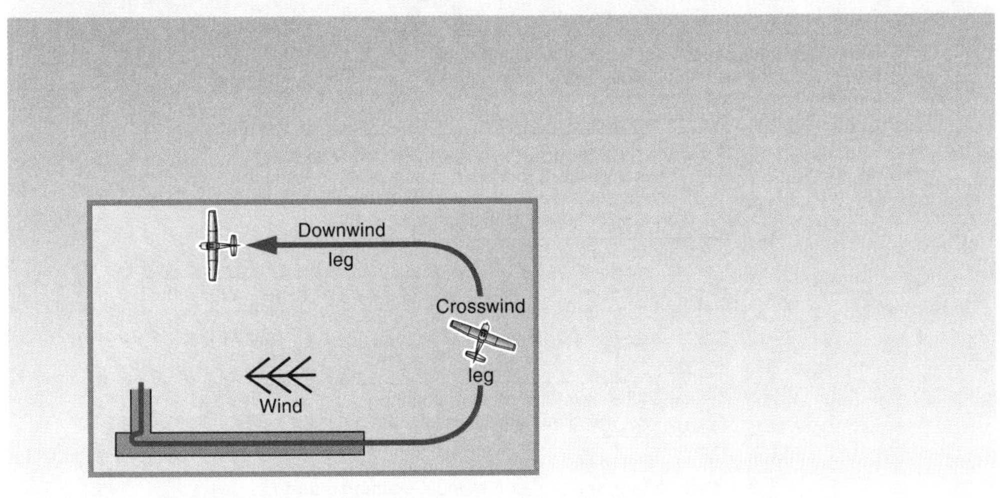
Downwind
leg
Crosswind
leg
Wind

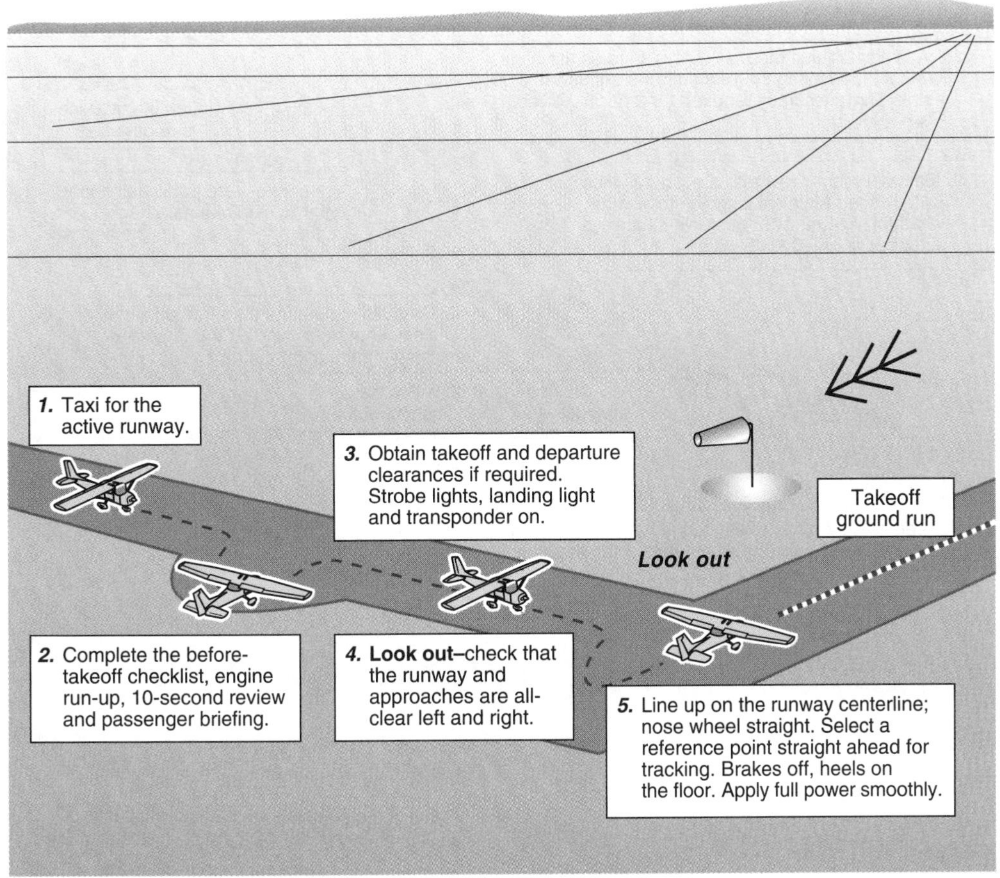
1. Taxi for the active runway.
2. Complete the before-takeoff checklist, engine run-up, 10-second review and passenger briefing.
3. Obtain takeoff and departure clearances if required. Strobe lights, landing light and transponder on.
4. **Look out**–check that the runway and approaches are all-clear left and right.
Look out
Takeoff ground run
5. Line up on the runway centerline; nose wheel straight. Select a reference point straight ahead for tracking. Brakes off, heels on the floor. Apply full power smoothly.

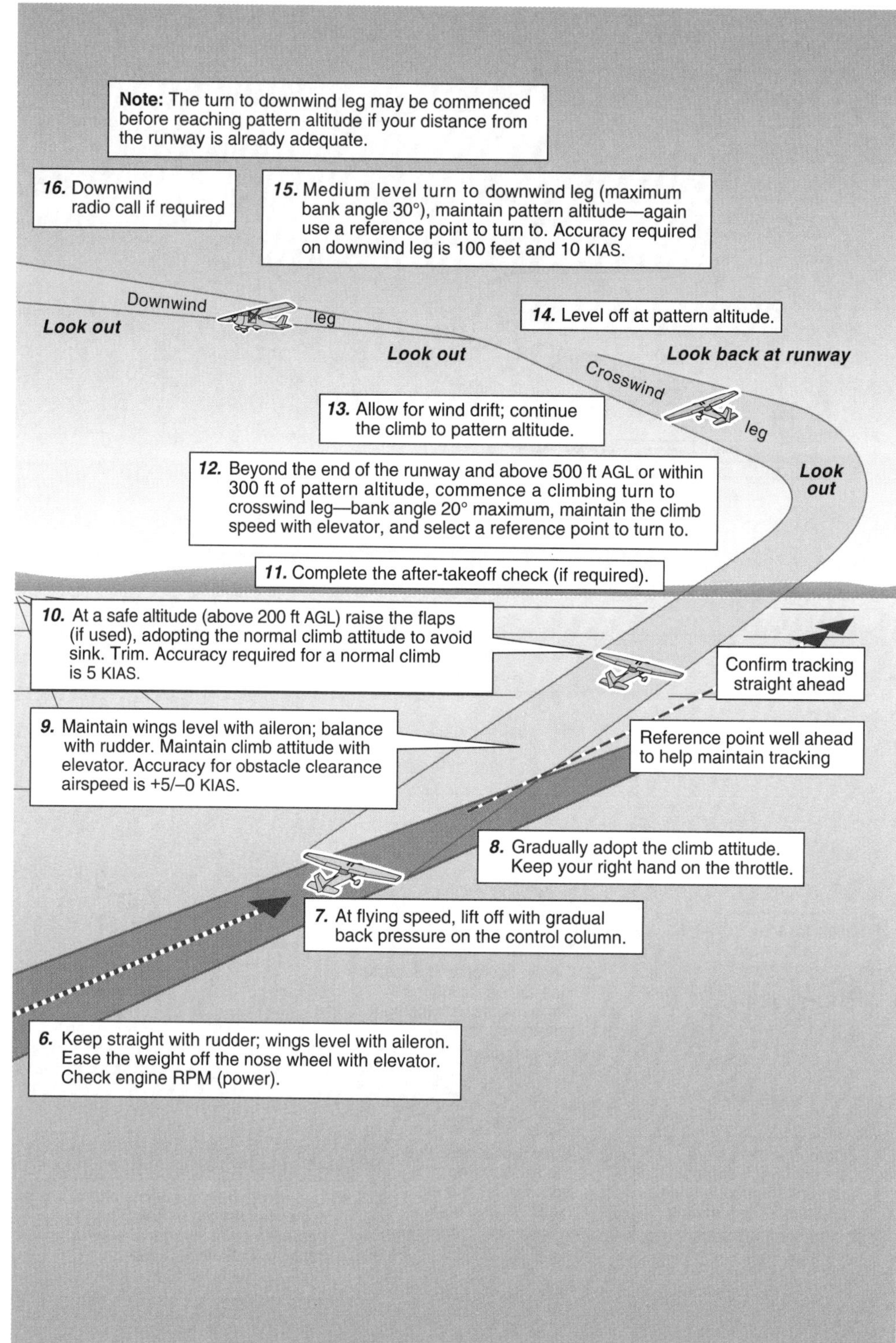

Note: The turn to downwind leg may be commenced before reaching pattern altitude if your distance from the runway is already adequate.
16. Downwind radio call if required
15. Medium level turn to downwind leg (maximum bank angle 30°), maintain pattern altitude—again use a reference point to turn to. Accuracy required on downwind leg is 100 feet and 10 KIAS.
Downwind leg
Look out
14. Level off at pattern altitude.
Look out
Look back at runway
Crosswind leg
13. Allow for wind drift; continue the climb to pattern altitude.
12. Beyond the end of the runway and above 500 ft AGL or within 300 ft of pattern altitude, commence a climbing turn to crosswind leg—bank angle 20° maximum, maintain the climb speed with elevator, and select a reference point to turn to.
Look out
11. Complete the after-takeoff check (if required).
10. At a safe altitude (above 200 ft AGL) raise the flaps (if used), adopting the normal climb attitude to avoid sink. Trim. Accuracy required for a normal climb is 5 KIAS.
Confirm tracking straight ahead
9. Maintain wings level with aileron; balance with rudder. Maintain climb attitude with elevator. Accuracy for obstacle clearance airspeed is +5/–0 KIAS.
Reference point well ahead to help maintain tracking
8. Gradually adopt the climb attitude. Keep your right hand on the throttle.
7. At flying speed, lift off with gradual back pressure on the control column.
6. Keep straight with rudder; wings level with aileron. Ease the weight off the nose wheel with elevator. Check engine RPM (power).

28 Traffic Patterns and Local Area Operations

OBJECTIVES

To describe:

- the procedure and terminology associated with a standard traffic pattern; and
- the technique to fly the pattern onto downwind (noting the attitudes, speeds and power settings for your airplane).

CONSIDERATIONS

Initial Climb and Departure

After takeoff, a straight climb is made on the upwind leg to at least 500 feet above ground level (AGL). During this initial climb the aircraft is in a delicate balance between climbing and accelerating, while the pilot retracts the flaps, perhaps adjust the power, turns off the boost pump and retrims. It is not difficult to fly, but it does require the pilot's full attention. The important aspect is to maintain the visual attitude immediately after liftoff and especially to keep the wings level; otherwise, the aircraft will wander off the runway centerline.

If the aircraft is departing the pattern, it will be turned to the departure heading and the climb will be continued. This turn is made at 500 feet AAL or higher. If the aircraft is remaining in the pattern, it will also turn at 500 feet, although this may be delayed to correct for wind or traffic ahead. Remember the turn can only be made in the pattern direction unless approved by ATC. If you wish to turn opposite to the pattern direction, then you must delay the turn until you are above 1,500 feet AGL or 3 nautical miles from the airport.

Energy, Momentum, Wind

Altitude is safety. It is important that this first turn is done above 500 feet AGL. Turning reduces climb performance. The initial climb and turn are also affected by wind, turbulence and downdrafts. Take into account any high terrain after takeoff and on the departure track. If there is an obstacle in the takeoff climb path that requires an early turn, try to avoid turning away from the wind as this reduces airspeed and climb angle. A turn into a head wind increases airspeed and steepens the climb angle. Try to avoid passing on the lee (downwind) side of a hill.

Normal Pattern

The traffic pattern is designed to simplify the operations of aircraft in the vicinity of an airport. The standard traffic pattern is 1,000 feet AGL—and with left turns. Some airports have other traffic pattern altitudes, perhaps because of controlled airspace above or high obstructions below; these usually fall within the range of 750 feet to 1,500 feet AGL.

Where the traffic pattern altitude differs from the standard, the nonstandard pattern altitude is found in the *Chart Supplement U.S.* For example, the *Chart Supplement U.S.* listing for Sycamore Strip, Texas, elevation 760 feet, shows a pattern altitude of "1560(800)." This indicates that the traffic pattern altitude is 800 feet AGL, which is (800 + 760 =) 1,560 feet MSL.

The traffic pattern is based on the runway in use, which is dictated by the tower at tower-controlled airports and chosen by the pilot at nontowered airports. It is usual to take off and land on a runway that is closest to being into wind.

All turns in traffic patterns at nontowered airports are normally to the left, giving the pilot in the left-hand seat a good view of the airport—unless the airport has approved traffic pattern indicators showing that right-hand turns are required. The *Chart Supplement U.S.* also includes this information, with "Rgt tfc" (right-hand traffic pattern) noted beside the specific runway.

Why Fly Patterns?

Aircraft are flown in a standard pattern to maintain a safe and orderly flow of traffic at an airport, to know where to look for other traffic, to position the aircraft accurately for final approach and to allow easy and safe access to the active runway. The preferred direction of takeoff and landing is into the wind so the duty runway will be the closest to that direction.

Repeated patterns (*closed traffic* or *circuits and bumps*) are a means of providing intensive training in takeoffs and landings. Usually an aircraft is landed and brought to a halt. Later you will be shown the *touch-and-go* where even more patterns can be achieved in a flight lesson. The standard pattern is the left-hand one, with all turns being made to the left. This gives a better view from the captain's seat than with turns to the right. At some airports and on some particular runways, however, the patterns may be right-handed to avoid built-up areas, hospitals, high terrain (especially for night patterns), or to avoid restricted areas or controlled airspace.

Left-hand patterns are usual.

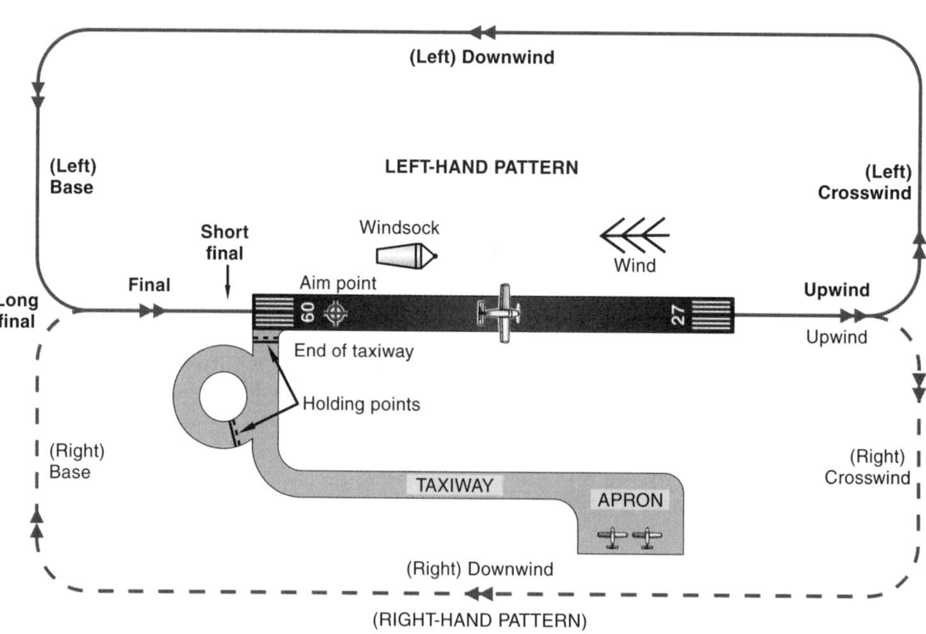

Figure 28-1 The pattern is rectangular.

The pattern is referenced to the runway on which it is based; for example, "join the pattern for runway three-six" refers to the pattern (left-hand unless otherwise advised) based on runway 36. The runway designation of three-six indicates that the runway direction is within 5° of magnetic north. The pattern is rectangular, based on the runway in use. It is also called a *circuit* because it used to have two straight legs and two curved ends—like a horse-racing or speedway track. The curved ends were modified to straight to provide more time to adjust the pattern so now we have four straight legs with rounded corners. In fact, there are five legs as the final leg is differentiated because it is a descending path to the runway.

Pattern Legs

The pattern has *five* legs:

- the takeoff and initial climb in the direction of the runway is called the *upwind* leg because to aircraft is flying toward the wind
- the next leg is called *crosswind*, which it would be if the wind was *aligned* to the runway;
- the next is *downwind*;
- the next, to differentiate from the crosswind leg, is called the *base* leg (because it is the basis of the final approach); and
- the *final* leg is just that (although it is aligned with the runway, it is very different from the upwind leg and so deserves an individual name).

Figure 28-2 Joining the pattern.

Local Area Operations

Much of your early training will be carried out away from the airport, which gives you a chance to develop good habits in departing and re-entering the traffic pattern. It should be noted that procedures for pattern departure and pattern entry vary between countries and, if flying overseas, you should be briefed on them. The procedures here refer to the United States. For flights away from the traffic pattern area, you need to be confident of your:

- local area knowledge (landmarks and airspace restrictions);
- pattern departure and entry procedures for your airport;
- altimetry procedures (vertical navigation);
- radio procedures;
- en route or regular checks to ensure satisfactory operation of the airplane; and
- ability to fly a particular heading using the magnetic compass.

APPLICATION

Pattern Procedure

If the aircraft is staying in the pattern, the turn is made onto the crosswind leg with an allowance for the fact that the wind will be trying to blow the aircraft sideways. The crosswind leg is flown so that the path of the aircraft *over the ground* is perpendicular to the runway and this usually requires the aircraft to be pointed partly into the wind (typically by 10°–20°).

The climb is made to pattern altitude, which, for most airports, is 1,000 feet AGL, and then the aircraft follows a level path. Pattern altitude at some airports may be different for various reasons (to avoid terrain or remain beneath certain airspace), but will usually lie in the range of 750 feet to 1,500 feet AGL.

From crosswind, a turn is made onto the downwind leg and the airplane is flown at pattern altitude parallel to the runway. This turn is important and can be difficult as it may be a climbing turn or a level turn depending on the aircraft's climb path and the wind at pattern altitude. At a general-aviation airport, a *downwind* radio call is made as you straighten on the downwind leg or as you fly abeam the upwind end of the runway. Otherwise, you will make a call turning base.

Abeam the threshold, reduce power and commence descent. Flap is lowered as required. At a suitable point (45° to the centerline from the threshold of the runway) a turn onto base leg is made. On the base leg, the pilot corrects for wind and adjusts the power to maintain the desired approach path. The turn onto the final approach is anticipated by imagining an extended centerline and adjusting the bank in the turn to roll out on final on the centerline. Any drift is allowed for by rolling out short of the final heading or turning slightly through the final heading. Ideally, the turn onto final should be completed above 500 feet AGL, and at least ¼ of a mile from the runway.

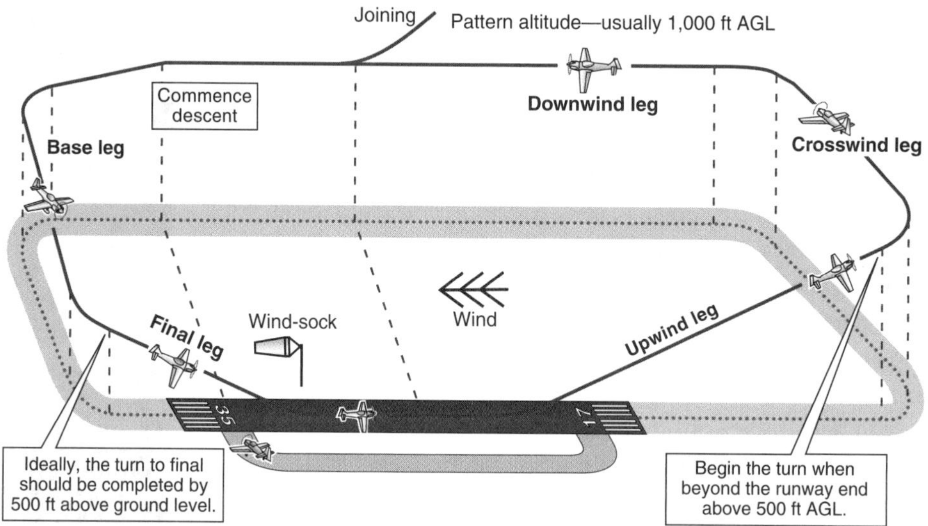

Figure 28-3 The normal pattern is flown at 1,000 feet AGL.

Effect of Wind on the Pattern

While flying a normal pattern, aim to fly a rectangular pattern *over the ground.* This means that, on any leg where there is a crosswind component, an allowance must be made for drift. This is most easily achieved by selecting a reference point on the ground well ahead of the airplane and making sure that the airplane tracks directly toward it. Note that the aircraft will not necessarily be pointing toward it: where an aircraft is pointing and where it is going may be two different directions.

With experience you will be able to anticipate the effect of the wind and make some allowance rather than waiting for the drift to become obvious and having to make a larger correction (one degree per knot of crosswind component is a rough but useful guide). The wind at pattern height may also differ from that on the ground. It will be stronger and typically steadier. Closer to the ground it will lose strength but may be unsteady. Simply adjust where the aircraft is pointing to achieve the desired path over the ground.

Operations at Nontowered Airports

Some airports without an operating control tower have a segmented circle visual indicator system to assist pilots in determining the traffic-pattern direction. The segmented circle is located in a position on the airport affording good visibility to pilots in the air and on the ground, and may be associated with:

- a wind direction indicator (wind sock, tetrahedron wind cone or wind-T);
- a landing direction indicator;
- landing strip indicators; and
- traffic pattern indicators.

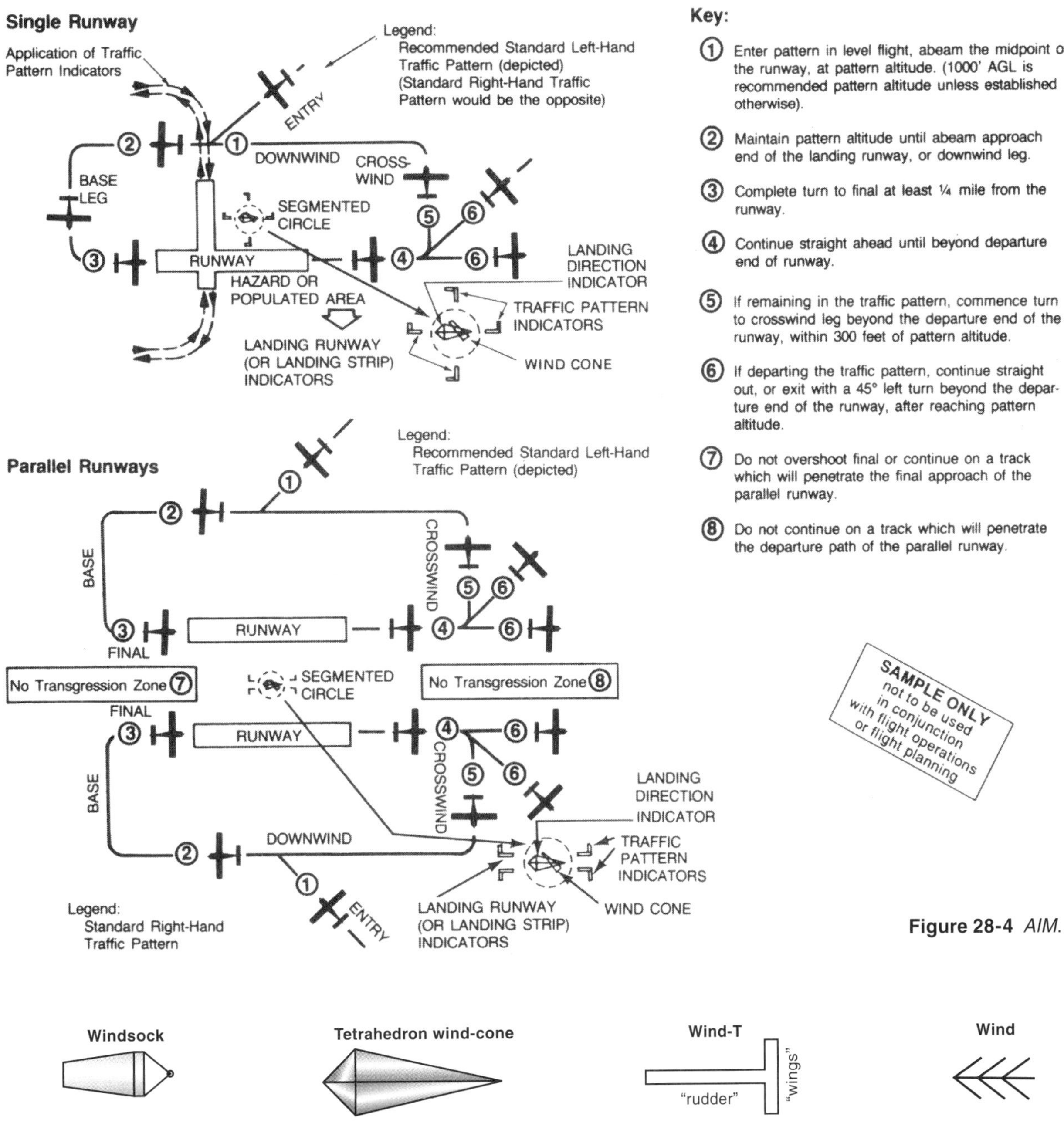

Figure 28-4 *AIM.*

Figure 28-5 Wind direction indicators.

Departing the Traffic Pattern

If, following takeoff, you wish to depart the traffic pattern, you should continue straight out on the upwind leg, or exit with a 45° left turn beyond the end of the runway, after reaching pattern altitude for a left-hand traffic pattern (a 45° right turn for a right-hand traffic pattern).

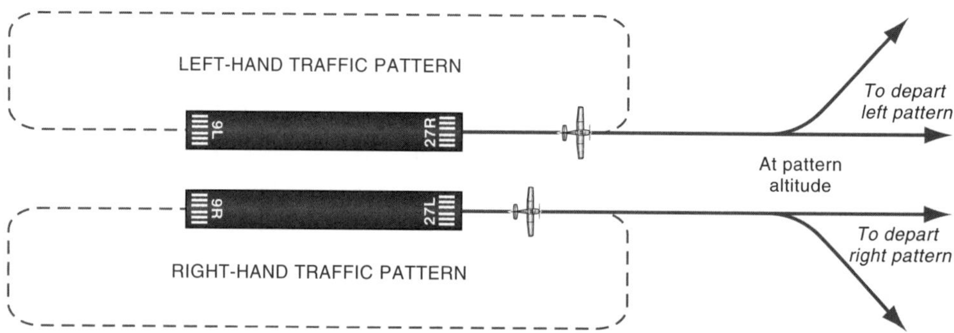

Figure 28-6 Departing the traffic pattern.

Figure 28-7 Departing.

At a tower-controlled airport, follow the instructions given by air traffic control, and make the necessary radio calls to obtain clearance. Follow any special procedures applicable to your airport.

If the tower is not active at your field, then you should plan a traffic pattern departure that will not conflict with other aircraft that are in the pattern or joining it. The recommended procedure for departing a nontowered airport is to either:

- extend the upwind leg as you climb out after takeoff and then, when clear of other pattern traffic, maneuver to set heading for the local training area (or the first leg of your cross country flight); or
- continue climbing out on the upwind leg and then, when at or above pattern altitude, turn 45° left and depart the pattern (if in a right-hand pattern, the turn would be 45° right).

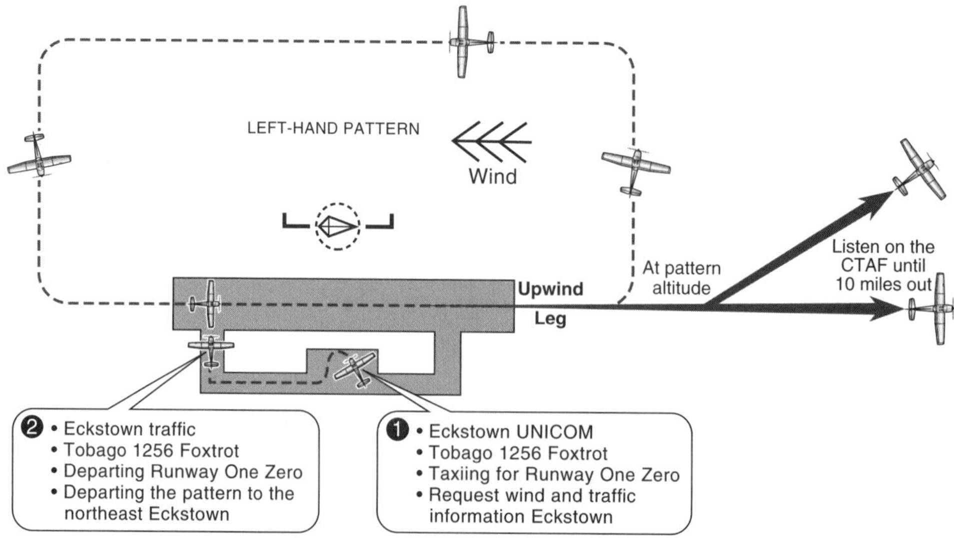

Figure 28-8 Departing the traffic pattern.

Ensure that the current altimeter setting is set in the pressure window so that the altimeter will read altitude above mean sea level (MSL). This enables you to determine accurately when you have reached the pattern altitude. If the airport has an elevation of 890 feet, and the pattern is to be flown at 1,000 feet above the airport elevation, then the traffic pattern altitude is reached when the altimeter indicates (890 + 1,000 =) 1,890 feet MSL. The elevations of mountains, radio masts, and so on are shown as altitude MSL on charts, so it is important for your own protection that your altimeter indicates correctly.

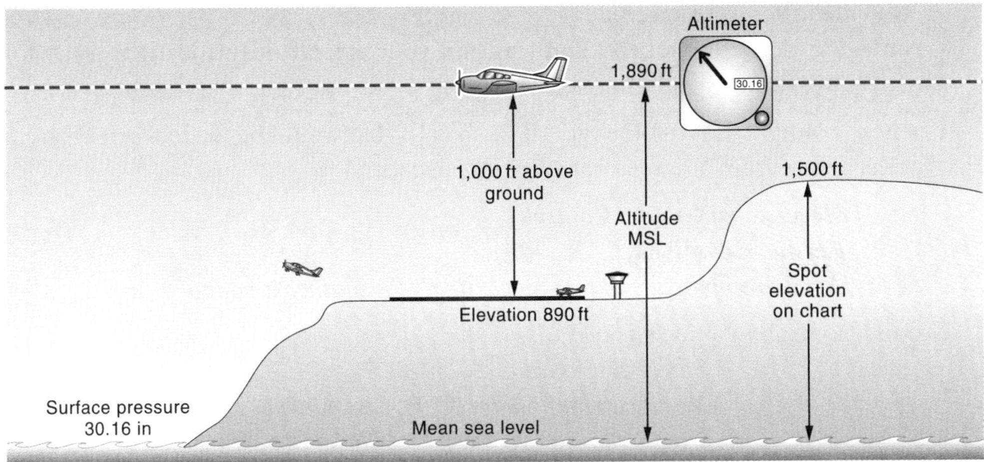

Figure 28-9 The altimeter reads altitude MSL with the current altimeter setting in the pressure window.

Radio Calls Departing Nontowered Airports

When departing from an airport that does not have an active control tower, you should make advisory radio calls on the common traffic advisory frequency (CTAF). This call may be to a UNICOM, MULTICOM frequency, or it may be on the tower frequency, even though the tower is not operating. The facility may respond; the calls may otherwise be "self-announce" calls to which there might be no response, depending upon who is listening.

The UNICOM frequency may be manned, so you can request wind and runway advisories on them. There may be no one else listening on the MULTICOM or tower frequency. Advisory radio calls should be made:

- before taxiing from the parking position; and
- before taxiing onto the runway for departure.

Some typical advisory calls departing a nontowered airport:

Pilot: *Ocean City traffic,*
Queen Air 7155 Bravo,
At Hangar two, taxiing to runway two six, Ocean City.

And:

Pilot: *Ocean City traffic,*
Queen Air 7155 Bravo,
Departing runway two six, departing the pattern to the southwest,
Climbing to five thousand five hundred, Ocean City.

Radio Calls Departing Tower-Controlled Airports

Obtain permission to taxi and take off at a tower-controlled airport. Two-way radio communication between the pilot and the tower is required at tower-controlled airports, unless specially authorized or in the case of radio failure.

Obtain permission to taxi and takeoff at a tower-controlled airport.

When you are departing from a tower-controlled airport, you should:

- listen to the ATIS if available;
- contact ground control before taxi and transmit your aircraft identification, position on field, taxi clearance request, flight status, direction of flight or destination, and ATIS identifier (if received);
- contact tower before takeoff and transmit your aircraft identification, ready for departure, runway, and direction of flight.

The next example shows some typical radio calls that would be made when about to taxi for departure from a tower-controlled airport:

Pilot: *Hagerstown Ground Control,*
Cessna 5345 Alpha,
At city ramp, ready to taxi, departing VFR southeast bound.

Ground Control: *Cessna 5345 Alpha,*
Hagerstown Ground Control,
Wind calm, altimeter 30.05, taxi runway zero two,
Contact tower 120.3 when ready for departure.

Pilot: *Cessna 5345 Alpha.*

Read back any "hold short of runway" instructions from ATC. After you have taxied to a point near the runway and completed the engine run-up, change frequency and call the tower:

Pilot: *Hagerstown Tower,*
Cessna 5345 Alpha, ready for departure runway two,
VFR southeast bound.

Tower: *Cessna 5345 Alpha,*
Hagerstown Tower, cleared for takeoff.

Pilot: *Cleared for takeoff, 45 Alpha.*

After takeoff, continue to monitor the tower frequency, and keep a good lookout for other traffic until well clear of the traffic area.

Joining the Traffic Pattern

Listen to ATIS prior to entering the terminal area, so you are prepared with the runway in use.

You should always know the elevation of the airport you intend to use—found on charts and in the Airport/Facility Directory—so that you can fly toward it at an appropriate altitude. Ensure that the altimeter pressure window is set to the current altimeter setting, so that the altimeter reads altitude MSL. If you are returning to an airport that has an automatic terminal information service (ATIS) broadcast on a specific VHF frequency, it is good practice to listen to the information broadcast when you are some 25 nautical miles out to obtain the weather conditions and the runway in use. When joining the traffic pattern at a tower-controlled airport, follow any ATC instructions that are given to you.

At an airport without an operating control tower, follow the standard recommended procedures that will avoid conflict with other aircraft. If possible, when at 10 miles out request an airport advisory (wind and runway in use) from UNICOM, FSS or on the CTAF, so that you can plan an efficient traffic pattern entry. If no advisory is received, then fly overhead the airport at least 500 feet above traffic pattern altitude and check the wind sock and segmented circle. Traffic pattern indicators, and the landing direction indicator, provide a visual indication to a pilot flying overhead as to the runway in use and the direction of the pattern. Then fly at least one-half mile outside the traffic pattern before descending to traffic pattern altitude.

Be at traffic pattern altitude at least one-half mile before reaching and entering the pattern from a 45° angle to the downwind leg.

Be 500 feet above traffic pattern altitude when crossing the airport.

Set the altimeter (local pressure) correctly.

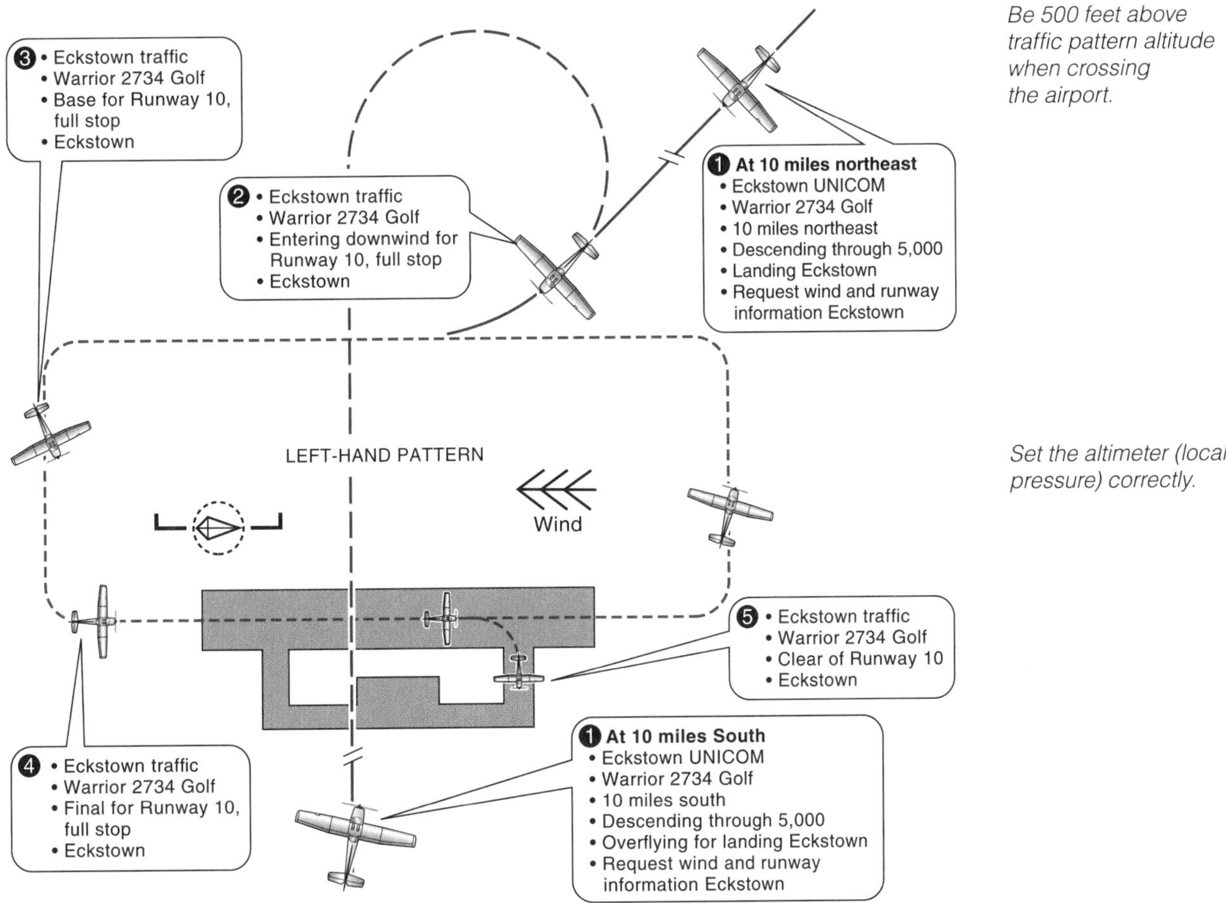

3 • Eckstown traffic
• Warrior 2734 Golf
• Base for Runway 10, full stop
• Eckstown
2 • Eckstown traffic
• Warrior 2734 Golf
• Entering downwind for Runway 10, full stop
• Eckstown
1 At 10 miles northeast
• Eckstown UNICOM
• Warrior 2734 Golf
• 10 miles northeast
• Descending through 5,000
• Landing Eckstown
• Request wind and runway information Eckstown
LEFT-HAND PATTERN
Wind
5 • Eckstown traffic
• Warrior 2734 Golf
• Clear of Runway 10
• Eckstown
4 • Eckstown traffic
• Warrior 2734 Golf
• Final for Runway 10, full stop
• Eckstown
1 At 10 miles South
• Eckstown UNICOM
• Warrior 2734 Golf
• 10 miles south
• Descending through 5,000
• Overflying for landing Eckstown
• Request wind and runway information Eckstown

Figure 28-10 Entering the pattern at a nontowered airport.

Obey the right-of-way rules in the traffic pattern and keep adequate spacing from other aircraft. Make small S-turns to assist with spacing or widen out if necessary, but do not make any unexpected or drastic maneuvers such as a 360° turn (except in an emergency of course).

On downwind and base legs, keep an eye out for other aircraft in the landing sequence, especially those that might be making a straight-in approach, possibly an IFR (Instrument Flight Rules) aircraft following a let down through the clouds.

On approach, an aircraft at the lower altitude has right of way, but should not take advantage of this right to cut in front of or overtake another aircraft.

Radio Calls Arriving at Nontowered Airports

When you are in flight and approaching a nontowered airport, you should make advisory radio calls:

- 10 miles out;
- entering downwind leg;
- on base leg;
- on final; and
- on leaving the runway after you have landed.

Some typical advisory calls inbound to a nontowered airport:

Pilot: *Ocean City traffic,*
Apache 225 Zulu, 10 miles south,
Descending through three thousand to enter downwind,
Runway one seven at Ocean City.

Pilot: *Ocean City traffic,*
Apache 225 Zulu,
Entering downwind runway one seven at Ocean City.

Pilot: *Ocean City traffic,*
Apache 225 Zulu, turning base runway one seven at Ocean City.

Pilot: *Ocean City traffic,*
Apache 225 Zulu, final runway one seven full stop at Ocean City.

Pilot: *Ocean City traffic,*
Apache 225 Zulu, clear of runway one seven at Ocean City.

Note: You can cancel a flight plan filed with FSS on the manned FSS frequency, but not on UNICOM or MULTICOM (which are non-FAA frequencies).

Radio Calls Arriving at Tower-Controlled Airports

When you are in flight and approaching a towered airport, you should:

- at 25 miles out, listen to the ATIS, and monitor the tower frequency; and
- at 15 miles out, contact the tower with aircraft type, identification, position, altitude and intentions, then respond to any instructions.

After landing and taxiing clear of the runway, you should contact ground control when directed, and advise "clear of the active." If you are unfamiliar with the airport, you should also request taxiing instructions. Some typical radio calls with the tower controller at a tower-controlled airport at 15 miles out:

Pilot: *Hagerstown Tower,*
Cessna 5345 Alpha,
Fifteen miles southeast at two thousand five hundred,
Landing Hagerstown.

Pilot: *Cessna 5345 Alpha,*
Hagerstown Tower,
Runway two in use, wind calm, altimeter 30.04,
Enter left downwind, report turning left base.

You join on the downwind leg of the left traffic pattern, and then call as instructed when turning to base leg:

Pilot: *Cessna 5345 Alpha,*
Turning left base runway two.

Tower: *Cessna 45 Alpha,*
Cleared to land.

Pilot: *Cleared to land 45 Alpha.*

The preferred procedure for closing a flight plan filed with FSS is to contact an FSS by phone or radio and request that your plan be closed. You can also close a flight plan by requesting an ATC facility (tower or ground) to do so with the FSS designated on your flight plan.

You land and then taxi straight ahead on the runway to the first safe taxiway, to clear the active runway. Clear of the runway, you change frequency and call ground control when directed to do so.

Pilot: *Hagerstown Ground Control,*
Cessna 5345 Alpha,
Clear of runway two,
Request taxi instructions to city ramp,
Unfamiliar with airport.

Ground Control: *45 Alpha, Taxi to city ramp, continue straight ahead,*
Turn right at the first intersection.

Pilot: *45 Alpha.*

TECHNIQUE

Climb-Out to Pattern Altitude

During the climb:

- look out, both at the horizon to check your attitude and your tracking, and to look for other aircraft;
- keep the wings level;
- maintain balance;
- hold the nose attitude in the correct position relative to the horizon for the climb-out, glancing at the airspeed indicator to confirm that climb speed has been achieved; and
- trim.

At a safe height (say, 200 or 300 feet AGL), retract the takeoff flaps (if used). During the climb following takeoff, look out to check your attitude and to check for other aircraft. Confirm that you have achieved the desired climb speed and adjust the attitude if necessary. After the airplane has settled into a steady climb, trim out any residual control pressure.

The procedure for aircraft that have a fuel pump switched on for takeoff is to switch it off at a safe altitude (say, 500 feet AGL). Then check that fuel pressure remains satisfactory. In more advanced airplanes with a retractable landing gear, the wheels will be raised once a positive climb is established after liftoff.

If your pilot's operating handbook calls for an after-takeoff check (with respect to flaps, power and fuel pump for instance), then it would be appropriate to perform this check when you are established in the climb-out (above 200 feet AGL). Allow for sink as the flaps are retracted. As you climb, look out to check your attitude and scan ahead, above and to either side. Check your reference point to confirm that you are tracking on the extended centerline of the runway and not drifting to one side. At 500 feet AGL, first scan the area into which you will be turning and then turn (usually left) onto the crosswind leg using a normal climbing turn (bank angle 15°). Balance with rudder and maintain climb speed with elevator. Selecting a new reference point will assist you to track correctly on this crosswind leg. Allow for drift.

Anticipate reaching pattern height and, as you approach it, start lowering the nose to the cruise attitude. To level off from a climb, use APPT:

A	**Attitude**	Lower the nose to the low-speed straight and level attitude.
P	**Pause**	Allow the speed to increase to the desired airspeed.
P	**Power**	Reduce power to maintain the desired airspeed.
T	**Trim**	Trim.

Downwind Leg

Check that the area is clear of other traffic and turn onto the downwind leg, selecting a reference point well ahead on which to parallel the runway. You may be required to make a radio call on the downwind leg as you pass abeam the upwind end of the runway (i.e. the climb-out end of the runway).

Allow for wind to achieve pattern over the ground.

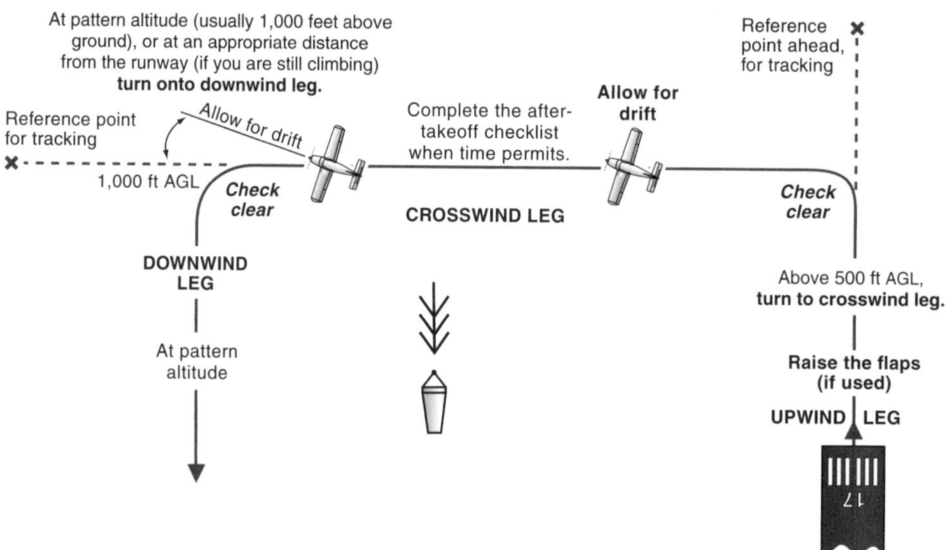

Figure 28-11 From takeoff to downwind.

AIRMANSHIP

Maintain a frequent lookout prior to entering the runway and in the pattern. The takeoff run, liftoff and climb-out to pattern altitude is one continuous maneuver that you should endeavor to fly smoothly, with firm control over the airplane.

Hold your heading accurately (keep the wings level and the airplane balanced and in trim), and adjust the pitch attitude to hold the climb-out speed as closely as possible, but certainly within 5 knots.

Fly an accurate pattern and follow the basic rules of the air. Know the attitudes, configurations and power settings for your airplane.

Use the airplane lights to make yourself visible in the terminal area.

Use your rotating beacon, strobe lights, landing lights and position lights, as appropriate, to make your airplane as visible as possible to other aircraft in the vicinity of an airport. This will reduce the risk of conflict.

When on the ground and clear of the runway, switch the strobe and landing lights off to avoid annoying other pilots.

Keep a particularly good lookout in the airspace around an airport, because this is where most near-misses and mid-air collisions occur. Obey the right-of-way rules.

Always depart and enter the traffic pattern at a nontowered airport in accordance with the recommended standard procedures, or the procedures recommended for that airport. Announce your intentions in advance. At tower-controlled airports, follow the instructions given by ATC.

FURTHER POINTS

Orientation

Flying magnetic headings can assist your orientation in the vicinity of the airport.

In poor visibility you may not be able to see the airport from your local training area. To help you to continually know where you are, you should become familiar with all the local landmarks—for example, water towers, railroads, highways, towns, villages, churches, other airports, radio towers—that will lead you to your home field, and you should also know the approximate magnetic heading to steer to return home. Flying magnetic headings can assist your orientation in the vicinity of the airport.

The magnetic compass suffers errors when the airplane is turning or otherwise accelerating, and gives accurate headings only when the airplane is in straight flight at a steady airspeed. Therefore, to maintain an accurate magnetic heading, fly straight at a constant speed, making use of external reference points on the horizon if you can.

If a turn is needed, select a new external reference point and turn toward it. Allow the compass to settle down, and then check the heading. When you use the heading indicator (HI), ensure that it is aligned with the magnetic compass.

If you become uncertain of your position, you should ask for assistance from ATC or FSS. At all costs, stay clear of controlled airspace, unless you have the necessary clearances.

Periodic Checks

While flying the airplane for long periods, either en route, in the local training area, or for prolonged periods in the traffic pattern area, periodic checks (say every 15 minutes or so) should be made of the various systems that are vital to safe flight.

Your flight instructor will ensure that you perform the appropriate check, which will contain items such as those included in the following FREHA check:

F	**Fuel Selection:**	on and sufficient.
	Fuel Tank:	usage monitored.
	Mixture:	rich or leaned as required; carburetor heat set.
	Fuel Pump:	on (if fitted and if required) and fuel pressure checked.
R	**Radio:**	frequency correctly selected, volume and squelch satisfactory, and make any necessary radio calls.
E	**Engine:**	oil temperature and pressure, power set (propeller RPM), check of other systems (ammeter, suction gauge).
H	**Heading Indicator:**	aligned with magnetic compass (only realign the HI with the magnetic compass in steady straight and level flight).
A	**Altitude:**	checked and correct altimeter setting.

Perform these checks at regular intervals on every flight and also just prior to entering the traffic pattern (where your workload generally increases).

Emergency Radio Transmissions

In an emergency, squawk 7700 on your transponder and make a MAYDAY call.

As well as the more usual traffic-type radio calls, you may occasionally hear distress or urgency signals. If you ever have to make an emergency call or a distress call, you should also squawk 7700 on your transponder. This will alert the radar controller.

Mayday mayday mayday,
Cessna November One Three Two Papa Kilo,
five miles south of Honeygrove
engine failure,
descending through two thousand feet,
heading two eight zero,
five persons on board.

The use of the word *mayday* (an anglicized version of the French *m'aidez*—"help me") signifies a distress signal and it takes priority over all other calls. The above mayday call informs ATC that the pilot of the airplane registered N132PK has the serious problem of a failed engine.

Do not forget the priorities of a pilot in command: aviate, navigate and communicate.

While ATC may offer helpful suggestions, you (the pilot in distress) must not be distracted from your main duty, which is to fly the airplane as safely as possible. Remember that an airplane does not need a radio to fly. Another type of call that you may hear (or make) is the pan-pan call.

Pan-pan pan-pan pan-pan,
Cessna November One Three Two Papa Kilo,
unsure of position in poor visibility east of Orange County,
maintaining two thousand feet,
heading two four zero.

The use of the term *pan-pan* signifies that this is an urgency signal. It informs ATC that the pilot of N132PK is requesting assistance, but the use of pan-pan indicates that the airplane is in no immediate danger. Squawk 7700 on your transponder to draw the attention of radar controllers to you. A pan-pan call is also appropriate if you wish to report that another airplane or a ship is in distress.

Hopefully, you will never have to make a distress or urgency call of this nature but, if you do, remember to fly the airplane first and make radio calls second. If you hear another pilot make such a call, then impose a temporary radio silence on yourself for a suitable period to avoid jamming these important transmissions and the ATC responses.

Radio Failure

If you ever experience two-way radio communications failure (a rare event), you must continue to fly the airplane carefully, then exercise good judgment in determining a suitable course of action.

Check Your Radio

If your radio ceases to work, carry out the following checks:

- correct frequency selected;
- headphones and microphone still plugged in (try both);
- volume up and squelch adjusted; and
- change back to the previous frequency or another local frequency or to the emergency frequency 121.5 MHz and try to establish contact.

If you suffer a complete loss of radio communications while within a radar environment—that is, under the control of an ATC facility that has you identified on its radar screens—you can use the IFR transponder procedure of squawking 7600. This will draw the attention of the radar controllers to your predicament.

Operating in a radar environment, squawk 7600 on the transponder if you experience communication problems.

> **Note:** Exercise judgment in the use of this IFR procedure. It would be appropriate to use if, for example, you are operating on a VFR clearance in radar-controlled airspace. If the failure occurs outside of a radar environment, the appropriate procedure would be to remain outside this airspace. If you are in Class D airspace, then you would receive appropriate light signals from the control tower (see below), remaining outside the Class D airspace until you have determined the direction and flow of traffic. At a nontowered airport you would want to keep a good lookout.

Remain VFR and Land

You can land at a nontowered airport at any time without a radio, and you may land at a tower-controlled airport without radio in an emergency.

If you have just taken off, then stay in the traffic pattern and return for a landing, looking for light signals at a tower-controlled airport. Transmit blind, which means transmit the usual radio calls on the usual frequency, in case your transmitter is functioning but your receiver has failed.

If you are arriving at an airport, transmit blind, and establish the traffic pattern in use before entering it. This can be done by observing other aircraft or by overflying the airport at least 500 feet above the traffic pattern altitude and checking the wind sock and traffic pattern direction indicator. Then join the traffic pattern normally, making the usual radio calls blind, and keeping a good lookout for other aircraft and for light signals from an active control tower.

If your receiver is functioning, you will be able to hear messages. You can acknowledge radio messages or light signals from the tower by:

- rocking your wings in daylight (in flight);
- moving the ailerons or rudder in daylight (on the ground); and
- by blinking the landing light or position lights at night.

Light Signals

Light signals from the tower may be given following a radio failure.

If radio contact cannot be maintained at a tower-controlled airport, the tower controller can pass instructions to the pilot by means of light signals.

On the Ground

When you are on the ground, the signals are:

- flashing green, which means cleared for taxi;
- steady green, which means cleared for takeoff;
- steady red, which means stop;
- flashing red, which means taxi clear of the landing area (runway) in use;
- flashing white, which means return to starting point on airport; and
- alternating red and green, which means warning: exercise extreme caution.

In Flight

When you are in flight, the signals are:

- steady red, which means give way to other aircraft and continue circling;
- flashing red, which means airport unsafe: do not land;
- alternating red and green, which means warning: exercise extreme caution;
- flashing green, which means return for a landing (to be followed by a steady green at the proper time); and
- steady green, which means cleared to land.

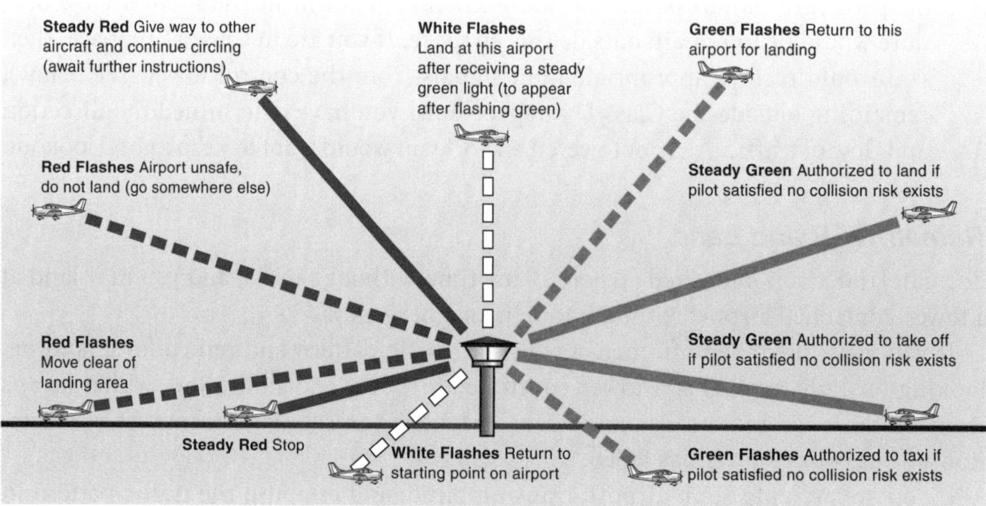

Figure 28-12 Light signals.

Minimum Weather Conditions

Traffic pattern operations are governed by two basic regulations:

Minimum Safe Altitudes

Minimum safe altitudes are found in 14 CFR §91.119.

14 CFR Part 91.119 states that the minimum altitude, except when necessary for takeoff or landing, is:

- sufficient altitude to glide clear if an engine fails; or
- over a congested area: 1,000 feet above the highest obstacle within a 2,000-foot horizontal radius of the aircraft; or
- over other than congested areas: 500 feet above the surface.

With this in mind, the traffic pattern would have a minimum altitude above the surface of 500 feet AGL, but this is not recommended. Good operating practice suggests a 1,000 feet AGL traffic pattern minimum unless otherwise noted in the *Chart Supplement U.S.*

Basic VFR Weather Minimums

Basic VFR weather minimums are found in 14 CFR §1.155.

14 CFR Part 91.155 states the minimum weather conditions for VFR flight in controlled and uncontrolled airspace in terms of:

- visibility; and
- distance from clouds.

Basic VFR minimums in controlled airspace are:

- a flight visibility of three statute miles; and
- 500 feet below clouds (and 1,000 feet above clouds, though this is not a consideration for traffic patterns) and 2,000 feet horizontally from clouds.

This means that a traffic pattern in Class C, D and E airspace has weather minimums of:

- flight visibility three statute miles; and
- cloud ceiling 1,000 feet AGL (so that at absolute minimum traffic pattern altitude of 500 feet AGL you are still 500 feet below the cloud ceiling).

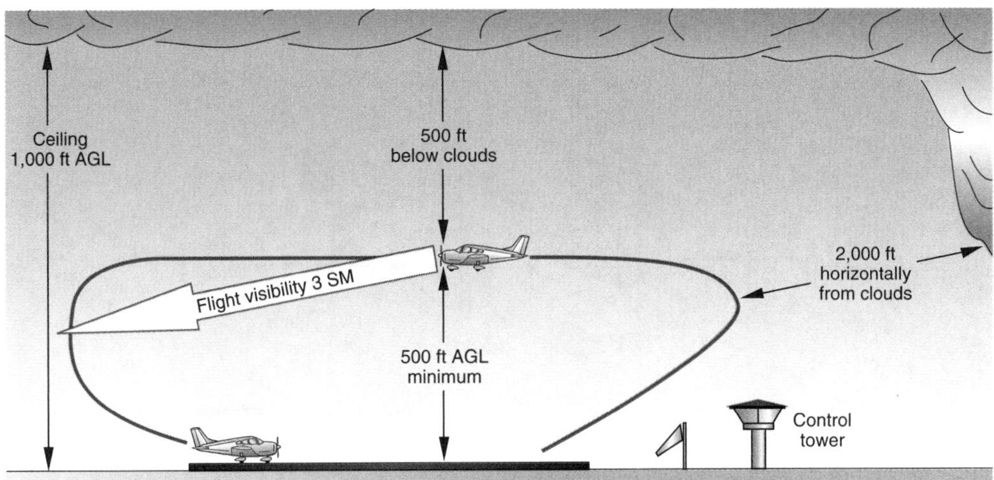

Figure 28-13 Basic VFR minimums in Classes C, D and E airspace.

The AIM recommends a 1,500 foot AGL ceiling to meet VFR weather minimums.

Control towers usually activate their airport beacon in daylight hours if weather conditions fall below the basic VFR minimums of three statute miles visibility and a cloud ceiling of 1,000 feet AGL. Note that these are minimums, not "recommended." The *AIM* recommends a traffic pattern minimum of 1,000 feet AGL for the 500-feet-below-clouds rule to be satisfied, which means a recommended ceiling of at least 1,500 feet AGL.

Exceptions in controlled airspace are:

- *In Class B airspace*, all aircraft are under radar control, and so the distance-from-clouds rule is relaxed to remain clear of clouds. This means that the bare minimum 500 feet AGL traffic pattern could be achieved with a low ceiling—but this is not recommended.
- With a *special VFR* clearance in controlled airspace, the requirements are reduced to:
  - a flight visibility of one statute mile (down from three); and
  - clear of clouds.

Basic VFR minimums outside controlled airspace below 1,200 feet AGL (that is, in Class G airspace) are:

- a flight visibility of one statute mile; and
- clear of clouds.

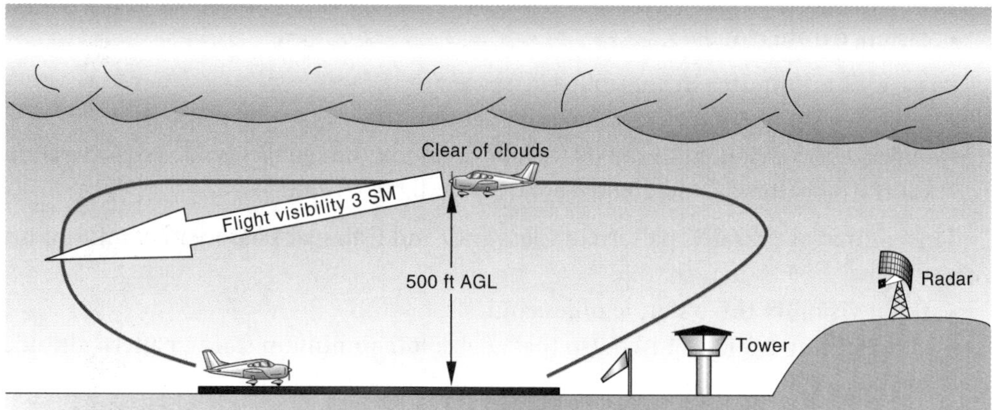

Figure 28-14 Reduced VFR minimums in Class B airspace.

Figure 28-15 Reduced VFR minimums with a special VFR clearance in controlled airspace (Classes B, C, D, and E).

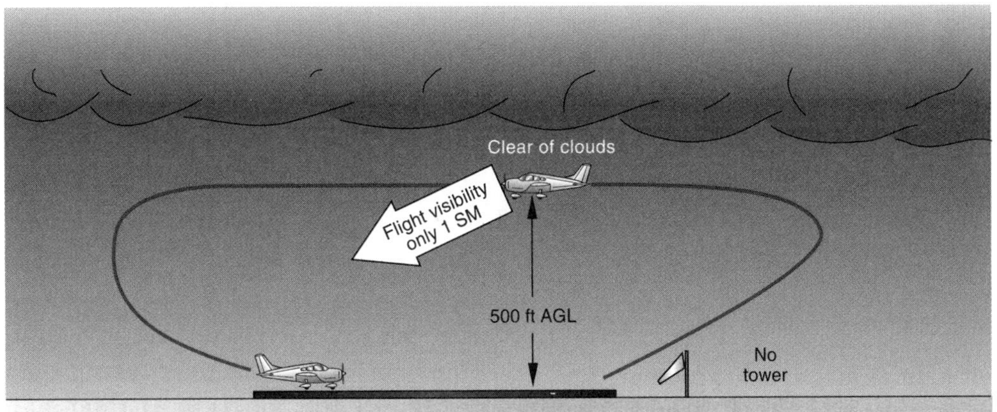

Figure 28-16 VFR minimums in Class G airspace.

These are the same minimums as for a special VFR clearance in controlled airspace.

Be aware that an instrument aircraft operating in Class E airspace above you could be executing an instrument approach procedure that allows it to descend to the published minimum descent altitude (MDA) or decision height (DH) that is in the Class G airspace below. This is where you are operating, possibly in poor weather conditions. Consequently a potential collision risk exists between your VFR aircraft and the IFR aircraft that is descending into your Class G airspace, even though both of you are operating legally. Listen on the CTAF and talk to other pilots to establish their position.

Recommended Traffic Pattern Minimums

It cannot be emphasized too strongly that the minimums discussed here are the absolute legal minimums for VFR traffic patterns. Be careful and conservative when deciding whether or not to operate in such poor conditions. The recommended minimums are a 1,000 feet AGL traffic pattern, with three statute miles visibility, distance from clouds as required by the airspace classification or special VFR clearance, and in sight of the surface. In particular, student pilots are required by the regulations (Part 61) to fly solo in minimum conditions of:

- flight or surface visibility of three statute miles or more by day; and
- with visual reference to the surface.

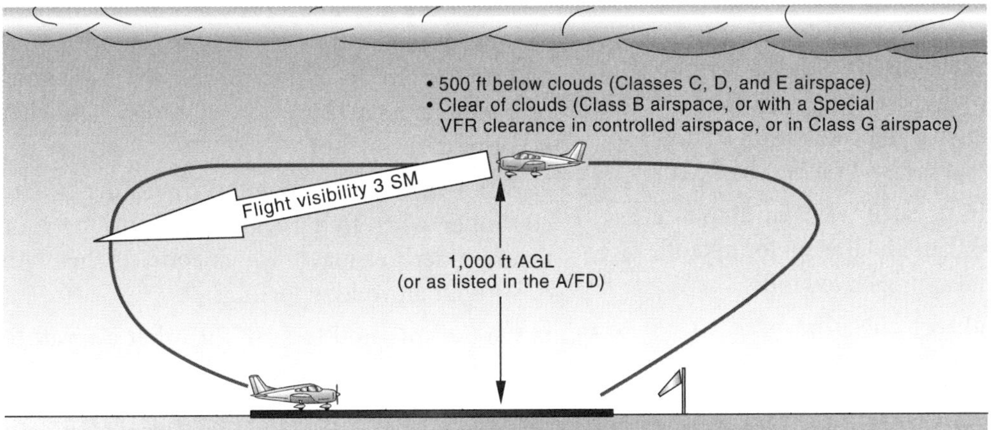

Figure 28-17 Recommended VFR traffic pattern minimums.

REVIEW 28

Traffic Patterns and Local Area Operations

1. In which direction are all turns made in the standard traffic pattern?
2. If visual markings or light signals at an airport without an operating control tower indicate that turns should be made to the right, which traffic pattern should you fly?
3. If you saw the following visual markings at an airport with crossing runways 9–27 and 36–18, which runway would you interpret as being in use? Is this with a left-hand traffic pattern or right-hand traffic pattern?

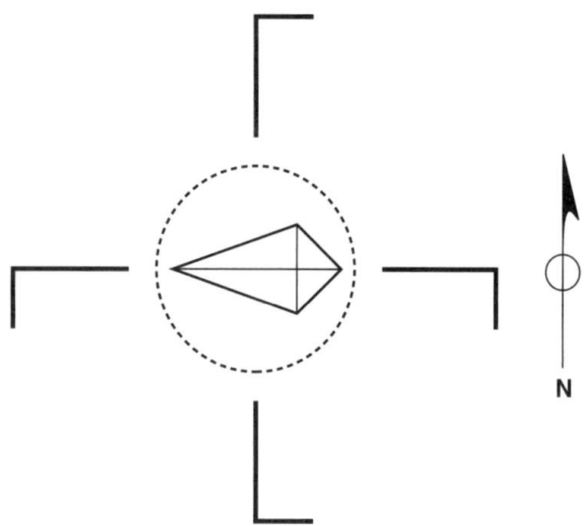

4. In the above case, is the traffic pattern for runway 9 left-handed or right-handed? Is the traffic pattern for runway 36 left-handed or right-handed? Is the traffic pattern for runway 18 left-handed or right-handed? In which of the following sectors could this be designed to keep traffic away from a built-up area of high obstruction: NW, NE, SE or SW?
5. Which aircraft has right-of-way: an airplane which is about to taxi out and line up for takeoff, or an aircraft on final approach to land?
6. Does the before-takeoff checklist need to be completed prior to takeoff?
7. If the airport elevation is 1,200 feet MSL, and traffic pattern altitude is 800 feet AGL, you could commence your turn after takeoff onto the crosswind leg when the altimeter indicates how many feet MSL? This is how many feet AGL? You would level off when the altimeter indicates how many feet MSL? How many feet AGL is this? What are the altitude and airspeed tolerances on downwind leg?
8. A typical downwind leg is displaced what distance from the runway?
9. What are the minimum weather conditions required for VFR flight at a tower-controlled airport (include ceiling in feet AGL and visibility in statute miles)?
10. Given the following information, say aloud a 10-second review you might give to your flight instructor before lining up for takeoff: wind at 15 knots, straight down the runway, liftoff speed 50 knots, obstacle-clearance speed 55 knots, V_X 60 knots, V_Y 70 knots, ground run 1,000 feet, 50-foot point by 1,600 feet, traffic pattern altitude 1,000 feet above the airport (airport elevation 800 feet), a clear field suitable for an emergency landing slightly to the right of the climb-out flight path, a nonstandard right-hand traffic pattern to avoid the town.
11. To make your airplane more conspicuous in flight to other pilots and to birds, which lights could you switch on? To make you more conspicuous on radar screens, it is also usual to switch what on prior to lining up?
12. Unless otherwise instructed by an air traffic controller, when flying VFR you should set your transponder to squawk which code? Is this with or without altitude reporting?
13. Is the best method to scan for other aircraft to move your eyes in a series of short movement?

14. If the engine cuts out at 200 feet AGL just after takeoff, should your first actions be to raise or lower the nose? Should you land straight ahead or turn back to the airport?
15. Name three variables that are allowed for in a takeoff performance chart or table.
16. What effect will an airplane experience at less that about one wingspan above the ground? What effect will the cushioning beneath the wings have on the quality of the flight? What effect does this have on drag?
17. How will climbing into a head wind affect the climb gradient over obstacles?
18. How will climbing into a tail wind affect the climb gradient over obstacles?
19. When taking off after a large airplane has just taken off or landed, do you need to avoid the wake turbulence caused by its wing-tip vortices?
20. During your takeoff ground run, a dog runs onto the runway and into your takeoff path. Describe how you would abort the takeoff.
21. At what altitude is the usual traffic pattern flown? In which direction are the turns?
22. Traffic patterns that are not 1,000 feet AGL for some reason—say because of controlled airspace above, or high obstructions below—will generally lie within what range (in feet AGL)? Where is information on nonstandard traffic patterns published?
23. Is two-way radio communication required at tower-controlled airports?
24. Is two-way radio communication required at nontowered airports?
25. At a tower-controlled airport, which frequency, if it is available, would you use when taxiing? Do you need to read back any instruction to hold short of runway?
26. At a tower-controlled airport, when would you switch from ground frequency to tower frequency?
27. At an airport without an operating control tower, you should be able to obtain an airport advisory regarding wind, runway in use, and traffic from which of the following: UNICOM, MULTICOM, the local FSS, or on tower frequency?
28. When departing from an airport without an operating control tower, you should make which two radio calls on the ground on the CTAF? What does CTAF stand for?
29. Are taxi and takeoff clearances required at an airport without an operating control tower?
30. Draw a diagram showing two methods of departing the traffic pattern at an airport without an operating control tower. Show the altitudes at which you would turn from the takeoff direction.
31. The airport elevation is 1,230 feet MSL. The traffic pattern altitude is 1,000 feet above airport elevation. How many feet MSL is this? What is the lowest altitude to overfly the airport and remain clear of the traffic pattern?
32. There are five radio calls you are recommended to make approaching an airport without an operating control tower. Where would you make them?
33. Approaching a tower-controlled airport, how many miles out should you listen to the ATIS and monitor the tower frequency? How many miles out would you contact the tower?
34. You receive a landing clearance and then land at a tower-controlled airport. Having taxied clear of the runway, when do you contact ground control on the ground frequency?
35. If you are returning from a cross-country VFR flight for which you filed a flight plan with FSS, what is the preferred method of canceling your flight plan? Will the tower or ground automatically cancel it after you have landed safely? Where can you relay your request to cancel your flight plan?

36. You appear to be catching up to an aircraft ahead of you in the traffic pattern. Which of the following are suitable solutions: slow down, make gentle S-turns, widen out, or make a complete 360° turn?

37. In terms of altitude, which aircraft has right of way on approach? Can it take advantage of this to cut in on or overtake another aircraft?

38. Your radio fails totally and you are unable to reestablish two-way radio communications. What should you do?

39. In flight, you observe a steady red light signal directed at you from the tower. What does this mean?

40. In flight, you observe a flashing green light signal directed at you from the tower. What does this mean?

41. In flight, you observe a steady green light signal directed at you from the tower. What does this mean?

42. After landing and taxiing clear of the runway, you observe a steady red light signal directed at you from the tower. What does this mean?

43. After landing and taxiing clear of the runway, you observe a flashing green signal directed at you from the tower. What does this mean?

44. How can you acknowledge light signals from the tower in daylight when you are on the ground?

45. What is the recommended traffic pattern altitude? Where is this published?

46. Student pilots are only permitted to fly solo if two weather conditions are satisfied. What are they?

Answers are given on page 582.

Visual Approach and Landing

29

Visual Approach

OBJECTIVES

To describe:

- the pattern used for training;
- factors affecting approach and landing performance;
- environmental factors that the pilot must take into account during the approach; and
- the piloting technique and visual references used to complete a safe, consistent approach.

CONSIDERATIONS

The approach begins with entry to the pattern. During training, you will practice closed patterns, but this is just a means of providing a greater number of takeoffs and landing within a given training session. Once you are qualified as a pilot, you will rarely conduct closed patterns except for practice or if you need to go around.

A closed pattern is used to practice takeoffs and landings.

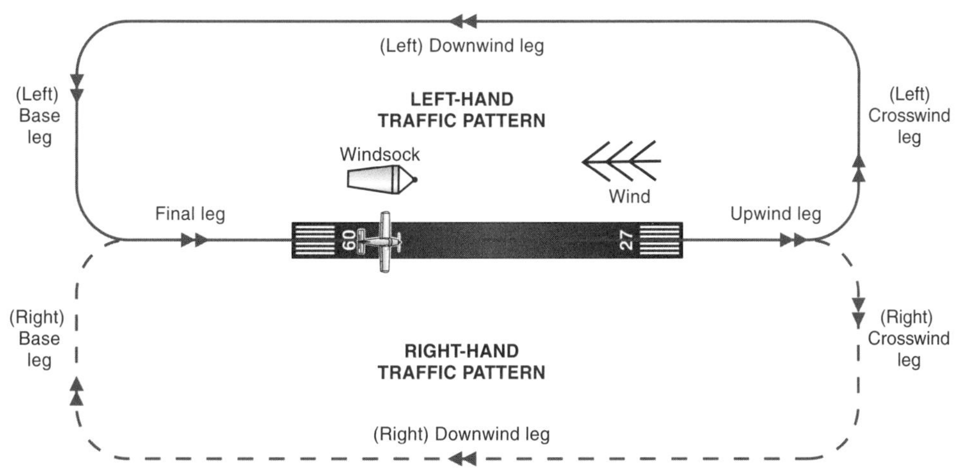

Figure 29-1 The traffic pattern.

Landing Distance

If necessary, consult the landing distance chart to confirm that the runway is adequate for the conditions and for the airplane weight. High elevations and high temperatures decrease air density and increase the landing distance required, as does a tail wind component, a downslope, or a contaminated runway.

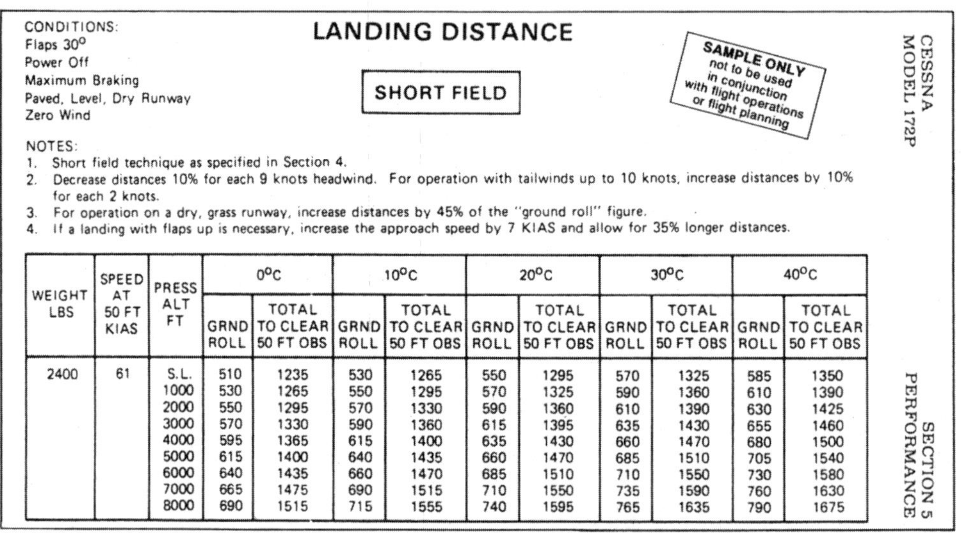

CONDITIONS:
Flaps 30°
Power Off
Maximum Braking
Paved, Level, Dry Runway
Zero Wind

LANDING DISTANCE

SHORT FIELD

SAMPLE ONLY not to be used in conjunction with flight operations or flight planning

CESSNA MODEL 172P

NOTES:
1. Short field technique as specified in Section 4.
2. Decrease distances 10% for each 9 knots headwind. For operation with tailwinds up to 10 knots, increase distances by 10% for each 2 knots.
3. For operation on a dry, grass runway, increase distances by 45% of the "ground roll" figure.
4. If a landing with flaps up is necessary, increase the approach speed by 7 KIAS and allow for 35% longer distances.

WEIGHT LBS	SPEED AT 50 FT KIAS	PRESS ALT FT	0°C		10°C		20°C		30°C		40°C	
			GRND ROLL	TOTAL TO CLEAR 50 FT OBS	GRND ROLL	TOTAL TO CLEAR 50 FT OBS	GRND ROLL	TOTAL TO CLEAR 50 FT OBS	GRND ROLL	TOTAL TO CLEAR 50 FT OBS	GRND ROLL	TOTAL TO CLEAR 50 FT OBS
2400	61	S.L.	510	1235	530	1265	550	1295	570	1325	585	1350
		1000	530	1265	550	1295	570	1325	590	1360	610	1390
		2000	550	1295	570	1330	590	1360	610	1390	630	1425
		3000	570	1330	590	1360	615	1395	635	1430	655	1460
		4000	595	1365	615	1400	635	1430	660	1470	680	1500
		5000	615	1400	640	1435	660	1470	685	1510	705	1540
		6000	640	1435	660	1470	685	1510	710	1550	730	1580
		7000	665	1475	690	1515	710	1550	735	1590	760	1630
		8000	690	1515	715	1555	740	1595	765	1635	790	1675

SECTION 5 PERFORMANCE

Figure 29-2 Cessna 172 Skyhawk Landing Distance chart (sample extract, reduced).

Your preflight planning will include ensuring the landing distance available is adequate.

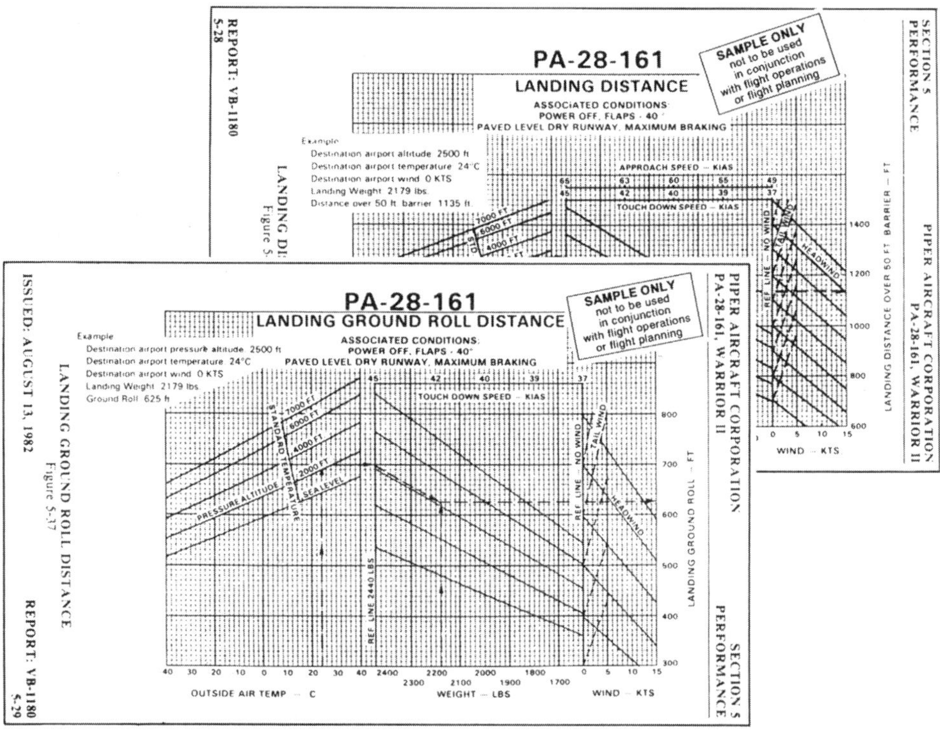

Figure 29-3 Sample extracts of the Piper Warrior Landing Distance, and Landing Ground Roll Distance charts (reduced).

Check NOTAMs for changes to runway lengths or runway unservicability.

Early in your training, your flight instructor will take the responsibility for ensuring that you have adequate runway length. Later in your training you will need to check NOTAMs (notices to airmen) to ensure that runway lengths have not been temporarily reduced, say because of work in progress to repair the runway surface or because of temporary obstructions in the takeoff or approach paths.

Ensure that you know if the full length of the runway is available for landing. A displaced threshold showing the start of the landing portion of the runway will be indicated by arrows or chevrons to a thick solid line across the runway. If arrows are used, that part of the runway can be used for takeoff but not for landing. If chevrons, rather than arrows, are used then that part of the runway is not available for any use.

If the runway is totally unusable, it will have a large cross (×) at each end.

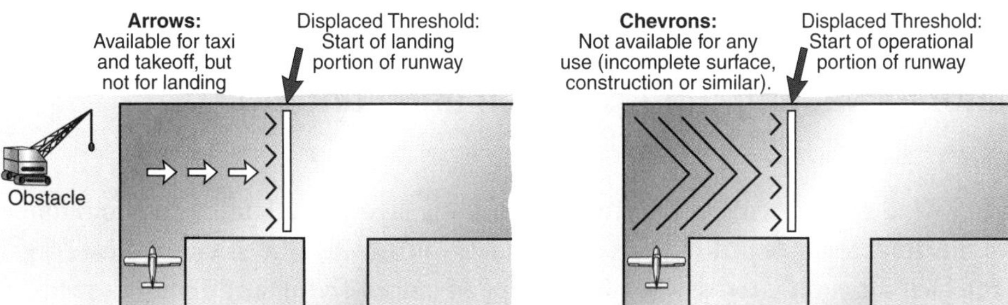

Figure 29-4 Displaced threshold markings.

Figure 29-5 Closed runway (or taxiway).

LAHSO

At airports with crossing runways, there may be land and hold short operations (LAHSO) in effect.

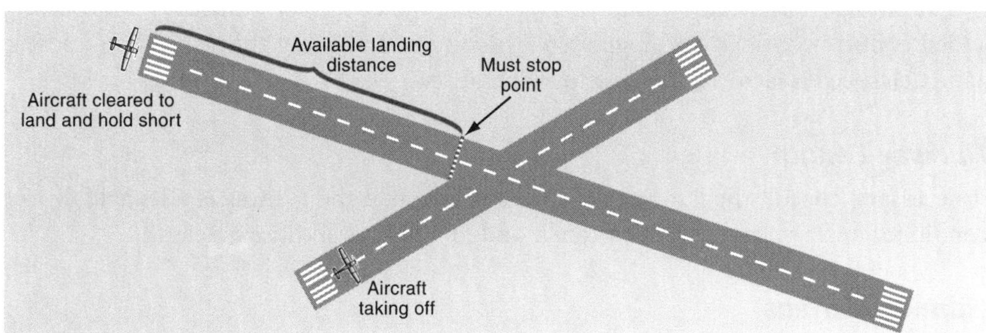

Figure 29-6 LAHSO runway restrictions.

Approach Speed

Touching down at the lowest speed puts least strain on the landing gear and airplane structure, and uses least runway. There must, however, also be a safe margin above the stall speed in the landing configuration (V_{SO}) and with the landing weight. For these reasons, the approach airspeed is usually 1.3 V_{SO}. This applies to aircraft of all sizes, from the smallest training airplane to the largest Boeing 747. If your airplane stalls at 50 knots in the landing configuration, then your approach speed will be 1.3 × 50 = 65 knots. If the B747 stalls at 100 knots in the landing configuration, then its approach speed will be 1.3 × 100 = 130 knots.

You should aim to fly the chosen approach speed as accurately as possible (within one or two knots in steady wind conditions), and certainly within plus or minus five knots, down to the point at which you commence to flare. At this point you will make the transition to the landing attitude and remove the power, with the airspeed bleeding off prior to touchdown. The wheels will touch at a speed significantly less than the approach speed. Note that, in gusting winds, it may be advisable to carry a few extra knots in the approach (usually one half of the gust factor) to allow for gusts and lulls affecting the airspeed.

Factors Affecting the Approach and Landing

Wind

Allow for wind effect when turning final.

A head wind component on the final approach is favorable. A tail wind component is generally unacceptable unless there are obstacles or runway slope that predicates against an into-wind landing. Crosswind landing is advanced flying and requires specialized training. A crosswind component on the final approach gives added difficulty in interpreting the aim point and flight path. A crosswind component on the final approach means that there is also a head wind or tail wind component on base. A tail wind on the base leg can be dangerous as it tends to blow the aircraft through the extended runway centerline during the final turn and there is a temptation to tighten the turn. Plan to turn earlier than usual under these conditions. Landing into wind is desirable because:

- for a given airspeed on approach, a head wind gives the lowest ground speed;
- there is no tendency to drift sideways;
- the approach is steep for the same airspeed giving better obstacle clearance;
- higher power is required and the added slipstream allows better directional control;
- the aircraft is more directionally stable on the ground; and
- the landing distance is reduced.

The stronger the steady wind, the greater are the effects. An unsteady wind brings added control workload and a greater difficulty in achieving the aim point, and the approach speed is factored to allow for wind gusts.

Runway Length

If necessary, consult the landing chart to confirm that the runway is adequate for the conditions and airplane weight. A touch-and-go requires additional length.

Runway Surface

For once, usually adverse factors may be in your favor. Long grass, wet grass, puddles and mud can help provided they do not cause the wheels to skid or are deep enough to damage the landing gear. Be especially protective of the nose wheel by holding the control column fully back after touchdown.

Runway Slope

Slope has significant effect, both for and against. Do not accept a downward-sloping runway unless there is a strong head wind.

Approach Path

The landing performance of an aircraft depends on the final approach being at the correct speed and the correct angle. If there are obstacles, the approach path is steeper and the aim point has to be further into the field. Thus the landing distance is increased. An attempt to duck under the approach path, to touchdown as early as possible, carries a risk of an airspeed increase and a higher rate of descent.

Power and Density Altitude

High elevations and high temperatures decrease air density and increase the landing distance required (because the TAS and GS are higher for the same IAS).

Landing Weight

Increased weight means a higher approach speed to maintain a safe margin above the increased stall speed. The energy, that the brakes have to absorb in the landing roll, is a function of weight and the square of the ground speed. Thus weight has a compounding effect on landing distance required.

Flaps

Flaps are an important factor for landing.

Using flaps provides:

- a lower stalling speed, thus permitting a lower approach speed while retaining an adequate margin over the stall;
- a steeper flight path at a given airspeed because of the increased drag;
- a lower nose attitude at a given airspeed, providing a better view of the approach and landing path;
- a shorter hold-off and landing run because of the increased drag and the lower airspeed.

The degree of flap used will depend on the airplane and the wind conditions actually prevailing. In strong and gusty winds, it may be preferable to use less than full flaps for better controllability and power response. Your flight instructor will advise you the optimum technique for your aircraft type.

APPLICATION

Flying the Pattern

If joining the pattern, enter in level flight abeam the midpoint of the runway, at pattern altitude. Maintain pattern altitude until abeam the approach end of the runway. Complete the prelanding checks and keep a good lookout, both for other aircraft and to check your position relative to the runway. The aircraft is *flown* with reference to the horizon and the instruments but is *positioned* relative to the runway.

Prelanding Check

Completing the prelanding check by about the midpoint on the downwind leg allows you to concentrate fully on your base turn, approach and landing. Memorize the prelanding checklist for your airplane. It will include such items as:

- brakes off;
- landing gear down (if required) (wait for three greens);
- mixture rich;
- correct fuel tank(s) selected, contents sufficient for a go-around and further pattern (otherwise declare an emergency for a priority landing), fuel pump on (if fitted), fuel pressure normal and fuel primer locked; and
- hatches (doors) and harnesses (seat belts) secure.

Commencing Descent

The descent point for a normal approach is commenced abeam the landing threshold. The descent should be judged and the power/flap adjusted so that you will roll out onto the final approach no lower than 500 feet height above airport (HAA) and at least ¼ of a mile from the threshold. Look outside and, if the altitude feels low, then adjust attitude and power or go around. With a little experience, you will get a feel for just where to commence descent to achieve the correct height on the final approach. The availability of power and flap also gives you the ability to control your descent flight path as you wish. Flap settings are recommended in the pilot's operating handbook, confirmed by your flight instructor.

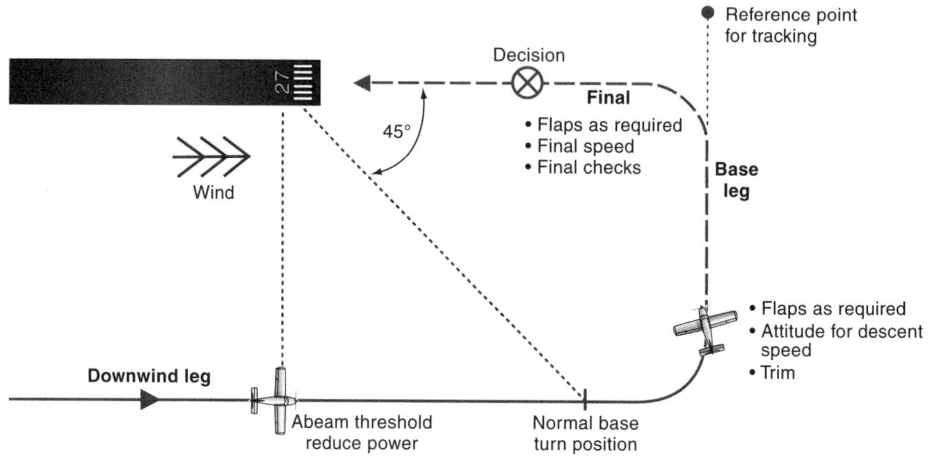

Figure 29-7 Positioning in the pattern and turning base.

Base Turn

A descending turn from downwind onto the base leg is made when the aircraft is at 45° to the threshold centerline. Some instructors will advise an earlier turn but this changes the perspective of the runway and makes the judgment of the approach less consistent.

Allow for drift on the base leg, so that the wind does not carry the airplane too far from the field, and maintain the rectangular pattern. The amount of drift can assist you in estimating wind strength: the greater the drift angle on the base leg, the stronger the head wind on the final approach. Be careful if there is a tail wind component on the base

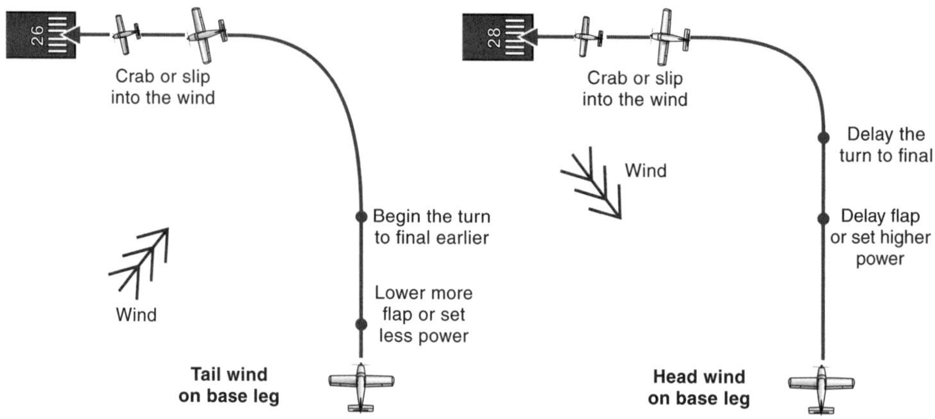

Figure 29-8 Turning onto the final approach.

leg as there would be with a crosswind from the left in a left-hand pattern. It will try to blow you through the centerline and may cause you to tighten the turn. Anticipate the tendency and turn earlier. It is always easier and safer, to reduce the bank after turning early than to tighten the turn.

Wind Effect

The wind often changes in strength and direction near the ground.

A tail wind on the base leg will increase the airplane's speed over the ground and the turn should be commenced a little early to avoid flying through final approach. Conversely, if there is a head wind on the base leg, the turn onto final can be delayed. If any crosswind exists on the final approach, then lay off drift so that the airplane tracks along the extended centerline of the runway, ensuring that the airplane is in balance.

Steep turns near the ground should be avoided. If you overshoot the turn onto the final approach, rather than steepen the turn, fly through final and rejoin it from the other side without exceeding a medium bank angle. However, if you are at an airport with parallel runways, enter a climbing turn and, if you must cross to the other runway, make a radio call.

Wind Shear and Turbulence on the Final Approach

It is usual for the wind to change in strength and direction near the ground due to friction and other causes. A sudden reduction in the head wind component will cause a reduction in indicated airspeed, which can result in a temporarily increased sink rate. Turbulence on the final approach also causes airspeed and descent rate fluctuations. If a strong wind gradient is suspected, then consider flying the approach using a lower flap setting (or no flap at all) and a higher approach speed than normal. The airplane will be more stable and more responsive compared to when full flap is lowered and a slow airspeed flown.

Figure 29-9
Position the airplane on centerline and allow for drift.

TECHNIQUE

Final Approach

The turn onto the final approach is a medium, descending turn in which you should:

- limit the bank angle to 30°, maintaining balance with rudder pressure;
- aim to be lined up on the final approach at or above 500 feet HAA;
- maintain flight path and airspeed with elevator and throttle; and
- make early corrections, with aileron and rudder, to maintain centerline.

Complete the final-approach check (PUF) as follows:

- *propeller* full fine;
- *undercarriage* (landing gear) down; and
- *flaps* full (carburetor heat cold).

Confirm that the runway is clear and that you are cleared to land. The runway perspective (symmetry) will indicate whether you are aligned with the runway. If you (your eyes) are on centerline, the centerline will be vertical to the horizon, regardless of the heading and attitude of the aircraft. If not, then make a correction in the form of a coordinated turn to carry your eyes across to the extended centerline—the centerline will move across to the vertical position. At this low airspeed, coordinated rudder input is important to help point the nose where you wish to go. Your eyes should be on the centerline—don't make any allowance for your offset seating. Your eyes are only 18 inches from the center of the cockpit and this is quite acceptable at this stage. Concentrate on maintaining an accurate eye-path on centerline and remember the nose of the aircraft may be pointing slightly to one side to achieve and to maintain this.

Judging the Approach Path

We have considered how to establish the alignment of the aircraft and its position relative to the extended centerline of the runway. Now we'll examine how to judge the vertical path down to the point where the aircraft is flared for landing.

The pilot uses the shape of the runway (the aspect), the width (when the runway perspective becomes familiar), the features and texture of the surface (to judge altitude and distance) and the altitude above terrain (allowing for any known slope).

Runway Perspective

The perspective of the runway seen as you roll out on final approach will depend on the position of the airplane and the dimensions of the runway. You will come to recognize the *picture* to aim for. If the aircraft is too high, then the runway will appear longer and narrower than usual and a steep flight path will be required to arrive near the aiming point for the round-out. If the airplane is too low, then the runway will appear shorter and wider than usual and the airplane will have to be "dragged in" with power

Either of these situations can be remedied and the earlier the better! Adjust the rate of descent and the flight path (using power and attitude) so that the runway assumes its normal perspective as soon as possible. This may require firm and positive action, but the sooner you do it, the more likely you are to make a good landing.

Take positive action with power and attitude to stay on-slope and on-speed.

Figure 29-10 Ideally, the aim point remains fixed in the windshield.

Note that the aspect of the runway is not constant. It should have a consistent shape for the start of the final approach, but then it will widen and appear flatter as you continue on the approach. Only the position of the aim point remains constant.

Fly a Stabilized Approach

A stable approach sets you up for a good landing.

The approach path to the runway is three-dimensional. A good approach requires tight control of the flight path and of the airspeed (a stabilized approach), and this will set the scene for a good landing. Landing flap should be selected by at least 300 feet HAA and the airplane retrimmed. Approach at the selected indicated airspeed (IAS) on a suitable approach path and on the extended runway centerline. This will require positive and firm action on your part.

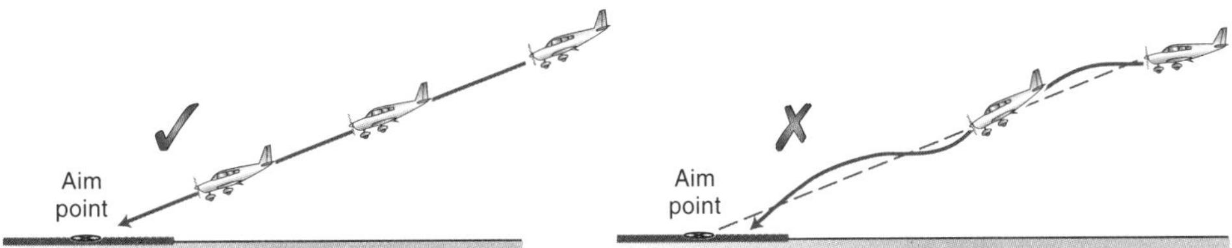

Figure 29-11 Fly a stabilized approach.

The sooner a correction is made the less the amount of the correction. You will notice an experienced pilot making almost continuous small corrections. The approach speed chosen will depend on the flap selected and the prevailing conditions (wind strength and direction, or the suspected presence of gusts, wind shear, turbulence or wake turbulence).

Aim Point

Ideally, the aim point should remain fixed in the windshield, the runway appearing larger and larger as it is approached and the field of view expanding from the aim point. If the airspeed is constant and the flap position is not changed then the aim point stays at a fixed position in the windshield. The shape of the runway will change from the point at which you lined up for the final approach. Note though that the aim point does not move relative to the horizon. It remains a constant distance below the horizon.

The aim point remains a constant distance below the horizon.

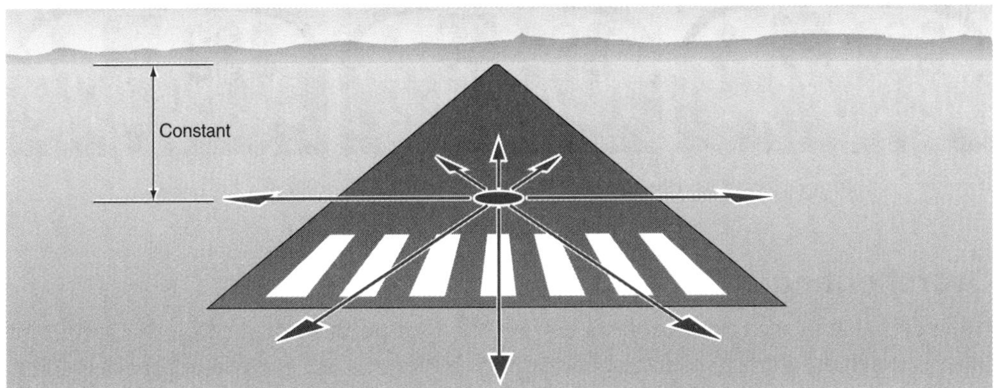

Figure 29-12 The aim point stays in a constant position.

If the aim point moves progressively up the windshield, then the airplane is undershooting. Conversely, if the aiming point moves progressively down the windshield, then the airplane is overshooting. In either case, you must take positive action to modify the approach path.

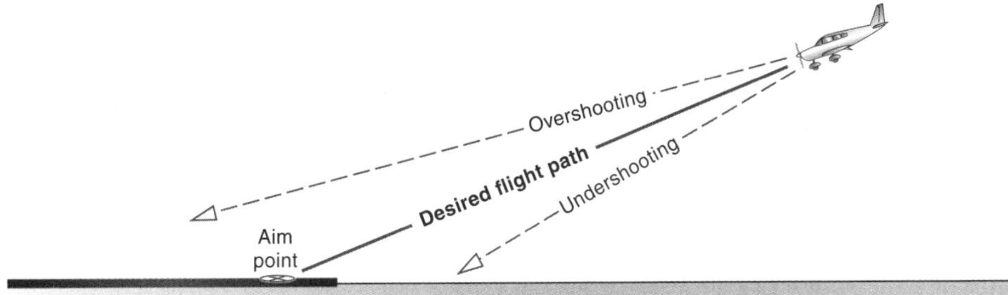

Figure 29-13 Fly the airplane down the desired approach path.

Airspeed Control

Power plus attitude equals performance. Any change in power will require a change in pitch attitude if the same airspeed is to be maintained.

- If power is added, raise the nose to maintain airspeed.
- If power is reduced, lower the nose to maintain airspeed.

Similarly, any change in attitude will require an appropriate adjustment of power to maintain the same airspeed. Keeping the airplane in trim during the approach will make your task considerably easier

Undershooting

If the actual approach path projects to a point short of the aim point (indicated by the aim point moving up the windshield toward the horizon and the runway appearing shorter and wider earlier), then it is likely that there is a head wind that must be countered for by adding power. Regain the desired flight path by adding power and raising the nose to maintain airspeed until the runway shape (aspect) is correct for that distance on the final approach.

If undershooting, add power and raise the nose to regain the desired flight path.

Figure 29-14 Undershooting: to correct, add power and raise the nose.

Overshooting

If the actual approach path projects beyond the aim point (indicated by the aim point moving down the windshield further away from the horizon), steepen the approach path by:

- increasing flap and adjusting the pitch attitude; or
- reducing power and lowering the nose to maintain airspeed.

An early correction will mean that you can regain the normal path quite early. When the path is correct, the power will have to be reintroduced if it had been reduced. If it progresses this far, go around.

If overshooting steepen the descent by lowering the nose and reducing power to maintain airspeed.

Figure 29-15 Overshooting: to correct, reduce power and lower the nose, or increase flap and lower the nose (or go around).

Flight Path Corrections

You will make many corrections to the approach flight path (eventually, it is like riding a bicycle in that you will make the corrections almost automatically). Most approach paths fluctuate between a slight overshoot and a slight undershoot, and continual minor corrections to both attitude and power are required.

You will make many corrections to the approach flight path.

Turbulence in the Traffic Pattern Area

Friction affects the air flowing over the earth's surface, leading to the wind at ground level being different to that at pattern altitude and higher. Any change in wind speed and/or direction is called wind shear, and it can cause turbulence.

Uneven heating of the earth's surface will cause vertical convection currents, also leading to turbulence. You experience this as a bumpy ride with a fluctuating airspeed.

In turbulent conditions, it is advisable to carry a few extra knots on the approach to give you better controllability. A flapless approach should be considered, since it will make the airplane more responsive to a power increase (due to the lower drag).

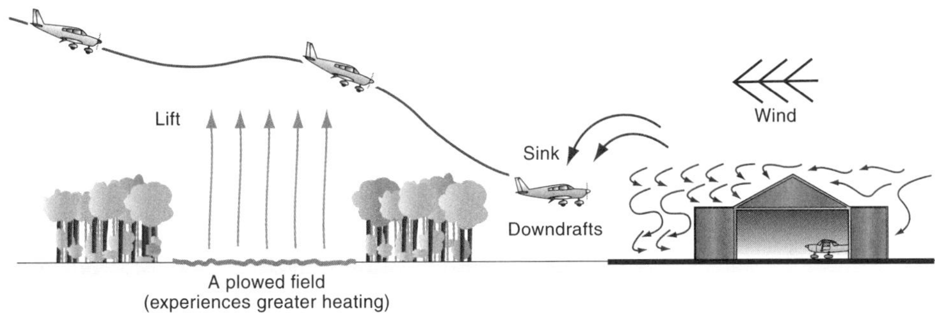

Figure 29-16 Turbulence has various causes.

Wake Turbulence

Significant wake turbulence can form behind the wing tips of large airplanes flying at high angles of attack (e.g. during takeoff and landing). The vortices that cause the turbulence drift downward and with the wind. They are best avoided! Never be afraid to delay a takeoff or approach if you suspect that wake turbulence from another aircraft (fixed-wing or rotary) could be a problem.

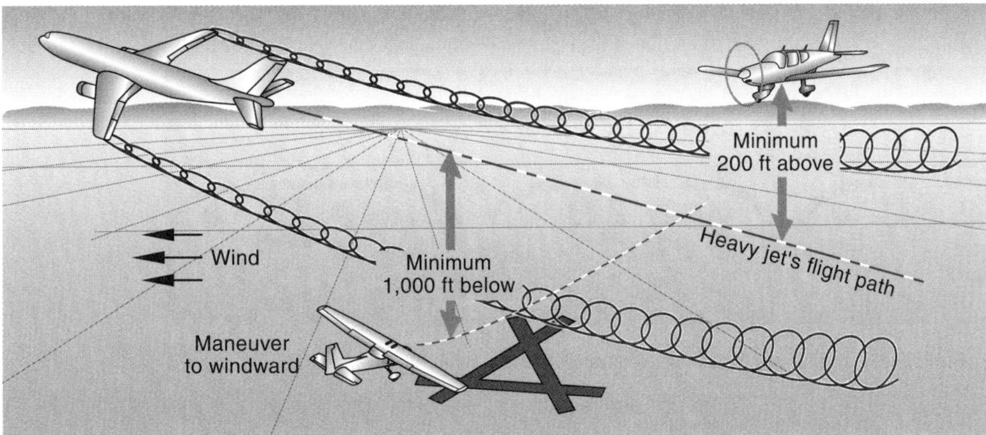

Figure 29-17 Avoiding wake turbulence from large aircraft.

AIRMANSHIP

Fly a neat traffic pattern, on altitude and on speed. Commence descent once on the base leg to position the airplane for a turn that will have you lined up on the final approach at or above 500 feet AGL. Use flap as appropriate. Fly a stabilized approach on slope, on the extended centerline and on speed. Maintain firm, positive and tight control of all three. Although you will be very busy, remain aware of other aircraft. Keep a good lookout.

Go-Around

If at any stage during the approach or landing you feel uncomfortable about the situation, carry out a go-around (also known as a baulked approach, overshoot or discontinued approach). This maneuver is covered in Chapter 31.

REVIEW 29

Visual Approach

1. Specify three items you would consider before landing on an unfamiliar runway.
2. Which wind direction on landing will provide the shortest landing distance if you land with landing flaps?
3. What effect do landing flaps have on the steepness of the approach? What effect do landing flaps have on the landing speed? What effect do they have on forward view?
4. In the approach to land, what should you use to positively control flight path and airspeed?
5. Will a before-landing checklist assist you to check the necessary item?
6. The power-off stalling speed with the flaps in the landing position is at which end of which arc on the airspeed indicator?
7. Is stalling speed with power on greater than with power off?
8. In gusty wind conditions, do you need to add a gust correction factor to your normal approach speed?
9. Is a good landing more likely if you fly a stable approach?
10. Within what accuracy should you fly your selected approach speed?

Figure 29-18 The aim point stays constant on a stabilized approach.

Answers are given on page 583.

30
Normal Landing

OBJECTIVES

To describe:
- the types of normal landing used in flight training;
- the procedure and technique for each;
- the process of landing the aircraft safely, consistently and gently;
- the visual references, judgments and technique to transition from flight to ground; and
- corrective measures for landing difficulties.

Figure 30-1
The landing is easiest from a stabilized approach.

CONSIDERATIONS

Types of Normal Landing

Full Stop, Stop-and-Go and Touch-and-Go

A normal landing brings the aircraft to a full stop as it turns off the runway. For training purposes, to save time and money, some variations are used. These are the stop-and-go and the touch-and-go. The stop-and-go consists of a landing to a full stop on the runway followed by an immediate takeoff using the remaining length of the runway. It can only be done on runways of adequate length for both the landing and the takeoff. Additionally, the runway is occupied for a prolonged period and other traffic may be affected.

The touch-and-go is a continuous maneuver where, after touchdown, the flaps and perhaps trim are reset, the power is increased and the aircraft enters a takeoff. It can only be done safely on runways with enough length for the landing, the change of configuration and trim, the introduction of power and the subsequent takeoff. The workload during a touch-and-go is higher than a normal landing. This exercise involves:
- flying an accurate pattern based on the runway used;
- making a powered (or power-assisted) approach; and
- an into-wind landing (there may always be sight drift).

APPLICATION

Short Final

A good approach leads to a good landing.

Aim to be lined up on final at least 400 feet above the airport elevation.

A good landing is most likely following a good approach, so aim to be well established in a stabilized approach with the airplane nicely trimmed by the time you reach short final, the last part of the approach. Short final for a training airplane may be thought of as the last 200 feet. Do not allow significant deviations in flight path, tracking or airspeed to develop. Carburetor heat will normally be returned to cold on short final in case

Figure 30-2 Typical attitudes in the approach and flare.

maximum power is required for a go-around; however, if icing conditions exist, follow the guidance provided in your pilot's operating handbook.

Throughout the final approach and landing, have your:

- left hand on the control column to control attitude; and
- right hand on the throttle to control power.

Landing

The landing starts with a flare commencing when the pilot's eyes are about 15 feet above the runway. The pilot uses texture, height of peripheral objects, width of the runway and the perceived height of the horizon as cues to commence the flare and to judge the rate of rotation to achieve an almost level path over the runway. The landing is not complete until the end of the landing roll.

Once you reach the flaring height, forget the aim point because you will fly over and well past it before the wheels actually touch down. It has served its purpose and you should now look well ahead. Pick a point at the center of the far end of the runway. Transfer your visual attention to this point and slowly retard the throttle.

Reduce the rate of descent as you near the ground.

A normal landing is similar to the approach to the stall, with attitude being increased to keep the aircraft flying at the reducing airspeed. Touchdown will occur just prior to the moment of stall. Do not rush and try not to be tense. The aircraft will land when it is ready. This method of landing allows the lowest possible touchdown speed (significantly less than the approach speed), with the pilot still having full control.

The landing consists of four phases:

- flare (or round-out);
- hold-off;
- touchdown; and
- landing roll.

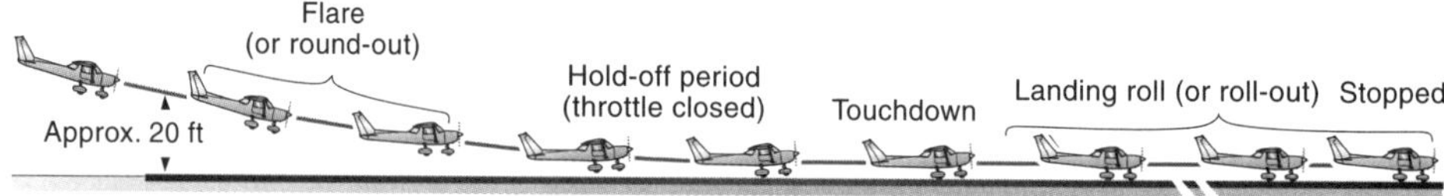

Figure 30-3 The landing.

Judgment in the Flare and Landing

To assist in judging the height of the wheels above the ground and the rate at which the airplane is sinking, your eyes should remain focused outside the cockpit from shortly before commencing the flare (when airspeed is no longer important) until the end of the landing roll. To achieve the best depth perception and develop a feel for just where the main wheels are in relation to the ground, it is best to look well ahead.

Flare

During the flare (round-out) the power is reduced and the nose is gradually raised to reduce the rate of descent. A small rate of sink is checked by a slight attitude change, a high rate of sink requiring a greater and quicker backward movement. A greater descent rate may require the pilot to add power momentarily to arrest the descent.

Figure 30-4 Flare.

Hold-Off

The hold-off should occur with the airplane close to the ground (with the wheels within a foot or so). The throttle is closed and the control column progressively brought back to keep the airplane flying a level path with the wheels just off the ground. If sinking, apply more back pressure; if moving away from the ground, relax the back pressure. The airspeed will be decreasing to a very low figure, but this is of no concern to you. You should be looking well ahead from the beginning of round-out until touchdown. Any sideways drift caused by a slight crosswind can be counteracted by lowering the upwind wing a few degrees and keeping straight with rudder.

Figure 30-5 Hold-off.

Touchdown

On touchdown, the main wheels should make first contact with the ground (which will be the case following a correct hold-off). The nose wheel will want to drop immediately but should be kept off the ground using the control column while the speed decreases. This may require a significant rearward pressure to allow it to touch gently.

Hold the airplane off for as long as possible just above the runway. Touchdown on the main wheels.

Landing Roll

During the landing roll the airplane is kept straight down the centerline using rudder and the wings kept level with aileron. Look at the far end of the runway. The nose wheel is gently lowered to the ground before elevator control is lost. Brakes (if required) may be used once the nose wheel is on the ground. Remember that the landing is not complete until the end of the landing roll when the airplane is stationary or has exited the runway at taxiing speed.

After-Landing Check

Once clear of the runway, stop the airplane, set fast idle RPM (1,000 to 1,200 RPM as recommended) and complete the after-landing check. It will contain such items as:

- flaps retracted;
- fuel pump off (if fitted); and
- external lights and transponder off

You may need to make a radio call on the UNICOM, CTAF or ground frequency.

Common Faults in the Landing

Every pilot learns how to land through experience. It is inevitable that many landings will be far from perfect, but progress will be made when you can recognize faults and correct them. Three very common faults are:

- the *balloon* (when the airplane moves away from the ground due to over-rotation before touchdown);
- the *bounce* (when the airplane moves away from the ground after touchdown, perhaps after several touchdowns, due to overcontrol after touchdown); and
- the *hang-up* (rounding out too high).

Balloon

A balloon can be caused by one or more of:

- too much or too rapid back pressure on the control column (over rotation);
- too much power left on;
- too high an airspeed; and
- a wind gust.

To correct for a small balloon:

- relax some of the back pressure on the control column;
- allow the airplane to commence settling (sinking) again;
- add power if the sink develops;
- when approaching the hold-off height, continue the backward movement of the control column; and
- complete the landing normally.

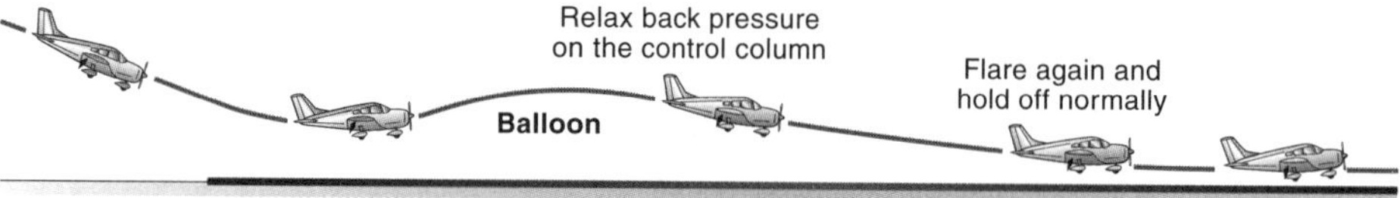

Figure 30-6 Correcting for a small balloon.

A large balloon during the landing may call for a go-around—certainly for inexperienced pilots!

Large Balloon. A large balloon may call for a go-around, certainly for an inexperienced pilot. As experience is gained, it may be possible to reposition the airplane (possibly using power) for the flare and landing, but this uses up lots of runway. The decision to attempt a recovery from a large flare will therefore depend on the extent of your experience and on the runway length remaining.

Bounced Landing

A bounce can be caused by one or more of:

- a failure to flare sufficiently or not quickly enough;
- touching down on the nose wheel (possibly caused by looking over the nose);
- touching down too fast;
- excessive backward movement of the control column on touchdown; and
- flaring too late.

An inexperienced pilot should consider an immediate go-around following a bounce. With experience, however, a successful recovery from a bounce can be made (provided that the runway length is adequate) by relaxing the back pressure and adding power if

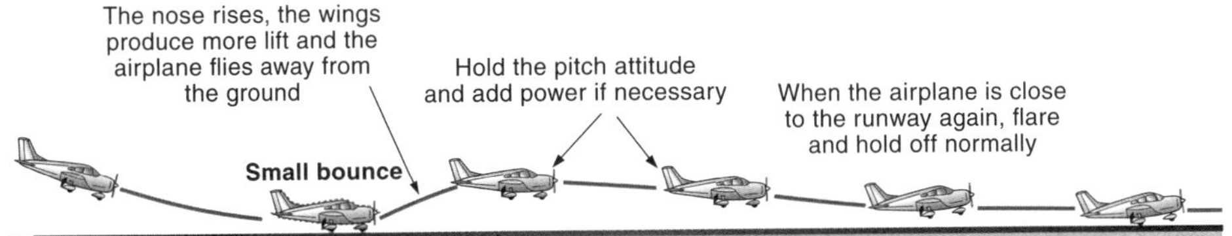

Figure 30-7 Recovery from a bounced landing.

necessary to reposition the airplane suitably to recommence the landing. Avoid pushing the nose down as a second bounced landing may result.

Avoid a second touchdown on the nose wheel—a series of kangaroo hops down the runway is not a desirable way to land an airplane! Prior to touchdown, make sure that the airplane is in the correct nose-high attitude (even if it is the second touchdown).

Rounding Out and Holding Off Too High (Hang-Up)

The hold-off is best completed with the main wheel tires a foot or so off the ground. Any more than this and a landing somewhat heavier than usual will result. If you recognize before impact that you are too high, add power; this will break the descent rate somewhat and allow a less heavy touchdown. Immediately the wheels touch the ground, close the throttle, otherwise the airplane may not decelerate. Holding off too high usually results from either:

- not looking far enough into the distance, with the result that the ground rushing by is blurred and depth perception is poor; or
- a second attempt to land following a balloon or bounce.

The more experienced you become, the less likely you are to find yourself bouncing, ballooning or rounding out too high. Part of the average student pilot's experience is recovering from misjudged landings, but this phase will not last too long.

Touch-and-Go

The number of practice patterns per hour can be greatly increased by doing a touch-and-goes. This involves a normal approach and landing and then, when established in the landing roll and after the nose wheel has been gently lowered onto the ground (and with sufficient runway length remaining):

Be sure to reset the flaps and perhaps the trim on the touch-and-go.

- move the flap to the takeoff setting;
- apply full power and perform a normal takeoff.

In a touch-and-go takeoff, the trim may not be set for takeoff and so there will be a reasonable amount of forward pressure required on the control column to hold the nose in the climb attitude. Once established in the climb away from the ground, this pressure can be trimmed off.

If the landing is misjudged and excessive runway is used, then bring the airplane to a stop as in a normal landing, rather than continue with a doubtful takeoff on possibly insufficient runway with a degraded obstacle clearance in the climb-out.

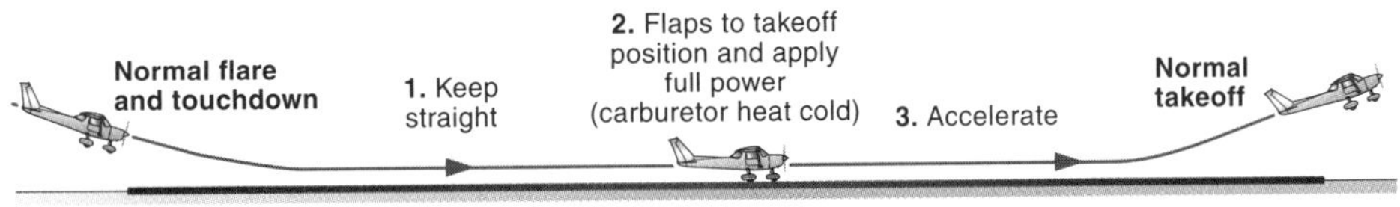

Figure 30-8 The touch-and-go.

REVIEW 30

Normal Landing

1. You should try to touch down at or within how many feet beyond a specified aim point on the runway?
2. On which wheels should you touch down?
3. After touchdown on the main wheels, you should lower the nose wheel onto the ground gently. True or false?
4. During the landing roll, how do you keep straight? How do you keep the wings level?
5. A preceding heavy jet airliner has touched down on the runway; you are on final approach to land, and the surface wind is a light quartering tail wind. Is this more dangerous from the point of wake turbulence than a strong head wind? If the runway is extremely long, should you aim for the runway threshold or well down the runway?
6. How will the length of a runway that slopes upward appear compared to a level runway? How does this affect how you will feel on slope? What sort of approach are you at risk of making to a upward sloping runway?
7. How will the length of a runway that slopes downward appear compared to a level runway? How does this affect how you will feel on slope? What sort of approach are you at risk of making to a downward sloping runway?
8. What impression will a wide runway give you during the flare? What influence may a wide runway have on the flare?
9. What impression will a narrow runway give you during the flare? What influence may a narrow runway have on the flare?

Figure 30-9 Look to the new aim point at the far end of the runway.

Answers are given on page 583.

TASK

Powered Approach and Normal Landing

Aim: To make an approach with power and land into wind.

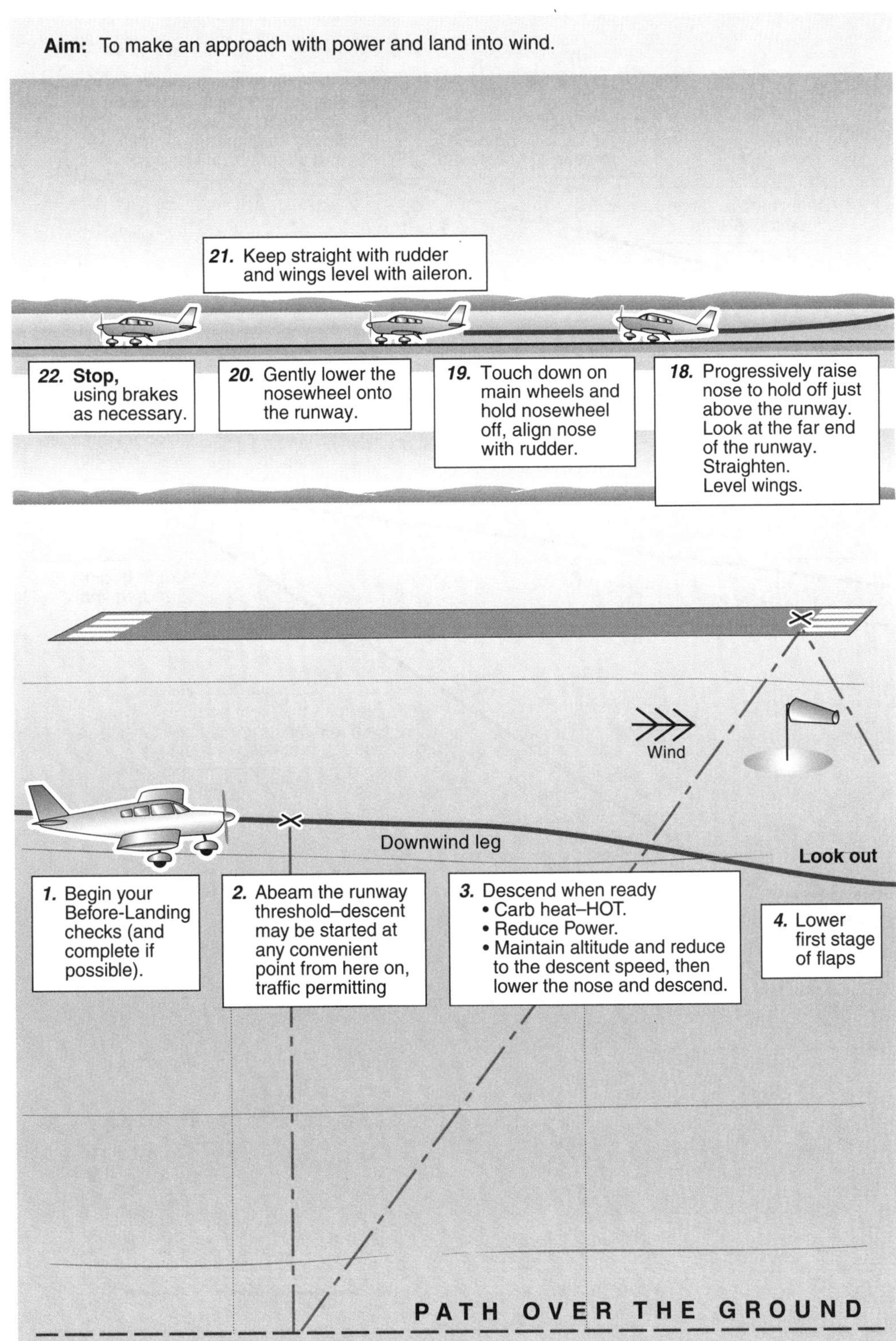

21. Keep straight with rudder and wings level with aileron.
22. Stop, using brakes as necessary.
20. Gently lower the nosewheel onto the runway.
19. Touch down on main wheels and hold nosewheel off, align nose with rudder.
18. Progressively raise nose to hold off just above the runway. Look at the far end of the runway. Straighten. Level wings.
Wind
Downwind leg
Look out
1. Begin your Before-Landing checks (and complete if possible).
2. Abeam the runway threshold–descent may be started at any convenient point from here on, traffic permitting
3. Descend when ready
• Carb heat–HOT.
• Reduce Power.
• Maintain altitude and reduce to the descent speed, then lower the nose and descend.
4. Lower first stage of flaps
PATH OVER THE GROUND

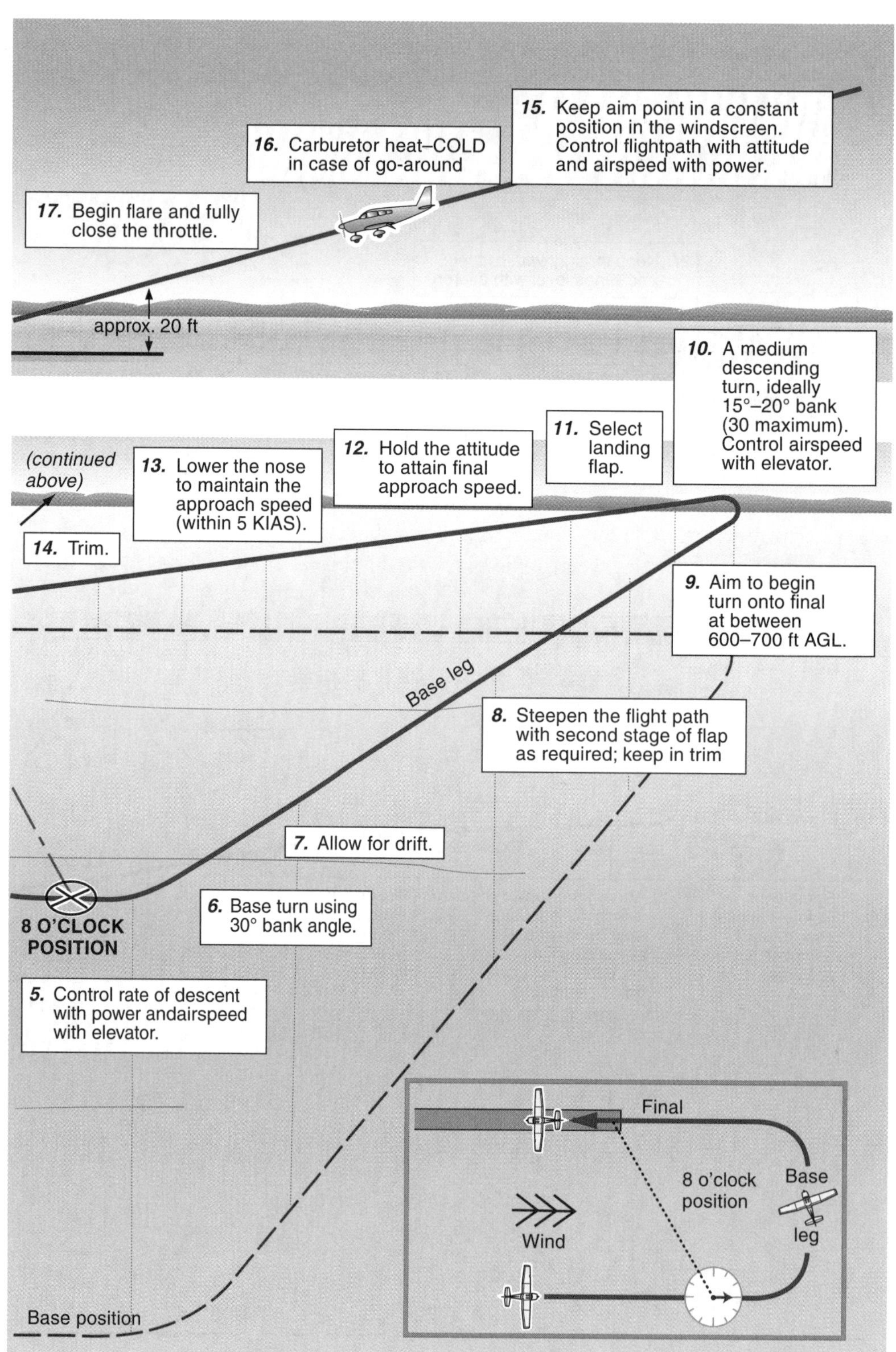
15. Keep aim point in a constant position in the windscreen. Control flightpath with attitude and airspeed with power.
16. Carburetor heat–COLD in case of go-around
17. Begin flare and fully close the throttle.
approx. 20 ft
10. A medium descending turn, ideally 15°–20° bank (30 maximum). Control airspeed with elevator.
11. Select landing flap.
12. Hold the attitude to attain final approach speed.
(continued above)
13. Lower the nose to maintain the approach speed (within 5 KIAS).
14. Trim.
9. Aim to begin turn onto final at between 600–700 ft AGL.
Base leg
8. Steepen the flight path with second stage of flap as required; keep in trim
7. Allow for drift.
8 O'CLOCK POSITION
6. Base turn using 30° bank angle.
5. Control rate of descent with power andairspeed with elevator.
Base position
Final
8 o'clock position
Base leg
Wind

31 Go-Around

OBJECTIVES

To describe:

- the circumstances under which a go-around may be safer than a continued landing; and
- the technique to transition from a powered approach with flaps (and landing gear) extended to a positive climb with flaps (and landing gear) retracted.

Figure 31-1 Raise the flaps in stages.

CONSIDERATIONS

Why Go Around?

It may be necessary to perform a go-around for various reasons:

- the runway is occupied by an airplane, a vehicle or animals;
- you are too close behind an airplane on final approach that will not have cleared the runway in time for you to land;
- the conditions are too severe for your experience (turbulence, wind shear, heavy rain, excessive crosswind, etc.);

The go-around is a climb away from a discontinued approach to land.

Figure 31-2 Going around.

- your approach is unstable (in terms of airspeed or flight path);
- you are not aligned with the centerline or directional control is a problem;
- the airspeed is far too high or too low;
- you are too high at the runway threshold to touch down safely and stop comfortably within the confines of the runway;
- you are not mentally or physically at ease; and
- a mishandled landing (balloon or bounce).

Effect of Flaps

Full flap causes a significant increase in drag. This has advantages in the approach to land: it allows a steeper descent path, the approach speed can be lower and the pilot has a better forward view. Full flap has no advantages in a climb: in fact establishing a reasonable rate of climb may not be possible with full flap extended. For this reason, when attempting to enter a climb from a flapped descent, consideration should be given to raising the flap. It should be raised in stages to allow a gradual increase in airspeed as the climb is established.

APPLICATION

Establish a Descent for a Practice Go-Around

Full flaps makes a climb-out difficult so reduce the flaps in stages as you climb away: avoid sinking.

Follow the usual descent procedures and lower an appropriate stage of flap. Initially, it may be desirable to practice the go-around maneuver with only an early stage of flap extended (or perhaps none at all), as would be the case early in the approach to land. A go-around with full flap requires more attention because of the airplane's poorer climb performance and generally more pronounced pitching moment as the power is applied and flaps retracted.

TECHNIQUE

Initiating a Go-Around

Act decisively!

A successful go-around requires that a positive decision be made and positive action taken. A sign of a good pilot is a decision to go around when the situation demands it, the maneuver being executed in a firm, but smooth manner. The procedure to use is similar to that already practiced when entering a climb from a flapless descent: power, attitude, trim (PAT). The additional consideration is flap, which is raised when the descent is stopped and the climb (or level flight) is initiated.

To initiate a go-around, move the carburetor heat to cold and smoothly apply full power (counting 1-2-3 fairly quickly is about the correct timing to achieve full power). Be prepared for a strong pitch-up and yawing tendency as the power is applied. Hold the nose in the desired climb attitude for the flap that is set, balance and then trim. The initial pressure and retrimming may be quite significant, especially with full flap.

Full flap creates a lot of drag and only marginal climb performance may be possible. In this case level flight might be necessary while the flap setting is initially reduced. If only partial flap is extended, a reasonable climb can be entered without delay.

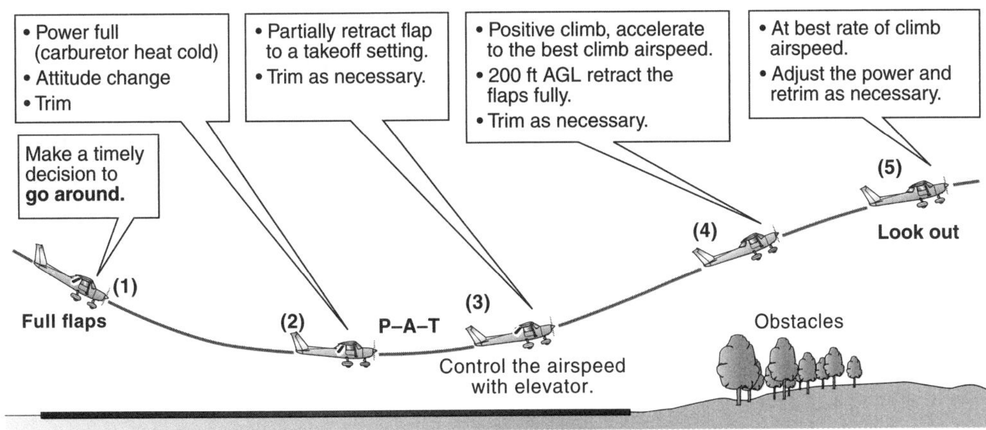
• Power full
(carburetor heat cold)
• Attitude change
• Trim
• Partially retract flap to a takeoff setting.
• Trim as necessary.
• Positive climb, accelerate to the best climb airspeed.
• 200 ft AGL retract the flaps fully.
• Trim as necessary.
• At best rate of climb airspeed.
• Adjust the power and retrim as necessary.
Make a timely decision to go around.
(1)
Full flaps
(2)
P–A–T
(3)
Control the airspeed with elevator.
(4)
(5)
Look out
Obstacles

Figure 31-3 The go-around.

As the airplane accelerates to an appropriate speed, raise the flap in stages and adjust the pitch attitude to achieve the desired speeds and climb performance. Trim as required.

Keep the airplane straight and the wings level as you climb away.

AIRMANSHIP

Make a positive decision to go-around, then perform it decisively. Exert firm, positive and smooth control over the airplane. Firm pressure must be held on the control column and rudder pedals when the power is applied. Correct trimming will assist you greatly. Ensure that a safe airspeed is achieved before each stage of flap is raised. Once established comfortably in the climb-out, advise the air traffic service unit (and the other aircraft in the traffic pattern) by radio that you are going around.

Go-around straight ahead, or to the side opposite from the pattern.

It is usual, once established in the go-around, to move slightly to one side of the runway so that you have a view of airplanes that may be operating off the runway and beneath you. The dead side, away from the pattern direction, is preferred. However, stay on the centerline if there are parallel runways.

Following the go-around, delay turning onto crosswind leg until at least at the upwind end of the runway to avoid conflicting with other traffic in the pattern.

Communicate—when you are established in the climb-out.

REVIEW 31

Go-Around

1. Write down the recommended go-around procedure for your airplane.
2. Sketch a typical go-around and write down the main points of how to fly the maneuver.
3. When you apply full power for a go-around, in which direction will there be a natural tendency for the nose to pitch? Do you need to positively hold the nose in the correct pitch attitude for the climb?
4. With the application of full power, as well as the nose wanting to pitch, to which side will there be a tendency to yaw? How do you counteract this yaw?
5. Will trimming off unwanted elevator pressure in the climb-out make the go-around easier?
6. What are the target speeds in the go-around in the following situations:
   - for a takeoff flap setting;
   - for a clean climb over obstacles; and
   - for a clean climb to altitude?
7. If you go around because of an aircraft taking off just ahead of you, in relation to the extended runway centerline, where should you climb?
8. During the go-around, which has the greater priority between flying the airplane or making an advisory radio call?
9. What should you do if the runway is occupied by another airplane, a vehicle or animals when you are on short finals?
10. What should you do if you are too close behind another airplane also on final approach that will not have cleared he runway in time for you to land?
11. What should you do if you are too high over the runway threshold for a safe landing within the confines of the runway?
12. What should you do if you find on final approach that conditions are too severe for your experience?
13. What should you do if everything looks good on final approach—that is, you are on speed, on flight path, aligned with the extended runway centerline, checklists complete and no conflicting traffic?

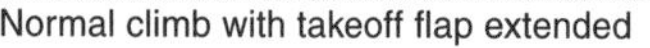
Normal climb with takeoff flap extended

Normal climb without flap

Figure 31-4 Establish climb attitude for flap position.

Answers are given on page 583.

TASK

Go-Around

Aim: To enter a climb from a flapped approach.

With the Airplane Established in a Flapped Descent

1. Make a firm decision to *go around.*
2. **P** – Power—throttle open fully (carburetor heat cold), landing gear retracted.

   A – Attitude—raise nose to level attitude. Partly retract flaps.

   T – Trim.
3. Raise the flaps slowly, in stages.
   Target speeds:
   • takeoff flap setting: obstacle-clearance airspeed;
   • clean: V_X +5/–0 knots initially, then V_Y ±5 knots for a normal climb-out.
4. Adjust the pitch attitude (higher as flaps are retracted), to maintain speed and rate of climb; avoid sinking.
5. Retrim for the climb-out.
6. Maintain your tracking, either along the extended runway centerline or to one side of it, for better vision of other traffic.
7. Continue in a normal pattern.

Look ahead for other traffic during the maneuver, especially before turning crosswind.

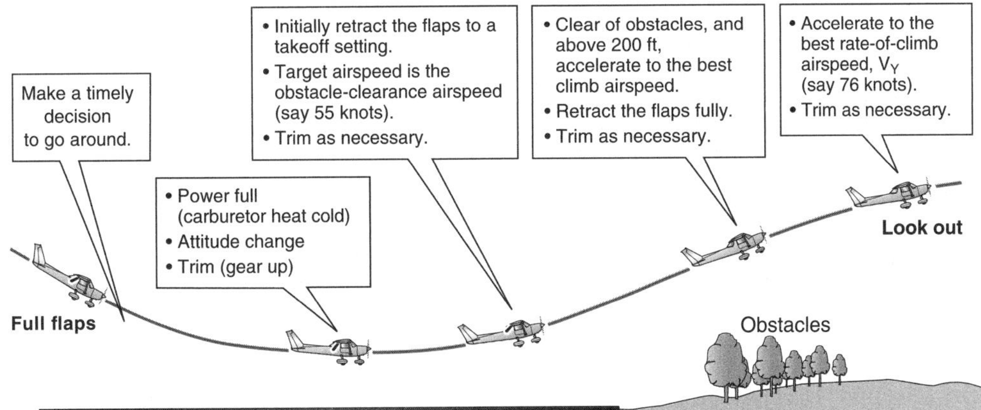

Emergency Operations

32
Fire and Engine Malfunctions

OBJECTIVES

To describe:

- appropriate responses to abnormal circumstances or equipment malfunctions;
- the mental self-preparation of a conditioned response to those serious emergency scenarios where limited time is available to react; and specifically
- to correct response to engine failure after takeoff (EFATO).

CONSIDERATIONS

For all in-flight situations, there will be a procedure for your aircraft. For the basic training airplane, it is mostly the airspeeds that vary, while the techniques and the priorities remain the same for all types. The procedures in the event of engine problems and fires were discussed earlier. Before your first solo, it is appropriate to consider and in some cases rehearse some of the correct responses to in-flight emergencies (sometimes called *abnormal operations*). There is no one set of procedures that will cover all possible situations and eventualities. The following points are designed to serve as a basis for discussion. Your instructor will advise the procedures for your aircraft and your operating environment.

There are additional procedures to be learned before your first area solo and these relate to *forced* landings in an unprepared field and *precautionary* search and landing to avoid weather or fading light. These are explained as separate exercises. The pilot's response to the in-flight situation is governed primarily by how much time there is to act. A fire must be addressed immediately, as must an engine failure on takeoff. A radio failure or electrical problem, however, can be considered and the checklist consulted. Let's consider the more significant and the more common scenarios:

If any problem occurs in flight, the most essential task is to maintain flying speed and control the airplane flight path. The emergency must be handled in conjunction with this primary task.

- in the traffic pattern; and
- in the training area.

Every flight exercise includes a discussion of the pilot's actions in the event of a malfunction or abnormal operation. These are classified as emergency actions or simply emergencies. They are applicable to every stage of aircraft operation and would be very useful if equivalently taught for motor vehicles. The pilot's operating handbook for the aircraft will specify the drills to be followed in coping with certain emergencies. For example:

- engine fire on start-up or while taxiing;
- electrical fire;
- cabin fire;
- flat main tire; and
- brake failure.

The more serious emergencies are considered in detail in the appropriate sections of this manual. However, since you are about to commence flight training, and become the pilot in command, you should have a basic awareness of emergency procedures even at this early stage.

Fire

For a fire to occur, three things are required:

- fuel (AVGAS, oil, papers, fabric, cabin seating, etc.);
- oxygen (present in the air); and
- an ignition source (cigarettes, matches, electrical sparks, etc.).

During your preflight inspection, you should check the lower surfaces of the airplane structure, and the ground beneath, for any evidence of fuel leaks.

The usual way to extinguish a fire is to eliminate one or more of these items, such as blanketing a fire with dry chemical from a fire extinguisher to starve the fire of oxygen. It is, of course, preferable that fire is prevented by keeping fuel and possible sources of ignition separate. For example, when refueling an airplane, ensure that there is no smoking in the vicinity, that the airplane and refueling equipment are adequately grounded to avoid the possibility of static electricity causing a spark, and that no fuel is spilled. As a precaution, however, a fire extinguisher should be readily available. Know how to use it!

Engine Fire During Start-Up

The best procedure in this situation is to keep the engine turning with the starter, but to move the mixture control to idle cutoff (or the fuel selector to off) to allow the engine to purge itself and the induction system of fuel. The fire will probably go out. If not, then further action should be taken:

- turn off the fuel;
- turn all switches off;
- put the brakes on; and
- abandon the aircraft, taking the extinguisher.

Electrical Fire

In the event of an electrical fire, an immediate landing is advisable. Do no reset any popped circuit breakers.

A distinctive smell often indicates that the fire is electrical. Switch off any associated electrical circuits. If required, a fire extinguisher can be used, but ensure that cabin ventilation is sufficient and the windows are open to remove smoke and toxic fumes from the cabin once the fire is out. An immediate landing is advisable.

Whether or not to shut the engine down in flight is a command decision and will, of course, mean a forced landing without power. A typical drill for an electrical fire is:

- turn off the master switch (to remove power from the electrical services);
- turn off all other switches (except ignition);
- set the cabin heat to off;
- use the fire extinguisher as required (and open fresh air vents);
- if on the ground, shut down the engine and evacuate or, if in flight, decide whether to keep the engine running to make an early landing or shut down the engine and make an immediate forced landing.

Cabin Fire

A cabin fire may be caused by such things as a cigarette igniting a seat or other matter. The source of the fire should be identified and the fire eliminated using the fire extinguisher. In flight, maintain flying speed and a suitable flight path while the emergency is resolved; opening a door or window may intensify the fire. After landing, consider an immediate evacuation after securing the airplane (shut down the engine, turn switches and fuel off, put the brakes on).

Emergency Egress

Emergency egress (escape) from the aircraft on the ground should be practiced, especially if you later carry passengers, which may include children or people with limited physical ability. Your aircraft may have more than one door and may have additional escape panels. Ask to be shown how to use all means of emergency exits.

Discontinued (Aborted) Takeoff and EFATO

There are two emergencies in the takeoff for which you should be prepared (even though they may never happen):

- the discontinued takeoff while still on the ground (pilot-initiated); and
- engine failure after takeoff (EFATO), fortunately not as common these days as it once was.

Prior to opening the throttle on each takeoff, it is a good idea to run through both of these procedures in your mind.

Discontinued Takeoff

Be prepared for two emergencies on takeoff: engine failure and a discontinued takeoff.

A pilot may decide to abort a takeoff during the ground run for many reasons, such as:

- an obstruction on the runway;
- restricted flight controls;
- engine failure or loss of power;
- engine or fuel problems;
- faulty instrument indicators (e.g. airspeed indicator zero);
- any doubt that the airplane is capable of flying;
- an insecure seat that feels as if it might slip backward; or
- any other condition that may, in your opinion, make the takeoff inadvisable.

This accelerating-and-then-stopping maneuver is known by various names, including the following:

- *accelerate-stop*;
- *discontinued takeoff*;
- *aborted takeoff*; or
- *abandoned takeoff*.

Aborting the Takeoff

You must make a firm and conscious decision to abort the takeoff, and then act positively:

- close the throttle fully;
- keep straight with rudder;

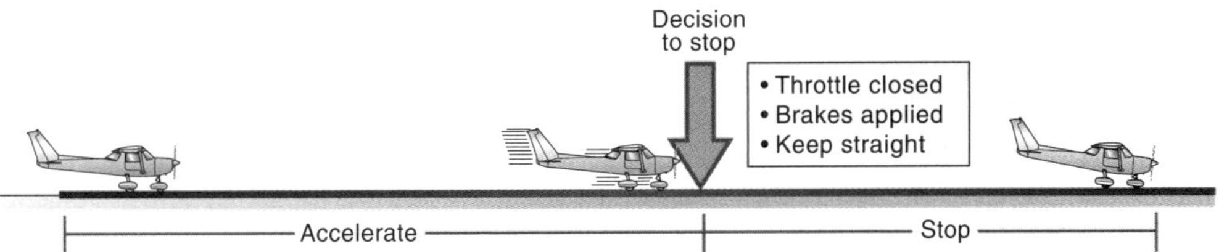

Figure 32-1 The aborted takeoff.

- brake firmly (immediate maximum braking if required), avoid locking the wheels;
- maintain directional control;
- clear the runway;
- stop the airplane, set the brakes to park, and establish the cause of the problem;
- shut down the engine if necessary (preferably clear of the runway); and
- notify ATC and seek assistance if required.

Fire or Engine Failure on Takeoff

On Takeoff Before Liftoff. Any major problem on takeoff is a reason to abort if the aircraft can be stopped in the available length of the runway. In the case of fire or engine failure (or significant loss of power), there is no choice even if the aircraft runs off the far end of the runway.

Immediate actions are:

- close the throttle;
- commence braking while keeping straight or steer for a clear path between obstacles;
- set the mixture control to idle cut-off;
- turn the fuel off;
- turn switches off; and
- abandon the aircraft and wait (especially if there is any indication of fire, any smoke, smells, vapor, if the brakes are overheated or if the aircraft is damaged).

If there is time to call aborting do so. Otherwise, do your best to stop and clear the runway and then advise the tower.

Before first solo it is appropriate to practice the correct response to engine failure after takeoff so that in this rare situation you have a reasonable chance of landing safely. This practice is not approved for some airfields and should only be considered on runways of more than adequate length.

The automatic reaction to a felt loss of thrust must be to immediately lower the nose to the glide attitude and pick somewhere to land in the forward windshield. In some aircraft this maneuver must be rapid, whereas in others the momentum is sufficient to allow a gentler change of attitude.

APPLICATION

Immediately lower the nose to the gliding attitude to maintain flying speed.

If engine power is lost in the climb-out following takeoff, the options open to the pilot will vary according to how high the airplane is, the nature of the terrain ahead, the wind conditions and so on. An event such as engine failure close to the ground requires prompt and decisive action by the pilot. No matter when the engine fails in flight, the first priority is to maintain flying speed. Immediately lower the nose to the gliding attitude to maintain flying speed.

A controlled descent and landing, even on an unprepared surface, is preferable by far to an unwanted stall in the attempted climb-out or turn back. Close the throttle, in case the engine comes back to life at an inopportune time. *Do not turn back to the field.* The altitude at which the failure occurs determines how you maneuver but, in general, you should plan to land fairly well straight ahead. Altitude is rapidly lost in descending turns and, from less than 500 feet HAA, it is doubtful that you would make the runway. Look for a landing area ahead (within the windshield) and within gliding distance.

Make yourself familiar with suitable emergency landing areas in the vicinity of your airfield, so that in the unlikely event of engine failure you already have a plan of action in mind. Take into account the wind velocity. Following engine failure, and having established the glide, quickly select the best landing area from the fields available ahead. Make only gentle turns (with, say, a maximum of 15° angle of bank).

Land straight ahead.

Gliding turns at low level can be dangerous due to:

- high rates of descent; and
- a tendency for the pilot to raise the nose to stop a high rate of descent and inadvertently stalling or spinning the airplane.

Complete checks and make a mayday call if time permits. Any attempt to switch fuel tanks or restart the engine depends on time being available. Maintaining flying speed is vital, more important than any radio call or even starting the engine. If the selected field looks rough and you think damage may result then, when committed to carrying out the landing:

- switch the ignition off;
- select the fuel off; and
- unlock the doors (or as advised in the pilot's operating handbook) in anticipation of a rapid evacuation.

After landing:

- Stop the airplane and set the brakes to park.
- Check that the fuel is off, ignition off, and electronics off.
- Evacuate.

After liftoff on a long runway, you may have sufficient runway remaining to land on. This is one reason why it is good airmanship to start such a takeoff using the full length of the runway. One of the most useless things in aviation is runway behind you!

One of the most useless things in aviation is runway behind you.

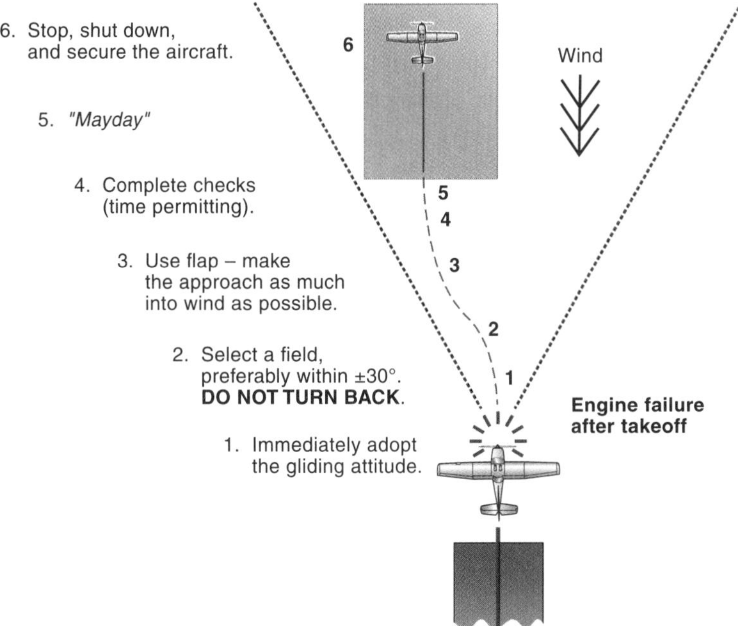

6. Stop, shut down, and secure the aircraft.
5. "Mayday"
4. Complete checks (time permitting).
3. Use flap – make the approach as much into wind as possible.
2. Select a field, preferably within ±30°. DO NOT TURN BACK.
1. Immediately adopt the gliding attitude.
Wind
Engine failure after takeoff
6
5
4
3
2
1

Figure 32-2 Engine failure after takeoff.

The use of flaps will depend on time and the closeness of a landing field. The flare will be the same as a glide approach as there is no power and little propeller slipstream over the elevators.

For the practice, use power to cushion the flare if the rate of descent is excessive or the airspeed too slow.

Engine Failure in the Pattern

Crosswind and Downwind Legs

If you have passed 500 feet and started to turn onto the crosswind leg then you have a little time to consider a greater number of options for landing, including landing downwind on the airfield. The attitude change, though, must still be immediate, especially if the aircraft is banked. If you wish to continue turning, the attitude must be even lower.

On the later part of the crosswind leg or when on the downwind leg, you may be able to establish a glide approach to an alternative runway. Declare a mayday.

Base Leg and Final Approach

When established on the base leg or final for a powered approach and the engine fails, you can no longer reach the runway. Don't even think about it. The aircraft will not glide as far as a powered approach. You may be able to cut the corner and reach some part of the airfield, but your path must be adjusted substantially. Importantly, adjust the attitude first to maintain glide speed and then see where the aircraft will reach. In some aircraft, the technique will be to fly the pattern so you can reach the runway from the base leg; that is, make every approach a glide. This is acceptable for aircraft where the engine reliability is suspect, but it is not the most precise way to control the approach and landing.

Engine Abnormalities: Partial Loss of Power or Oil Pressure

If there is any abnormal engine indications, RPM fluctuations, or rough running, in the pattern area, declare an emergency (pan-pan or mayday), continue the pattern to land and maintain your place in the pattern. Turn onto the base leg early so that you can reach the threshold even if there is a total loss of power. Turn the boost pump on, check the fuel contents and change tanks if necessary, select mixture to full rich and carburetor heat to hot. Broadcast your call sign, symptoms, position and intentions. *Do not go-around.*

It is important to be looking ahead and to know what attitude to set rather than be looking for airspeed. Learn to select the flaps by feel so that you do not have to look for the selector.

Do not attempt to turn for a landing area unless you are certain that the altitude above terrain is adequate.

REVIEW 32

Fire and Engine Malfunctions

1. Where are the emergency procedures for your airplane contained?
2. Any signs of fire in flight warrant what sort of call?
3. What sort of type is the fire extinguishers for your airplane?
4. If you have an electrical fire and turn off all electronics, what services would you lose in your airplane?
5. What are the three immediate actions to abort a takeoff?
6. If the engine fails after liftoff and there is insufficient runway to land ahead, where would you choose to land?
7. What is the glide speed for your airplane?
8. What is the single most important action for EFATO?

Figure 32-3 Choose a clear area and land ahead.

Answers are given on page 584.

TASK

EFATO (Practice)

Aim: To demonstrate and practice the immediate actions following engine failure after takeoff.

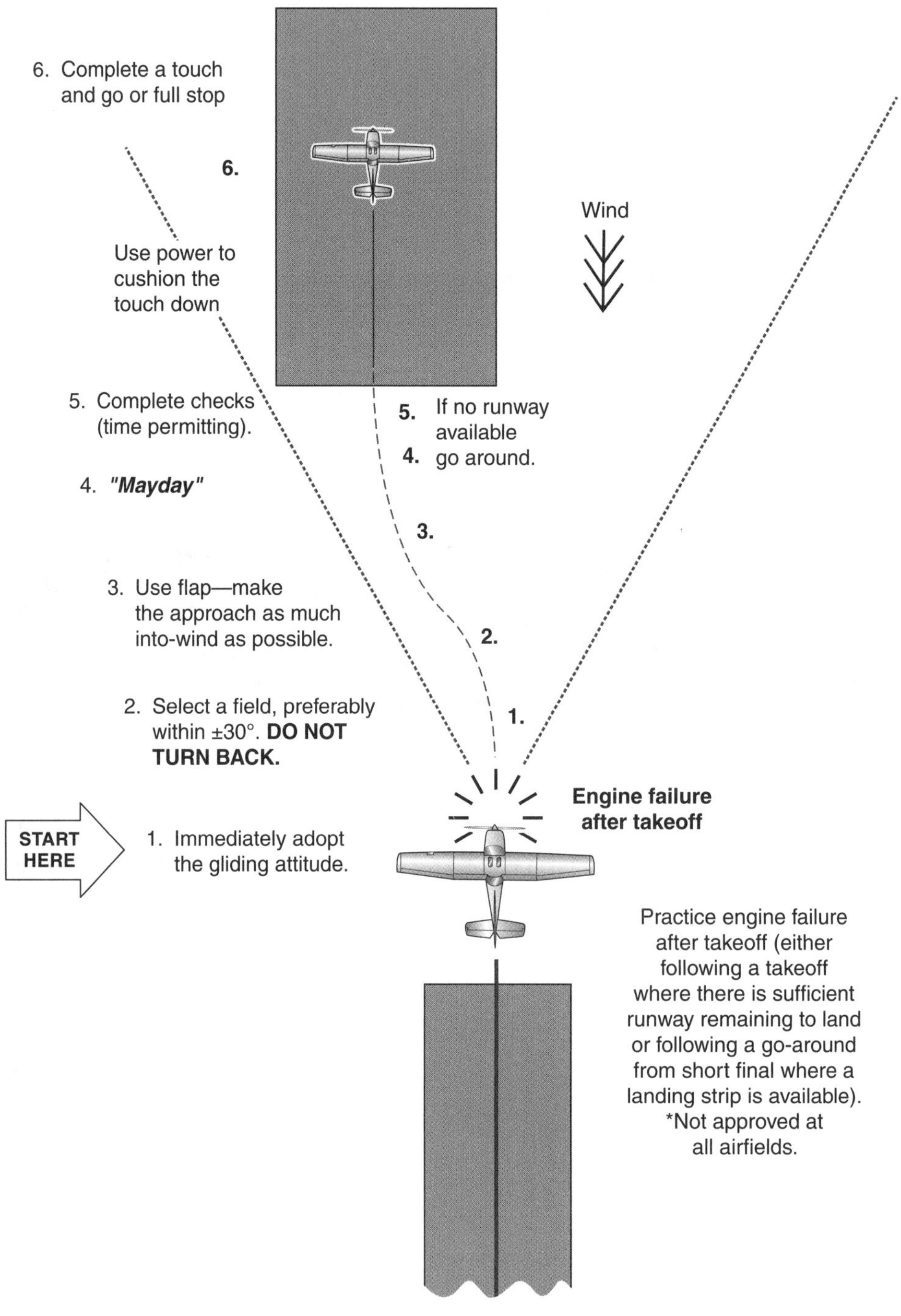

6. Complete a touch and go or full stop
6.
Use power to cushion the touch down
Wind
5. Complete checks (time permitting).
4. *"Mayday"*
5. If no runway available
4. go around.
3.
3. Use flap—make the approach as much into-wind as possible.
2.
2. Select a field, preferably within ±30°. **DO NOT TURN BACK.**
1.
Engine failure after takeoff
START HERE
1. Immediately adopt the gliding attitude.
Practice engine failure after takeoff (either following a takeoff where there is sufficient runway remaining to land or following a go-around from short final where a landing strip is available). *Not approved at all airfields.

33

Power-Off (Glide) Approach

OBJECTIVE

To describe the procedure and technique to carry out an approach and landing with idle power.

CONSIDERATIONS

The glide approach and landing made without the assistance of power is very good for developing your judgment and is good practice for emergency forced landings following an engine failure. On a glide approach, the flight path angle to the runway is deliberately on the steep side so that it can be controlled by the use of flaps or sideslip. For this reason a displaced aim point at least one-third of the runway length in from the actual threshold is chosen. When attainment of this aim point becomes certain, then flaps and slips are used to refine the aim point and to bring it closer to the actual threshold.

Approach Flight Path

The flight path on a power-off approach is steep and the flare more pronounced.

On a normal, engine-assisted approach, power is used to control the rate of descent and the airspeed to the aim point on the runway. Without power, the descent rate is greater and the pitch attitude of the airplane must be lower to maintain the desired approach speed. The result is a steeper approach path to the runway and so the airplane must be positioned higher on the final approach than normal. The lower nose attitude and the steeper path in the glide, especially with full flap, will mean that the change of pitch attitude required in the flare will be greater and must be initiated earlier, especially since there is little slipstream over the elevators.

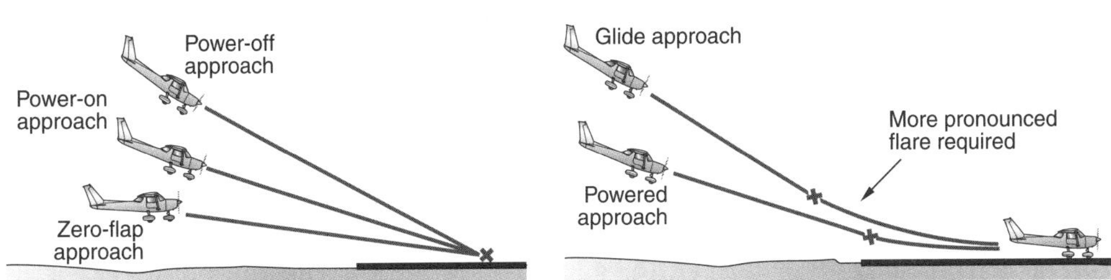

Figure 33-1 A glide approach is steep and the flare (attitude change) more pronounced.

APPLICATION

Base Turn Position

Turn base earlier in strong wind conditions.

To achieve the steeper approach path to the aim point on the runway, make the downwind leg shorter than normal, with the base leg flown closer to the field than in the normal power-assisted approach. In strong wind conditions, the base leg should be flown even closer to the field to ensure that you do not undershoot.

Descent Point

Delay the descent from pattern altitude for a planned power-off approach.

The descent point on base leg should be carefully chosen since the intention is, once power is removed, not to have to use it again. Use the amount of drift correction required on the base leg to estimate the wind strength for the final approach. Ideally, if you have judged the closer base leg correctly, descent may be commenced when you are certain of reaching the displaced aim point. Initially, aim well down the runway (say 500 feet) so that the airplane is definitely higher than normal on approach. The approach can later be steepened with flap, whereas it cannot be flattened without the use of power.

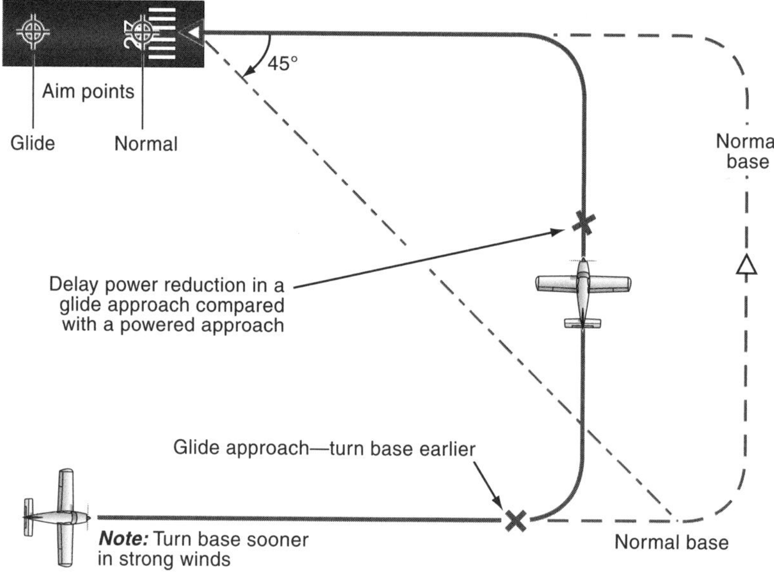

Figure 33-2 Turn onto the base leg earlier and delay descent for a glide approach.

TECHNIQUE

Controlling the Flight Path

Use of flaps in stages will steepen the glide path and bring the aim point nearer the threshold. It is preferable to be high on approach rather than too low. If you are high on approach, either:

- extend some flap, lower the nose to achieve the correct airspeed, and retrim;
- turn away from the field slightly or delay the turn onto the final approach;
- sideslip; or
- fly S-turns on final approach (but these can make the approach difficult to judge).

If you are in any doubt about reaching the aim point:

- delay the selection of flap; and/or
- cut in on the base leg to shorten the final approach.

If you are very low, use power to reposition the airplane on the glide path or to go around and start again.

Turns

Avoid steep gliding turns, since the descent rate will increase significantly and stalling speed will increase. Be prepared for an increased rate of descent and a steepening of the glide path in the medium turn onto to final approach.

Glide Distance

Do not try to stretch the glide.

Do not allow airspeed to get too low by trying to *stretch* the glide. It has the reverse effect. At very low airspeeds the flight path will steepen even though the nose position is high. Raising the flaps is not advisable, since it will initially cause the airplane to sink (unless you have selected full flap too early, in which case returning to part flap may be advisable). In a strong head wind, a slightly higher approach speed will give the airplane more *penetration* even though the descent rate is increased. Apply power and go around if the approach has been badly misjudged.

Landing Flap

Delay the selection of landing flaps until absolutely certain of reaching the field.

If the aim point with partial flap is 500 feet down the runway, selection of more flap will give you a new aim point nearer the threshold. Progressively lower the flap as required, but delay the selection of landing flap until you are absolutely certain that the runway will be reached comfortably. In a glide approach, err in favor of a slight overshoot of the aim point.

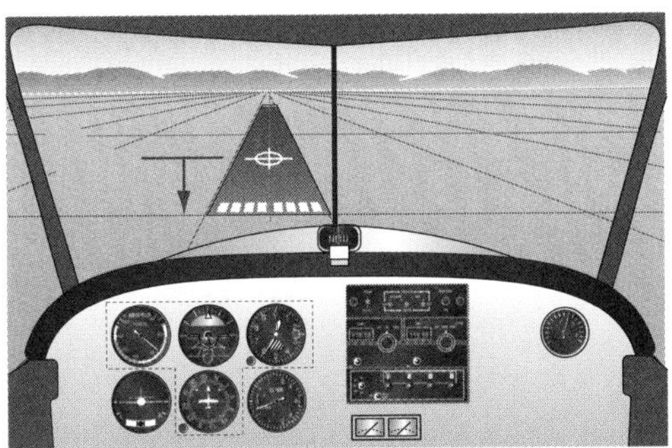

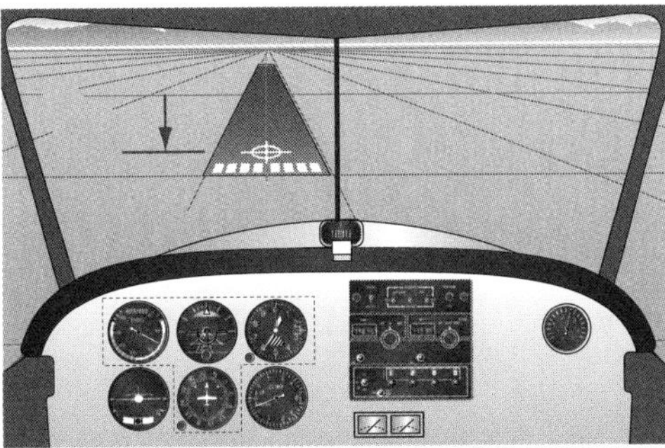

Figure 33-3 Bringing the aim point closer to the threshold by lowering additional flap.

Flare

Begin the flare slightly higher than normal.

With full flap and no power, the glide path will be steep and the nose attitude will be quite low to achieve the desired approach speed. The change of attitude in the flare will be quite pronounced and a gentle flare should be commenced a little higher than normal. Remember the elevators will not be as powerful.

REVIEW 33

Power-Off (Glide) Approach

1. How will the steepness of the power-off (glide) approach compare to the power-on approach? How will the nose attitude compare?
2. How will the rate of descent change when entering a gliding turn?
3. How should the distance from the runway of the descent point for a power-off gliding approach compare to that for the descent of a normal powered approach?
4. If you are high on a glide approach, what change to the flaps should you make?
5. How will the steepness of a glide compare to a glide with more flaps at the same airspeed?
6. What should you do if you are a little lower on approach than you want to be?
7. What should you do if you are hopelessly low on a practice glide approach?
8. How does the change in nose attitude when flaring the airplane after a power-off approach compare to that following a normal power-on approach?

Answers are given on page 584.

TASK

Glide Approach and Landing

Aim: To carry out a practice approach and landing without the use of power.

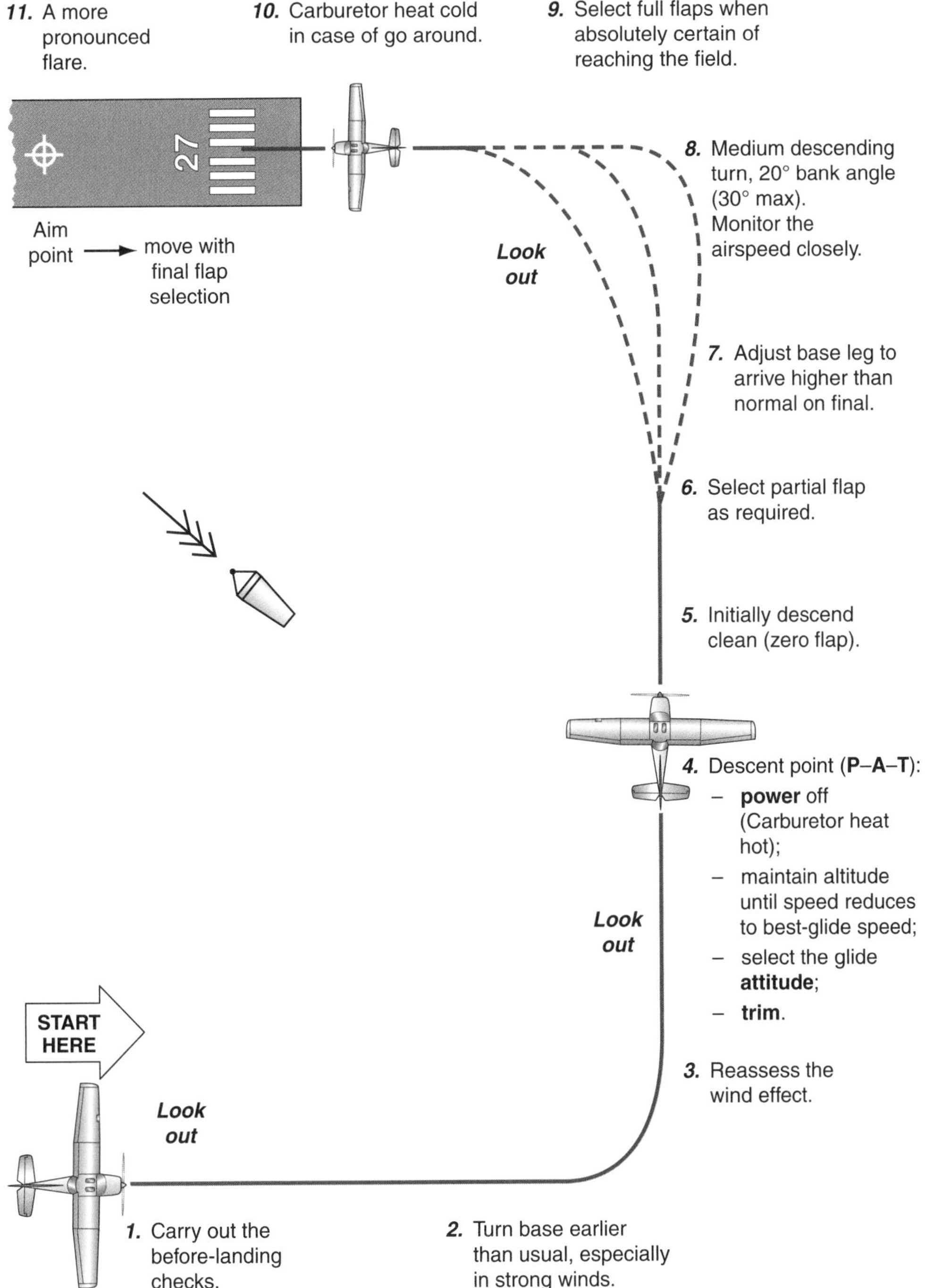

11. A more pronounced flare.
10. Carburetor heat cold in case of go around.
9. Select full flaps when absolutely certain of reaching the field.
27
8. Medium descending turn, 20° bank angle (30° max). Monitor the airspeed closely.
Aim point → move with final flap selection
Look out
7. Adjust base leg to arrive higher than normal on final.
6. Select partial flap as required.
5. Initially descend clean (zero flap).
4. Descent point (**P–A–T**):
– **power** off (Carburetor heat hot);
– maintain altitude until speed reduces to best-glide speed;
– select the glide **attitude**;
– **trim**.
Look out
START HERE
3. Reassess the wind effect.
Look out
1. Carry out the before-landing checks.
2. Turn base earlier than usual, especially in strong winds.

34

Zero-Flap Approach

OBJECTIVE

To describe the procedure and technique to approach and land without the use of flaps.

Zero-flap approaches are shallow.

CONSIDERATIONS

A flapless approach will be necessary if a failure of any part of the flap system occurs (a rare event) or, in some cases, in the event of an electrical failure. Landing with less than full flap may be suggested for some aircraft in strong and gusty winds. Crosswind landings are often made in such conditions. Compared to a normal approach and landing the main features of a flapless approach and landing are:

- flatter flight path requiring an extended base turn position (an extra 5 seconds or so);
- higher approach speed (due to the higher stalling speed) typically add 5 knots to all pattern speeds;
- higher nose attitude and reduced forward and downward view;
- little flare and a longer float (due to less drag), if the hold-off is prolonged;
- risk of scraping the tail if the nose is raised too high on touchdown; and
- longer landing roll.

Use a slightly higher airspeed but keep it under control with attitude and power.

APPLICATION

It is most important to control the flight path and airspeed fairly closely on a flapless approach. It is important to keep the airspeed on schedule. If too high or too fast, reduce power and raise the nose slightly to reduce airspeed; if the power is already at idle, consider a sideslip to increase the rate of descent and lose altitude. You may lose sight of the runway threshold on short finals. Trust your peripheral vision and maintain the attitude. A clean wing has less drag than a flapped wing, which means that excess speed takes longer to wash off; that is, a flapless airplane is slippery and the float in ground effect will be longer. This can lengthen the hold-off and float considerably. To avoid using too much runway and also to avoid the risk of scraping the tail, do not prolong the hold-off, particularly on a short runway. Once the aircraft is flared allow it to touch down and hold that attitude until ready to lower the nose. Once the nose wheel is on the ground, brakes can be used.

With zero flaps, the airplane is "slippery." Use a forward slip to steepen the approach without gaining airspeed.

Airspeed control is the most important element of flying a flapless approach and landing. Since the pattern is extended also be aware of other traffic that may turn inside you. You may lose sight of the threshold altogether from short finals. Don't lower the nose. Continue the approach and trust your peripheral vision to judge the flare.

REVIEW 34

Zero-Flap Approach

1. How does the steepness of the flight path for a zero-flap approach compare to that for a full-flap approach? How does the approach speed of a zero-flap approach compare to a full-flap approach?

2. How can you lose unwanted altitude on a zero-flap approach? What effect does this have on drag? What effect does this have on the steepness of the glide?

Answers are given on page 584.

TASK

Flapless Approach and Landing

Aim: To approach and land without the use of flaps.

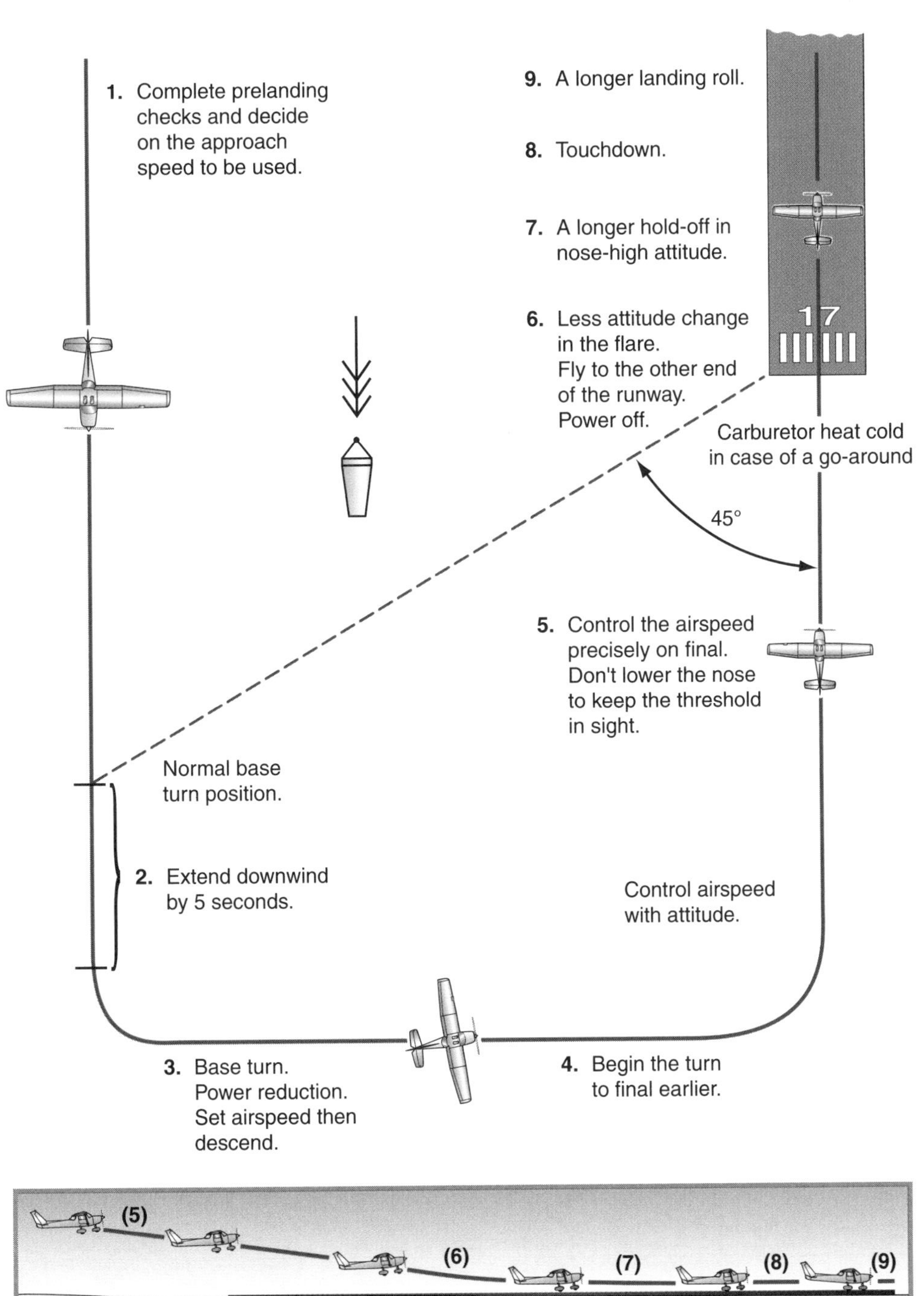

1. Complete prelanding checks and decide on the approach speed to be used.
9. A longer landing roll.
8. Touchdown.
7. A longer hold-off in nose-high attitude.
6. Less attitude change in the flare. Fly to the other end of the runway. Power off.
17
Carburetor heat cold in case of a go-around
45°
5. Control the airspeed precisely on final. Don't lower the nose to keep the threshold in sight.
Normal base turn position.
2. Extend downwind by 5 seconds.
Control airspeed with attitude.
3. Base turn. Power reduction. Set airspeed then descend.
4. Begin the turn to final earlier.
(5)
(6)
(7)
(8)
(9)

35

Forced Landings Following Engine Failure

OBJECTIVES

To describe:

- the pilot's immediate reactions to total engine failure or substantial loss of power;
- the mayday call;
- checks and procedures relevant to your airplane; and
- the pattern, key points, judgment and techniques to land safely off an airport in actual or practice circumstances.

Figure 35-1 Forced landing.

CONSIDERATIONS

Why Would an Engine Fail?

Always physically check the fuel prior to flying.

A forced landing due to a mechanical malfunction or a structural problem is a rare event with modern airplanes. However, occasionally it happens, so be prepared. Fuel starvation is often the cause of an engine stopping in flight. Fuel gauges can be inaccurate and fuelers have on rare occasions loaded incorrect or contaminated fuel. A visual inspection of the fuel tanks and of the fuel itself during your preflight inspection should prevent insufficient or incorrect fuel causing a forced landing.

Fuel management, plotting time, distance and fuel, checking consumption against planned figures, correct power settings and leaning procedures are all essential elements to avoid engine failure due to fuel starvation. Forgetting to switch from a near-empty fuel tank in flight to an alternative tank, incorrect use of the mixture control and failure to use carburetor heat can all lead to an engine stoppage. If the engine fails immediately after a fuel selection, revert at once to the previous selection.

Always check your fuel selection and be aware of the actual fuel situation. Use the mixture control and carburetor heat controls correctly.

Fuel contamination is another potential cause, as is insufficient oil. Actual forced landings also result from practice forced landings when the engine does not respond for a go-around. This is often the result of incorrect fuel or switch selections, insufficient clearing of the spark plugs and engine warming during the glide, carburetor icing or leaving the go-around far too late.

The minimum altitude during a practice forced landing is 500 feet AGL.

Performance data published in flight manuals are obtained from test results achieved by experienced test pilots flying new, calibrated airplanes under ideal conditions. Similar results will be difficult to achieve for an average pilot in a well-used airplane. The published fuel consumption and range figures also assume correct leaning of the mixture and critically depend on the cruise altitude selected. Always be aware of the real fuel situation. Never allow fuel starvation to force you into an unwanted landing.

Other possible causes of engine stoppage include faults in the magneto system, in ancillary equipment (e.g. a carburetor malfunction or a broken fuel line), mechanical failure (possibly due to insufficient oil) or an engine fire. This is not to say that you will have to cope with an engine stoppage each and every time you go flying. It is not unusual for a pilot to go through a whole career without a real engine failure, although simulated engine failures will have been practiced many times.

Forced landings without power can be made quite safely.

A well-trained pilot is well prepared for an engine failure at any time in flight or on the ground. A disciplined approach to checklists and the sequence of events during training is important, as the recall of procedures can be extremely difficult when faced with a real emergency. All pilots must be able to cope with an emergency landing without the use of engine power, probably on an unprepared surface. This can be done quite successfully. The low landing speed of a modern training aircraft and its robust construction allow it to be landed safely in quite small fields, provided the pilot positions the airplane accurately and especially avoids the risk of stalling. The intention is to survive without injury and a bonus is to have an undamaged airplane.

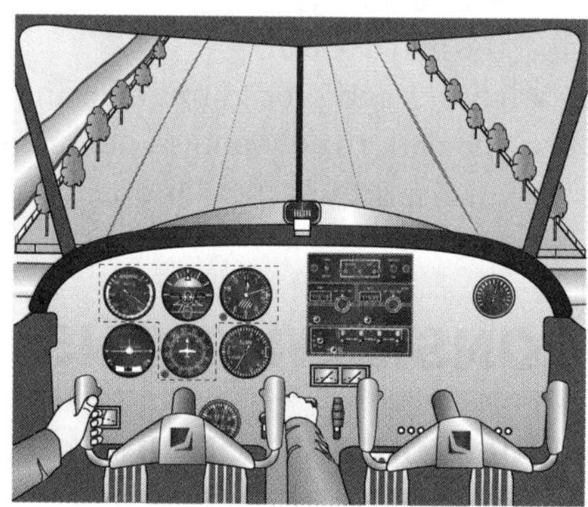

Figure 35-2 Safe forced landings can be made into small fields.

No new flying aspects are introduced with this exercise; it is simply a matter of putting together what you already know, gliding, gliding turns, glide approach, some radio calls and emergency checklist items and making a decision on a suitable field fairly quickly.

An airplane that glides at 700 feet per minute rate of descent will allow the pilot only 3 minutes from an altitude of 2,000 feet AGL. Always be aware that flying the airplane is the first priority, so maintain the best-glide airspeed and trim. Planning and executing the approach comes next, with an attempt (if you think it advisable) to restart the engine. This would only occur if you were fairly sure that the failure was a fuel or carburetor icing problem and that it had been cured. Partial power from an engine that has not completely failed may give you extra time and the possibility of gaining some extra distance, but do not rely on it. The engine may fail completely at a most inopportune moment and it spoils your judgment. Plan your approach and landing as if no power is available.

Emergency Equipment and Survival Gear

You must know the location and use of all emergency equipment and survival gear in your airplane. If your airplane is equipped with an emergency locator transmitter (ELT), know how it is used in the event of an accident (reference your POH). You must understand where and how to use any fire extinguishers in your airplane, and understand that this equipment must be maintained, just like the rest of your flight equipment. If you keep a basic first aid kit and any kind of survival gear, including life vests or a raft, you will have to discuss their uses with your instructor.

Engine Failure at Altitude

Altitude above ground means time to a pilot, and the amount of time that you have available determines how quickly you need to react and how far you can glide. If the engine fails near the ground convert any excess speed into altitude (and more time) by a gentle climb. For an engine failure during the cruise, maintain altitude until the airspeed decays to gliding speed, or turn toward a known clear area, and then establish a glide with the airplane in trim. When the airplane is comfortably under control, perform some simple immediate actions and attempt an engine restart, provided that you think restarting the engine is a good idea. The usual immediate actions include:

- closing the throttle;
- turning on the fuel boost pump;
- changing fuel tanks;
- setting the mixture control to rich;
- turning off and locking the primer;
- turning on carburetor heat;
- checking the magnetos by selecting each individually to see if the engine restarts by itself; and
- moving the throttle to see if there is any response.

Engine Restart

An immediate engine restart may be possible.

Rectify the problem if possible.

If the propeller is still turning, rectification of the fuel or ignition problem (if that is the cause) will see the engine fire up again without any need to use the starter.

Following a mechanical failure or fire, the engine should be stopped immediately. If the failure is partial, resulting in reduced or intermittent running, then use the engine at your discretion. There is a likelihood that it may fail at a critical stage, so it may be best not to rely on it and simply assume a total failure. Following a failure due to faulty operation by the pilot, restart the engine in the glide.

Practice Forced Landing (PFL)

So far we have covered the genuine engine-failure situation. In practice, however, we only simulate an engine failure and, once having demonstrated that we could have made a safe landing, go around off the approach from a safe altitude (say 500 feet AGL in the low flight training area).

To ensure that the engine will respond at the time of go-around:

- ensure that the mixture is rich, move the carburetor heat to hot (prior to reducing power) and switch the fuel boost pump on (also propeller to maximum RPM);
- clear the plugs and warm the engine (by increasing momentarily to a moderate RPM and back to idle) for a few seconds every 500 or 1,000 feet on descent; and
- when applying power for the go-around, check the mixture is rich and set carburetor heat to full cold (most engine manufacturers recommend applying power first, then moving carburetor heat to cold).

Simulate the trouble check, mayday call and safety check; that is, call them out at the appropriate time in your glide descent, but do not action them. For example, call out "fuel off, magneto switches off", but do not move the switches.

APPLICATION

Forced Landing Scenario

Many scenarios are possible and your actions will depend on the situation at the time, the altitude above ground at which the failure occurs, the surface wind and the availability of suitable landing fields (possibly even an airport). We will consider a very general situation that is capable of modification to suit your precise set of conditions.

If the engine fails at a reasonable altitude (say 3,000 feet or more above ground level), a basic pattern that may be followed is:

- convert excess speed to maintain altitude or to turn;
- establish best-glide attitude and speed and then trim;
- carry out the immediate actions;
- select a suitable field and plan the pattern;
- make a distress (mayday) radio call;
- attempt to resolve the emergency (while maintaining a safe glide) using the trouble checks;
- brief the passengers for the landing (brace position and unlock the door or remind them of emergency egress routes); and
- carry out a safety check before landing.

Always Note the Surface Wind

While flying, it is good practice to be aware of the surface wind, to note the terrain and choose forced landing fields within gliding range as you proceed along track. This saves a significant amount of time and stress if the engine does fail. If you fly as if the instructor is next to you and is about to close the throttle and ask for a forced landing then you will always be ready.

Don't be too blasé about the reliability of the modern engine. They are reliable but they also occasionally fail. Many ultralight pilots have developed a habit of flying from one place to another via a series of suitable landing fields—just as all pilots did in the dawn of aviation. A forced landing into wind is generally safer because of the lower ground speed on touchdown and the shorter landing roll. However, a crosswind landing into a longer field could be preferable.

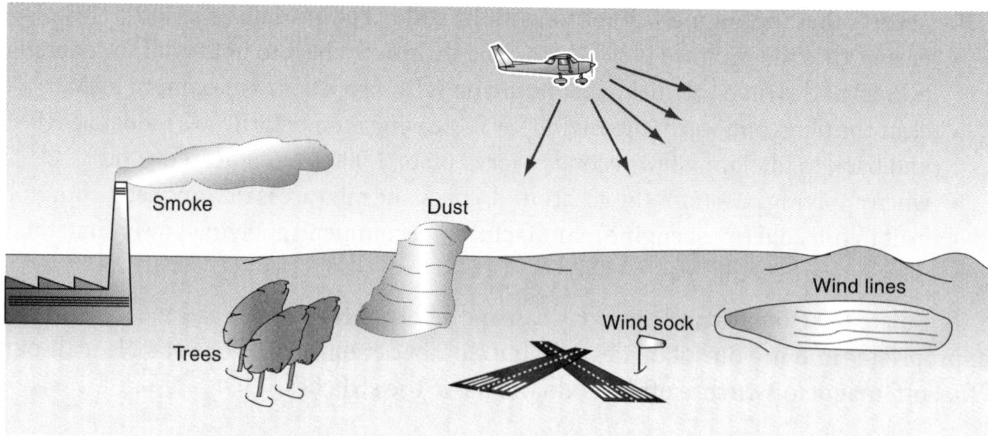

Figure 35-3 Always be aware of the surface wind direction.

Indicators of surface wind include:

- ATIS;
- smoke/dust from tractors;
- a wind sock;
- moving cloud shadows on the ground (especially if the clouds are low);
- the drift angle and speed of the airplane over the ground; and
- wind lanes on water (ripples or waves that flow downwind).

There is a story that horses and cattle always stand with their tails pointing into the wind, but you shouldn't rely on it.

Estimating Available Gliding Distance

Fly at the recommended gliding speed to achieve the best gliding range.

A typical training aircraft has a best lift-to-drag ratio of approximately 12:1, which means that, when flown at the correct gliding speed, 12,000 feet (or 2 nautical miles) can be gained horizontally for each 1,000 feet lost in altitude. Losing 1,000 feet vertically in 12,000 feet horizontally is an angle of depression (down from the horizontal) of about 5° (easy to work out using the 1-in-60 rule). Remember that this best lift-to-drag ratio only occurs at one angle of attack, which equates to one airspeed for the particular weight. Any error in speed reduces the gliding distance. Your instructor will stress the importance of flying an accurate attitude, and therefore airspeed, during the forced landing.

To estimate gliding range, in still air, conservatively, lower your arm about 5° from the horizontal. You should be pointing at a position on the ground to which a glide in still air is possible. Of course, the closer the chosen field is, the more certain you are of reaching it comfortably. However, there could be a need to turn and to maneuver, and there are changing winds at different levels. A safer approach is to allow double this angle, say 10°, when selecting a field and remember that you want to arrive next to that field at an altitude of at least 1,500 feet AGL. From 3,000 feet above the ground, you can only expect to travel three nautical miles to a suitable field—anything further is risky.

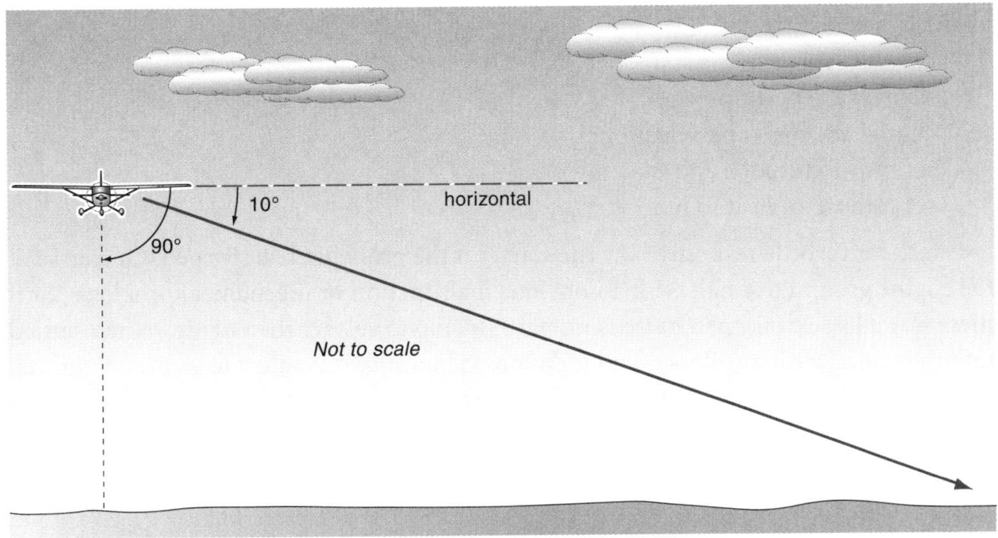

Figure 35-4 An approximate estimate of gliding range in nil wind and without turning.

A head wind will reduce the gliding distance; a tail wind will increase it. A windmilling or stopped propeller will also decrease it. In your training so far, you have become familiar with the glide path achievable with the engine idling and the propeller turning over. Selecting coarse pitch also reduces propeller drag in the case of an actual failure.

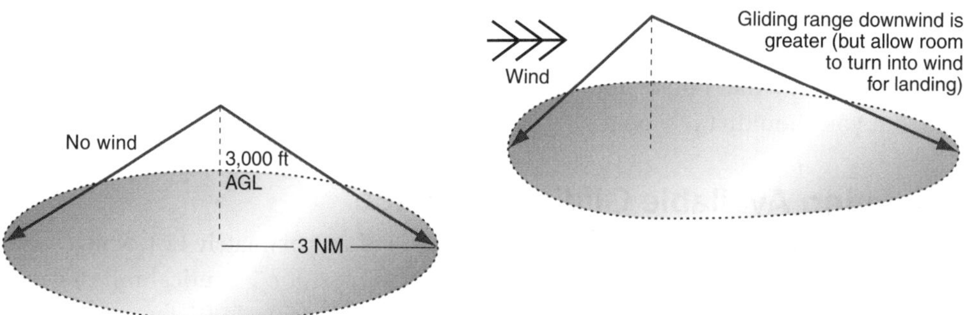

Figure 35-5 Wind affects gliding distance over the ground.

If the engine has failed, the propeller (either stopped or windmilling) will cause a significant increase in drag. The nose of the airplane will have to be lowered to maintain airspeed and the rate of descent will increase. The increased drag will mean a steeper glide path and a reduced gliding range. The propeller will probably continue turning unless the airspeed is reduced significantly below glide speed. It will probably stop during the landing flare, but don't be distracted by this.

Selecting a Suitable Field

Choose a forced-landing field well within your gliding range.

Following an engine failure, maintain altitude until the airspeed reduces and then adjust the attitude to maintain the best-glide speed for the particular weight. Trim the aircraft accurately and let the natural stability help you to maintain best speed. Carry out the following immediate actions:

- close the throttle;
- turn on the boost pump;
- change the fuel tank selection;
- set the mixture to full rich; and
- set carburetor heat to hot.

Check for throttle response. Try the starter if the propeller has stopped. Of course, if the engine ground to a halt with an obvious malfunction or mechanical problems, or if there was a loss of oil, then there is no point trying to restart the engine. When settled into the glide, select a suitable field for a forced landing. It is safest to select a field well within your gliding range and to fly a pattern around it, rather than to try a long straight glide to a distant field. The closer field makes correct judgment of the glide easier and gives you more flexibility and room to correct if your original estimates are not perfect.

The easiest place to look for a field is out of the left window. But do not fail to look out to the right, just in case a perfectly suitable field is available there. Maneuver the aircraft if necessary, and look beneath it. Ideally, select a field downwind of your present position, since that is where the gliding range of the airplane will be greatest.

Make all turns toward the field and do not turn your back on it: it is possible to lose sight of the field and waste time reidentifying it.

The forced landing field should be:

- well within gliding range;
- large and preferably surrounded by other suitable fields;
- clear of obstacles on the approach and overshoot areas;
- level or slightly uphill;
- a suitable surface; and
- close to civilization (communication and assistance may be valuable).

Make all turns toward the field.

Apply the mnemonic WOSSSSS:

WOSSSSS Forced Landing Check

W	Wind
O	Obstacles (on approach such as trees, rocks, power lines)
S	Size and shape of field (in relation to the wind)
S	Surface and slope
S	"Shoots" (undershoot and overshoot areas)
S	Sun (position relative to planned final approach)
S	S(c)ivilization (proximity for assistance after landing)

Of course, the ideal surface is a runway at an airport; however, pasture or stubble may be satisfactory (although wet grass, often indicated by dark green areas, may be a disadvantage). Crops and beaches in general should be avoided as landing surfaces, the preferred order being pasture, stubble, plowed fields, beaches, standard crops. Avoid roads if possible, because of the danger of vehicles, power lines and roadside posts or signs although, especially after heavy rain, a quiet, straight country road might be the best option.

Practice Forced Landing

Keep a good lookout. Other aircraft may be practicing glide approaches to the same field in the training area, possibly from the other direction in calm wind conditions. Ensure that the climb-out area following the go-around is clear of obstacles. Check this well before you descend to a point where the go-around could become marginal.

Practicing forced landings requires steady concentration. It is practicing for an emergency and has its own peculiar risks. You are calling out items associated with a real forced landing, yet operating the airplane so that it will function normally when you carry out a go-around from a safe altitude.

Be quite clear that, while practicing, you should not do anything that would endanger the airplane (e.g. do not actually shut down the engine). Go around so that you do not descend below 500 feet AGL.

TECHNIQUE

Planning the Approach

Use key points in planning the approach.

The basic plan that you formulate depends mainly on your altitude above the ground. Various patterns and key points around a field can assist you in flying a suitable glide descent. Each flight training organization and each flight instructor will have a preferred technique, but the aim is the same in every case: consistently good positioning for a glide approach and landing. We discuss various planning techniques. Your flight instructor will give you sound advice on which to use.

Method A: 1,000 Feet AGL Close Base Leg Technique

The basic aim using this technique is to arrive at 1,000 feet AGL on a close base leg, from which a comfortable glide well into the field can be made. If the engine is stopped, the drag from the propeller will steepen the glide path compared to the glide angle when the engine is idling (as in the practice maneuver), so allow for this possibility.

A close base leg provides flexibility.

A wide base leg allows little room for error, but a close base leg gives flexibility in the case of overshooting or undershooting the field, allowing adjustments to be made quite easily. According to your position when the engine fails, choose either a left or right 1,000-foot base area, with a long base leg and a short final approach. Left turns provide a better view of the field for the pilot. Noting a ground reference point near the 1,000-foot position will assist in reidentifying the turning-base point if you are distracted.

A suitable distance for the downwind leg is approximately ½ nautical mile from the selected landing path. In flying a square pattern around the selected field, approximately 1,000 feet per leg will be lost, and this must be considered in your planning.

Stay close to the field and make all turns toward it.

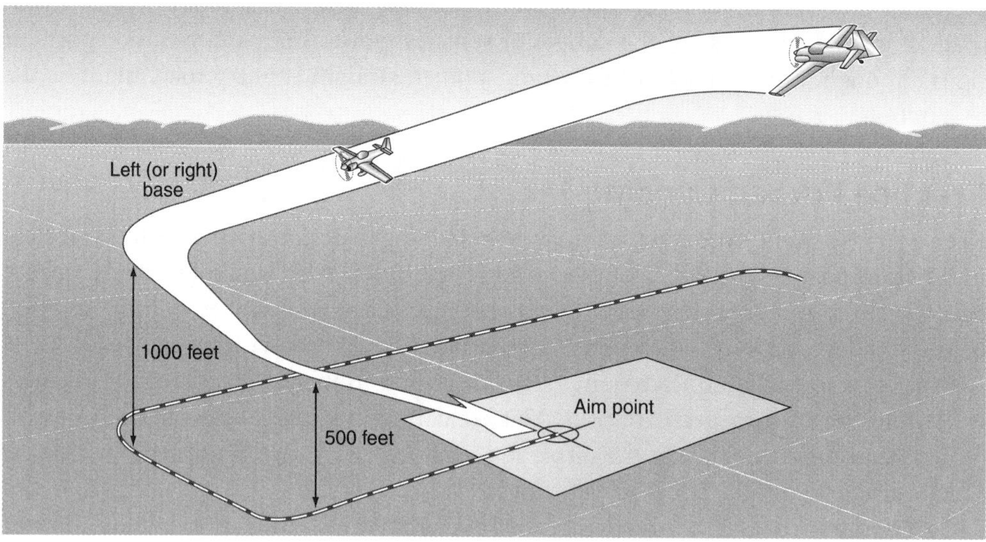

Figure 35-6 A basic pattern plan for a forced landing.

Method B: High Key and Low Key Technique

The other technique uses two reference points (called *high* and *low key points*) to check the progress of the landing pattern and provides more options for cutting corners and correcting the approach. The advantage of using the high key and the low key is that they are closely related to the selected landing strip and therefore are easily reidentified:

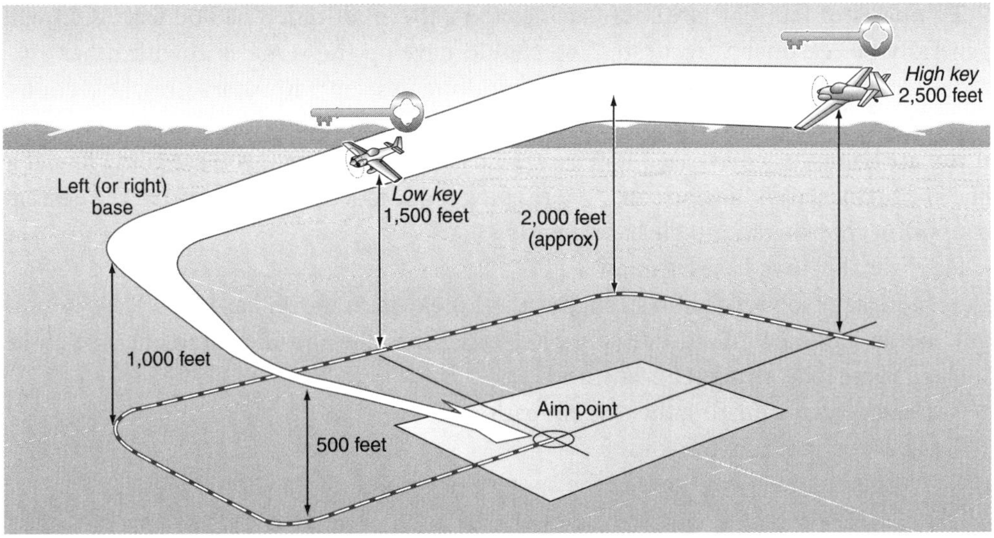

Monitor the descent to the key points, and plan on a long base and a short final.

Figure 35-7 The high key and the low key.

- *low key* is 1,500 feet AGL (about ½ nautical mile) abeam the landing threshold (a similar position to where the airplane would be using Method A if they flew a downwind leg); and
- *high key* is 2,500 feet AGL in line with and about ½ nautical mile upwind of the upwind end of the selected landing strip.

Assess the wind during the descent.

The first objective in the descent is to glide to the high key, keeping the field in sight. The purpose of the high key is simply to assist your judgment in reaching the low key, which is the more important key point. If you cannot reach the high key then you may find that you can glide direct to the low key without any definite consideration of the high key. If not, then you have no choice but to head directly for the base position. Monitor descent to the key points and plan the base leg and final approach. If too high, widen out; if too low, cut in.

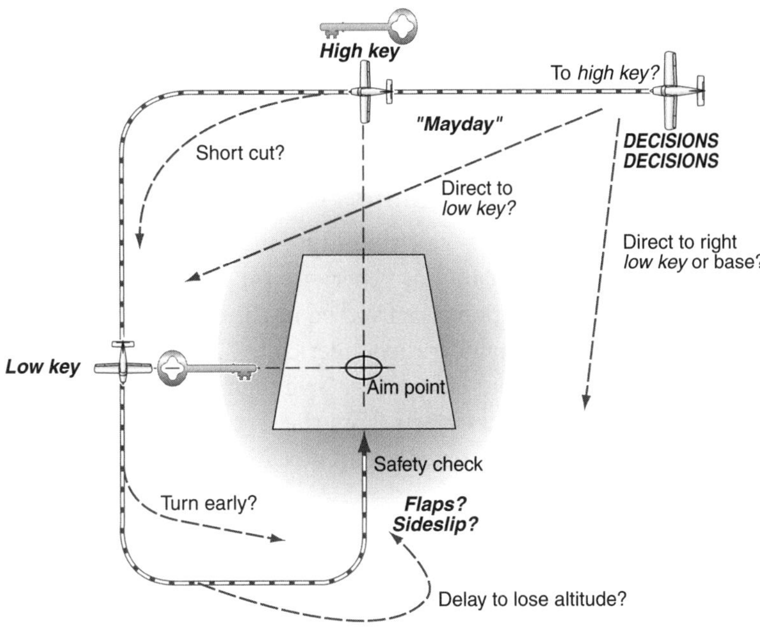

Figure 35-8 Monitor the descent to the key points.

Estimates of familiar altitudes (such as the pattern altitude of 1,000 feet AGL) will generally be reasonably accurate. You should develop the same skill with other altitudes. You are now following an almost spiralling descent with short straight sections. Throughout the pattern, the aim point will stay a constant distance below the horizon, if you are going to achieve it. If it becomes closer to the horizon, you are going low; if it become further from the horizon, you are going high. Assess the wind during the descent to assist in choosing a suitable base point.

A reasonably long base leg allows:

- more time to judge wind strength (using the drift angle on base);
- better judgment of altitude (since it is easier to judge altitude out to one side of the airplane than straight ahead); and
- flexibility in adjusting the descent path:
  - cutting in if too low; and
  - widening out, lengthening the base leg or extending flap, if too high.

A short final approach allows for a glide path steeper than expected.

Rectifying the Problem

Attempt to rectify the engine problem if there is time.

When established in the glide, there may be time to look for the cause of the engine failure and to remedy it. The pilot's operating handbook will contain a list of the appropriate items to check.

It will include:

- fuel;
- boost pump;
- primer;
- mixture;
- carburetor heat;
- oil temperature and pressure;
- magneto switches; and
- throttle response.

Control the flight path.

If the propeller is rotating, then turning the fuel and ignition on should be enough to restart the engine; otherwise, the starter may be required. While attempting to rectify the problem, the continuing descent toward the key points should be monitored and the suitability of the field confirmed.

If you decide that your chosen field is unsuitable, then select another as early as possible.

Radio Calls and Passenger Briefing

Advise others of your planned forced landing.

Make a distress call. The mayday call should be made on the area or flight service frequency that you have been using, or otherwise on 121.5 MHz as this frequency is monitored. Keep radio conversations brief and do not be distracted from your main duty, which is to fly the airplane. Squawk transponder code 7700.

Advise your passengers of your intentions. Give them firm directions. Request them to remain calm, to remove sharp objects from their pockets, to remove spectacles and ensure that their seat belts are fastened securely. Unlatch the door or remind them of the escape route.

Use of soft clothing or pillows will protect them if a sudden deceleration or impact is expected. Harnesses should remain fastened until the airplane stops.

Approaching Low Key at 1,500 Feet AGL

As the low key is approached, all of your attention needs to be focused on positioning the airplane for the approach and landing. Further attempts to restart the engine would only distract you from this task.

Do not be distracted from your main duty, which is to fly the airplane.

Secure the airplane, placing it in a safer condition for a landing on an unprepared field by carrying out a safety check to ensure:

Secure the airplane for touchdown on a rough surface.

- fuel is off;
- mixture is off; and
- switches are off (magnetos off, master switch off unless flaps are electrically operated).

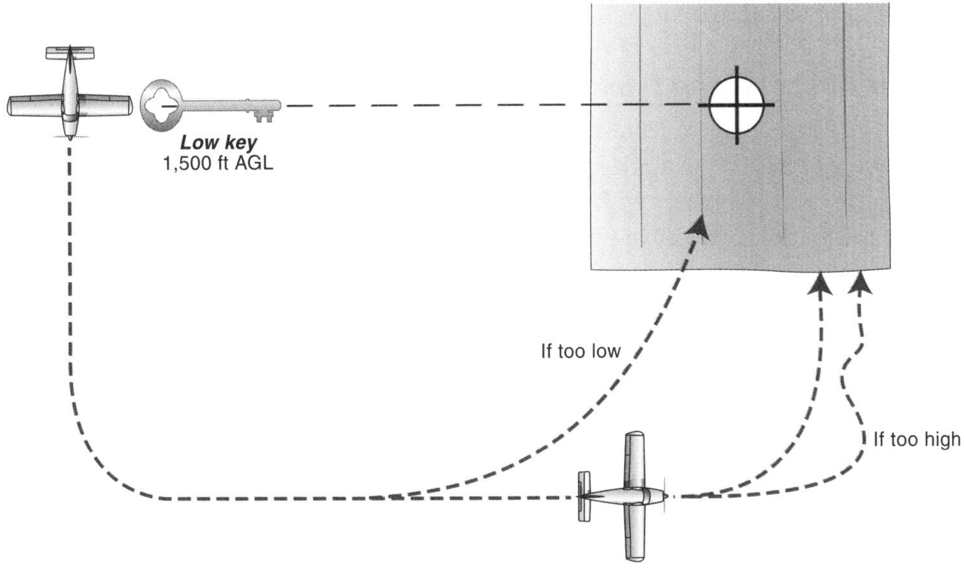

Figure 35-9 Position for a long base leg and a short final approach.

Turning to Base Leg

From the low key abeam the touchdown point, extend downwind according to the wind. The stronger the wind, the shorter the extension of the downwind leg, bearing in mind that it is preferable to be a little high on the final approach than to be too low.

Extend downwind according to the wind.

If the surface wind is:

- greater than 20 knots, commence base turn at the low key point abeam the aiming point for landing, i.e. at about 1,500 feet AGL;
- between 10 and 20 knots, commence base turn when the aiming point for landing appears about one-half chord length behind the trailing edge (for a low-wing airplane), which will occur at about 1,300 feet AGL; and
- less than 10 knots, commence base turn when the aim point for landing appears about one chord length behind the trailing edge (for a low-wing airplane), which will occur at about 1,100 feet AGL.

When to Use Flaps

A typical technique is to lower:

A long base leg and a short final give you the greatest flexibility.

- the first stage of flap at the base turn (if confident of reaching the aim point);
- the second stage when turning onto the final approach (assured of reaching the aim point); and
- full flap on the final approach (to bring the aim point closer to the threshold).

If the airplane appears to be high on the base leg then either:

- lengthen the base leg (go past the centerline and turn back);
- widen the base leg (turn away from the field slightly and then have a longer final approach);
- extend part flap;
- sideslip; or
- S-turn (turn away and back).

If the airplane becomes low on base leg, then you can:

- shorten the base leg;
- cut in toward the field for a shorter final approach; and
- delay the use of flap.

Monitor Airspeed and Bank Angle

Monitor airspeed and bank angle closely in the gliding turn to final.

It is most important that you maintain the correct gliding speed, especially when turning. A gliding turn near the ground should not be steep because:

- stalling speed increases with increasing bank angle and wing loading; and
- the rate of descent in turn increases with bank angle.

Be very conscious of your airspeed during the turn onto the final approach and limit the angle of bank to 15°–20° (30° maximum). Do not allow the airplane to approach the stall! Turn onto the final approach so that reaching the aim point or beyond is assured. It is better to land too far in than to undershoot the field and hit a fence or some other obstacle.

Final Approach

Once certain that you can reach the aim point, continue extending flap in stages to steepen your approach and bring the aim point closer to the near end of the field. Ensure that the master switch is off once electrically operated flaps have been placed in the landing position. If you are too high on the final approach:

- extend flap;
- make shallow S-turns;
- sideslip (but keep up your airspeed); and
- dive off excess altitude (but avoid this also if possible).

Figure 35-10 Extending more flap brings the aim point closer.

If you are too low on final approach, delay extending flap. Do not fall into the trap of trying to stretch the glide by raising the nose. Airspeed will fall and the flight path will in fact be steeper. Moreover, there will be no excess airspeed with which to stop the rate of descent. The impact will be short and firm.

In an extreme case, you may have to land in a closer field. It is better to land in a shorter field under complete control than to stall trying to reach a better one. As a last ditch attempt crank the engine with the starter motor—it will reduce propeller drag at least. Stay in control.

Landing

A forced landing with full flap is generally safest because:

- the touchdown speed is low (due to the lower stalling speed);
- the landing run is shorter; and
- the stress on the airframe will be less if the field is rough.

Hold the nose wheel off during the landing.

Touch down on the main wheels, holding the (less robust) nose wheel off with full up elevator. Brake as necessary but you may skid on wet grass. Unseen obstacles and ditches could be a problem. If collision with an obstacle is imminent (say the far fence), apply full rudder and braking on one side only to initiate a skidding turn. Otherwise, maneuver to pass between obstacles even if the wings are damaged. They will absorb energy and slow you down.

Down and Stopped

Secure the airplane and evacuate.

A forced landing is not complete until the airplane is stopped, the passengers evacuated, the airplane made secure and assistance obtained. Therefore, as soon as the airplane stops, evacuate the aircraft and move at least 100 feet away.

When certain there is no risk of fire, return to the aircraft, turn on the master switch (if there is no smell of fuel) and make a general radio broadcast that you are down safely. Then secure the airplane (check all switches are off, fuel is off and control locks are in).

Set the brakes to park. Chock and lock the airplane. Seek assistance and telephone the chief flight instructor and the appropriate authorities. If possible, leave someone in charge of the airplane.

AIRMANSHIP

When practicing forced landings without the use of engine power:

- Look out, especially in the latter stages of the glide approach.
- Clear the engine by increasing the RPM at least every 1,000 feet on descent.
- Do not descend below the authorized break-off altitude.
- Know your checks thoroughly and execute them in the correct sequence.
- Do not turn your back on the field. Keep it in sight at all times.
- Do not make unnecessary changes in your field selection.
- Make command decisions in a calm but firm manner.

REVIEW 35

Forced Landings Following Engine Failure

1. Following a sudden engine failure in flight, what should your first action be?
2. When maneuvering for a forced landing after engine failure, which airspeed do you maintain as closely as possible by altering the pitch attitude?
3. Should you be aware of the wind direction and have a suitable emergency landing area picked out at all times?
4. At which airspeed will you travel the furthest through the air in a glide?
5. You should make an emergency call on the frequency currently in use or on the emergency frequency. What is the emergency frequency?
6. In a radar environment, you can alert a radar controller to your emergency situation by squawking which code on your transponder?
7. There are three likely problems that could cause an engine to fail in flight. What are they?
8. Recall the items in your emergency forced landing checklist.
9. If the flaps are not available and you find yourself too high on final approach to the forced landing area, you could steepen the descent and lose excess altitude by using which technique?
10. During a simulated forced landing, do you need to clear the engine periodically and keep it warm during the prolonged descent?
11. While practicing forced landings after simulated engine failure, is it possible that you could still suffer a genuine engine failure?
12. You have suffered an engine failure in Mooney 8536C, five miles south of Eltville at an altitude of 7,000 feet MSL. You are descending through 6,000 feet MSL on a heading of south and plan to land in a farmer's grass-covered field. You have been using the Chicago FSS frequency. How would you construct your mayday call?
13. Before simulating engine failure, what do you select mixture and carburetor heat to?
14. Rehearse a complete mayday call.
15. State the minimum height by which you must go-around.
16. List the go-around actions.

Figure 35-11 Control the touchdown.

Answers are given on page 584.

TASK

Practice Forced Landing

Aims: To carry out a safe approach and landing following engine failure.

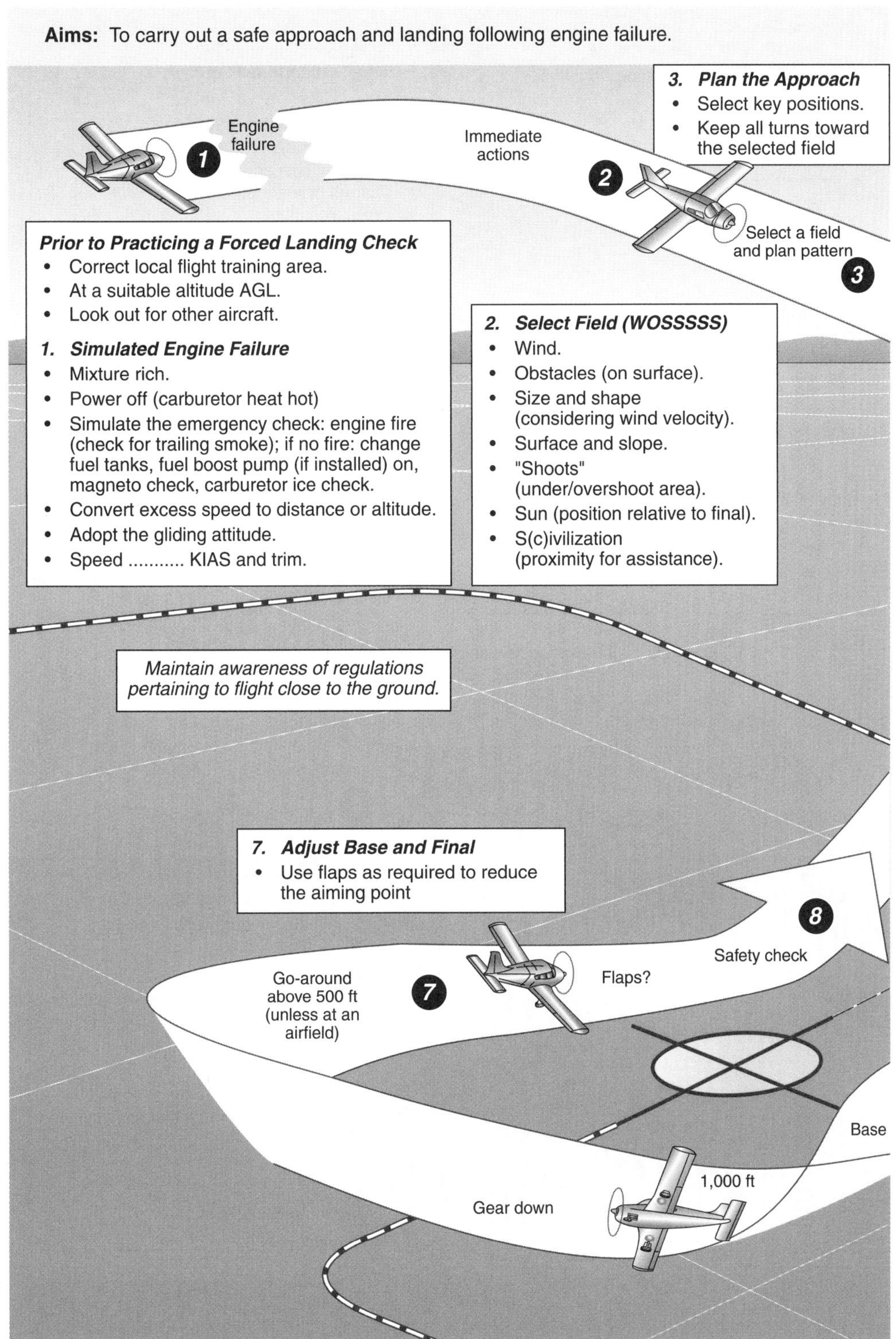

3. Plan the Approach
• Select key positions.
• Keep all turns toward the selected field
Engine failure
Immediate actions
1
2
Select a field and plan pattern
3
Prior to Practicing a Forced Landing Check
• Correct local flight training area.
• At a suitable altitude AGL.
• Look out for other aircraft.
1. Simulated Engine Failure
• Mixture rich.
• Power off (carburetor heat hot)
• Simulate the emergency check: engine fire (check for trailing smoke); if no fire: change fuel tanks, fuel boost pump (if installed) on, magneto check, carburetor ice check.
• Convert excess speed to distance or altitude.
• Adopt the gliding attitude.
• Speed .... KIAS and trim.
2. Select Field (WOSSSSS)
• Wind.
• Obstacles (on surface).
• Size and shape (considering wind velocity).
• Surface and slope.
• "Shoots" (under/overshoot area).
• Sun (position relative to final).
• S(c)ivilization (proximity for assistance).
Maintain awareness of regulations pertaining to flight close to the ground.
7. Adjust Base and Final
• Use flaps as required to reduce the aiming point
8
Safety check
Go-around above 500 ft (unless at an airfield)
7
Flaps?
Base
1,000 ft
Gear down

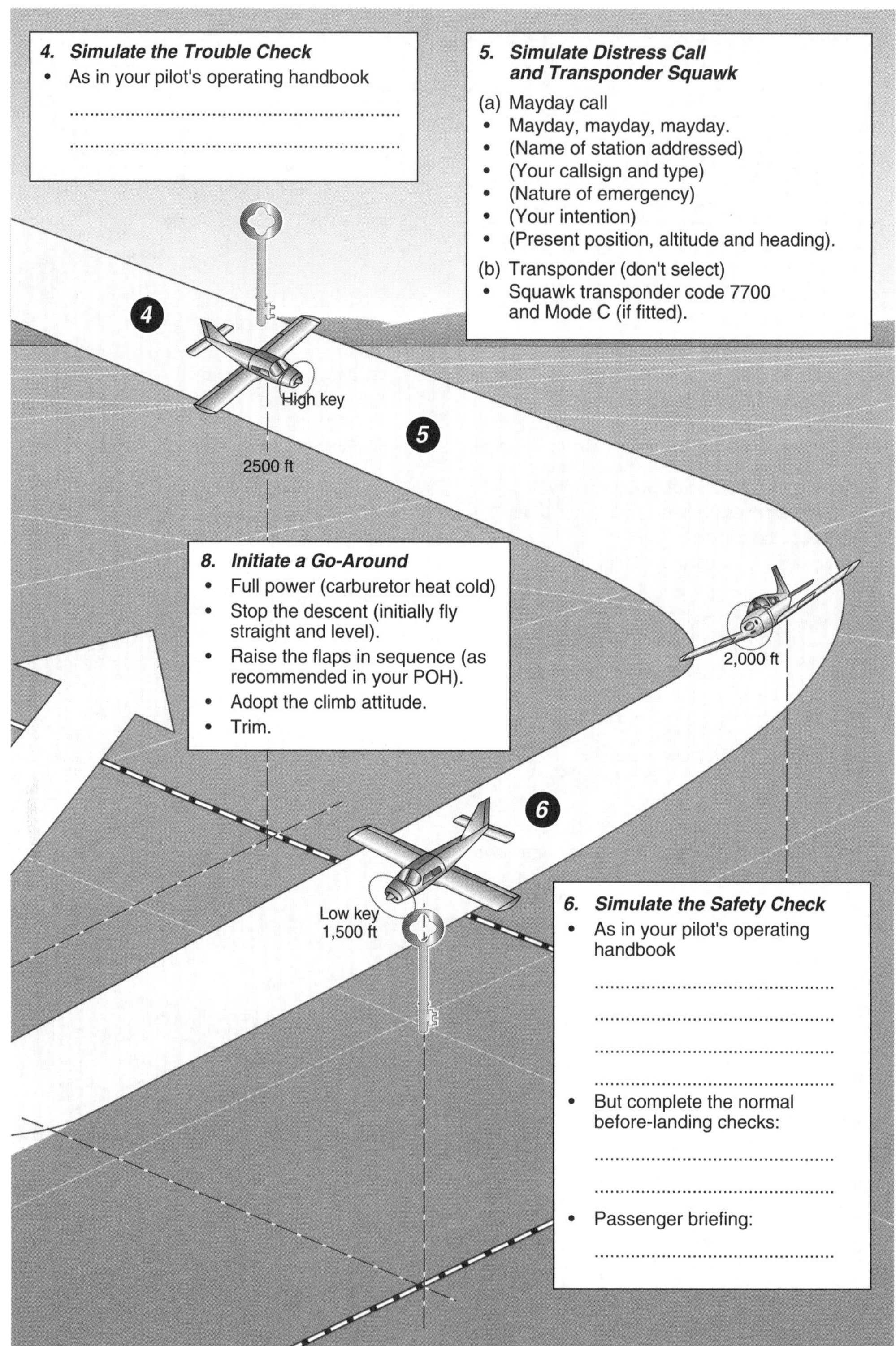
4. Simulate the Trouble Check
• As in your pilot's operating handbook
....
....
5. Simulate Distress Call and Transponder Squawk
(a) Mayday call
• Mayday, mayday, mayday.
• (Name of station addressed)
• (Your callsign and type)
• (Nature of emergency)
• (Your intention)
• (Present position, altitude and heading).
(b) Transponder (don't select)
• Squawk transponder code 7700 and Mode C (if fitted).
4
High key
5
2500 ft
8. Initiate a Go-Around
• Full power (carburetor heat cold)
• Stop the descent (initially fly straight and level).
• Raise the flaps in sequence (as recommended in your POH).
• Adopt the climb attitude.
• Trim.
2,000 ft
6
Low key
1,500 ft
6. Simulate the Safety Check
• As in your pilot's operating handbook
....
....
....
....
• But complete the normal before-landing checks:
....
....
• Passenger briefing:
....

36

Forced Landing into Water (Ditching)

OBJECTIVES

To describe the factors relevant to a forced landing into water.

CONSIDERATIONS

Make emergency calls before ditching.

Ditching means landing on water. The aim is to land safely on water. There may be circumstances where you have limited power. Use any fuel or partial power to reach land or a ship.

Being forced to ditch in the ocean or a lake is a remote possibility; however, it is worthwhile having a suitable procedure in the back of your mind. Try to land in shallow water, near a beach, near a ship or in a shipping lane if possible. Make a mayday call as soon as the ditching is inevitable.

Landing Direction

If the water is smooth, or smooth with a very long swell, then land into wind.

If there is a large swell or rough sea, then land along the swell, even if you have to accept a crosswind. This avoids the danger of nosing into a big wave. Waves generally move downwind except near a shoreline or in fast-moving estuaries, but swells may not bear any relationship to surface wind direction.

Clues to wind direction and strength include:

- wave direction;
- wind lanes (the streaked effect being more apparent when viewed downwind);
- gust ripples on the water surface; and
- airplane drift.

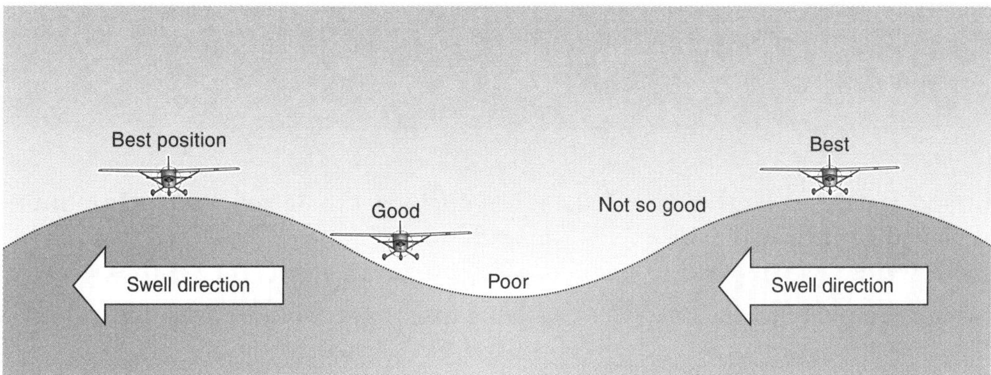

Figure 36-1 Touch down on top of a swell, or just after it.

APPLICATION

If your engine is running, use a powered approach for ditching. From altitude, water generally appears to be calmer than it is. Fly low and study the water surface before ditching. Generally ditch with an early stage of flap set, using a low speed, a high nose attitude (tail down) and a low rate of descent controlled by power (if available). Power gives you a lot more control over the touchdown point, so avoid running out of fuel prior to ditching. Touch down with as low a flying speed as possible, but do not stall.

Alert the Passengers

Used a powered approach for ditching, if possible.

Warn the passengers. Buckle up and don life jackets, if available, but do not inflate them until in the water, as they may restrict the evacuation. Remove headsets and anything else that may get in the way during the evacuation.

Be prepared for a double impact: the first when the tail strikes the water, the second (and greater) when the nose hits the water. The aircraft may also slew to one side.

Evacuation (if possible) should be carried out as calmly as possible, life jackets being inflated outside the cabin. The pilot in command should supervise.

REVIEW 36

Forced Landing into Water (Ditching)

1. If the wind is light and there is a large swell running, should you plan to ditch along the swell, into the swell or into the wind?
2. Which is the area of a swell to avoid when ditching?
3. When ditching, should you use power to minimize the rate of descent?
4. When ditching, should you touch down at as low a flying speed as possible or by stalling in?

Answers are given on page 584.

37 Precautionary Landing

OBJECTIVES

To describe:
- the preparation, judgment and assessment techniques prior to landing on an untested surface; and
- the piloting technique to minimize risks associated with landing on unfamiliar terrain.

Figure 37-1 Landing at an unfamiliar field.

CONSIDERATIONS

Why Land on an Unfamiliar or Unprepared Field?

A pilot may be faced with the decision to land away from an airfield for a number of reasons. These include:
- suspected engine or airframe problems;
- sudden deterioration in weather, with low cloud and decreasing visibility making further flight unsafe; or
- deficient flight planning or navigation.

Occasionally, an unscheduled landing is necessary.

Being totally lost, having insufficient fuel or insufficient daylight remaining are good enough reasons to consider making a precautionary landing in a field. It is far better to land in a field of your choice under controlled conditions than to be forced into a landing in an unsuitable field under poor conditions and perhaps with limited time available.

Potential incapacitation of the pilot due to, say, food poisoning or nausea is best coped with on the ground. Land sooner rather than later, but ensure that the field chosen for landing is suitable.

If you are about to land at an unfamiliar field, then you should conduct a precautionary inspection before landing, unless there is other aircraft activity at the field.

Decision to Land

Make an early decision to land.

If any doubt exists as to the advisability of continuing the flight, make the decision to land while there is still time to do so with the airplane under full control and before conditions deteriorate to a dangerous level. It is better to land before you run out of either fuel, daylight or visibility, even if the landing is in a field rather than at an airport.

Estimate what time you have available, and act accordingly.

Estimate what time you do have available. Slowing the airplane down and possibly lowering some flap may help enormously. Slow flight gives you more time to observe the ground and to plan, as well as making the airplane more maneuverable. The turning radius is reduced at slow speeds (same angle of bank) and the forward view from the cockpit is improved. However, do not fly so slowly as to risk symptoms of the stall. Do not fly at less than your normal traffic pattern and approach airspeeds.

APPLICATION

Low Flying in Bad Weather or Reduced Visibility

Poor visibility, a descending cloud base or rising ground may require some unplanned low flying. If you are caught out in really marginal conditions, maintain as much separation from the ground as possible, but avoid entering cloud (an estimated 100 feet beneath it is adequate). You may not have a clear horizon, so keep the attitude indicator in your visual scan and check your airspeed as you maneuver.

Use any aircraft systems that can assist you in coping with bad weather, such as carburetor heat (if required), pitot heaters, window demisters, etc. Make your airplane more visible by switching on the rotating beacon, landing light and strobes. Reassure your passengers and use them to help you look. If safe visibility and distance from cloud cannot be maintained, then consideration should be given to either:

- diverting to an area where better weather exists;
- landing at a nearby airfield, or requesting radar guidance if navigation is a problem; or
- making a precautionary landing in a field.

Bad-Weather Traffic Pattern

Avoid flying into cloud.

A pattern in bad weather (i.e. poor visibility and/or a low cloud base) should be flown so that visual contact with the field is not lost. This may require a tight pattern flown at low level in the precautionary configuration. Aim for a pattern altitude of at least 500 feet AGL if possible, but do not enter cloud. Maintain a clearance of at least 300 feet vertically from obstacles.

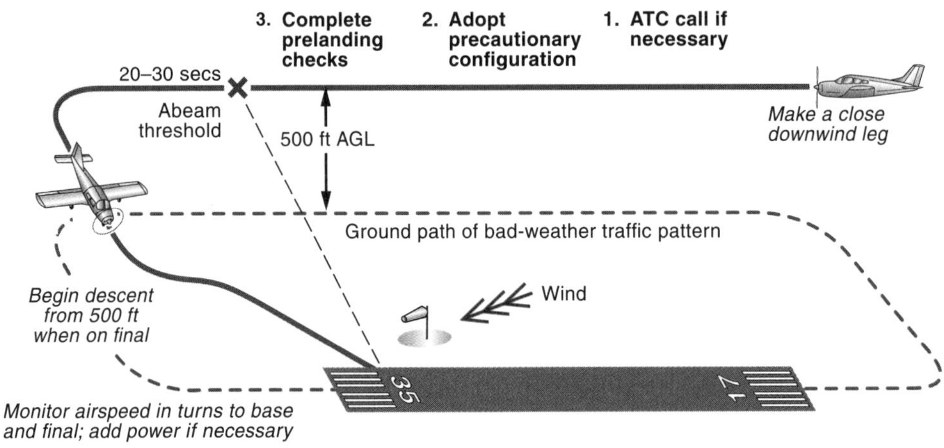

Figure 37-2 The bad-weather traffic pattern.

Search for a Suitable Landing Area

Once the decision to land has been taken, immediately search for a suitable landing area. Ideally, choose an airport; otherwise, select the most suitable landing field. Consider advising air traffic control of your intentions by radio on the normal frequency and, if not satisfactory, on the emergency frequency 121.5 MHz.

Items to consider when selecting a field include:

- its alignment with respect to the surface wind;
- size (large is better than smaller);
- obstacles in the approach or go-around areas;
- surface slope (a downslope is not good);
- surface conditions and obstructions;
- proximity to civilization.

If no suitable field is obvious, then searching downwind will allow you to have a higher ground speed and so cover more area.

Airplane Configuration and Pre-Descent Checks

Consider adopting the slower precautionary configuration.

If low cloud, poor visibility or a restricted maneuvering area is involved, then adopt the *precautionary* (or bad-weather) configuration. Use the optimum stage of flap, which may be just the first stage. Check your flight manual for the configuration for your aircraft. If there is none recommended consider using the same configuration as the base leg and final approach for a normal approach but, perhaps, with less than full flap. Extending some flap allows:

- slower speeds (due to reduced stalling speed);
- a smaller turn radius and a higher rate of turn for the same angle of bank (due to the reduced speed);
- better view from the cockpit (due to lower nose attitude);
- improved elevator and rudder response due to higher power and greater slipstream effect over the tail (possibly);
- higher power and quicker engine response; and
- reduced likelihood of carburetor icing at higher power (carburetor heat hot).

Staying in this configuration allows you to fly the whole sequence (descents, straight and level, and climbs) at a constant airspeed, thereby removing one variable. Fly the attitude for the desired speed, and control descent, level flight and climb-out with the use of power. It is preferable to fly this pattern with the landing gear down as there is a possibility of forgetting to lower it on the final pattern of this non-standard procedure.

Before descent, reduce to flap-operating speed, lower the first stage of flap, select the boost pump on, change to the fullest fuel tank, set mixture to rich, carburetor heat on, pitot heat on, lights on and transmit your position, passengers on board (POB) and intentions.

TECHNIQUE

Field Inspection

Inspect the selected landing area.

Several inspection runs should be made in the precautionary configuration and a traffic pattern and altitude established. With no restrictions, a normal pattern should be suitable. Take particular note of the wind velocity and anticipate the effect on your pattern, approach and landing. Try to establish a pattern into wind and, if possible, avoid a tail wind component on the base leg.

In bad weather, a low and close pattern (e.g. 500 feet AGL) may be advisable. The altitudes at which the pattern are flown and the number of inspection runs carried out depend on the situation—it's your decision, Captain.

Ensure you keep cross-referring to the attitude while looking down at the field. Keep your visual scan active, including monitoring airspeed.

Keep your cockpit workload to a minimum in low-level flight. Flying low to inspect a surface means accurate flying and a good lookout. Keep the airplane in trim or, if anything, trim slightly nose-up so that the airplane will have no tendency to descend while your attention is directed outside.

Three Inspection Patterns

If there are no restrictions caused by time, fuel or weather, and three inspection patterns are considered necessary, a suitable plan might be:

Pattern 1

At 1,500 feet AGL check for other aircraft and establish a normal traffic pattern, note landmarks and magnetic headings. Some flight instructors may consider this preliminary pattern superfluous. Complete low-flying checks before descent.

Pattern 2

To select and make a preliminary evaluation of the actual landing path descend for a 500-foot pattern. You are now entering a region of increased risk. At less than 1,000 feet AGL you are potentially amongst power lines, transmission towers and antennas. Check the path is clear before descending. Make a 500 feet AGL run slightly right of the landing path to give you a good view of the approach path and the landing surface through your left cockpit window. Check the climb-out path is clear before inspecting the runway. Look for large obstacles and obstructions, ditches, animals, wires, fences, wet patches or greener growth (soft ground), etc. Check the runway length by counting "one potato, two potato" etc. The length is approximately 130 feet per potato (at 80 knots) so you need to count 15 potatoes for a 2,000-foot runway. Return to 500 feet pattern altitude at the end of the field.

Pattern 3

Look out for power lines.

Descend on the final approach leg to a lower, but still safe, level of, say, 200 feet to the right of the landing path. Make a run alongside the landing path for a closer inspection of the landing surface itself. Return to 500 feet pattern altitude. If uncertain of the surface you can make an additional run alongside the landing strip at 100 or even 50 feet, but the relative speed is greater and not much more will be obvious. Make each inspection run alongside the selected landing path at a constant altitude and not as a slow descent that necessitates a frantic climb at the far boundary to avoid obstacles.

Pattern 4

Complete a further 500-foot pattern, with a normal final approach path, followed by a short-field landing. To practice this procedure safely, it must be flown under the following conditions:

- in an area where low flying is permitted;
- in an area where there are no power lines or obstructions;
- in weather conditions that allow low, slow flight (no wind, icing and turbulence); and
- to a surface that has been surveyed as safe for landing (otherwise go-around from short finals).

Use carburetor heat as recommended for your airplane.

AIRMANSHIP

Fly the airplane into a position for a normal engine-assisted approach. Consider making a short-field landing to minimize stress on the airplane during the touchdown and landing roll if the field is rough. Complete the appropriate prelanding checks. If time is not a consideration, be prepared to go around if not totally satisfied with the approach.

Be aware of the usual illusions caused by the wind effect when low flying. Keep your turns accurate and balanced in spite of the deceptive appearance of the ground if there is a strong wind. Add power to maintain airspeed in the turn if necessary and monitor the airspeed indicator.

Even though three preliminary patterns are shown, adapt the procedure according to your requirements. Make your command decision quickly and efficiently, and then do it. Adapt your plan to suit the conditions (e.g. low cloud, imminent darkness, low fuel). Possibly a 500 feet AGL, close-in pattern with only one inspection run might be called for, with no delay in making a landing. When practicing the precautionary search and landing:

- Ensure that you are in the correct local flying area and keep a good lookout for other aircraft.
- Consider and obey any regulations or local rules (such as no descents below 500 feet AGL, do not frighten animals, etc.).
- Align the heading indicator with the landing direction (either on 360° or 180°) to help with orientation.

Your flight instructor will give you plenty of practice at this procedure in many different situations. Adapt to each situation as you see fit. In actual circumstances, tell flight service your intentions or any other aircraft that is in the area.

REVIEW 37

Precautionary Landing

1. What do you call an inspection of an unfamiliar airfield before deciding whether or not to land?
2. What items would you consider when selecting a field for a precautionary landing?
3. Which sort of landing should you make if it is difficult to determine just how rough the surface of the proposed landing area is?
4. In conditions of low clouds and poor visibility and strong winds that cause you to adopt a precautionary landing procedure and fly low, will there be visual illusions to be careful of? If so, what are these caused by?
5. How does flying downwind, how does the ground speed compare to the airspeed? What illusion does this cause with regard to airspeed? What might the unwary pilot be trapped into doing?
6. When flying crosswind at a low level, can the drift caused by the crosswind give a visual illusion of slipping or skidding? Can this lead an unwary pilot into applying unnecessary rudder?

Answers are given on page 584.

TASK

Precautionary Landing

Aim: To carry out a safe approach and landing at an unfamiliar field, or on an unprepared surface, with engine power available.

For the purpose of this exercise, the scenario is a cloud base of 600 ft AGL, poor visibility and 20 minutes flight time available before night sets in.

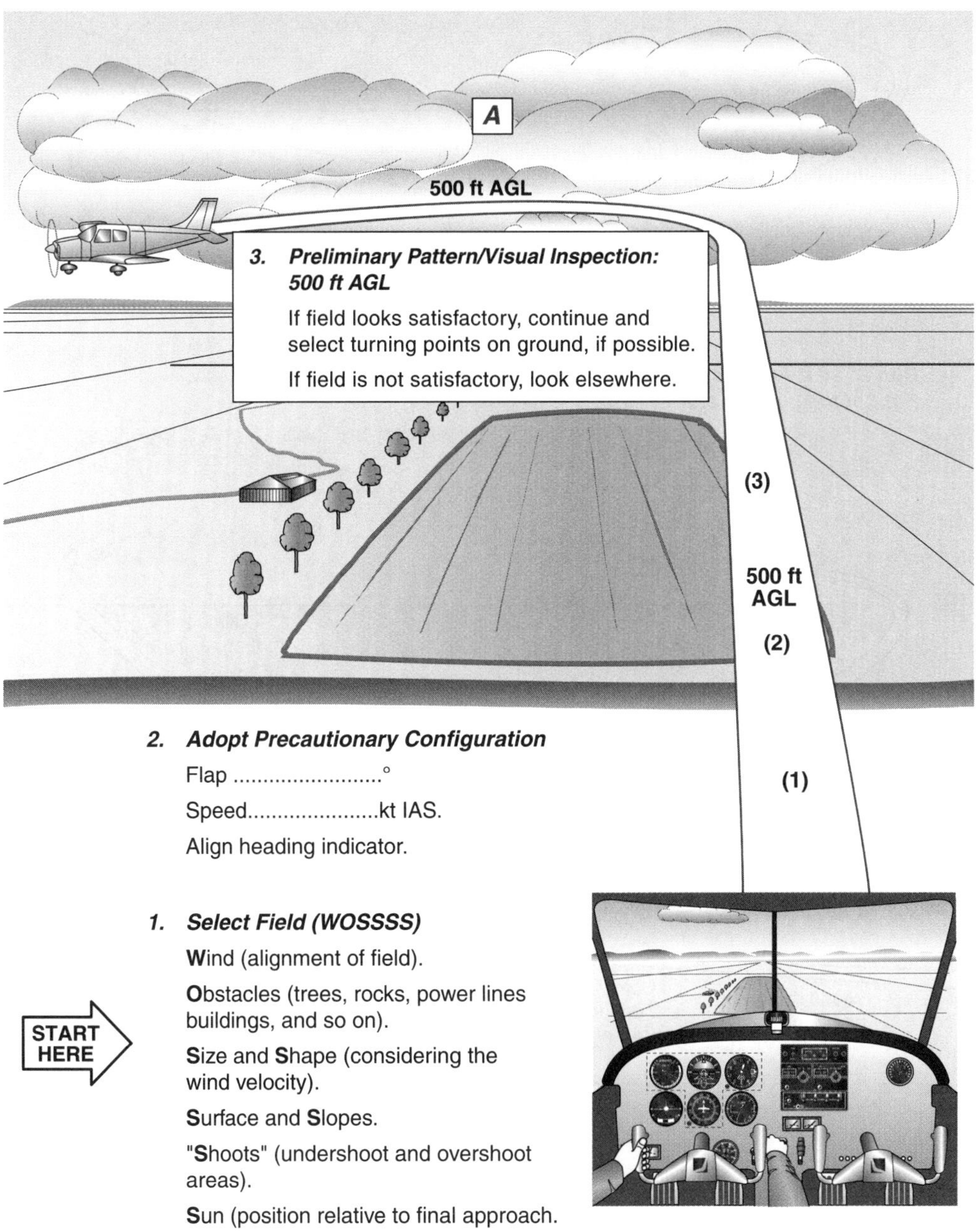

A
500 ft AGL
3. Preliminary Pattern/Visual Inspection: 500 ft AGL
If field looks satisfactory, continue and select turning points on ground, if possible.
If field is not satisfactory, look elsewhere.
(3)
500 ft AGL
(2)
(1)
2. Adopt Precautionary Configuration
Flap ....°
Speed......................kt IAS.
Align heading indicator.
1. Select Field (WOSSSS)
Wind (alignment of field).
Obstacles (trees, rocks, power lines buildings, and so on).
Size and Shape (considering the wind velocity).
Surface and Slopes.
"Shoots" (undershoot and overshoot areas).
Sun (position relative to final approach.
S(c)ivilization.
START HERE

Run 1. 200 ft AGL to the right of the landing path

Look for: Large obstacles.
Obstructions.
Ditches.
Transmission wires.
Fences, animals or vehicles.

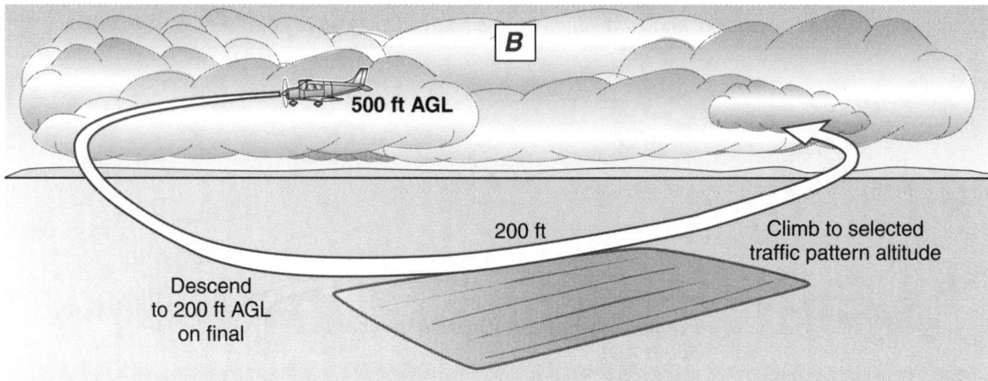

Run 2. 50 ft AGL just right of the landing path

Inspect landing surface closely.

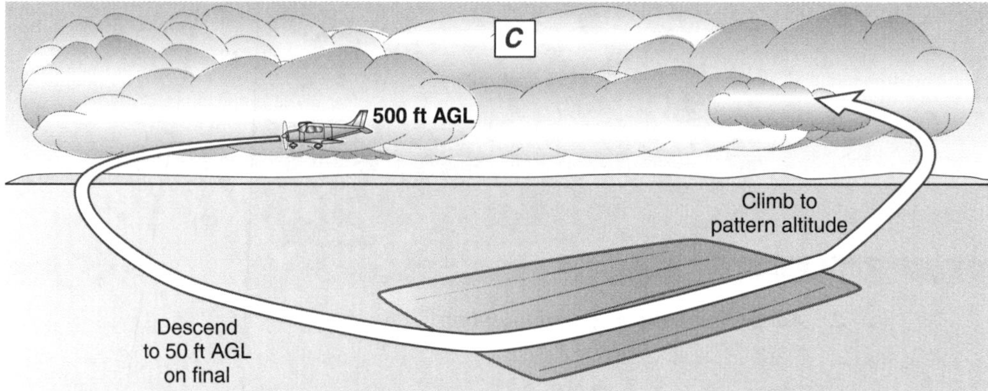

Run 3. Short, soft-field approach and landing

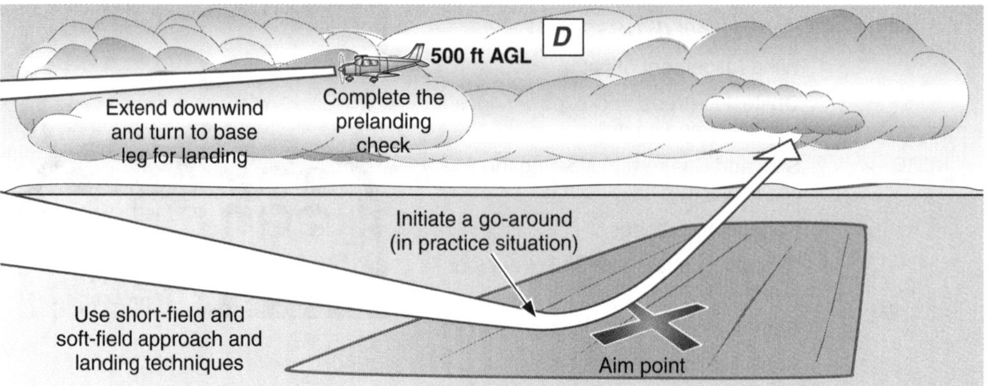

Crosswind Takeoff and Landing Operations

38

Crosswind Takeoff

OBJECTIVES

To describe:

- the influence of a sideways component of wind on the takeoff run, liftoff and initial climb;
- the assessment of the crosswind component from the total wind velocity; and
- the technique to takeoff and climb in a crosswind while maintaining centerline and safe margins of control.

Figure 38-1 Crosswind takeoff.

CONSIDERATIONS

Do not operate in crosswind conditions that exceed airplane or personal limits.

Not all airports have a runway that faces upwind on a given day. For this reason, takeoffs and landings on runways where there is a crosswind component are frequent events. Every airplane type (from the smallest trainer up to the Airbus A340 and Boeing 747) has a maximum crosswind component specified in the flight manual and pilot's operating handbook. If the actual crosswind component on the runway exceeds the limit for the airplane or what you feel is your own personal limit, then use a different runway (which may even mean proceeding to a different airport).

Crosswind Strength

The crosswind component on a runway can be estimated from the wind strength and the angle that the wind direction makes with the runway. As a rough guide:

- a wind 30° off the runway heading has a crosswind component of ½ the wind strength;
- a wind 45° off the runway heading has a crosswind component of approximately ⅔ the wind strength;
- a wind 60° off the runway heading has a crosswind component of approximately 9⁄10 the wind strength; and
- a wind 90° off the runway heading is all crosswind.

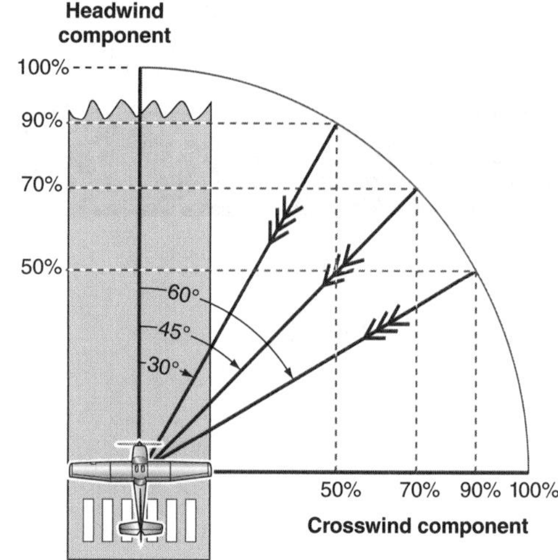

Figure 38-2 Estimating crosswind component.

APPLICATION

Weathervaning

Keep straight with active rudder control.

In a crosswind, an airplane will tend to weathervane upwind because of the large keel surfaces behind the main wheels. Provided that the crosswind limit for your airplane is not exceeded, it will be possible to keep straight on the ground with the rudder without too much difficulty. A crosswind from the right will require left rudder to counteract its effect, with most rudder at slow speeds and then less as the airflow over the rudder increases. Use whatever rudder is required to keep straight. Holding the nose wheel firmly on the ground until liftoff will assist in directional control.

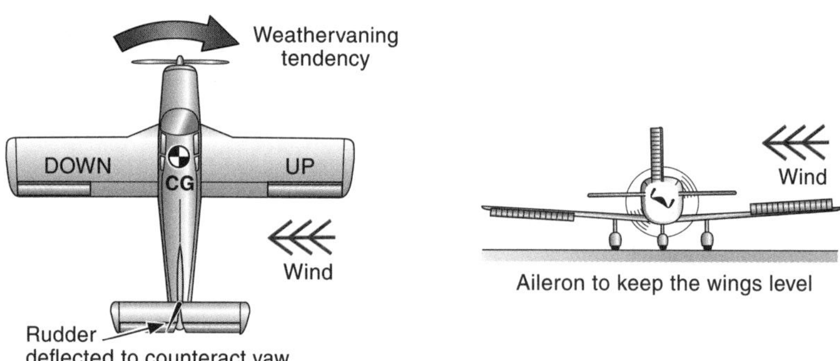

Figure 38-3 Keep straight with rudder; and wings level with ailerons.

TECHNIQUE

Takeoff Run

A crosswind blowing under the upwind wing will tend to lift it. Counteract this effect and keep the wings level with aileron; that is, move the control column upwind. While full deflection might be required early in the takeoff run, this can be reduced as the faster airflow increases control effectiveness. You do not have to consciously think of aileron movement; just concentrate on keeping the wings level.

Keep the wings level with aileron control.

A right crosswind, for example, requires right control column and left rudder (crossed controls). A glance at the wind sock before you open the throttle for the takeoff run will allow you to anticipate this and position the controls correctly.

The controls are crossed in a crosswind takeoff.

As speed increases, the amount of aileron and rudder required will reduce until, at liftoff, there will probably be some rudder still applied, but little or no aileron. There is no need to consciously think about this; just:

- keep straight with rudder; and
- keep the wings level with the ailerons.

Liftoff

Allow the aircraft to accelerate. Use as much rudder as necessary but avoid braking. In a crosswind takeoff, hold the airplane on the ground during the ground run (with slight forward pressure on the control column) and then lift off cleanly and positively. It may be advisable to delay liftoff until 5 knots or so past the normal rotation speed to achieve a clean (no skip) liftoff.

Hold the airplane firmly on the ground during the takeoff run until liftoff speed (not beyond).

Drift After Takeoff

As the airplane enters the air mass after liftoff, it will tend to move sideways with it. Any tendency to sink back onto the ground should be resisted to avoid the strong sideways forces that would occur on the landing gear.

Once well clear of the ground, the aircraft will naturally yaw upwind (weathervane) to counteract the drift. Keep the wings level. Any remaining crossed controls are removed once airborne by centralizing the balance ball and keeping the wings level. Climb out normally on the extended centerline of the runway.

Lift off cleanly to avoid drift.

After liftoff, establish coordinated flight (relax the rudder) and apply a wind correction angle.

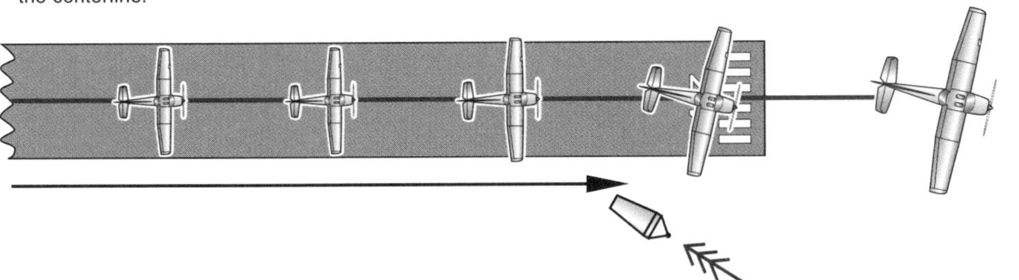

1. Hold the airplane firmly on the runway (slight forward pressure); turn the control wheel into the wind to keep the wings level, with opposite rudder to stay on the centerline.
2. Lift off cleanly and establish the climb attitude.
3. Remove crossed controls as you yaw into wind to allow for drift.
4. Normal climb-out, maintaining the extended runway centerline by allowing for drift

Figure 38-4 The crosswind takeoff.

AIRMANSHIP

Maintain an exceptionally good lookout and give way to airplanes using the upwind runway and standard traffic pattern, which may conflict with your pattern. Exert firm, positive control during this maneuver and ensure a clean liftoff.

Traffic Separation

The crosswind pattern is a rectangular pattern over the ground and is based on a runway with a crosswind component. The standard names are still given to the various legs of the pattern, even though the actual wind effect experienced on each of those legs may differ from what the name of the leg suggests.

Adjustments should be made to allow for the wind effect in the pattern, such as laying off drift and modifying the turns. Since the wind at pattern altitude may differ in direction and strength from that at ground level, make use of ground features to assist in correct tracking around the pattern. When flying in a crosswind pattern, be aware that other aircraft may be operating in a standard into-wind pattern and that their pattern may conflict.

Airplanes in the standard pattern will generally have right of way, so the main responsibility for avoiding conflict is with the pilot in the crosswind pattern. A crosswind pattern might sometimes be flown at a different level to avoid conflict with the standard pattern.

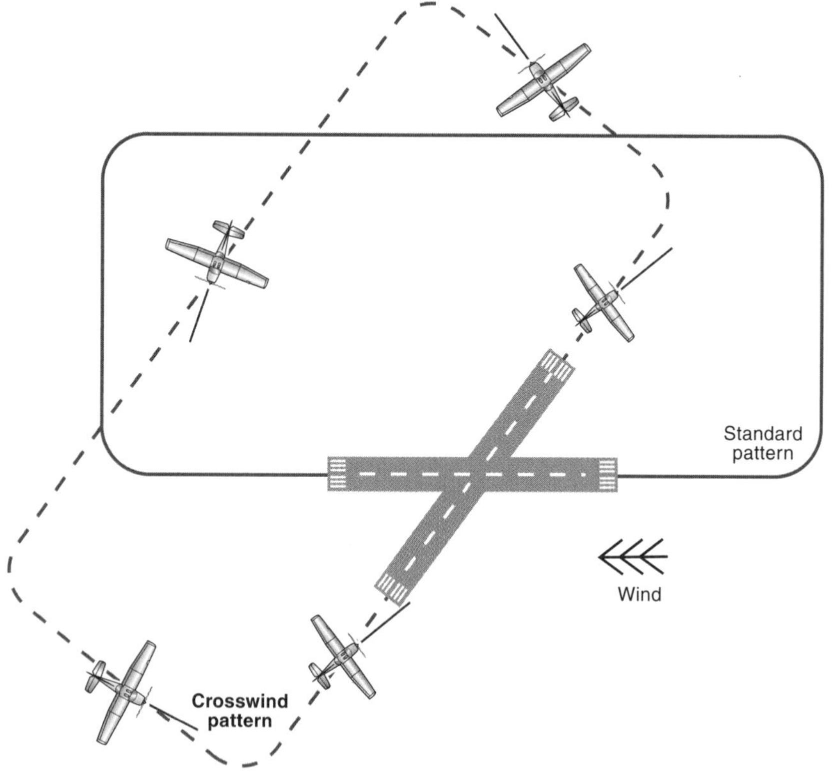

Figure 38-5 Counter drift to maintain a rectangular pattern.

REVIEW 38

Crosswind Takeoff

1. What will be the crosswind component caused by a 10-knot wind at 90° to the runway direction?
2. What will be the crosswind component caused by a 10-knot wind at 60° to the runway direction?
3. What will be the crosswind component caused by a 10-knot wind at 45° to the runway direction?
4. What will be the crosswind component caused by a 10-knot wind at 30° to the runway direction?
5. What will be the crosswind component caused by a 20-knot wind at 45° to the runway direction?
6. What will be the crosswind component caused by a 20-knot wind at 60° to the runway direction?
7. What will be the crosswind component caused by a 20-knot wind at 30° to the runway direction?
8. What will be the crosswind component caused by a 20-knot wind at 90° to the runway direction?
9. A crosswind limitation will be found in which section in the pilot's operating handbook? A maximum demonstrated crosswind will be found in which section?
10. What flap setting is recommended for the crosswind takeoff taking into account the runway length?
11. In which direction will a crosswind cause an airplane on the ground to weathervane?
12. In crosswind conditions, which control surface is used to keep the airplane on the ground aligned with the runway centerline?
13. In crosswind conditions, which control surface is used to keep the wings level when the airplane is one the ground?
14. At the start of the takeoff ground run, how will the amount of rudder and aileron deflection compare to that just before liftoff, when the airspeed is higher?
15. During the takeoff run in strong crosswind conditions, should you hold the airplane on the ground or should you lift off early?
16. It is more important to lift off cleanly and positively in a crosswind takeoff. Why?
17. Will the controls be crossed immediately after liftoff in crosswind conditions?
18. When clear of the ground in a crosswind takeoff, should you remove any crossed controls? How will this be indicated by the balance ball?
19. When clear of the ground in a crosswind takeoff, should you apply a wind correction angle, so that your flight path is along the extended runway centerline?

Figure 38-6 Anticipate the effect of wind.

Answers are given on page 584.

TASK

Crosswind Takeoff

Aim: To take off on a runway with a crosswind component that is below the limit for the airplane.

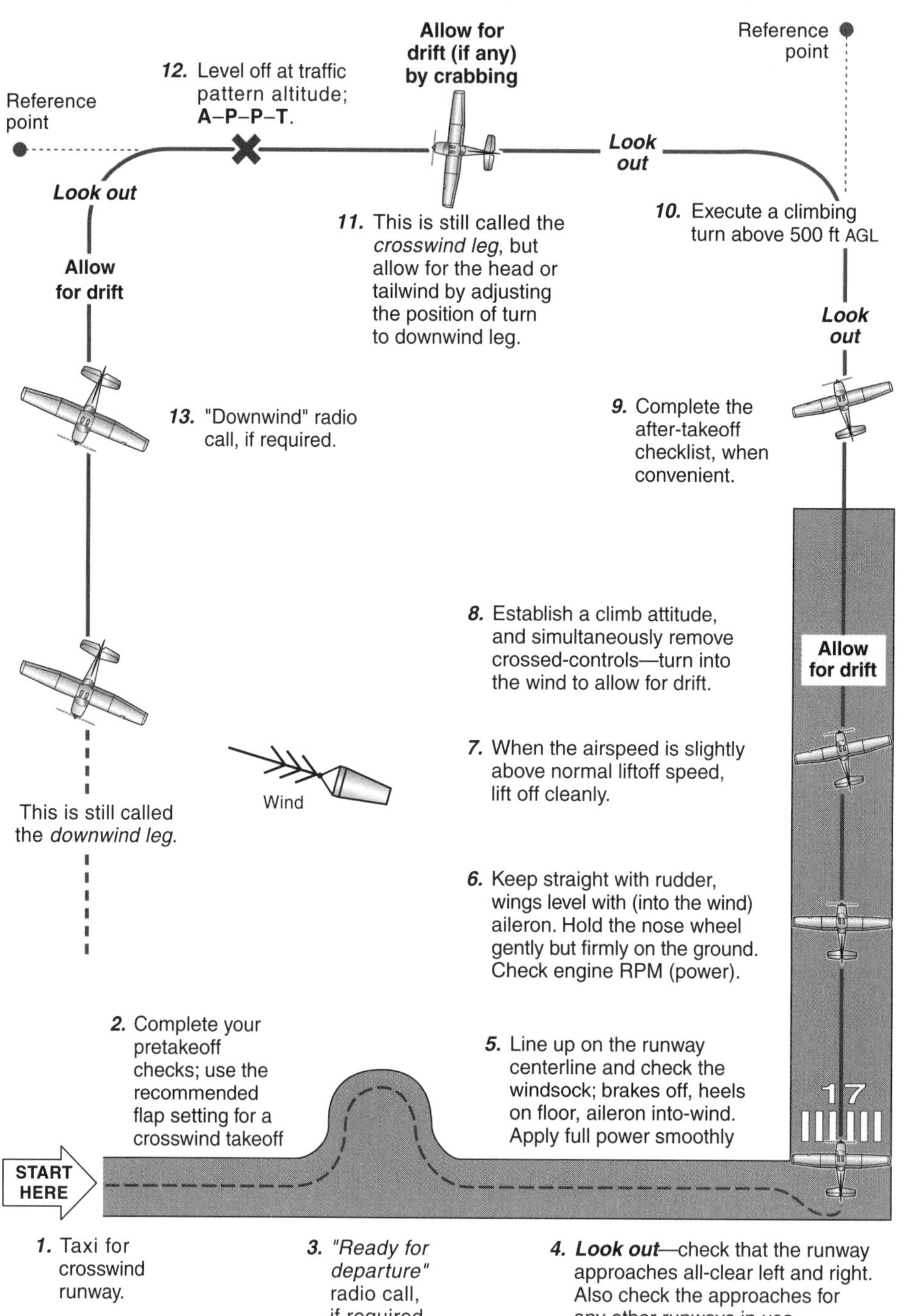

Allow for drift (if any) by crabbing
Reference point
12. Level off at traffic pattern altitude; A–P–P–T.
Reference point
Look out
Look out
Allow for drift
11. This is still called the crosswind leg, but allow for the head or tailwind by adjusting the position of turn to downwind leg.
10. Execute a climbing turn above 500 ft AGL
Look out
13. "Downwind" radio call, if required.
9. Complete the after-takeoff checklist, when convenient.
8. Establish a climb attitude, and simultaneously remove crossed-controls—turn into the wind to allow for drift.
Allow for drift
7. When the airspeed is slightly above normal liftoff speed, lift off cleanly.
Wind
This is still called the downwind leg.
6. Keep straight with rudder, wings level with (into the wind) aileron. Hold the nose wheel gently but firmly on the ground. Check engine RPM (power).
2. Complete your pretakeoff checks; use the recommended flap setting for a crosswind takeoff
5. Line up on the runway centerline and check the windsock; brakes off, heels on floor, aileron into-wind. Apply full power smoothly
17
START HERE
1. Taxi for crosswind runway.
3. "Ready for departure" radio call, if required
4. Look out—check that the runway approaches all-clear left and right. Also check the approaches for any other runways in use.

39

Crosswind Approach and Landings

OBJECTIVES

To describe:

- the anticipation required for a crosswind approach;
- the compensatory inputs required; and
- the techniques available and recommended to safely land an airplane up to its demonstrated crosswind limit.

Figure 39-1 Crosswind approach.

CONSIDERATIONS

Crosswind Pattern

Ensure that the crosswind component on the selected runway does not exceed the limit for the airplane (or your own personal limit).

Planning for the crosswind approach and landing starts early in the pattern, even as you turn onto the crosswind leg shortly after takeoff. A tail wind on the crosswind leg will tend to carry you wide; a head wind will hold you in too close. Adjust each leg of the pattern to position the aircraft suitably with respect to the runway.

Fly the pattern according to the wind to achieve a rectangle over the ground.

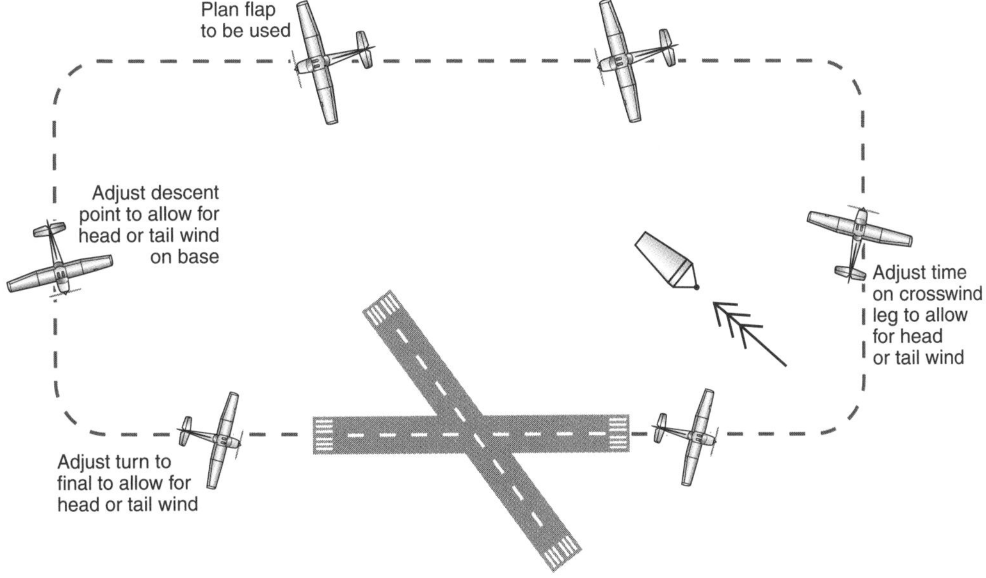

Plan flap to be used
Adjust descent point to allow for head or tail wind on base
Adjust time on crosswind leg to allow for head or tail wind
Adjust turn to final to allow for head or tail wind

Figure 39-2 Flying the crosswind pattern.

Tail Wind on Base Leg

Anticipate the effect of a tail wind on base leg.

A tail wind on base leg will increase your speed over the ground and tend to carry you past the runway. For this reason, you should show some anticipation and:

- commence descent early;
- begin the turn onto the final approach early; and
- continue the turn onto the final approach beyond the runway heading to allow for drift.

If you fly through the final approach, avoid any tendency to overbank (a bank angle of 30° is a reasonable maximum). Simply rejoin the final approach from the other side.

Head Wind on Base Leg

When flying into a head wind on base leg, you can afford to delay your turn to final.

A head wind on base leg will decrease your speed over the ground, and so you can:

- delay descent until later than usual;
- delay the turn onto the final approach until almost in line with the runway; and
- stop the turn short of runway heading to anticipate the expected drift.

If you turn too early then you may not reach the final approach, and a positive turn will have to be made upwind to become established. If you turn too late and fly through the final approach, fly the runway heading and the wind will most probably carry you back onto the extended centerline. Once in line with the runway, lay off drift to track directly down the final approach.

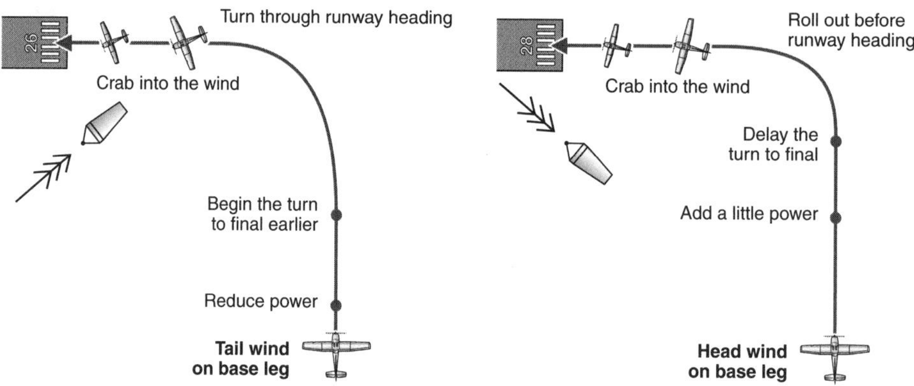

Figure 39-3 Allow for wind effect when turning final.

APPLICATION

Tracking On Final

Positively control tracking down final.

Because of the crab angle needed to maintain the extended centerline, the runway will appear to one side of the nose, but will still look symmetrical. On the final approach for a crosswind landing, you should have a view directly down the runway centerline. If the airplane drifts downwind, then make a very definite turn upwind and regain the final approach without delay. (Do not just aim the nose of the airplane at the runway!) Keep the airplane in balance.

Figure 39-4 An upwind approach and a crosswind approach both on centerline.

Figure 39-5 Correct centerline displacement early on final approach.

Wind strength often decreases near the ground, so continual adjustments to heading will have to be made to maintain your track down the final approach. This is especially the case in strong and gusty conditions.

Once tracking is under control, then achieving a stabilized descent path and a workmanlike landing becomes a simpler task. It is particularly true in the crosswind case that a good landing requires a good approach.

Crosswind Landing

Align the Axis (Wheels)

While an airplane is airborne, the fact that its longitudinal axis is not aligned with the runway is not significant. However, it would be uncomfortable to touch down in this situation, since the wheels are not aligned with the path of the airplane down the runway in a crosswind. A strong sideways force on the landing gear could do structural damage or, in an extreme case, tip the airplane over. On touchdown, the wheels should be aligned with the runway direction. The trick in a crosswind landing is to:

Following a crosswind approach, align the wheels with the runway prior to touchdown.

- align the axis of the airplane (the wheels) with the runway direction prior to touchdown; and to
- avoid any sideways drift across the runway before the wheels touch down.

To do this requires the coordinated use of the controls (ailerons, rudder, elevator and power). As your skills develop with practice, you will gain great satisfaction from consistently performing good crosswind landings.

There are three accepted crosswind landing techniques:

- the crab method;
- the wing-down method; and
- the combination method (incorporating the best features of each of the above), being a crab approach and a wing-down landing.

Your flight instructor will teach you his or her preferred method.

General Considerations

Strong crosswinds are often accompanied by gusts and turbulence, and consideration should be given to using only partial or zero flap and a slightly higher approach speed than normal to give you better controllability. The flare in a crosswind landing is normal, but the hold-off should not be prolonged (otherwise sideways drift could develop). The airplane should be placed on the ground, wheels aligned with the runway, while the flight controls are effective and with the airplane tracking along the runway centerline.

Once on the ground, directional control is more easily achieved if the nose wheel is lowered onto the ground at an early stage in the landing roll. Forward pressure on the control column may be required. You must retain firm control throughout the whole maneuver until the airplane is stopped or at least has slowed to taxiing speed. During the landing roll:

- keep straight with rudder (the crosswind causes an upwind weathervaning tendency);
- lower the nose wheel to the ground to assist in directional control;
- keep the wings level with progressive upwind aileron as the airspeed decreases (the crosswind will tend to lift the upwind wing), maybe with full control movement required by the end of the landing roll.

TECHNIQUES

Crab Method

In the crab method, drift should be laid off all the way down the final approach and through the flare. This will keep the airplane tracking down the centerline, but the wheels will not be aligned with the landing direction.

Just prior to touchdown, yaw the airplane straight with smooth and firm rudder pressure to align its longitudinal axis (and the wheels) with the centerline of the runway. Keep the wings level with ailerons.

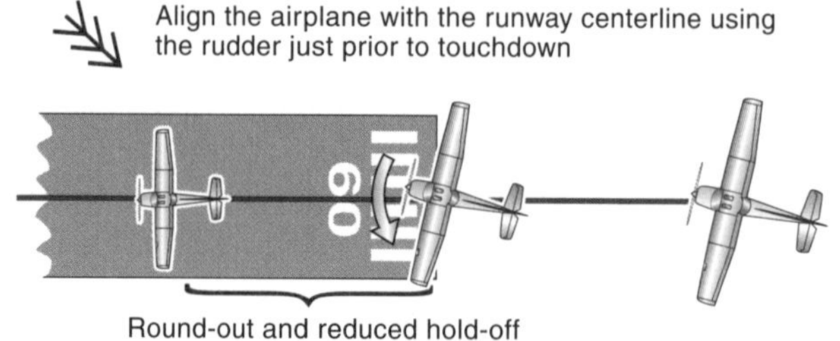

Align the airplane with the runway centerline using the rudder just prior to touchdown
09
Round-out and reduced hold-off

Figure 39-6 In crab method, align the airplane just prior to touchdown.

The hold-off period should not be prolonged and the main wheels of the airplane should be lowered onto the runway before any sideways drift has a chance to develop. Do not allow the nose wheel to touch first as this could cause a bounce as well as overstress the structure; however, the nose wheel should be lowered to the ground early in the landing roll to aid in directional control.

Judgment and Timing

Judgment and timing are important when using the crab method. Failing to remove the crab angle prior to landing will result in the wheels touching down sideways; removing it too early will allow a sideways drift to develop and, as well as landing downwind of the centerline, the wheels will still touch down with a sideways component. In both cases, the landing will feel heavy and the landing gear will be unnecessarily stressed. A reasonable touchdown can only be achieved with fine judgment in removing drift and contacting the ground. If any sideways drift looks like developing before touchdown, it can be counteracted by:

- a small amount of upwind wing-down; and
- keeping straight with rudder.

This technique is really a lead-in to the next method of crosswind landing, the wing-down or sideslip method.

Figure 39-7 Sideslipping crosswind approach.

Wing-Down Method

Control drift with bank, and heading with rudder.

This method can be employed in the latter stages of the approach. In some places, it is taught to be used all the way down the final approach; in others, it is used just for the last few feet. At this stage of your training, we will discuss this method as applying to the last 300 feet or so. It is sometimes recommended for high-wing aircraft, which are susceptible to the upwind wing being lifted, or for aircraft where the rudder power is limited. Check your aircraft's flight manual. The airplane is made to track down the extended centerline, not by crabbing, but by slipping. The airplane tracks toward the runway in a sideslip.

Figure 39-8 Wing-down landing.

To initiate a sideslip:

- lower the upwind wing a few degrees; and
- apply opposite rudder pressure to stop the airplane turning and to align its longitudinal axis with the runway centerline.

The airplane is out-of-balance and so the balance ball will not be centered. The stronger the crosswind, the more wing-down and the more opposite rudder required.

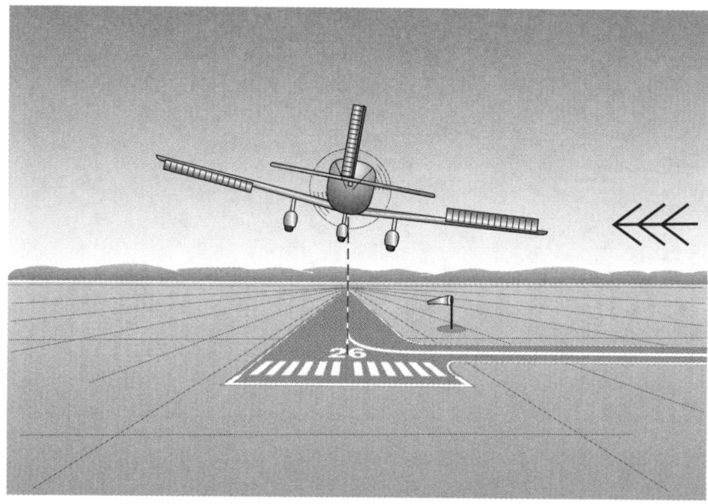

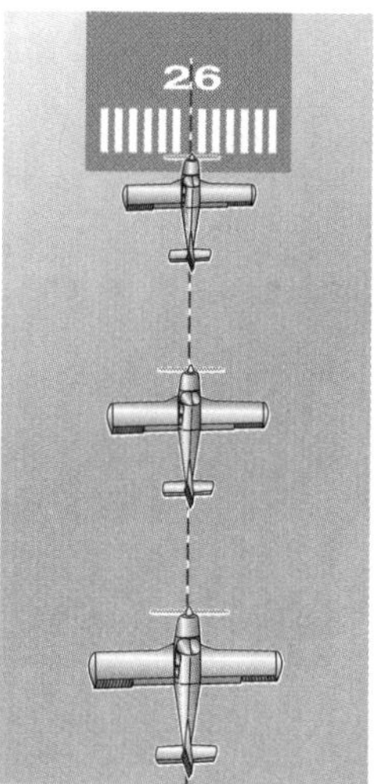

Figure 39-9 The wing-down crosswind technique.

Drift Control

If the airplane starts to drift downwind across the runway, you have applied insufficient bank, so:

- lower the wing a few degrees further; and
- keep straight with rudder.

If the airplane starts to slip upwind across the runway, you have applied too much wing-down, so:

- reduce the bank a few degrees; and
- keep straight with rudder.

In gusty conditions especially, you will be continually varying the degree of wing-down and opposite rudder to remain aligned with the runway centerline. During this whole process, adjust the pitch attitude to maintain airspeed.

Touchdown

The bank and opposite rudder is held on through the flare and the aircraft is rolled just before touchdown. It is preferable to keep some bank until touchdown, which will occur on the upwind main wheel.

Throughout the maneuver the airplane will be tracking straight down the runway with its longitudinal axis aligned with the centerline. No sideways drift across the runway should be allowed to develop.

Figure 39-10
View from the cockpit in a left crosswind.

When the wing-down main wheel touches first, there may be a tendency for the airplane to yaw upwind, but the airplane can easily be kept straight with rudder. The other main wheel will touch down naturally, after which you should lower the nose wheel onto the ground to allow more positive directional control. In the landing roll:

- keep straight with rudder, holding the nose wheel on the ground; and
- keep wings level with upwind aileron, with full control deflection possibly required as the airplane slows down.

Advantages of the Wing-Down Method

In the ground roll, keep straight with rudder and wings level with aileron.

Less judgment and timing is required in the actual touchdown using this method, since the airplane is aligned with the runway centerline throughout the flare and hold-off. There is no crab angle to remove and no sideways drift. It is of less importance if the airplane touches down a little earlier or a little later than expected, whereas with the crab method good judgment in aligning the airplane just before touchdown is required.

Combination Method

Crab into the wind on approach.

A distinct disadvantage of the wing-down technique being used all the way down the final approach is that the controls are crossed and the airplane is out of balance (the ball is not centered). This is both inefficient and uncomfortable. It is also more difficult to judge the aircraft's attitude and aim point in a sideslipping approach. Additionally, larger aircraft with swept wings expose themselves to a risk of scraping the engine pods on landing. A more comfortable approach can be flown if drift is laid off to maintain the extended runway centerline by crabbing and the airplane is flown in balance (ball centered, pilot and passengers comfortable).

Before touchdown, yaw the nose straight with rudder and prevent sideways drift with wing-down.

Remember to flare!

During the flare the aircraft is straightened with rudder and the upwind wing is lowered to prevent drift. This prevents any side load on the landing gear and makes the touchdown more tolerant. At just what point you transfer from the crab to the wing-down depends on your experience and the wind conditions. Initially, it may be better to introduce the wing-down at about 100 feet above ground level but, as you become more experienced, this can be delayed until in the flare below 20 feet.

During the ground roll, keep straight with rudder and wings level with aileron.

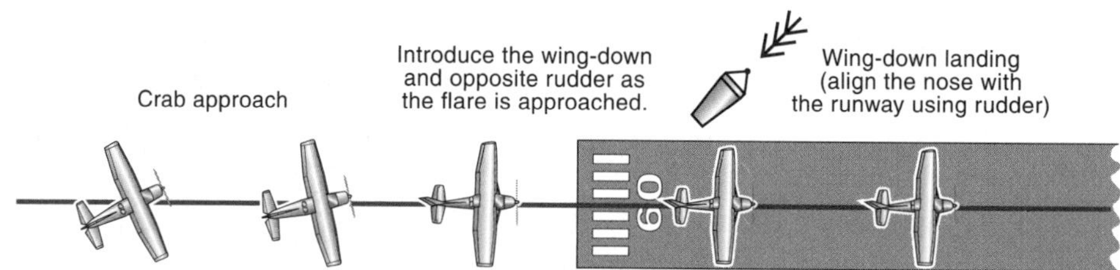
Crab approach
Introduce the wing-down and opposite rudder as the flare is approached.
Wing-down landing (align the nose with the runway using rudder)
09

Figure 39-11 The combination (recommended) method of crosswind landing.

AIRMANSHIP

Be prepared for a go-around.

Be firm and positive in your handling of the airplane. Be decisive! Remember that your crosswind pattern may conflict with the standard traffic pattern, so keep a good lookout. If at any stage you feel distinctly unhappy about the approach and landing, go around and start again.

REVIEW 39

Crosswind Approach and Landing

1. In strong and gusty crosswind conditions, what flap setting makes the airplane easier to control? Why?
2. For what flap setting will the airplane respond most quickly to power changes? Why?
3. Name the three methods of handling a crosswind landing.
4. To counteract the wind drift on long final in crosswind conditions, you should apply which angle? What is another name for this angle?
5. What is required for a good landing?
6. When making a crosswind landing, what must you still remember to do?
7. When making a crosswind landing, should you touch down with the airplane aligned with the runway centerline?
8. When making a crosswind landing, should you touch down without sideways drift across the runway?
9. When using the wing-down method in a crosswind landing, which wing should you lower? How do you keep aligned with the runway centerline?
10. When using the wing-down method in a crosswind landing, on which side is the main wheel that should touch down first if the crosswind is from the right? On which side is the main wheel that should touch down first if the crosswind is from the left?
11. During the landing roll, which control surface is used to keep straight? During the landing roll, which control surface is used to keep the wings level?
12. What effect does lowering the nose wheel onto the ground have on directional control?
13. During the landing roll, what will happen to the effectiveness of the ailerons as you slow down?

Answers are given on page 585.

TASK

Crab Method of Crosswind Landing

Aim: To carry out a crosswind approach and landing by crabbing into wind until just prior to wheel contact on touchdown.

1. *On Final Approach*

Track down extended runway centerline by heading the airplane into the wind.

Control airspeed with elevator, flight path with power and keep coordinated with rudder. The wings should be level except when adjusting your crab angle.

2. *During the Flare*

Reduce power and raise the nose normally.

Maintain your track above the runway centerline by crabbing into wind.

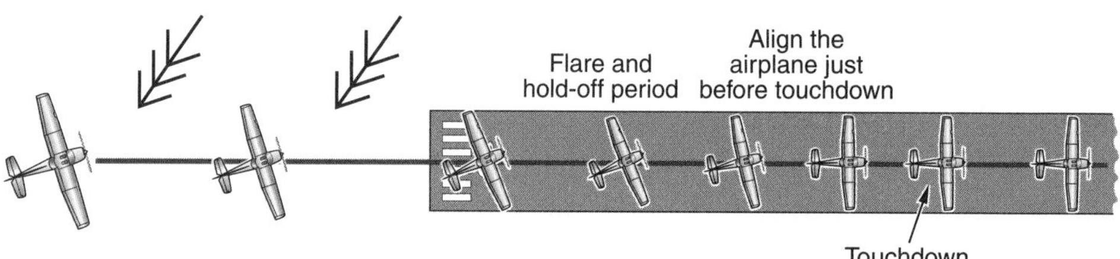

3. *Just Prior to Touchdown*

Align the airplane with the centerline with smooth and firm rudder pressure.

Hold wings level with aileron.

4. *The Landing Roll*

Keeping straight with rudder, lower the nose wheel onto the ground.

Keep wings level with progressive use of aileron into the wind.

Hold the nose wheel on the ground to obtain positive steering.

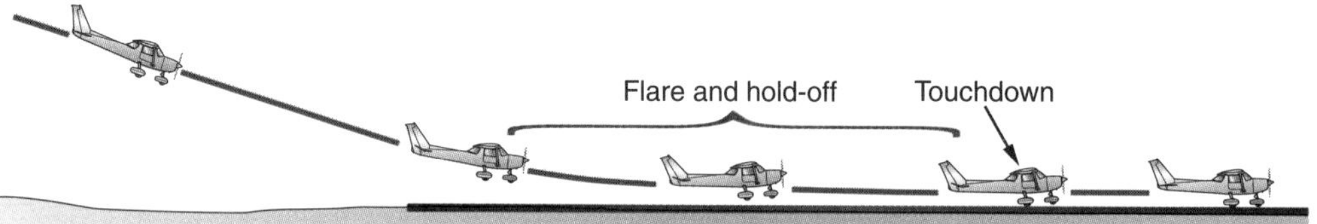

TASK

Wing-Down Method of Crosswind Landing

Aim: To land the airplane in a crosswind following a wing-down approach.

1. ***On Final Approach, Aligned with Runway Centerline***

   Lower the upwind wing and use rudder to remain aligned with the runway centerline.

   Control airspeed with power, flight path with altitude and centerline with bank and (opposite) rudder.

2. ***During the Flare***

   Reduce power and raise nose normally.

   Maintain your track along the runway centerline with wing-down aileron.

   Keep wheels aligned with opposite rudder.

The wing-down crosswind landing:
Stop the wind drift with aileron.
Keep the nose aligned with the runway centerline with rudder.

3. ***The Touchdown***

   The touchdown will be on the upwind wheel because of that wing being lower. This is okay.

   The other main wheel will follow naturally.

4. ***The Landing Roll***

   Keep straight with rudder.

   Lower the nose wheel to the ground.

   Maintain wings-level with aileron progressively deflected into the wind.

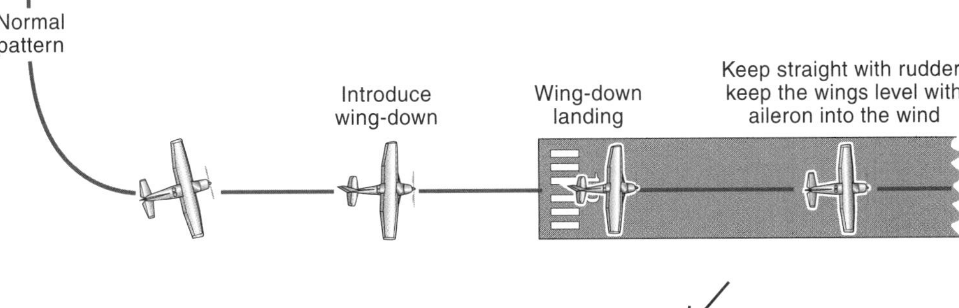
Normal pattern
Introduce wing-down
Wing-down landing
Keep straight with rudder; keep the wings level with aileron into the wind

TASK

Combination Method of Crosswind Landing

Aim: To land the airplane in a crosswind using a crab approach followed by a wing-down landing.

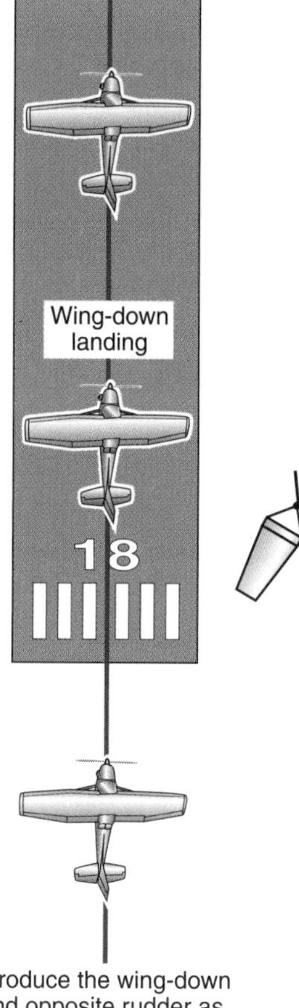

5. *The Landing Run*

Keep straight with rudder.

Lower nose wheel to the runway.

Keep the wings level with progressive aileron into wind—full control-wheel movement may eventually be required.

4. *The Touchdown*

Touch down on the upwind main wheel and allow the other main wheel to follow.

Maintain directional control with rudder.

3. *During the Flare*

Reduce power and raise the nose normally.

Maintain a track along the centerline with wing-down, and keep the nose aligned with opposite rudder.

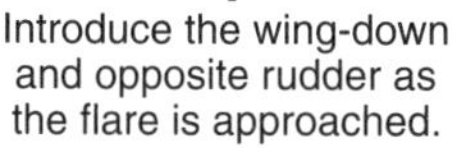

2. *At or Approaching Flare Height*

Use smooth rudder pressure to align airplane with runway centerline and stay aligned.

Lower the upwind wing to prevent sideways drift.

Introduce the wing-down and opposite rudder as the flare is approached.

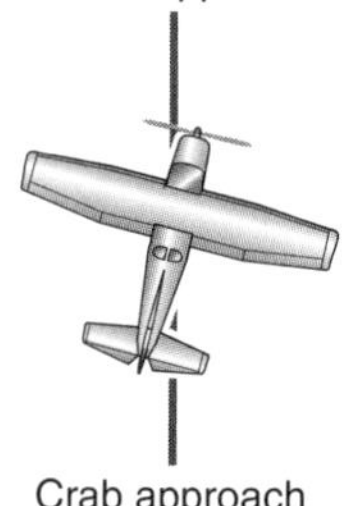

1. *On Final Approach*

Adjust the heading to track (crab) down final along the extended runway centerline.

Keep the wings level, and balance with rudder pressure.

Crab approach

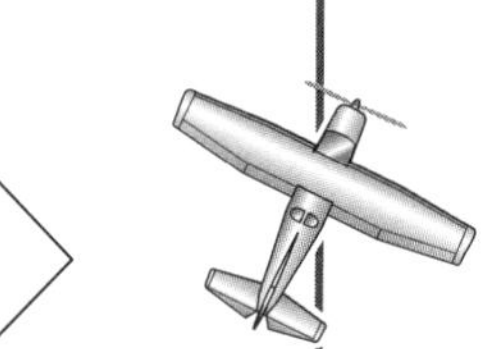

Maximum Performance Takeoff and Landing Operations

40

Short-Field Operations

OBJECTIVES

To describe:

- the factors to be considered in establishing the minimum takeoff and landing distance for your aircraft; and
- the optimum configuration and technique to achieve the minimum takeoff and landing distance for your aircraft.

CONSIDERATIONS

Prior to using any airport or landing area, you must evaluate:

- wind direction;
- the takeoff and landing surface (length and condition); and
- obstructions and other hazards in the takeoff and approach paths.

What is a Short Field?

A short field is one in which the runway length available or the obstacle-clearance gradients are only just sufficient to satisfy takeoff and landing requirements. Even if a runway is long, obstacles in the approach sector may reduce the distance available for landing, and obstacles in the takeoff sector may reduce the distance available for takeoff.

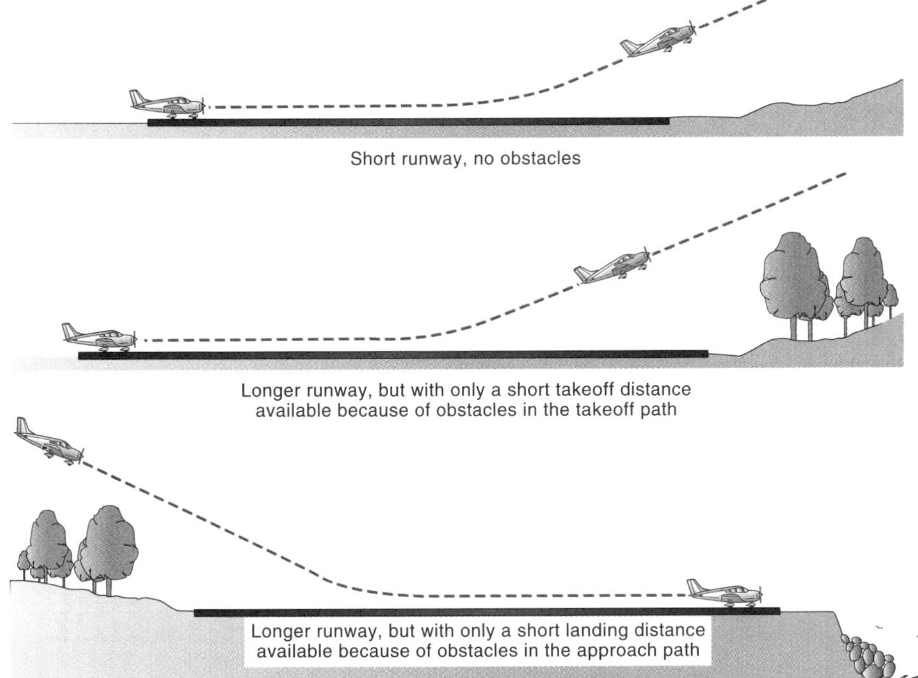

Short runway, no obstacles
Longer runway, but with only a short takeoff distance available because of obstacles in the takeoff path
Longer runway, but with only a short landing distance available because of obstacles in the approach path

Figure 40-1 Short-field operations.

APPLICATION

Short fields require maximum performance from the pilot to achieve maximum performance from the airplane.

Maximum performance is required when taking off or landing on a short field, and this means maximum performance from both the airplane and the pilot. In a two-pilot cockpit, you should brief the other pilot on your intentions.

For takeoff, *maximum performance* means using the recommended short-field flap settings and maximum power to minimize your ground run. For a climb-out over obstacles, you must hold the pitch attitude to achieve the steepest climb path:

- obstacle-clearance airspeed for that flap setting; or
- best-angle climb airspeed for zero flaps (V_X).

A typical situation could be the following: recommended 10° flaps for takeoff, with the liftoff at 50 knots, achieve obstacle-clearance airspeed 54 knots by 50 feet above the runway level, and maintain this speed until clear of obstacles. If it was a zero-flap takeoff, the steepest climb to clear obstacles is achieved at V_X, which is 60 knots. Because these speeds are quite near the stalling speed (perhaps only 15% greater), there is not much tolerance allowed. You should not fly slower than these speeds, because you risk a stall, and you should not fly faster than 5 knots above them as this will flatten the climb-out path; the tolerance is +5/–0 knots.

When clear of obstacles, you can lower the nose and accelerate to the best rate-of-climb airspeed, V_Y, which could be 76 knots. If you used flaps for the takeoff, you will raise them now. Because V_Y is well away from the stall, the tolerances are a little greater, plus or minus 5 knots.

For landing, maximum performance means a steep approach if there are obstacles to be cleared in the approach path, followed by an immediate touchdown at minimum speed, and braking to minimize the after-landing ground run. This short-field performance can best be achieved using a full-flaps, power-on approach.

Performance Charts

Refer to the appropriate performance charts for your airplane.

The takeoff and landing performance charts for your airplane should be consulted to ensure that a short field in a confined area is indeed adequate for the planned operations under the existing conditions. An inspection on foot of the proposed takeoff and landing surface and the surrounding area may be necessary. During the inspection, remember that the takeoff is not complete until all obstacles are cleared, so not only the takeoff surface but also the surrounding area need to be considered.

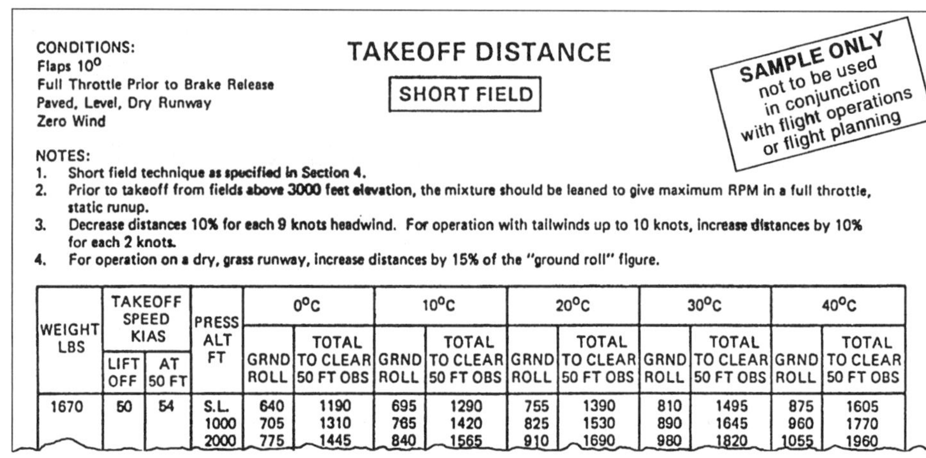

TAKEOFF DISTANCE

SHORT FIELD

CONDITIONS:
Flaps 10°
Full Throttle Prior to Brake Release
Paved, Level, Dry Runway
Zero Wind

SAMPLE ONLY not to be used in conjunction with flight operations or flight planning

NOTES:
1. Short field technique as spucified in Section 4.
2. Prior to takeoff from fields above 3000 feet elevation, the mixture should be leaned to give maximum RPM in a full throttle, static runup.
3. Decrease distances 10% for each 9 knots headwind. For operation with tailwinds up to 10 knots, increase distances by 10% for each 2 knots.
4. For operation on a dry, grass runway, increase distances by 15% of the "ground roll" figure.

WEIGHT LBS	TAKEOFF SPEED KIAS		PRESS ALT FT	0°C		10°C		20°C		30°C		40°C	
	LIFT OFF	AT 50 FT		GRND ROLL	TOTAL TO CLEAR 50 FT OBS	GRND ROLL	TOTAL TO CLEAR 50 FT OBS	GRND ROLL	TOTAL TO CLEAR 50 FT OBS	GRND ROLL	TOTAL TO CLEAR 50 FT OBS	GRND ROLL	TOTAL TO CLEAR 50 FT OBS
1670	50	54	S.L.	640	1190	695	1290	755	1390	810	1495	875	1605
			1000	705	1310	765	1420	825	1530	890	1645	960	1770
			2000	775	1445	840	1565	910	1690	980	1820	1055	1960

Figure 40-2 Consult the performance charts.

TECHNIQUE

The Short-Field Takeoff

There are generally two considerations in the short-field takeoff:

- achieving a minimum ground run; and
- avoiding obstacles in the climb-out.

A short-field takeoff is a normal takeoff, except that you should pay special attention to the following points to achieve the shortest ground run and steepest climb-out.

- Check the performance charts.
- Take off as much into-wind as possible. Use the recommended flap setting for takeoff.

Take advantage of a head wind.

- Adjust the mixture control as recommended in the pilot's operating handbook for the existing condition—usually full rich, except when at airport elevations above 3,000 feet, when some leaning.
- Position the airplane at the end of the runway, aligned with the runway centerline to ensure that you have maximum runway available.
- Apply maximum power smoothly and positively, with the brakes applied, and holding the control column back to reduce loads on the nose wheel; check that maximum power is being delivered.
- Release the brakes as full power is reached—although, if loose stones could damage the propeller, a rolling start is preferred.
- Track down the runway centerline during the takeoff ground run, keeping the wings level with the ailerons.
- Lift off at the minimum recommended flying speed.

Anticipate turbulence and downdrafts.

- Set the nose attitude for the airspeed that will give you the steepest climb over any obstacles: with flaps, use the obstacle-clearance airspeed; without flaps, use the best angle-of-climb airspeed, V_X +5/–0 knots.
- At a safe altitude, and when clear of obstacles, retract the flaps, and lower the nose to the pitch attitude required for the best rate-of-climb airspeed, V_Y +5/–0 knots.
- Remain aligned with the extended runway centerline in the climb-out, unless other obstacles preclude this. Avoid turning downwind.

Climb out well clear of obstacles.

- Finally, complete the after-takeoff checklist.

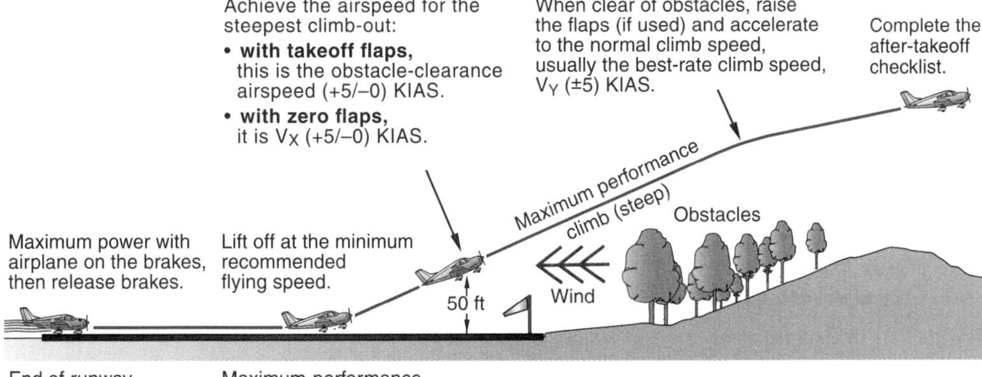

Figure 40-3 The maximum performance short-field takeoff.

The Short-Field Landing

Don't land if a later takeoff is doubtful.

The short-field landing is used when the landing area:

- has marginal landing distance available; or
- has obstacles in the approach path that reduce the usable length.

Land as directly into the wind as possible.

Land as much into wind as possible for a steeper approach and a shorter landing roll. Position the airplane as for a normal approach—the preferred technique being a power-on approach at a low speed with an aim point as close to the threshold as practicable. The airplane should touch down without float as soon as the throttle is closed.

Fly as slow an approach speed as is safe.

Full flaps is the preferred configuration if the wind conditions are suitable, since this allows a lower approach speed and there will be less float prior to touchdown due to the extra drag. In gusty conditions, you might add one-half of the gust value to the approach speed—for instance, with gusts of 10 knots, add 5 knots. The recommended approach speed for a short-field landing may be less than for the normal approach—check your pilot's operating handbook. Fly a stabilized approach along the extended runway centerline at the selected airspeed (+5/–0 knots).

Frequent, small adjustments to power and attitude will be required to maintain the desired flight path and airspeed. Correct the approach path as early as possible to arrive at the flare with power on.

Fly the approach path to clear all obstacles.

Obstacles in the approach path may require use of an aim point further into the field, or an approach a little steeper than usual. Having cleared the obstacles, do not reduce power suddenly, otherwise a high sink rate and a heavy touchdown may result since at a low speed the airplane has less-effective controls and a reduced flaring capability.

If there are no obstacles in the approach path, then slightly undershooting on the approach may be considered, with power being used to ensure that you reach the threshold safely.

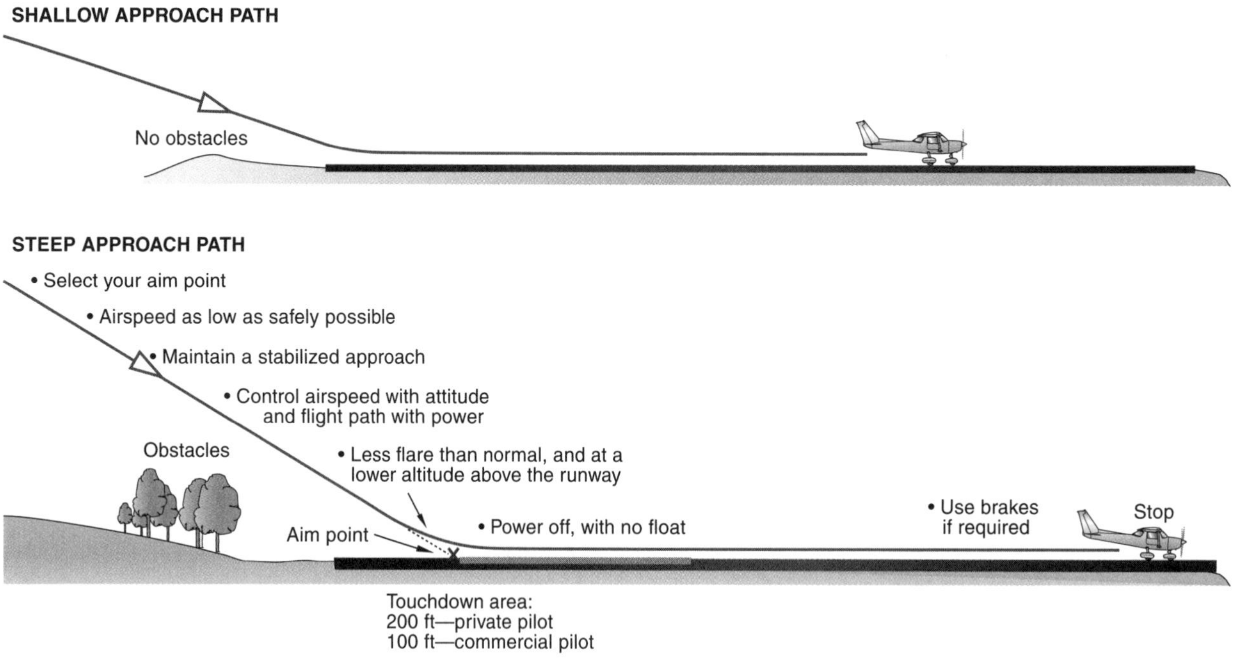

SHALLOW APPROACH PATH
No obstacles

STEEP APPROACH PATH
• Select your aim point
• Airspeed as low as safely possible
• Maintain a stabilized approach
• Control airspeed with attitude and flight path with power
Obstacles
• Less flare than normal, and at a lower altitude above the runway
Aim point
• Power off, with no float
• Use brakes if required
Stop
Touchdown area:
200 ft—private pilot
100 ft—commercial pilot

Figure 40-4 Ensure that you clear all obstacles in the approach path.

Aim to cross the airport boundary with power on at the selected speed, and at the minimum altitude consistent with adequate obstacle clearance. If airspeed is too high in the landing, the float may be significant, and unnecessary runway distance wasted.

Touch down with the longitudinal axis of the airplane aligned with the runway centerline. Whereas the tolerance for touchdown on a long runway is in the area from the aim point to 500 feet beyond it, for the maximum performance landing it is:

- not before the specified aim point; and
- at or within 200 feet beyond the specified point, for private pilots, and within 100 feet beyond the specified point, for commercial pilots.

Since the nose will be higher than in a normal landing—because of the lower speed and higher power—hardly any flare is needed. The flare should be started closer to the ground than normal. Some power should be left on at the commencement of the flare if the speed is low—the airplane will touch down as soon as the throttle is closed.

If a crosswind exists, apply crosswind, as well as short-field, techniques.

- If a high sink rate develops, add power to prevent a heavy landing. Power may be required all the way to the ground—if so, close the throttle as soon as the wheels touch.
- If an especially short landing roll is required, brakes may be used when all the wheels are firmly on the ground. Apply brakes smoothly and positively to stop in the shortest distance consistent with safety. Maintain positive directional control along the centerline in the after-landing ground run. Early in the landing roll, the wings will still be producing some lift and so all of the weight will not be on the wheels. Excessive braking at this time may cause skidding.

Do not hold the airplane off for a prolonged period. Allow touchdown and start braking.

AIRMANSHIP

Do not attempt the takeoff if you have any doubt about your ability to safely complete the maneuver. The options you may have include:

- waiting until evening when it is cooler;
- waiting until the wind is down the runway; and
- off-loading some baggage or passengers and making separate flights to a nearby airport with a longer runway (shuttle service).

Figure 40-5 Weigh up all the factors.

REVIEW 40
Short-Field Operations

1. Name two factors that could lead to a maximum performance takeoff being required?
2. For a maximum performance takeoff from a short field with obstacles in the climb-out path, should you use the full length of the runway? What sort of start, rolling or standing, do you make for a maximum performance takeoff? Which of the steepest climb gradient or the fastest rate of climb should you climb away at?
3. For a takeoff with flaps, the steepest climb gradient can be achieved at which of the following speeds: the published obstacle-clearance speed for that flap setting, V_X or V_Y? What is the accuracy required?
4. What is V_X defined as? What is the require accuracy? If the published V_X is 56 knots, what is the required accuracy?
5. What is V_Y defined as? Is the steepest climb the same as the quickest climb to altitude? How does the nose attitude for V_Y compare to that for V_X? What is the required accuracy for V_Y? If the published V_Y is 70 knots, what is the required accuracy?
6. If you lost power at 200 feet after a maximum performance takeoff, what would your initial actions be?
7. What are two factors that lead to a maximum performance landing being required?
8. Which approach gradient, steep or shallow, would you fly if the landing distance is short because of obstacles in the approach sector? At what flap setting is this best achieved? At what airspeed is this best achieved?
9. If the landing distance is short, and there are no obstacles in the approach sector, is there a need to fly a steep approach?
10. What should the airspeed be for a maximum performance landing? What length, short or prolonged, should the flare be? Should the brakes be used?
11. On a maximum performance approach, the recommended airspeed should be maintained to an accuracy of how many knots? How is the flight path and airspeed positively controlled?
12. For a maximum performance landing, can the point of touchdown be before the aim point you have specified during the approach? How many feet beyond the specified aim point can the touchdown be for private and commercial pilots?
13. Which sort of approach, power-on or power-off, gives you the most control over the approach and the touchdown point?

Figure 40-6 Short-field takeoff.

Answers are given on page 585.

41
Soft-Field Operations

OBJECTIVES

To describe:

- the negative factors associated with a soft-field takeoff and landing; and
- the optimum technique for takeoff and landing from a soft surface.

Figure 41-1 Soft-field operations.

CONSIDERATIONS

As with any airport, before using a soft field you must evaluate:

- the wind direction;
- the takeoff and landing surface (condition and length); and
- obstructions or other hazards in the takeoff and approach paths.

What is a Soft Field?

A soft field could be an area which has a soft surface such as sand or snow, a wet grassy surface or a rough surface. A soft field may be quite long and without obstacle-clearance problems in the climb-out or approach paths. It may also be short, which means the short-field consideration of obstacle clearance also becomes important. For this exercise, however, we assume a long takeoff surface and no obstacle-clearance problems.

When operating from a soft surface, you want the wings to support the weight for as long as possible, keeping the airplane's weight off the wheels since the wheels may have a tendency to dig in. Your aim should be to achieve the shortest ground run possible on a soft surface, both in the takeoff and the landing. Only use a soft field if you are totally satisfied that a safe takeoff and landing can be made.

Soft surfaces create extra frictional drag and stress on the wheels, degrading the acceleration in the takeoff run, and increasing the deceleration in the landing roll. Takeoffs will require more distance than usual, and landings less. Consult the performance charts for the exact requirements for your airplane.

APPLICATION

Planning the Takeoff

Keep rolling on a soft surface.

The main concern in a soft-field takeoff is to transfer the weight from the wheels to the wings as soon as possible, and to achieve a short ground run. Consequently the optimum flap setting and maximum power should be used.

At high-altitude airports, especially in hot conditions, adjust the mixture control as recommended by the manufacturer.

TECHNIQUE

Taxiing Out

Transfer the weight from the wheels to the wings early in the takeoff run.

Try to avoid stopping on the soft surface; complete your engine run-up and pretakeoff checklist before taxiing, as the wheels may tend to sink into the soft surface. Taxi onto the takeoff surface at a speed consistent with safety and, when aligned with the takeoff path, smoothly apply full power, holding the control column fully back.

The Soft-Field Takeoff

While still rolling, smoothly apply maximum power and check the engine instruments to ensure that maximum power is being delivered. During the takeoff ground run, keep the weight off the nose wheel with the control column held back. Maintain positive directional control along the center of the takeoff path. Lift the airplane off the ground as soon as possible—at a lower speed than in a normal takeoff—and accelerate to the appropriate climb speed close to the surface and in ground effect. Because the airplane can fly in ground effect at a lower speed than when it is well away from the ground, do not climb more than about 10 feet above the ground until a safe flying speed is attained, at which time a normal climb-out can proceed.

Accelerate in ground effect.

If flaps were used for takeoff, hold the recommended obstacle-clearance airspeed until all obstacles have been cleared. Hold V_X, the best-angle climb airspeed, until all obstacles are cleared. Because of the proximity of these low speeds to the stall, do not fly any slower—the speed tolerance is +5/–0 knots. When any obstacles have been cleared, the airplane can be accelerated and the flaps raised at a safe altitude. The normal climb speed will be V_Y, the best-rate climb airspeed, with a tolerance of plus or minus 5 knots.

Apply elevator back pressure to raise the nose wheel off the ground as soon as possible.
Lift off at an early stage.
Accelerate in ground effect.
Initiate a climb-out.

Figure 41-2 The soft-field takeoff.

Apply drift correction if necessary. Maintain a straight track along the extended takeoff path, until a turn is necessary, by using a reference point ahead, or by an occasional quick glance over your shoulder at the takeoff area. Complete the after-takeoff checklist.

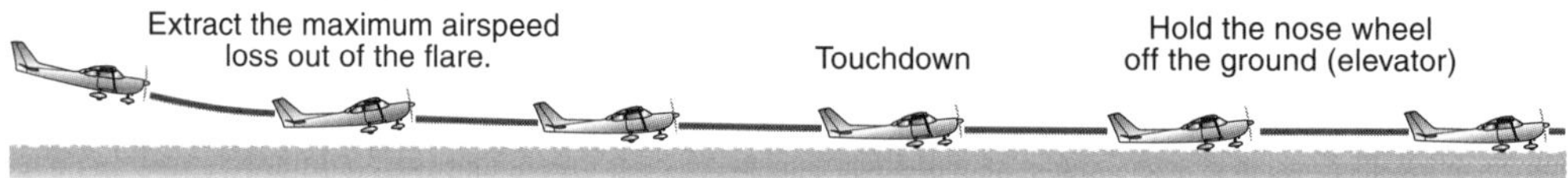
Extract the maximum airspeed loss out of the flare.
Touchdown
Hold the nose wheel off the ground (elevator)

Figure 41-3 The soft-field landing.

The Soft-Field Landing

Since the tendency on a soft field is for the nose wheel (and, to a lesser extent, the main wheels) to dig in, the aim should be to:

- land as slowly as possible; with
- the nose held up as long as possible during the landing roll.

Don't land if you can't takeoff later.

The Approach

Extending full flaps reduces the stall speed, so the touchdown can be made at a very low speed. If field length is not a problem, a normal approach can be flown, with a slightly modified flare at the selected aiming point. Fly a stabilized approach along the extended landing path at the recommended airspeed right through to the touchdown zone (tolerance plus or minus 5 knots). Promptly correct any deviations from the desired flight path and airspeed.

Approach with full flaps, if conditions permit.

Touchdown

Some power can be left on to start the flare, as the nose is raised higher than normal in a prolonged float. Try to touch down smoothly, with a minimum descent rate, with the airspeed as slow as possible, with no drift and the wheels aligned with the landing direction. The higher the nose attitude and the lower the speed on touchdown, the better.

Touch down as gently and as slowly as possible.

As the main wheels touch, hold back-elevator to keep the nose wheel off the soft surface for as long as possible, and then gently lower it. Use rudder to achieve and maintain good directional control in the ground roll. Brakes are usually not required in soft-field landings, because the soft surface will tend to slow the airplane down. Using the brakes will put additional stress on the landing gear, and may cause the nose wheel to dig in. On occasions, power may be required toward the end of the landing roll on a soft surface to keep the airplane moving, so that you can taxi to the parking area and not become bogged in the soft surface.

Hold the nose wheel off and avoid using the brakes.

Keep rolling on a soft surface.

Parking

If possible, park the airplane on a hard surface to make it easier to taxi away on the next flight. Complete the normal shutdown checklist and secure the airplane.

Ensure that you park on a hard surface.

REVIEW 41

Soft-Field Operations

1. What three items regarding a runway would you evaluate before using it?
2. When operating on a soft surface, what is the risk for the wheels?
3. Which flap setting shortens the ground run during takeoff?
4. How do you reduce the risk of the nose wheel digging in during the takeoff run on a soft field?
5. How do you reduce the risk of the wheels digging in at the start of the takeoff run on a soft field after taxiing out and aligning the airplane?
6. How does the liftoff in soft-field takeoff compare to that of a normal takeoff? How is ground effect used in a soft-field takeoff?
7. To clear obstacles in the takeoff path if flaps are used, you should initially climb at which airspeed? Which airspeed should be used if the takeoff is clean? What is the tolerance for both these speeds?
8. When clear of obstacles, you can raise the flaps at a safe altitude and accelerate to which speed? What is its tolerance?
9. When settled in the climb, which checklist should you complete?
10. How does the speed at touchdown for a soft-field landing compare to that for a normal landing? How is the risk of the nose wheel digging in reduced in a soft-field landing?
11. What wind direction and flap setting would you plan on landing with for a soft-field landing?
12. What is the accuracy you should fly your selected approach speed to?
13. How do you reduce the risk of the wheels digging in during and at the end of the landing roll on a soft surface?
14. How does the amount of power needed to taxi on a soft surface compared to a hard surface?
15. On which type of surface should you try to park?

Answers are given on page 585.

Performance Maneuvers

42
Steep Turns

OBJECTIVES

To describe:

- the factors to be considered when turning an aircraft at bank angles beyond 45°;
- the techniques for safely and efficiently completing a steep turn and to correct for deviations in pitch and bank; and
- the use of a steep descending spiral to lose altitude in a confined area.

CONSIDERATIONS

A steep turn is a turn in which the bank angle is 45° or more. For this exercise a bank angle of 45° will be used. A steep turn is a high-performance maneuver that requires good coordination and positive attitude control.

Increased Lift

A steep turn requires increased lift (increased angle of attack), and this requires back pressure on the control column.

In straight and level flight, the lift produced by the wings balances the weight of the airplane. In turns, the lift force is tilted and consequently the lift generated by the wings must be increased to provide not only a vertical component to balance the weight but also a horizontal component (known as the centripetal force) to pull the airplane into the turn. In a 60°-banked turn, for example, the total lift produced by the wing must be double the weight, if altitude is to be maintained. Thus at the same airspeed the angle of attack must be doubled. This requires, as you will see, a significant pull force on the control column. The tighter the turn, the greater the angle of attack and the greater the force required. If the force is not maintained, the nose will drop and the aircraft will descend.

Increased lift in a turn is generated by an increased angle of attack.

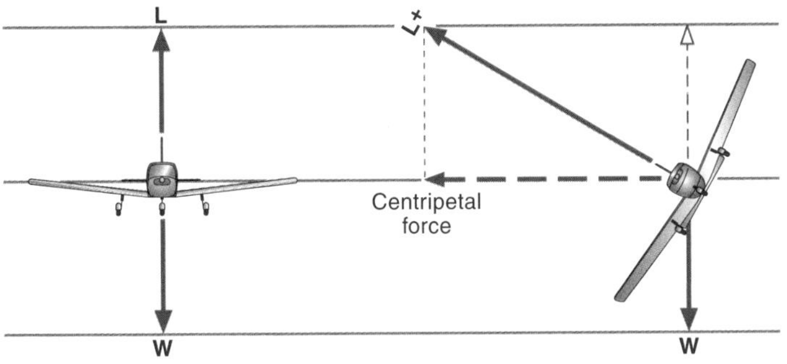

Figure 42-1 A steep turn requires increased total lift.

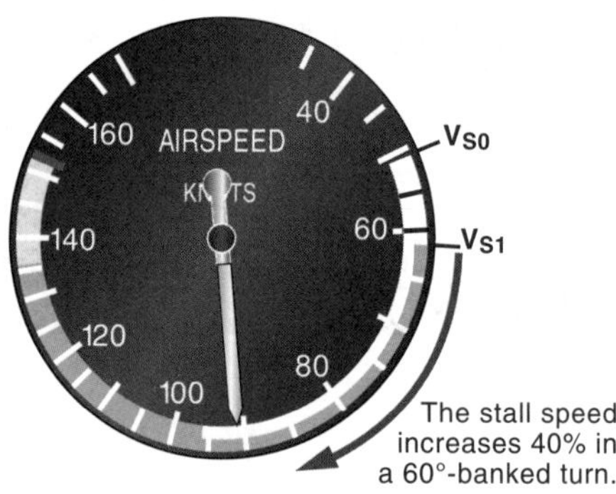

Figure 42-2 Be alert to the stall-speed increase in a steep turn.

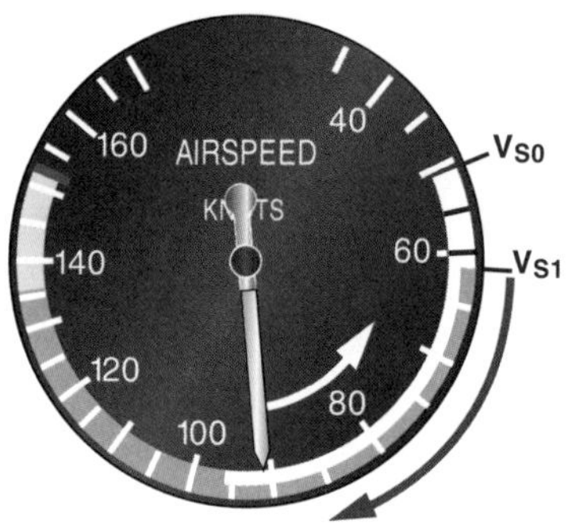

Figure 42-3 Use power to maintain airspeed in a steep turn—anticipate.

Load Factor

During a turn, you will experience an increased load factor (which is the ratio of lift to weight) or g-force. The symbol for load factor is n. The normal load factor is one (+1g) when the airplane is either stationary on the ground or in steady, straight and level flight. You experience this as 1g, your normal weight. In a 60°-banked turn, the load factor is 2 and you will feel twice your normal weight because the lift generated by the wings is now double the airplane's weight. The human body soon becomes accustomed to these g-forces. For the 45°-banked turn the load factor will be +1.4g.

The steeper the turn, the greater the angle of attack required to generate sufficient lift, and consequently the stalling angle of attack will be reached at a higher airspeed than when the wings are level. In a 60°-banked turn, for example, the stalling speed is some 40% greater (for example, an airplane that stalls at 50 knots straight and level will stall at 70 knots when pulling 2g).

The greater the load factor, the higher the stalling speed. Feeling a g-force is a signal that the airplane structure is under additional stress and that stalling speed has increased. At any hint of stalling in a steep turn, some of the back pressure on the control column should be released. This will reduce the angle of attack and move the wings away from the stalling angle. Reducing the bank angle or adding power (if there is any in reserve) will also assist in avoiding a stall in this situation.

Increased Drag

The greater angle of attack used to generate the increased lift required in a steep turn also creates additional induced drag. This must be balanced by increased thrust if the airplane is to maintain airspeed. Whereas it is acceptable to lose a few knots in medium turns, it is very important to maintain airspeed in steep turns because of the higher stalling speed. As well as coordinating the use of aileron, rudder and elevator (as in medium turns), power now becomes an added ingredient as the maximum achievable bank angle in a steady steep turn is determined by the amount of power available.

APPLICATION

Maximum-Performance Turns

A maximum-performance steep turn at a particular airspeed is flown like a normal steep turn except that power is progressively applied as the bank angle is increased, until maximum power is reached. The ability to maintain altitude and airspeed in this maneuver depends on the amount of power available. For most training airplanes, the performance limit is reached at about 65° of bank. Turning performance is measured in terms of:

- the rate of turn (the greater, the better); and
- the radius of turn (the smaller, the better).

At a constant airspeed, turning performance increases with bank angle. At a constant bank angle, turning performance is better at low airspeeds. Therefore, the best turning performance can be achieved at a relatively low airspeed and a high bank angle (providing the airplane is not stalled or the airframe overstressed).

Overstressing

The lift that can be generated by the wings with full rearward movement of the control column is far greater at high airspeeds than at low airspeeds and results in greater load factors occurring. For example, pulling the control column fully back at 150 knots will increase the g-loading considerably more than at 50 knots. At high airspeeds, therefore, there is a danger of overstressing the airframe by exceeding the maximum allowable load factor. (This is +3.8g for most training airplanes in the normal category. Some aircraft with reduced weight may be classified as utility category and may be approved for +4.5g.)

Maneuvering Speed (V_A)

Large elevator deflection at high airspeed can cause the wings to generate so much lift that the airplane's limiting load factor is exceeded. At low airspeeds, the airplane will stall before the limiting load factor is reached; that is, the airframe is protected.

The airspeed at which the aircraft would stall at the load-factor limit is called the maneuvering speed (V_A). The best aerodynamic turning performance can be achieved at this speed provided sufficient power is available to overcome the induced drag.

For most training airplanes, the engine performance is the limiting factor in maximum-performance, steep turns. Turning performance can then only be improved by accepting a loss of altitude in the turn. V_A for maximum weight is specified in the flight manual. At airspeeds less than maneuvering speed (V_A), full elevator deflection will not overstress the airframe. At lesser weights, when stalling speed is lower, the actual V_A will be reduced proportionally with the change in weight. If the weight reduces by 9 percent, V_A is reduced by 3 percent (the square root of the change in weight). The aircraft's approved

It is safer to be below V_A before beginning a steep turn.

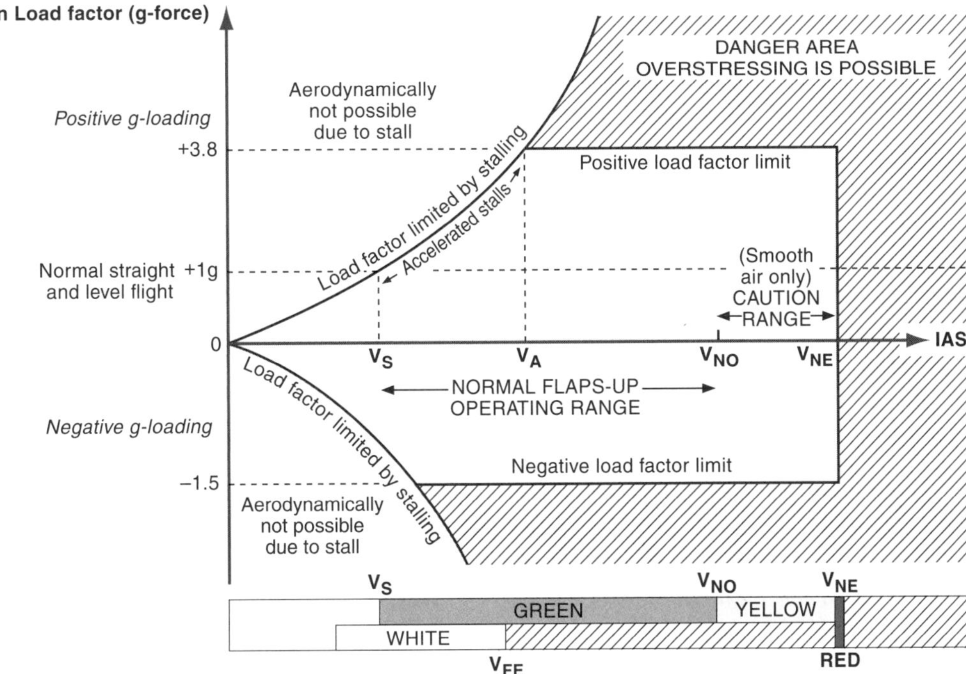

Figure 42-4 The V-n diagram of airspeed (V) versus load factor (n).

flight envelope is commonly displayed as a V-n diagram (a diagram of allowable speed range and load-factor limits).

The g-forces in a 45° steep turn are nowhere near as great as in a 60°-banked turn. For this reason, you may find it easier to practice steep turns at a 45° bank angle initially, progressing to 60° bank angle turns later on. Prior to practicing steep turns, your training organization may require you to carry out the pre-aerobatic HASELL check.

TECHNIQUE

Rolling into a Steep Turn

Be on-speed, on-altitude, and in-trim before rolling into a steep turn.

Trim the airplane for straight and level flight at the desired airspeed and altitude. Look out for other airplanes and select a reference point on the horizon for the roll-out. Roll into the turn just as you would for a medium turn except that as the bank angle passes through 30°:

- smoothly increase power;
- progressively increase the back pressure on the control column to hold the nose up;
- adjust the bank angle and back pressure to place the nose in the correct position relative to the horizon; and
- balance with rudder.

Do not apply too much back pressure entering the turn or the airplane will climb: just gradually increase it as you steepen the bank, to prevent the nose dropping. The back pressure required in a steep turn will probably be much greater than you had anticipated.

Note the attitude when established in the turn. This will allow you to set the steep turn whenever you wish. Do not trim as the turn is only a transient maneuver.

Maintaining a Steep Turn

Add power to maintain altitude and airspeed.

The secret of flying an accurate steep turn is to hold the nose in the correct position relative to the horizon (even if it takes a lot of back pressure), ensuring the airspeed is maintained by adding sufficient power.

Keep a very good lookout during the steep turn to monitor the nose position and the approach of your roll-out reference point, as well as to look for other aircraft, especially in the direction of your turn.

An occasional glance at the instruments will confirm that the turn is proceeding satisfactorily, but do not sacrifice your outside reference by concentrating on the instruments. In just a second or two, you can quickly check:

- altitude on the altimeter and vertical speed indicator;
- airspeed on the airspeed indicator;
- bank angle on the attitude indicator; and
- balance on the balance ball.

Adjusting the bank angle and nose position is a continuing requirement throughout the steep turn and keeps the pilot quite busy. That is why it is such a good training maneuver! The sooner the corrections are made, the smaller they can be and the better the steep turn.

If altitude is being gained in the steep turn, it means that the vertical component of the lift force is too great, and so either:

- steepen the bank angle; and/or
- relax some of the back pressure.

If altitude is being lost then the vertical component of the lift force is insufficient. To regain altitude:

- reduce the bank angle slightly;
- raise the nose with back pressure; and
- once back on altitude, reapply the desired bank angle and back pressure.

If the nose drops below the horizon during a steep turn, trying to raise the nose with back pressure may only tighten the turn rather than raise the nose. If you feel you are having to pull hard and that the nose is not coming up, reduce the bank or even roll to wings-level, raise the nose to the climb attitude, climb back to your desired altitude and start again.

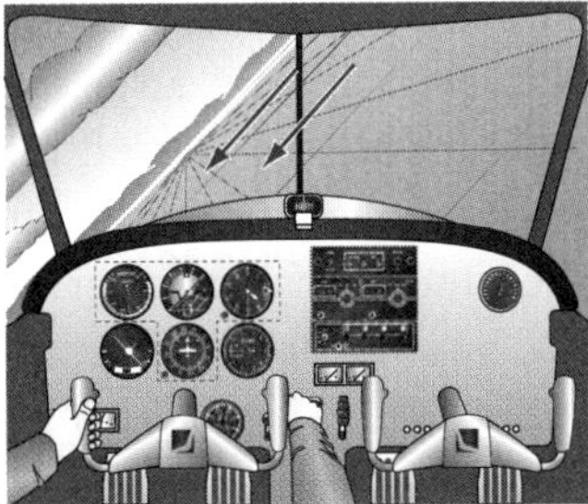

Figure 42-5 Typical attitudes while flying the maneuver.

Prestall Buffet

If the airplane turns through more than 360°, you may in fact strike your own slipstream and feel some turbulence. This is not stall buffet, but the sign of a well-executed steep turn. If, however, stall buffet is felt, then release some of the back pressure to reduce the angle of attack before the stall actually occurs and, to avoid losing altitude, you will have to decrease the bank angle as back pressure is released.

Accuracy

When practicing steep turns aim to achieve an accuracy of ±200 feet and bank angle within 5°. As your training progresses, try to pass through your own wash. The important thing is to make the correction as soon as a trend becomes obvious. This will contain any deviations.

Rolling Out of a Steep Turn

This is the same as rolling out of a medium turn, except that:

- greater anticipation is required to roll out on your reference point (allow ⅓ to ½ of the bank angle);
- there is a great deal more back pressure to be released, otherwise altitude will be gained; and
- after the airspeed has been regained, power must be reduced to cruise power.

Remember to keep the airplane in balance with rudder.

Concentration is required in the roll-out, especially to avoid gaining altitude since you may be a little reluctant to relax all of the back pressure. For rolling out of a 45°-banked turn, relaxing back pressure as you pass the 30° point is usually sufficient.

For rolling out of a 60°-banked turn, the release of back pressure is so great that it may feel as though you have to push the control column forward.

Remember to reduce the power as you release the back pressure, otherwise airspeed will rapidly increase. After some practice at steep turns to the left and right, your flight instructor may suggest that you roll from a steep turn one way immediately into a steep turn the other way.

Steep Spirals (Emergency Descent)

The steep spiral is a combination of:

- a steep descending turn (to lose altitude quickly); and
- turns around a point (to remain over a ground reference point).

The practical purpose of a steep spiral over a ground reference object could be to lose altitude rapidly over a selected emergency landing field. To maintain a constant ground radius around a ground reference object, you need to vary the bank angle. It will be steepest when the wind is from behind you, and shallowest when you are heading into the wind. Consider lowering the gear to contain airspeed.

The steep descending turn, as an air maneuver with a constant bank angle, will allow the wind to carry the airplane with it. The steep spiral, based on a ground reference point, uses a varying bank angle to counteract this wind drift.

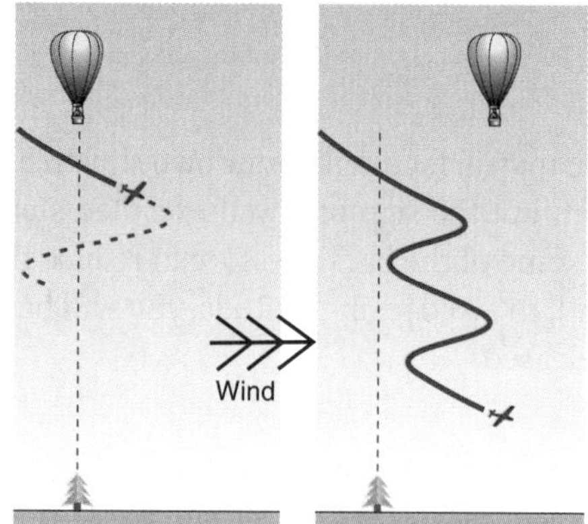

Figure 42-6 The descending path moves with the wind.

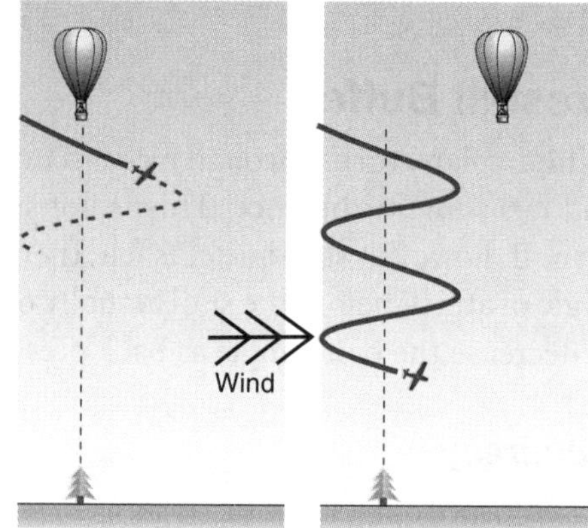

Figure 42-7 The steep spiral remains centered on a ground object.

Use the aircraft's POH to determine the best way to make a rapid descent from altitude. The examiner wants to see that you recognize the need to descend, as well as establish the recommended emergency descent airspeed (±5 knots), demonstrate situational awareness, and follow an emergency checklist. Be prepared to discuss reasons why you might need to execute an emergency descent (e.g. engine fire, electrical fire, loss of pressurization).

Since the stalling speed increases in a turn, it is usual to fly at a greater airspeed than the best-glide airspeed when performing a steep spiral. Altitude loss is quite rapid in the steep-spiral maneuver. Depending on the airplane used, it could be as much as 1,000 feet per 360° turn, so in three complete turns you may lose 3,000 feet. The objective is to roll out toward a distant reference point or on a specified heading after three or more 360° turns, no lower than 1,500 feet AGL. In a prolonged spiral, you may decide to warm the engine by opening the throttle. This is best done as you turn through the upwind direction where the bank angle is shallowest.

Throughout the maneuver, divide your attention between airplane control, flight path over the ground and orientation. Keep a lookout for other airplanes, especially below.

If you are using this maneuver to position yourself for either a practice or a real power-off forced landing, then a suitable roll-out point could be 1,500 feet AGL or higher, in a position from where you can successfully complete a traffic pattern to a simulated or actual forced landing—discussed later.

AIRMANSHIP

Practice steep turns in an appropriate area and keep a very good look out for other aircraft. Note various landmarks that will assist in orientation during and after the turn. It is easy for an inexperienced pilot to become disoriented in steep turns that involve large changes of heading.

Handle the power smoothly and monitor the gauges to ensure engine limitations are not exceeded. Exert smooth, but firm, control over the airplane.

If the nose attitude drops or the bank angle or airspeed increases uncomfortably, roll to wings level and raise the nose to the level attitude. (Reduce power if necessary.)

REVIEW 42

Steep Turns

1. Steep turns should be practiced no lower than how many feet AGL? If ground level is 2,200 feet MSL, how many feet MSL should you not go below on your altimeter when practicing steep turns?
2. In a steep turn, what effect does applying back pressure on the control column have on lift? What effect does this have on drag? How does this affect the amount of power needed?
3. How does the load that the wings carry in a steep turn compare to that in straight and level flight? How does the stalling speed change in a steep turn compare to a less steep turn? In terms of weight, how does the pilot feel?
4. During a steep turn, what pressure can you expect to hold on the control column? What power will be required during a steep turn?
5. What is the change in the load factor in the a steep turn?
6. What are the accuracy limits for steep turns, including altitude, bank angle (for both private and commercial pilots), airspeed and roll-out heading?
7. What effect does increasing the bank angle have on the radius of the turn?
8. What effect does reducing the airspeed have on the radius of the turn?
9. What is the banking tendency in a steep turn? Which wing travels faster?
10. In steep gliding turn, what will happen to the rate of descent?
11. What should you initially do if the airspeed becomes excessive in a steep descending turn? What change do you then make to the nose attitude before reestablishing the desired steep turn?
12. What effect will simply exerting back pressure on the control column without reducing the bank angle have on a steep turn? What risk does this pose?
13. In an emergency descent, is the rate of descent high or low?

Answers are given on page 585.

TASK
Steep Turns

Aim: To perform a steep turn, maintaining constant altitude and airspeed.

Required Accuracy:
- Altitude ±100 feet
- Bank angle 45° ±5° for private pilots, and 50° ±5° for commercial pilots
- Airspeed ±10 KIAS
- Nominated roll-out heading ±10°
- No tendency to stall nor to reach excessive speeds

1. Entry

Complete the HASELL check.

Clear the area and look out.

Select a reference point on the horizon.

Nominate the number of turns and the roll-out reference point or heading.

Nominate bank angle, airspeed and altitude, and then stick to them.

Roll into the turn with ailerons.

Coordinated with rudder to keep ball centered.

Apply back pressure to maintain altitude.

Add power progressively to maintain airspeed.

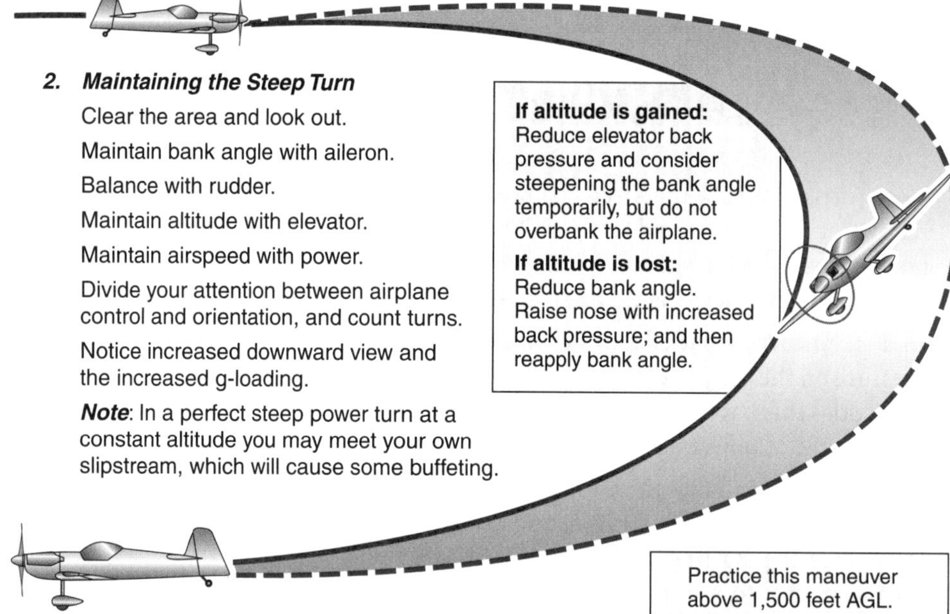

2. Maintaining the Steep Turn

Clear the area and look out.

Maintain bank angle with aileron.

Balance with rudder.

Maintain altitude with elevator.

Maintain airspeed with power.

Divide your attention between airplane control and orientation, and count turns.

Notice increased downward view and the increased g-loading.

Note: In a perfect steep power turn at a constant altitude you may meet your own slipstream, which will cause some buffeting.

If altitude is gained:
Reduce elevator back pressure and consider steepening the bank angle temporarily, but do not overbank the airplane.

If altitude is lost:
Reduce bank angle.
Raise nose with increased back pressure; and then reapply bank angle.

Practice this maneuver above 1,500 feet AGL.

3. Roll Out

Locate roll-out reference point (anticipate by one-half the bank angle).

Roll out of the turn with aileron and balance with rudder.

Release the elevator back pressure to maintain altitude.

Progressively reduce power to maintain the desired cruise airspeed.

Immediately make fine adjustments to be precisely on heading, altitude and airspeed.

Note: Try 720° turns (twice around) both left and the right, rolling straight from one to the other. You must reduce power and lower the nose a little as you pass through wings level, before reapplying bank angle, back pressure and power.

TASK

Steep Spirals (Emergency Descent)

Aims: To descend in a spiral, maintaining a constant-ground-radius turn over a reference point.

Select a suitable field or road pattern with sides about one mile long and fly about one-half to one-quarter mile from the boundary for good vision and to keep the bank angle in turns to less than 45°.

1. Entering a Steep Spiral

Climb to a suitable starting altitude.

Select a suitable ground reference point that is prominent (tree, road intersection).

Complete the HASELL pre-aerobatic check.

Clear the area and look out.

Select a roll-out point or roll-out heading, specifying the number of 360° descending turns you will make.

Plan the steep spiral downwind so that the first turn will be steepest (maximum 55° bank angle).

Reduce power (carburetor heat on, throttle closed, mixture rich) and enter straight glide.

Add some speed to the best wings-level glide speed to retain an adequate margin over the increased stalling speed in a turn (add 20 knots for a 60° steep descending turn). Hold this speed throughout the maneuver.

Roll into the turn with aileron and coordinated rudder (maximum 50° to 55°), adjusting the bank angle as necessary to maintain the specified ground radius.

Set the pitch attitude to maintain the increased airspeed.

2. Maintaining a Steep Spiral

Clear the area.

Monitor the ground reference point and your ground track around it (maintain a constant ground radius).

Expect to reduce the bank angle as you turn from downwind to upwind, and then increase the bank angle again as you turn downwind once again.

Keep balanced with rudder.

Maintain the target airspeed (±10 KIAS)–if the airspeed increases, reduce the bank angle, raise the nose with elevator control and reapply the desired bank angle.

Periodically warm the engine by briefly advancing the throttle to normal cruise power (upwind is best, where the bank angle is shallowest).

Divide your attention between airplane control, flight path over the ground, and the orientation (note the roll-out reference point or the heading on each turn, and count the turns).

Check your altitude (and roll out early, if necessary, to avoid going below the minimum safe altitude).

Be prepared for the wind to decrease and change in direction as you descend, but maintain a constant ground radius by varying the bank angle.

3. The Roll-Out

Clear the area.

Roll out using aileron and rudder, starting about 20° before the selected reference point or heading.

Select the desired pitch attitude with elevator for a straight glide, straight and level, or climb, (carburetor heat off, throttle increased).

Maintain airspeed with elevator.
Maintain a constant ground radius with bank angle.
If desired, reduce rate of descent with power.

TASK

Steep Spirals (Emergency Descent)

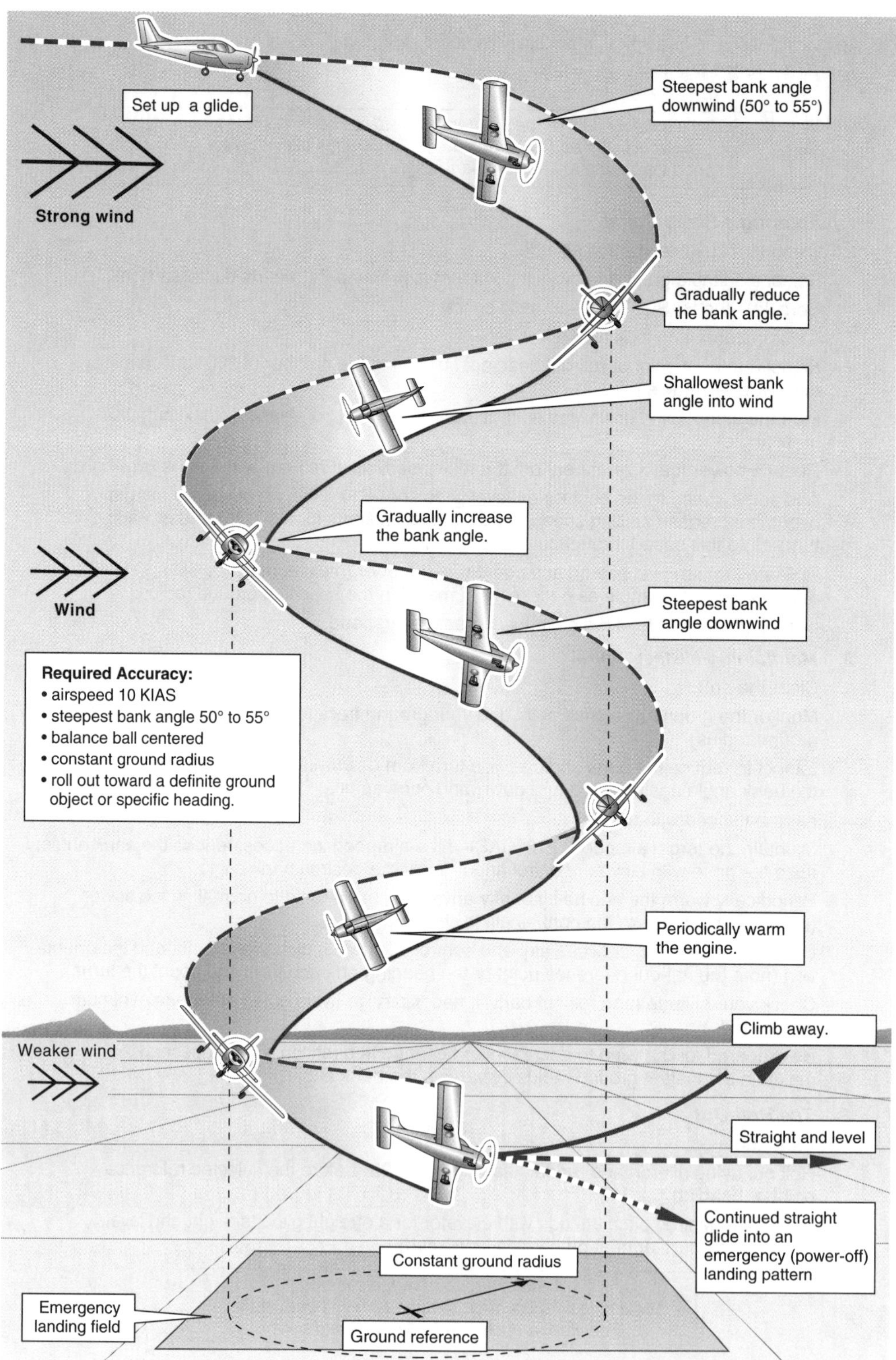
Set up a glide.
Steepest bank angle downwind (50° to 55°)
Strong wind
Gradually reduce the bank angle.
Shallowest bank angle into wind
Gradually increase the bank angle.
Wind
Steepest bank angle downwind
Required Accuracy:
• airspeed 10 KIAS
• steepest bank angle 50° to 55°
• balance ball centered
• constant ground radius
• roll out toward a definite ground object or specific heading.
Periodically warm the engine.
Climb away.
Weaker wind
Straight and level
Continued straight glide into an emergency (power-off) landing pattern
Constant ground radius
Emergency landing field
Ground reference

43
Unusual Attitude Recoveries

OBJECTIVES

To describe:
- the instrument and physical indications of an unusual or divergent attitude or airspeed; and
- the technique to safely recover positive control from unusually high and low nose attitude conditions.

CONSIDERATIONS

An unusual attitude may result from a steep turn that has been allowed to steepen, a mishandled stall entry or recovery, a spiral descent due to poor visibility or lack of a clearly defined horizon, or inattention to attitude and airspeed in a climbing turn. They are also taught as part of a pilot's flight training when the recovery is made purely on instruments, or during aerobatic training where recovery from extreme nose-high and nose-low situations may be required. All recoveries are routine once learned.

Potentially hazardous attitudes are nose high with decreasing airspeed and nose low with increasing airspeed.

What is an Unusual Attitude?

The two fundamental unusual attitudes are:
- nose high with a decreasing airspeed (leading to a possible stall and departure from controlled flight); or
- nose low with an increasing airspeed (leading to a tightening spiral with risk of structural damage or failure and, ultimately, impact with the ground), the more common of the two.

It is important to understand what is happening to the aircraft in both these situations.

APPLICATION

Nose-High Unusual Attitude

Imagine the aircraft has somehow reached a very nose-high attitude, probably also with a high angle of bank, and the airspeed is rapidly approaching the stalling speed. As long as any back pressure is released, the aircraft will not stall because the critical angle of attack cannot be exceeded without back pressure, no matter what the attitude has become. If the pilot lets go of the controls, the aircraft would eventually settle to a nose-low, airspeed-increasing situation. However, this would result is a significant loss of altitude.

Nose high and decreasing airspeed: beware of a stall or spin.

To regain level flight with no altitude loss and without risking a stall, the angle of attack is reduced, full power is immediately applied (with rudder to balance) to stop the airspeed decay, and the wings are rolled level—in that order.

Nose-Low Unusual Attitude

The most common loss of control scenario is either a steep turn that has been allowed to become a descending steep turn with increasing bank angle and airspeed, or a subtle but dangerous tightening of a turn on instruments or with a poor visual horizon and the pilot not flying with reference to the attitude indicator or is not believing the attitude indicator. As the bank increases the nose drops, sideslip tends to yaw the nose further below the horizon, and the airspeed increases. The noise increases and the g-forces build. The problem now is that the aircraft is trimmed for a lower speed and so, as the airspeed increases, the elevator trim is trying to pitch the nose up. However, in a steeply banked turn this nose-up pitching moment is tightening the turn. There is also a tendency for the bank angle to be increasing and for the airspeed and g-force to increase further.

Nose low and increasing airspeed: beware of an overspeed or a spiral dive.

In both cases, the aircraft develops an ever steepening and accelerating turn that may ultimately lead to structural failure or, if the pilot overreacts, actually cause the structural failure during the attempted recovery. It has to be handled gently.

The recovery is very simple if the horizon is visible and the aircraft has spare altitude in which to recover. The power has to be removed to contain the airspeed, the wings have to be rolled level to stop the turn (but this must be done before applying any back pressure and indeed may require some forward pressure due to the high airspeed) and then the aircraft is gently recovered from the dive. It takes time and altitude, with a quick recovery being even more dangerous.

TECHNIQUE

Nose High and Decreasing Airspeed

If the nose is well above the horizon and the speed is low and/or decreasing, a stall is a possibility. To recover from a nose-high unusual attitude:

- ease the control column forward and push the nose toward the horizon;
- apply maximum power;
- apply sufficient rudder to prevent further yaw; and
- roll the wings level with coordinated use of rudder and ailerons.

If the aircraft has already stalled, or if a spin develops then recover using the recommended incipient- or full-spin recovery.

Nose Low and Increasing Airspeed

If the nose is low, especially if power is applied, exceeding the maximum allowable airspeed (V_{NE}, shown on the ASI as a red line) is a danger that could overstress the airplane. A steep bank angle and a low nose attitude may develop into a spiral dive.

To recover from a nose-low, high-airspeed unusual attitude:

- reduce power (close the throttle quickly and completely);
- roll the wings level with aileron and rudder, but don't allow the nose to pitch up;
- ease out of the ensuing dive; and
- as the airspeed reduces below V_{NO} and the nose passes through the horizon, reapply power and climb away.

A nose-low, increasing-speed attitude, if not corrected, can develop into a spiral dive, which can be recognized by:

- a high g-loading;
- a rapidly increasing airspeed (that distinguishes it from a spin); and
- a rapid loss of altitude, probably with the rate of descent increasing.

The recovery from the spiral dive is the same as that for a nose-low, high-speed situation, but it is especially important to avoid excessive elevator deflection when easing out of the dive, otherwise the limit load factor for the airplanes could be exceeded, overstressing the airframe. It is permissible to use the ailerons firmly to roll the wings level, provided the g-force is reduced by relaxing any back pressure and, if necessary, even applying some forward pressure to stop excessive pitch up.

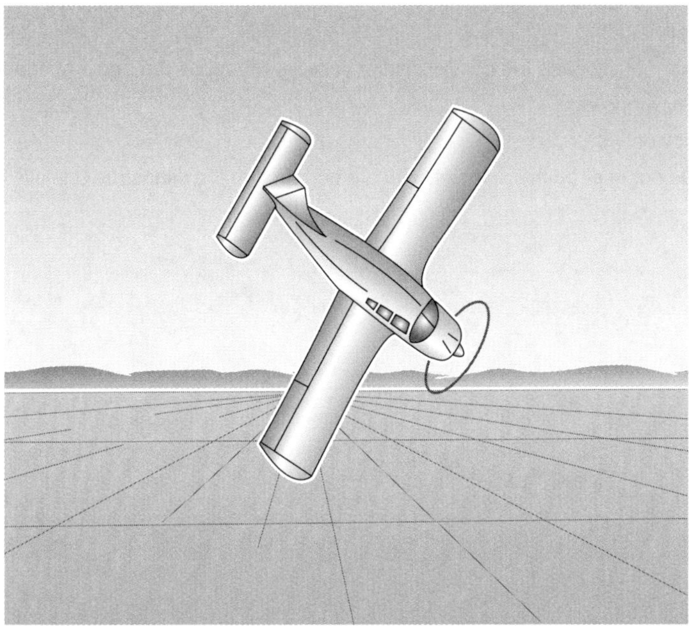

Figure 43-1 Extreme nose low. Recover carefully.

REVIEW 43

Unusual Attitude Recoveries

1. What is the risk associated with a high-nose and low-speed situation?
2. Describe how you would recover from a nose-high and low-airspeed unusual attitude.
3. If a nose-low and high-speed situation occurs, what is there a risk of? If a steep bank occurs, this could cause structural damage or what other outcome?
4. Describe how you would recover from a nose-low and high-airspeed unusual attitude.
5. If the airspeed becomes too high in a steep descending turn, what should you do?
6. When recovering from a spiral dive, it is important to avoid excessive deflection of which control when easing out of the dive? What does this prevent?

Answers are given on page 586.

TASK

Recovery from Unusual Attitudes

Aim: To recognize and recover from an unusual airplane attitude.

1. ***Nose High and Low Airspeed***

   This is recognized primarily from the airspeed indicator and sloppy controls.

   Recovery:

   • Simultaneously ease the control column forward to reduce the angle of attack.

   • Roll the wings level.

   • Add power.

   Note: Do not use the ailerons until you are certain that the wings are unstalled.

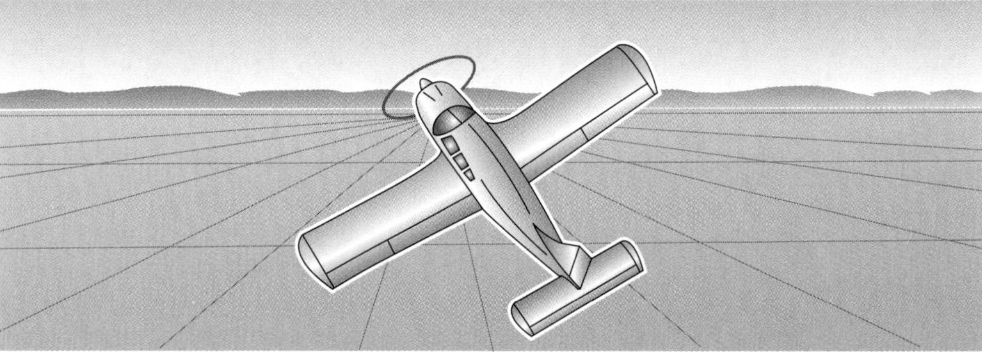

2. ***Nose Low and High Airspeed***

   This is recognized primarily from the airspeed indicator and vertical speed indicator.

   Recovery:

   • Reduce power.

   • Roll the wings level with aileron and coordinate with rudder.

   • *Ease* out of the dive.

   • Add power after nose passes through the horizon.

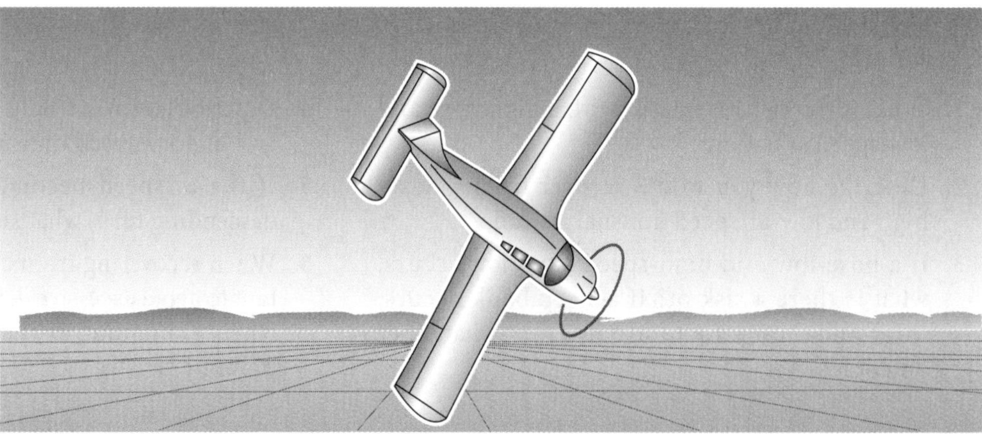

44 Chandelles

OBJECTIVES

To perform a chandelle—a maximum performance climbing turn with a heading change of 180°—gaining as much altitude as possible and rolling out just above stall speed.

CONSIDERATIONS

Power, Momentum and Altitude

The airplane enters the chandelle at a high speed with lots of momentum, and high power. When the turn is commenced, the airplane is pulled into a climbing turn to convert this energy into altitude.

The chandelle is a 180° zoom and turn that converts power and momentum into altitude.

As altitude is gained, the airspeed dissipates. The purpose is to achieve the 180° turn with as much altitude gain as possible, and roll out wings-level just above the stall speed. Maintain that airspeed momentarily, avoiding the stall, then resume straight and level flight with a minimum loss of altitude.

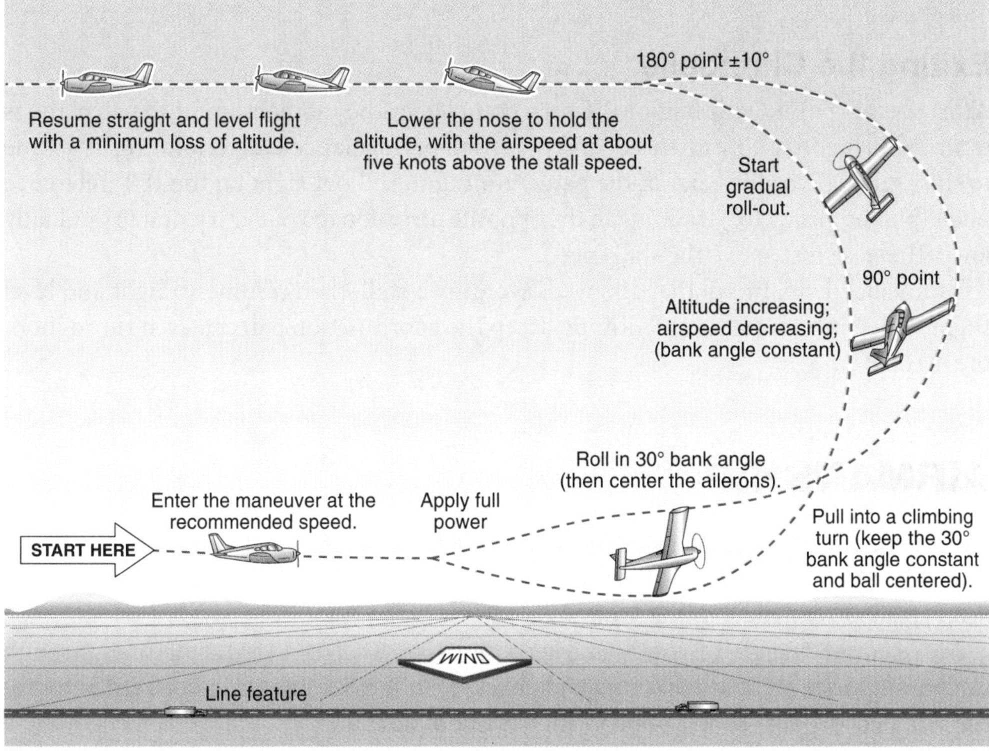

Figure 44-1 The chandelle (to the left).

The high power and falling airspeed will probably require some right rudder pressure to keep the balance ball centered. The first half of the chandelle, from 0° to 90°, is flown with a constant bank angle and steadily increasing pitch attitude. Most of the airplane's power and momentum is converted to altitude, the consequence being that the airspeed drops at about 1 to 2 knots per second.

TECHNIQUE

Practice this maneuver at least 1,500 feet above ground level and use speeds less than maneuvering speed V_A to avoid any risk of overstressing the airframe, even with full control deflection. V_A is found in the pilot's operating handbook, in the section on limitations, and is a lower airspeed at lower weights.

Entering a Chandelle

Roll into a turn then pull up into a chandelle.

The chandelle is entered at a recommended speed, which should not exceed V_A. If the recommended airspeed cannot be attained in straight and level flight with cruise power (as may be the case with some low-powered training aircraft), you may enter a straight shallow dive to accelerate.

Roll to about a 30° bank angle—certainly no more and maybe a little less, otherwise the airplane may not climb too well—and hold it steady by centering the ailerons. This should only take a few seconds. The airplane will start to turn away from its original heading.

Simultaneously raise the pitch attitude with back pressure on the control column, and smoothly apply the recommended power (usually full power for airplanes with fixed-pitch propellers, and climb power for constant-speed propellers). Hold the bank angle constant at about 30°.

Exiting the Chandelle

To exit the maneuver, smoothly roll out of the chandelle and level off in low-speed level flight.

After the 90° point, with half of the turn completed, the momentum of the airplane is diminishing with falling airspeed, and the climb performance is deteriorating. It is time to start gradually rolling out of the bank, aiming to roll out right on the 180° reference point (plus or minus 10°) traveling in the opposite direction to your entry, and to gradually lower the nose just above the stall speed.

Momentarily maintain that airspeed, avoiding a stall, then resume straight and level flight with a minimum loss of altitude. Keep the coordination ball centered throughout the maneuver.

AIRMANSHIP

Fly balanced.

Start the maneuver flying crosswind and make the 180° chandelle turn into the wind, minimizing the horizontal distance between the entry path and the exit path, which will keep you approximately in the same area.

Make power changes smoothly, and keep the balance ball centered at all times through the power, airspeed, and bank angle changes. Divide your attention between smooth, coordinated airplane control, and keeping a good lookout.

REVIEW 44
Chandelles

1. What is the aim of the chandelle in terms of altitude? What is the heading change in a chandelle?
2. How does the airspeed of the airplane at the bottom of a chandelle compared to that at the top?
3. The altitude during a chandelle must be how many feet AGL or higher?
4. If the ground in the vicinity of where you are practicing chandelles is 1,800 feet MSL, your minimum altitude should be how many feet MSL? How many feet AGL is this?
5. What is the maximum speed of entry for a chandelle?
6. Is a good lookout essential during a chandelle?
7. What is the maximum bank angle that should the be used in a chandelle? If this angle is exceeded what will happen?
8. Do you add power in a correctly flown chandelle?
9. How should the balance ball behave during the chandelle?
10. In a well-flown chandelle, how many degrees from the entry heading should you roll the wings level? How many knots above the stalling speed should you exit the chandelle? What change in airspeed needs to be made on exiting the chandelle and resuming straight and level flight?
11. In what direction in relation to wind should you start the chandelle? To minimize ground coverage, in what direction is the turn made in relation to the wind?

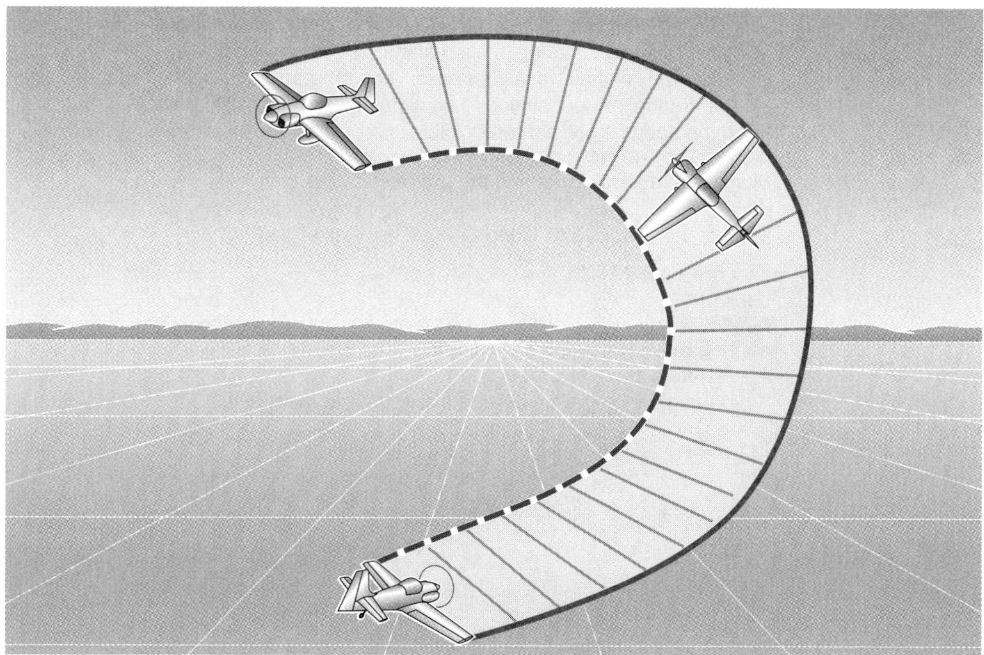

Figure 44-2 The chandelle.

Answers are given on page 586.

TASK

Chandelle

Aim: To fly a chandelle, which is a maximum-performance climbing turn with a heading change of 180°, gaining as much altitude as possible and rolling out just above stall speed.

1. ***Entry***
   Complete the HASELL check.
   Clear the area and look out.
   Start the maneuver tracking crosswind and perform the chandelle climbing turn into the wind to minimize drift and stay in the same area.
   Establish the recommended entry speed (which should not exceed the maneuvering speed V_A) by adding power in straight and level flight, or by lowering the nose into a straight shallow dive to accelerate.
   At the entry speed, roll to approximately 30° bank (certainly no more, and maybe a little less). The airplane will start to turn.
   Establish the 30° bank angle, and then simultaneously raise the pitch attitude gradually with elevator and smoothly apply recommended power, keeping the ball centered with rudder.
2. ***The first 90° turn***
   Keep the bank angle constant at 30°.
   Continue raising the nose attitude with elevator (airspeed will be reduced at about 1 to 2 KIAS per second).
   Keep the ball centered with rudder.
   Monitor reference points and the progress of turn.
   Look out.
   Keep the bank angle constant at 30° to the 90° point.
3. ***The Chandelle from 90° to 180° (the second 90° of the turn)***
   Maintain power and maintain pitch attitude.
   Airspeed will continue to fall (as power and momentum is converted to altitude).
   Start a gradual roll-out aiming to be wings-level at the 180° point.
   Keep the balance ball centered with rudder pressure (probably right rudder with high power and low airspeed).
   Monitor reference points and the progress of the turn.
   Look out.
   Monitor the airspeed as it approaches the stall speed.
4. ***The roll-out at 180°***
   Look out.
   Aim to roll out with wings level 180° from the entry direction (±10°) at an airspeed about 5 KIAS above the stall speed.
   Accelerate without loss of altitude.
   Keep the balance ball centered throughout the maneuver.

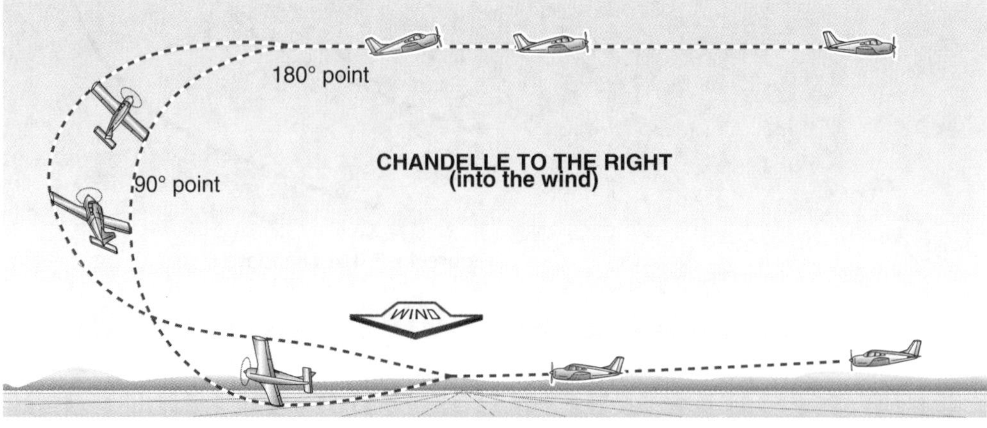

45 Lazy Eights

OBJECTIVE

To describe the technique for aircraft control and balance through a lazy eight. Lazy eights are a good coordination exercise and they are also fun.

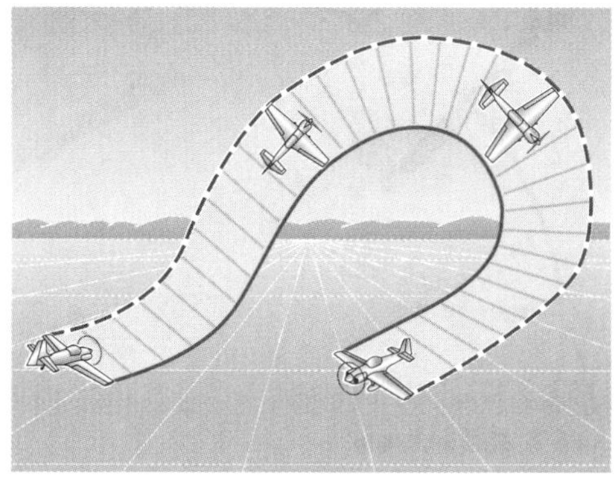

Figure 45-1 Wingover.

CONSIDERATIONS

The lazy eight is a series of S-patterns (wingovers) across a line feature, but not at constant altitude: the high speed at entry is traded for a higher altitude at the top of a climbing turn, which should occur halfway through each turn of the S-pattern. The airspeed will be lowest at this point, but must be above the stall.

The higher altitude is then traded for speed in a descending turn, planned to finish at the 180° point at the original entry speed and altitude, with the wings level as you roll into a climbing turn in the opposite direction.

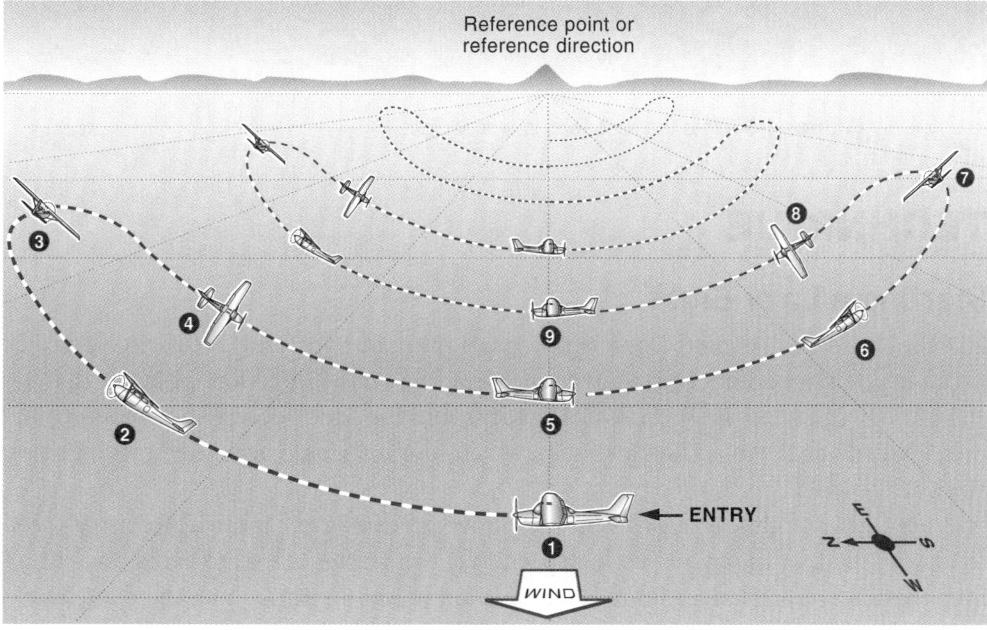

Figure 45-2 The lazy eight.

Speed is traded for altitude (and vice versa) in a lazy eight.

The Name

The nose traces a lazy eight (horizontal 8) over half the horizon.

The lazy eight is so-named because the nose of the airplane slowly makes a figure-eight shape along half of the horizon. Compare figure 45-3 below with figure 45-2 which shows the flight path of the airplane in a lazy eight.

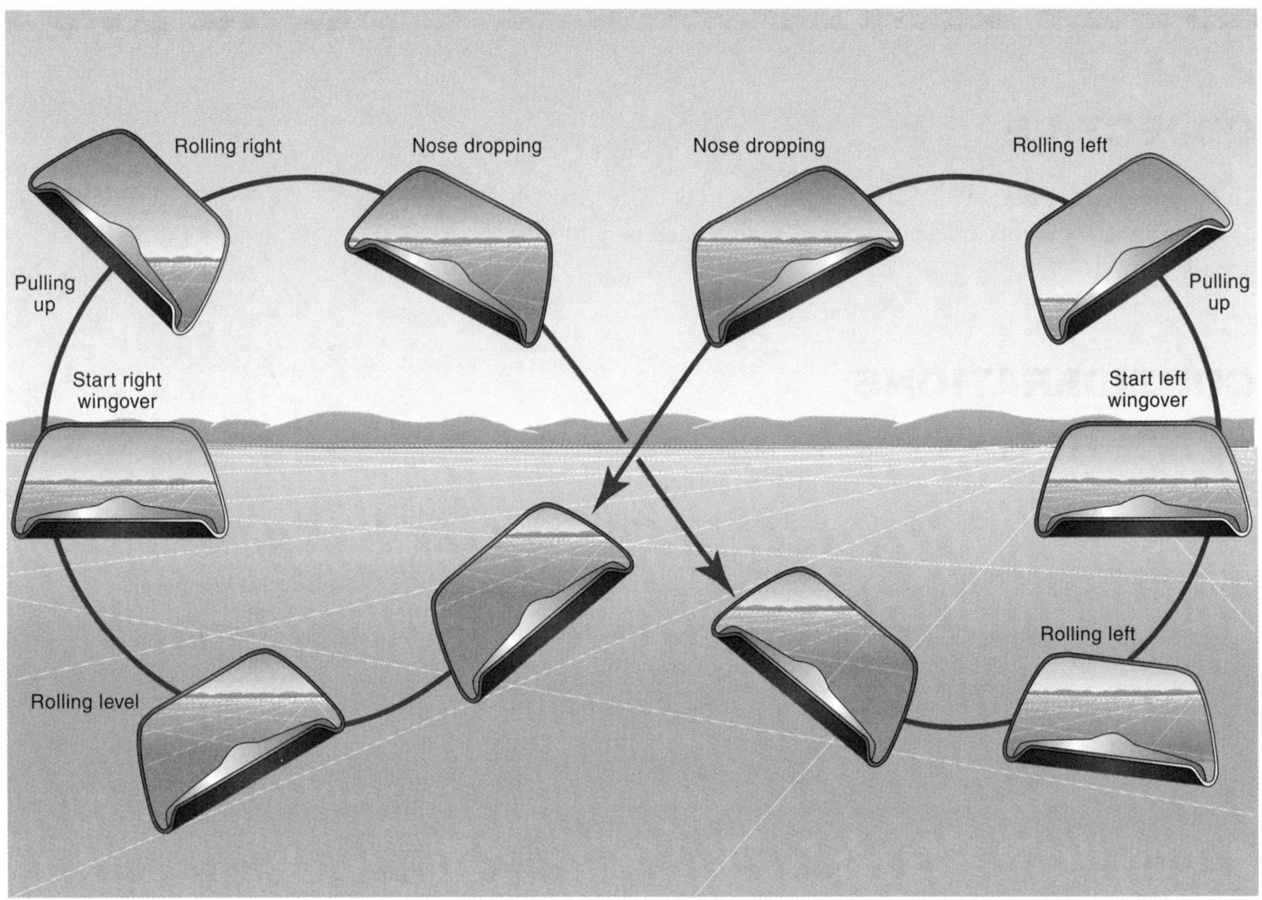

Figure 45-3 What the pilot sees in a lazy eight.

TECHNIQUE

Starting a Lazy Eight

Enter the lazy eight crosswind and turn into the wind.

Like the chandelle, it is good airmanship to start the maneuver flying crosswind, and pick a distant reference point or take a reference heading on the direction indicator that lies on your upwind wing tip. By making the turns into the wind you will cover less ground than if you made the turns downwind, in which case you would be carried much further away by the wind.

Practice lazy eights at least 1,500 feet above ground level, and use an entry speed of cruise speed, or the maneuvering speed (V_A), whichever is less, to avoid any risk of overstressing the airplane. Aim to leave constant power on throughout the maneuver.

You should carry out the pre-aerobatic HASELL check prior to practicing lazy eights.

First Climbing Turn

Trim the airplane for straight and level flight at the recommended entry airspeed, and fly crosswind at your entry altitude. Select a distant reference point on your upwind wing tip, or note the heading on your heading indicator (or both).

Raise the nose into the climbing attitude, and then gently roll in bank, keeping the coordination ball centered with rudder pressure.

Pass the 45° reference point with maximum pitch-up for the maneuver, the bank angle slowly increasing through 15°. The airspeed will be decreasing.

After the 45° reference point, keep the bank angle slowly increasing to a maximum of 30° bank at the top of the turn, but start lowering the nose so that it is on the horizon at the 90° point, looking at the distant reference point.

Make a climbing turn through a 90° heading change.

The airspeed will be at its lowest value, but still some knots above the stall. Take note of your altitude and airspeed. (To keep the coordination ball centered at this point, you may need some bottom rudder and opposite aileron.)

Descending Turn

Continue the coordinated turn with the bank angle momentarily at its maximum value of 30°. Lower the nose into a descending turn, slowly decreasing the bank angle to pass through the 135° reference point with bank angle reducing through 15° and the lowest nose attitude in the whole maneuver—well below the horizon.

Next, commence a descending turn from 90° through 180° of heading change.

Continue the coordinated turn from the 135° reference point to the 180° reference point, raising the nose and decreasing the bank angle so as to be in level flight passing through the 180° reference point, and (ideally) at the original entry airspeed and altitude.

Second Climbing Turn

Raise the nose and roll in the opposite direction to commence the climbing turn for the second wingover to complete the second half of the S-pattern, and keep the maneuver going.

Continue into a climbing turn in the opposite direction.

Accuracy

The nose attitude and bank angle should be constantly changing throughout the lazy-eight maneuver.

You should aim to cross the low points of the lazy eight within 100 feet of the entry altitude, within 10 knots of the chosen entry airspeed, and with a heading tolerance at the 180° and 360° points of plus or minus 10°.

You should also aim to reach the high points of the maneuver within 100 feet of the same high altitude, and within 10 knots of the same low airspeed.

If you find yourself gradually losing altitude in consecutive lazy eights, add some power (and vice versa). Try and keep everything as smooth and symmetrical as possible.

AIRMANSHIP

Practice in an appropriate area, and no lower than 1,500 feet AGL. Divide your attention between coordinated airplane control, orientation, and keeping a good lookout.

Fly smoothly and balanced, maintaining a good lookout.

REVIEW 45

Lazy Eights

1. During the lazy eight, by how many degrees should the direction change?
2. In relation to the wind, in what direction should you enter the lazy eight? In relation to the wind, in what direction should you make the first turn to minimize ground coverage?
3. At which reference point should the highest pitch attitude occur? What should the bank angle be at this point? At this point how should the bank angle be changing?
4. At the 90° reference point in the lazy eight, what should the bank angle be? Where should the nose point in relation to the horizon? At which limit will the airspeed be for the maneuver? At which limit will the altitude be for the maneuver?
5. At which reference point should the lowest pitch attitude occur in the lazy eight? What should the bank angle be at this point? How should the bank angle be changing at this point?
6. Is the lazy eight a coordinated maneuver? If so, should the ball be kept in the center at all times?
7. The required lazy-eight accuracy is to pass through the 180° reference point within how many feet of the entry altitude? This is within how many knots of the entry airspeed? How many degrees within the specified bank angle is this? The heading tolerance is 180° plus or minus how many degrees?
8. Is the objective in a lazy eight to fly the maneuver with constant power set or with power continually changing?
9. Passing through the 180° reference point, what should be the pitch attitude? What should be the bank angle? What is the change in attitude that is made at this point?
10. Where during the second turn should the highest pitch attitude occur?
11. At the top of the second turn of the lazy eight, within how many feet of the previous highest altitude should you aim to be? At this point, within how many knots of the previous lowest airspeed should you aim to be?
12. If you find yourself becoming higher and faster at the low points of consecutive lazy eights, what could you do?

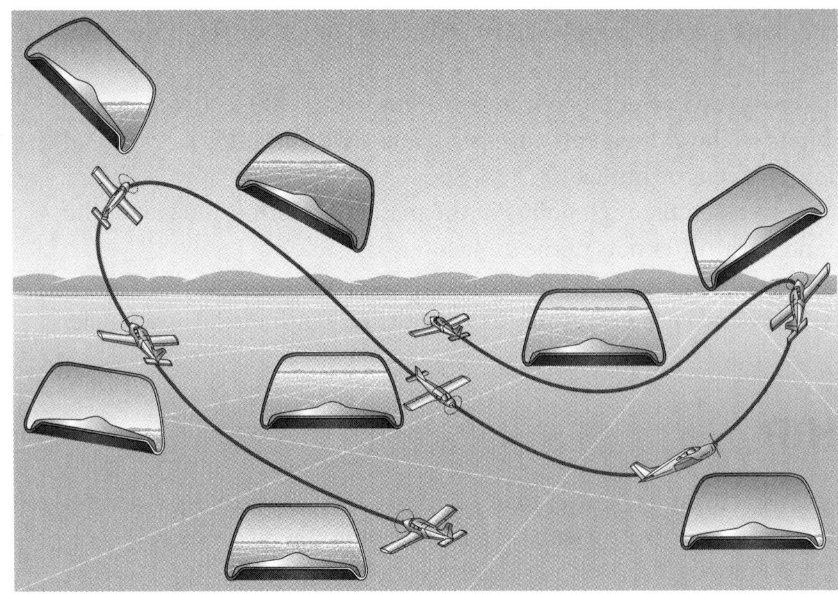

Figure 45-4 Lazy eight.

Answers are given on page 586.

TASK

Lazy Eight

Aim: To fly a series of lazy eights, each consisting of two gentle wingovers in opposite directions.

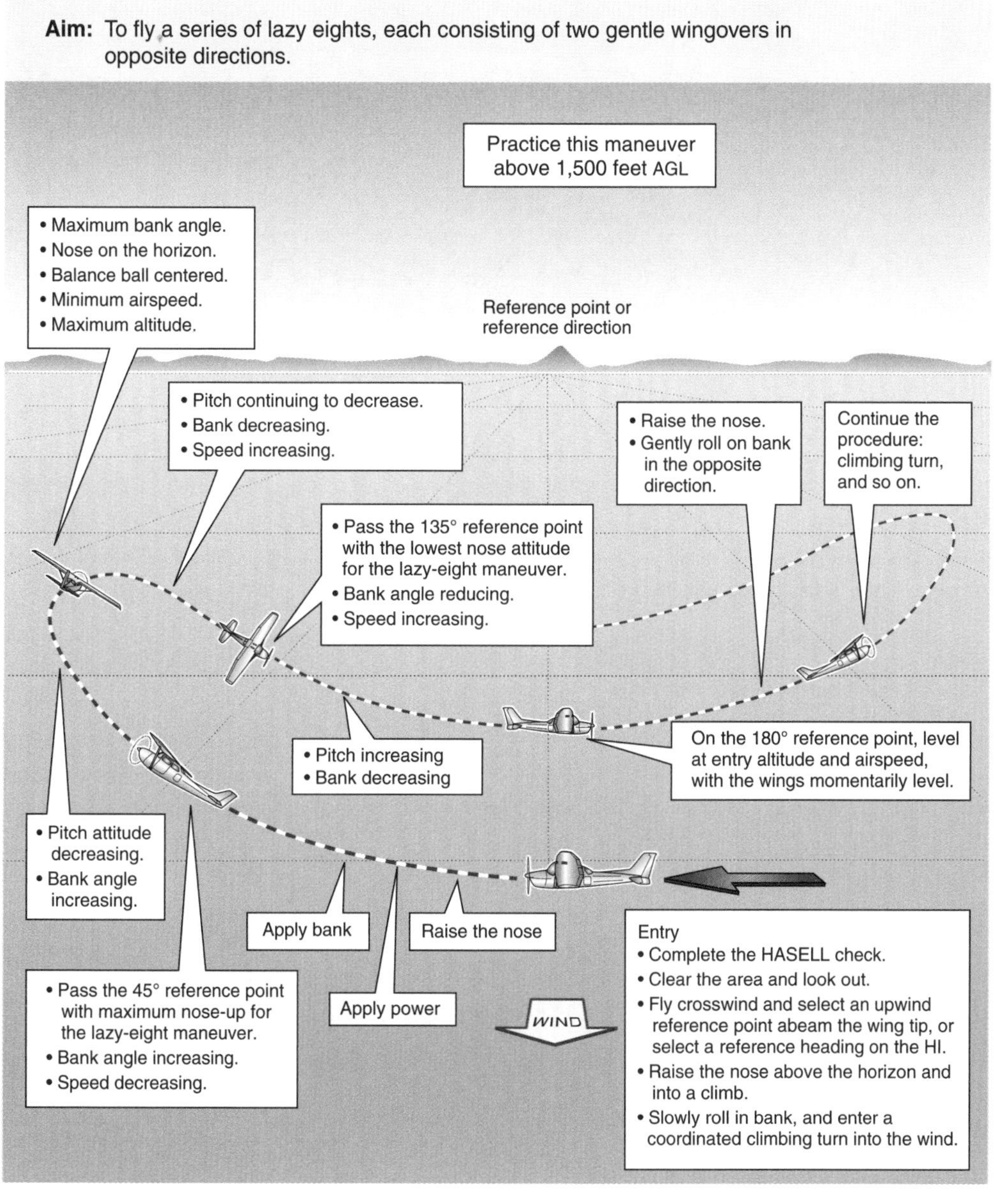

Practice this maneuver above 1,500 feet AGL
• Maximum bank angle.
• Nose on the horizon.
• Balance ball centered.
• Minimum airspeed.
• Maximum altitude.
Reference point or reference direction
• Pitch continuing to decrease.
• Bank decreasing.
• Speed increasing.
• Raise the nose.
• Gently roll on bank in the opposite direction.
Continue the procedure: climbing turn, and so on.
• Pass the 135° reference point with the lowest nose attitude for the lazy-eight maneuver.
• Bank angle reducing.
• Speed increasing.
On the 180° reference point, level at entry altitude and airspeed, with the wings momentarily level.
• Pitch increasing
• Bank decreasing
• Pitch attitude decreasing.
• Bank angle increasing.
Apply bank
Raise the nose
Apply power
• Pass the 45° reference point with maximum nose-up for the lazy-eight maneuver.
• Bank angle increasing.
• Speed decreasing.
WIND
Entry
• Complete the HASELL check.
• Clear the area and look out.
• Fly crosswind and select an upwind reference point abeam the wing tip, or select a reference heading on the HI.
• Raise the nose above the horizon and into a climb.
• Slowly roll in bank, and enter a coordinated climbing turn into the wind.

Required Accuracy:

- Constantly change pitch and roll.
- Entry altitude ±100 feet and entry airspeed ±10 KIAS, at 180° and 360° reference points ±10°.
- High altitude ±100 feet, and low airspeed ±10 KIAS at top of wing-overs (at 90° reference point), and so on.

Ground Reference Maneuvers

46

Low Flying and Wind Awareness

OBJECTIVES

To describe:

- the actual and apparent effect of wind on an aircraft at low level; and
- the technique for safely flying various ground reference maneuvers that compensate for the effects of wind.

CONSIDERATION

Wind Effects in Straight Flight

Zero Wind

An airplane flying in stabilized straight and level flight will fly through an airmass in the direction it is headed.

If the airmass is stationary—no wind—the track over the ground will be the same as the path of the airplane through the air, and the ground speed—the speed at which the airplane passes over the ground—will be the same as the airspeed.

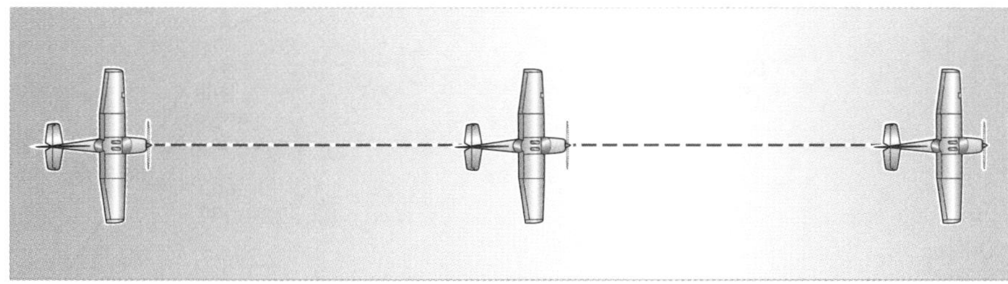

Figure 46-1
Flying in zero-wind conditions.

Flying into a Head Wind

The wind carries the airplane within it.

In a head wind, the airmass will carry the airplane back with it, causing the ground speed to be less even though the airspeed remains unchanged. The effect on ground speed is most apparent visually when you are flying fairly low, which for purposes of practicing will be in the range of 500 feet to 1,000 feet AGL.

Reduced ground speed

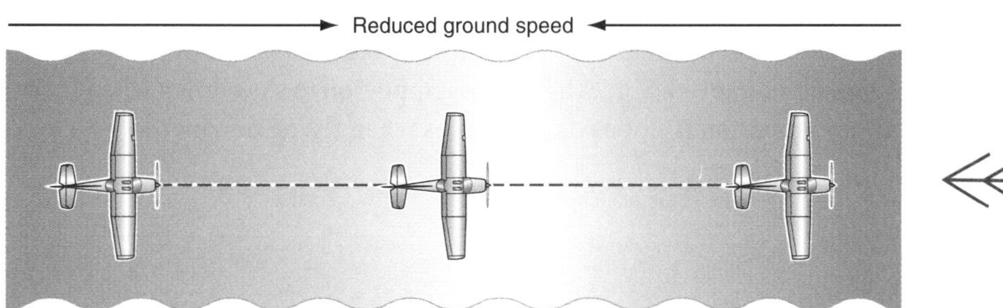

Figure 46-2
Flying in a head wind.

Flying with a Tail Wind

In a tail wind, the airmass will carry the airplane forward with it, causing the ground speed to be greater even though the airspeed remains unchanged.

A tail wind causes a false impression of high speed—check the ASI regularly.

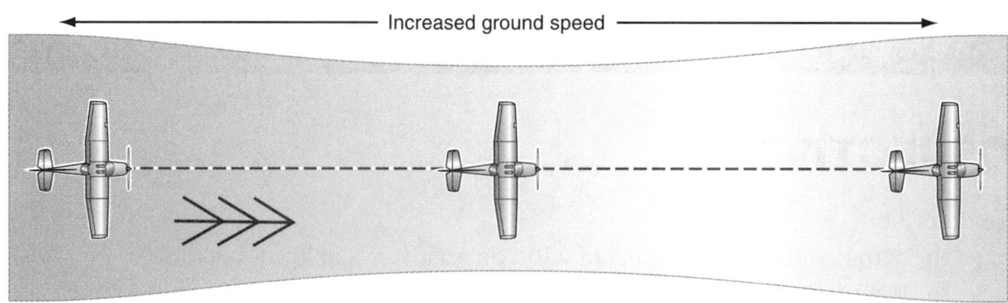

Figure 46-3 Flight with a tail wind.

There is a danger of a visual illusion in the tail wind situation. An airplane flying with an airspeed of 80 knots in a 35-knot tail wind, for instance, will have a ground speed of 115 knots. The proximity of the ground will give an illusion of speed much greater than 80 knots, but you must resist any temptation to slow down. Reducing the ground speed to what feels like 80 knots would require an airspeed of 45 knots, which may be below the stalling speed. This temptation to slow down may exist if you are flying a rectangular pattern around a small field: the downwind leg at the high ground speed will not take long, and you may feel a little rushed and tempted to slow things down—don't! Increase the speed of your thinking instead.

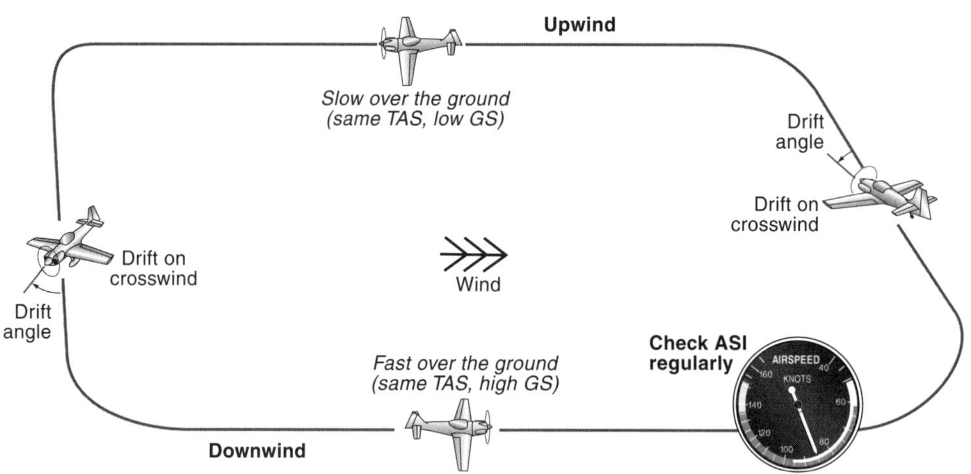

Figure 46-4 Monitor the airspeed carefully when flying downwind close to the ground.

In a head wind, the reverse is the case. The ground speed is lower than the airspeed, giving an impression of slow speed. Since there is no temptation to slow down when flying into a head wind, this situation is not as dangerous as when flying downwind.

Flying in a Crosswind

If you fly a straight path through an airmass that is moving sideways, your path over the ground will be in a different direction to the airplane's heading. This is known as drift, or wind drift, and is illustrated in figure 46-6. If you want to track between two ground reference points, and initially steer the desired course as heading, you will be carried downwind. You could continually turn to head directly at your target, but this will result in a curved path to the target point—an inefficient procedure called *homing* to a point, and best avoided.

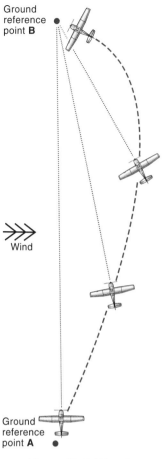

No crosswind

Crosswind

Heading

Drift

Track

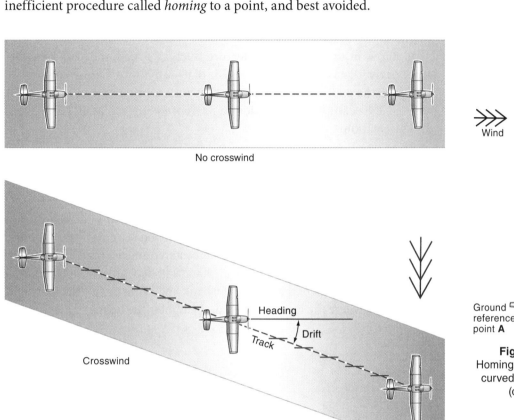

Figure 46-6 The airplane in a crosswind is carried laterally (sideways) over the ground.

Ground reference point **B**

Wind

Ground reference point **A**

Figure 46-5 (Above) Homing results in an inefficient curved track over the ground (curve of pursuit).

It is much more efficient to fly a path through the air that is directed somewhat into the crosswind, and allow the crosswind effect to keep you on the desired ground track. The difference between the ground track and the airplane heading is called the *wind correction angle* (WCA) or *crab angle*. The slower your airspeed, or the stronger the crosswind, the more crab angle that will be required.

Apply a wind correction angle (WCA) into a crosswind.

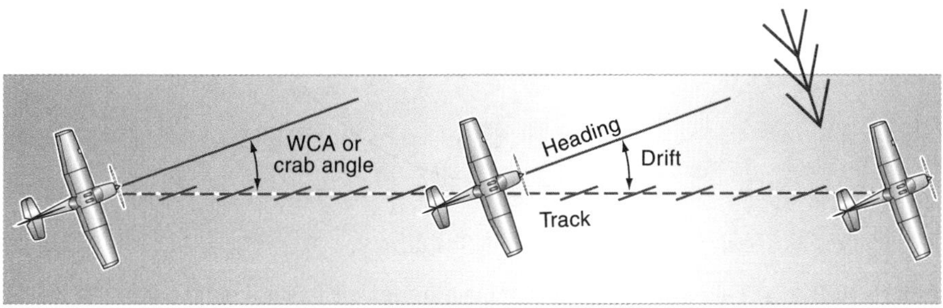

Figure 46-7 Apply a wind correction angle, or crab angle, in a crosswind.

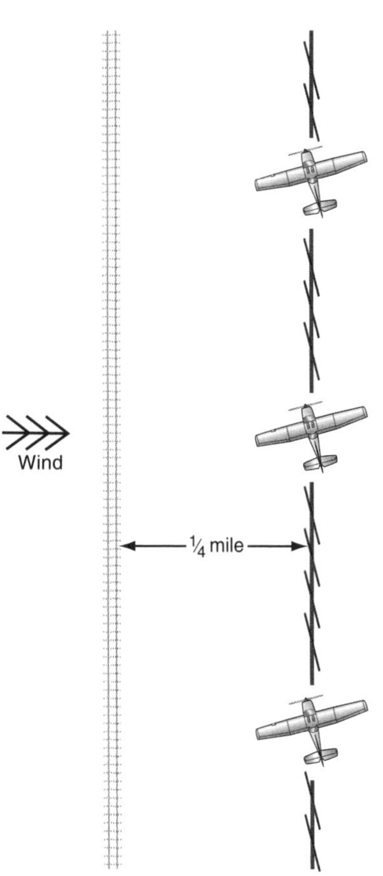

Figure 46-8
Inspecting a line feature.

Sideways drift over the ground from a crosswind causes false impressions of coordinated flight. In strong crosswinds, especially if the airspeed is low, the airplane will experience a large drift angle over the ground. This will give an illusion of slip or skid, even though the balance ball is centered.

The false sensation of slip or skid, especially when turning, can tempt an inexperienced pilot to use rudder to counteract it, which would make the airplane uncoordinated, and degrade its performance. Confirm coordination with the ball. Since airspeed tends to reduce in a turn, it is also good airmanship when flying low to have your hand on the throttle to adjust power to maintain the airspeed if necessary.

If you want to inspect a line feature (such as a road, railroad, pipeline, fence or river), it is best to fly to one side of it—usually to the right of it, since this gives the pilot in the left seat the best view. One quarter mile is usually sufficient. Selecting a distant ground reference point can assist in tracking and orientation.

Wind Effects in Turning Flight

Turning When There Is No Wind

If you fly at a constant bank angle at a steady speed in zero-wind conditions, your path over the ground will be the same as your circular path through the air. The maneuver illustrated below is centered above a road intersection.

The turning performance of the airplane will depend on two factors:

- bank angle, where the greater the bank angle, the tighter the turn; and
- speed, where the lower the speed, the tighter the turn.

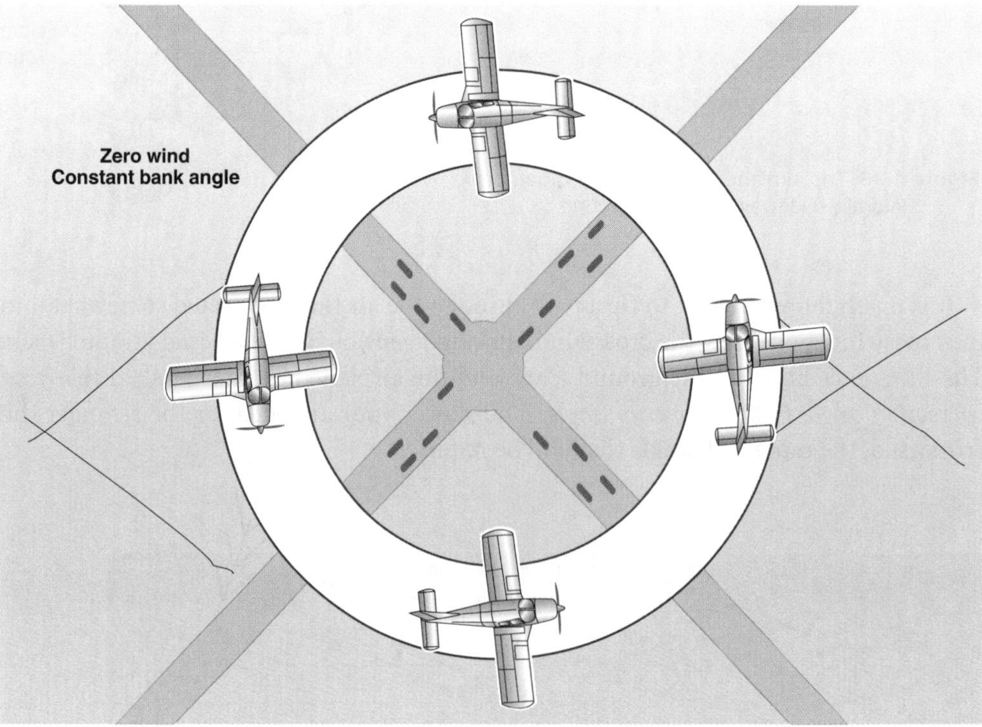

Figure 46-9 In still air, a constant bank angle provides a circular ground path.

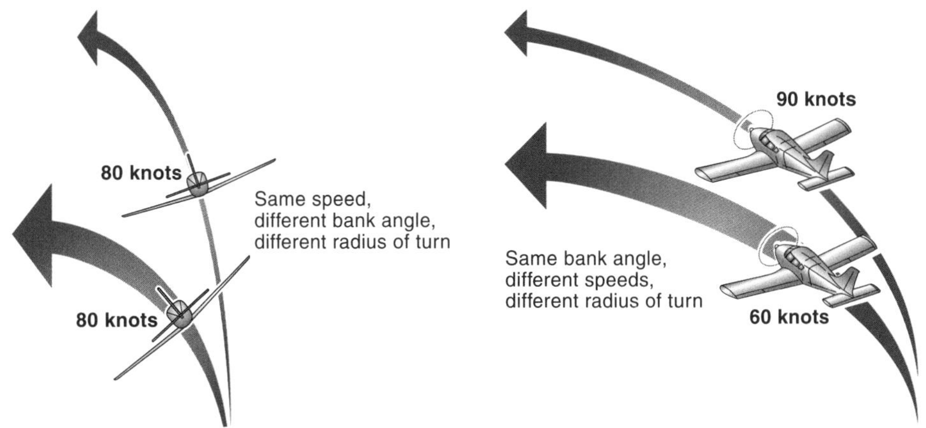

Figure 46-10 (Left) increase the bank angle to tighten the turn, or (right) decrease the speed to tighten the turn.

The ground radius increases with higher ground speeds.

As the ground speed increases, hold the ground radius constant by increasing the bank angle.

So, if you want a turn of smaller radius, you can either increase the bank angle or decrease the speed (but don't forget that stall speed increases in a turn).

APPLICATION

Turning in a Wind

If you hold a constant bank angle and a constant airspeed, the wind will carry the airplane downwind, and the result will be a circular path through the air but a distorted looping pattern over the ground.

The ground radius of the turn will be greatest when the ground speed is greatest, which is when the airplane is headed directly downwind, and least when the ground speed is least, which is when the airplane is headed directly into the wind.

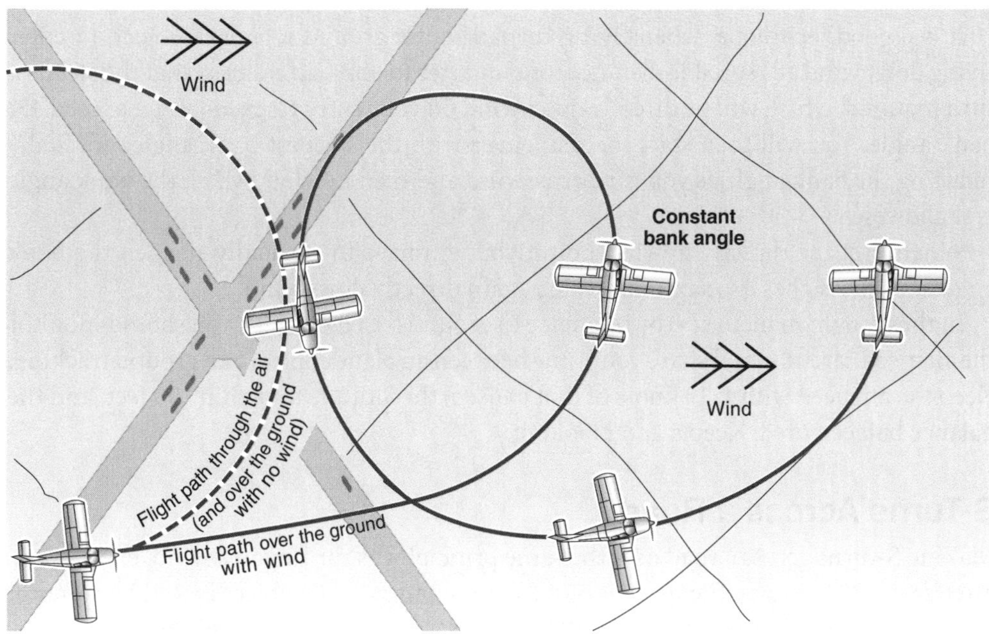

Figure 46-11 Distorted ground track for a constant bank angle turn in a wind.

To achieve a constant ground radius, and fly a circular path around a ground reference point, you will have to vary the bank angle. The lower the speed over the ground, the shallower the bank angle. The higher the speed over the ground, the steeper the bank angle. Therefore you will need to have:

- the steepest bank angle when headed directly downwind; and
- the shallowest bank angle when headed directly upwind.

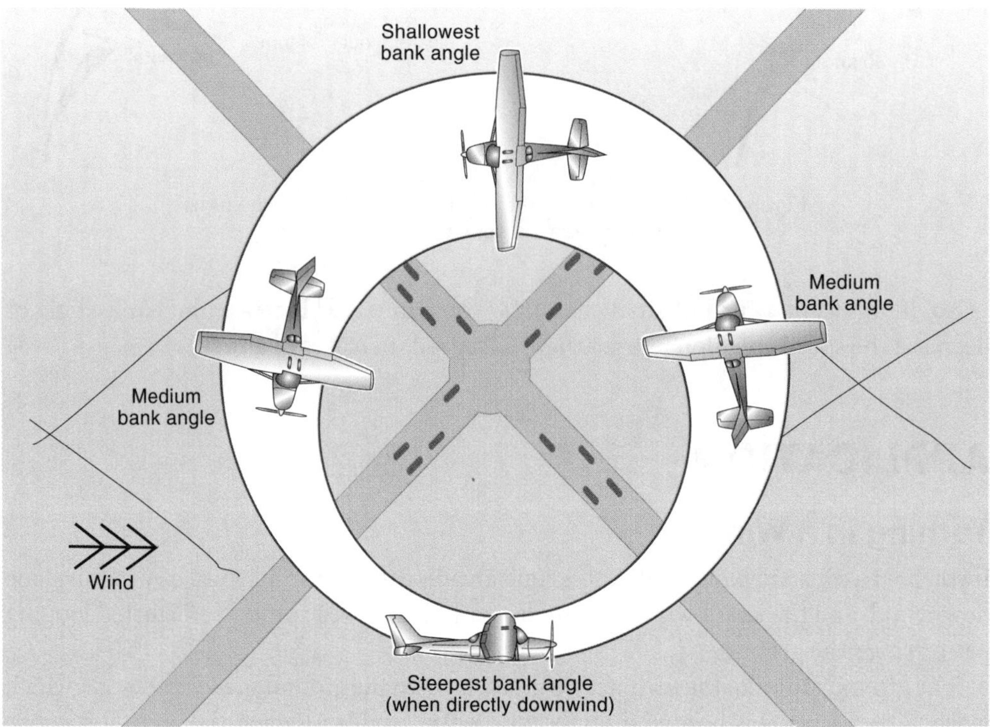

Figure 46-12 Turns around a point—a circular ground path.

Always monitor airspeed.

It is a good technique, when flying turns about a ground reference object, to enter flying downwind at a suitable distance (one-quarter to one-half mile) so that the steepest turn required, which will be directly downwind on your entry track, does not exceed 45° bank angle. You will then start the maneuver with the steepest bank angle, gradually reducing the bank angle as you turn crosswind and then upwind, where the bank angle is shallowest.

When past the directly upwind point, you will have to gradually steepen the bank angle until it reaches its maximum value again directly downwind.

In these flight maneuvers (by reference to ground based objects), you should monitor the airspeed carefully and share your time between airplane control and ground tracking. Keep the airspeed within 10 knots of that chosen, the altitude to within 100 feet, and the balance ball centered. Keep a good lookout.

S-Turns Across a Road

Making S-turns across a road uses the same principles as turning in a wind, except that, after each 180° of turn, the direction of turn is changed. The object is to fly a series of equally sized semicircles either side of a road that lies perpendicular to the wind.

The ground radius of each semicircle is adjusted by changing the bank angle, which will be steepest when flying downwind. You will briefly level the wings passing overhead the road as you reverse the direction of the turn.

The bank angle will be shallowest when heading upwind, with the wings being leveled again as you cross the road and reverse the direction of turn.

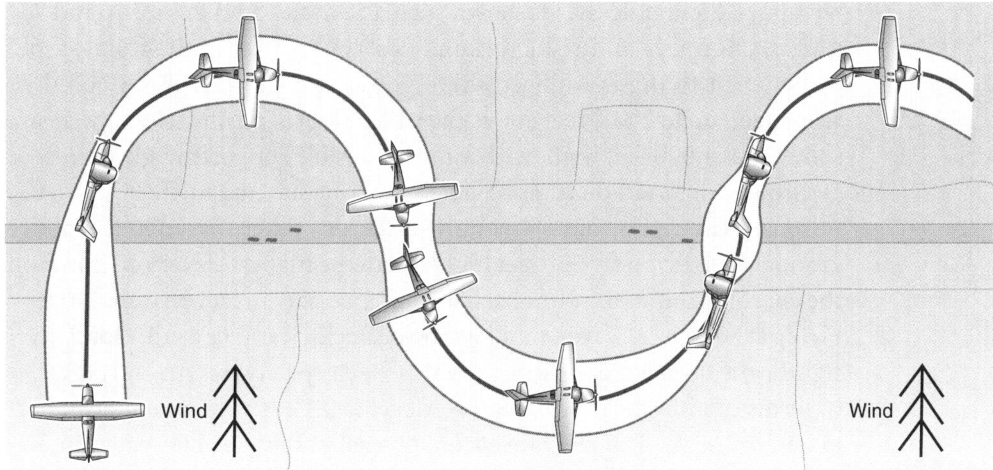

Figure 46-13 S-turns across a road.

Low Flying

A low level is generally considered to be 500 feet above ground level (AGL) or lower. Low-level flying may be necessary:

Low-level flying is 500 feet AGL or below.

- in poor weather conditions such as low cloud and/or poor visibility; or
- to inspect a field in preparation for a forced landing with power available (known as a *precautionary landing*).

Pilot Responsibilities

Do not fly below 500 feet AGL, except when taking off or landing. There are other restrictions regarding flight over built-up areas (1,000 feet above the highest obstacle within a horizontal radius of 2,000 feet from the aircraft), and so on. For the purpose of training, it is usual to select an altitude 600 feet to 1,000 feet AGL in a suitable area.

Low clouds, or some other unforeseen situation, may force you below the minimum legal levels. As a visual pilot, you are not qualified to enter clouds and this should be avoided at all costs. If low clouds are encountered, it is better to fly slowly beneath them closer to the ground and turn back as soon as possible, rather than to enter clouds. This is because, in clouds, all visual contact with the ground and the horizon will be lost, and the consequences for an untrained pilot are usually fatal!

Be aware that radio communication, which depends on line-of-sight transmission, may be poor at low levels. Around the country there are some areas that have been set aside for local low-level training. Other aircraft may be operating there at the same time as you, so maintain a good lookout for them (and for obstructions such as TV towers and transmission lines). Do not forget that balloons, helicopters, sailplanes, hang-gliders and ultralight aircraft may also be operating at low levels.

Obstacle Clearance

A close study of maps of the area is advisable prior to flight—special attention should be given to the elevation of the ground above sea level, the nature of the terrain, and the position of obstacles.

You have a limited field of vision when flying low, and ground features move rapidly through it. You need to anticipate any ground features and recognize them quickly. Obstacles such as overhead cables, radio and TV towers, chimneys and rising ground deserve particular attention—especially when flying in valleys where power transmission lines could be suspended up to 2,000 feet above the valley floor. Transmission towers are sometimes 1,000 feet high, with almost invisible supporting guy-wires.

Ground obstructions can be noted prior to starting to fly at low level. Aeronautical charts may show only obstacles higher than 300 feet above ground level. If you fly 500 feet higher than the highest elevation shown on the chart for the area, your obstacle clearance may in fact be only 200 feet. Flying at 300 feet AGL you may have no obstacle clearance at all, especially if significant altimeter errors are present. Charts specify terrain and obstacles in terms of altitude above mean sea level (MSL). If you are using a chart to determine vertical clearance from obstacles, then the current altimeter setting should be set in the pressure window so that the altimeter reads altitude MSL.

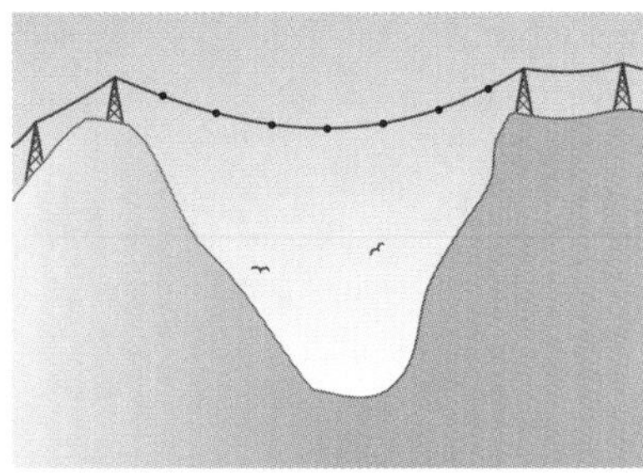

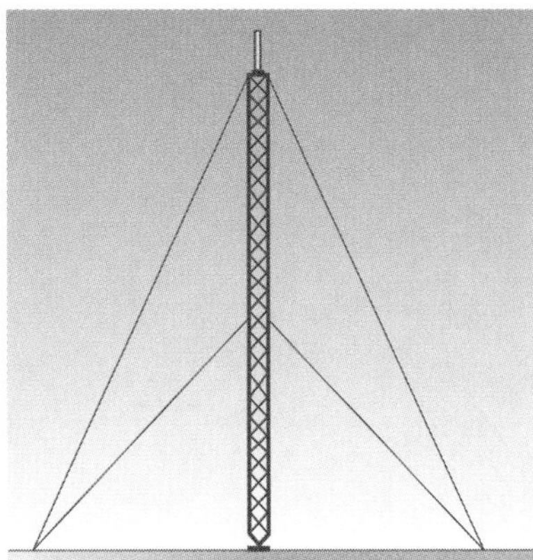

Figure 46-14
Elevated cables and radio towers are a hazard to low-flying aircraft.

If there are air currents running down a slope, then be certain that your airplane has the performance to outclimb them. For instance, if your airplane climbs at 700 feet per minute (fpm), and the downdraft is at 600 fpm, then your climb over the ground is quite shallow, in fact only 100 fpm. If the ground is rising, you may not clear it. Raising the nose will not help: it will lead to a loss of airspeed, and a poorer climb performance if you are already at the best climb speed.

Figure 46-15
Be cautious of small unmanned aircraft systems (UAS, or drones) operating at and below 400 feet AGL.

Some common sense rules for obstacle-clearance are:

- anticipate rising ground and climb early to remain at the desired altitude above it;
- ensure that the airplane can actually out-climb the rising ground, especially if a wind is blowing down its slope;
- avoid areas of rising ground associated with a lowering cloud base;
- always be prepared to turn back.

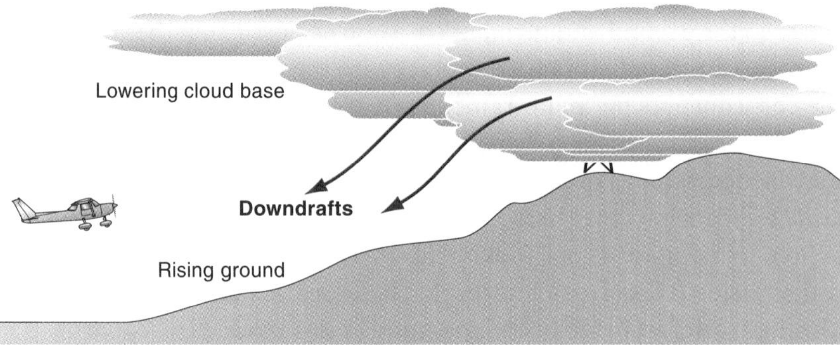

Figure 46-16 Avoid a lowering cloud base, rising ground and downdrafts.

Ground Features

Features with significant vertical dimensions are good landmarks for low-level navigation. Isolated hills and peaks, high monuments, factory chimneys and radio or television towers fall into this category.

Select ground features suitable for low flying.

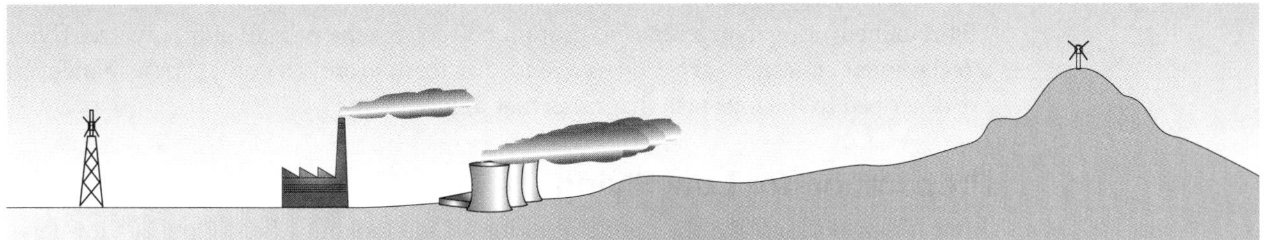

Figure 46-17 Choose landmarks suitable for low-level flying.

Misleading Visual Effects

The dangers when low flying are:

- the illusion of a high speed when flying downwind, so monitor your airspeed indicator so as not to be tricked into reducing power and slowing down; and
- the illusion of slipping or skidding when flying crosswind, so keep the balance ball centered.

Be careful of the visual illusions caused by wind when low flying.

Obstacle Avoidance

Begin any turns early enough to be certain of remaining downwind of them. If you try to turn upwind of them, there is a risk that the wind will carry you back into the obstacles.

Remain downwind of obstacles but be aware of downdrafts and turbulence.

Turbulence and Wind Shear

The air is often more turbulent near the ground than at higher altitudes for various reasons, the main ones being:

- surface friction slowing down strong winds;
- changes in wind speed and direction (wind shear); and
- uneven heating of the earth's surface creating convection currents.

The possibility of turbulence at low level is another reason why it is good airmanship to keep your hand on the throttle most of the time when low flying, to enable an immediate response to airspeed variations if they occur.

Airplane Configuration

In good visibility and over open country, the normal cruise configuration of clean wings may be suitable for low-level flying. In poor visibility, or in confined areas where good maneuverability is required, however, a precautionary configuration of some flaps extended may be preferable.

Using the precautionary configuration allows:

- better vision because of the lower nose attitude with flaps extended;
- a lower cruise speed because of the reduced stalling speed;
- better maneuverability and smaller radius turns because of the lower airspeed; and
- better response to elevator and rudder, because the extra power required causes a greater slipstream effect.

A disadvantage of having flaps extended for long periods, however, is the increased fuel consumption and consequent reduced range capability of your airplane.

TECHNIQUE

Flight maneuvering by reference to ground objects, for the private pilot, involves flying a rectangular course, S-turns across a road, and turns around a point. These maneuvers are described in the four task diagrams that follow.

Preparation for Low Flying

Keep in trim when low flying.

Since it is important that the pilot maintains a good lookout when flying at a low level, a low flying check of items in the cockpit should be completed prior to descending. The FREHA check, outlined previously, may be adequate:

F	**Fuel Selection:**	on and sufficient.
	Fuel Tank:	usage monitored.
	Mixture:	rich or leaned as required; carburetor heat set.
	Fuel Pump:	on (if fitted and if required) and fuel pressure checked.
R	**Radio:**	frequency correctly selected, volume and squelch satisfactory, and make any necessary radio calls.
E	**Engine:**	oil temperature and pressure, power set (propeller RPM), check of other systems (ammeter, suction gauge).
H	**Heading Indicator:**	aligned with magnetic compass (only realign the HI with the magnetic compass in steady straight and level flight).
A	**Altitude:**	checked and correct altimeter setting.

Additional check items prior to low-level flight should include:

- the security of the airplane (doors and harnesses), and take steps to make the airplane more visible (landing lights, rotating beacon and strobe lights on, if appropriate);
- check the surface wind direction (use smoke, dust, wind lines on lakes, and so on);
- adopt the chosen configuration (clean, or with some flaps extended in the precautionary configuration); and
- trim.

A good lookout is essential! Study the ground even before you begin the descent to a low level, to ensure that adequate clearance above obstacles can be maintained. Also look out for other aircraft. Beware of rising ground, especially if a wind is blowing down its slopes!

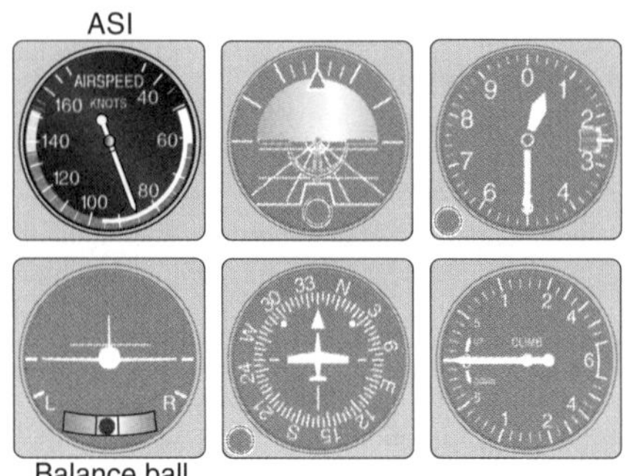

Figure 46-18 Monitor the airspeed and balance ball when flying at low level.

Allow for Momentum

The airplane will take time to respond to any control movements because of its inertia, which is a resistance to change. Begin climbs and turns early to avoid obstacles. Turn downwind of obstacles, rather than upwind of them, to avoid being blown back onto them. Avoid harsh maneuvers (such as steep turns or high-g pull-ups) that may lead to accelerated or high-speed stalls.

Trim

An airplane that is correctly trimmed is easier to fly and more likely to maintain altitude. Since your attention is directed out of the cockpit for most of the time in low-level flying, a well-trimmed airplane is essential. A slight nose-up trim will help ensure that an unintentional descent does not occur.

Low Flying in Bad Weather

Do not enter cloud.

Poor visibility, a descending cloud base or rising ground may require some unplanned low flying. You are obliged to remain in visual meteorological conditions (VMC), but if you are caught out in really marginal conditions, maintain as much separation from the ground as possible, but avoid entering clouds. In reality, you should never find yourself in this situation! Always plan carefully, and exert strong discipline over your flight to avoid this sort of situation. If you are caught out in bad weather, however, use any aircraft systems that can assist you in coping with it, such as carburetor heat (if appropriate), pitot heaters, and so on. Make your airplane more visible by switching on the rotating beacon, strobe, and landing lights.

If the legal requirements of minimum visibility and distance from clouds cannot be satisfied, then consideration should be given to either:

- diverting to an area where better weather exists;
- landing at a nearby airport;
- requesting radar guidance if navigation is a problem; or
- making a precautionary landing in a field.

The Bad-Weather Traffic Pattern

At a tower-controlled airport in bad weather, the controllers may pick the traffic pattern they wish you to fly. ATC may switch on the airport beacon in daylight if conditions are less than VFR (visibility less than three miles and/or cloud ceiling less than 1,000 feet). At nontowered airports in bad weather, while ideally you would fly the standard traffic pattern, this may not be possible. You will have to devise your own safe pattern in terms of track, altitude, airplane configuration and airspeed. A traffic pattern in bad weather—poor visibility and/or a low cloud base—should be organized so that visual contact with the field is not lost. This may require a tight pattern flown at low level in the precautionary configuration. Aim for a traffic pattern altitude of at least 500 feet AGL, if possible, but do not enter clouds! Maintain a clearance of at least 300 feet vertically from obstacles.

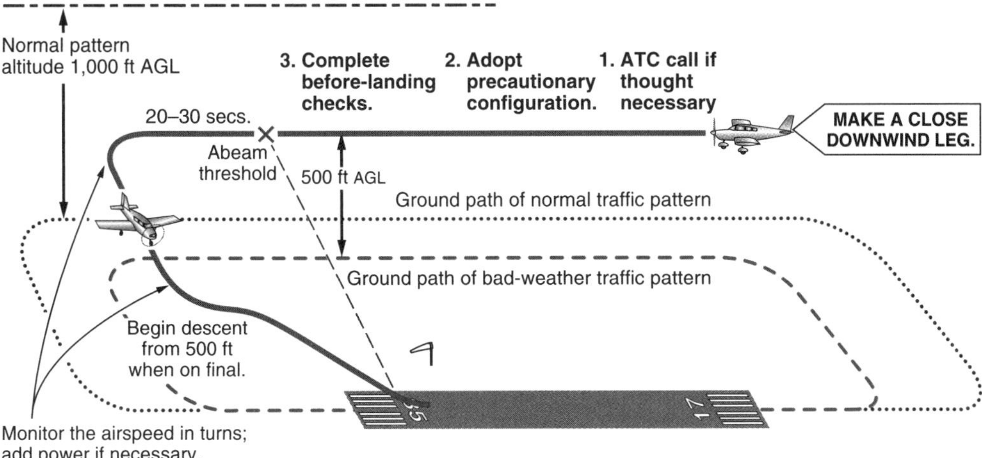

Figure 46-19 The bad-weather traffic pattern at a nontowered airport.

AIRMANSHIP

Keep a good lookout for other aircraft and also for birds. Avoid congested areas and maintain a suitable altitude (at least 500 feet AGL). Also, avoid annoying people or farm animals. Select a suitable area with good ground references. Beware of false impressions caused by the wind effect, best counteracted by reference to the airspeed indicator and the balance ball. Be aware of false horizons. Share your time appropriately between:

- airplane control;
- maintaining and adjusting the path over the ground, keeping coordinated with rudder pressure; and
- maintaining a visual scan so that you can see-and-avoid other aircraft or obstacles.

Apply the necessary wind drift corrections in straight flight by adjusting heading, and in constant ground radius turns by adjusting bank angle (but not to exceed 45°). Entering a maneuver with the wind behind you will mean that the first turn will be the steepest. Turbulence may be greater at low levels, so ensure that you are strapped in securely. Hold the chosen speed to within 10 knots and altitude to within 100 feet. Avoid bank angles in excess of 45°.

REVIEW 46

Low Flying and Wind Awareness

1. What is the speed of an airplane through the air called?
2. What is the speed of an airplane over the ground called?
3. In a head wind, how will the ground speed compare to the airspeed?
4. How could your impression of the airspeed be affected by a tail wind? Which instrument must you check? What change in airspeed should you avoid?
5. To maintain a desired track over the ground, what do you apply? What is this also known as?
6. Are the flying characteristics of an airplane, such as the stall, determined by its airspeed or its ground speed?
7. What illusion could sideways drift over the ground cause when a wind correction angle is applied in a crosswind? How is this illusion counteracted?
8. For a given airspeed, how does the turn radius alter at a steeper bank angle?
9. How does the turn radius alter at a higher speed for a given bank angle?
10. To maintain a constant ground radius about a reference ground object, do you vary the bank angle?
11. When flying a turn with a constant ground radius in a wind, when is the ground speed the greatest? What is the relative bank angle at this point?
12. When flying a turn with a constant ground radius in a wind, when is the ground speed the least? What is the relative bank angle at this point?
13. A low level is considered to be how many feet AGL or below?
14. Most low-level maneuvers are carried out at how many feet AGL?
15. Will aeronautical charts always show transmission towers and other obstacles less than 300 feet high?
16. What is the required accuracy in ground reference maneuvers for private pilots (including nominated altitude, nominated airspeed, bank angle and balance ball position)?
17. In poor weather conditions, you notice that an airport beacon is operating even though it is daylight. What does this indicate?

Answers are given on page 586.

TASK

Low Flying and Wind Awareness

Aims: a. To fly the airplane safely at a low level.
b. To observe the misleading visual effects caused by a strong wind at low levels.

1. ***Prior to Descending to Low Level***

   Complete FREHA check (refer to full version earlier in the text):

   F – Fuel system checks.
   R – Radio correctly set.
   E – Engine and systems for normal operation.
   H – Heading indicator aligned correctly and position on the chart checked.
   A – Altitude and altimeter pressure settings checked.

   Additional considerations:

   – Security of the airplane (doors and harnesses, etc.) and its visibility (landing lights, beacons, strobes on).
   – Note surface wind direction.
   – Airplane configuration (clean or early stage of flap).
   – Trim.
   – Decide on suitable IAS for the operation.

   Awareness of low flying regulations.

   > *Look out for obstacles and other aircraft, including balloons, ultralight airplane, gliders and sailplanes, parachutists, airships, towers, masts, hang-gliders, large birds and flocks of birds.*

2. ***Descent to Low Level***

   Begin the descent, hand on throttle, and keep a good lookout.

   Fly no lower than 500 ft AGL (or as advised by your flight instructor).

   Estimate terrain clearance visually, with back-up from the altimeter and know the elevation of the terrain.

3. ***Establish Cruise Flight at the Desired Level***

   Establish the airplane at your chosen airspeed and altitude.

   Trim.

   Consider increasing power in any medium turns to maintain airspeed.

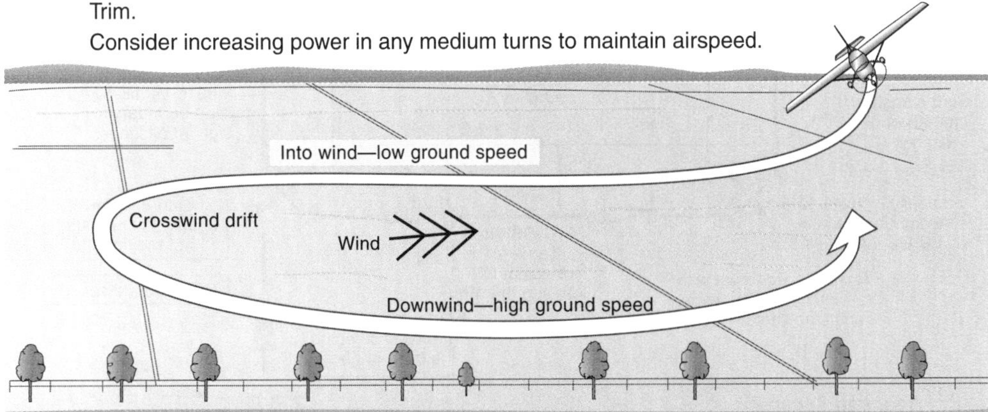

4. ***Observe the Various Effects of Wind—Look Out***

   These are more noticeable as you near the ground:

   For the same IAS, there is a low ground speed upwind—check the ASI

   At same IAS, there is a high ground speed downwind, so do not reduce power without checking ASI first.

   Noticeable drift on crosswind legs—check ball centered.

   Significant downwind drift in turns (check ball) and do not fly close to obstacles.

TASK

Rectangular Pattern

Aim: To fly a rectangular pattern at constant altitude and constant airspeed around the edges of a field, allowing for wind effects.

Practice at 600 to 1,000 feet AGL. Select a suitable field or road pattern with sides about one mile long and fly about one-half to one-quarter mile from the boundary for good vision and to keep the bank angle in turns to less than 45°.

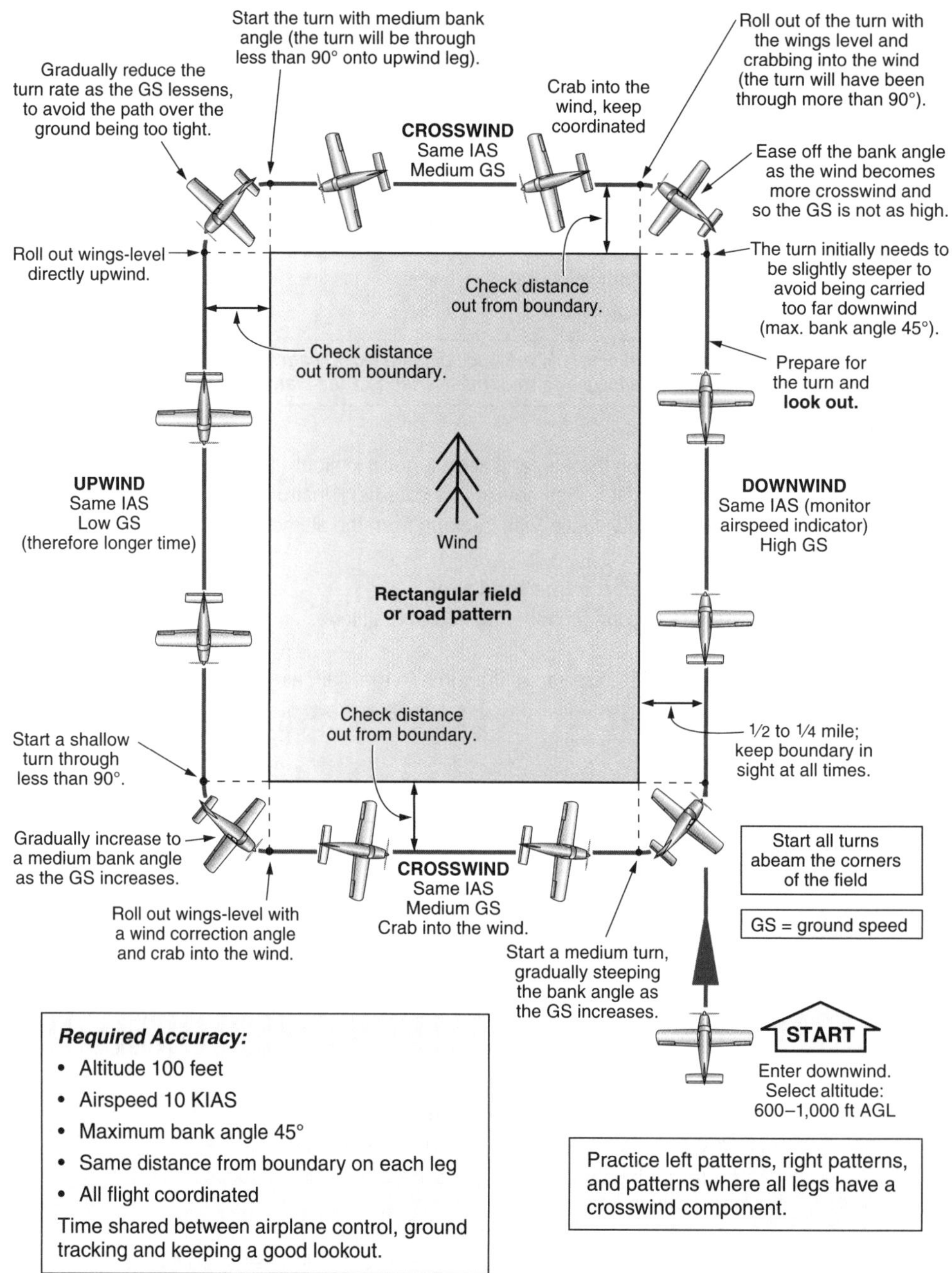

Start the turn with medium bank angle (the turn will be through less than 90° onto upwind leg).
Gradually reduce the turn rate as the GS lessens, to avoid the path over the ground being too tight.
CROSSWIND
Same IAS
Medium GS
Crab into the wind, keep coordinated
Roll out of the turn with the wings level and crabbing into the wind (the turn will have been through more than 90°).
Ease off the bank angle as the wind becomes more crosswind and so the GS is not as high.
Roll out wings-level directly upwind.
Check distance out from boundary.
The turn initially needs to be slightly steeper to avoid being carried too far downwind (max. bank angle 45°).
Check distance out from boundary.
Prepare for the turn and look out.
UPWIND
Same IAS
Low GS
(therefore longer time)
Wind
DOWNWIND
Same IAS (monitor airspeed indicator)
High GS
Rectangular field or road pattern
Check distance out from boundary.
1/2 to 1/4 mile; keep boundary in sight at all times.
Start a shallow turn through less than 90°.
Gradually increase to a medium bank angle as the GS increases.
CROSSWIND
Same IAS
Medium GS
Crab into the wind.
Start all turns abeam the corners of the field
GS = ground speed
Roll out wings-level with a wind correction angle and crab into the wind.
Start a medium turn, gradually steeping the bank angle as the GS increases.
START
Enter downwind.
Select altitude:
600–1,000 ft AGL

Required Accuracy:

- Altitude 100 feet
- Airspeed 10 KIAS
- Maximum bank angle 45°
- Same distance from boundary on each leg
- All flight coordinated

Time shared between airplane control, ground tracking and keeping a good lookout.

Practice left patterns, right patterns, and patterns where all legs have a crosswind component.

TASK

Turns Around a Point

Aim: To fly a constant-ground-radius turn about a ground reference point, and to maintain a constant altitude and constant airspeed.

Practice this maneuver no lower than 500 feet AGL (typically 600 to 1,000 feet AGL). Practice in both directions, for at least two turns.

Select a suitable ground reference point (house, crossroads, and so on).

Clear the area and keep a good lookout.

Select a roll-out point, or choose a roll-out heading.

Choose an altitude and airspeed.

Enter downwind and commence turn (maximum bank angle 45).

Gradually reduce bank angle as you turn from downwind to upwind.

Monitor ground track, and alter bank angle to maintain it.

Gradually increase bank angle as you turn from upwind to downwind.

Fly at least two turns and a roll out on desired heading.

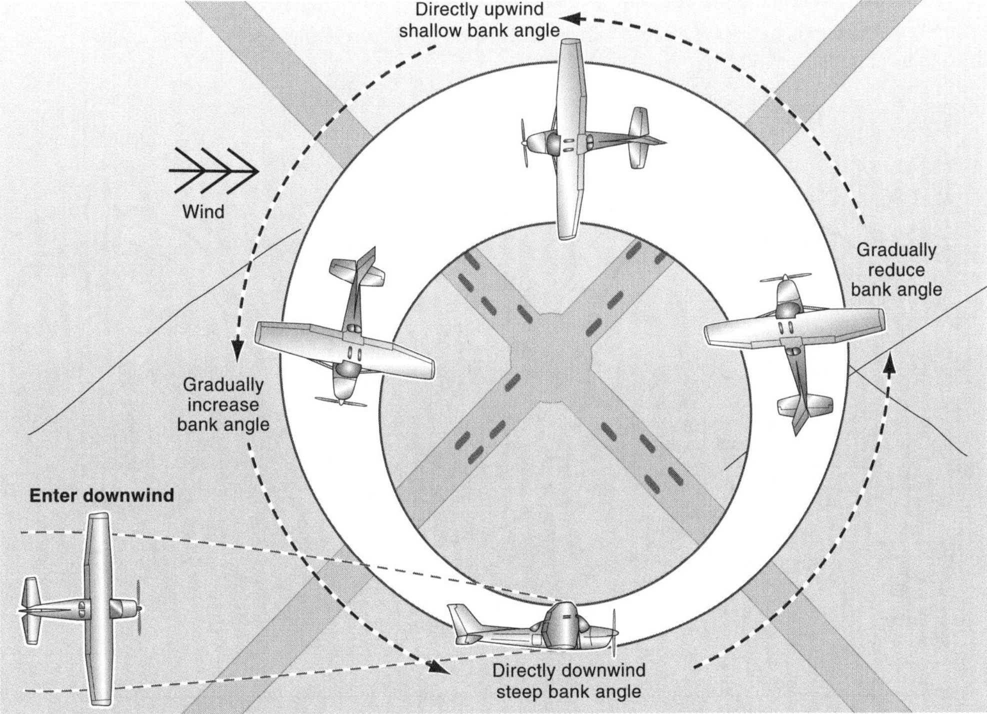

Required Accuracy:

- Altitude 100 feet
- Airspeed 10 KIAS
- Balance ball centered

Divide attention between airplane control, ground tracking and keeping a good lookout. Also practice entering at points other than direct downwind.

TASK

S-Turns Across a Road

Aims: To fly a series of S-turns across a line feature, with semicircles of equal ground-size, and to maintain a constant altitude and a constant airspeed.

Practice this maneuver no lower than 500 feet AGL (typically 600 to 1,000 feet AGL).

Select a suitable road, highway, railroad or other line feature that lies crosswind.

Clear the area and keep a good lookout.

Select a roll-out point, or choose a roll-out heading.

Choose an altitude and airspeed.

Approach the line feature from the upwind side, so that the initial turn will be the steepest bank angle (do not exceed 45).

Crossing the reference feature, apply the steeper bank angle, gradually decreasing it as you turn upwind.

Level the wings crossing the feature upwind, and apply a shallow bank angle in the opposite direction.

Gradually increase bank angle as you turn downwind.

Level the wings as you cross the feature downwind, and then apply a steep bank angle in the opposite direction.

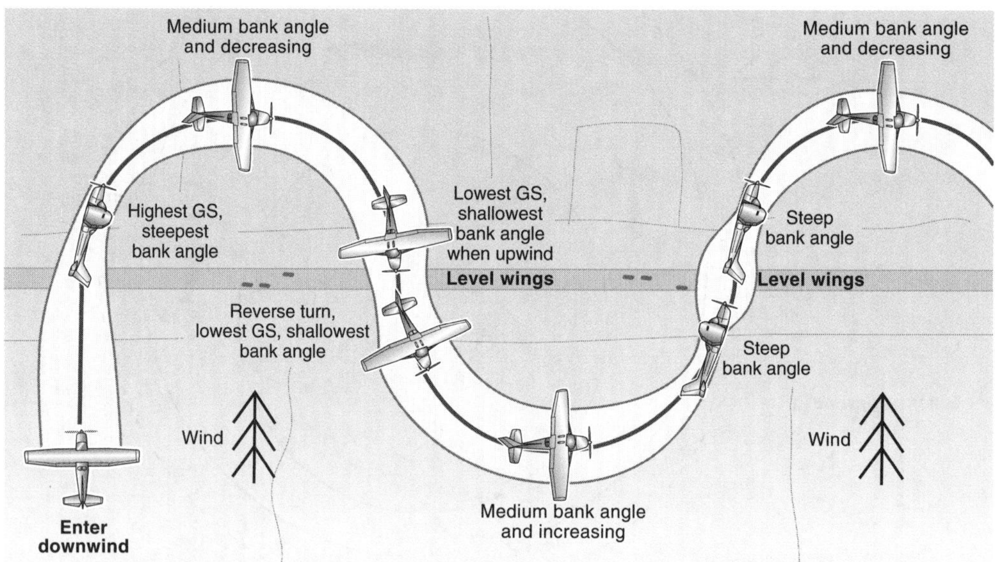

Required Accuracy:

- Altitude 100 feet
- Airspeed 10 KIAS
- Balance ball centered

Do not exceed 45 bank angle.

Time-share between airplane control, ground tracking and keeping a good lookout. Also practice entering at points other than direct downwind.

47

Eights-On-Pylons

OBJECTIVES

To describe:

- the method to calculate pivotal altitude; and
- the technique to control the aircraft's attitude, altitude and speed to center the turns on the pylons.

CONSIDERATIONS

Eights-on-pylons is an approximate figure-eight flown around two pylons, with the wing tip pivoting on the pylons. The aim is not to fly a perfect figure-eight pattern over the ground, but to keep the wing tip pinned on the pylon. Eights-on-pylons is a three-dimensional maneuver, with altitude, airspeed and bank angle varying gradually throughout the maneuver (especially in strong winds). Using two pylons, you will fly alternating left and right 360° turns, making an approximate figure-eight pattern about the pylons.

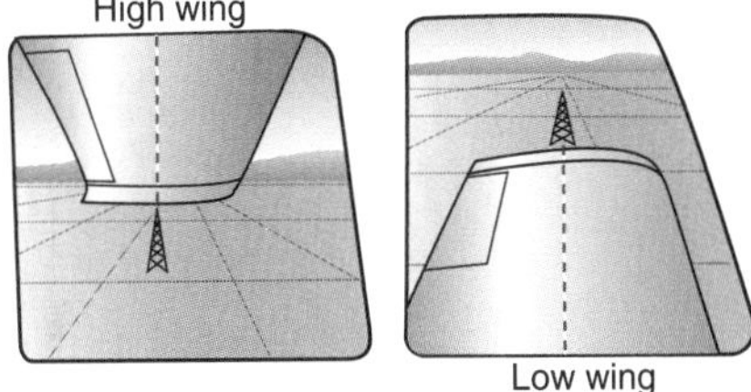

Figure 47-1
What you want to see out of the side window—the wing tip "pinned" on the pylon.

Bank Angle

Bank and put the wingtip on the pylon.

The eights-on-pylons maneuver is easier to understand if you consider the turn pivoted on one of the pylons first—that is, only one-half of the complete eight. The closer you are to the pylon, the steeper the bank angle needed to put the wing tip on the pylon, as shown below.

- At a given altitude, the closer you are to a point above the pylon, the steeper the bank angle has to be to place the wing tip on the pylon.
- At a given speed, the radius of turn will depend upon the bank angle—the steeper the bank angle, the tighter the turn. You can see this effect in figure 47-2, where, at 100 knots, the shallower bank angle results in a wider turn and the steeper bank angle results in a tighter turn—with all of the turns being centered on a point above the pylon.

Speed

The radius of a turn depends on bank angle and speed.

The radius of turn depends not only upon bank angle, but also upon speed: the higher the speed, the wider the turn at a given bank angle. If the airplane in the previous illustration was flying at the same altitude, but faster, say 120 knots instead of 100 knots, the turns would all be wider and so would no longer be centered on a point above the pylon. The airplane would fly away from the pylon—in other words, the pylon would appear to drift gradually behind the wing tip. You could steepen the bank angle to reduce the turn radius, but the wing tip would then no longer be pinned on the pylon.

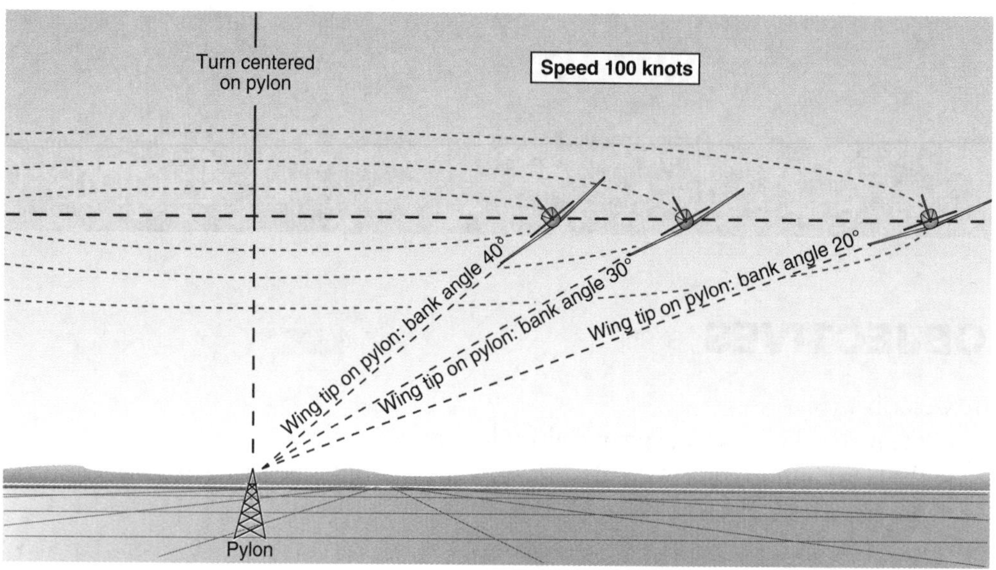

Figure 47-2 Near the pylon the bank angle has to be steeper to put the wing tip on the pylon.

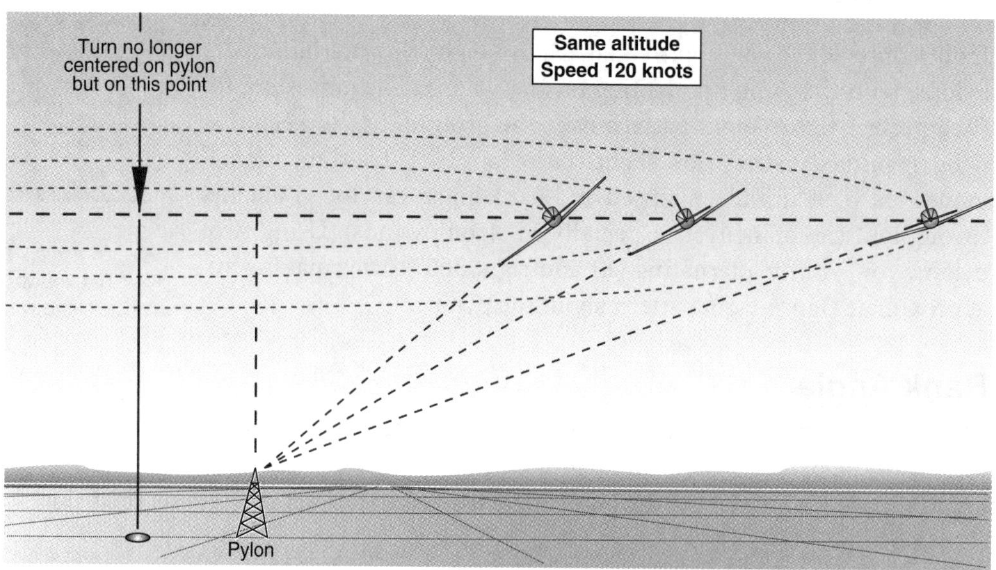

Figure 47-3 The higher the speed, the wider the turn (compare with previous figure).

Speed and Altitude

At higher speeds, fly at a higher altitude.

At the higher speed, you can still (1) place the wing tip on the pylon, and (2) center the turn on a point above the pylon, if you fly at a higher altitude and steepen the bank angle. Conversely, at a lower speed, you should fly at a lower altitude and a shallower bank angle. The particular altitude for each speed is known as the *pivotal altitude*. It is only at this vertical distance above the pylon that you can place the wing tip on the pylon and pivot about it as the turn proceeds. See figure 47-5.

Altitude Terminology

To make clear the important distinction between vertical distance above ground level (AGL) and above mean sea level (MSL), you could use the term *pivotal height* for the vertical distance of the airplane above ground level, and *pivotal altitude* for the vertical distance above mean sea level; this latter value is what you fly on the altimeter (with sea level pressure set in the pressure window). This follows the practice you will encounter later, in your instrument rating training, where *height* is used to refer to the vertical distance above a ground reference—for example, HAA, height above airport, and HAT, height above touchdown. To follow common usage in this maneuver, however, refer to the vertical distance above ground level as the *pivotal altitude AGL*, and the value you fly on your altimeter, set on sea level pressure as the *pivotal altitude MSL*. Be sure that you use the MSL pivotal altitude on your altimeter.

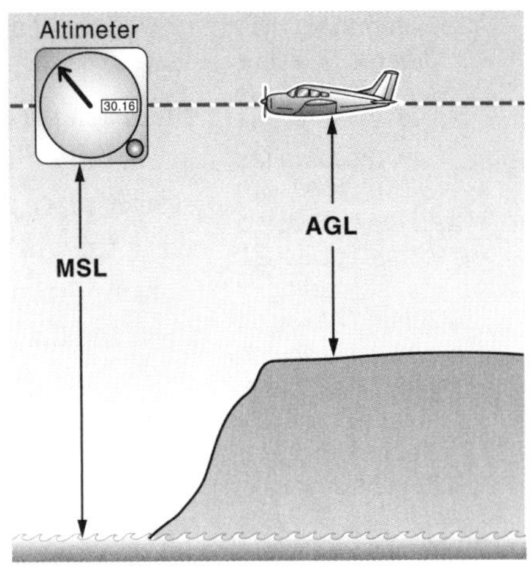

Figure 47-4 Altitudes above mean sea level and above ground level.

Calculating Pivotal Altitude AGL

If you fly at the pivotal altitude for your speed, then you only need to place the wing tip on the pylon and you will pivot about it (regardless of the bank angle needed to place the wing tip on the pylon). You can determine the pivotal altitude above the level of the pylon—that is, above ground level—using the (fairly simple) formula:

Each ground speed has its own pivotal altitude above the pylon.

$$\text{Pivotal altitude AGL} = \frac{(\text{ground speed in knots})^2}{11.3} \text{ feet AGL}$$

For example, at a ground speed of 100 knots:

$$\text{pivotal altitude AGL} = \frac{100^2}{11.3} = \frac{10{,}000}{11.3} = 885, \text{ (890 feet AGL to nearest 10 feet)}$$

At a ground speed of 120 knots:

$$\text{pivotal altitude AGL} = \frac{120^2}{11.3} = 1{,}274 \text{ (or 1,280 feet)}$$

At a ground speed of 80 knots:

$$\text{pivotal altitude AGL} = \frac{80^2}{11.3} = 566 \text{ (or 570 feet)}$$

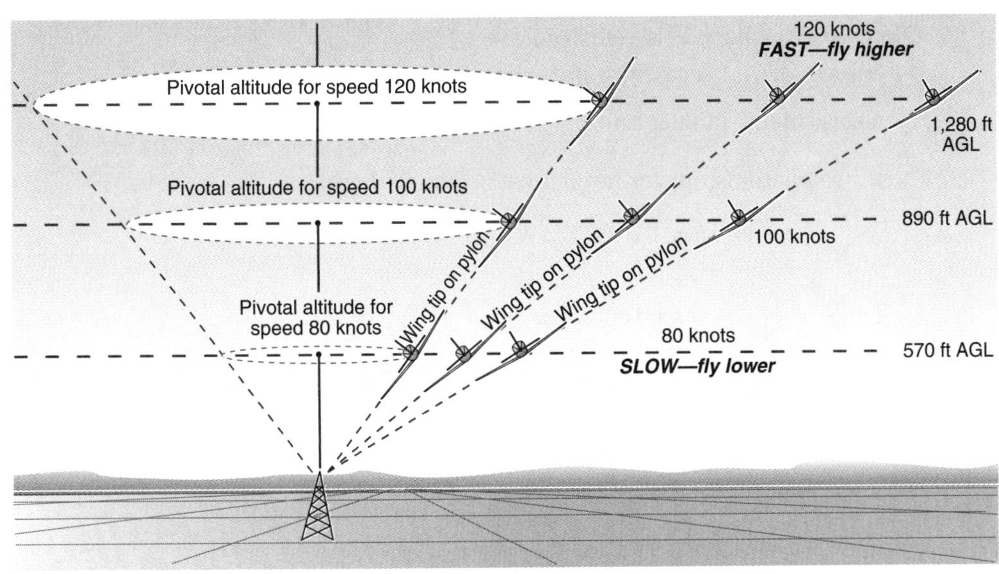

Figure 47-5 Pivotal altitudes AGL for different speeds.

It is important that, in order to use your altimeter when it is set on mean sea level pressure (as it usually is), you add the calculated pivotal altitude AGL to your estimation of the ground elevation above mean sea level. For example, a calculated pivotal altitude of 890 feet AGL, plus a ground elevation of 1,200 feet MSL, equals 2,090 feet MSL, which you would fly on the altimeter.

For those interested, a simple mathematical proof of this formula is given below.

What is interesting to note, and the crucial point to understand for this maneuver, is that each speed has its own pivotal altitude AGL. It does not depend on the bank angle at all, but only ground speed. If you are at the correct pivotal altitude for that speed, you simply place the wing tip on the pylon, using whatever bank angle is necessary, and the wing tip will pivot on the pylon as the turn progresses. The distance from the pylon is not important. The greater the distance, the shallower the bank angle required to place the wing tip on the pylon. If you are at the correct pivotal altitude for the speed, the turn will automatically center on the pylon.

The Formula for Pivotal Altitude AGL

The following discussion is for those who are mathematically inclined.

1. Consider the airplane is at the pivotal altitude AGL (H) and turning with bank angle θ (theta).
   a. The wing tip as seen by the pilot lies on the pylon.
   b. The turn of radius (R) is centered directly above the pylon.

   From this large triangle: $\tan\theta = \frac{H}{R}$

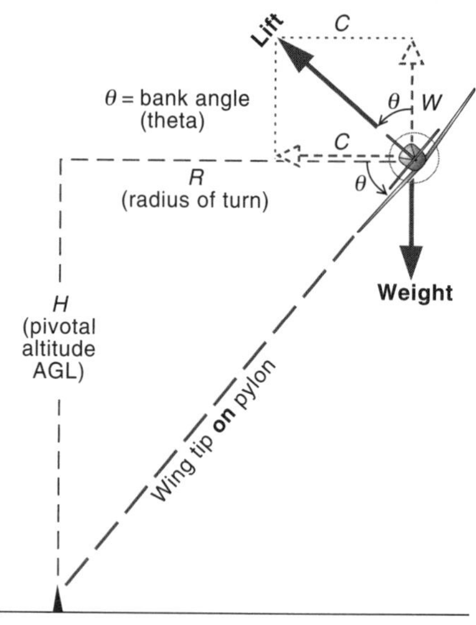

Figure 47-6 Pivotal altitude AGL.

2. The forces acting on the airplane are:
   a. The vertical component of the lift force which counteracts the weight W (where $W = mg$, m being the mass in pounds, and g being the acceleration due to gravity: 32.2 feet per second^2).
   b. The horizontal component of the lift force, also known as the centripetal force (C), which pulls the airplane into the turn of radius R. From physics, we know that, where V is velocity in feet per second, in this case ground speed.

   From this small triangle: $\tan\theta = \frac{C}{W}$

3. These two relationships for tan θ must be equal, therefore:

$$\frac{H}{R} = \frac{C}{W} \qquad \text{where } C = \frac{mV^2}{R} \text{ and } W = mg$$

$$\therefore \frac{H}{R} = \frac{mV^2}{R} \times \frac{1}{mg} \qquad \text{cancel m's, cancel R's}$$

$$\therefore H = \frac{V^2}{g} \qquad \text{where V is velocity in feet per second}$$

Result

H, the pivotal altitude AGL, depends only on speed *V* (in fact V-squared), since g is a constant. There is no mention of bank angle *q*. If the speed (*V*) increases, the pivotal altitude AGL (*H*) must therefore be greater for the wing tip to pivot on the pylon. Conversely, if the speed (*V*) decreases, the pivotal altitude AGL (*H*) must be lower for the wing tip to pivot on the pylon. Then for a speed in knots (rather than in feet per second), use the formula given opposite. Then, to obtain the pivotal altitude MSL, which we can use on our altimeter, simply add the calculated pivotal altitude AGL (that is, *H*) to the estimated elevation MSL of the pylon.

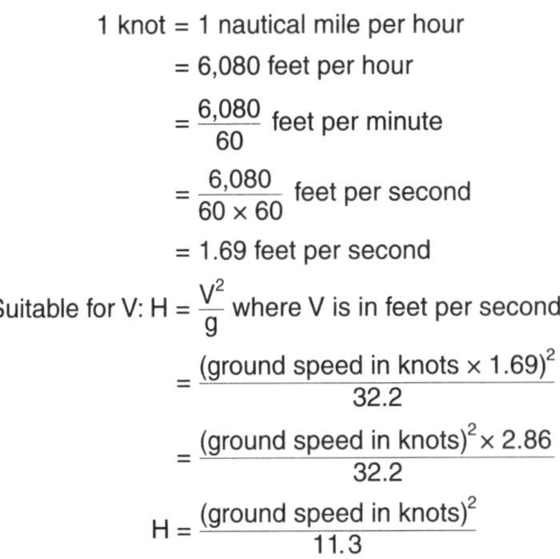

$$
\begin{aligned}
1 \text{ knot} &= 1 \text{ nautical mile per hour}\\
&= 6{,}080 \text{ feet per hour}\\
&= \frac{6{,}080}{60} \text{ feet per minute}\\
&= \frac{6{,}080}{60 \times 60} \text{ feet per second}\\
&= 1.69 \text{ feet per second}\\
\text{Suitable for V: } H &= \frac{V^2}{g} \text{ where V is in feet per second}\\
&= \frac{(\text{ground speed in knots} \times 1.69)^2}{32.2}\\
&= \frac{(\text{ground speed in knots})^2 \times 2.86}{32.2}\\
H &= \frac{(\text{ground speed in knots})^2}{11.3}
\end{aligned}
$$

Flying the Maneuver in Zero Wind

Flying at a constant airspeed in a zero-wind situation, the ground speed of the airplane around a ground object (the pylon) will remain constant. Ground speed will equal airspeed all the way around the turn.

Calculate the Pivotal Altitude MSL

First, calculate the pivotal altitude AGL for your ground speed using the formula (or read it off a card that you have prepared earlier, to simplify the task in the air); add this figure to your estimate of the elevation of the pylon above sea level to obtain the pivotal altitude MSL, to use on your altimeter. Plan on using the normal cruise speed.

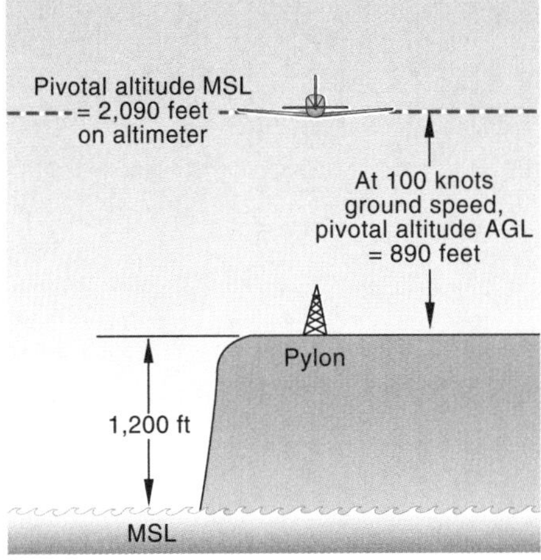

Figure 47-7
Calculating the pivotal altitude MSL.

Entering the Maneuver

Fly abeam the pylon at a distance where you can place the wing tip on the pylon without having to exceed 40° bank angle. The recommended maximum bank angle is 30° to 40° at the steepest point, which is downwind. *Fly abeam pylon at, or slightly above, pivotal altitude.*

Bank Angle

Passing abeam the pylon, roll into the turn and place the wing tip on the pylon. If you are close to the pylon, the bank angle will be steep; if you are further away, the bank angle will be shallow. This will not affect the maneuver since, if you are at the correct pivotal altitude for that speed, the turn will be centered above the pylon, provided you keep the wing tip on the pylon. The turns will be of different radii, but you will pivot about the pylon.

Fly abeam pylon at, or slightly above, pivotal altitude. Roll into the turn and place the wingtip on the pylon.

Accuracy of the Maneuver

It is likely that your estimation of pivotal altitude is not exact, since it involves an estimation of the pylon's elevation above sea level if you want to use your altimeter, or it involves an estimation of your vertical distance above the pylon if you want to eyeball it. This does not create a problem—you simply begin the maneuver, then adjust your altitude if necessary. If you are too high, you will tend to turn inside the pylon. From the cockpit, the pylon will appear to move gradually forward of the wing tip. Do not try to chase it using rudder; this will put the ball out of the center. Correct it by dropping down to a slightly lower altitude (use forward pressure on the control column). Conversely, if you are too

If the calculated pivotal altitude is not correct, climb or descend as appropriate.

low, your turn will gradually take you wide of the pylon, which will appear to gradually slip back behind the wing tip. The solution is to climb to a slightly higher altitude (using back pressure on the control column). See figure 47-8.

TECHNIQUE

1. Enter the maneuver at the estimated pivotal altitude MSL.
2. Abeam the pylon, place the wing tip on the pylon using the ailerons; keep coordinated with rudder—balance ball centered.
3. Adjust the altitude if necessary.
   - If the pylon moves forward, apply forward pressure to descend.
   - If pylon moves back, apply back pressure to climb.

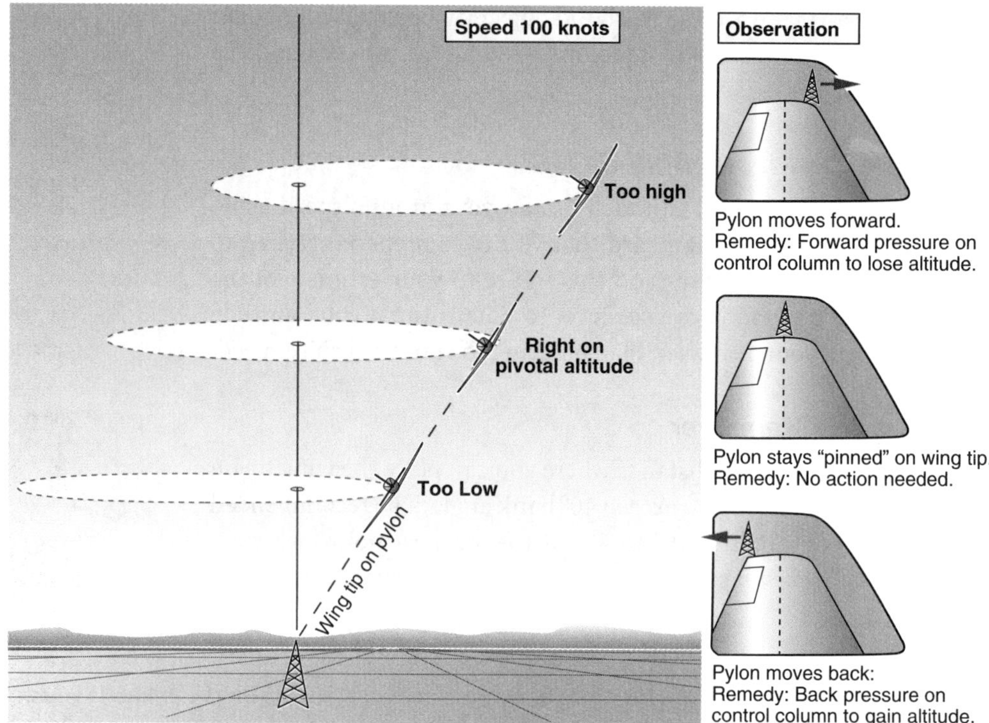

Figure 47-8 Adjusting the altitude—apply elevator in the direction in which the pylon is moving, to move wing tip toward the pylon.

Control in the Maneuver

It was suggested earlier to enter the maneuver at, or slightly above, your estimated pivotal altitude MSL. This is because it is easier to lose a little altitude without having to change power than it is to gain it.

A benefit of this technique is that, in descending without reducing power, you will gain a little airspeed, which will mean a slightly higher pivotal altitude than earlier, and so you will not have to descend quite as far.

Conversely, in climbing without adding power, you will lose a little speed, so the pivotal altitude will be slightly lower than before, and hence you will not have to climb quite as far. This does not require any calculation—you simply observe the movement of the pylon relative to the wing tip, and pin it with movements of the control column:

- aileron to keep it level with the wing tip; and
- elevator to stop it moving fore or aft.

Follow the pylon with the control column (if it moves back, bank more to catch it).

Note that, theoretically there is a second technique, but one that is not recommended. If you are not right at the pivotal altitude for your current speed, then alter the speed (rather than the altitude). This will require power changes and trim changes, making it more difficult to fly accurately.

If you are flying in strong wind conditions, large power changes will be required to alter the airspeed in an attempt to keep the ground speed constant. To keep it constant in a 20-knot wind, for instance, will require a 40-knot airspeed increase as you turn from flying downwind to flying upwind—the power demand may exceed the capability of the airplane.

Flying the Maneuver in a Wind

To fly a complete 360° turn in a 20-knot wind at a constant airspeed, say 100 knots, your ground speed will vary between 120 knots downwind and 80 knots upwind.

Adjust the altitude as wind causes the ground speed to change.

The eights-on-pylons maneuver depends on ground speed (since you are placing the wing tip on a ground object), so you will have to vary the altitude as you turn around the pylon.

- A higher altitude downwind, when the ground speed is higher.
- A lower altitude upwind, when the ground speed is lower.

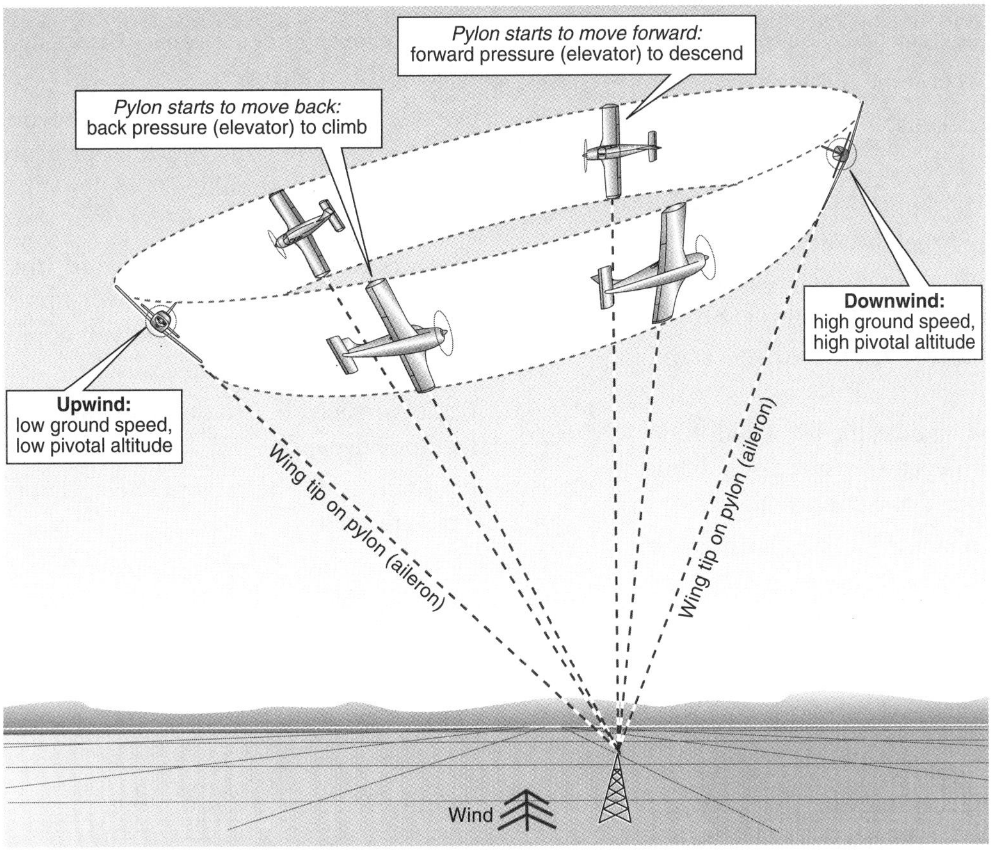

Figure 47-9 Use control column pressures to control pivotal altitude in a wind.

The accepted entry technique is to fly diagonally crosswind (and downwind) between the pylons. The wind coming from behind will give you a high ground speed, and consequently a higher pivotal altitude AGL. At 120 knots, it will be 1,280 feet AGL. Fly over the midpoint between the pylons, using a wind correction angle (WCA) to allow for drift. Wait until your wing tip is abeam the pylon (or even a little past it), and then roll into the turn using coordinated aileron and rudder, and place the wing tip on the pylon.

In your initial turn, you can expect the pylon to move forward gradually as your ground speed reduces (and your pivotal altitude AGL reduces). Apply forward pressure to descend. Flying into the wind with a ground speed of 80 knots, the pivotal altitude AGL is 570 feet, but you will have picked up a little airspeed in the descent, so the pivotal altitude will not be quite so low.

Keep the wing tip pinned on the pylon as you descend. In the second half of the turn, as you go from upwind to downwind again, the higher ground speed will mean a higher pivotal altitude and you will have to gradually climb to keep the wing tip pinned on the pylon. The pylon will start to move back, so apply back pressure to climb.

REVIEW 47
Eights-On-Pylons

1. What is the aim of the eight-on-pylons maneuver?
2. Is eights-on-pylons a constant-altitude maneuver?
3. Is eights-on-pylons a constant-airspeed maneuver?
4. How is the bank angle controlled?
5. What is the name of the altitude at which the turn is centered above a pylon when the airplane is banked to place the wing tip on the pylon?
6. What does AGL stand for? What does MSL stand for?
7. Which of the following does the pivotal altitude AGL above the pylon depend on: speed only, bank angle only or both speed and bank angle?
8. What is a simple formula for calculating the pivotal altitude AGL?
9. If the airspeed is 90 knots, what is the pivotal altitude AGL, to the nearest 10 feet, in a zero-wind situation?
10. If the airspeed is 100 knots, what is the highest pivotal altitude AGL, and the lowest, in a 10-knot wind? What pivotal altitudes MSL would you expect to use on your altimeter if the pylons are at approximately 800 feet MSL?
11. What is the recommended steepest bank angle acceptable for this maneuver?
12. If the pylon is gradually moving back from your line of sight down the wing tip, what pressure on the control column should you apply? What change in altitude will this cause?
13. If the pylon is gradually moving forward from your line of sight down the wing tip, what pressure on the control column should you apply? What change in altitude will this cause?
14. On which of airspeed or ground speed does the pivotal altitude depend?
15. How does increasing the ground speed change the pivotal altitude?
16. How does decreasing the ground speed change the pivotal altitude?

Answers are given on page 586.

TASK

Eights-On-Pylons

Aim: To pivot the wing tips on two pylons as you fly a figure-eight based on them. Altitude, bank angle, and airspeed will vary throughout this maneuver, but the wing tips should stay fixed on the pylon in each turn.

Estimate the wind strength and direction and calculate the pivotal altitude MSL for your entry downwind (highest ground speed), adding the estimated pylon elevation to the pivotal altitude AGL obtained from the formula.

$$\text{Pivotal altitude AGL} = \frac{(\text{ground speed in kts})^2}{11.3} \text{ feet AGL}$$

Ground Speed	Pivotal Altitude AGL
120 knots	feet AGL
110 knots	feet AGL
100 knots	feet AGL
90 knots	feet AGL
80 knots	feet AGL

Fly crosswind and select two suitable pylons perpendicular to the wind. Since the maneuver depends upon the pivotal altitude AGL, it is made easier if you select two pylons at approximately the same elevation.

Look out for hazards and other aircraft.

Position the airplane to enter the eight at normal cruise speed, flying diagonally across the midpoint, with the wind from the side and behind (so the GS will be high) at, or just above, your calculated pivotal altitude MSL.

Wait until you are just past the right pylon and roll into a right turn (recommended bank angle 30° to 40° at the steepest point) to position the wing tip on the pylon.

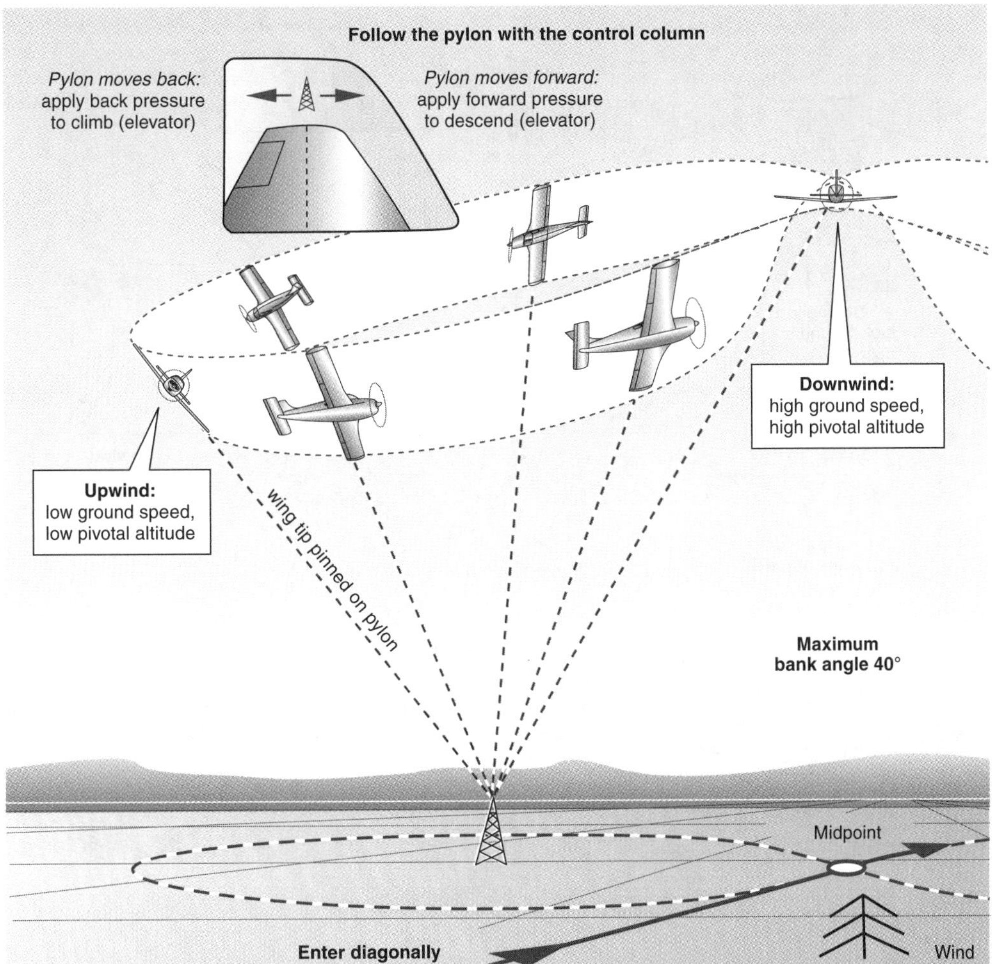

Follow the pylon with the control column
Pylon moves back: apply back pressure to climb (elevator)
Pylon moves forward: apply forward pressure to descend (elevator)
Downwind: high ground speed, high pivotal altitude
Upwind: low ground speed, low pivotal altitude
wing tip pinned on pylon
Maximum bank angle 40°
Midpoint
Enter diagonally
Wind

If too high (as expected) the pylon will move forward of your line-of-sight along the wing tip. Apply forward pressure to descend. Expect the lowest altitude upwind. Prevent up–down movement of the pylon using aileron; prevent fore–aft movement of the pylon using elevator. Follow the pylon with the control column.

In the second half of the turn around the pylon, the ground speed will gradually increase. As the pylon starts to move back, apply back pressure to climb, to keep the wing tip pinned on the pylon.

Approaching the midpoint between the two pylons, roll the wings level for 3 to 5 seconds, then roll in the other direction and place the wing tip on the second pylon. Keep coordinated with rudder.

Prevent the pylon moving forward by using forward pressure on the elevator; prevent the pylon moving back by using back pressure on the elevator. Follow the pylon with the control column.

Throughout the maneuver, divide your attention between coordinated airplane control, keeping the wing tip pivoting on the pylon, and looking out for hazards and other aircraft.

Fly at least three patterns (with each one getting better).

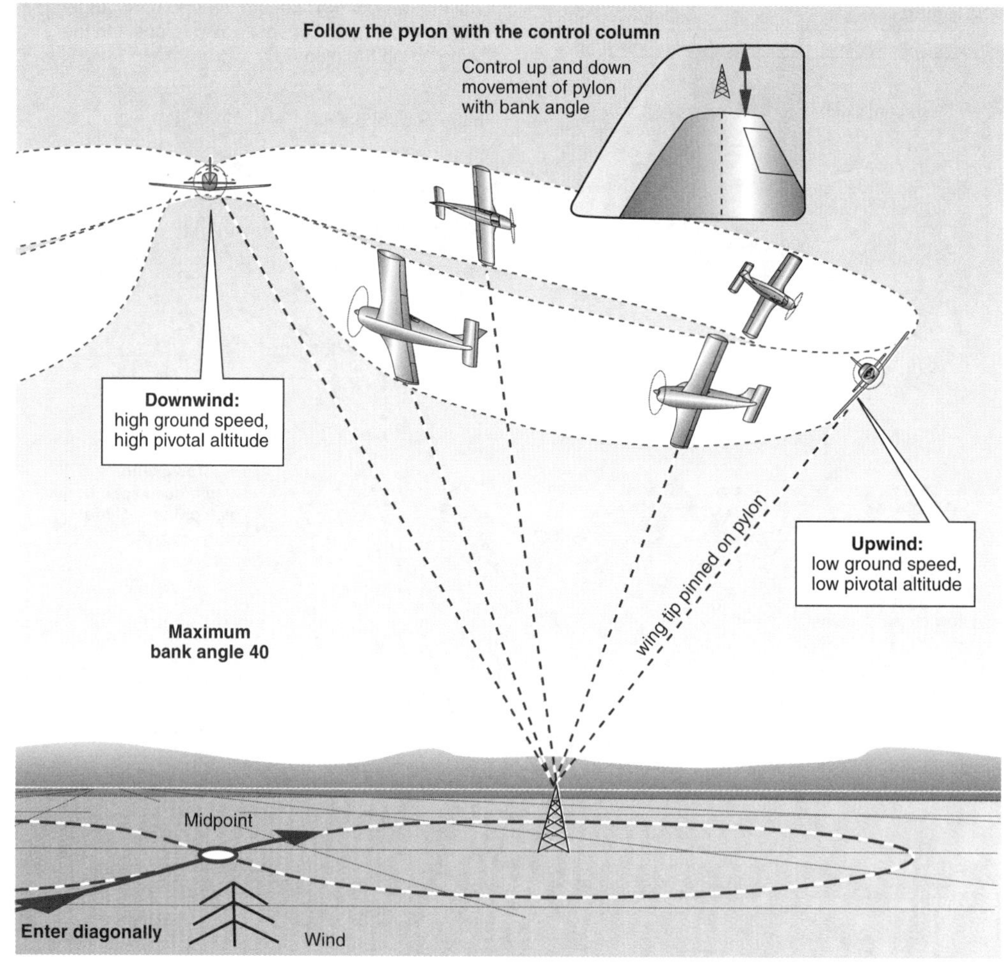
Follow the pylon with the control column
Control up and down movement of pylon with bank angle
Downwind: high ground speed, high pivotal altitude
Upwind: low ground speed, low pivotal altitude
wing tip pinned on pylon
Maximum bank angle 40
Midpoint
Enter diagonally
Wind

Expanding Your Horizons

48

First Solo Flight

OBJECTIVES

To describe:

- the thoughts and feelings you may experience immediately before and during your first solo flight; and
- the positive attitude, confidence and justifiable reward associated with flying alone for the first time.

CONSIDERATIONS

You are able to fly solo when the instructor believes, with some confidence, that you can fly safely with a degree of consistency and you have mastered the presolo maneuvers defined in the regulations. (Three consistently safe traffic patterns and landings in a row is the yardstick used by one school.) Most important is evidence that you are taking control and responsibility for your own actions—that you are walking on your own two feet.

The instructor is looking to see you make corrections for inaccuracies without waiting to be told and without asking for instructions, responding to radio calls without question and saying what you intend to do rather than asking what is next. These are the signs of aviation maturity, of being in command. They are no different from other life skills, just applied at a higher altitude.

First solo is a great experience!

First solo is an unforgettable experience that you will remember and treasure all your life. When your instructor tells you to stop after turning off the runway, steps out of the airplane, secures the harness and then leaves you to your first solo flight, you are being paid a big compliment. Your instructor is confident that you can safely complete a solo traffic pattern. You have demonstrated sufficient awareness, skill and consistency to be trusted to take the aircraft up by yourself.

You may feel a little apprehensive (or very confident), but remember that the instructor is trained to judge the right moment to send you solo. Your instructor has a better appreciation of your flying ability than anybody (including you—especially you).

Your instructor will have observed your progress and have assessed your consistency, safety and predictability. It is not the occasional brilliant landing that is looked for, but a series of consistently safe ones. Your instructor will choose the conditions and the traffic so that they are not more demanding than you are used to.

Student pilots must receive and log flight training in specific maneuvers before conducting a solo flight—these maneuvers are defined in 14 CFR §61.87.

You know instinctively when you are ready to fly solo. In some cases, you may feel you are ready before time. Your instructor knows when the time is right. Trust in that.

Your instructor will also advise the control tower that this is a first solo and the controller will keep a watchful eye open for this new fledgling. The controller will anticipate wind changes and try not to change the active runway while you are flying your first solo traffic pattern.

Presolo Written Exam

Before going solo, you must have passed a written examination administered and graded by the flight instructor who endorses your logbook for solo flight. The written examination will include questions on the applicable Federal Aviation Regulations, and the flight characteristics and operational limits of your airplane. By answering the review questions of each exercise during your training, and by gradually completing the specific airplane type questions in Appendix 1, you will be well prepared for the questions on the flight characteristics and operational limits of your airplane.

These next review questions prepare you for the regulations questions. They direct you into your current copy of the regulations to indicate the level of knowledge you require prior to going solo. Since regulation numbering changes from time to time, the part has been identified—for example, Part 91 and Part 61—but not the individual section, which you can easily find using the table of contents page in your book of regulations.

APPLICATION

Fly your first solo traffic pattern in the same manner as you flew the pattern before the instructor stepped out. The usual standards apply to the takeoff, pattern and landing. Follow exactly the same pattern and procedures. Maintain a good lookout, fly a neat pattern, establish a stabilized approach and carry out a normal landing. Be prepared for better performance of the airplane without the weight of your instructor on board. If at any stage you feel uncomfortable, go around. Many students comment on how much better the airplane flies without an instructor and how much quieter it is!

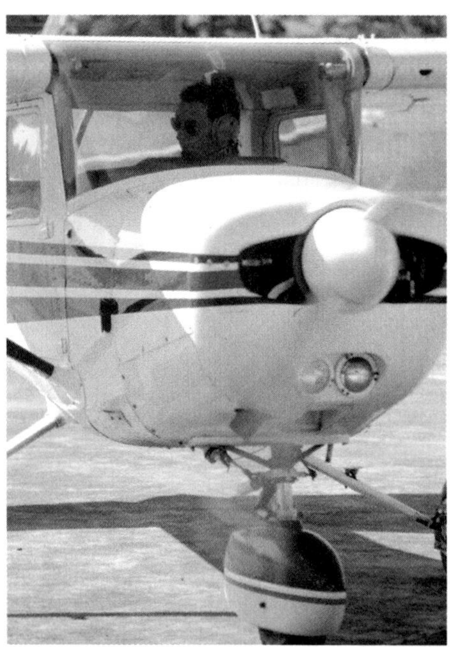

Figure 48-1 First solo.

Be in control. Do not be blown with the wind. The tower will try to avoid any interruptions or runway changes while you are airborne but, if there is a need for you to hold overhead the field or to change runway, then take your time, think through the best plan of action, ask for instructions if you are in doubt and then complete a normal pattern and landing.

If an emergency occurs, such as engine failure (and this is an extremely unlikely event), carry out the appropriate emergency procedure that you have been taught. If your radio fails simply complete the pattern and land normally. Be aware of other traffic. You have been taught to go around and it may happen even on your first solo. Simply complete another pattern.

Your flight instructor, when sending you solo, not only considers you competent to fly a pattern with a normal takeoff and landing, but also considers you competent to handle an abnormal situation. One takeoff, one pattern and one landing are the rites of passage to the international community of pilots. Welcome.

CONGRATULATIONS!

Solo Flights

Your initial solo flights will be in the traffic pattern area practicing takeoffs and landings but, quite soon, you will be proceeding solo to the local training area to practice other maneuvers.

Further refinement and consolidation of the basic skills that you now possess will follow, with solo periods being interspersed with dual periods. The dual flights allow your flight instructor to refine your skills and further develop your accuracy and consistency. In the very important solo flights, you will develop the skills of a captain, making your own decisions and acting on them. Remember that ultimately you are the pilot in command, the decision-maker.

Start to question if the weather is entirely suitable, whether you are getting the most value from the flight, and if there are better areas to explore. These mental processes form a healthy basis for your future command decisions.

Figure 48-2 Congratulations!

REVIEW 48

First Solo Flight

Refer to your personal copy of the regulations and *AIM* when completing these questions. Use the table of contents or the index to find each particular topic covered.

Federal Aviation Regulations Part 91 General Operating and Flight Rules

Responsibility and Authority of Pilot in Command

1. Who is directly responsible for, and is the final authority as to, the operation of an aircraft?
2. In an in-flight emergency requiring emergency action, which of the following statements is true?
   - The pilot in command may deviate from any rule of this part (Part 91) to the extent required to meet that emergency.
   - The pilot in command must not deviate from any rule of this part (Part 91).
   - The pilot in command may deviate from any rule of this part (Part 91) but only after receiving prior permission of ATC.
3. Each pilot in command who deviates from any rule of Part 91 in an in-flight emergency shall send a written report of that deviation to the administrator under which of the following circumstances:
   - immediately;
   - within 24 hours; or
   - upon the request of the administrator?

Civil Aircraft Airworthiness

4. Who is responsible for determining whether the aircraft is in a condition for safe flight?
5. The pilot in command needs to discontinue the flight when unairworthy mechanical, electrical, or structural conditions occur. True or false?

Preflight Action

6. Each pilot in command, before beginning a flight, needs to become familiar with all available information concerning that flight. True or false?

Use of Safety Belts

7. The pilot in command must ensure that all persons on board have been notified to fasten their safety belt and shoulder harness, if installed, under which of the following circumstances:
   - at all times in flight; or
   - before takeoff or landing?

Operating Near Other Aircraft

8. No person may operate an aircraft so close to another aircraft as to create a collision hazard. True or false?

Right of Way Rules

9. An airplane at 2 o'clock at the same altitude is converging on your flight path. Does it have right of way?
10. Each pilot has the responsibility to see and avoid other aircraft, regardless of who has right of way. True or false?
11. Which aircraft has right of way:
    - glider;
    - balloon;
    - an aircraft in distress; or
    - a landing aircraft?
12. Which aircraft has right of way:
    - a landing aircraft; or
    - an aircraft about to taxi onto the runway for takeoff?
13. When two aircraft are approaching to land, the one at which altitude has right of way: higher or lower?
14. An aircraft can take advantage of this rule to cut in front of another or overtake it. True or false?

Minimum Safe Altitudes

15. Except when necessary for takeoff or landing, no person may operate an aircraft below which of the following altitudes:
    - 3,000 feet AGL;
    - 1,000 feet AGL; or
    - an altitude allowing, if a power unit fails, an emergency landing without undue hazard to persons or property on the surface?
16. Except when necessary for takeoff and landing, how many feet above the highest obstacle is the minimum altitude that any person may operate an aircraft over a congested area? What is the horizontal radius from the highest obstacle to which this minimum altitude applies?
17. Except when necessary for takeoff and landing, how many feet AGL may a person operate an aircraft over a non-congested area, excluding over open water or sparsely populated areas? In the case of open water or sparsely populated areas, what is the minimum distance that an aircraft may be operated from any person, vessel, vehicle or structure?

Altimeter Settings

18. For operations at an airport, the pressure window of the altimeter should be set to which of the following:
    - the current altimeter setting for that airport; or
    - 29.92 in. Hg?
19. If you are about to take off at an airport where there is no reported altimeter setting, which of the following should you do:
    - not take off; or
    - set the airport elevation in the altimeter?

Operation at Airports with Operating Control Towers

20. Are two-way radio communications required at airports with operating control towers?
21. At airports with an operating control tower, clearances are required from ATC for which of the following circumstances:
    - for you to taxi;
    - for you to take off and land; or
    - for you to taxi, take off and land?
22. When approaching to land at an airport with an operating control tower, should you remain at or above the glide slope of a visual approach slope indicator (VASI) until a lower altitude is necessary for a safe landing?

Compliance with Clearances and Instructions

23. In which of the following circumstances should you follow any ATC clearance or instruction:
    - at all times; or
    - at all times, except in an emergency when you, as pilot in command, think an alternative course of action is necessary?
24. If you deviate from an ATC clearance in an emergency, when should you advise ATC of that deviation:
    - as soon as possible, for instance by radio; or
    - only after you have landed?
25. If you do not deviate from the regulations, but are given priority by ATC in an emergency, you shall submit a report of that emergency to the manager of that ATC facility according to which of the following:
    - immediately;
    - after landing;
    - within 48 hours; or
    - within 48 hours if requested by ATC?

ATC Light Signals

26. Following a radio failure in flight at a tower-controlled airport, the tower directs the following light signals toward you: steady red, followed by flashing green, followed by steady green when you are on final, and, on short final, a flashing red (as another aircraft, unauthorized, taxis onto the runway). What do they mean?

Operating on or in the Vicinity of an Airport

27. When approaching to land at an airport without an operating control tower, in which direction should all turns be made unless the airport displays approved markings indicating otherwise?
28. When departing from an airport without an operating control tower, do you need to comply with any traffic pattern established for that airport?

Basic VFR Weather Minimums

29. What are the basic VFR weather minimums inside controlled airspace (Classes C, D and E) by day in terms of the following:
    - flight visibility (statute miles);
    - feet below clouds;
    - feet above clouds; and
    - feet horizontally from clouds.

Federal Aviation Regulations Part 61 Certification: Pilots, Flight Instructors and Ground Instructors

Requirement for Certificates, Ratings and Authorizations

30. As pilot in command, which you are when you fly solo, are you required to have your pilot certificate and medical certificate in your personal possession?

Duration of Medical Certificate

31. A third-class medical is issued to a 38-year-old student pilot; at the end of which month does it expire? That same pilot's student pilot certificate is valid for what period of time?

Solo Flight Requirements for Student Pilots

32. Before going solo, do you need to have passed a written examination administered and graded by the flight instructor who endorses your logbook for solo flight? If so, will the written examination include questions on the applicable regulations and the flight characteristics and operational limits of your airplane?
33. Must you have received instruction in emergency procedures and equipment malfunctions prior to going solo?
34. To fly solo, how many days prior to the solo flight must your logbook be endorsed by an authorized flight instructor for solo flight in the specific make and model of aircraft you will fly?

General Limitations

35. Can a student pilot act as pilot in command of an aircraft that is carrying a passenger?
36. How many statute miles during daylight hours must the flight or surface visibility be for a student pilot to act as pilot in command of an aircraft?
37. May a student pilot act as pilot in command of an aircraft when the flight cannot be made with visual reference to the surface?

Operations at Airports Located in Class B Airspace

38. Does a student pilot require special instruction and a logbook endorsement before going solo at a specific airport in Class B airspace?

Answers are given on page 587.

49

Cross-Country Flight

OBJECTIVES

To achieve the following:

- to access and assemble all data pertinent to a planned flight;
- to plan a flight to take account of weather, daylight, fuel, airspace and terrain;
- to select an optimum route and cruising levels;
- to describe the in-flight procedures and technique for visual navigation;
- to describe the use of navigation aids; and
- to discuss the procedures in the event of in-flight diversion or uncertainty of position.

CONSIDERATIONS

Cross-country flying is a significant step forward in your training which, so far, has been restricted to the local training area and has concentrated on:

- basic flying skills (climbing, turning, straight and level, landing, and so on); and
- basic procedures (traffic patterns, forced landings, flight maneuvers by reference to ground objects, and so on).

Flying to another airport, perhaps quite distant, requires the additional skills and knowledge that are summarized here in this chapter.

Figure 49-1 Cross country.

APPLICATION

Start-Up and Taxi

Obtain the airport information from the ATIS or by radio, if available. If in any doubt about the exact time, confirm it with ATC and ensure that your clock is set correctly. Ensure that your navigation equipment is accessible, but will not restrict the controls in any way. Have your charts prefolded.

Following normal procedures, start the engine, switch on the radio and make the appropriate radio calls if required. At tower-controlled airports, you will require a taxi clearance from the tower, perhaps on a separate ground frequency. At airports without an operating tower, you should announce your intentions on the CTAF—the common traffic advisory frequency (which may be FSS, UNICOM, MULTICOM or tower frequency).

Taxi to the takeoff position. At tower-controlled airports, read back any instructions to hold short of a runway. Complete all of the normal preflight checks.

Takeoff and Set Heading

At tower-controlled airports, you require a clearance to line up on the runway and take off. At airports without an operating control tower, you are totally responsible, but you should announce your intentions on the CTAF and have a good look around (especially in the approach paths from either direction) before taxiing onto the runway for departure.

When aligned on the runway, but not accelerating, check that the magnetic compass is reading correctly and that the heading indicator is aligned with it.

Following takeoff, the easiest method of setting heading is from directly overhead the airport, at which time you would mentally note your actual time of departure.

You can also set your heading en route, by climbing out straight ahead before turning to intercept the course at some short distance en route. A radar controller (possibly on a departures frequency) may give you radar vectors as headings to steer to get you on course. Ensure that you do not violate any regulations (such as entering clouds as a VFR pilot)—in the case of radar vectors, keep clear of the clouds and request a revised clearance or instructions. When on course, you should estimate what the actual time of departure from overhead the airport would have been.

To use the magnetic compass precisely, you should refer to the compass deviation card in the cockpit so that the magnetic heading can be modified if necessary to the slightly

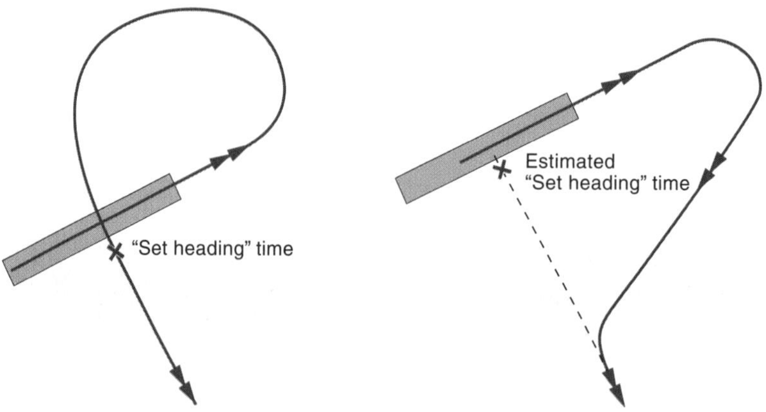

Figure 49-2 Two methods of setting heading.

more accurate compass heading. (Deviation is usually less than 3° and so is not really operationally significant.)

When well clear of the traffic pattern, enter the ATD (actual time of departure) on the flight log, and estimate the arrival time at the destination and at selected points en route. Advise FSS of your departure time. The current altimeter setting (obtainable by radio) should be set in the pressure window of the altimeter so that altitude above mean sea level is indicated. Look well ahead to ensure that visual flight and the required separation from clouds can be maintained and, if not, consider making a diversion.

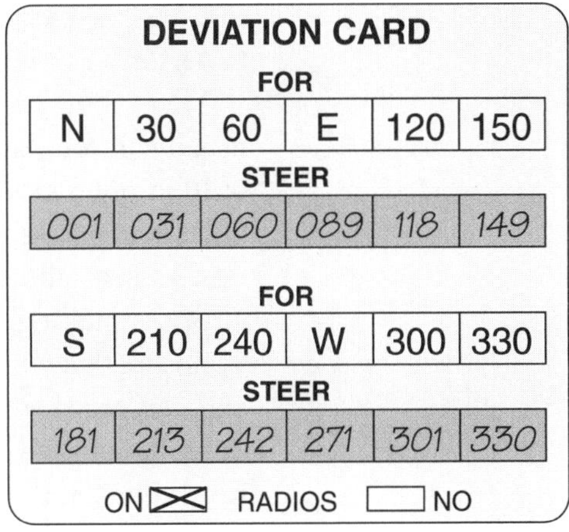

DEVIATION CARD

FOR	N	30	60	E	120	150
STEER	001	031	060	089	118	149

FOR	S	210	240	W	300	330
STEER	181	213	242	271	301	330

ON [X] RADIOS [ ] NO

Figure 49-3 A deviation card.

When established outbound from the airport:

- arrange the chart so that your planned course runs up the page, making it easier for you to read chart to ground;
- confirm that the heading indicator is aligned with the magnetic compass; and
- positively check a definite ground feature or group of features within the first 10 miles to ensure that you are indeed on course, and that no gross error has been made—misreading the compass or misaligning the heading indicator is always a possibility.

Set course and advise FSS of your departure time.

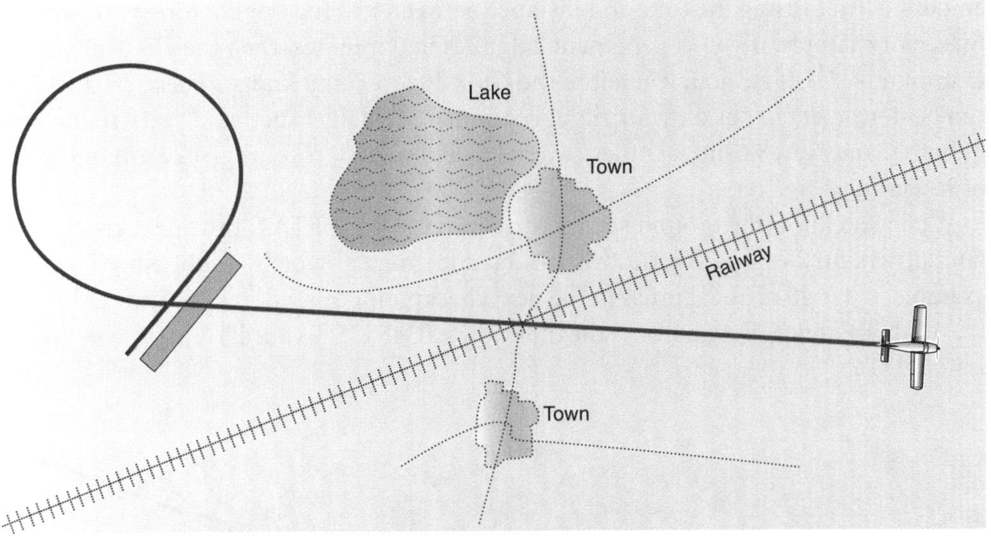

Figure 49-4 Check that tracking is correct soon after you set your heading.

En Route Visual Navigation

En route visual navigation involves pilotage and dead reckoning.

Pilotage is flying with visual reference to ground features, such as following a highway or river between two towns, and requires constant sighting of the ground. Dead reckoning is deducing the current position of the airplane by calculations of speed, course, time, wind effect and previous known position, and requires only periodic identification of ground features.

It is important to maintain steady headings for known times when flying cross-country to simplify your dead reckoning. You should navigate by means of precomputed headings, ground speeds and elapsed times (adjusted as necessary in flight). You should aim to hold altitude and heading as accurately as possible, but certainly within the limits of cruise altitude plus or minus 200 feet, and within 10° of the selected heading. The 200-foot tolerance on altitude is a little more lenient than usual, since you have navigational tasks to perform as well as manipulate the airplane.

There is no need to refer to the chart all the time, but be sure to keep it handy (and usually on your lap). It is best to select certain ground features that will occur at intervals of 10 minutes or so (which, at a ground speed of 100 knots, puts them about 17 nautical miles apart) to verify that you are on or near your planned course. Selecting checkpoints this far apart allows you to divide your time for the other duties, which include flying the airplane, making radio calls and carrying out periodic checks of the airplane systems.

Know from the chart which features to expect ahead.

Ensure that you use the appropriate checklists throughout the flight—the climb, cruise and descent checklists—and use recommended cruise procedures. At the appropriate time, look ahead for the next checkpoint that should be coming into view—in other words, look at the chart, note the features that should shortly come into view and then look outside with the expectation of seeing them. Read from chart to ground, then use features to either side of course and well ahead to confirm your position. You must identify landmarks by relating the surface features to chart symbols. Aim to stay within 3 nautical miles of the flight-planned route at all times, and to arrive at en route checkpoints and the destination within five minutes of the initial or revised ETA.

Ground Speed Checks

Make regular checks of the ground speed and revise your ETAs.

The actual ground speed is easily calculated from the distance traveled in a particular amount of time, using the time and distance between two fixes or crossing two position lines. For example, if you cover 5 nautical miles in 3 minutes, then the GS is 100 knots (3 minutes = $\frac{1}{20}$ of an hour, therefore the GS = 20 × 5 = 100 knots). These calculations can be done mentally or on your flight computer. Mentally is better, if you can manage it. In the same way, 8 nautical miles covered in 5 minutes ($\frac{1}{12}$ hour) gives a ground speed of 96 knots.

When you know the ground speed, you can revise your ETA for the next checkpoint (and others further on). Again, this can be done mentally or by flight computer. For example, if it is 40 nautical miles to the next checkpoint, this will take 5 times as long as the 8 nautical miles, 25 minutes. If the time now is 0345 UTC, your ETA at the checkpoint is 0410 UTC.

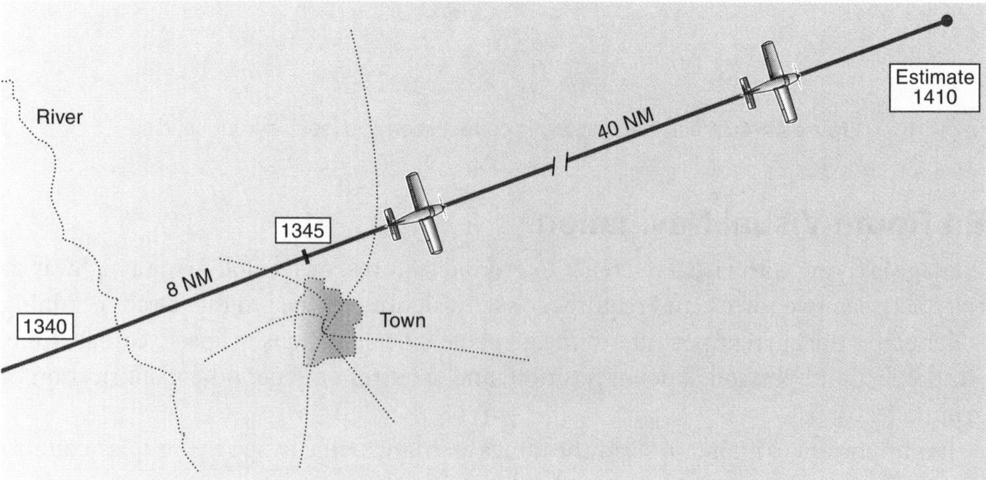

Figure 49-5 Calculate the ground speed and revise your ETAs.

Checking the actual time at the one-quarter, one-half and three-quarter points makes the mental calculation of the next ETA easy. Also, it is good airmanship to log the times at fixes (or mark them on the chart), so that you have some record of what positions the airplane passed over, and when.

Your aim should be to arrive at en route checkpoints and the destination at the initial or revised ETA, certainly within five minutes of it. If this does not look possible, then advise FSS of a further revised ETA.

Off-Course Corrections

Adjust heading as necessary.

It is usual to find that the actual ground track differs from the planned course plotted on the chart, possibly because the winds aloft are different to those forecast. Whatever the cause, it is a simple calculation to revise the heading to rejoin the planned course.

There are various means of doing this and your flight instructor will inform you of the preferred method. It can be done by flight computer, or it can be done mentally (which leaves your hands free for other duties and avoids having your head in the cockpit for too long). It is good airmanship to log the heading changes and the times at which they were made.

In each of the three methods shown in figure 49-6, the same result from a known tracking error (TE) and a calculated closing angle (CA) is obtained—a turn of 12° to the right. Having regained course, turn 4° left to maintain it. Your aim should be to stay within 3 nautical miles of the flight-planned course at all times.

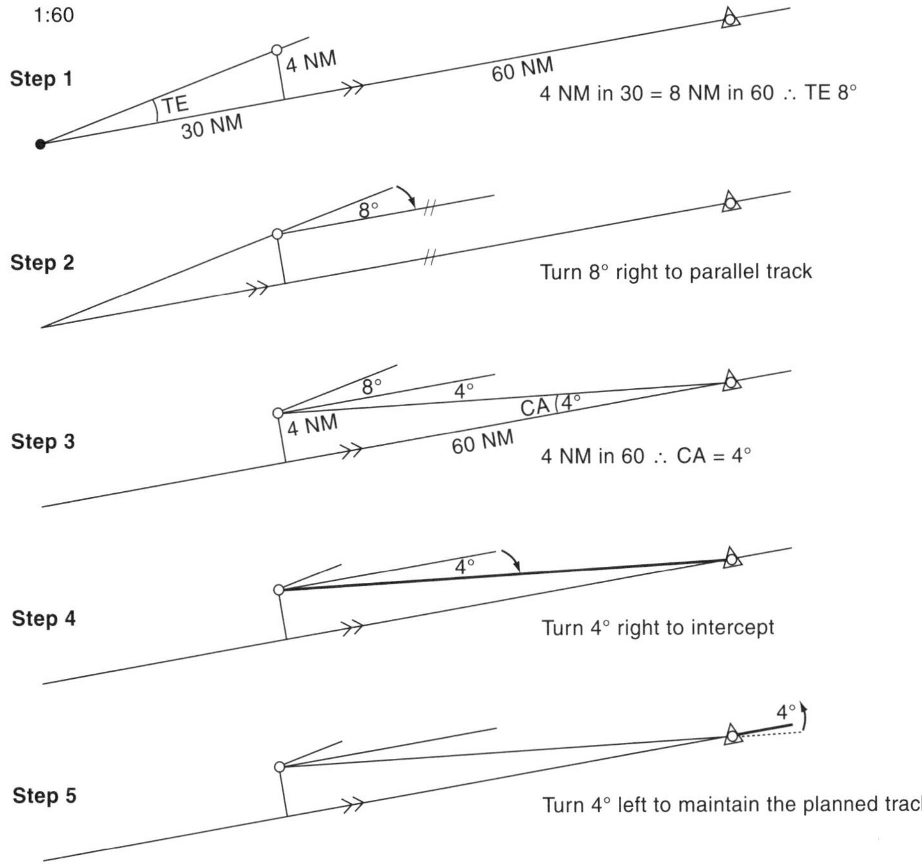

Figure 49-6 Various methods of revising heading.

Regular Airplane Checks

The correct operation of the airplane and its systems should be checked on a regular basis (say each 15 minutes, or just prior to arrival overhead a checkpoint). A suitable periodic check is the FREHA check detailed on page 304 and page 456. Also, leaning the mixture correctly is vital for fuel efficiency and obtaining the range you have planned for.

Turning Points

Just prior to reaching a turning point, check that the heading indicator is aligned with the magnetic compass (part of the FREHA check). Take up the new heading over the turning point, log the time and calculate the ETA for the next checkpoint. Then, within 10 nautical miles of passing the turning point, confirm from ground features that you are on the planned course, and that no gross error has been made. Monitor fuel usage at each turning point.

Use of the Radio

The radio is a very useful aid to a pilot. En route and outside controlled airspace, you will normally select the local FSS frequency to enable immediate contact with the nearest FSS. It is good airmanship to pass accurate and frequent position reports to FSS, update ETAs, and to advise any change in plans, such as a diversion or if you will arrive more than 30 minutes after planned ETA (to prevent unnecessary search and rescue procedures from commencing).

A position report should include your:

- aircraft identification;
- position and time;
- altitude or flight level, and type of flight plan (for example, VFR);
- next reporting point and ETA;
- next succeeding reporting point (name only);
- pertinent remarks, such as weather conditions.

Pilot: *Sacramento, Cessna 1238 Sierra,*
Sacramento at zero two two eight,
Niner thousand five hundred, VFR,
Estimate Manteca at zero two four seven Zulu, Panoche next,
Light turbulence, high cirrus above.

Make use of the radio to obtain in-flight weather advisories from Flight Service by contacting 122.2 Mhz. Initial contact can be made with Flight Service by referring to the facility name and your aircraft identification, followed by over—for example, "Seattle Radio, November One Two Three Four Alpha, over." In addition to receiving weather advisories in this way, you are encouraged to report your current weather (good or bad) as this may be of assistance to other pilots.

You can also tune to a hazardous in-flight weather advisory service (HIWAS) broadcast or a transcribed weather broadcast (TWEB) by selecting the VOR or ADF receiver to the appropriate station, shown on sectional charts.

En Route Radio Navigation

Radio navigation aids can be useful on a cross-country VFR flight, provided you select, identify and check the operation of each aid before using it. The main radio navigation aids for en route use are the VOR and DME (VORTAC), GPS, and the NDB.

You should be able to locate your position relative to the radio navigation facility, intercept and track along the selected radial or bearing, locate your position using cross-radials or cross-bearings, recognize station passage, and recognize a signal loss and take appropriate action. Illustrated in figure 49-7 is how you could intercept a magnetic course (MC) of 030° to a particular VORTAC—that is, inbound on the 210 radial—by setting 030 with the omni bearing selector (OBS) and initially steer-ing a magnetic heading of 050° until the course deviation indicator (CDI) centers. You then determine a heading that will keep the CDI centered, which may take a little trial and error. Passing overhead the VOR station, the CDI will flicker, and the flag will change from *to* to *from*, at which time the new course—outbound from the VOR station—should be set with the OBS.

Use radio navigation aids for tracking and for ground speed checks.

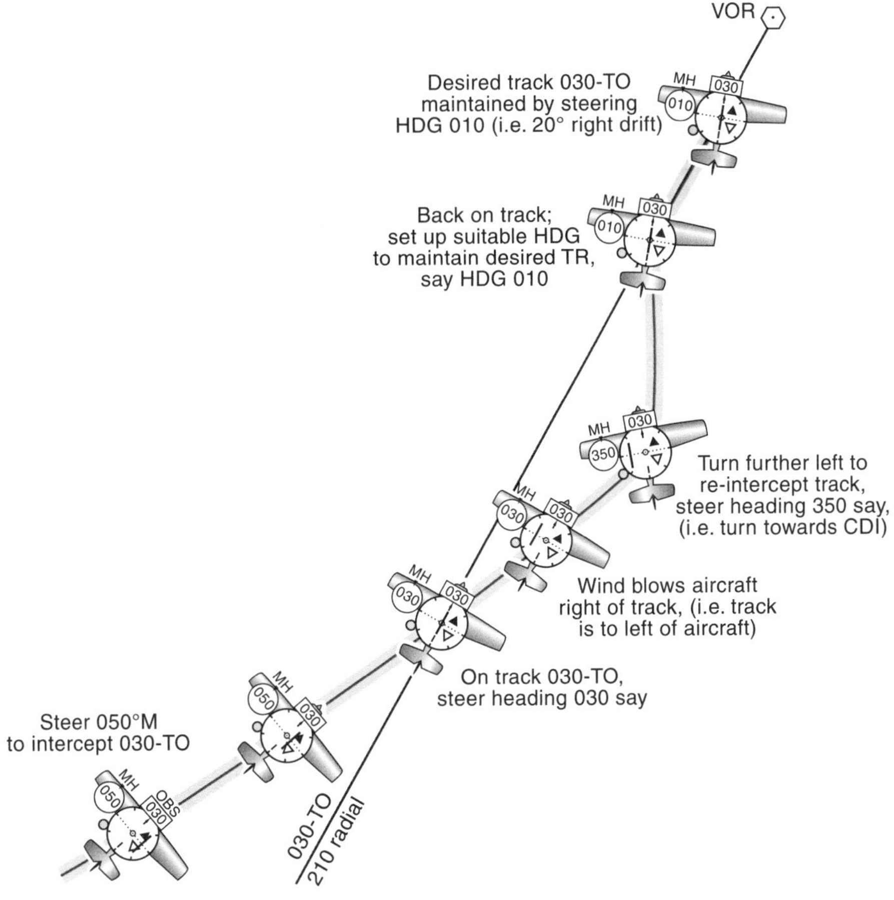

Figure 49-7 Intercepting and tracking MC030 to a VORTAC.

Ground speed checks are also made easy by using DME distances when some distance away from the VORTAC and tracking directly to or away from it.

The ADF can also be tuned into en route NDBs and used for tracking or orientation purposes, as shown in figure 49-8.

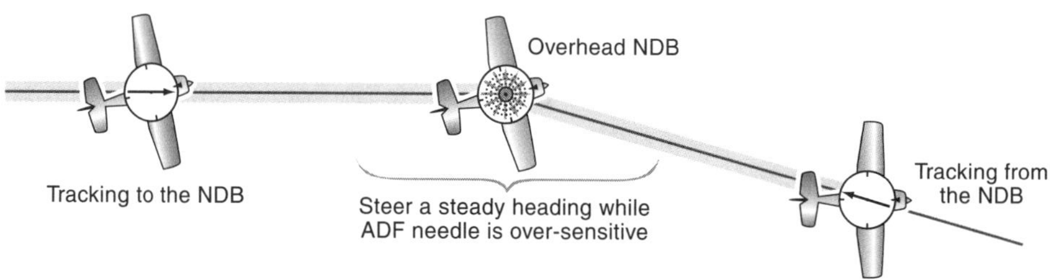

Figure 49-8 Do not overcorrect when close to the NDB.

Many aircraft now have a GPS installed which, like other area navigation (RNAV) systems, allows a pilot to navigate between preset waypoints that can be determined. (See figure 49-10.)

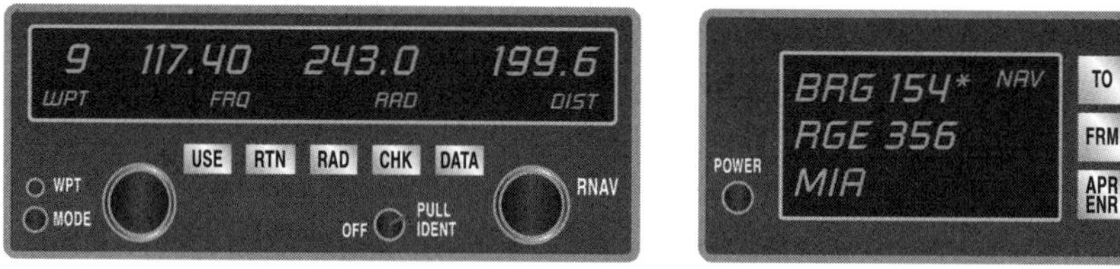

Figure 49-9 Typical RNAV and GPS displays.

Always be prepared for basic navigation, even with sophisticated electronic equipment on board.

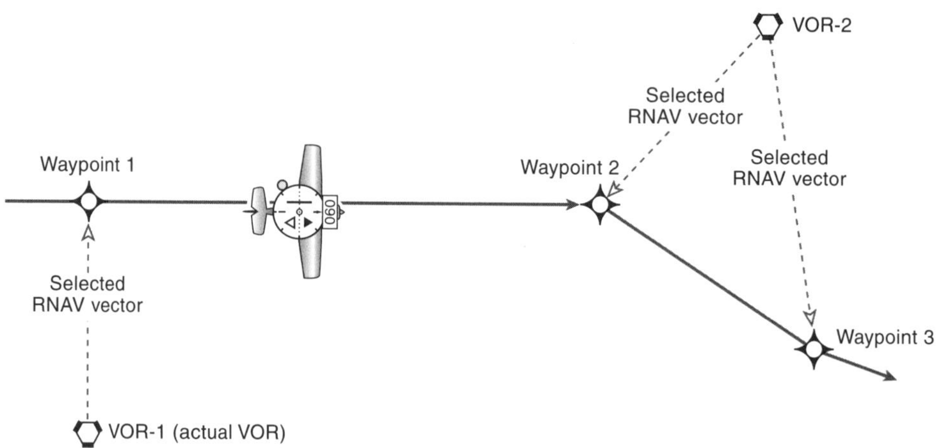

Figure 49-10 Tracking between waypoints.

Ensure that you know how to operate your particular equipment, and know its limitations, before you rely on it to support your visual navigation.

Occasionally electronics and electrical systems fail, and you have to rely on basic VFR navigation, which is pilotage and dead reckoning. Do not neglect these just because your current aircraft has sophisticated radio navigation equipment!

Arrival at the Destination

If flying high, plan to commence descent some distance from the airport so that you arrive at a suitable altitude to join the traffic pattern. Do not forget to move the mixture control to rich in the descent.

Plan an efficient descent. Note down the ATIS or recorded weather information and plan your traffic pattern entry.

Listen to the ATIS (if provided) or the recorded weather information—Automated Surface Observing System (ASOS) or Automated Weather Observing System (AWOS)—well before arriving in the traffic pattern. Follow the procedures for pattern entry appropriate to that airport. When approaching an airport without an operating control tower, you should announce your intentions on the CTAF when 10 miles out, entering downwind, base and final, and when leaving the runway. Approaching a tower-controlled airport, it is usual to be in contact with the tower by 15 miles out.

Normal procedures at a nontowered airport are to join downwind at 45° to the traffic pattern. After landing, make the appropriate radio calls, taxi in, shut down, complete appropriate checklists, and make sure that you secure the airplane before leaving it.

Unless hangared or about to be flown again, tie the airplane down, with chocks in position, but release the parking brakes so that the airplane can be moved easily by hand if necessary without having to unlock the doors.

Fueling may be a consideration, especially if you are leaving the airplane overnight. Full tanks minimize condensation of water in the tanks, as well as saving you having to call the fueler out early the next morning.

Close the flight plan directly with FSS (the preferred method) or ask an ATC facility to relay your cancelation to the FSS designated on your flight plan. A control tower will not automatically close your flight plan, since not all VFR flights file flight plans—you need to request it.

Diversions

A successful cross-country flight does not necessarily mean arriving at the destination. Sometimes conditions are such that continuing to the destination would expose your flight to unnecessary risk. Weather forecasters are not infallible.

If the actual weather conditions ahead deteriorate to such a degree that onward visual flight would be unsafe (or less safe than you wish it to be), then to divert is good airmanship. You should learn to recognize adverse weather conditions, and to divert promptly to an appropriate airfield using a suitable route.

Other reasons for diverting could be an airplane malfunction, pilot fatigue, a sick passenger, or impending darkness. Never be afraid to divert if you feel it is the appropriate thing to do.

There will always be pressures to press on from, for example, passengers wanting to get home, a sense of failure if you do not make it to the planned destination, or the inconvenience of having to overnight away from home unexpectedly.

When faced with an operational decision of what to do, forget all of these secondary problems! They are irrelevant to your decision of whether to divert or not, which should be made purely on flight safety and nothing else.

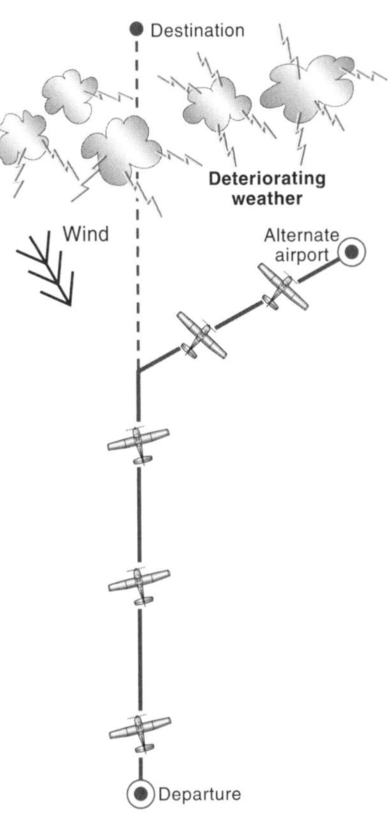

Figure 49-11
Divert earlier rather than later.

Having decided to divert, perhaps in difficult conditions such as turbulence, there is a basic diversion procedure that you should follow.

- Maintain positive and authoritative control of the airplane at all times—altitude within 200 feet, heading within 10° and airspeed within 10 knots.
- Make your decision to divert earlier rather than later.
- Select an appropriate airport within range—request weather and other information from flight watch on 122.0 MHz.
- If possible, plan to divert from a prominent ground feature ahead, so that the diversion is started from a known point; if time does not permit, divert immediately and look for good checkpoints—make use of radio navigation aids.
- Mark the diversion course on the chart and estimate course direction and distance—estimate the direction in degrees true with reference to the latitude-longitude grid and estimate the distance with your thumb (from the top joint of your thumb to the tip is typically about 10 nautical miles at a chart scale of 1:500,000).
- At the prominent feature, take up the estimated diversion heading, which you have calculated from the estimated course, allowing for magnetic variation and wind drift. Your heading is extremely important at this stage—even more important than distance (within reason).
- Log the time at the diversion point and log your new heading.
- Refer to the chart and look for a positive ground feature soon after altering heading to ensure that no gross error has been made.
- When time permits, measure the course direction and distance accurately—ideally this would be done prior to the actual diversion.
- Estimate the ground speed, time interval and the ETA at the diversion airfield or next turning point.
- Estimate the fuel consumption to the diversion airfield (plan to arrive with at least 30 minutes reserve by day and 45 minutes by night, at cruise rate).
- Inform the nearest FSS or ATC center by radio of your actions (new destination, cruising altitude and ETA).
- Continue with normal navigation until you reach the diversion airfield.
- Obtain the ATIS, join the traffic pattern normally, land, close your flight plan—consider if the original destination airfield should be advised—and then advise your home base of the situation.

Never be afraid to divert if you feel it is the appropriate thing to do.

Low-Level Navigation

If a diversion is necessary because of a lowering cloud base, you may find yourself involved in low-level navigation. Low-level flying itself has been covered in a previous exercise, but navigational aspects worth noting are:

- If possible, perform any required checks before descent to a low level.
- Consider using the precautionary configuration (which allows slower flight, a better forward view, better maneuverability, but poorer fuel consumption).
- Your field of vision at low level is small and the speed that ground features pass through it is greater.
- Check-features need to be close to your course to fall within this field of vision and must be prominent in profile (when seen from the side).
- Anticipate reaching the ground features, because they may not be in your field of vision for long.
- Keep your eyes out of the cockpit as much as possible.

Uncertainty of Position

You can prevent becoming uncertain of your position, always knowing (at least approximately) where you are, by flying accurate headings, looking out for prominent landmarks, monitoring time and making use of available radio navigation aids.

Being temporarily uncertain of your position is not the same as being lost.

One position line is useful, but two position lines that cut at a good angle enables you to immediately fix your position accurately. With a VOR, you would select what you think is a nearby station, identify it, and turn the OBS until the CDI centers, then note whether the bearing is to or from the VOR.

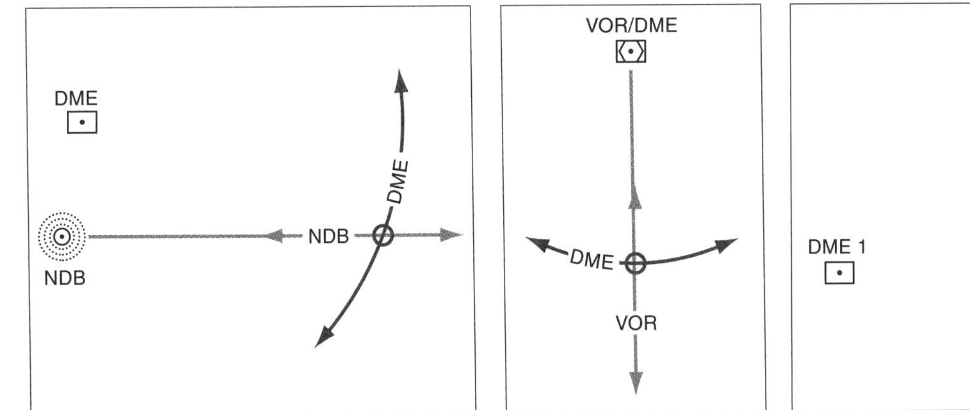

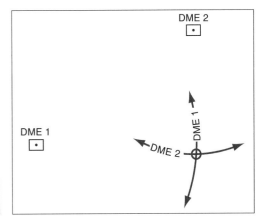

Figure 49-12 Three examples of using two radio navigation aids to fix your position.

A simultaneous DME reading from a VORTAC is all you need to fix your position. Without DME, you could select your VOR receiver to another VORTAC and obtain a bearing of it by centering the CDI. Nearby NDBs may also be useful.

A DR (dead reckoning) position can be calculated which, hopefully, can shortly be backed up with a positive fix over or abeam a ground feature.

If, at any time, you feel uncertain of your position:

- Log your heading—compass and heading indicator (HI)—and the time.
- If the HI is incorrectly set, then you have the information needed to make a reasonable estimate of your actual position. Realign the HI with the compass, and calculate a heading and time interval to regain the planned course.
- If the HI is aligned correctly with the compass, then the nonappearance of a landmark, while it will perhaps cause you some concern, need not indicate that you are grossly off course. You may not have seen the landmark for some perfectly legitimate reason (bright sunlight, poor visibility, a change in features not reflected on the chart, or clouds).
- Consider a precautionary landing if the onset of bad weather, fuel exhaustion, or darkness is imminent.
- Request assistance from FSS or ATC. In a radar environment, it may be quite easy to be identified using your transponder. Also, some airports have VHF direction-finding antennas that can determine the direction your voice transmissions are coming from. If you feel it is appropriate, make an urgency call (pan-pan pan-pan pan-pan) on the frequency in use or on the emergency frequency 121.5 MHz.
- If still unable to fix your position, follow the procedure below.

Lost

Becoming lost is usually the result of some human error. Careful preflight planning followed by in-flight attention to the simple navigational tasks will ensure that you never become lost. You may become temporarily uncertain of your exact position, but this is not being lost because you can calculate an approximate dead-reckoning position.

If you are in a radar environment, say within 100 nautical miles of a major city airport, ATC may be able to locate you on radar and provide radar headings to a suitable airport.

Procedure to Follow

If you ever become lost, formulate a plan of action. Do not fly around aimlessly.

If you become lost, carry out the following procedure.

- It is important that you initially maintain the heading (if terrain, visibility and what you know of the proximity of controlled airspace permit) and carry out a sequence of positive actions.
- If a vital checkpoint is not in view at your ETA, then continue to fly for 10% of the time since your last positive fix.
- Start from the chart position of your last known fix, check the headings flown since that last fix, and ensure that:
  - the magnetic compass is not being affected by outside influences such as a camera, portable radio, or other metal objects placed near it;
  - the gyroscopic heading indicator is aligned with the magnetic compass;
  - magnetic variation and the wind correction angle have been correctly applied to obtain your headings flown; and
  - an estimate of the course direction on the chart against that shown on the flight plan is correct.
- When lost, read from ground to chart—that is, look for significant ground features or combinations of features and try to determine their position on the chart.
- Establish a most probable area in which you think you are. There are several ways in which this can be done, and we recommend you consult your flight instructor for his or her preferred method. Two suggested methods follow.

Establishing your Most Probable Area

Method 1. Estimate the distance flown since the last fix and apply this distance, plus or minus 10%, to an arc 30 degrees either side of what you estimate is the probable ground track.

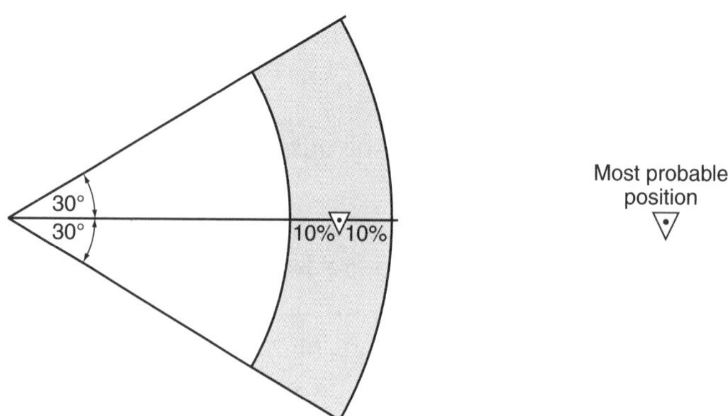

Figure 49-13 Estimating the most probable area that you are in.

Method 2. Estimate your most probable position and draw a circle around it of radius equal to 10% the distance flown since the last fix.

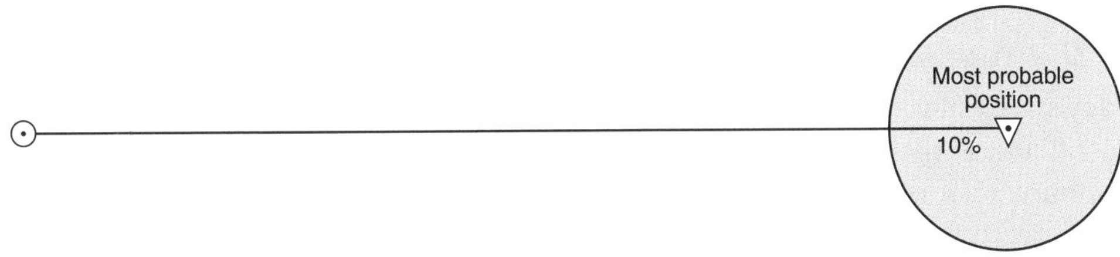

Figure 49-14 Another means of estimating the most probable position.

Establish a safety altitude to ensure there is adequate clearance above all obstacles in what you consider the general area to be, being especially careful in conditions of poor visibility or low clouds, or when near or over mountains.

Check large features within this area of the chart with what can be seen on the ground. Try and relate features seen on the ground with those shown on the chart—that is, read from ground to chart.

Confirm the identification of any feature by closely observing secondary details around the feature.

When you do positively establish a fix, recheck your heading indicator and recommence normal navigational activity. Calculate the heading, ground speed, and time interval for the next check feature, and set course for it.

If you are still unable to fix your position, you should consider taking one of the following actions:

- increase your most probable area by from 10% to 15% or even 20% of the distance flown from the last fix;
- climb to a higher altitude to increase your range of vision, and for better line-of-sight VHF radio reception;
- turn toward a prominent line-feature known to be in the area, such as a coastline, large river, railroad or highway, and then follow it to the next town, where you should be able to obtain a fix;
- steer a reciprocal heading, and attempt to return to your last fix; or
- seek navigational assistance from the FSS or ATC center with which you are in radio contact. It is wise to take this step prior to reaching the desperation stage.

A radar advisory service may be available. If not, information that may be requested to establish your position is the time and position of your last fix, with headings and times flown since then.

Important Points

Some important points for cross-country flying are as follows.

Fly the airplane at all times maintaining an awareness of time, especially with respect to sunset and your fuel state.

- If you want to cover as much ground as possible with the fuel available, you should fly the airplane for best range.
- Keep a navigation log.
- Remain positively aware of time. Keep your eye on the fuel and on the amount of time remaining until last light. If last light is approaching, remember that it will be darker at ground level than at altitude and, if you are flying in the tropics, that it will become dark quickly following sunset.

- If you decide to carry out a precautionary search and landing, allow sufficient time and fuel to accomplish this because two or three inspections might have to be made before finding a suitable landing area.

Why Did You Become Lost?

If at any stage you became lost, try to determine the reason systematically (either in flight or post flight) so that you can learn from the experience.

Common reasons for becoming lost include:

- incorrectly calculated headings, ground speeds and time intervals—hence the need to make mental estimates of approximate answers to these items;
- an incorrectly synchronized heading indicator—that is, the gyroscopic HI was not aligned correctly with the magnetic compass (the HI should be aligned every 10 or 15 minutes against the compass);
- a faulty compass reading (caused by transistor radios, cameras and other metallic objects placed near the compass);
- incorrectly applied magnetic variation;
- incorrectly applied wind drift;
- an actual wind velocity significantly different to the forecast, and not allowed for in flight by the pilot;
- a deterioration in weather, a reduced visibility, or an increased cockpit workload;
- an incorrect fix or misidentification of a check feature;
- a poorly planned diversion from the original planned course; and
- not paying attention to carrying out normal navigational tasks en route.

With regular checks of the HI alignment with the compass, reasonably accurate flying of heading, and with position fixes every 10 or 15 minutes, none of the above errors should put you far off course. It is only when you are slack and let things go a bit too far that you becomes lost.

System and Equipment Malfunctions

Prior to setting out on a cross-country flight, you should be prepared to handle certain system and equipment malfunctions. These may be simulated on your training exercises by your flight instructor.

Consider these possible malfunctions, read your POH, discuss them with your flight instructor and make your own notes. A discussion of such items will occur on your practical flight test at the preflight stage or in flight.

In a real situation where you feel apprehensive, you could declare an emergency (by radio on the frequency in use or on the emergency frequency 121.5 MHz), and squawk the emergency code 7700 on your transponder.

Emergencies are thought of as:

- distress situations, such as fire, mechanical failure, structural damage, immediate assistance required (a mayday call is appropriate); and
- urgency situations, such as lost or doubtful of position, problems with fuel endurance or weather, another aircraft in trouble (a pan-pan call is appropriate).

Be able to provide answers applicable to your airplane type for the following:

Carburetor or Induction Icing	Cause:	Ice forming in the carburetor.
	Indications:	RPM decrease (fixed-pitch prop), rough running, engine stoppage.
	Action:	Apply full carburetor heat.
Partial Power Loss	Cause:	. . . .
	Indications	. . . .
	Action	. . . .
Rough-Running or Overheating Engine	Cause:	. . . .
	Indications	. . . .
	Action	. . . .
Loss of Oil Pressure	Cause:	. . . .
	Indications:	. . . .
	Action:	. . . .
Fuel Starvation	Cause:	. . . .
	Indications:	. . . .
	Action:	. . . .
Engine Compartment Fire	Cause:	. . . .
	Indications:	. . . .
	Action:	. . . .
Smoke or Fumes in Cockpit	Cause:	. . . .
	Indications:	. . . .
	Action:	. . . .
Electrical System Malfunction	Cause:	. . . .
	Indications:	. . . .
	Action:	. . . .
Electrical Fire	Cause:	. . . .
	Indications:	. . . .
	Action:	. . . .
Wing Flaps Malfunction	Cause:	. . . .
	Indications:	. . . .
	Action:	. . . .
Landing Gear Malfunction	Cause:	. . . .
	Indications:	. . . .
	Action:	. . . .
Door Opening in Flight	Cause:	. . . .
(Note: Noise level may be very high. Do not let	Indications:	. . . .
this distract you from controlling the airplane.)	Action	. . . .
Trim Inoperative	Cause:	. . . .
	Indications	. . . .
	Action:	. . . .
Airframe and Pitot-Static Icing	Cause:	. . . .
	Indications:	. . . .
	Action:	. . . .
Vacuum System Malfunction (and Associated Instruments)	Cause:	. . . .
	Indications:	. . . .
	Action:	. . . .
Loss of Pressurization	Cause:	. . . .
	Indications:	. . . .
	Action:	. . . .
Emergency Descent	Cause::	. . . .
	Indications:	. . . .
	Action:	. . . .
Use of Emergency Exits	Cause:	. . . .
	Indications:	. . . .
	Action:	. . . .
Other Malfunctions	Cause:	. . . .
	Indications:	. . . .
	Action:	. . . .

REVIEW 49

Cross-Country Flight

1. Is it good airmanship to brief passengers on safety and the route to be flown before engine start?
2. Within how many miles of a non-towered airport is it usual to listen to and advise intentions on the CTAF? What does the abbreviation CTAF stand for?
3. What is flying along ground features such as roads or rivers known as?
4. What is maintaining calculated headings for known times, with a periodic check against prominent ground features, known as?
5. For accurate navigation is it very important to fly accurate headings?
6. What are the tolerances expected in cross-country flying, including altitude, heading, airspeed and arrival at your ETA, as revised in position reports?
7. Should available radio navigation aids be used to back up your visual navigation?
8. On what frequency can Flight Service be contacted?
9. The HIWAS is available on many VORs and NDBs. What does HIWAS stand for? Is this detailed on sectional charts?
10. For the benefit of other pilots, it is good airmanship to occasionally report your current weather, bad or good, to flight service stations of which service? What is this called?
11. Weather and other information at some airports is available on an ATIS or which other recorded systems? What does ATIS stand for?
12. Is it good airmanship to plan an efficient descent to arrive overhead the destination airport near to, but at least 500 feet above, the traffic pattern altitude?
13. If bad weather ahead forces you to divert to an alternate airport, should you advise FSS of your change in plans?
14. Is it important for navigational purposes to keep a record of any major heading changes and the time and position where they were made?
15. How many minutes within your ETA should you close your flight plan with FSS? What is the reason for this?
16. At a tower-controlled airport, will the tower automatically close a VFR flight plan after the aircraft has landed safely?
17. When practicing planning for cross-country flight, within a period of how many minutes should you try to complete planning for a cross-country flight?

Answers are given on page 587.

50

Instrument Flight

OBJECTIVES

To describe:

- human sensory limitations with respect to flight without a clearly defined visual horizon;
- techniques from which the pilot can assemble flight path, speed and situational information;
- piloting techniques for flight on instruments; and
- recovery techniques from unusual altitudes and with partial instrument failure.

Figure 50-1 Instrument flight.

CONSIDERATIONS

Instrument flying is, in some ways, easier and is definitely more accurate than visual flight. It is easier because no lookout is required. You must fly with a safety pilot or in controlled airspace with traffic separation. By its very nature instrument flight does not allow adequate visual lookout and it is not expected. Instrument flight is more accurate because the attitude reference is better.

Figure 50-2 Control and performance.

However, you do have to overcome some limitations of the human senses. As an instrument pilot, you must learn to trust what you see on the instruments. We normally use our sight to orient ourselves with our surroundings, supported by other bodily senses that can sense gravity, such as feel, weight and balance. Even with the eyes closed, however, we can usually manage to sit, stand and walk on steady ground without losing control. This becomes much more difficult standing on the tray of an accelerating or turning truck, or even in an accelerating elevator.

In in airplane, which can move and accelerate in three dimensions, singularly or simultaneously, the task becomes almost impossible without having a visual reference. In this case, the eyes work as usual, but the reference they now use is mechanical not natural. You must trust the attitude indicator in terms of its information but, like all mechanicals, it may suffer from unreliability (the pilot nevertheless uses it but treats it suspiciously by cross-checking the other instruments, especially the standby AI or turn coordinator). The starting point in your instrument training will be learning to trust your eyes to derive information from the instruments and to override any other sensations.

You must learn to trust what you see on the instruments.

Fundamental Skills

There are two types of flight instrument:

- the control, or reference, instruments (the gyro and engine instruments, which the pilot uses to set attitude and thrust); and
- the performance instruments (which show the consequences of the pilot's inputs).

The pilot controls the aircraft by setting attitude and thrust. Thus the control instruments are the attitude indicator, the directional gyro or heading indicator, the turn and balance indicator and the thrust or power instruments. The rest of the flight instruments show the result of what has been set. These instruments lag and need to be interpreted.

The pilot can be reactive or proactive (or inactive). The easiest and best way to fly is to be proactive; that is, set an attitude and a thrust value and wait for the instruments to confirm the accuracy of the first settings. In this way, you are always in control. The settings will become very accurate with experience but may need refining when you are first learning. Simply make an adjustment and wait for further confirmation.

The alternative option of seeing the instrument values and then adjusting means that you are reacting to what has already happened when, as a pilot, you should be making things happen. Since the instruments lag, they will cause you to lag behind the airplane. This is called *flying the performance instruments* and is a second-class (second-hand), belated technique. The fundamental processes in instrument flight are:

- airplane control (directing the airplane along the desired flight path at the desired airspeed using the technique of setting a pitch and bank attitude and a thrust value);
- instrument scanning to gather data (for verification and for results of control inputs);
- data processing (understanding and assembling the various data);
- making a further adjustment; and
- confirming the result.

Taking time to hold the attitude constant and making the effort to trim accurately are important aspects of instrument flight.

Cockpit

Instrument flying is much easier if you are comfortable in the cockpit and know your airplane well. Adjust the seat position prior to flight to ensure that you can reach all of the controls easily, and so that you have the correct eye position.

Minimum Safe Altitude

Stay above the minimum safe altitude unless visual.

One thing that your eyes cannot do in clouds or on a dark night is see the ground. You should therefore calculate a minimum safe altitude at all times to ensure that you remain well above any obstructions—normally plan to remain at least 1,000 feet above the highest obstacle within four nautical miles of your planned course (2,000 feet in mountainous areas).

APPLICATION

Attitude Flight

Attitude flight is the technique of selecting a precise attitude, and a nominated power or thrust to achieve the desired flight path. This flight path is reflected by the performance of the airplane in terms of flight path (lateral and vertical) and airspeed. The performance instruments show the results of the selected flight path. Attitude flight is the best way to fly all aircraft, and the only way to fly a high-performance airplane. For a given weight and configuration, a particular attitude combined with a particular power setting will always result in a similar flight path through the air, be it a straight and level flight path, a climb, a descent or a turn. Any change of power or attitude will result in a change of flight path or airspeed.

Power + attitude = performance.

Airplane attitude has two aspects: pitch and bank. That is, the attitude is measured by the nose position against the horizon and the bank angle. Pitch attitude is the angle between the longitudinal axis of the aircraft and the horizontal—*fuselage reference line* (FRL) or *deck angle* are terms that are sometimes used. Bank angle (or bank attitude) is the angle between the lateral axis of the airplane and the horizontal.

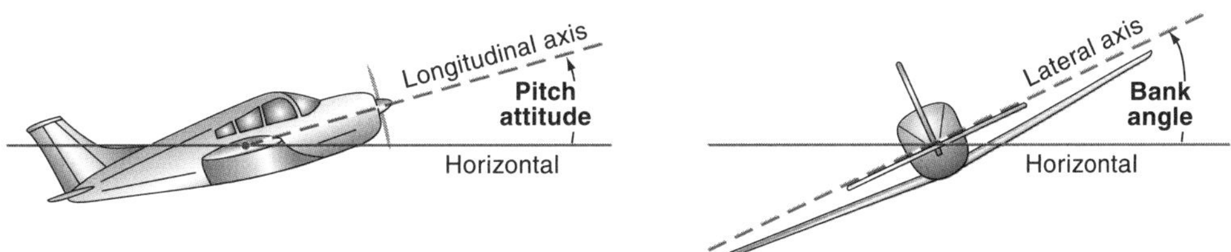

Figure 50-3 Pitch attitude and bank angle.

The pitch attitude is the geometric relationship between the longitudinal axis of the airplane and horizontal. Pitch attitude refers to the airplane's inclination to the horizontal; that is, where it is *pointing* and not to where the airplane is actually *going*. The angle of attack, however, is the angle between the chord line and the relative airflow. The angle of attack, therefore, is closely related to flight path through the air but has nothing to do with the horizon.

Pitch attitude and angle of attack are different, but they are related in the sense that, for the same flight path, if the pitch attitude is raised, then the angle of attack is increased. Conversely, if the pitch attitude is lowered, the angle of attack is decreased.

Pitch attitude is not angle of attack.

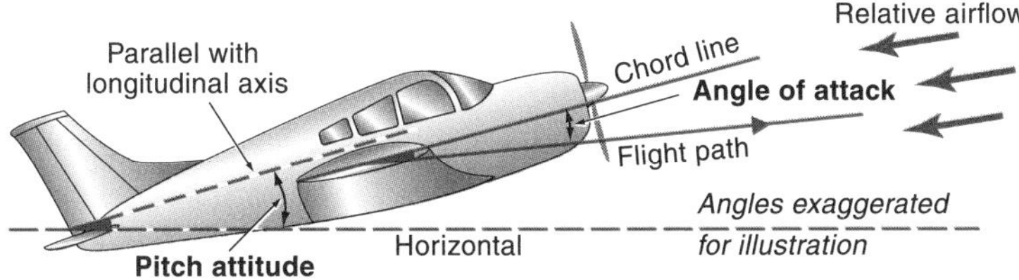

Figure 50-4 Pitch attitude and angle of attack are not the same.

Attitude Flight on Instruments

Attitude flight on instruments is an extension of visual flying, with your attention gradually shifting from external visual cues to the instrument indications in the cockpit, until you are able to fly accurately on instruments alone.

You select pitch attitude using the elevator. In visual conditions, you select the desired pitch attitude by referring the nose position to the external natural horizon. In instrument flight, pitch attitude is selected with reference to the attitude indicator, using the position of the center dot of the aircraft symbol relative to the horizon bar.

Figure 50-5
The primary instrument panel.

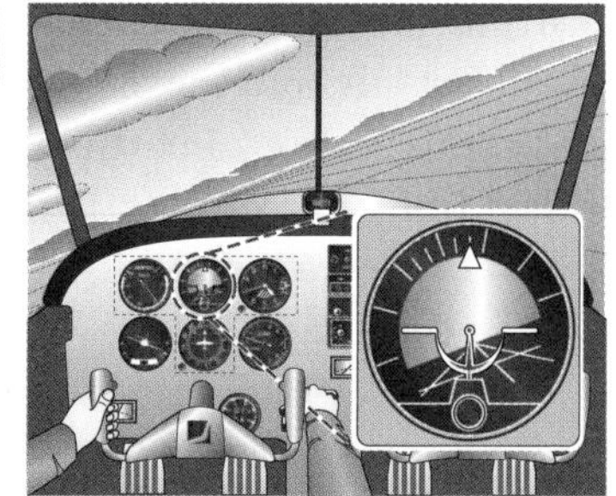

Figure 50-6 Nose-low pitch attitude, and wings-level; nose-high pitch.

You select bank angle using the ailerons. In visual conditions, you refer to the angle made by the external natural horizon in the windshield. On instruments, you select bank angle on the attitude indicator, either by estimating the angle between the wing bars of the miniature airplane and the horizon bar, or from the position of the bank pointer on a graduated scale at the top of the attitude indicator.

Most of your attention during flight, both visual and on instruments, is concerned with achieving and holding a suitable attitude. A very important skill to develop when flying on instruments, therefore, is to check the attitude indicator every few seconds. There are other tasks, of course, to be performed, and there are other instruments to look at as well, but the eyes should always return regularly and frequently to the AI, the focal point of the radial scan. To achieve the desired performance (in terms of flight path and airspeed), you must not only place the airplane in a suitable attitude with the flight controls, you must also apply suitable power with the throttle. Just because the airplane has a high pitch attitude does not mean that it will climb: it requires climb power as well as climb attitude to do this. With less power, it may not climb at all.

Attitude flying is the name given to the technique of controlling the airplane's flight path and airspeed by setting a precise attitude and power. The technique used in attitude flying is the same visually or on instruments and applies day or night. It is *the* way to fly.

Sensory Illusions

Sensory illusions can confuse you.

Most of the time, people live in a +1g situation, with their feet on the ground. (+1g is the force of gravity.) Usually there is little or no lateral or longitudinal acceleration. However, some variations do occur in everyday life such as when driving a car or traveling in a lift. Accelerating a car, hard braking, or turning on a flat bend will all produce lateral or longitudinal g-forces on the body different to the vertical pull of gravity alone. Passengers, with their eyes closed, could perhaps detect this by bodily feel or by their sense of balance.

A right turn on a flat road, for instance, could be sensed as a feeling of being thrown to the left, but it is impossible to detect a turn if the curve was perfectly banked for the particular speed. A straight road sloping to the left (and causing the passenger to lean to the left) might give the passenger the false impression that the car is turning right, even though it is in fact not turning at all. The position-sensing systems of the body, using nerves all over the body to transmit messages of feel (touch) and pressure to the brain, can be fooled in this and other ways.

The organs within the inner ear used for balance and to detect accelerations can also be deceived. For instance, if you are sitting in a car traveling around a suitably banked curve, the sensing system in your ears falsely interprets the g-force, holding you firmly and comfortably in the seat, as a vertical force, as if you were moving straight ahead rather than in a banked turn. These organs have other limitations, one being that a constant velocity is not detected, neither is a very gradual change in velocity. If you are sitting in a train, for instance, and there is another train moving slowly relative to you on an adjacent track, it is sometimes difficult to determine which train is moving, or if indeed both are moving.

False impressions of motion can also be caused by unusual g-forces caused by, for instance, rapid head motion, or lowering the head as the aircraft rolls into a turn. If you happen to drop your pencil while instrument flying, don't just lower your eyes and lean down to look for it in one motion. Take it very carefully step by step to avoid any feelings of vertigo, and keep the attitude constant while you do so.

Because an airplane moves in three dimensions, it is possible to accelerate and decelerate in three dimensions, and this can lead to more complicated illusions. Pulling up into a steep climb, for instance, holds a pilot tightly in his seat, which is exactly the same feeling as in a steep turn. With your eyes closed, it is sometimes difficult to say which maneuver it is.

Another example is decelerating, which may give a false impression of pitching down. Be aware that your sense of balance and bodily feel can lead you astray in an airplane, especially with rapidly changing g-forces in maneuvers such as this. The one sense that can resolve all of these illusions is sight. If the car passenger could see out, or if the pilot had reference to the natural horizon and landmarks, then the confusion would be easily dispelled.

Unfortunately, in instrument flight you do not have reference to ground features, but you can still use your sense of sight to scan the instruments, and obtain substitute information from your surrogate horizon. Therefore, an important instruction to the budding instrument pilot is to believe your eyes and what the instruments tell you.

While sight is the most important sense, and must be protected at all costs, also make sure that you avoid anything that will affect your balance or position-sensing systems.

Avoid alcohol, drugs (including smoking in the cockpit) and medication. Do not fly when ill or suffering from an upper respiratory infection (e.g. a head cold or flu). Do not fly when tired or fatigued, stressed or dehydrated. Do not fly with a cabin altitude higher than 10,000 feet MSL without supplemental oxygen. Avoid sudden head movements and avoid lowering your head or turning around in the cockpit.

Despite all these don'ts, there is one very important do: trust what your eyes tell you from the instruments—if the instruments disagree, believe the majority.

Scanning the Instruments

Scanning the instruments with your eyes, interpreting their indications, and applying this information is a vital skill to develop if you are to become a competent and confident instrument pilot.

Power is selected with the throttle, and can be checked on the engine instruments. Pitch attitude and bank angle are selected using the control column, with reference to the attitude indicator. With both correct power and attitude set, the airplane will perform as expected. The more accurate the settings the more accurate the response. The attitude indicator and the power indicator, because they are used when controlling the airplane, are known as the *control* or *reference* instruments.

Figure 50-7 Instrument scan.

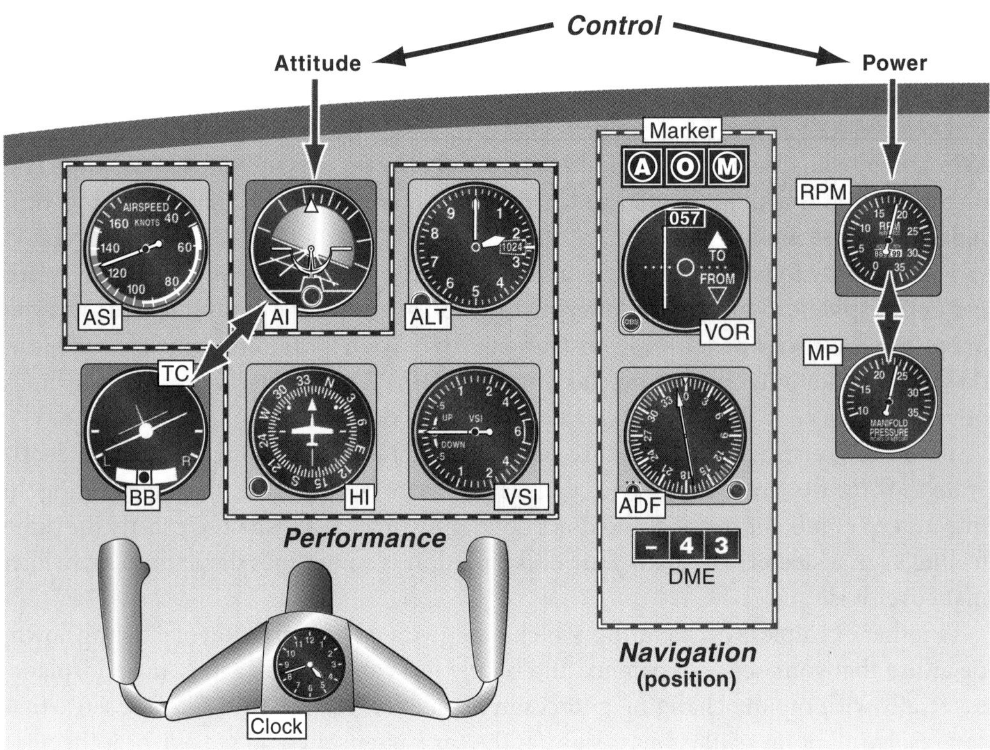

Figure 50-8 Layout of a typical instrument panel.

Once the power and attitude have been set, the resulting performance (flight path and speed) of the airplane, sometimes called the *velocity vector*, can be confirmed and adjusted by reference to the *performance* instruments—the altimeter for altitude and altitude trends, the airspeed indicator for airspeed and airspeed trends, the VSI for rate of climb and descent, and so on.

Scanning is an art that will develop naturally during your training, especially when you know what to look for. The primary scan is that of the six basic flight instruments, concentrating on the AI and radiating out to the others as required. This is called *selective radial scan*. The cycle is to set an attitude and power, cross-check the immediate response of the other instruments to confirm the AI is correct and then, as they settle, to check the stable response and, if necessary, to make an adjustment. Having scanned the instruments, interpreted the message they contain, built up a picture of where the airplane is and where it is going, you can control it very precisely yet very easily.

Controlling the Airplane

During instrument flight, the airplane is flown using the normal controls according to the picture displayed on the instrument panel. From this picture, you will, with practice, know what control movements (elevator, aileron, rudder and throttle) are required to either maintain the picture as it is, or change it. In most flight conditions, the power is set at a predetermined value and it is only the attitude that the pilot varies. This adjustment may be to achieve a certain airspeed, vertical path, rate or direction.

When maneuvering the airplane, a suitable control sequence to follow (the same as in visual flight) is:

- Visualize the desired new flight path and airspeed.
- Set the attitude and the power to achieve the desired flight path and airspeed.
- Hold the attitude on the AI, allowing the airplane to settle down into its new performance, and allowing the lagging pressure instruments to stabilize.
- Make small adjustments to attitude and power until the actual performance equals the desired performance.
- Trim (which is essential, if you are to achieve accurate and comfortable instrument flight). Heavy loads can be trimmed off earlier in the sequence to assist in control, if desired, but remember that the function of trim is to relieve control on the pilot, and not to change aircraft attitude.

Change

Check, Hold, Adjust, Trim

Figure 50-9 Control input—correction sequence.

Some helpful hints follow:

- Derive the required information from the relevant instrument; for example, derive heading from the heading indicator, altitude from the altimeter, etc.
- Respond to deviations from the desired flight path and airspeed. Use the AI as a control instrument, with power as required. For instance, if you are 50 feet low on altitude, then raise the pitch attitude on the AI slightly and climb back up to altitude.

Do not accept steady deviations: it is just as easy to fly at 3,000 feet as it is to fly at 2,950 feet. Instrument flight is in the mind. It is a test of self-discipline as much as flying ability. Be as accurate as you can and then you will become more accurate, more consistently and more easily. If you don't strive, you won't achieve. The instruments are like the score in a computer game. They show the results of your effort and skill.

- Do not over control. Avoid large, fast or jerky control movements, which will probably result in continuous corrections, overcorrections and then recorrections. This can occur if attitude is changed without reference to the AI, or it might be caused by the airplane being out-of-trim, or possibly by a pilot who is fatigued or tense.
- Do not be distracted from a scan of the flight instruments for more than a few seconds at a time, even though other duties must be attended to, such as checklists, radio calls and navigation tasks. Rather, integrate these tasks into an expanded scan of information.
- Be relaxed. Easier said than done at the beginning, but it will come with experience.

Figure 50-10 Stabilized flight.

Developing a Scan Pattern

The performance of an airplane is, as always, determined by the power set and the attitude selected. In visual flying conditions, the external natural horizon is used as a reference when selecting pitch attitude and bank angle. The power indicator in the cockpit is only referred to occasionally such as when setting a particular power for cruise or for climb.

In instrument conditions, when the natural horizon cannot be seen, pitch attitude and bank angle information is still available to the pilot in the cockpit from the attitude indicator.

Relatively large pitch attitude changes against the natural horizon are reproduced in miniature on the attitude indicator. In straight and level flight, for instance, the wings of the miniature airplane should appear against the horizon line, while in a climb they should appear one or two bar widths above it. In a turn, the wing bars of the miniature airplane will bank along with the real airplane, while the artificial horizon line remains in line with real horizon. The center dot of the miniature airplane represents the airplane's nose position relative to the horizon.

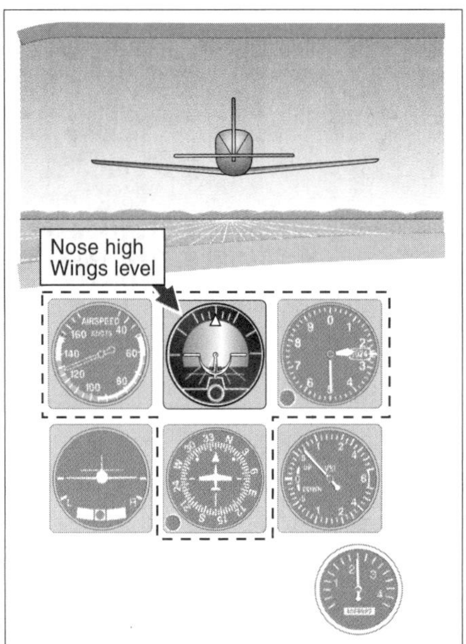

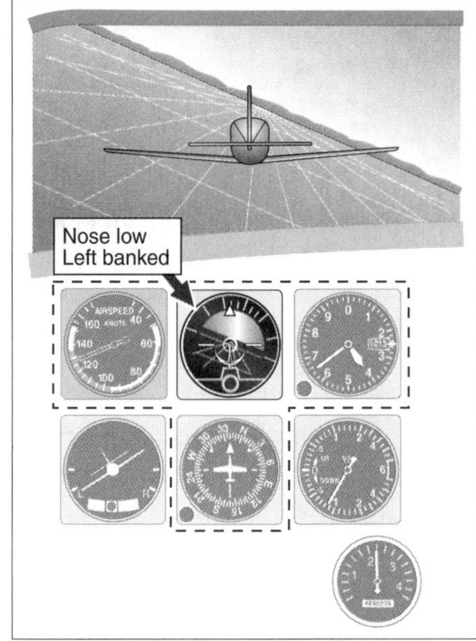

Figure 50-11 The AI is the master instrument for pitch attitude and bank angle.

Simple Scans

Balance (Coordination)

The AI, while it shows pitch attitude and bank angle directly, does not indicate balance (coordination) or yaw. Balance information can be obtained simply by moving the eyes from the attitude indicator diagonally down to the left to check that the balance ball in the turn coordinator is indeed being centered with rudder pressure. The eyes should then return to the AI.

Heading

Directional information can be obtained from the heading indicator (HI) or from the magnetic compass. From the AI, the eyes can be moved straight down to the HI to absorb heading information, before returning to the AI. Each eye movement to obtain particular information is very simple, starting at the attitude indicator and radiating out to the relevant instrument, before returning again to the AI.

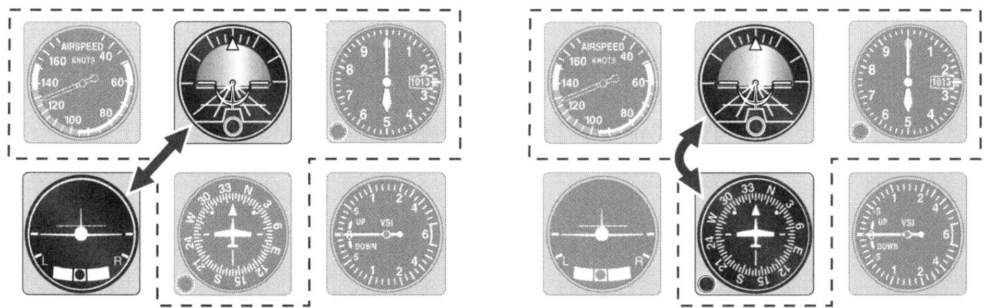

Figure 50-12 A simple scan for balance (coordination) (left) and a simple scan for heading (right).

Airspeed

Airspeed information is also very important, and this is easily checked by moving the eyes left from the AI to the airspeed indicator (ASI), before returning them to the AI.

Altitude

The altimeter is the only means of determining the precise height of the airplane, in visual as well as in instrument conditions. To obtain height information, the eyes can move from the AI to the right where the altimeter is located, before moving back to the AI.

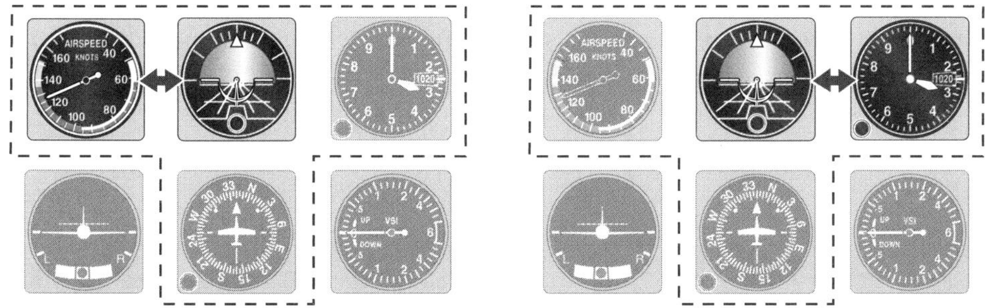

Figure 50-13 A simple scan for airspeed (left) and a simple scan for level flight path (attitude) (right).

Vertical Speed

The rate of change of altitude, as either a rate of climb or a rate of descent in feet per minute, can be monitored on the vertical speed indicator (VSI) by moving the eyes from the AI diagonally down to the right to the VSI, before returning them to the AI. The VSI, since it is often used in conjunction with the altimeter, is located directly beneath it on most instrument panels.

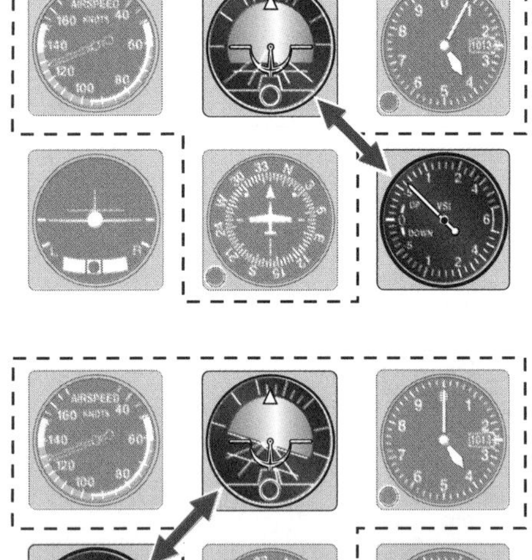

Figure 50-14 A simple scan for vertical speed information (top) and a simple scan for turn rate (bottom).

Turning

A turn is entered using the AI to establish bank angle and the ball to confirm balance. Additional information on the turning rate is available from the turn coordinator once the bank angle is established. The normal rate of turn in instrument flying is 3° per second, known as *rate one* or *standard rate*, and this is clearly marked on the turn coordinator.

With these six basic flight instruments, plus the power indicator, it is possible to fly the airplane very accurately and comfortably without any external visual reference, provided the instruments are scanned efficiently, and the pilot controls the airplane adequately in response to the information that is derived from them.

Control and Performance

Control the airplane to achieve the desired performance. The attitude selected on the attitude indicator and the power set on the power indicator determine the performance (flight path and speed) of the airplane. Hence these two instruments are known as the *control* instruments.

The attitude indicator is located centrally on the instrument panel directly in front of the pilot, so that any changes in attitude can be readily seen. Because continual reference to the power indicator is not required, it is situated slightly away from the main group of flight instruments, easy to scan occasionally, but not in the main field of view.

The other flight instruments are performance instruments that display how the airplane is performing (as a result of the power and attitude selected) in terms of:

- altitude or vertical performance on the altimeter and VSI;
- heading or turning performance on the HI, compass and turn coordinator; and
- airspeed on the ASI.

They each have a delayed response, so they indicate what *has* happened. Their *trend* gives an indication of what is happening.

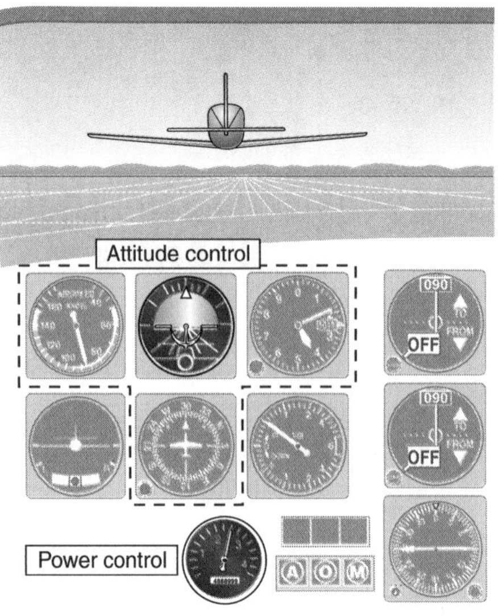

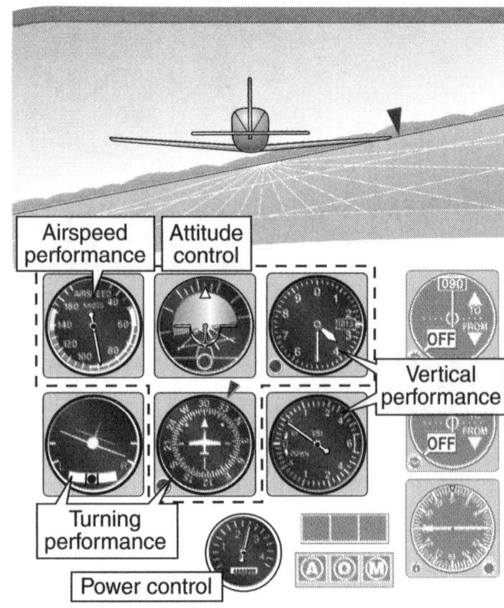

Figure 50-15 Use the control instruments to select attitude and power (left). The performance instruments show the result (right).

Figure 50-16 The vertical path reference instruments (left) and the bank/turn reference instruments (right).

Changes in pitch attitude are shown directly on the AI, and are reflected on the altimeter, VSI and ASI. Changes in bank angle are shown directly on the AI, and are reflected on the turn coordinator and the HI. The quality of flight is shown by the balance ball.

Selective Radial Scan

Of the six main flight instruments, the attitude indicator is the master instrument. It gives you a direct and immediate picture of pitch attitude and bank angle. It will be the one most frequently referred to (at least once every few seconds in most stages of flight). The eyes can be directed selectively toward the other instruments to derive relevant information from them as required, before returning to the AI. This eye movement radiating out and back to selected instruments is commonly known as the selective radial scan.

For instance, when climbing with full power selected, the estimated climb pitch attitude is held on the attitude indicator, with subsequent reference to the airspeed indicator to confirm that the selected pitch attitude is indeed correct. If the ASI indicates an airspeed that is too low, then lower the pitch attitude on the AI (say by a half bar width or by one bar width), allow a few seconds for the airspeed to settle, and then check the ASI again.

The key instrument in confirming that the correct attitude has been selected on the AI during the climb is the airspeed indicator. Because it determines what pitch attitude changes should be made on the AI during the climb, the airspeed indicator is the primary performance guide for pitch attitude in the climb. It is supported by the AI and the VSI.

Approaching the desired cruise level, however, more attention should be paid to the altimeter to ensure that, as pitch attitude is lowered on the AI, the airplane levels off at

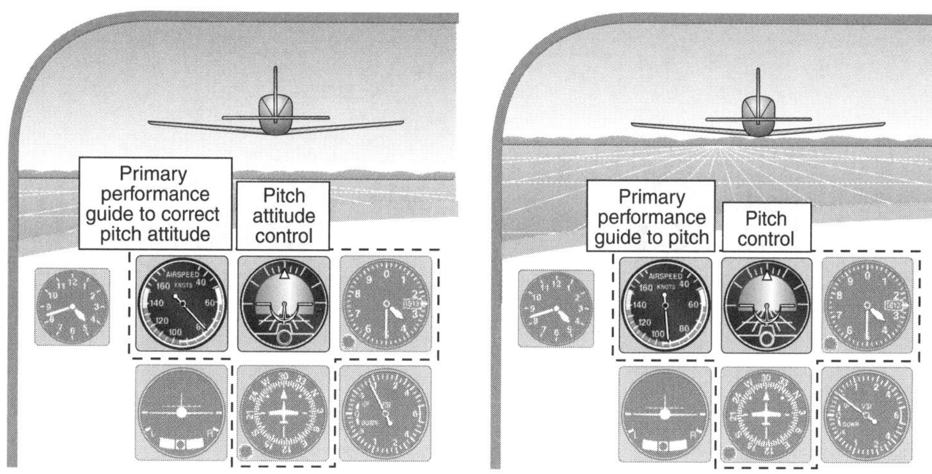

Figure 50-17 ASI is the primary instrument in the climb to confirm or to correct the pitch attitude.

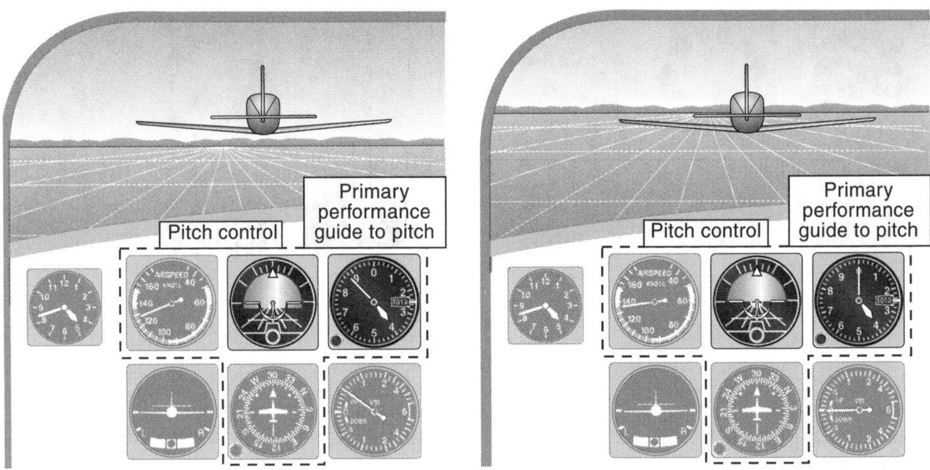

Figure 50-18 The altimeter is the primary instrument in the cruise to confirm or to correct the pitch attitude.

the desired altitude. When cruising, any minor deviations from altitude detected on the altimeter can be corrected with small changes in pitch attitude. Because the altimeter is now the instrument that determines if pitch attitude changes on the AI are required to maintain level flight, the altimeter is the primary performance guide for pitch attitude in the cruise. It is supported by the AI and the VSI.

If climb power is still set after the airplane has been leveled off at cruise altitude, then the airplane will accelerate, shown by an increasing airspeed on the ASI. At the desired speed, the power should be reduced to a suitable value.

While it is usual simply to set cruise power and then accept the resulting airspeed, it is possible to achieve a precise airspeed by adjusting the power. Because the ASI indications will then determine what power changes should be made during level flight, the airspeed indicator is the primary performance guide to power requirements in the cruise.

Heading is maintained with reference to the heading indicator (HI), any deviations being corrected with gentle balanced (coordinated) turns. Because the indications on the HI will determine what minor corrections to bank angle should be made on the attitude indicator during straight flight, the heading indicator is the primary performance guide

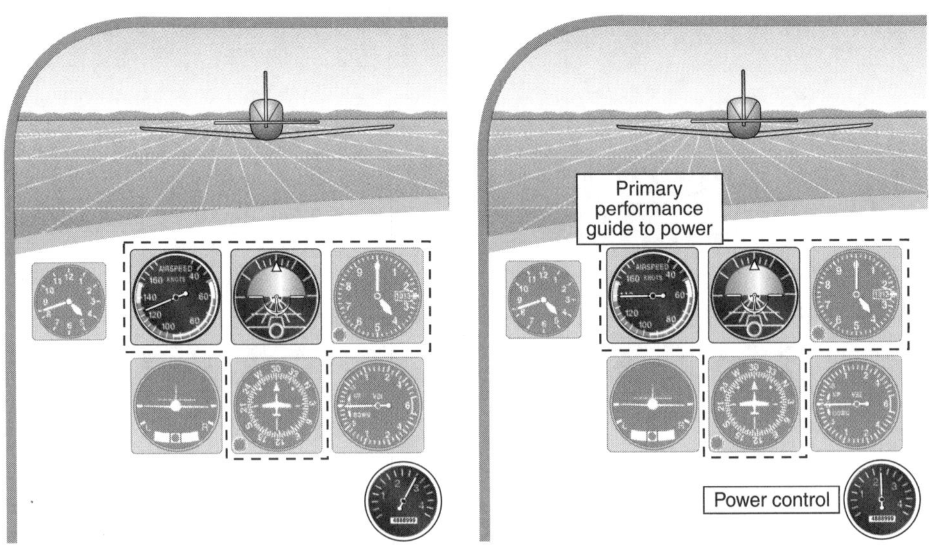

Figure 50-19 The ASI is the primary instrument in the cruise to confirm or to correct the power.

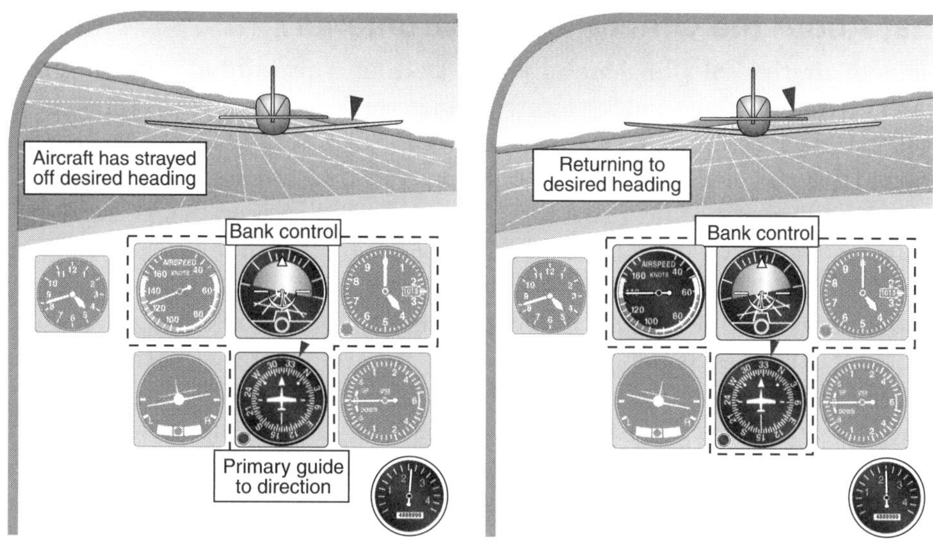

Figure 50-20 The HI is the primary instrument in straight flight to confirm or correct bank.

to zero bank angle in maintaining a constant heading for straight flight. It is supported by the turn coordinator and the AI. The ball should be centered to keep the airplane in balance, avoiding any slip or skid and providing coordinated, straight flight.

Basic-T Scan

A basic scan suitable for straight and level flight (where altitude, direction and airspeed need to be monitored) is centered on the AI, and radiates out and back, following the basic-T pattern on the panel, to the relevant performance instrument:

- the HI to confirm heading (and correct with shallow turns on the AI);
- the altimeter to confirm altitude (and correct with pitch changes on the AI); and
- the ASI to confirm airspeed (and, if desired, correct with power changes).

If cruise power is set and left alone, with the resulting airspeed being accepted (often the case in a normal cruise), then scanning the ASI need not be as frequent, and the scan can concentrate on the AI, HI, and altimeter.

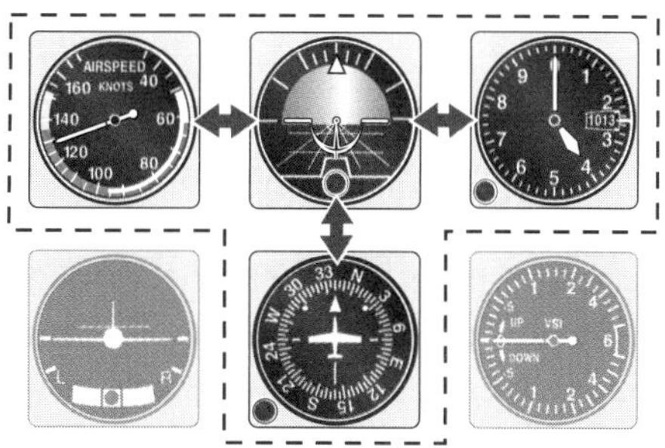

Figure 50-21
The basic-T scan in cruise flight.

Additionally, once established and well trimmed on the cruise, the airplane will tend to maintain height because of its longitudinal stability, making it less essential to scan the altimeter continually compared to when the airplane is out of trim. The airplane may not be as stable laterally as it is longitudinally, however, and so the HI should be scanned quite frequently to ensure that heading is maintained. Non-IMC-rated pilots are already well-practiced at scanning the altimeter regularly, since it is the only means of accurately maintaining altitude, but they may not be used to scanning the HI quite so frequently as is necessary in instrument conditions. This skill must be developed.

What About the Other Flight Instruments?

In smooth air, the VSI will show a trend away from cruise altitude often before it is apparent on the altimeter, and can be used to indicate that a minor pitch attitude correction is required if altitude is to be maintained. The VSI provides supporting pitch information to that provided by the altimeter, although it is of less value in turbulence which causes the VSI needle to fluctuate. If the wings are held level on the AI, and heading is being maintained on the HI, then it is almost certain that the airplane is in balance (coordinated), with ball centered. Normally, the balance ball does not have to be scanned as frequently as some of the other instruments, but it should be referred to occasionally, especially if heading is changing while the wings are level, or if the *seat of your pants* tells you that the airplane is skidding or slipping.

The turn coordinator will show a wings-level indication during straight flight, and provides supporting information regarding bank. In a standard-rate turn, the turn coordinator is the primary performance guide to confirm that the bank angle is correct.

Scan Technique

Keep the eyes moving and continually return to the AI.

Starting with your eyes focused on the AI, scan the performance instruments that provide the information required. Relevant information can be obtained from different instruments, depending on the maneuver. Primary pitch information (to confirm whether or not the pitch attitude selected on the AI is correct) is obtained from the altimeter during cruise flight, but from the ASI during climbs and descents.

There is no need to memorize particular scan patterns, since they will develop naturally as your training progresses. Do not allow the radial scan to break down. Avoid fixation on any one instrument because the resulting breakdown in the radial scan will cause delayed recognition of deviations from the desired flight path and airspeed.

Fixation on the HI, for instance, can lead to heading being maintained perfectly, but in the meantime altitude and airspeed may change, tendencies which would have been detected (and corrected for) if the altimeter, VSI and ASI had been correctly scanned. Keep the eyes moving, and continually return to the AI. Occasionally, the eyes will have to be directed away from the main flight instruments for a short period, such as when checking the power indicator during or following a power change, or when periodically checking the oil temperature and pressure gauges, fuel gauges, the ammeter, or the suction (vacuum) gauge, or when realigning the heading indicator with the magnetic compass. Do not neglect the radial scan for more than a few seconds at a time, even though other necessary tasks have to be performed.

Avoid omitting any relevant instrument. For instance, after rolling out of a turn, check the HI to ensure that the desired heading is being achieved and maintained. The wings might be level and the airplane flying straight, but you may be on the wrong heading.

Use all available resources. For instance, with correct power set and the correct attitude selected on the AI, it is possible to maintain height, at least approximately, using only the AI and the power indicator but, if precision is required, then the altimeter must be included in the scan as the primary reference for altitude. Furthermore, do not forget that supporting instruments can provide additional information to back up primary instruments. For instance, altitude is indicated directly on the altimeter, but any tendency to depart from that height may first be indicated on the VSI (especially in smooth air), which makes it a very valuable supporting instrument to the altimeter.

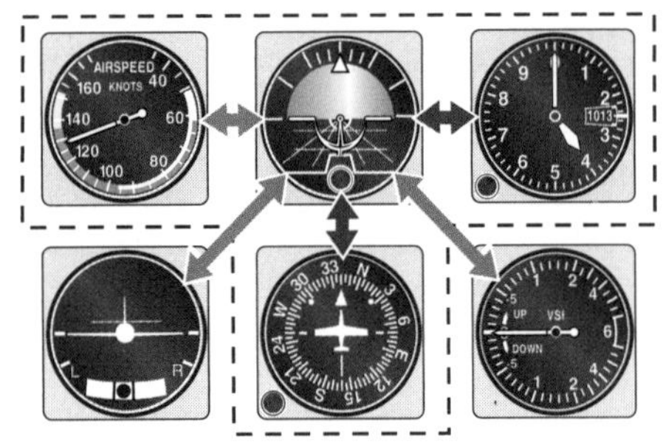

Figure 50-22 A suitable scan during straight and level flight.

Other Scans

Circular Scan

It is necessary on some occasions to have a fast scan, such as on final approach of an instrument approach. On other occasions, however, the scan can be more relaxed; for instance, when cruising with the autopilot engaged, it may be suitable just to have a fairly relaxed circular scan.

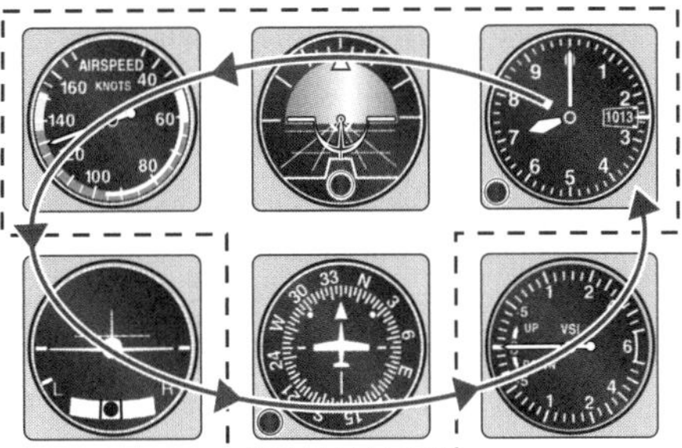

Figure 50-23 A circular scan.

Vertical Scan

If you are performing other tasks while flying a constant heading, such as map reading, then a very simple scan to make sure things do not get out of hand is a vertical scan from the AI down to the HI and back again.

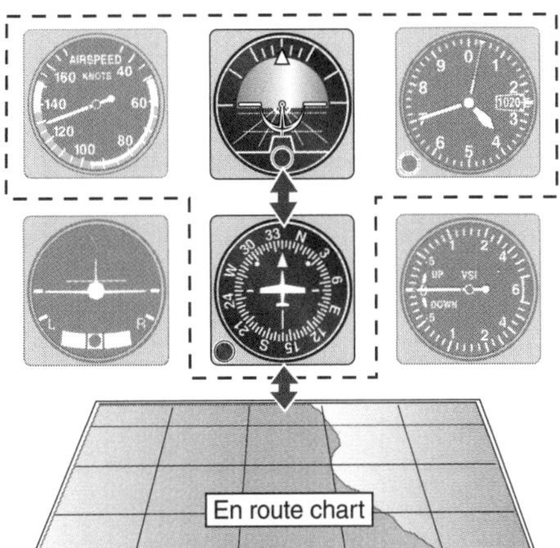

Figure 50-24 The vertical scan.

Inverted-V Scan

If at any time, you suspect an instrument failure, then a very efficient means of establishing what instrument or system has failed is to commence an inverted-V scan, centered on the AI and radiating to the turn coordinator and the VSI. Each of these instruments normally has a different power source—the vacuum system for the AI, the electrical system for the turn coordinator, and the static system for the VSI—so a false indication on one should not be reflected on the others. Confirmation of attitude and flight path can then be achieved using the other instruments. With practice, you will develop scans to suit every situation.

Figure 50-25 The inverted-V scan.

AIRMANSHIP

Never proceed into instrument conditions without a flight instructor unless you are properly qualified (with a valid instrument rating) in a suitably equipped airplane, and within the limitations of your ability and licence rating privileges. Always calculate a minimum safe altitude before entering instrument conditions. Keep in practice. Use smooth and coordinated control movements. Use PC-based simulators to improve scan and orientation.

Type Performance Table

To help you adjust to a new airplane type, we have included a type performance table (shown below). You will be able to fill this table in as you become familiar with the power settings and attitudes required to achieve the required performance in the various phases of flight.

Attitude can be shown on the AI by inserting a horizon line. The table allows for aircraft with retractable landing gear—if yours has a fixed landing gear, then just pencil the wheels in on the chart, and only fill in the powers and attitudes that you need.

Aircraft Type............................. Performance Table

	Configuration Flaps Gear	Power MP RPM	Attitude	Performance Airspeed/VSI	V-speeds
Takeoff	..............° Down				Obstacle-clearance speed = ...knots
	..............° Up				
Climb	0° Up				V_{S1} = ... (stall speed, clean) V_X = ... (best angle) V_Y = ... (never exceed)
Cruise					V_A = ... (man'g speed) V_{NO} = ... (normal max) V_{NE} = ... (never exceed)
Cruise Descent (500ft/min)					
Slow speed cruise **1. Clean**					
2. Flaps and landing gear extended	..............° Down				V_{FE} = ... (flaps extended)
Approach. Flaps and landing gear extended	..............° Down				V_{LO} = ... (landing gear extended) V_{SO} = ... (landing flaps & gear extended)

REVIEW 50

Instrument Flight

Figure 50-26 Instrument approach.

1. An instrument pilot must learn to doubt what your eyes see on the instruments. True or false?
2. What are the three fundamental skills in instrument flying?
3. What is looking at the instruments in a systematic manner to extract the information you need known as?
4. What are two control instruments?
5. What are the performance instruments for altitude?
6. What are the performance instruments for direction?
7. What is the performance instrument for airspeed?
8. When flying on instruments do you need to know approximately how far you are above the ground and any nearby obstructions?
9. How many feet above the highest obstacle is a suitable minimum safe altitude when flying using instruments? Within how many nautical miles of the highest obstacle does this minimum safe altitude apply? In designated mountainous terrain, how many feet above the highest obstacle is the minimum safe altitude raised to?
10. What is the required accuracy when flying on instruments?
11. What is the primary guide to balance—that is, no slip or skid—in all flying?
12. During a climb, you can check that the climb attitude set on the attitude indicator is correct by checking which instrument?
13. During a descent, you can check that the descent attitude set on the attitude indicator is correct by checking which instrument?
14. During straight and level flight, you can check that the attitude set on the attitude indicator is correct by checking which instrument?
15. During a standard-rate turn, you can check that the bank attitude set on the attitude indicator is correct by checking which instrument?
16. Which side rudder will you have to apply to keep the balance ball centered when applying full power in a conventional training airplane? When reducing power in a conventional training airplane, which side rudder will you have to apply to keep the balance ball centered?
17. Which way does the nose tend to pitch when power is added?
18. What are two potentially hazardous flight attitudes?
19. When practicing recoveries from unusual flight attitudes on instruments, what bank angle and what degree of pitch up or down should you not exceed?

Answers are given on page 587.

TASK

Straight and Level on Instruments

Aim: To maintain a steady cruise, straight and level, by sole reference to the flight instruments.

1. Establishing Straight and Level Flight

Select power for level flight.

Set pitch attitude for level flight by positioning the miniature airplane against the horizon line of the attitude indicator.

Hold the attitude and allow airplane to stabilize.

Monitor: AI-ALT-AI-HI-AI-ASI-AI-VSI-AI-TC-AI-ALT, etc.

Trim the airplane carefully so that it will fly "hands-off."

2. Raising the Nose at Constant Power

Place the miniature airplane a little above the horizon line on the AI (say one-half or one bar width) and hold.

The ASI will show a gradual decrease and finally settle on a lower indicated airspeed (IAS).

The altimeter, after some lag, will start showing an increase in altitude.

The VSI, after some initial fluctuations, will settle on a steady rate of climb.

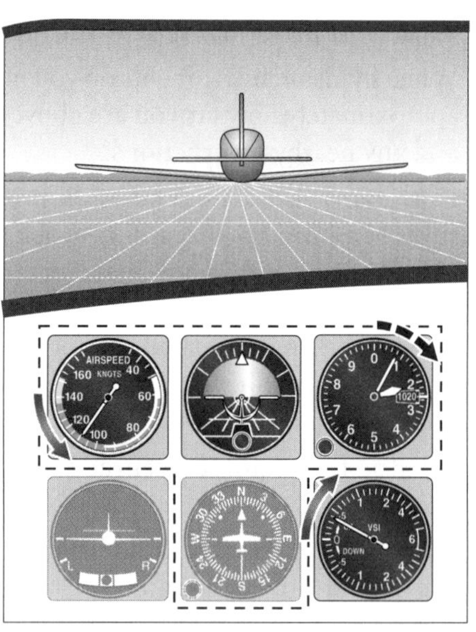

3. *Lowering the Nose at Constant Power*

Place the miniature airplane a little below the horizon line on the AI and hold this attitude.

The ASI will show a gradual increase and finally stabilize at a higher IAS. Note that a relatively large airspeed change will occur after a small change in attitude.

The altimeter, after some lag, will start showing a gradual decrease in altitude.

The VSI will eventually stabilize on a steady rate of descent.

4. *Maintaining Straight and Level at Constant Power*

Required accuracy: ***• airspeed ±10 knots*** ***• heading ±10°*** ***• altitude ±100 ft***

Correct variations in:

Altitude by making very small changes in the position of the miniature airplane relative to the horizon line on AI. Within ±100 ft is acceptable.*

Heading by using small bank angles and checking that the airplane is coordinated. Within ±10° is acceptable.*

Airspeed by adjustments in power, followed by, as a consequence, a small change in attitude. Within ±10 knots is acceptable.*

Keep in trim.

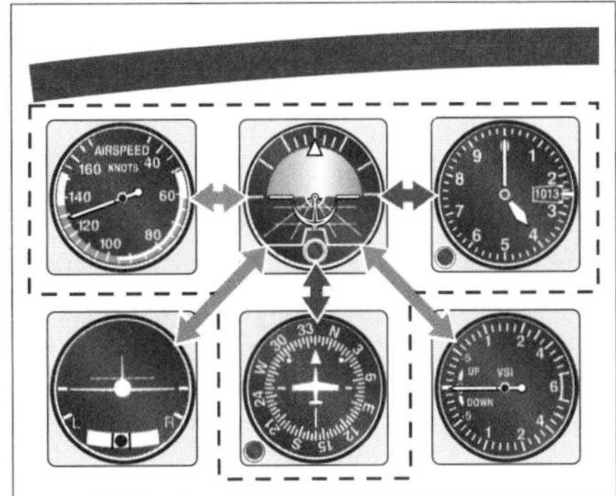

**Aim to have airspeed, altitude and heading precisely on the desired numbers. If they are not or if they are tending to deviate, take corrective action immediately.*

5. Changing Airspeed, Straight and Level

(a) To increase airspeed at a constant altitude:

Add power with the throttle (coordinate with rudder and forward pressure on the control column).

Gradually lower the pitch attitude to avoid climbing (monitor VSI and altimeter), and allow the airspeed to increase to the desired value.

Adjust power to maintain desired airspeed, and hold the attitude constant.

Trim.

(b) To decrease airspeed at a constant altitude:

Reduce power with the throttle (coordinate with rudder and hold nose up with elevator back pressure).

Gradually raise the pitch attitude to avoid descending and allow the airspeed to reduce to the desired value.

As the desired airspeed is approached, adjust power to maintain it, and hold the pitch attitude constant.

Trim.

Different pitch attitudes for different speeds

Normal cruise

High-speed flight

Slow flight

TASK

Climbing and Descending on Instruments

Aim: To climb, cruise and descend, and to change from one to another, with reference only to the flight instruments.

1. Climb, Cruise and Descent at a Constant Airspeed

Climb, cruise and descent speeds are usually different. However, by using a constant airspeed in these initial maneuvers, we simplify the task by removing one of the variables.

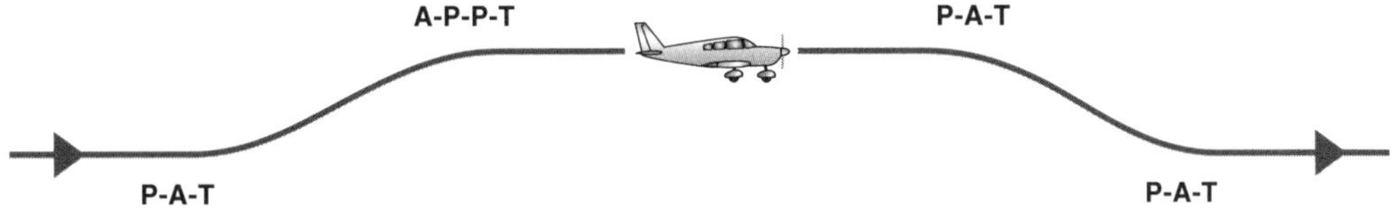

(a) From straight and level, enter a climb at a constant airspeed:

Settle into straight and level cruise flight and note airspeed.

Smoothly open throttle to full power (coordinate with rudder).

Simultaneously raise the nose slightly to maintain airspeed, and hold the pitch attitude.

Note the VSI shows a rate of climb and altimeter a gain in altitude.

Adjust the attitude to maintain airspeed.

Trim.

(b) From a climb, level off and maintain a constant airspeed:

Lower the nose to maintain a constant airspeed.

Reduce to the normal cruise power setting (as before), coordinate with rudder.

Note the VSI returns to zero and the altimeter a constant altitude.

Trim.

(c) From straight and level, commence a descent:

Reduce power (by 600 RPM or so), coordinate with rudder.

Lower the nose to maintain a constant airspeed.

Note the VSI shows a rate of descent and the altimeter shows a decreasing altitude.

Trim.

(d) From a descent, enter a climb:

Smoothly open the throttle to full power (coordinate with rudder) and simultaneously allow nose to rise to the climb attitude.

Hold the attitude to maintain the desired airspeed.

Note the VSI shows a rate of climb and the altimeter a changing altitude.

Trim.

Required accuracy:
• airspeed ±10 knots • heading ±10° • level off at desired altitude ±100 ft

2. ***Initiating a Climb at Normal Climb Speed***

Usually the normal climb speed is less than the cruise speed. As in normal visual flight, a climb is initiated in the sequence P-A-T: Power–Attitude–Trim.

Procedure:

Settle in straight and level flight and note the airspeed.

Increase power to the climb figure (coordinate with rudder).

Raise the nose to the climb attitude.

Hold the new attitude as airspeed decreases to the desired climbing speed. The VSI will show a rate of climb and the altimeter an increase in altitude.

Make minor pitch attitude adjustments to achieve and maintain the correct climb airspeed.

Trim.

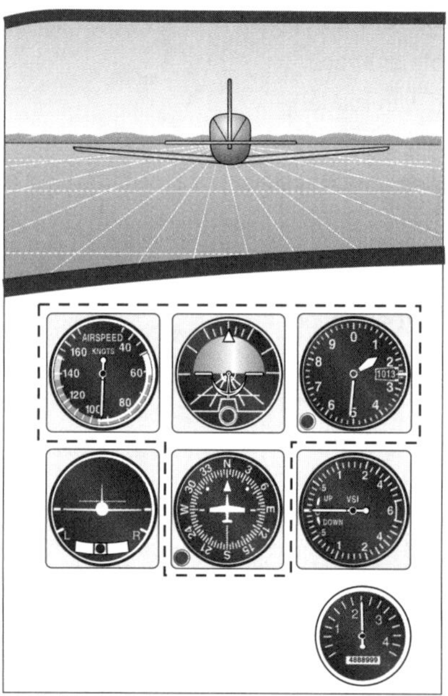

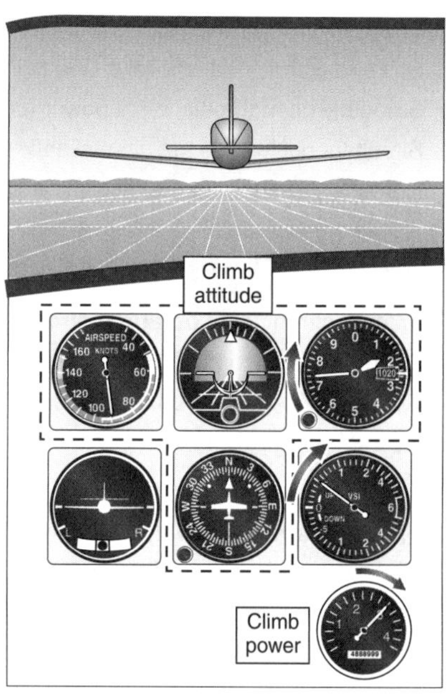

Required accuracy:* • *airspeed ±10 knots* • *heading ±10°

Note: If desired, you can trim earlier in the sequence, while holding the new attitude as airspeed decreases, to off-load some control-column pressure. However, a final trim adjustment will need to be made. Do not use trim to change the attitude; pitch attitude must only be changed with elevator. The trim is used solely to relieve sustained control pressures.

A steady climb is maintained with reference to all flight instruments, with the ASI confirming that you are indeed holding the correct attitude for climbing, as set on the AI.

3. *Leveling Off from a Climb*

As in normal visual flight, leveling off from a climb follows the A-P-T sequence: Attitude–Power–Trim. Since the cruise speed is normally greater than the climb speed, the airplane is allowed to accelerate before the power is reduced from climb to cruise power.

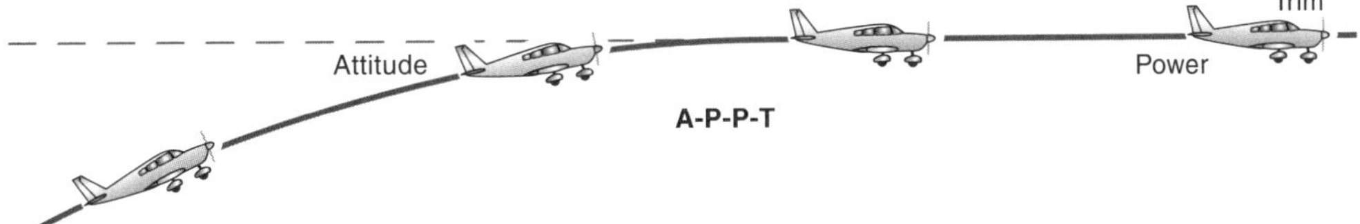

To level off at the desired altitude:

Smoothly lower the nose to the low speed cruise position slightly before the desired altitude is reached—a suitable amount of lead being approximately 10% of the rate of climb. (For example, at 500 ft/min rate of climb, begin lowering the nose 50 ft prior to reaching the desired altitude).

Allow the airspeed to increase toward the cruise figure.

Reduce power to cruise RPM as the cruise speed is reached.

Make minor adjustments to maintain altitude, heading and airspeed.

Trim.

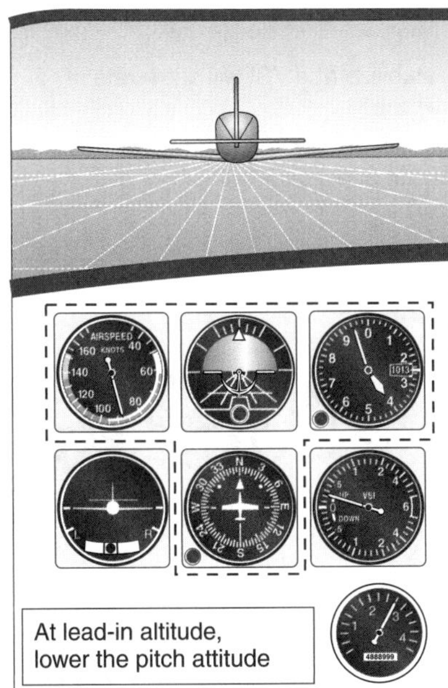

At lead-in altitude,
lower the pitch attitude

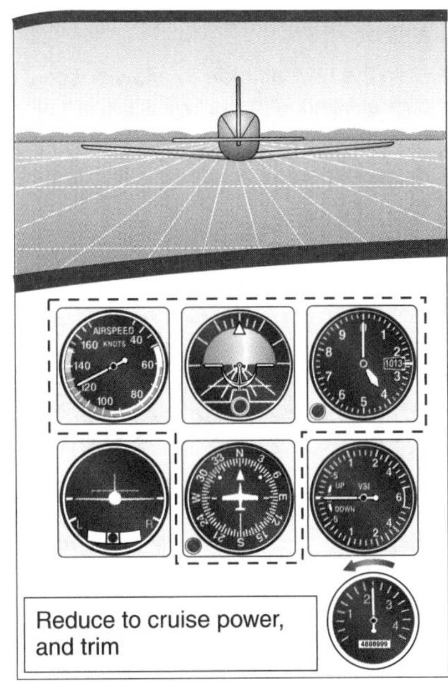

Required accuracy: ***• airspeed ±10 knots*** ***• heading ±10°*** ***• altitude ±100 ft***

Note: Steady, straight and level flight is maintained by reference to all flight instruments, with the altimeter confirming that you are holding the correct attitude for straight and level, as shown on the attitude indicator.

4. *Initiating a Descent on Instruments*

As in normal visual flight, a descent is initiated in the order P-A-T: Power–Attitude–Trim. Descent speed is usually less than cruise speed – decelerate to descent speed at the cruise altitude before lowering the nose to descend.

The standard rate of descent in instrument flying is 500 ft/min. This may be achieved by a reduction of 600 RPM or so from the cruise power-setting. However, you may remove more power and descend at a greater rate, if desired. Also, a glide descent may be made, with the throttle fully closed.

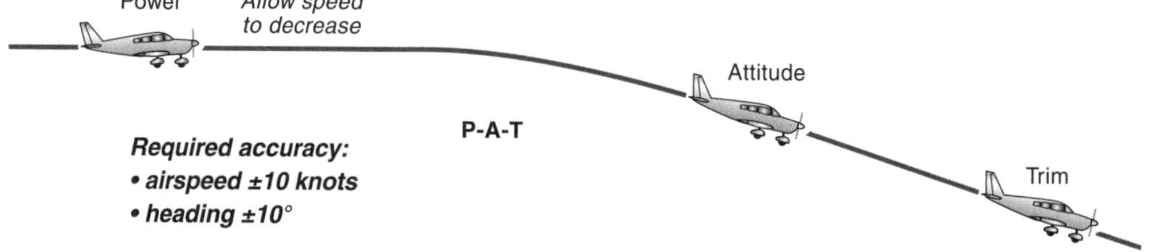

Procedure:

Reduce power (coordinate with rudder and exert back pressure on the control column as necessary to maintain altitude).

Allow the airspeed to decrease toward the desired descent speed.

Approaching the descent speed, smoothly lower the nose to the estimated descent attitude.

Hold the new attitude to allow descent speed to stabilize (the VSI will show rate of descent and altimeter will show an altitude decrease).

Make minor adjustments to achieve the desired descent airspeed and rate of descent (control airspeed with pitch attitude and rate of descent with power).

Trim.

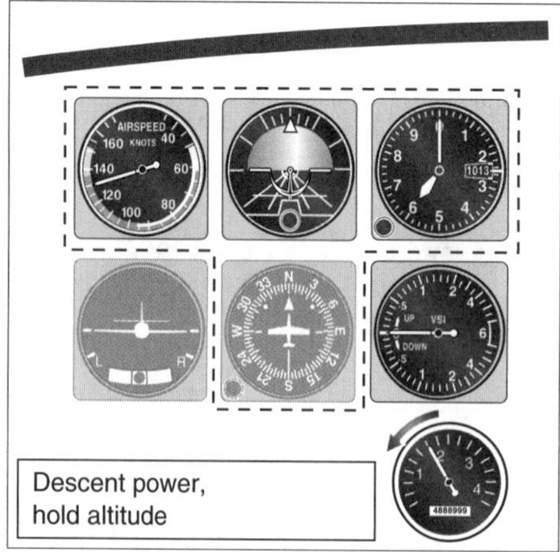

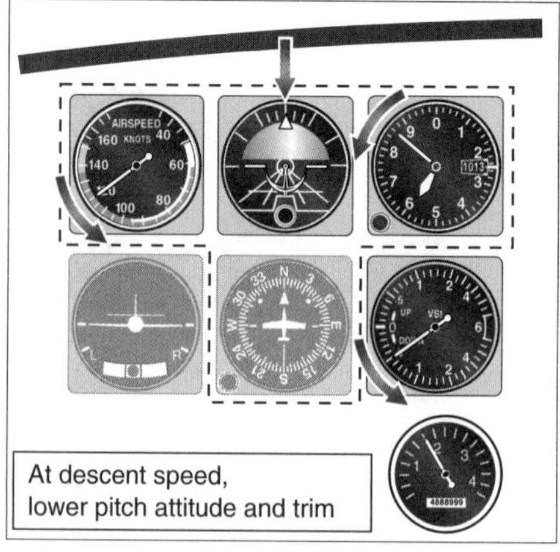

At descent speed,
lower pitch attitude and trim

Note: A steady descent is maintained with reference to all flight instruments, with the ASI confirming you are holding the correct attitude for descent as shown on the attitude indicator.

5. *Controlling the Rate of Descent at a Constant Airspeed*

To achieve any desired rate of descent while maintaining a constant airspeed, both the power and attitude must be adjusted.

The rate of descent is indicated to the pilot by:
• the vertical speed indicator (primarily); or
• the altimeter and clock.

(a) To increase the rate of descent:

Reduce power.

Lower the pitch attitude to maintain airspeed.

Trim.

(b) To decrease the rate of descent:

Increase power.

Raise the pitch attitude to maintain airspeed.

Trim.

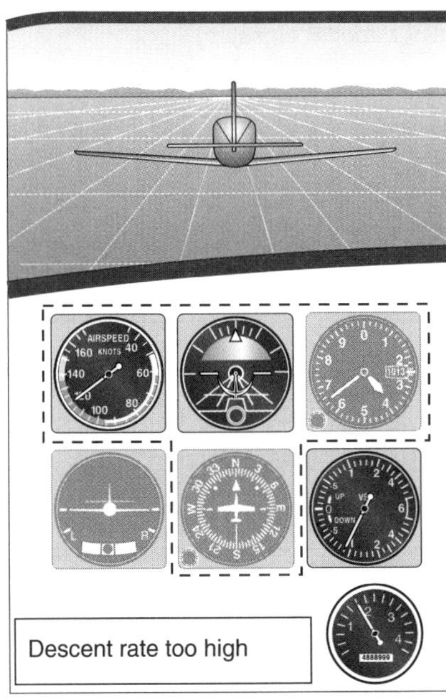
Descent rate too high

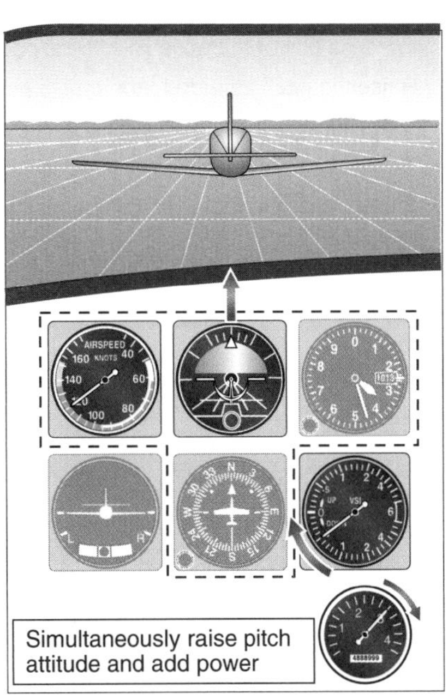
Simultaneously raise pitch attitude and add power

Required accuracy: • airspeed ±10 knots • heading ±10° • desired rate of descent ±100 ft/min

6. Leveling Off from a Descent

As in normal visual flight, leveling off from a descent follows the sequence P-A-T: Power–Attitude–Trim.

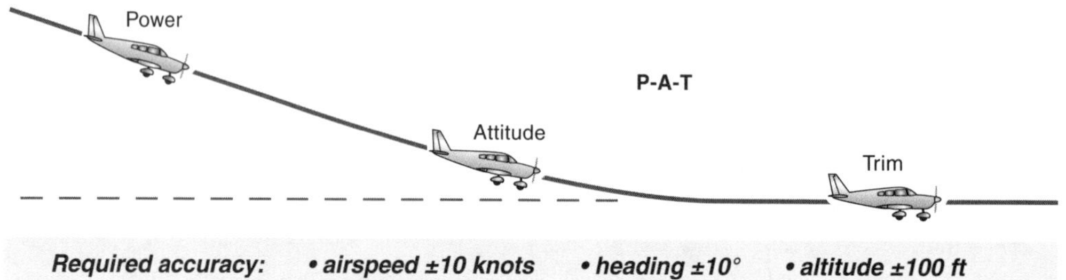
Power
P-A-T
Attitude
Trim

Required accuracy: • airspeed ±10 knots • heading ±10° • altitude ±100 ft

To level off at a specific altitude, increase the power and gradually raise the nose towards the cruise position just before that height is reached—the amount of lead being approximately 10% of the rate of descent. For example, at 500 ft/min rate of descent, start increasing power and raising the nose 50 ft prior to reaching the desired altitude.

Increase power to cruise RPM (and coordinate with rudder pressure).

Raise the pitch attitude to the cruise position.

Make minor adjustments to maintain altitude.

Trim.

Steady, straight and level flight is maintained with reference to all flight instruments—with the altimeter confirming that you are holding the correct attitude for straight and level as shown on the attitude indicator.

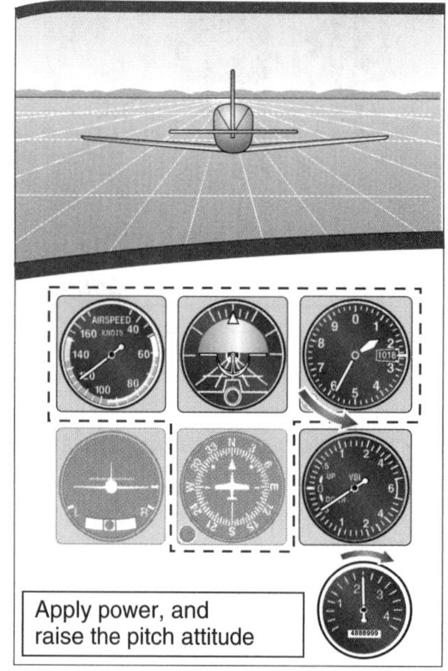
Apply power, and
raise the pitch attitude

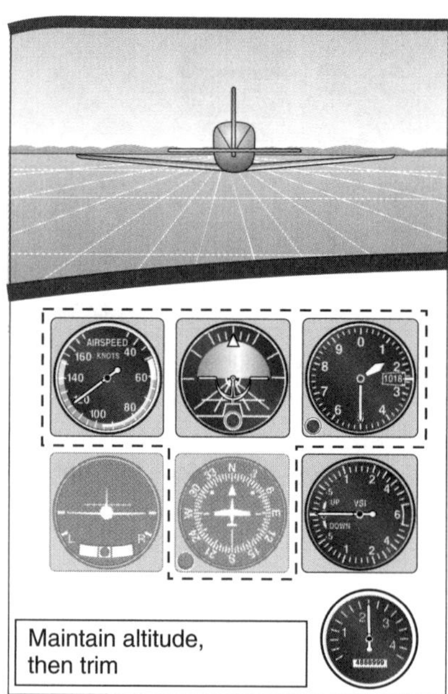
Maintain altitude,
then trim

7. ***Climbing Away from a Descent***

The procedure is the same as leveling off from a descent, except that climb power and climb attitude are selected instead.

Be prepared for strong nose-up and yawing tendencies as climb power is applied. Even though the climb attitude is higher than the descent attitude, it may initially require forward pressure to stop the nose rising too far. Rudder will of course be required to coordinate the increase in slipstream effect.

Trim off any steady pressure remaining on the control column.

Procedure:

Apply climb **power**, balance with rudder.

Set the desired pitch **attitude** for the climb.

Positive rate of climb: select gear and flaps up.

Trim.

Required accuracy:
- ***airspeed ±10 knots***
- ***heading ±10°***

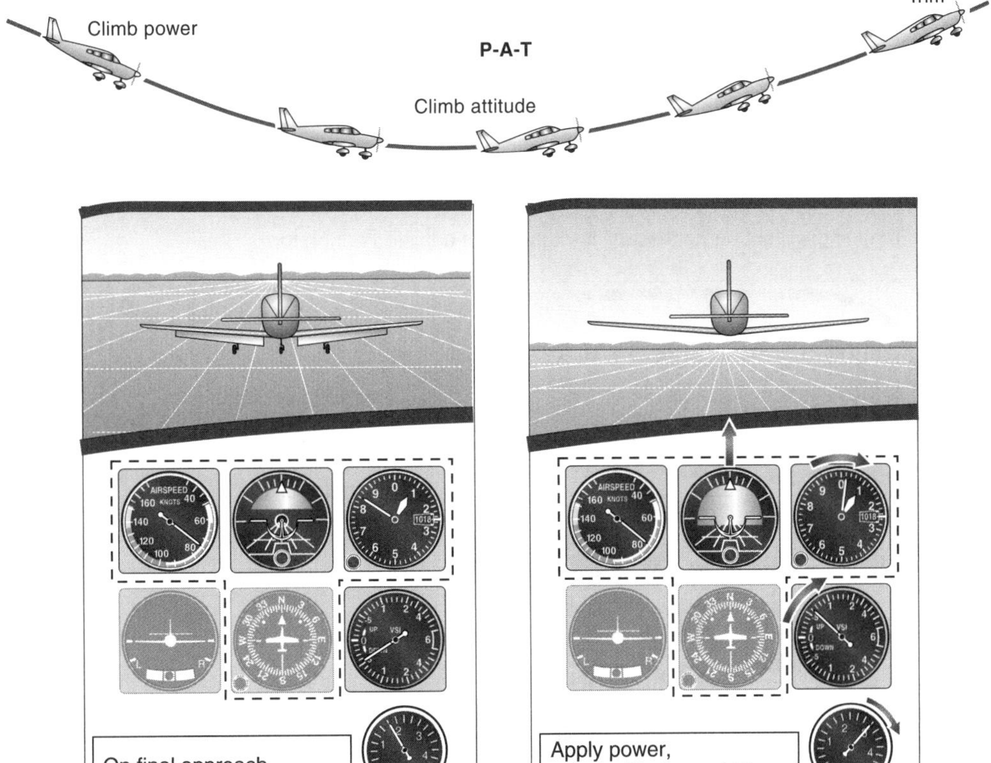

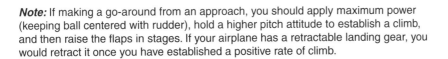

Note: If making a go-around from an approach, you should apply maximum power (keeping ball centered with rudder), hold a higher pitch attitude to establish a climb, and then raise the flaps in stages. If your airplane has a retractable landing gear, you would retract it once you have established a positive rate of climb.

TASK

Turning on Instruments

Aim: To turn the airplane solely by reference to the flight instruments.

1. A Standard-Rate Level Turn

The required bank angle for a standard-rate turn will equal one-tenth of the airspeed, plus half of that. For example, at 80 knots, the bank angle required will be (8 + 4) = 12°.

Trim for straight and level flight.

To enter and maintain the turn:

Roll into the turn using aileron, and coordinate with rudder pressure.

Hold a constant bank angle and keep the balance ball centered.

Hold the correct pitch attitude to maintain altitude using elevator.

Do not use trim in a turn, since turning is normally only a transient maneuver (although you may trim for a sustained turn).

The rate of turn is indicated to the pilot by:

The turn coordinator (standard rate = 3° per sec, or 360° in 2 min), or the heading indicator and clock.

To stop the turn on a desired heading:

Anticipate and begin recovery from the turn about 5 prior to reaching the desired heading.

Roll the wings level, and coordinate with rudder.

Lower the pitch attitude to that required for straight and level flight.

Trimming will not be necessary, if trim was not adjusted during turn.

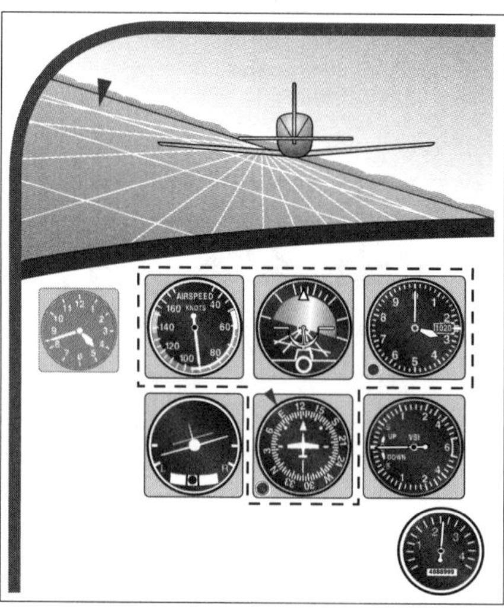

A standard-rate level turn to the left

Required accuracy:

- ***altitude ±100 ft***
- ***bank angle ±5°***
- ***heading ±10°***
- ***airspeed ±10 knots***

Note: A standard-rate turn may also be achieved by using the clock and the heading indicator. By holding the calculated bank angle you should achieve a turn rate of 3° per second, which will give a 45° heading change in 15 seconds, a 90° heading change in 30 seconds, a 180° heading change in one minute and 360° heading change in two minutes (hence the 2 **MIN** that is marked on many turn coordinators).

2. *A 30°-Banked Level Turn*

At the speeds achieved by most training aircraft, a 30°-banked turn is greater than standard rate. A steeper bank angle requires greater back pressure to maintain altitude, so the airspeed will decrease a little further—by about 5 or 10 kt. If you wish to hold the airspeed constant, then a little power will be required. The pitch attitude will be slightly higher than for straight and level flight.

The rate of turn can be estimated from the turn coordinator, or by using the clock and heading indicator (bearing in mind that the turn coordinator may be limited by stops at about twice standard rate, so that steeper bank angles will not be accompanied by an increased rate of turn).

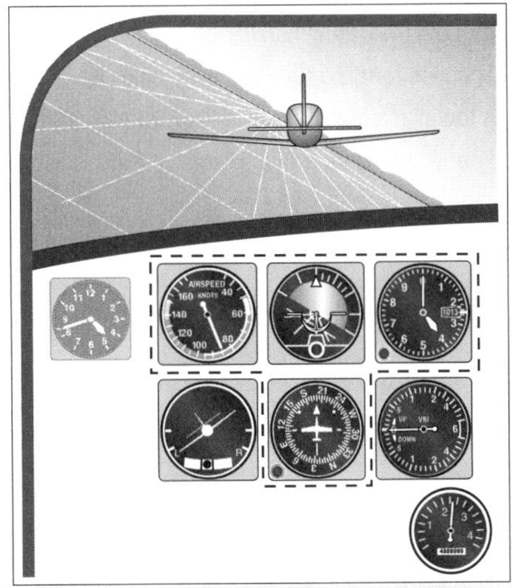

***Required accuracy:* • altitude ±100 ft • bank angle ±5° • heading ±10° • airspeed ±10 knots**

3. *The Climbing Turn*

The climbing turn will normally be entered from a straight climb. To ensure adequate climb performance, do not exceed a 20° bank angle in a typical training airplane.

The pitch attitude will have to be lowered slightly to maintain a constant airspeed in a climbing turn. (In climbing and descending turns, speed is maintained with the elevator, whereas in level turns it is altitude that is maintained with the elevator.)

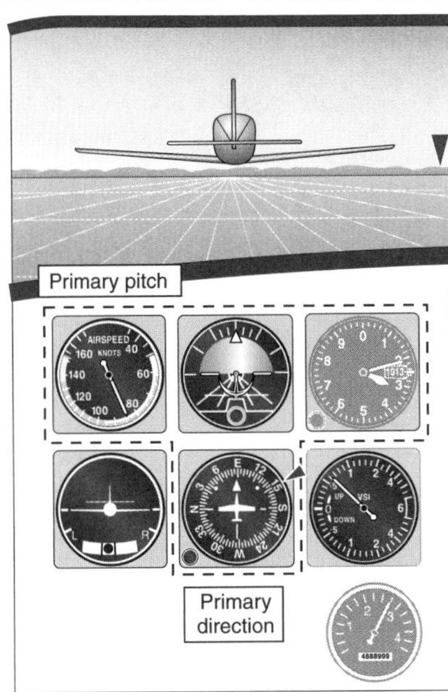

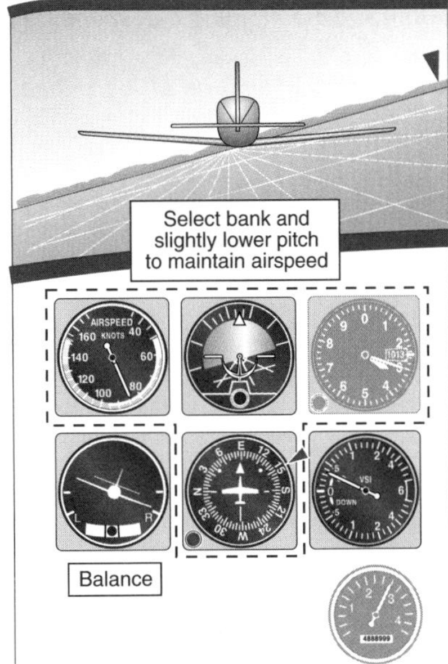

Entering and maintaining a climbing turn to the right

***Required accuracy:* • altitude ±100 ft • bank angle ±5° • heading ±10° • airspeed ±10 knots**

4. Descending Turns

The descending turn will normally be entered from a straight descent.

A lower pitch attitude will be required in the turn to maintain airspeed.

The rate of descent will increase in a turn; it can be controlled with power, if you wish.

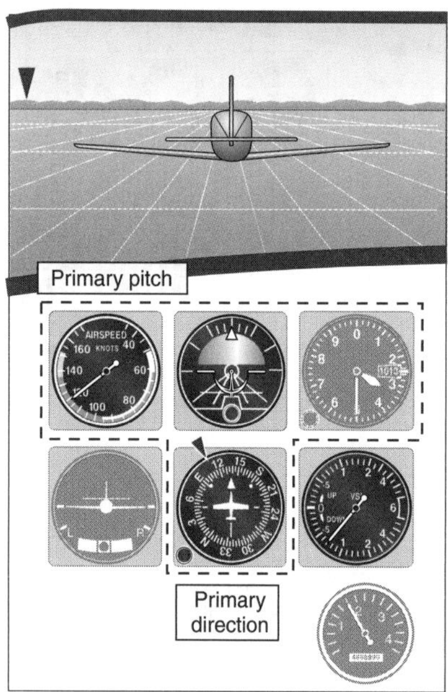

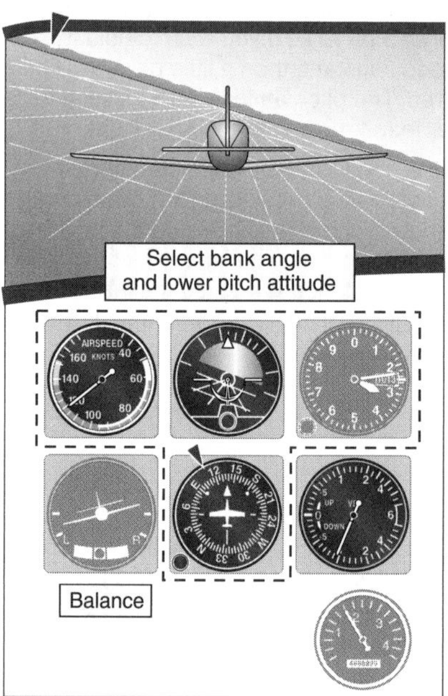

Entering and maintaining a descending turn to the left

Required accuracy: • altitude ±100 ft • bank angle ±5° • heading ±10° • airspeed ±10 knots

TASK

Recovery from Unusual Attitudes

Aim: To recognize a potentially hazardous flight attitude from instrument indications and recover before a hazardous attitude develops.

An **unusual attitude** is considered to be a potentially hazardous attitude where either:

- the airplane's nose is unusually high with the airspeed decreasing; or
- the airplane's nose is unusually low with the airspeed increasing; the airplane may also be banked.

The **easiest recovery** from an unusual attitude is not to get into one! In extreme attitudes, the attitude indicator (a gyroscopic instrument) may tumble, depriving you of your most important instrument. Most of its information can be derived, however, from other sources:

- Approximate **pitch attitude** can be determined from the airspeed indicator (increasing or decreasing airspeed) and the altimeter and vertical speed indicator (descent or climb). A decreasing airspeed indication and a decreasing rate of climb would indicate an unusually high nose-up attitude; conversely, a rapidly increasing airspeed and rate of descent would indicate a nose-low attitude.
- **Turning** can be detected on the turn coordinator. The heading indicator (a gyroscopic instrument) may have tumbled and the magnetic compass will probably not be giving a steady reading if there is any significant turn occurring. The turn coordinator is gyroscopic but will not topple.

1. ***Nose High and Steep Bank—Beware of Stall***
   Recovery Procedure:

(a) **If close to the stall:**
Simultaneously lower the nose to the level pitch attitude (referring to the AI); and apply full power (coordinate with rudder).
As speed increases, level the wings (refer to the AI).

(b) **If not close to the stall:**
Select straight and level flight (refer to the AI):

- control wheel forward;
- roll wings-level with aileron (ailerons can be used as the wings are not stalled) coordinating with rudder; and
- add power as necessary.

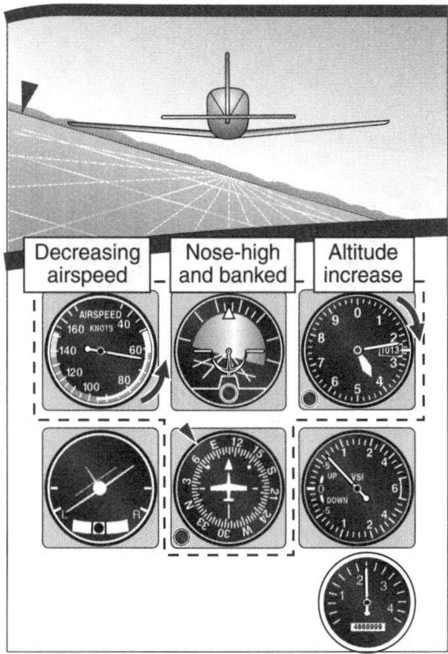

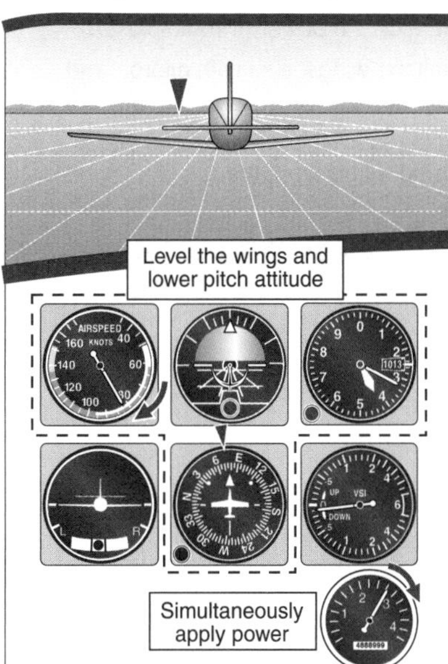

A nose-high unusual attitude and recovery

Note: Do not exceed 45° bank angle or 10° pitch from level flight when practicing recovery from unusual flight attitudes on instruments. Recover to a stabilized level flight attitude or climb using prompt coordinated control movements applied in the proper sequence. Avoid any excessive load factors, and do not exceed airspeed limits, or stall the plane.

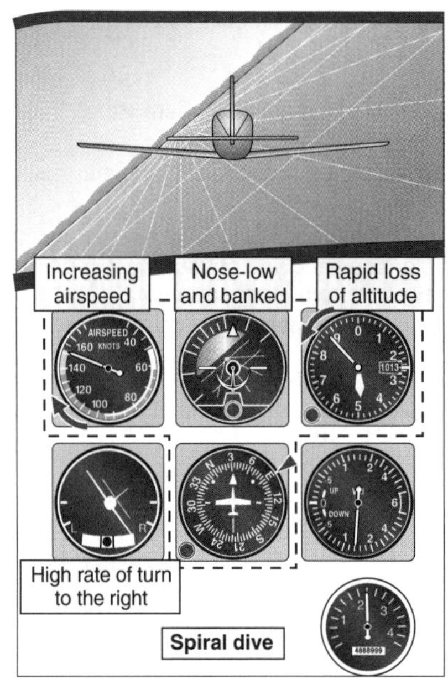

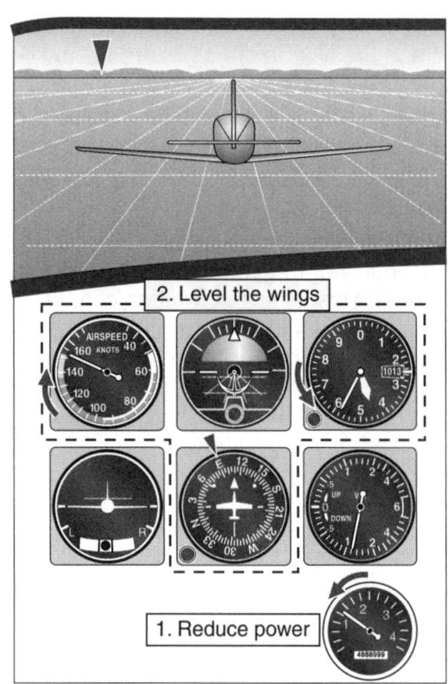

2. ***Nose Low and High Airspeed***
   Beware of an overspeed or a spiral dive.

   Recovery Procedure:

   Reduce the power (throttle closed).

   Roll the wings level with aileron and rudder.

   Ease out of the ensuing dive into straight and level attitude (AI).

   Reapply power.

   Regain altitude, if necessary.

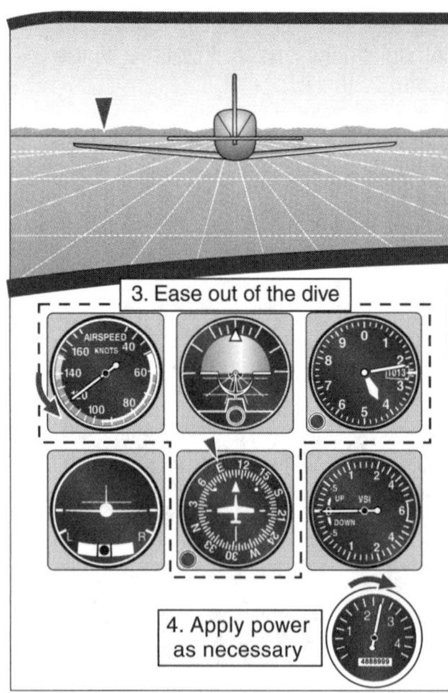

A nose-low unusual attitude and recovery

Note: Do not exceed 45° bank angle or 10° pitch from level flight when practicing recovery from unusual flight attitudes on instruments. Recover to a stabilized level flight attitude or climb using prompt coordinated control movements applied in the proper sequence. Avoid pulling any excessive g-loadings, and do not exceed airspeed limits, or stall the plane.

51
Night Flight

OBJECTIVES

To describe:
- the human limitations with regard to night visual perceptions;
- all aspects of lighting used to assist the pilot at night; and
- the procedures and techniques for night flight.

Figure 51-1 Sunset.

CONSIDERATIONS

Nighttime

Night is considered to occur between the end of evening civil twilight, which, in temperate zones, occurs about 20 minutes after sunset, and the beginning of morning civil twilight, which occurs about 20 minutes before sunrise. The period of twilight that occurs between the sun setting or rising and darkness can sometimes be quite lengthy, especially in areas of high latitude near the Poles, such as Alaska, Canada, Scandinavia and Russia, and can be very short in the tropics.

Certain aspects of flight have to be considered when flying at night, such as:
- adaptation of your eyes to night vision;
- additional personal equipment;
- additional aircraft equipment and lighting;
- airport lighting; and
- navigating at night.

To have night-flying privileges, you must receive at least three hours of flight instruction at night, including at least 10 takeoffs and landings, and a night cross-country flight.

The FAA requires private pilot applicants to have logged a dual night cross-country as part of the minimum requirements (with exception of pilots flying in Alaska who may choose to have "*NIGHT FLYING PROHIBITED*" listed on their certificate).

Personal Pilot Equipment

Carry your own flashlight at night.

As well as your normal daytime equipment, you must carry a serviceable flashlight. A good white beam is essential for your external preflight checks. A fairly weak red light is best for use in the darkened cockpit, since it will not destroy your night vision; however, it will make red items on your charts difficult or impossible to see. It is important that your personal equipment is well organized, since things are always more difficult to find when it is dark—especially when you have to fly the airplane with little external visual reference. Fold your charts with the course line visible, so that they are immediately available for use. Carry spare batteries for your flashlight or a second flashlight. Ensure the flashlight is fully charged if rechargeable.

Figure 51-2
Required instruments.

Aircraft Equipment and Lighting

The cockpit instrumentation required for VFR daytime flight is also required for VFR night flight. This includes:

- certain flight instruments;
- certain engine gauges; and
- fuel quantity gauges.

Surprisingly, an artificial horizon is not required, although it will be very useful at night. Aircraft with retractable landing gear must also have a landing gear position indicator, and those with a constant-speed propeller must have a manifold pressure gauge.

The additional equipment required for VFR night flight includes:

- approved position lights (red, green, and white);
- an approved anticollision light system (usually a red rotating beacon and white strobe lights);
- landing light(s), if the aircraft is for hire;
- an adequate source of electrical power (engine-driven alternator and onboard battery); and
- spare fuses stored in an accessible place.

Figure 51-3
Rotating beacon.

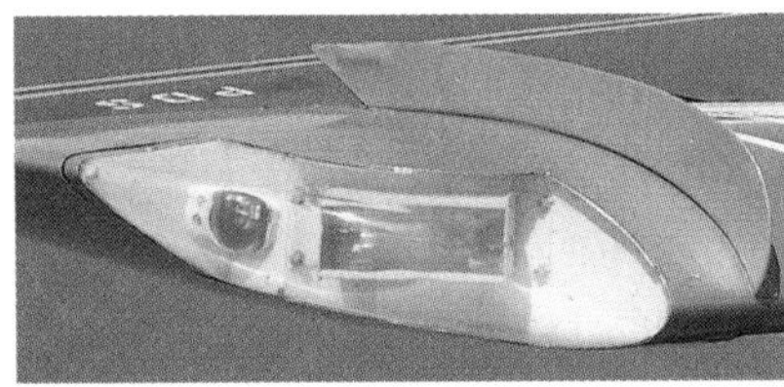

Figure 51-4
Navigation light and strobe.

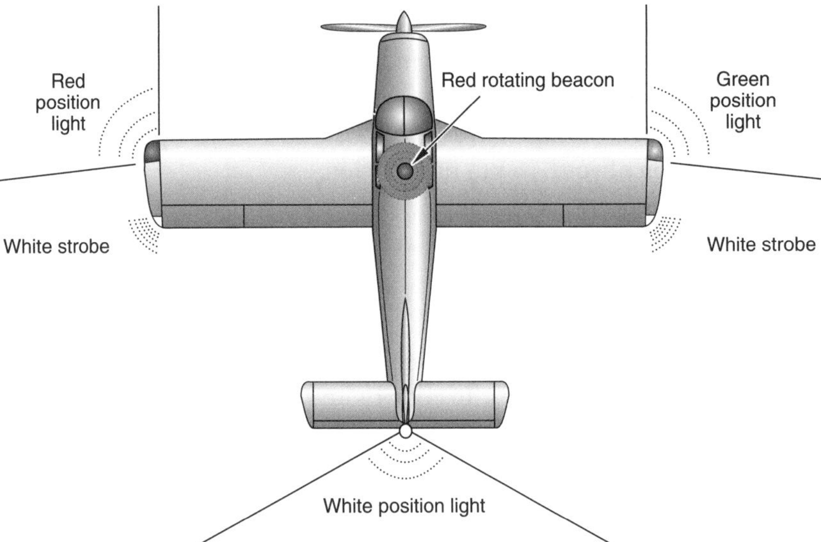

Figure 51-5 Required lights.

Airport Lighting

The main aeronautical lighting provided at an airport to assist you to maneuver your airplane at night consists of:

- taxiway lighting;
- runway lighting;
- the airport beacon;
- approach lighting;
- visual approach slope indicators (VASI); and
- red warning lights on significant obstacles.

Figure 51-6
Airport lighting.

You may be night flying at an airport with fairly simple lighting, or you might be at a sophisticated international airport with advanced lighting, especially approach lighting. In this section you should read about taxiway lighting (blue edge or centerline green), simple runway lighting (white), and airport beacons (alternating green and white), but only take what you need from the advanced approach lighting and runway lighting descriptions. Definitely read about pilot-controlled airport lighting. Particulars of lighting at specific airports are shown on aeronautical charts and in the *Chart Supplement U.S.*

Airport Beacons

The airport beacon is designed to help the pilot visually locate the airport from some distance away. Some airport beacons rotate, others transmit pulses of light, the effect being the same—flashes of one or two alternating colors, which are:

- green–white–green–white at civil airports; and
- green–white–white–green–white-white at military airports.

Obstruction Lights

Many obstructions that could be hazardous to aircraft are marked at night by flashing red or white lights, and/or steady red lights.

Taxiway Lights

Taxiway lights are centerline green or sideline blue.

Taxiways are lit in one of two ways for the guidance of pilots, with either:

- two lines of taxiway blue edge lights; or
- one line of centerline green taxiway lights.

At some airports, there is a mixture of the two types, centerline green on some taxiways, and blue edge on others. Centerline green lights will be flush with the taxiway surface (or almost so) and can be taxied over. On the other hand, sideline blue taxiway

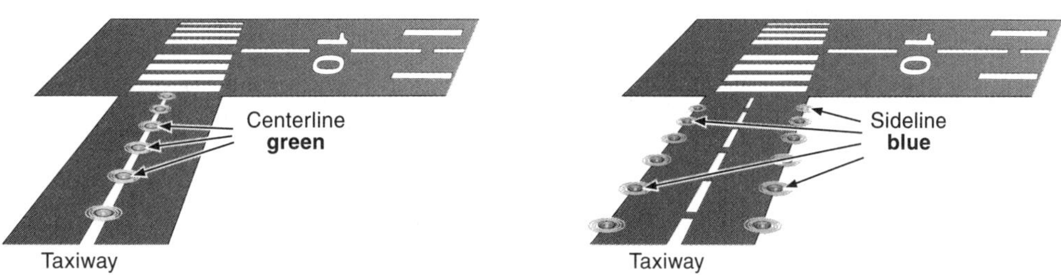

Figure 51-7 Taxiway lighting.

lights (and the white runway edge lights) may not be flush, and are also used to indicate boundaries, so do not taxi across them.

At certain points on the taxiway, there may be red stop-bars installed, to indicate the position where an airplane should hold position—for instance, before entering or crossing an active runway.

Runway Lighting

Runway lighting defines the boundaries of the actual landing area. Some advanced systems on precision instrument approach runways provide you with distance-down-the-runway information, but this is not vital for a visual pilot who can see the end of the runway and its lights.

Runway Edge Lights. Runway edge lights are white, and outline the edges of runways during periods of darkness or restricted visibility.

Runway End Lights. The runway end lights each have two colors, showing green at the near end to aircraft on approach, and red to airplanes stopping at the far end.

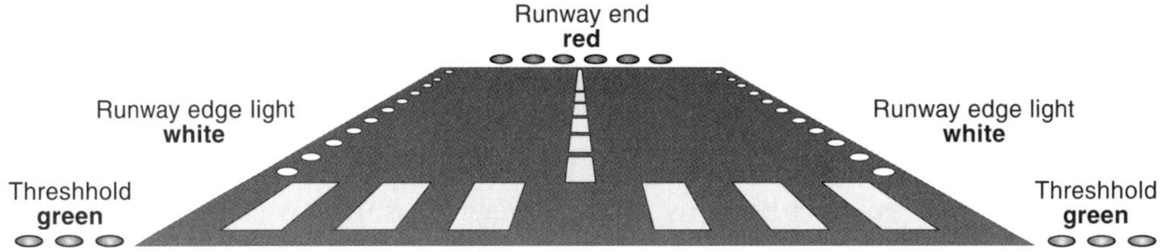

Figure 51-8 Basic runway lighting at night.

> **Note for Private Pilot Applicants:** This is the extent of the airport lighting at basic airports. You may now bypass the rest of this lighting section, except for pilot-controlled lighting systems (page 536), and move on to the topic of Night Vision—unless you wish to know about some of the sophisticated lighting available at major airports, so that you will not be phased by the extent and intensity of the lighting on your first approach to a precision instrument runway at night.

Advanced Runway Edge Lights. Runway edge lights are classified according to the intensity or brightness they are capable of producing:

- high intensity runway lights (HIRL);
- medium intensity runway lights (MIRL); and
- low intensity runway lights (LIRL).

Runway edge lights are white, except on instrument runways where amber replaces white for the last 2,000 feet (or last-half on runways shorter than 4,000 feet), to form a caution zone for landings in restricted visibility. When the pilot sees the white edge lights replaced by amber, some idea of how much runway is left for stopping is gained.

Runway End Identifier Lights. Runway end identifier lights (REIL) consist of a pair of synchronized white flashing lights located each side of the runway threshold at the approach end. They serve to identify:

- a runway end surrounded by many other lights;
- a runway end that lacks contrast with the surrounding terrain; and
- a runway end in poor visibility.

In-Runway Lighting. Some precision approach runways have additional in-runway lighting embedded in the runway surface as follows:

- touchdown zone lights (TDZL) are bright white lights either side of the runway centerline in the touchdown zone (from 100 feet in from the landing threshold to 3,000 feet or the half-way point, whichever is the lower);
- runway centerline light systems (RCLS) are flush centerline lighting at 50 feet intervals, starting 75 feet in from the landing threshold to within 75 feet of the stopping end; RCLS also includes runway-remaining lighting, where the centerline lighting seen by a stopping airplane is:
  - initially all white;
  - alternating red and white from 3,000 feet-to-go point to 1,000 feet-to-go; and
  - all red for the last 1,000 feet; and
- taxiway turn-off lights are a series of green in-runway lights spaced at 50 feet intervals defining a curved path from the runway centerline to a point on the taxiway.

Approach Lights

At many airports, an approach lighting system (ALS) extends out from the approach end of the runway to well beyond the physical boundaries of the airport, possibly into forested or built-up areas. Approach lights do not mark the boundaries of a suitable landing area; they simply act as a lead-in to a runway for a pilot on approach to land.

ALS lighting is a standardized arrangement of white and red lights, consisting basically of extended centerline lighting, with crossbars sited at specific intervals back along the approach path from the threshold, out to a distance of:

- 2,400 to 3,400 feet for precision instrument approach runways; or
- 1,400 to 1,500 feet for nonprecision instrument approach runways.

Figure 51-9 Approach lights.

Approach light systems assist an instrument pilot to transition from instrument flight to visual flight for a landing.

The approach lighting provides you with a visual indication of how well the airplane is aligned with the extended runway centerline as well as helping you to estimate the distance the airplane has to fly to the touchdown point on the runway.

There are various types of approach light systems in use, the sophistication of the system depending upon the importance of the airport and the frequency and type of operations. Some approach lighting systems include sequenced flashing lights (SFL), or runway alignment indicator lights (RAIL), which appear to the pilot as a ball of white light traveling toward the runway at high speed (twice per second), along the extended centerline.

The runway threshold is marked with a row of green lights, and some runway thresholds have flashing strobes either side to act as runway end identifier lights (REIL).

Visual Approach Slope Indicator (VASI)

VASIs provide approach-slope guidance by day and by night.

In conditions of poor visibility and at night, when the runway environment and the natural horizon may not be clearly visible, it is often difficult for a pilot to judge the correct approach slope of the airplane toward the touchdown zone of the runway. A number of very effective visual slope indicators provide visual slope guidance on approach. Especially at night, you should not fly a shallower approach than the typical 3° VASI slope.

Lateral guidance is provided by the runway, the runway lights or the approach light system. The slope guidance provided by a VASI is to the touchdown zone, which will probably be some 1,000 feet in from the runway threshold.

Two-Bar Red-on-White VASI. The typical two-bar VASI has two pairs of wing bars alongside the runway, usually at 500 feet and 1,000 feet from the approach threshold. It is sometimes known as the red/white system, since these two colors are used to indicate whether you are right on slope, too high or too low. You will see:

- if high on slope, all bars are white;
- if right on slope, the far bars are red and the near bars are white; and
- if low on slope, all bars are red.

During the approach, the airplane should be maintained on a slope within the white sector of the near bars and the red sector of the far bars. If the airplane flies above or below the correct slope, the lights will change color, there being a pink transition stage between red and white.

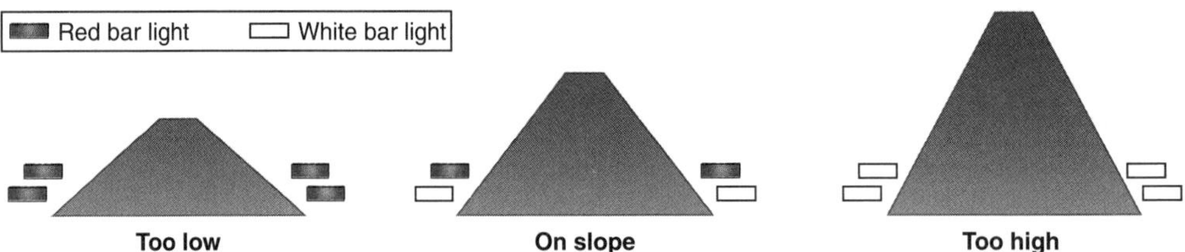

Figure 51-10 Perspectives on approach using a two-bar red-on-white VASI.

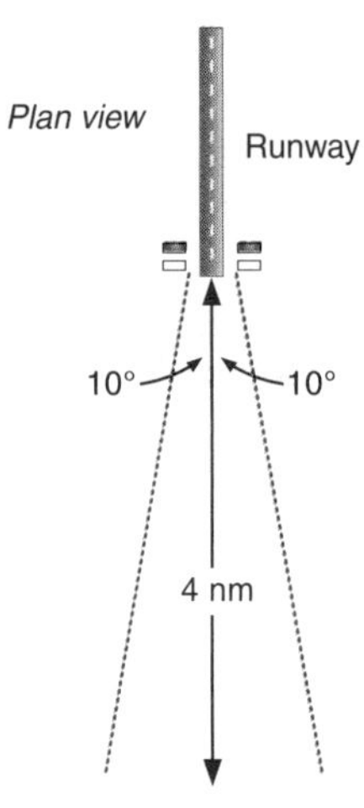

Figure 51-11
The extent of useful VASI information.

The plane of the VASI approach slope only provides guaranteed obstacle clearance in an arc 10° left or right of the extended centerline out to a distance of 4 nautical miles from the runway threshold, even though the VASI may be visible in good conditions out to 5 nautical miles by day and 20 nautical miles by night. Before relying solely on the VASI for descent guidance, therefore, the airplane should be within 4 nautical miles and inside this arc, preferably aligned with the extended runway centerline.

There are other operational considerations when using the red/white VASI. At maximum range, the white bars may become visible before the red bars, because of the nature of red and white light. In haze or smog, or in certain other conditions, the white lights may have a yellowish tinge about them. When extremely low on slope, the two wing bars (all lights red) may appear to merge into one red bar: at close range to the threshold, this would indicate a critical situation with respect to obstacle clearance, and the pilot should take urgent action to regain slope or make a missed approach. Some VASI systems use a reduced number of lights, in which case they may be known as an abbreviated VASI or AVASI.

Three-Bar VASI. The three-bar VASI has an additional wing bar at the far end, intended to assist the pilots of long-bodied airplanes such as the Boeing 747 or the McDonnell Douglas MD-11. A VASI shows the deviation of the pilot's eyes from the approach slope, and not the deviation of the wheels. Since the wheels of an airplane with a very long fuselage will be much further behind and below the eyes, it is essential that the eyes follow a

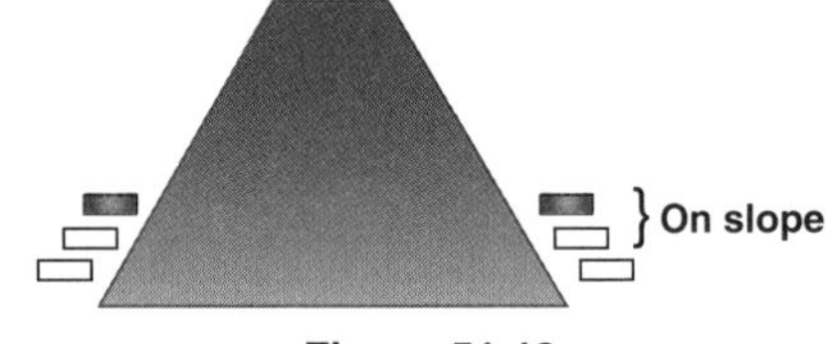

Figure 51-12
Correct view for the pilot of a long-bodied airplane using the three-bar VASI.

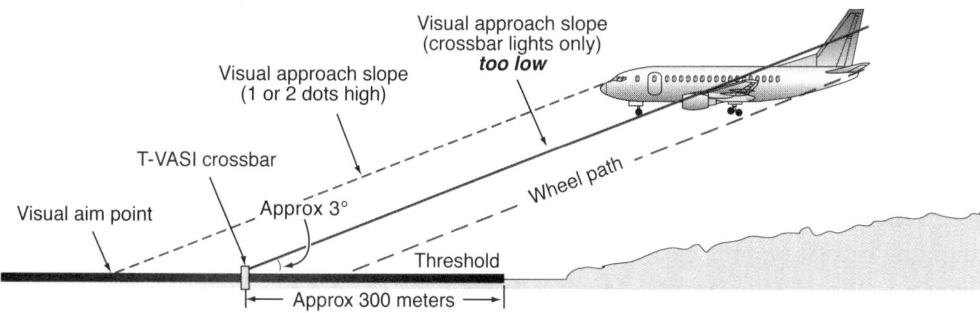

Figure 51-13 A three-bar VASI ensures adequate wheel clearance over the threshold for long-bodied aircraft.

parallel but higher slope to ensure adequate main wheel clearance over the runway threshold. The additional wing bar on the three-bar VASI, placed further into the runway, makes this possible.

Pilots of such airplanes should use the second and third wing bars, and ignore the first. When the pilot's eyes are positioned on the correct slope for a long-bodied airplane, they will see the top bar red, the middle bar white (and ignore the lower bar which is also white).

Pilots of smaller airplanes should refer only to the two nearer wing bars, and ignore the further "long-bodied" wing bar. When on slope, the indications will be the following:

- top bar red and ignored;
- middle bar red; and
- lower bar white.

Figure 51-14
Correct view for the pilot for smaller airplane using the three-bar VASI.

Precision Approach Path Indicator (PAPI). PAPI is a development of the VASI, and also uses red/white light signals for guidance in maintaining the correct approach angle, but the lights are arranged differently and their indications must be interpreted differently. PAPI has a single wing bar, which will consist of four light units on one or both sides of the runway adjacent to the touchdown point. There is no pink transition stage as the lights change from red to white. If the airplane is on slope, the two outer lights of each unit are white and the two inner lights are red. Above slope, the number of white lights increase; below slope, the number of red lights increase.

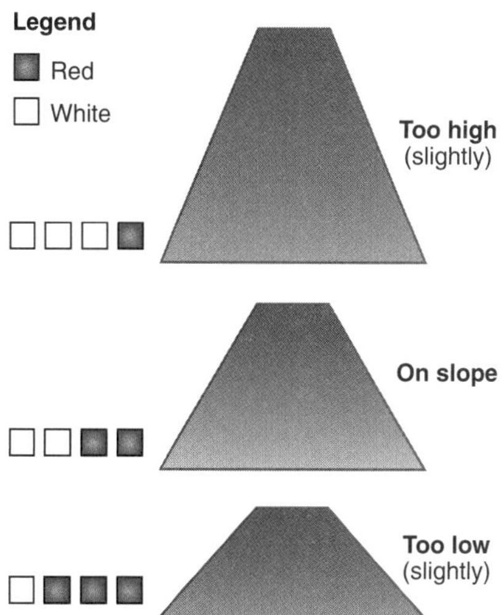

Figure 51-15
Slope guidance using PAPI.

Pulsating Visual Approach Slope Indicator (PVASI). PVASI consists of a single light unit, positioned on the left side of a runway adjacent to the touchdown point, which projects three or four different bands of light at different vertical angles, only one of which can be seen by a pilot on approach at any one time. The indications provided by a typical PVASI are:

- fast-pulsing white for well above the glide slope (or glide path);
- pulsing white for above the glide slope;
- steady white for on the glide slope (or alternating red/white for some systems);
- pulsing red for below the glide slope; and
- fast-pulsing red for well below the glide slope.

Pilot Control of Some Lighting Systems

The approach lights and runway lights at an airport are controlled by:

- the control tower personnel (when the tower is active); or
- the pilot (at certain airports).

The pilot may request ATC to turn the lights on (or off), or to vary their intensity if required. On a hazy day, with restricted visibility but a lot of glare, maximum brightness might be necessary; on a clear dark night, a significantly lower brightness level will be required. At selected airports, when ATC facilities are not manned, airborne control of the lights by the pilot is possible using the VHF COM. The *Chart Supplement U.S.* specifies the type of lighting available, and the VHF COM frequency used to activate the system (usually the CTAF).

Some airport lighting systems can be controlled directly by the pilot.

To use an FAA-approved pilot-controlled lighting system, simply select the appropriate VHF frequency on the VHF COM, and depress the microphone switch a number of times. A good technique involves keying the mike seven times within five seconds, which will activate the lights at maximum intensity, and then subsequently keying it a further five or three times for medium or low intensity respectively, if desired. For more detailed information, refer to the *Aeronautical Information Manual.*

All lighting is activated for 15 minutes from the time of the most recent key transmission. If pilot-controlled lights are already on as you commence an approach, it is good airmanship to reactivate them and thereby ensure that they will stay on for the duration of the approach and landing.

Night Vision

There are two aspects of vision that are important to a pilot flying in a night sky:

- dark adaptation; and
- peripheral vision.

The Structure of the Eye

Light rays pass through the pupil of the eye and are focused by the lens onto the retina, which is a light-sensitive layer at the back of the eye. It sends electrical signals along the optic nerve to the brain, allowing us to see. The central part of the retina contains cone cells, which are most effective in daylight and least effective in darkness. They allow us to see color, small details, and distant objects. The outer band of the retina contains rod cells, which are responsible for your peripheral—that is, off-center—vision and are effective in both daylight and darkness. They are sensitive to movement, but not to detail or color, and so only register black, white and gray.

Adaptation of the Eyes to Darkness

It takes the eyes about 30 minutes to adapt to a dark environment, as most of us have experienced when we enter a darkened cinema (late) and stumble across other patrons in an attempt to find an empty seat. The rate at which dark adaptation of the eyes occurs depends to a large extent upon the contrast between the brightness of light previously experienced and the degree of darkness of the new environment.

While bright lighting within the previous few minutes has the strongest effect, bright light experienced for some period within the preceding few hours will also have an effect. Bright lighting should therefore be avoided prior to night flying.

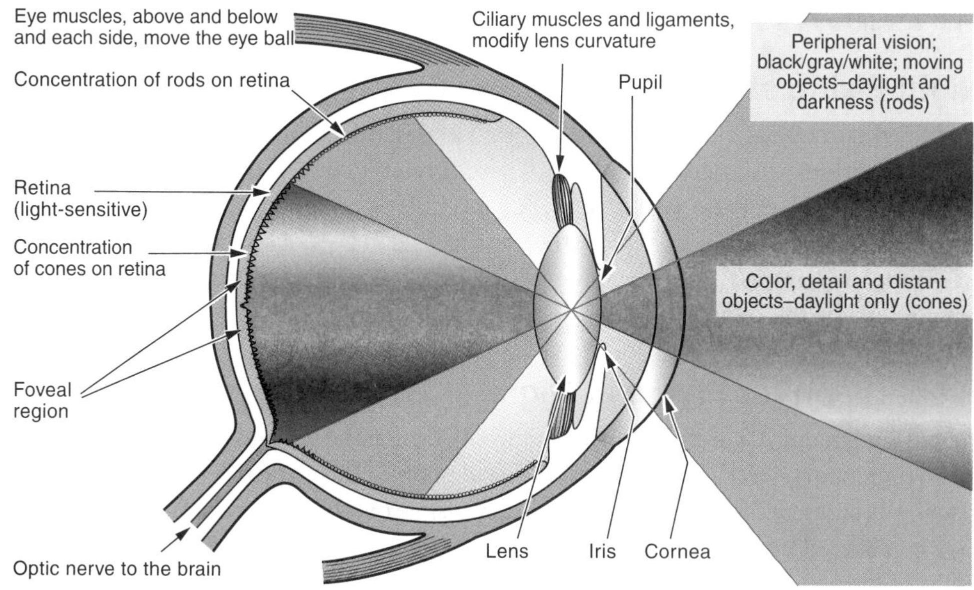

Figure 51-16 Structure of the eye.

Generally, this is difficult to achieve, since flight planning in a well-lit room and preflight inspections with a strong flashlight or on a well-lit tarmac will almost always be necessary. The best that can be achieved in many cases is to dim the cockpit lighting prior to taxiing, and to avoid looking at bright lights during those few minutes prior to takeoff.

Bright lighting should be avoided prior to night flying.

Night vision can also be affected by the lack of oxygen, so ensure that you use oxygen when flying above 10,000 feet MSL. On a more mundane level, avoid cigarette smoke in the cockpit at night, since it will displace oxygen in your blood to an appreciable extent, and consequently reduce your night vision by an amount comparable to an extra 5,000 feet in altitude. In the long term, a good diet containing foods with vitamins A and C can improve your night vision.

Electrical storms should be avoided by at least 10 miles and, if you are not an instrument-rated pilot in a suitably equipped airplane, then you should stay on the ground.

Since bright lights will impair your outside vision at night, it is good airmanship to keep the cockpit lighting at a reasonably low level, but not so low that you cannot see your charts, or find the fuel selector.

There are some occasions, however, when bright cockpit lighting can help preserve your vision. This can occur on an instrument flight, for instance, if flying in the vicinity of electrical storms. Nearby lightning flashes can temporarily degrade your dark adaptation and your vision, particularly if it is in contrast to a dim cockpit. Bright lighting in the cockpit can minimize this effect and, although your external vision will not be as good as with dim cockpit lighting, you will avoid being temporarily blinded by the lightning flashes.

Scan off center at night.

Scanning for Other Aircraft at Night

Because only the rod cells in your eyes are sensitive in darkness, objects will be more readily visible in your peripheral vision. You will see objects better when your eyes are looking to one side of them at night, rather than straight at them as in daylight.

Figure 51-17 Peripheral viewing at night.

APPLICATION

Night Flying at an Airport

Night flying requires a combination of visual and instrument flying skills. The takeoff run at night, for instance, is made with visual reference to the runway. Shortly after takeoff, however, outside visual reference might be very poor, and transferring your attention from outside the cockpit to the instruments in the cockpit at or before that time is essential. In contrast, flying by day and in good weather conditions, your attention can remain outside the cockpit.

Preparation for Flying at Night

Night flying requires careful attention to preflight preparation and planning. In contrast to daylight hours, weather conditions in the vicinity of the airport are difficult to assess visually at night. While stars might be clearly visible overhead one minute, the next they may be covered unexpectedly by low clouds, which could have a significant effect on flight in the area.

Study the available weather reports and forecasts.

Study the available weather reports and forecasts, paying special attention to any item that could affect visibility and your ability to fly at a safe operating altitude.

Some of the main items to consider are:

- cloud base and amount;
- weather such as rain, snow, fog and mist;
- temperature–dewpoint relationship, where the closer they are, the more likely it is that fog will form as the temperature drops further; and
- wind direction and strength, to assess the most suitable runway, the possibility of fog being blown in, and the likelihood of wind shear caused by the diurnal effect (a light surface wind with a strong wind at altitude, less vertical mixing).

Check any special procedures for night flying at that airport and in the vicinity.

Minimum Weather Conditions

The basic VFR minimums apply for night flying:

- flight visibility of three statute miles; and
- distances from clouds of 500 feet below (and 1,000 feet above) and 2,000 feet horizontally.

What this means in the traffic pattern at night is:

- a flight visibility of at least three statute miles; and
- a cloud ceiling of at least 1,000 feet AGL, so that you can fly in the traffic pattern at 500 feet AGL and still have a 500-foot clearance from clouds above.

The exception here is in *Class G airspace at nontowered airports*, where the reduced day minimums (flight visibility at least 1 statute mile, cloud ceiling at least 500 feet AGL) do not apply; however, the above basic VFR minimums are relaxed in terms of flight visibility only—it is reduced from 3 statute miles to a minimum flight visibility of 1 statute mile, provided you operate in the traffic pattern within ½ statute mile of the runway.

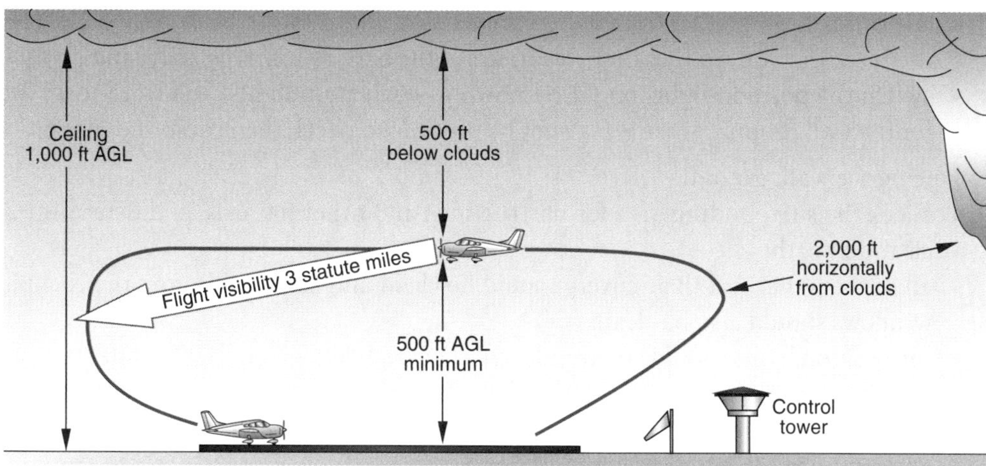

Figure 51-18 Basic VFR minimums at night are flight visibility at least 3 statute miles, and cloud ceiling at least 1,000 feet above the airport elevation.

Cross-Country

For a cross-country flight at night, carry the appropriate aeronautical charts, and have them suitably prepared and available for quick use in the cockpit. The better the preflight preparation of the charts, the lower the in-flight workload. Note that, if red light is to be used in the cockpit, then red print on the chart will not be easily seen.

All lines drawn on your charts should be in heavy black, since even white light in the cockpit will probably be dimmed to ensure that good external night vision is retained. If you are instrument-qualified, carry the instrument approach charts for the expected airports of operation, as well as for any other suitable airports nearby just in case unexpected cloud cover rolls in and an in-flight diversion becomes necessary.

Note on the chart any well-lit landmarks that may be useful, including airport beacons, towns, major roads, railroad yards, and so on, as well as any radio navigation aids available for use. Be especially aware of significant lit or unlit obstructions.

Try to choose well-lit checkpoints and use the radio navigation equipment and autopilot.

Check your personal equipment, including the normal daylight items such as a navigation computer, a plotter (or a protractor and scale rule) and pencils. A definite requirement for night flying is a serviceable flashlight, which is essential for your external preflight checks, and very useful in the cockpit in case of electrical failure.

The External Preflight Check

A strong flashlight is essential if the external preflight check is to be carried out successfully at night. Not only must the airplane be checked, but the surrounding area should also be scanned for obstructions, rough ground and other aircraft. Tie-down ropes and wheel chocks are also difficult to see (and remove) at night.

All normal external checks should be made, although some additional items must also be included at night. These should be incorporated into the external preflight check if any night flying at all is to occur, even though the takeoff might be made in daylight.

Additional items, such as the position lights, need to be checked prior to night flight.

A check of the aircraft lights is important. A typical technique during the preflight check is to position yourself near (or in) the cockpit and:

- place the master switch on;
- check the instrument lighting and dimmers (if fitted);
- check the cabin lighting;

- check the taxi light, landing light, strobe lights and rotating beacon by switching them on, then off, so that they do not drain the battery unnecessarily; and
- switch the position lights on (also known as navigation lights) and leave them on for the walkaround, since it may not be possible to check them from the cockpit.

During the walkaround:

- check the surrounding area for obstructions and other hazards, and determine a clear taxi path;
- all of the lights and their covers should be clean and serviceable, and the cockpit windows should also be clean;
- the position lights should be carefully checked (red–left, green–right, white–tail), as position lights are essential for night flying (the taxi light is essential for safe taxiing, but the landing lights, while useful, are not essential for flight because good takeoffs and landings can be made without them); and
- for a neat external check, a test of any electrical stall-warning device can be made at this time, before returning to the cockpit and placing the master switch back to off, to minimize electrical drain on the battery.

Take great care during the preflight check at night, focusing the torch on each specific item as it is checked, and also running its beam over the airplane as a whole. Ensure that the windshield is clean and free of dust, dew, frost or ice.

If ice or frost is present, check the upper leading edge of the wing (the main lift-producing part of the airplane) to ensure that it is also clean. Any ice, frost or other accretion should be removed from the airplane (especially from the lift-producing surfaces such as wings and horizontal stabilizer) prior to flight. Do not forget to remove the pitot cover, otherwise there will be no airspeed reading on the ASI.

Internal Preflight Check

Carry out the internal preflight check. Ensure that spare fuses, if required, are available. Place all items that might be required in flight in a handy position, especially the flashlight, which should be placed where you can lay your hands on it in complete darkness. While handy, it should still be secure, otherwise it could become a dangerous missile in the cockpit during turbulence. A red lens on the flashlight is useful, as red light will not diminish your night vision as much as white light.

Cabin lighting should be set at a suitable level. Dim the cabin lights so that external vision is satisfactory, and reflection from the canopy minimized, but do not have them so dim that you cannot see the controls or fuel selector. Check and set individual instrument lighting, if fitted. It is unwise to commence night flying immediately after being in a brightly lit environment. Allow your eyes time to adjust to natural night light. Complete the preflight checklist, making sure that the additional night items are covered.

Cockpit and Cabin

Do not start up until you have the cockpit well organized with:

- your equipment stowed for easy in-flight access, especially the flashlight;
- lighting set adequately; and
- passenger briefing, and so on, completed.

Make sure that you have the parking brake set before starting the engine, especially since any movement of the airplane will be more difficult to detect than during daylight hours. To avoid draining the battery, any unnecessary electrical services should be off until after start-up. Ideally, the anti-collision beacon should be turned on just prior to engine start, to warn any person nearby that the airplane is active.

Keep a sharp lookout before starting the engine—a spinning propeller is deadly, and may be difficult to see at night. With dim cabin lights, an open window and a loud warning that you are about to start the engine ("clear") and the flashing of the taxi lights or landings lights several times, the risk will be minimized. Complete the prestart checklist if applicable, then start the engine normally.

- When the engine is running, check outside to make sure that the airplane is not moving.
- The alternator/generator should be checked to ensure that it is functioning correctly, with the ammeter showing a positive reading after the start-up.
- Adjust the engine RPM if necessary to achieve a suitable charging rate. If the anti-collision beacon was off for the start-up, it should now be turned on for added safety.
- Confirm that the position lights are on; they are required to be on when the aircraft moves at night, since this is how other pilots determine which way your airplane is pointed.
- Complete the after-start checklist, if applicable.
- Adjust cockpit lighting to assist your eyes in adapting to the darkness outside.

TECHNIQUE

Taxiing at Night

The responsibility for all movement of the airplane, on the ground and in the air, lies with the pilot. Take advantage of any assistance provided by a marshaler, but remember that you carry the final responsibility. Use the taxi light, but avoid blinding the marshaler or pilots of other airplanes, if possible. The taxi light not only assists you to see obstructions and avoid them, it also makes it more obvious to other people that your aircraft is moving, or about to.

Taxi slowly and carefully. Taxiing at night requires additional attention for the following reasons:

Request a progressive taxi if you are operating at an unfamiliar airport.

- distance at night is deceptive and stationary lights may appear to be closer than they really are;
- speed at night is deceptive, and there is almost always a tendency to taxi too fast, since there are fewer ground references. Consciously check taxi speed by looking at the wing tip area (where reflected light off surface objects will help you to judge speed), and slow down if necessary; and
- other aircraft and any obstacles will be less visible at night; an airplane ahead on the taxiway may be showing just a single white tail-light that can be easily lost in the multitude of other lights, therefore, keep a good lookout.

When stopped, double check that the parking brake is set.

Follow taxi guidelines or lights. Taxiway lighting will be either two lines of sideline blue along the taxiway edges, or one line of centerline green. Yellow taxi guide lines may be marked on hard surfaces, and will be visible in the taxi light. Stay in the center of the taxiway to preserve wing tip clearance from obstacles.

The ground reflection of the wing tip position lights, especially on a high-wing airplane, are useful in judging the clearance between the wing tips and any obstacles at the side of the taxiway.

If there is any doubt about your taxi path, slow down or stop. If you stop, set the parking brake. In an extreme situation, say on a flooded or very rough taxiway, it may be advisable to even stop the engine, seek assistance, or check the path ahead on foot. The landing lights may be used to provide a better view ahead, but they will draw additional electrical power, and their continuous use on the ground may not be advisable (refer to your pilot's operating handbook).

Pay attention to the welfare of other pilots. Some taxiways run parallel to the runway, so avoid shining your bright lights into the eyes of a pilot taking off or landing, or taxiing, either by switching them off, or positioning the airplane conveniently. Avoid looking into the landing lights of other aircraft yourself, since this could seriously degrade your night vision.

Following the start-up and prior to takeoff, all of the vital radio navigation equipment should be checked—including the VHF COM, VHF NAV, DME, ADF, marker lights and transponder. The altimeter should be checked for the correct altimeter setting, and an indication close to airport elevation. During the taxiing run, the instruments should be checked.

Turning left:

- HI and magnetic compass decreasing;
- ADF tracking;
- the turn coordinator indicates a left turn, and the balance ball indicates that the airplane is skidding right; and
- AI steady.

Turning right:

- HI and compass increasing;
- ADF tracking;
- turn coordinator shows a right turn, and ball indicates skidding left; and
- AI steady.

At the Holding Point

The holding point or holding bay may have special lights or markings. Do not enter the runway until you are ready, you have a clearance (if appropriate), and the runway and its approaches are clear of conflicting aircraft.

While completing the pretakeoff checks at the holding position, ensure that your taxi and landing lights do not blind other pilots. Ensure that the parking brake is on—an airplane can easily move during the power check, and at night there are few visual cues to alert the pilot. During the pretakeoff checks, do not have the cabin lighting so bright that it impairs your night vision. (The flashlight can be used if bright light is needed temporarily.) Check outside regularly to confirm that the aircraft is stationary.

Pay special attention to the fuel selection, since the fuel selector may be in a poorly lit area. Correct trim will ensure that you have no unusual control forces to contend with when airborne. Ensure that any item required in flight is in a handy position. Complete the before-takeoff checklist thoroughly. Checking the heading indicator for alignment with the magnetic compass while the airplane is stationary is especially important at night, since it will be used for heading guidance, both in the traffic pattern and on cross-country flights.

A final check of cockpit lighting should be made. Ensure that it is adjusted to a suitable minimum, bright enough to see the major controls and instruments in the cockpit, but not so bright as to seriously affect your outside vision.

A 10-second review prior to lining up of your proposed flight path, and also proposed actions in the event of engine failure, shows good airmanship.

The Night Takeoff

When ready to line up for takeoff, make any required radio call, and look carefully for other traffic on the ground and in the air. Clear the approach path to the runway, checking both left and right.

Check the wind sock for wind direction and strength. Conditions are often calm at night, making either direction on the runway suitable for operations—so ensure that the approach areas at both ends of the runway are clear.

The landing lights of an approaching airplane are generally quite visible, but sometimes a pilot will choose to practice a night landing without using them, in which case the airplane will be more difficult to see unless it has strobe lights.

Do not waste runway length when lining up for takeoff, especially on a short runway. Line up in the center of the runway, check that the HI agrees with the runway direction and, with the brakes off and your feet well away from the brakes and on the rudder pedals, smoothly apply maximum power.

Directional control during a night takeoff is best achieved with reference to the runway edge lighting, using your peripheral vision, since your eyes should be focused well ahead of the airplane toward the far end of the runway. Runway centerline markings may also assist you. Avoid over-controlling during the ground run, keeping straight with rudder, and wings level with ailerons. If a problem occurs during the takeoff ground run prior to liftoff, close the throttle and apply the brakes as necessary, keeping straight with rudder.

Visual reference to the ground is quickly lost after liftoff.

The takeoff is the same by night as it is by day. Fly the airplane away from the ground at the normal liftoff speed, and adopt the normal climb-out attitude. The big difference is that, at night, visual reference to the ground is quickly lost after liftoff, and any tendency to settle back onto the ground will not be as easily noticed. As soon as the airplane is positively airborne, therefore, fly instruments.

Transfer your attention to the instruments before losing the last visual references, which typically will be the last set of runway lights. The first 300 to 400 feet of the climb-out will probably have to be totally on instruments until you are high enough to regain usable visual references.

Maintain the takeoff pitch attitude and wings-level on the attitude indicator, then establish a normal climb. Climb power and climb attitude will result in a positive climb away from the ground, reflected by a positive climb rate on the VSI and a gradually increasing altimeter reading.

The airspeed indicator should be checked periodically to ensure that a suitable airspeed is being maintained on the climb-out, with minor adjustments being made on the attitude indicator as necessary. When clear of the ground and comfortable in the climb-out, the HI is cross-checked for heading.

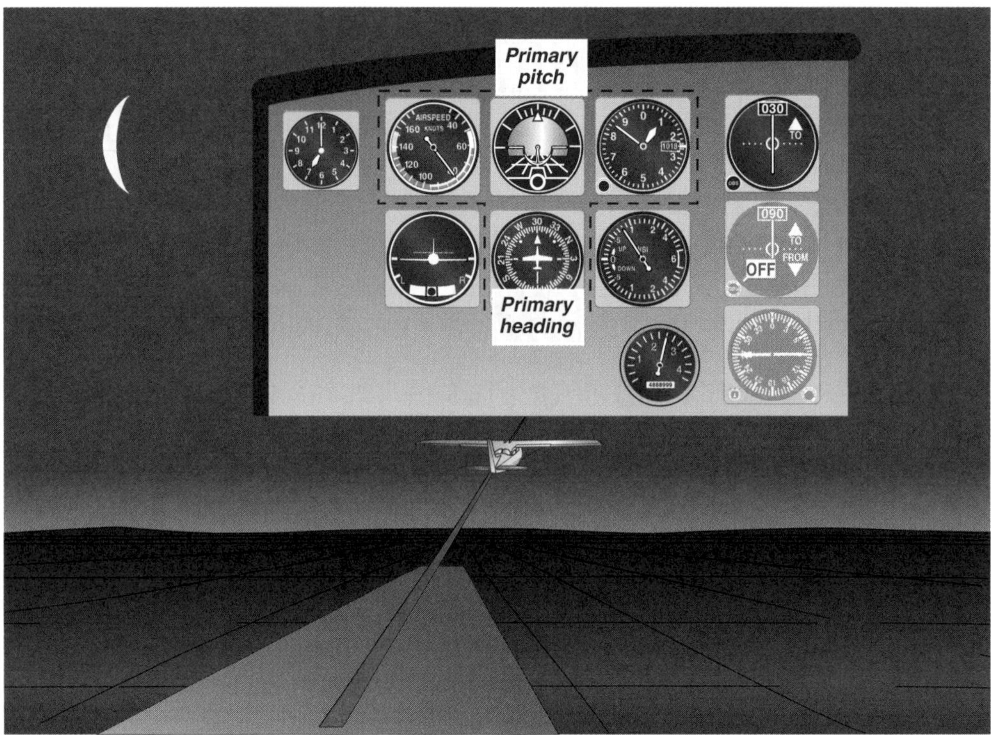

Figure 51-19 Transfer to the instruments after liftoff, and maintain a positive climb.

Retractable Gear

In a retractable-gear airplane, the landing gear should not be raised until a positive climb is indicated on both the altimeter and the VSI, and perhaps until insufficient runway remains ahead for a safe landing in case of engine failure (a very rare event these days with well-maintained aircraft and well-trained pilots).

Flaps

The flaps should not normally be raised until at least 200 feet above the airport, and no turns should be made until a safe altitude is reached. Normally, a steady, straight climb is maintained until within 300 feet of pattern altitude before turning onto the crosswind leg.

Landing Lights

With little or no natural external horizon visible, the instruments become very important. If glare from the landing lights is distracting in the cockpit, turn them off when established in the climb. Mist, haze, smoke or cloud will reflect a lot of light.

Engine Failure

The actions to follow in the event of a problem during the takeoff run were covered above. If an engine failure occurs during the climb-out, follow the normal daylight procedures. Lower the nose to the gliding attitude to ensure that a stall does not occur, and use the landing lights to assist in ground recognition. Maintain control of the airplane. If sufficient altitude is available, restart the engine and climb away.

The Night Traffic Pattern

The traffic pattern at night is usually the same as that by day, except that it is flown mainly on instruments, with occasional reference to the airport lighting to assist in positioning the airplane suitably. The normal techniques of attitude flying apply. There is often a tendency to overbank at night, so special attention should be paid to bank angle.

When the airplane makes the first turn, the runway and airport lights will be easily seen and should be referred to frequently. Well-lit landmarks may also be useful for positioning in the traffic pattern.

Allow for drift on the crosswind leg, and level the airplane off using normal instrument procedures when you reach the pattern altitude. Maintain this altitude accurately, and carefully scan outside before making any turns. A good lookout for other aircraft must be maintained at all times, and the usual radio procedures followed. Look for the position lights of other airplanes, and respond with appropriate heading or altitude changes to avoid collisions.

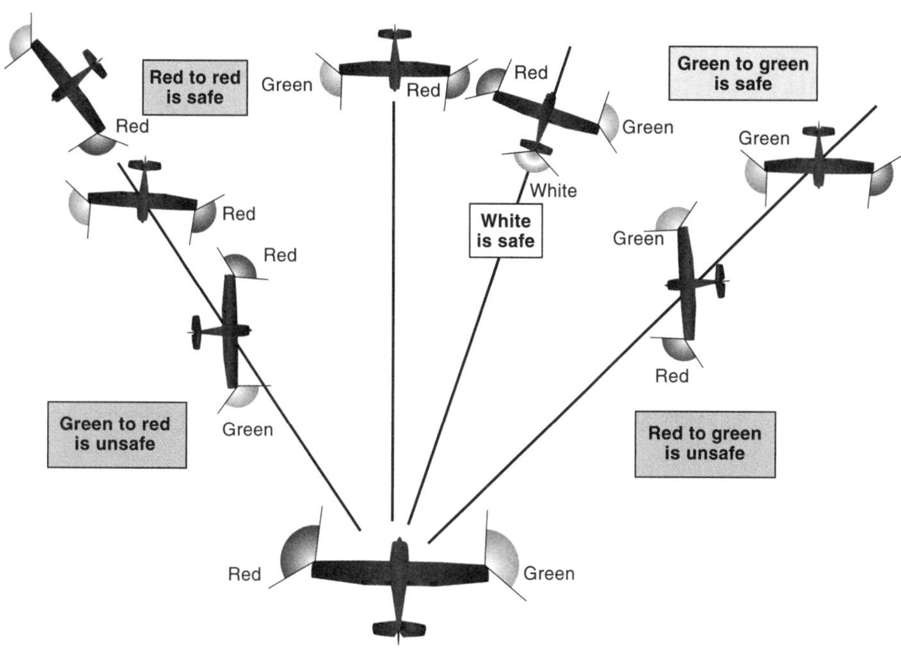

Figure 51-20 Using the observed position lights of other traffic to avoid collision.

While green to red is not safe, green to red will be the situation with two airplanes flying parallel on downwind. An especially careful lookout will need to be maintained. The usual right-of-way rules apply.

Listening to radio transmissions will help you maintain a picture of what else is happening in the traffic pattern.

The turn from downwind to base leg should be made at the normal position, with reference to the runway lights and any approach lighting, and the descent planned so that the turn to final commences at about 600 to 700 feet above the airport elevation—ideally with a 20° bank angle, and certainly no more than 30°.

When on final, confirm that you are in fact lined up with the runway, and not just a well-lit road—check that your heading agrees approximately with the runway direction, and make use of any radio navigation aids you have available.

The Night Approach

A powered approach is preferable at night.

Make a powered approach at night, rather than a glide approach; in modern training aircraft, the powered approach is generally used by day also. Power gives the pilot more control, a lower rate of descent and, therefore, a less steep approach slope. The approach to the aim point should be stable, using any available aids, such as the runway lighting and a VASI if available.

Using the runway edge lighting only, correct tracking and slope is achieved when the runway perspective is the same as in daylight. For correct tracking, the runway should appear symmetrical in the windshield.

Guidance on achieving the correct approach slope is obtained from the apparent spacing between the runway edge lights. If the airplane is getting low on slope, the runway lights will appear to be closer together. If the airplane is flying above slope, then the runway lights will appear to be further apart. Attention should also be paid to the airspeed indicator throughout the approach, to ensure that the correct airspeed is being maintained.

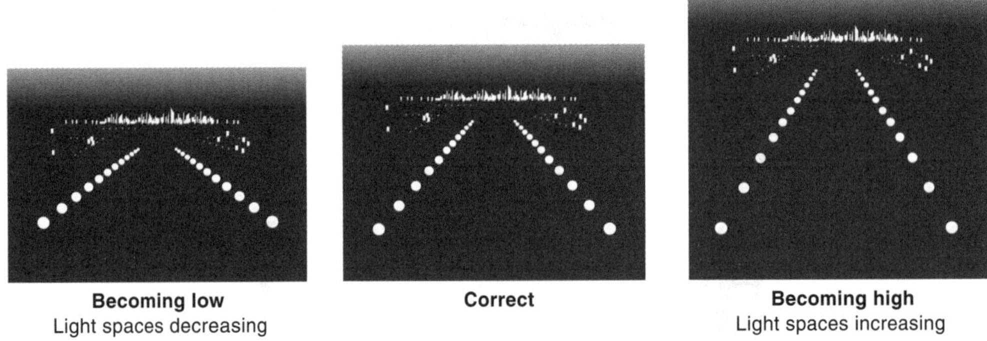

Figure 51-21 Perspectives on approach using runway edge lighting.

If no VASI is available, then the aim point during the approach should be a point selected somewhere between two to four runway-edge lights along the runway from the approach threshold. If there is a VASI available, however, the aim point provided by this system should be used. Because it is an approach aid and not a landing aid, the VASI should be disregarded when below about 200 feet above the airport, and attention placed on the perspective of the runway edge lighting in anticipation of the flare. Following the landing flare and hold-off period, the airplane will touch down some distance beyond the aim point used during the approach.

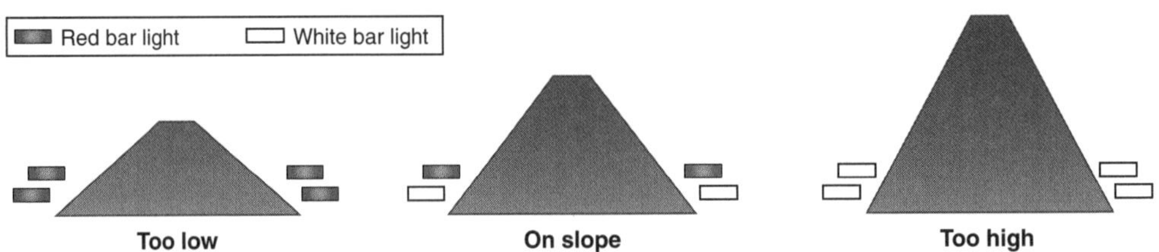

Figure 51-22 Perspectives on approach using VASI.

Tracking

Stay on centerline during the approach. Any tendency to drift off the extended centerline can be counteracted with coordinated turns, and drift can be laid off if a crosswind exists. Be prepared for wind changes as the descent progresses—the difference between the wind at 1,000 feet above the airport and at ground level is likely to be more pronounced at night than by day. It is common for the wind strength to decrease and the wind direction to back—change direction counterclockwise—as the airplane descends.

Stay on slope during the approach. Any variations in slope should be corrected with coordinated use of power and attitude. The aim point should stay, on average, in the same position in the windshield. Stay on airspeed during the approach. Check your airspeed on the airspeed indicator, and do not be afraid to use power. Overcome any tendency to fly too fast (a common fault at night). Occasionally check the altitude. Use the landing light as desired (not essential).

A VASI, if available, should be used as an approach guide.

Approaching the threshold, the runway lights near the threshold should start moving down the windshield, and certain runway features may become visible in the landing lights. The VASI guidance will become less valuable below about 200 feet and should not be used in the latter stages of the approach, and certainly not in the flare and landing. The VASI is an approach guide only—it has no value in the flare and touchdown. It is pilot judgment that counts in the landing.

The Flare, Hold-Off and Landing at Night

Use the runway lighting as your main guide in the flare.

The airplane should be flown on slope toward the aim point, where the landing flare will begin. The best guide to the flare (or round-out) height and holding the airplane off is the runway perspective given by the runway edge lighting.

As the airplane descends toward the runway, the runway edge lighting that you see in your peripheral vision will appear to rise.

The appearance of the ground can sometimes be deceptive at night so, even with the landing light on, use the runway lighting as your main guide in the flare, both for depth perception as well as tracking guidance. For this reason, your first landings may be made without using the landing light. When using the landing light, however, do not stare straight down the beam, but to one side.

There is a common tendency to flare a little too high in the first few night landings, but this tendency can soon be modified with a little practice. The runway perspective on touchdown should resemble that on liftoff, and an appreciation of this is best achieved by looking well ahead toward the far end of the runway. Avoid trying to see the runway under the nose of the airplane—this will almost certainly induce a tendency to fly into the ground without flaring.

Gradually reduce the power to idle as you enter the hold-off phase and touchdown.

As you flare for the landing, the power should gradually be reduced entering the hold-off phase, and the throttle fully closed as the airplane settles onto the runway at touchdown. Keep straight with rudder during the landing ground roll and, in any crosswind, keep the wings level with aileron. Use back elevator as necessary to keep weight off the nose wheel.

Stay on the centerline until the airplane has slowed to taxiing speed, using brakes if necessary. Speed is deceptive at night—you are usually moving faster than you think, so be careful and slow down. Taxi clear of the runway, stop the airplane, set the parking brake, and complete the after-landing check.

The Go-Around at Night

The technique is the same as by day, except that a go-around by night is performed primarily by reference to instruments, rather than external features such as the horizon (which may not be discernible).

A go-around by night is performed primarily by reference to the instruments.

Whereas the eyes may be concentrated on the runway lighting during the latter stages of the approach, these lights are no longer necessary during a go-around and, when full power is applied and the pitch attitude raised to the go-around attitude, it is possible that they may no longer be in view.

There will be a strong pitch/yaw tendency as go-around power is applied, and this must be controlled with reference to the flight instruments. Hold the desired pitch and bank attitudes on the AI, monitor vertical performance on the altimeter, monitor airspeed on the airspeed indicator, and hold direction on the heading indicator. Keep the balance ball centered with rudder pressure.

Do not change configuration (flaps/gear) until established in the go-around, with a positive rate of climb indicated on both the altimeter and the VSI.

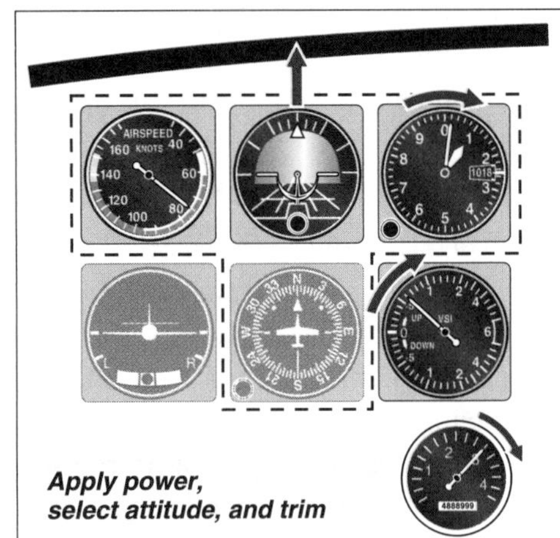

Figure 51-23 The go-around at night.

Wind Variations with Altitude

The surface wind at night may differ significantly from the wind at altitude. The term *surface wind* refers to the wind measured 30 feet above open-and-level ground—the height of most wind socks. The wind well away from the influence of the surface—typically some thousands of feet above it by day, and possibly only 500 feet above it by night—is known as the *gradient wind.*

There will be some vertical mixing in the air mass near the earth's surface, depending upon a number of things, including heating, which will cause thermal eddies in the lower layers. During a typical day, the earth's surface is heated by the sun. The earth's surface, in turn, heats the air near it, causing the air to rise in thermal eddies and mix with the upper air. This vertical mixing in the lower levels of the atmosphere brings the effect of the gradient wind closer to the ground. With vigorous heating (such as over land on a sunny day), the friction layer is deep, and so the stronger upper winds are brought down to lower levels.

The Surface Wind at Night

If the thermal eddying is weak—such as at night—then the vertical mixing is less and the friction layer shallower. With less warming and mixing, the effect of a strong gradient wind may not reach the ground, resulting in a surface wind that is lighter at night than by day. A light daytime wind of 10 knots may become practically calm by night, even though the upper winds have not changed.

A consequence of a reduced wind speed is a reduced coriolis effect, hence the surface wind will back compared with the wind at altitude—that is, the wind direction will move counterclockwise as the airplane descends. (The effect is reversed in the southern hemisphere.)

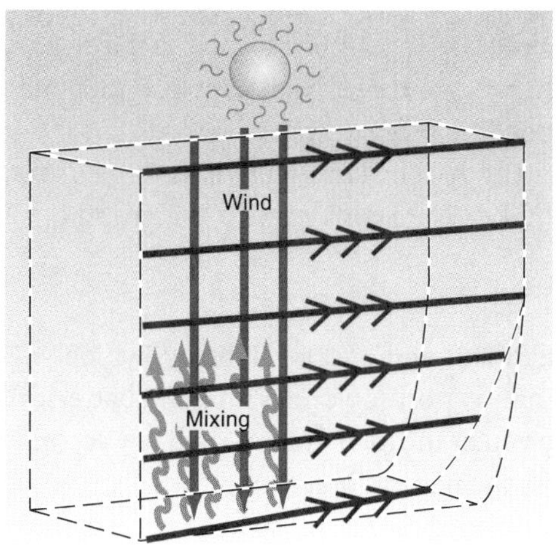

Wind stronger and does not back as much

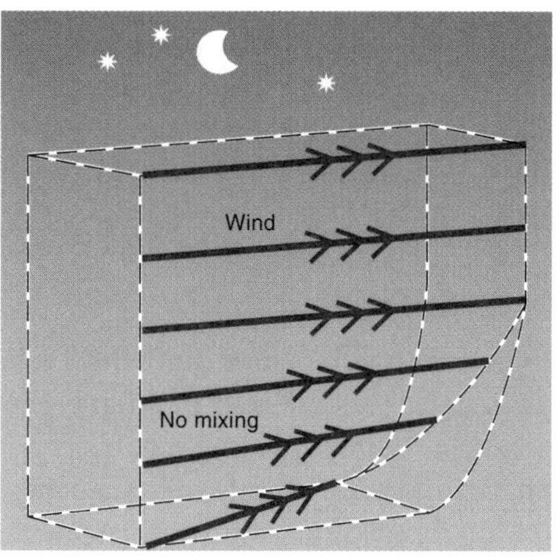

Wind weaker and backs more

Figure 51-24 The diurnal (daily) variation of wind.

The Climb-Out at Night

Expect stronger and sharper wind changes as you climb out by night. The difference in wind strength between the surface and at altitude will usually be more marked at night and, if there is a sudden transition from the lower winds in the shallow friction layer to the undisturbed upper winds at a particular altitude, say at about 500 feet, then wind shear could be experienced as the airplane passes through this level.

A surface wind of 5 knots on takeoff may suddenly become 20 knots at some low altitude on a clear night—possibly with a significant change in direction as well—yet it may be only 10 knots at 1,000 feet AGL on a clear and sunny day.

Emergencies at Night

Engine Failure

A forced landing at night away from an airport is obviously a more dangerous event than by day, when better vision will allow the easier selection of a suitable field. Moonlight may help at night, but do not count on it! Normal daylight procedures should be followed if the engine fails at night, with the emphasis on keeping the airplane at flying speed and restarting the engine.

Flying the airplane at a low forward airspeed—lower than normal gliding speed but consistent with retaining full control—will help achieve a lower rate of descent and allow more time for remedial action and for carrying out a forced landing if necessary.

A mayday call should be made promptly on the frequency in use, or on the emergency frequency 121.5 megahertz, to alert the rescue services. Squawk 7700 on the transponder if time permits.

Make a common-sense estimate of your altitude above the ground and keep a good lookout.

Time available for action will depend upon your altitude above the ground, so reference to the altimeter is important. With the correct altimeter setting set in the pressure window, the altimeter will read altitude MSL. If sufficient altitude and time is available, glide the airplane (at a safe speed) back toward the airport, while you continue troubleshooting the problem.

The full procedures for rectifying the problem and restarting the engine should be carried out if time permits. Fuel selection is a major item to consider. If, however, a landing has to be made, then consideration should be given to landing upwind, using only a partial flap setting (rather than full flaps) to avoid a steep nose-down gliding attitude with a high descent rate, and to minimize the amount of flare required prior to touchdown.

Well-lit roads will almost certainly have light poles and overhead wires, so they may not be suitable for landing, even though they look like nice runways.

It is preferable to touch down in a fairly flat attitude. The landing light may be useful during the last few hundred feet, especially to make visual contact with the ground.

Electrical Failure

An electrical failure may cause the loss of instrument and cockpit lighting, which will necessitate the use of your flashlight (kept in a handy position and with good batteries). A sudden failure of lighting should only deprive you of the instruments for a few seconds but, in this time, make use of visual cues such as the natural horizon.

If discernible, the natural horizon will generally be of more value when the airplane is well above the ground. Close to the ground, shortly after takeoff for instance, there may be insufficient ground lighting to provide a horizon and, in any case, the ground lights could possibly be on a sloping hillside giving a false horizon, or there could be so few that the airplane will quickly fly over them anyway. Scan the flight instruments!

If the electrical failure is only partial, then alternative lighting may be available in the cockpit from another light source. If a bulb has blown, interchange it. Panic action is not required—calm and careful consideration is. Do not be distracted from controlling the attitude of the airplane.

The attitude indicator, if it is electrical, will gradually run down if electrical power is removed, but it could remain useful for a brief period. Attention should be paid to the airspeed indicator, however, to ensure that flying speed is maintained. The first step following a failure of any kind is: fly the airplane!

When flying the airplane is under control, try to rectify the problem, and follow the appropriate emergency procedures or checklists. For an electrical failure, check the switching, monitor the alternator/generator or battery discharge rate, and check circuit breakers and fuses (if convenient) without disturbing your control of the airplane. If the electrical failure is only partial, but with a high discharge rate, then off-load the alternator or battery by switching off nonessential services, such as some radios, the landing lights, and so on. A landing as soon as reasonably possible on a suitable runway should be considered.

A return to the airfield should be planned, making a radio call if possible, and keeping a good lookout for other aircraft. If it is only a radio failure, then ATC can perhaps be alerted by flying a traffic pattern, descending, and then flying above the landing runway, flashing the landing light and/or position lights on and off. Without radio, light signals from the ATC personnel on the ground may be used—the main ones being:

- continuous red—give way to other aircraft and continue circling;
- red flashes—do not land (the airport is not available for landing);
- green flashes—return to the airport vicinity, but wait for permission to land; and
- continuous green—you may land.

If your position lights have failed, then the airplane should be landed normally as soon as it is safe to do so, unless ATC authorizes the continuation of the flight. ATC should be informed of the lack of position lights as soon as possible, so that other aircraft can be warned. Loss of the position lights will not affect control of the airplane in any way—in fact, the pilot generally cannot even see these lights—however it will affect the ability of other airplanes to see you and remain clear. A normal traffic pattern and landing should be made.

If the landing light has failed, then this is of little importance. It is not required for a pilot to make a normal, safe landing. You should, from time to time, practice night landings without using the landing light.

Failure of Airport Lighting

Most airports have a standby power supply that will operate within seconds of an airport power failure. There is a possibility, although remote, that a complete power failure could occur. Airplanes in the vicinity of an airport without any runway lighting at night should hold at a safe altitude and maintain a good lookout. Radio contact should also be maintained, preferably with ATC on the ground, but if that is not possible, with other aircraft in the traffic pattern or with ATC on an alternative frequency.

If the lighting is not returned to service, then consideration should be given to diverting (at a safe altitude) to a nearby airport where runway lighting is available. Radar service may be available to assist in tracking. A lowest safe altitude of 1,000 feet above the highest obstacle—2,000 feet in mountainous terrain—within four nautical miles either side of the diversion course should be allowed for, possibly higher if conditions permit.

Lost

If you become temporarily uncertain of your position, follow the same procedures as you would during daylight hours. Radio navigation aids, if available in the vicinity, should always be taken advantage of if you know how to use them. If you are really lost, then do not hesitate to ask for navigational assistance from ATC. The choice of alternate airports will be more limited at night, of course, since runway lighting and a navigation aid will be necessary.

It is always advisable to carry sufficient fuel at night for an unexpected diversion to an alternate field.

Night Navigation

Navigating at night follows the same basic principles as navigating by day, except that ground features are more difficult to see, distances are more difficult to estimate, and the likelihood of encountering unexpected clouds or areas of restricted visibility is greater.

The best ground features to use at night are usually the light patterns of towns, and the beacons of any nearby airports. Cities like Los Angeles are generally too large for distinctive light patterns to be meaningful to a novice night flyer, but small towns, especially if they have areas of darkness around them, are generally good. Busy freeways delineated by a stream of car headlights may also be useful ground features for navigation.

On moonlit nights, reflections off the surface of lakes and other large bodies of water may make them very visible—especially when viewed against the moon—although this should not be relied upon for navigation purposes, in case clouds cover the sky unexpectedly. On clear and calm nights, the reflections of stars off mirror-like water surfaces may give the impression of surface lights.

Flying over dark unlit ground or water can be disconcerting, and can lead to disorientation. Concentrate on the flight instruments.

Airport beacons, which are installed at various civil and military airports, are good landmarks. During the airport's hours of operation, the controllers will switch the airport beacon on at night, and also by day in bad visibility (below VFR minimums). Flashing lights, especially marine beacons on dark patches of water, can sometimes cause disorientation.

The runway lights themselves may be difficult to pick out, especially if the airport is surrounded by brightly lit streets. Use the airport beacon as a guide to the airport, and monitor your HI so you can determine the orientation of the runway.

Radio navigation aids are very useful at night, if you know how to use them correctly. For instance, positive identification of a runway by using the localizer is helpful. Some aids experience errors at night—for instance, NDB night effect, which may be greatest during the periods around dawn and dusk.

In general, you can expect major en route VORs and NDBs to be operating continuously, but some aids associated with a particular airport may not be available outside specified hours of operation. This could also apply to a radar service or an ILS. It is better to check first, and be sure.

Availability of Airports

Many airports close down at night. It is always advisable to check which airports are available at night, and which are not. Call an FSS briefing office if you are unsure. Check not only your planned departure and destination airports, but also those airports which might be useful as alternates in case of a diversion. You must be certain that runway lighting will be available for your landing.

Flight Planning

Good flight planning is especially important at night, since there will be fewer visible ground features to assist in determining navigation errors, as well as less assistance available from ATC or FSS in the form of communications or radar.

A weather briefing is essential before every night flight.

The weather takes on special importance at night. All relevant information should be studied carefully, especially the airport forecasts for your destination, as well as those for a number of alternates and your airport of departure. Remember that the temperature/dewpoint spread provides some clue as to the possibility of mist or fog forming when the temperature falls during the night. Also, fewer weather observers on duty at night will mean fewer weather updates. Make use of automated weather services (HIWAS, ATIS, ASOS and AWOS).

Attention should be paid to the possibility of low clouds, mist or fog, and also to the wind strength and direction, at altitude as well as at the surface. The presence of clouds might be indicated by surface lights or the stars and moon disappearing. If you inadvertently enter clouds, concentrate on the flight instruments and make a medium or shallow 180° turn to the reciprocal heading—this should bring you back into the clear within a short time.

Mist or fog might be indicated by lights and stars appearing fuzzy. Remember that vertical visibility through mist and fog is much better than slant visibility. Even though you can see the airport clearly from overhead, the slant visibility on approach might make an approach and landing impossible.

A suitable route should be chosen that utilizes the best features available at night—the lights of small towns, airport beacons, operating radio navigation aids, marine beacons, freeways—even if this route is slightly longer than the direct route. Rugged or high terrain is best avoided, and a safety altitude to ensure adequate terrain clearance should be calculated. A vertical clearance of at least 1,000 feet above the highest obstacle within 4 nautical miles of your planned course is recommended. Take along adjoining sectional charts, since you can see long distances at night, and far-distant towns might still be good landmarks.

Courses should be marked on the chart with conspicuous black lines, to ensure that they will be clearly seen in a dimly lit cockpit. The flight log should also be filled in with a dark pencil or pen, so that it is easily read in dim lighting. Red lines will not be visible in red lighting, and certain colors on the map may not be as distinguishable by night, which may lead to some difficulties.

Care should be taken in measuring courses and distances, and then in calculating headings and ground speeds. Always recheck! Dead reckoning is very important at night, and a correct flight log is a much better starting point than an incorrect one.

Calculate an accurate fuel log, ensuring that there is sufficient fuel available for a successful diversion and landing, with adequate reserves remaining.

It is recommended that a flight plan be submitted for a night cross-country flight, since this increases your protective search-and-rescue cover.

Headings and Airspeed

Fly accurate headings and airspeed.

Distance at night can be deceptive, since there will be fewer ground features visible and available for comparison in terms of size and location. The usual tendency at night is to underestimate distance. What appears to be about 5 miles may in fact be 10. Altitude and speed may also be difficult to estimate, so careful attention should be paid to the altimeter and to the airspeed indicator.

The airplane should be navigated, according to a predetermined flight log, by flying planned heading and true airspeed. From time to time occasional track corrections and revised ETAs may be required, using reliable pinpoints and radio navigation aids. Accurate heading and time-keeping is essential, and changes should only be made when you are absolutely certain that a change is required.

If you become lost on a night cross-country flight, follow the normal daylight procedures. Use available visual features and radio navigation aids to fix your position, or request assistance from ATC or FSS—they may be able to provide a radar fix or a DF bearing. However, with good flight planning and accurate flying in terms of airspeed and heading, you will always know where you are, even at night.

REVIEW 51

Night Flight

1. What are the two types of light-sensitive cells on the retina of the eye?
2. Which kind of light-sensitive cells mainly occupy the central part of the retina? Are these cells sensitive to color? Are they good for small detail? Which of central vision or peripheral vision are they used for?
3. Which kind of light-sensitive cells mainly occupy the outer band of the retina? Are these cells sensitive to color? Are they good for small detail? Which of central vision or peripheral vision are they used for?
4. What is another name for peripheral vision?
5. Which of peripheral vision or central vision is better at night?
6. Approximately how many minutes does it take for your eyes to adapt fully to darkness?
7. How long does it take for bright light to impair your dark adaptation?
8. Does smoking in the cockpit affect your night vision?
9. Will a good diet improve your night vision?
10. What is the best light to use in a cockpit to avoid impairing your night vision?
11. If you use red light in a darkened cockpit, will you be able to see red markings or features on your navigation chart?
12. Should you carry a flashlight with you at night?
13. When should the position lights be turned on?

Figure 51-25 Sunset—a great time to fly!

14. Sketch a diagram showing the placement in your cockpit of the instruments required for night flight.
15. What is the color of the position light on the left wing? What is the color of the position light on the right wing? What is the color of the rear-facing position light on the tail?
16. Is an approved anti-collision light system required at night?
17. Do you need to always use the landing light when landing at night?
18. For night flight, the airplane, must the airplane have spare fuses stored in an accessible place?
19. What color are centerline taxiway lights? What color are sideline taxiway lights?
20. What color is runway edge lighting? What color are the runway threshold lights when seen from the approach side? What color are the runway end lights at the far end of the runway?
21. What sequence will a civil airport beacon flash?
22. What does VASI stand for? Approximately how many degrees slope to the runway will VASI provide?
23. A two-bar VASI will show what color on top of white when the airplane is on slope?
24. What does a two-bar VASI showing red-on-red indicate?
25. What does a two-bar VASI showing white-on-white indicate?
26. Describe how to switch on pilot-controlled runway lights to maximum intensity. When activated, they should stay on for how many minutes?
27. What tendency caused by the lack of ground references should you avoid when taxiing at night?
28. On takeoff at night, what should you do as soon as the airplane is airborne?
29. What tendency should you avoid with regard to airspeed on final approach to land?
30. To assist in orientation at night, do you need to keep the HI aligned with the magnetic compass?
31. How does the extent of the use of the flight instruments when flying VFR at night compare to that when flying by day?
32. If you see a red position light from another aircraft out to the right, is the situation safe?
33. If you see a green position light from another aircraft out to the left, is the situation safe?
34. Is red-to-green safe?
35. What is the usual tendency with regard to estimating distances at night? Is a town that appears to be 10 nautical miles distant likely to 20 nautical miles distant or 5 nautical miles distant?
36. How does the strength of the wind on the runway at night usually compare the that during the day? Why?
37. Are sharp changes in wind speed and direction as you climb out after a takeoff more likely at night? Why?
38. Is it good airmanship to carry sufficient fuel for diversion to another airport at night in case the lighting at your airport fails or the weather deteriorates unexpectedly?

Answers are given on page 588.

52 Unmanned Aircraft Systems (UAS)

OBJECTIVES

To achieve the following:

- An understanding of unmanned aircraft regulations and operational limitations.
- For manned aircraft pilots to recognize and safely operate with unmanned aircraft sharing the National Airspace System.
- To know what to do in the event of an accident or incident with an unmanned aircraft.

INTRODUCTION

An unmanned aircraft (UA), or drone, is an aircraft operated without the possibility of direct human intervention from within or on the aircraft. An unmanned aircraft system (UAS) is an unmanned aircraft plus its associated elements that are required for safe operation, such as a data link, ground control station, and any necessary ground support equipment. As a manned aircraft pilot, you will share the National Airspace System (NAS) with unmanned aircraft—more specifically, small unmanned aircraft (sUA). To meet the criteria of an sUA, the unmanned aircraft must weigh less than 55 pounds (25kg), including everything that is onboard or otherwise attached to the aircraft.

While military unmanned aerial vehicles (UAV) have been around since the early 1900s, civil unmanned aircraft are relatively new to aviation and have seen a rapid growth in operations conducted within the NAS. Much like the rules and regulations manned aircraft pilots abide by for the safety of the NAS, the FAA has developed rules and regulations that commercial operators and remote pilots of civil sUA must abide by. These are outlined in 14 CFR Part 107, Small Unmanned Aircraft Systems. If operators intend to fly their drone or model aircraft solely for recreational (i.e., hobbyist) purposes, they should abide by the statutory exception and safety guidance outlined in Advisory Circular 91-57.

Remote pilot or remote pilot-in-command: a person who holds a Remote Pilot Certificate with an sUAS Rating under 14 CFR Part 107 and has the final authority and responsibility for the operation and safety of an sUAS operation.

Figure 52-1 shows the difference between a conventional sUA that you might see in a commercial operation under Part 107 and a recreational remote controlled aircraft. While

Figure 52-1 Conventional sUA versus remote controlled airplane

a model aircraft is a more fragile structure built from lightweight materials, conventional sUA tend to be built from sturdier materials and feature sophisticated technology, like cameras and lithium batteries.

The Administrator may issue a certificate of waiver authorizing a deviation from any regulation specified in §107.205 if the Administrator finds that a proposed sUAS operation can safely be conducted under the terms of that certificate of waiver.

Drones have evolved so much over the years that many commercial operators have now received a certificate of waiver (or exemptions) for the operation of autonomous unmanned aircraft within the NAS. An autonomous operation is a flight during which an unmanned aircraft operates without pilot intervention in the management of the flight, and/or is pre-programmed for tasks apart from human-pilot control. This technology is being used for the commercial delivery of goods and even the delivery of urgent medication and vaccines.

REGULATIONS

See 14 CFR Part 48, Registration and Marking Requirements for Small Unmanned Aircraft, for the current regulations regarding sUA registration and identification.

There are two main types of drone operations: recreational and commercial—those operating for hire or for a business, such as surveillance, media, delivery, or emergency services. In both types of operation, the unmanned aircraft is required to be registered with the FAA and to be marked with a registration number, similar to a tail number you would see on an airplane. This registration number is used to identify the unmanned aircraft and trace it back to its owner.

If a pilot intends to operate an unmanned aircraft for commercial purposes, they must adhere to the regulations outlined in 14 CFR Part 107 and obtain a Remote Pilot Certificate with Small Unmanned Aircraft Systems Rating. This can be accomplished by completing an FAA Knowledge Exam or, if the operator already holds a pilot certificate issued under 14 CFR Part 61, by completing a free online course offered by the FAA. The purpose of both the exam and free course is to make sure that the remote pilot-in-command has an understanding of the regulations and aeronautical knowledge to be able to safely operate a drone within the NAS.

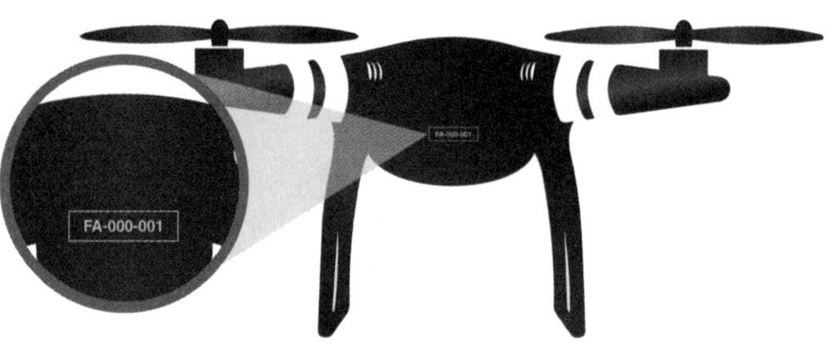

How to label your UAS
Find registration number on the confirmation screen and in your user profile.

Registration # FA-000-001

Figure 52-2 An unmanned aircraft marked with a registration number.

OPERATIONAL LIMITATIONS

The remote pilot must ensure that the drone operation poses no undue hazard to people, aircraft, or property in the event of a loss of control of the aircraft for any reason.

Small unmanned aircraft are restricted to ground speeds no faster than 87 knots (100 mph) and operational altitudes at and below 400 feet AGL, unless flown within a 400-foot radius of a structure and not flown higher than 400 feet above the structure's immediate uppermost limit (as seen in figure 52-3). As a manned aircraft pilot, it is important to stay vigilant and use the see-and-avoid concept when operating at low altitudes, during such times as ground reference maneuvers, departure and landing, and off airport operations.

Similar to manned aircraft, sUA conducting operations during civil twilight must be equipped with anti-collision lighting that is visible for at least three statute miles. The

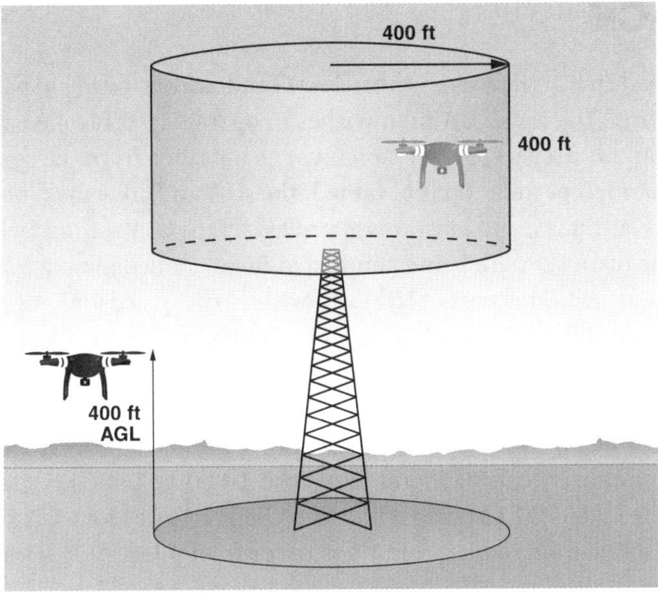

Figure 52-3 Flying in the vicinity of a structure.

purpose of this is to allow the remote PIC and/or visual observer (VO) to better see the sUA and to allow other aircraft operating within the NAS to more easily identify the sUA during civil twilight, night, and times of reduced visibility. When identifying sUA anti-collision lights from the cockpit, you should look for two factors:

A visual observer (VO) is a person acting as a flight crewmember who assists the sUA remote PIC to see and avoid other air traffic or objects aloft or on the ground.

1. The regularity of the lights should be blinking or a strobe effect.
2. The color of the lights should be white or red.

While navigation lights are not required under Part 107, some operators may still choose to install such lights on their sUA. These lights will be a solid white, green, or red. However, as a manned aircraft pilot, you should not rely on navigation lights installed on sUA to determine the direction of travel in the same way as you would a manned aircraft. Mainly because of the maneuverability of sUA and their ability to travel in all directions—forward flight, reverse flight, left, and right—as well as their ability to quickly change their direction of travel.

Figure 52-4 Scan for unmanned aircraft anti-collision lights.

AIRSPACE

A UAS NOTAM may also be referred to as a drone NOTAM (DROTAM) or UAS Operating Area (UOA) NOTAM. These terms are interchangeable, and the process for filing one is still done by using 1800WXBrief.com or by calling 1-800-WX-BRIEF.

Small unmanned aircraft may operate in Class G and uncontrolled airspace without prior permission from ATC. If an sUA pilot wishes to operate in controlled airspace, such as Class B, C, D, and E airspace, permission must be obtained from the controlling facility (ATC) beforehand. If permission is obtained, the sUA and crew may then operate at the specified times, altitudes, and locations approved by the controlling facility.

If operations of an sUA are being conducted in controlled airspace, a UAS NOTAM will typically be issued. This type of NOTAM will also be issued for UAS operations being conducted outside of Part 107 regulations. For example, a UAS NOTAM will be issued for an sUAS that has received prior permission and a waiver to operate at altitudes greater than 400 feet AGL to conduct a search and rescue mission. These types of NOTAMs can be obtained just like any other NOTAM, via a thorough weather briefing using 1800WXBrief.com or by calling Flight Service at 1-800-WX-BRIEF. Figure 52-5 shows an excerpt of the UAS NOTAM map with a specified NOTAM for a UAS Operating Area of a one-half statute mile radius from the surface to 400 feet AGL within the outlined latitude and longitudes.

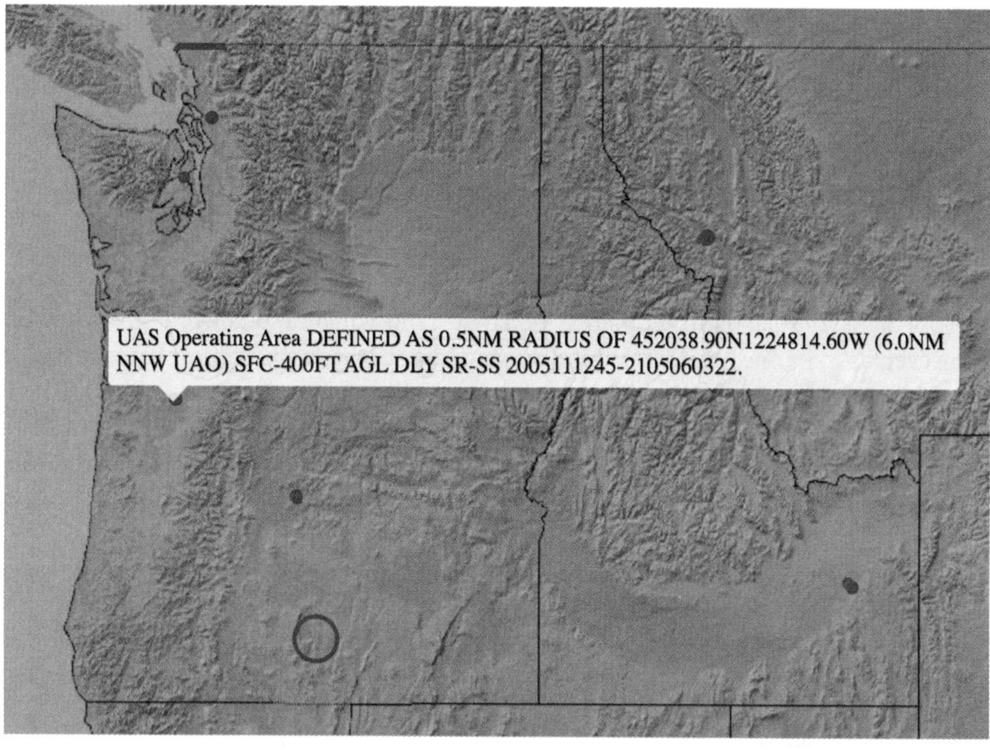

Figure 52-5 UAS NOTAM excerpt over the Pacific Northwest.

Airport Operations

No person may operate an sUA in a manner that interferes with operations and traffic patterns at any heliport, seaplane base, or airport—such as approach corridors, taxiways, runways, or helipads. For example, an unmanned aircraft hovering 200 feet above a runway may cause a manned aircraft holding short of the runway to delay takeoff or a manned aircraft on the downwind leg of the pattern to delay landing. While the unmanned aircraft in this scenario would not pose an immediate traffic conflict to the aircraft on the downwind leg of the traffic pattern or to the aircraft intending to take off, nor would it violate the right-of-way rules, the sUA nevertheless would have interfered with the operations of the traffic pattern at an airport.

VISUAL LINE OF SIGHT AND RIGHT-OF-WAY

The remote PIC, VO, or person manipulating the controls is required to maintain visual line of sight (VLOS) of the sUA at all times, allowing the crew to continually scan for other air traffic or hazards that may be in the vicinity. Furthermore, it is the responsibility of the sUA crew to give right-of-way and yield to all manned aircraft operations. Precaution should still be taken by manned aircraft pilots to continually see-and-avoid any and all unmanned aircraft. As noted earlier, autonomous drone operations may exist as well as operations outside of VLOS if the operator has received the appropriate certificate of waiver from the Administrator. Because of such operations and even with enhanced safety procedures and anti-collision technology built into unmanned aircraft, it becomes particularly important for manned aircraft pilots to play a vigilant role in avoiding and maintaining a safe distance from unmanned aircraft. A manned aircraft pilot may have little to no way to tell if that unmanned aircraft is being operated outside of VLOS or autonomously.

WHAT TO LOOK FOR

Unmanned aircraft come in all shapes and sizes, from civilian to military, tiny to huge, and can be divided into two main categories: fixed-wing and rotor-wing. The rotor-wing category can further be broken down by classification based on the number(s) of rotors they utilize for flight. Common configurations you might see are multicopters (consisting of more than one rotor) like a quadcopter (consisting of four rotors) or hexacopter (consisting of six rotors). Common fixed-wing platforms consist of model airplanes and military UAVs. Depending on the type, they will have a variety of flight characteristic and speeds which require manned aircraft pilots to stay vigilant with scanning and see-and-avoid techniques. Below are some examples of the types of unmanned aircraft platforms operating in the NAS.

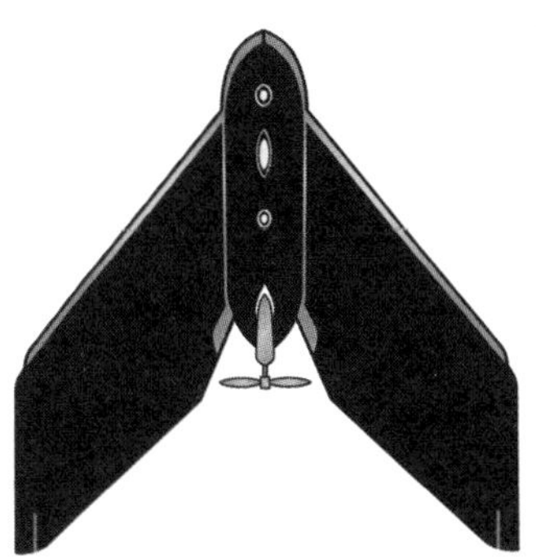

Figure 52-6
Fixed-wing unmanned aircraft.

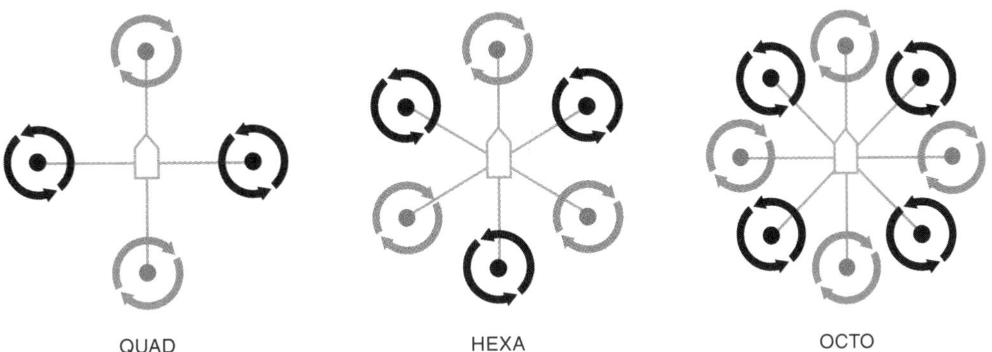

Figure 52-7 Common types of rotor-wing unmanned aircraft.

Figure 52-8 Various unmanned aircraft types operating in the NAS.

ACCIDENT OR INCIDENT WITH AN UNMANNED AIRCRAFT

Although typically small in size, a mid-air collision between an sUA and manned aircraft can cause substantial or even catastrophic damage. Unlike a bird of similar size and weight, which is made up of mostly soft tissue and water, an sUA is a much denser object and can inflict greater structural damage to the airframe and engine components.

If you should find yourself involved in an aircraft incident or accident (as defined in 49 CFR §830) you should make an immediate report to the nearest NTSB field office. A mid-air collision with a drone not resulting in substantial damage or serious injury would be classified to the NTSB as an incident. If you witness a drone operation not following FAA regulations or have a close call, you can report it to your local FAA Flight Standards District Office (FSDO). You should also report any dangerous or illegal operation of a drone you witness to the local law enforcement agency or first responders.

Figure 52-9 Quadcopter impacting the leading edge of a wing.

REMOTE ID

As of September 26, 2023, all UAS—unless otherwise authorized by the Administrator—must meet the requirements of 14 CFR Part 89, Remote Identification of Unmanned Aircraft. This requirement for remote identification, or remote ID, will apply to the majority of all unmanned aircraft operating within the NAS. Remote ID is the ability of an unmanned aircraft in flight to provide information such as identification, location, altitude, and its control station or takeoff (launch) location that can be received by other parties. This information can be used by the FAA and authorized public safety organizations to identify unsafe or illegal operations within the NAS and to identify an unmanned aircraft involved in accident or incident.

Remote ID helps the FAA, law enforcement, and other federal agencies to find the control station of a UAS that appears to be flying in an unsafe manner or where it is not allowed to fly.

REVIEW 52

Unmanned Aircraft Systems (UAS)

1. What is an unmanned aircraft (UA)?
2. Commercial operators of sUAS must abide by the regulations outlined in which Part of Title 14 CFR?
3. What is an autonomous UAS operation?
4. Who is the final authority in charge of an sUAS operation?
5. Name the two types of unmanned aircraft operations and explain the difference between them.
6. True or false? An sUAS operating under Part 107 are required to have operational navigation lights during civil twilight.
7. What is a UAS NOTAM and where can they be found?
8. True or false? It is the responsibility of the sUAS crew to give right-of-way and yield to all manned aircraft.
9. If you are involved in an incident or accident with an unmanned aircraft who should you notify?
10. If you witness an unsafe or criminal unmanned aircraft operation who should you notify?
11. What is the purpose of unmanned aircraft remote ID?

Answers are given on page 588.

Appendices

APPENDIX 1

Your Specific Airplane Type

Introduction

The basic principles of flight, engines, systems and performance apply to all airplanes, but there are differences between one airplane type and another. You should be thoroughly familiar with the type of airplane you are about to fly. For this reason, you should develop a sound knowledge of the specific airplane you are training in and that you will be flying during the flight test.

The primary source of this specific knowledge is the FAA-approved airplane flight manual (AFM), which is associated with the airplane's certificate of airworthiness, and the pilot's operating handbook (POH). You may be using an information manual based upon the pilot's operating handbook, but it must be kept amended for it to remain current. You will also learn more about specific airplane characteristics and operations in the textbook *Private and Commercial*, the second volume in this Pilot's Manual Series.

Having learned to fly one specific type of airplane, it is a relatively straightforward matter to be trained on another. You must display not only an ability to fly the airplane but also a sound knowledge of it, along the same lines as described here. You should also have an understanding of what maintenance a pilot is permitted to perform on the airplane. (Speak about this with your flight instructor.)

As part of the flight test for your private or commercial pilot certificate, you should be prepared to answer questions similar to those asked below, specifically related to the type of airplane that you will be flying. Since each specific type of airplane may require a different answer to the questions asked, no answers are provided here. You should research them in the primary reference documents mentioned above, discuss them with your flight instructor, and fill in the answers as your training progresses.

The Flight Manual

- The flight manual that I am using is for which type of airplane (manufacturer's name and model)?
- Is flight manual required to remain with the particular airplane? If so, where is it located?

Airworthiness Certificate and Other Documents (MAROW)

- Where is the airworthiness certificate is located? Does it need to be displayed at the cabin or cockpit entrance so that it is legible to passengers or crew?
- Where is the registration certificate located?
- Where are the operating limitations (flight manual, pilot's operating handbook, placards) located?
- Where is weight and balance information located?
- A list of required placards is found in which section of the pilot's operating handbook?
- Where is a copy of the checklists located?

Emergency Equipment

- Does the aircraft have a fire extinguisher? Where is it located? The type, and how to use it, can be found in which section of the pilot's operating handbook?
- What does ELT stand for? Does the aircraft have an ELT? If so, where is it located? Information on the ELT may be found in which section of the pilot's operating handbook? Does FAR Part 91 specify that the ELT battery expiry date must be marked on the ELT and entered in the aircraft maintenance record? How many nautical miles from the training airport is the limit to which a training aircraft without an ELT may proceed as specified in FAR Part 91?
- Does the aircraft have a first-aid kit? If so, where is it located?
- Does the aircraft carry survival gear? If so, where is this gear located?
- Does the aircraft have flotation devices? If so, what are these devices, and where are they located?
- Does the aircraft have a flashlight? If so, where is it located?

- Does the aircraft have a transponder? What is the code to squawk in an emergency situation?
- Is the aircraft fitted with seat belts? When must these be worn? See Part 91 under "Flight crewmembers at stations."
- Is the aircraft fitted with shoulder harnesses? When must these be worn? See Part 91 under "Flight Crewmembers at Station."
- Is the aircraft fitted with supplemental oxygen? This must be used during extended flights above how many feet MSL cabin altitude?

Weight and Balance Limitations

- What is the maximum takeoff weight?
- What is the maximum landing weight?
- What is the maximum passenger load (excluding the pilot)?
- What is the maximum number of persons on board (POB)?
- What is the maximum baggage weight that can be carried?
- What is the empty weight of the airplane?
- If you carry one adult passenger and full fuel, how much baggage can you carry?
- In which category (or categories) is the airplane permitted to fly?
- Do these weight limitations vary if the airplane is certificated to fly in the normal category and in another category, such as the utility category or the acrobatic category? Why are the weight limits less and the CG limits not as far rearward?
- Calculate the weight and balance situation—the gross weight and center of gravity position—given certain requirements, such as the number of passengers, the amount of fuel, the amount of baggage, and so on, using the airplane weight information found in the flight manual.

Airspeed Limitations

- The normal operating airspeed range is marked on the airspeed indicator with which colored arc?
- The caution airspeed range is marked on the airspeed indicator with which colored arc?
- The flaps-extended airspeed range is marked on the airspeed indicator with which colored arc?
- What is V_{NE}? What is its value in knots? How is it marked on the airspeed indicator?
- What is V_{NO}? What is its value in knots? How is it marked on the airspeed indicator?
- What is V_A? What is its value in knots? Is it marked on the airspeed indicator?
- If specified, what is V_B, otherwise known as rough-air airspeed? What is its value in knots? Is it marked on the airspeed indicator?
- What is V_{S1}, wings level and flaps up? What is it in knots? Is it marked on the airspeed indicator? If so, which speed end of which colored arc is it located?
- What is V_{FE}? What is its value in knots? Is it marked on the airspeed indicator? If so, which speed end of which colored arc is it located?
- The stalling speed with full flaps extended and the wings level is how many knots, known as V_{S0}?
- Do published stalling speeds assume the airplane is at maximum gross weight?
- Does stalling speed increase, decrease or remain unchanged if the airplane is at less than maximum weight?
- Does stalling speed increase, decrease or remain unchanged if significant power is applied?
- Does stalling speed increase, decrease or remain unchanged if the airplane is banked?
- Does stalling speed increase, decrease or remain unchanged if the airplane is maneuvering, such as when pulling out of a dive?
- In a 30°-banked turn, the stalling speed will increase by what percentage? This is how many knots?
- In a 60°-banked turn, the stalling speed will increase by what percentage? This is how many knots?
- What is the maximum speed in knots at which you may use abrupt and full elevator travel?

Aerodynamic Load Limitations

- What is the maximum load factor (flaps up)?
- What is the maximum load factor (flaps extended)?
- Are there any other handling limitations if, for instance, the airplane has a full load of passengers, of maximum baggage, or a maximum fuel load?

Authorized Operations

- Is the airplane certificated to fly during the day?
- Is the airplane certificated to fly during the night?
- Is the airplane certificated to fly under the Visual Flight Rules (VFR)?
- Is the airplane certified to fly under the Instrument Flight Rules (IFR).
- Is the airplane certificated for flight into known icing conditions.
- Are forward slips with flaps extended prohibited? Is there a placard regarding this near the flap control?

Takeoff Performance Limitations

- What is the maximum structural takeoff weight?
- Be able to use the takeoff chart(s) in the flight manual to calculate the performance figures—performance-limited takeoff weight or runway length required—given a specific situation.
- What is the takeoff distance required, under standard MSL conditions for a takeoff at maximum weight and a climb to clear a 50-foot obstacle?
- Compared with a takeoff at a sea-level airfield, will a takeoff at a high-elevation airfield require the same, more or less runway length?
- Compared with a takeoff in standard conditions, will a takeoff in high humidity require the same, more or less runway length?
- Compared with a takeoff under standard conditions, will a takeoff at a higher temperature require the same, more or less runway length?
- What is the obstacle-clearance speed with takeoff flaps extended? This is found in which section of the pilot's operating handbook?
- What are V_X and V_Y? What are they in knots? They are found in which section of the pilot's operating handbook?

Landing Performance Limitations

- What is the maximum structural landing weight?
- Be able to use the landing chart(s) in the flight manual to calculate the performance figures—performance-limited landing weight or runway length required—given a specific situation.
- What is the landing distance in feet required under standard MSL conditions for a landing at maximum weight approaching over a 50-foot obstacle?
- Compared with a landing at a sea-level airfield, will a landing at a high-elevation airfield require the same, more or less runway length?
- Compared with a landing at standard temperature, will a landing at a higher air temperature require the same, more or less runway length?
- The normal approach speed is how many knots?
- The maximum demonstrated crosswind component for landing is how many knots?

Cruise Flight (Maximum Range)

- Be able to use any tables or graphs in the flight manual to calculate range—that is, the distance the airplane can fly under given conditions.
- What is the recommended power setting (RPM) to achieve 65% power at 5,000 feet?
- What fuel flow in gallons per hour can you expect at 5,000 feet using the 65% best economy setting.
- What fuel flow in gallons per hour can you expect at 5,000 feet using 65% power and the best power setting.
- A gliding speed of how many knots will give you the best gliding range?

Maximum Endurance

- Be able to use any tables or graphs in the flight manual to calculate endurance—that is, the time that the airplane can remain airborne under given conditions. At 5,000 feet MSL, what are the maximum endurance figures (include expected fuel consumption)?

Flight Controls

- Understand how the elevator (or stabilator) system works—for example, will moving the control column back cause the airplane's nose to rise or drop? Is this a result of the elevator moving up or down?
- Understand how the aileron system works—will moving the control column to the left cause the airplane, at normal flying speeds, to roll toward the left or right? This done by moving the left and right ailerons in which directions?
- Understand how the rudder system works.
  - Where will moving the left rudder pedal in cause the right rudder pedal to move?
  - Will moving the left rudder pedal in cause the airplane's nose to yaw left or right? Is this due to the trailing edge of the rudder moving left or right?
  - What is the main function of the rudder in normal flight?
  - Is there an interconnection between the rudder and the aileron systems on this specific airplane?
- Understand how the trim system works:
  - Is there an elevator trim?
  - Is there a rudder trim?
  - Is there an aileron trim?
  - What type is the elevator trim?
  - What is the main function of a trimming device?
- Understand how the flap system works.
  - Is the flap system mechanical, electrical or hydraulic?
  - Are the flaps operated with a switch or lever?
  - Is the flap indicating system mechanical or electrical?
  - What is the flap range?
  - How is the flap position indicated?
- Does the airplane have a stall warning device?
- Is the stall warning device, if installed, interconnected with the flap system?

- Does the aircraft have leading-edge devices? If so, how are they operated?
- Does the aircraft have spoilers? If so, how are they operated?
- Does the aircraft have deicing or anti-icing capability on the wings and other aerodynamic surfaces?

The Propeller

- Is the propeller a fixed-pitch or constant-speed propeller?
- Will nicks, mud, insects or other contamination affect the performance of the propeller?
- Should new nicks or damage to the propeller be referred to a mechanic if possible prior to flight?
- Most training airplanes used for initial instruction have a fixed-pitch propeller, but if yours has a constant-speed propeller, then you should know how it works, how to control the RPM and manifold pressure with the propeller control and the throttle, and list the recommended settings and limits for RPM and manifold pressure.

Landing Gear and Brakes

- Is the airplane a tricycle landing gear or tail wheel type?
- Does the airplane have nose wheel steering?
- Are the rudder and the nose wheel steering interconnected?
- Can the rudder pedals be used to provide directional control when taxiing?
- Is the landing gear retractable? If retractable, what is it operated by? Does it have an emergency means of extension?
- Are shocks on the nose wheel during taxiing, takeoff and landing absorbed by a leaf spring, bungee or oleo-pneumatic strut?
- Are shocks on the main wheels during taxiing, takeoff and landing absorbed by a leaf spring, bungee or oleo-pneumatic strut?
- Are brakes fitted to just the main wheels, just the nose wheel or both the main wheels and nose wheel?
- How are the brakes operated from the cockpit?
- Are the wheel brakes operated mechanically or hydraulically?
- Are the wheel brakes disc or drum type?
- What is normal tire pressure in the main wheels and nose wheel?
- Know what defects in the tires are acceptable or unacceptable for flight, such as cuts, wear or bald spots.

The Electrical System

- How many volts does the DC electrical system operate at?
- Where is the battery located?
- Does the battery supply electrical power to the engine starter motor?
- When the engine is running, is electrical power supplied by an alternator or a generator?
- Is a serviceable battery required for the alternator to come on-line?
- When on-line, will the alternator recharge the battery?
- Understand how to manage the electrical system, for instance the indications and actions to be taken if the alternator (or generator) system fails or malfunctions.
- If the alternator (or generator) fails in flight, then should as much electrical load as possible be shed by switching nonessential services off? Which services would you switch off?
- A fully charged battery should supply emergency power for a period of approximately how long if required?
- Know the function and location of circuit breakers and fuses, and what to do if they pop or fail. How many times should you reset a popped circuit breaker?
- Is it possible to use external power when parked and, if so, what are the procedures? They can be found in which section of the pilot's operating handbook?
- Which of the following lights does the airplane have: rotating beacon, position lights, strobe, taxi light, landing light, cockpit lights, internal instrument lights, flashlight?
- Does the stall warning device, if installed, operate electrically or mechanically?
- If the electrical system of the aircraft totally fails (alternator not battery), know which of the following items become inoperative (also know the position of each in the cockpit):
  - flap switch or lever;
  - landing gear switch or lever;
  - VHF COM radio;
  - VHF NAV radio;
  - ADF;
  - GPS;
  - transponder;
  - rotating beacon;
  - taxi and landing lights;
  - flashlight;
  - ELT; and
  - magnetos and engine ignition system.

Flight Instruments

- Name the flight instruments operated by the pitot-static system and know whether they use pitot pressure, static pressure or both.
- Know the position of the pitot tube(s) and static vent(s), and any associated drains to eliminate water from the lines.
- Is there electric pitot-heat to prevent ice forming on the pitot tube which would cause incorrect instrument indications?
- Is there an alternate static source and, if so, where is it located? What is its purpose and what effect does it have on the instrument indications if the static source is changed by the pilot from normal to the alternate?
- Name the gyroscopic flight instruments.
- Name the flight instruments that are operated electrically.
- Name the flight instruments that are operated by the vacuum system, if fitted, and know how the vacuum system works (venturi or vacuum pump) and the maximum and minimum suction required for correct operation.
- How is the airspeed indicator operated?
- How is the attitude indicator (artificial horizon) operated?
- How is the altimeter operated?
- How is the vertical speed indicator operated?
- How is the heading indicator operated? Does it need to be periodically realigned with the magnetic compass?
- How is the turn coordinator (or turn indicator) operated?
- How is the clock operated?

Communication and Navigation Aids

- Does the aircraft have a VHF COM set; can it be used with the cockpit speaker and/or headphones?
- Does the aircraft have a VHF NAV set? Can this be used to receive signals from an NBD or VOR? Does it have DME capability?
- Does the aircraft have an ADF?
- Does the aircraft have a GPS navigation receiver?

Fuel

- The correct grade of fuel is what color? What additives, if any, are permitted?
- How many fuel tanks does your airplane have, where are they located, and what is their capacity in terms of usable fuel? How can you select fuel from each tank? Can you use fuel from both tanks simultaneously? Sketch from memory the fuel selector positions: off, left, right, and both.
- How can the airplane be fueled? Where are the filler caps and what precautions need be taken?
- Is it advisable to fill the fuel tanks prior to parking the airplane overnight? Why?
- Where are the fuel drains located and why are they used? When should fuel be drained?
- Where are the fuel tank vents located and why are they important?
- How can fuel quantity be measured, both on the ground and in flight? Is there a low-level warning?
- Does the engine have a carburetor or a fuel injection system? How does it work?
- Is the air that enters through the normal engine air intake filtered?
- Is the air that passes into the carburetor filtered when carburetor heat is hot?
- Does the engine require priming prior to start-up and, if so, how is it done?
- Does the airplane have fuel pumps and, if so, where are they located, what is their function, are they electrically or engine-driven, what are their maximum and minimum acceptable operating pressures, and when should they be used?
- Know the correct fuel management procedures, such as which tank(s) to use for takeoff and landing, when to use fuel pumps if fitted and when and how to switch tanks.

Engine Oil

- What is the correct engine oil for the airplane?
- Is the engine oil stored in a tank or sump? Where is this located?
- Explain how oil quantity can be measured. How many oil quantity indicators does the aircraft have?
- What is the minimum oil quantity prior to flight?
- What is the maximum quantity of oil?
- Is the oil used to lubricate, cool or both lubricate and cool the engine?

The Engine

- What is the make and model of the engine? How many horsepower can it produce? How many cylinders does it have? How are the cylinders arranged?
- Is the engine air-cooled or water-cooled?
- Cooling of the engine can be increased by opening the cowl flaps. Yes or no?
- What cockpit gauges are used to monitor engine operation?

- What is the normal and the maximum RPM?
- If the airplane is fitted with a fixed-pitch propeller, how is RPM controlled?
- If the airplane is fitted with a constant-speed propeller, how is RPM controlled? How is manifold pressure controlled?
- What are the minimum and maximum oil pressures?
- What is the normal oil pressure approximately?
- What are the minimum and maximum oil temperatures?
- What is the normal oil temperature approximately?
- Is the airplane fitted with a cylinder head temperature (CHT) gauge? If so, what are the CHT limits?
- During ground operations of the engine, it is usual to perform a magneto check, which should be done according to procedures specified by your training organization.
  - Specify the maximum acceptable RPM drop when one magneto is switched off, the maximum difference between the separate magneto drops, and (if permitted) the significance of the grounding check when both magnetos are switched off briefly.
  - What is the probable cause if the engine keeps running even though the magneto switch has been placed off?
- Specify the action to be taken if an engine fire occurs in flight.
- Is there a fire detection and warning system?
- Specify the action to be taken if an engine fire occurs on the ground.
- What equipment is no longer available if the engine fails in flight?
- What instruments are rendered inoperative if the engine fails in flight?
- What will moving the throttle in and out do?
- Explain the functioning of the mixture control and how to operate it correctly. If an exhaust gas temperature gauge (EGT) is fitted, explain how to use it.
- Under what conditions is it permissible to lean the mixture?
- To lean the mixture, should the mixture control be moved in or out?
- To enrichen the mixture, should the mixture control be moved in or out?
- Explain how to lean the mixture.
- What is the full out position of the mixture control called? Is it used to stop or start the engine?
- What are the indications if ice forms in the carburetor? For an engine with a fixed-pitch propeller? For an engine with a constant-speed propeller?
- How do you melt carburetor ice and prevent it forming again?
- What effect does applying carburetor heat have on the mixture? Does it lean, richen or not alter it?
- Does the hot air used to eliminate carburetor ice pass through a filter?
- Should you use carburetor heat when taxiing if it is not necessary?
- Is the engine normally aspirated, or supercharged or turbocharged to boost its performance on takeoff and at high altitudes?

Ventilation and Heating

- Know how to ventilate the cockpit adequately. What controls do you have?
- Know how to heat the cockpit adequately. What controls do you have? Is there a cockpit temperature gauge?
- Know how the heating system works and where the heated air comes from—for example, from over the exhaust muffs, allowing air to circulate near the exhaust system, thereby raising its temperature, before being channeled into the cabin.
- Exhaust fumes from the engine contain which dangerous gas, which is colorless and odorless and should be excluded from the cockpit?
- Will the presence of carbon monoxide in the cabin necessarily lead to unconsciousness?
- What precautions would you take if you suspect the presence of carbon monoxide in the cabin?
- What action would you take in the event of a fire occurring in the cabin?
- Is supplemental oxygen available for high-altitude flying? Where is it located, and how is it used. Information is found in which section of the pilot's operating handbook?
- Can the cabin be pressurized? If so, what controls and indicators do you have in the cockpit? What actions would you take in the event of a sudden decompression at high altitude? An emergency descent procedure is found in which section of the pilot's operating handbook?

Hydraulic System

- Does the aircraft have a hydraulic system? What equipment does it operate?
- What controls and indicators for the hydraulic system are in the cockpit?
- How are the hydraulic pumps driven?
- How is the hydraulic pressure regulated?
- What are the hydraulic pressure limits?

APPENDIX 2
Abbreviations

For explanations, refer to the Pilot/Controller Glossary in the *Aeronautical Information Manual* and the index to the Federal Aviation Regulations.

AAL	above aerodrome level
AC	advisory circular
ADS–B	automatic dependent surveillance – broadcast
AFM	aircraft flight manual
AGL	above ground level
AI	attitude indicator
AIM	Aeronautical Information Manual
ALS	approach light system
ALT	altitude
AM	amplitude modulated
AMSL	above mean sea level
ASI	airspeed indicator
ASOS	automated surface observing station
ATC	air traffic control
ATD	actual time of departure
ATIS	automatic terminal information service
ATS	air traffic services
AUW	all-up weight
AVGAS	aviation gasoline
AWOS	automated weather observing station
CDI	course deviation indicator
CFR	code of the federal regulations
CG	center of gravity
CHT	cylinder head temperature
CL	centerline
C_L	coefficient of lift
CoA	certificate of waiver or authorization
CRM	crew resource management
CSU	constant-speed unit
CTAF	common traffic advisory frequency
D	drag
DC	direct current
DG	directional gyro
DH	decision height
DME	distance measuring equipment
DR	dead reckoning
E	east
EFATO	engine failure after takeoff
EGT	exhaust gas temperature
ELB	emergency locator beacon
ELT	emergency locator transmitter
EPT	effective performance time
ETA	estimated time of arrival
ETD	estimated time of departure
ETE	estimated time en route
FAA	Federal Aviation Administration
FAR	Federal Aviation Regulations
FRL	fuselage reference line
FSS	flight service station
g	acceleration due to gravity
GA	general aviation
GAAP	general-aviation aerodrome procedures
GMT	Greenwich mean time
GPS	global positioning system
GS	ground speed
HAA	height above airport
HAT	height above touchdown
HDG	heading
HI	heading indicator
HIRL	high-intensity runway lights
HIWAS	hazardous in-flight weather advisory service
IAS	indicated airspeed
ICAO	International Civil Aviation Organization
IF	instrument flight
IFR	instrument flight rules
ILS	instrument landing system
ISA	international standard atmosphere
km	kilometer

kt	knot
LAHSO	land and hold-short operation
L/D	lift-drag ratio
LF	low frequency
LIRL	low-intensity runway lights
LSA	light-sport aircraft
LSALT	lowest safe altitude
MBZ	mandatory broadcast zone
MC	magnetic compass
MDA	minimum descent altitude
MEL	minimum equipment list
MF	medium frequency
MFD	multi-function display
MH	magnetic heading
MIRL	medium-intensity runway lights
MP	manifold pressure
MSL	mean sea level
N	north
NAS	National Airspace System
NDB	non-directional beacon
NM	nautical miles
NOTAM	notice to airmen
OBS	omni-bearing selector
PAPI	precision approach path indicator
PFD	primary flight display
PFL	practice force landing
PNR	point of no return
POB	persons on board
POH	pilot's operating handbook
PTT	press to transmit
PVASI	pulsating visual approach slope indicator
QNH	altimeter setting
RAIL	runway alignment indicator lights
RCLS	runway centerline light system
REIL	runway end identification lights
RNAV	area navigation
RPM	revolutions per minute
S	south
SAE	Society of Automotive Engineers
SFL	sequenced flashing lights
SSR	secondary surveillance radar
STBY	standby
sUA	small unmanned aircraft
sUAS	small unmanned aircraft system
T	thrust
TACAN	tactical air navigation
TAS	true airspeed
TCAD	traffic alert and collision-avoidance device
TCAS	traffic alert and collision-avoidance system
TDZL	touchdown-zone lights
TE	tracking error
TIS–B	traffic information service – broadcase
TPA	traffic-pattern altitude
TUC	time of useful consciousness
T-VASI	T-form VASI
UA	unmanned aircraft
UAS	unmanned aerial system
UAV	unmanned aerial vehicle
UHF	ultra high frequency
USG	United States gallon
UTC	coordinated universal time
V	voltage
V_A	maneuvering speed
V_B	turbulence-penetration speed
VASI	visual approach slope indicator
V_{FE}	maximum flaps-extended speed
VFR	visual flight rules
VHF	very high frequency
VLOS	visual line of sight
VMC	visual meteorological conditions
V_{NE}	never-exceed speed
V_{NO}	maximum speed—normal operations
VO	visual observer
VOR	very high frequency omnidirectional range
VORTAC	combined VOR and TACAN station
V_S	stalling speed
VSI	vertical speed indicator
V_{S0}	stalling speed in landing configuration
V_{S1}	stalling speed in clean configuration
V_X	speed for best angle of climb
V_Y	speed for best rate of climb
W	west
WCA	wind correction angle
Z	Zulu time

APPENDIX 3
Answers to Review Questions

Review 1
The Training Airplane

1. Refer to Figure 1-3 on page 4.
2. Raise.
3. Right.
4. With the rudder pedals.
5. Increase.
6. Rudder pedals.
7. In the wings.
8. Oil.
9. Refer to Figure 1-23 on page 12.
10. Mixture control.
11. The magnetos. More efficient combustion. Yes.
12. The battery (or external power).
13. By the alternator.
14. Ignition switch.
15. VHF radio. SQ stands for squelch. It eliminates background noise.
16.

Airspeed indicator

Attitude indicator

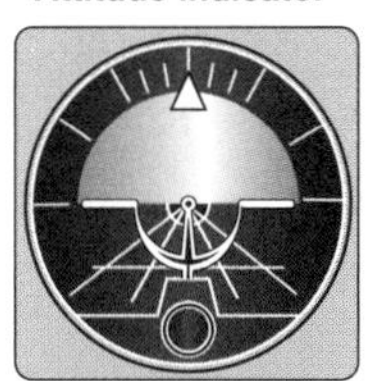

Altimeter

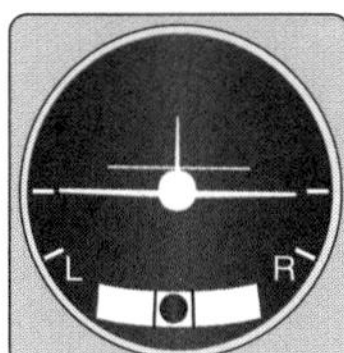

Turn coordinator

Heading indicator

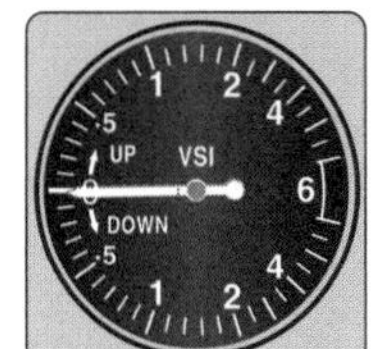

Vertical speed indicator

Review 2
Flight Preparation

1. Current medical and pilot certificates.
2. Maintenance record, airworthiness certificate, registration certificate, and documents showing the airplane's operating limitations and weight and balance data (MAROW).
3. Yes.
4. Yes.
5. Yes. Go/no-go decision (sensible).
6. Yes.
7. Yes.
8. Yes.
9. Yes in an appropriate area.
10. During cockpit preparation.
11. During cockpit preparation.
12. Yes. Must be.
13. Refer pages 28–33 as well as your flight instructor.

Review 3
Communications

1. The phonetic alphabet is a way for all pilots and air traffic controllers to avoid misunderstanding. Refer to the table on page 41 for the pronunciation of each individual letter.
2. Megahertz, which is the signal frequency in millions of cycles per second.
3. The magnitude of the maximum extent of the oscillation from the mean.
4. Somewhere in between.
5. To enable the pilot to fly while transmitting.
6. Yes.
7. It is the international distress signal.
8. Standby (SBY).
9. Fly the normal pattern, continue to make normal transmissions, look for a green light on final approach, look for traffic.
10. Emergency locator transmitter.
11. VHF COM is a radio transmitter and receiver; VHF NAV is a radio receiver used for navigation.

12. Up to 60 nautical miles.
13. The hand-held microphone is there for back-up only; the headset enables intercockpit communications, and unlike the hand-held microphone, keeps the pilot's hands free to fly to airplane.
14. Strength 2, readability 3.
15. True.
16. No radio call if all other indications are normal, but turn for home. If there were other unusual indications then a pan-pan would be declared.
17. Return via normal reporting points and lanes of entry. Make normal calls. Select 760 on the transponder. Enter the pattern from 500 feet above on the dead side and look for traffic. Follow a normal pattern for landing.
18. Reset the connections. Check radio and intercom turned on, volumes and squelch adjusted. If still quiet try the hand-held mike.
19. 121.5 MHz.
20. Go around for another pattern.

Review 4 Your First Flight

1. Check the answer with your instructor.
2. Check the answer with your instructor.
3. Check the answer with your instructor.
4. Check the answer with your instructor.
5. Check the answer with your instructor.
6. Check the answer with your instructor.
7. Knots.
8. Feet.
9. Check the answer with your instructor.
10. Normal walking pace.
11. Pitch and bank.
12. —

Review 5 Engine Starting

1. Yes.
2. Yes.
3. Battery, external power source, and hand cranking.
4. On.
5. Yes.
6. Yes. Yes.
7. Yes.
8. Yes. Oil pressure rises.
9. No.
10. Slightly cracked open.
11. Cylinders.
12. Accelerator pump. To the carburetor.
13. Mixture cutoff. Throttle wide open.
14. Section 9. Supplements.
15. No.
16. Never.
17. Yes.
18. No.

Review 6 Taxiing and Pretakeoff Checks

1. Yes.
2. Rudder pedals.
3. Top.
4. Absolutely.
5. When necessary. No.
6. Less.
7. With power or braking (not used together).
8. A fast walking pace.
9. Left. Right.
10. Yes (protect the propeller).
11. More power for a soft surface.
12. Yes.
13. Neutral or back.
14. Forward.
15. Into the wind.
16. Rudder and opposite braking.
17. Yellow.
18. Yes.
19. Stop then cleared to taxi.
20. Yes.
21. Yes. Common traffic advisory frequency.
22. Right.
23. Taking off or landing.
24. No.
25. Right.
26. The pilots.
27. Yes.
28. The pilot in command.
29. View of runway may be obstructed by nose of airplane.
30. At an angle, slowly. No.
31. No.
32. Low power.
33. Decrease. Left. Right.

34.

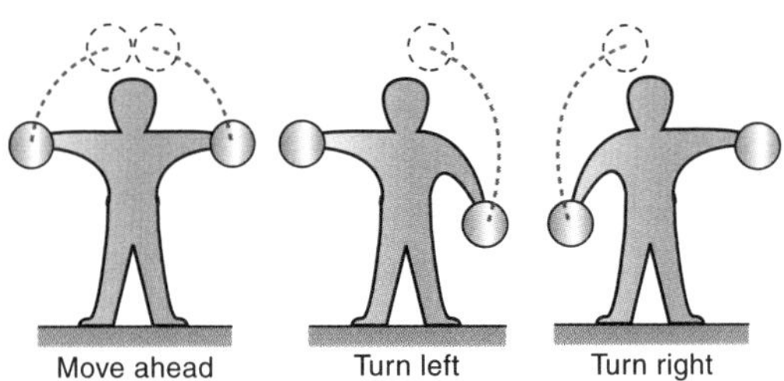

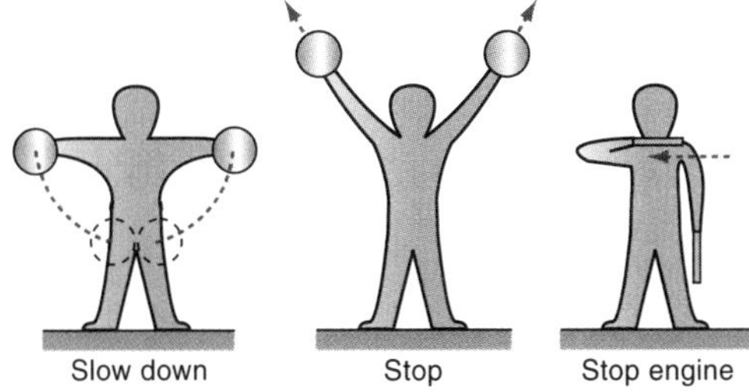

Review 7 Postflight Actions

1. Into any expected wind, but also for a clear taxi out.
2. Yes.
3. Yes.
4. A little slack but secure ties.

Review 8 Primary Controls

1. Elevators, ailerons, rudder and power.
2. Elevator.
3. Ailerons.
4. Rudder.
5. Rudder to center the ball.
6. Pitching motion about the lateral axis.
7. Rolling motion about the longitudinal axis.
8. Yawing motion about the vertical axis.
9. Pitching motion about the lateral axis.
10. Rolling motion about the longitudinal axis.
11. Yawing motion about the normal axis.
12. Prevent unwanted yaw or sideslip.
13. Causes the nose to yaw right or prevent it from yawing left.
14. Causes the nose to yaw left or prevent it from yawing right.
15. Left.
16. Right.
17. Left. Left.
18. Up. Down.
19. Down. Up.
20. Up. Raise.
21. Down. Lower.
22. Left.
23. Right.
24. Stability.
25. Firm pressure should be felt.
26. Right.
27. Indirect effect.
28. Up. Down. Left. Right. Adverse aileron yaw.
29. Down. Up. Right. Left. Adverse aileron yaw.
30. Ailerons.
31. Yes.
32. To the left. The nose will drop.
33. Left. Left.
34. Right. Right.
35. The airspeed will increase.
36. The airspeed will decrease.
37. Rudder pressure.
38. Trim.
39. Aileron trim. Rudder trim.
40. No. Attitude must be constant.
41. Never.
42. Not normally.
43. Back.
44. Forward.
45. The pressure should diminish. No.
46. Down. Aerodynamic force. Up. Back.
47. Yes, if to be sustained.
48. Yes.
49. Yes.
50. Perhaps.
51. Yes. No. Transient maneuver.
52. The greater the movement, the greater the effect.
53. The greater the airflow, the greater the effect. The greater the airspeed, the greater the airflow.
54. All of them.
55. Increasing power increases the amount of air.
56. Slipstream.
57. Fuselage and empennage.
58. Elevator and rudder.
59. No. It is less affected.
60. Spiral.
61. Clockwise. Left side. Left.
62. True.

Review 9
Secondary Controls

1. Yes. No.
2. No.
3. Extending flaps increases lifting ability.
4. Slower flight is allowed with flaps extended.
5. An increase.
6. A lot of drag. Steepens the descent.
7. Lower nose attitude. Better forward view.
8. Lower. Better. Shorter.
9. White.
10. V_{S0}. White. Low-speed.
11. Operate in small stages. After each stage.
12. Lift flaps.
13. Drag flaps.
14. No.
15. No. Low-speed end of the green band.
16. False. Airmanship means always operating the airplane within its limitations.
17. Forward. Back.
18. Slow.
19. Carburetor ice
20. Carburetor heat.
21. Drop. Less dense. Rise.
22. Yes.
23. No. Cold.
24. Red. Near the throttle.
25. To lean the mixture for optimum fuel usage at high altitudes and, when pulled fully out, to stop the engine.
26. Full rich.
27. Move mixture control slowly out to achieve peak EGT then slightly in.
28. Idle cutoff.

Review 10
Straight and Level Flight

1. Lift equals weight. Thrust equals drag.
2. Horizontal stabilizer and elevator.
3. Refer to figure 10-3, page 128.
4. Elevator.
5. In trim.
6. Hold the desired attitude with elevator and trim off any steady pressures.
7. Ailerons.
8. Rudder.
9. Altimeter. 100 feet.
10. Heading indicator. Magnetic compass. ±10°
11. Altimeter and vertical speed indicator. Lower.
12. Heading indicator and magnetic compass. Small coordinated turns.
13. Airspeed capability and rate of climb capability.
14. Airspeed capability and rate of climb capability.
15. Power and attitude.
16. Static stability.
17. Horizontal stabilizer.
18. Vertical stabilizer.
19. Wing dihedral and high keel surfaces improve stability.
20. Yes.
21. Yes.
22. Angle of attack and airspeed.
23. High angle of attack.
24. Low angle of attack.
25. Yes
26. Right rudder pressure.
27. Flying with crossed controls.
28. No. No.
29. Nose-down effect.
30. Nose-up effect.
31. Yes, plus the effect of the stabilizer.
32. Down. It holds the nose up.
33. Thrust-drag couple. The nose will drop.
34. Reduced. Reduced. The nose will drop.

Review 11
Climbs

1. Greater power required.
2. Maximum power.
3. Climb power. Climb attitude.
4. Yes.
5. Airspeed and rate of climb.
6. Airspeed indicator, vertical speed indicator and altimeter.
7. Up. Left. Forward pressure. Right pressure.
8. Small changes in pitch attitude.
9. Lower.
10. Raise.
11. Yes.
12. Obstacle-clearance speed. Plus 5/minus 0 knots.
13. V_X. Plus 5 or minus 0 knots.
14. Lower. ±5 knots.
15. The gradient will be shallower.
16. The gradient will be steeper.

17. Fuel rich.
18. ±10 knots. ±10°. Yes.
19. ±100 feet.
20. Performance decreases in warmer weather. Performance decreases at higher altitudes.
21. Decrease.
22. Higher.
23. Lower the nose and increase airspeed.
24. Full rich.
25. Airmanship.
26. Ceiling.
27. Airspeed indicator.
28. Greater than.
29. Performance decreases.

Review 12
Normal (Powered) Descents

1. No.
2. A power reduction. Lower nose attitude.
3. A power increase. Higher nose attitude.
4. 400 fpm.
5. 600 fpm.
6. 450 fpm.
7. 20 seconds.
8. Reduce power. Lower the nose.
9. 4 minutes.
10. Add power. Raise the nose.
11. Airspeed within 10 knots, heading within 10°, descent rate within 100 fpm, target altitude within 100 feet.
12. The aim point remains stationary.

Review 13
Use of Flaps in the Descent

1. Yes.
2. Lower nose attitude. Better forward view.
3. Operated in stages.
4. No, it reduces it.
5. Yes.
6. Yes.
7. The airplane will sink.

Review 14
Descents to an Aim Point

1. Undershooting. Add power. Raise the nose.
2. Overshooting. Reduce power. Lower the nose.
3. Undershooting. Add power and raise the nose.
4. Overshooting. Reduce power and lower the nose.

Review 15
Glide

1. Yes.
2. No. This is due to more drag for the same lift.
3. No. This is due to more drag for the same lift.
4. Nose attitude.
5. Lower the nose.
6. Flatter glide path. It does not affect rate of descent.
7. Steeper glide path. It does not affect rate of descent.
8. Up.
9. Rich mixture, carburetor heat to hot.
10. Airspeed within 10 knots, heading within 10° and target altitude within 100 feet.
11. Yaw right. Pitch down. Counteract with left rudder pressure and back pressure on the control column.
12. Yes. Do so by momentarily adding power.
13. Drop.

Review 16
Slips

1. Right. No.
2. Crossed controls.
3. No. Transient.
4. Forward slip.
5. Yes.
6. It may not be.
7. True.
8. Yes.
9. Yes.
10. Sideslip.
11. Yes.
12. No.
13. Yes.
14. Yes.
15. Rudder.
16. Lower the upwind wing.

Review 17
Medium Level Turn

1. Lift force.
2. Ailerons.
3. Neutralizing the ailerons.
4. Small movements.

5. Horizontal component.
6. Left.
7. Right.
8. Increase the lift. Drag will increase. Airspeed will decrease.
9. Higher.
10. The altitude remains the same.
11. The further the deflection, the greater the rate.
12. The longer the application, the steeper the angle.
13. No. Transient maneuver.
14. The load factor increases as bank angle increases.
15. The stalling speed increases.
16. Tighten the turn. It will increase rate of turn.
17. Tighter. Less time.
18. 20° and 45°.
19. Altitude within 100 feet, bank angle within 5°, roll-out heading within 10°. Always centered.

Review 18 Turning to Selected Headings

1. Heading indicator.
2. No.
3. In steady, wings-level flight.
4. In steady, wings-level flight.
5. ±100 feet. ±10°. With small coordinated turns.
6. Right.
7. Left.
8. Right.
9. Left.
10. Left.
11. Left.
12. Left.
13. Left.
14. Right.
15. Either way.
16. Right. 40 seconds.
17. Left. 30 seconds.
18. Left or right. 60 seconds.
19. Before the compass indicates your target heading.
20. After the compass indicates your target heading.
21. When the compass approaches selected heading.
22. When the compass approaches selected heading.
23. False. There is a tendency for the nose to drop.
24. Elevator.
25. Transient.
26. Reduce a little.
27. Elevator.
28. Power.
29. Elevator.
30. Aileron.
31. A regular lookout.

Review 19 Climbing Turn

1. It is tilted in the direction of the bank.
2. Horizontal.
3. Vertical.
4. It is reduced.
5. Climb performance decreases.
6. Vertical speed indicator and altimeter.
7. 200 feet per minute.
8. 15°.
9. Adjusting the nose attitude.
10. Airspeed.
11. Lower the nose attitude.
12. Ailerons.
13. Elevator.
14. Rudder.
15. Centered.
16. Left. Right.
17. Bank angle within 5°, climbing airspeed ±5 knots, balance ball centered and roll-out heading within ±10°.

Review 20 Descending Turn

1. A power increase.
2. A power reduction.
3. ±5 knots.
4. Elevator.
5. A lower nose attitude.
6. A lower nose attitude.
7. Turning onto the final approach leg for landing.
8. Centered.
9. Elevator.

Review 21 Gliding Turn

1. It is tilted in the direction of the bank and increased.
2. The rate increases.
3. Vertical speed indicator and altimeter.
4. Drag increases. Airspeed decreases unless the nose is lowered.

5. It is reduced.
6. Horizontal.
7. Centered.
8. Centered.

Review 22 Slow Flight and Stall Avoidance

1. Back side.
2. The lower the speed, the higher the power that is required.
3. Sloppy. No.
4. Low. Sloppy. The ailerons.
5. High. Firm and effective. Elevator and rudder.
6. Right.
7. The airspeed indicator, altimeter and balance ball.
8. 5–10 knots above the 1g stall speed.
9. Power + attitude (+ configuration).
10. Raise the nose.
11. Lower the nose.
12. Reduce power, gradually raising the nose to maintain altitude; when target speed is reached, increase power and continually adjust both power and attitude to maintain that speed; anticipate the need for right rudder to keep the balance ball centered as power is added; retrim.
13. Increase power; lower the nose to maintain altitude; keep the balance ball centered with rudder; adjust power as target speed is attained; retrim.
14. Reduce power, raising the nose to maintain altitude; lower flaps in stages, adjusting the attitude to avoid gaining altitude; add power to maintain the new speed; retrim.
15. Add power, holding the nose down to maintain altitude; raise the flaps in stages and hold the nose up to avoid sinking; reduce power to maintain altitude; retrim.
16. Trimming.
17. 1,500 feet AGL. 6,800 feet MSL.
18. For private pilots: altitude ±100 feet, airspeed +5/–0 knots, heading ±10°, bank angle ±10°. For commercial pilots: altitude ±50 feet, airspeed +5/–0 knots, heading ±10°, bank angle ±5°.
19. Right. The strong propeller slipstream due to the high power and the P-factor.
20. Lower end of the green arc.
21. Lower end of the white arc.
22. It is lower.
23. Increased.
24. Twice as heavy. 40%. No.
25. 7%.
26. Release back pressure and apply full power, level the wings and lower the nose, resume normal flight.
27. Just before (5–8 knots).
28. Immediately any symptoms are evident.

Review 23 Full Stall and Recovery

1. True.
2. The critical angle.
3. No. They are only a guide for your flight situation.
4. Straight and level at maximum weight with zero flap.
5. Lower than.
6. Green band.
7. The HASELL check:

   H Height
   A Airframe
   S Security
   E Engine
   L Location
   L Look out

8. 1,500 feet AGL. 3,800 feet MSL.
9. Reducing airspeed, less effective controls, operation of a stall warning device, onset of prestall buffet and relatively high nose attitude (also control position).
10. The actual stall can be recognized by the nose dropping and the airplane descending.
11. The main objective in any stall recovery is to reduce the angle of attack and restore smooth airflow over the wings.
12. The approach to the stall.
13. Just before the stall.

Review 24 Variations on the Stall

1. A higher nose attitude. A lower airspeed. The same angle of attack.
2. Nose-up trim. Pitch up. Forward pressure. Elevator-trim stall.
3. Higher stalling speed. Accelerated stall.
4. A stall that inadvertently occurs during a stall recovery.
5. Heading within 10°, altitude within 100 feet, climbing turn bank angle of 15° to 20°, descending turn bank angle 30° with tolerance of ±10°.
6. Lower wing. Bottom-rudder stall.
7. Upper wing. Top-rudder stall.
8. Crosswind approach and landing.
9. Top-rudder stall.

Review 25
Incipient Spin

1. The initial stages of a spin.
2. If the pilot is flying uncoordinated and the balance ball is way out of the center (especially with flaps extended and power applied).
3. Flying with crossed controls.
4. Fly slowly, bring the control column back and, just prior to the stall, apply full rudder.
5. Airspeed and the balance ball (and be conscious of back pressure).

Review 26
Stabilized Spin

1. Yes.
2. True.
3. True.
4. Autorotation.
5. Flatter.
6. False. It has a high angle of attack and low airspeed.
7. Less lift. More drag.
8. The incipient spin, the full spin and the recovery from the spin.
9. A stalled wing and a wing drop, which can be induced by yawing the airplane with rudder.
10. Ailerons.
11. Opposite to the spin.
12. Yes.
13. Neutralize the rudder.
14. Yes.
15. A too-steep uncoordinated climbing turn after takeoff and a too-slow uncoordinated turn onto the final approach.
16. 3,000 feet AGL. 4,800 feet MSL.
17. No, it is optional.
18. No, all airplanes are permitted to be stalled.
19. Yes, only some airplanes are permitted to be spun.
20. Low angle of attack. High airspeed maneuver. Wings are unstalled. It is not a spin.

Review 27
Normal Takeoff

1. Wind direction, runway (length available and condition) and obstructions and other hazards in the takeoff path.
2. The start of the runway.
3. Into the wind. Into the wind.
4. Reduction in some aircraft.
5. Full power. Mixture will be rich.
6. Yes.
7. Yes.
8. Yes.
9. No.
10. Yes. Common traffic advisory frequency.
11. Yes.
12. Landing light, strobe lights and transponder.
13. Yes. Smoothly and positively. A glance at the engine gauges.
14. Use the rudder to keep straight. Use ailerons to keep wings level.
15. Rotation.
16. Slight back pressure. To take the weight off the nose wheel.
17. Yaw left. Right rudder pressure.

Review 28
Traffic Pattern and Local Area Operations

1. To the left.
2. Right-hand traffic pattern.
3. Runway 27. Left-hand.
4. Runway 9: right handed. Runway 36: right handed. Runway 18: left handed. NW.
5. An aircraft on final approach to land.
6. Yes.
7. 1,700 feet MSL. 500 feet AGL. 2,000 feet MSL. 800 feet AGL. Altitude tolerance of ±100 feet, airspeed tolerance of 10 knots.
8. One-half to one mile.
9. 1,000 feet AGL and 3 statute miles.
10. The wind is about 15 knots from straight ahead. Liftoff speed for this takeoff is 50 knots, obstacle-clearance speed is 55 knots and, when the flaps are up, V_X is 60 knots and V_Y is 70 knots. I expect the ground run to be 1,000 feet, so we should lift off about half way down the runway, and be climbing through 50 feet at the 1,600-foot point, so we will be well above all obstacles. I will climb straight ahead to 1,000 feet above the runway, which will be 1,800 feet on the altimeter, and then turn right onto the crosswind leg. We will be remaining in the traffic pattern, so I expect to remain on tower frequency. If I have an engine failure on the ground I will close the throttle, apply the brakes, and bring the airplane to a stop. I will set the brakes and carry out any emergency procedure and inform others by radio. If I have an engine failure in flight, I will land on the remaining runway if sufficient remains, otherwise

I will land approximately straight ahead with only slight turns if necessary. There is a large field slightly right of the climb-out path that is suitable.

11. Strobe lights and landing lights. Transponder.
12. 1200. This is with altitude reporting.
13. Yes.
14. Lower the nose. Land ahead.
15. Aircraft weight, airport pressure altitude and outside air temperature.
16. Ground effect. Fly further. Less drag.
17. Increase.
18. Reduce.
19. Yes, by a few minutes.
20. Close the throttle, apply the brakes and keep straight.
21. 1,000 feet AGL. Turns are to the left.
22. 600 feet to 1,500 feet AGL. In the *Chart Supplement U.S.*
23. Yes.
24. No.
25. Ground frequency. Yes.
26. Before entering.
27. UNICOM and FSS (since they are staffed and the others are not).
28. Before taxiing from the parking position and before taxiing onto the runway for departure. Common traffic advisory frequency.
29. No.
30. Refer to figures 28-6 and 28-8 on page 294, and figure 28-9 on page 295.
31. 2,230 feet MSL. 2,730 feet MSL.
32. 10 miles out, entering the downwind leg, on the base leg, on final approach and leaving the runway.
33. 25 miles. 15 miles.
34. Call when directed to do so by the tower.
35. Contact FSS by phone or radio and request them to cancel your flight plan. The tower will not cancel it automatically upon landing. Relay cancellation request to the FSS nominated on the plan.
36. Slow down, make gentle S-turns and widen out.
37. Lower aircraft. No.
38. Transmit blind, listen up, establish the traffic-pattern direction before joining and landing, squawk 7600. (Note that this is an IFR procedure but would be appropriate for a VFR flight if, for example, operating on a VFR clearance in a radar environment.)
39. Don't land, give way to other aircraft and continue circling.
40. Return for a landing.
41. Cleared to land.
42. Stop.
43. Cleared to taxi.
44. By moving the ailerons or rudder (or by flashing your landing light).
45. 1,000 feet AGL. *Chart Supplement U.S.*
46. Flight or surface visibility of 3 or more statute miles by day with visual reference to the surface at all times.

Review 29 Visual Approach

1. Wind direction, landing surface (length available and condition) and obstructions and other hazards in the approach and takeoff paths.
2. Into a headwind.
3. Steeper approach. Slower speed. Forward view is better.
4. Power and attitude.
5. Yes.
6. Low-speed end of the white arc.
7. No.
8. Yes (half the gust factor).
9. Yes.
10. ±5 knots.

Review 30 Normal Landing

1. 500 feet (for private pilots) or 200 feet (for commercial pilots).
2. Main wheels.
3. True.
4. Keep straight with rudder. Keep wings level with ailerons.
5. Yes. Well down the runway (steeper approach).
6. Longer. High. Shallow approach.
7. Shorter. Low. Steep approach.
8. Too low. Higher than normal.
9. Too high. Lower than normal.

Review 31 Go-Around

1. Refer to your POH or flight instructor.
2. Refer to figure 31-3, page 335.
3. Up. Yes.
4. The left side. Counteract with right rudder.
5. Yes.
6.
   - Obstacle-clearance speed +5/–0 knots;
   - V_X +5/–0 knots; and
   - V_Y +5/–0 knots.
7. To one side of the extended runway centerline.

8. Fly the airplane.
9. Go around.
10. Go around.
11. Go around.
12. Go around.
13. Continue with the landing.

Review 32 Fire and Engine Malfunctions

1. Section 3, Emergency Procedures, of the pilot's operating handbook.
2. Mayday.
3. Refer to your POH.
4. All electrics and radios.
5. Throttle closed, brakes and keep straight.
6. A landing area ahead within the windshield.
7. Check with your instructor for specific glide speed.
8. Lower the nose.

Review 33 Power-Off (Glide) Approach

1. Steeper. Nose attitude will be lower.
2. It will increase.
3. Closer to.
4. Lower the flaps.
5. Steeper.
6. Delay the selection of more flaps.
7. Admit defeat, add power and do it better next time.
8. Greater attitude change (less elevator power).

Review 34 Zero-Flap Approach

1. Shallower flight path. Faster approach speed.
2. Forward slip. This increases drag. Steeper approach.

Review 35 Forced Landing Following Engine Failure

1. Adopt the gliding attitude.
2. Best-glide airspeed.
3. Yes.
4. At the best-glide airspeed.
5. 121.5 MHz.
6. 7700.
7. Fuel problem, ignition problem and carburetor icing.
8. Refer to you POH.
9. Forward slip.
10. Yes.
11. Yes.
12. Mayday, mayday, mayday. Chicago radio, Mooney eight five three six Charlie. Engine failure. Forced landing five miles south of Eltville. Passing six thousand feet. Heading one eight zero.
13. Mixture to rich, carburetor heat to hot.
14. Something like: Mayday, mayday, mayday. All stations. This is Cessna five four seven two Bravo.
15. 500 feet AGL.
16. Full power, balance, gear up, flaps to takeoff, climb attitude, positive climb, flaps up, climb power.

Review 36 Forced Landing into Water (Ditching)

1. Along the swell.
2. The advancing face of the swell.
3. Yes.
4. At as low a flying speed as possible under control.

Review 37 Precautionary Landing

1. Precautionary inspection.
2. Use the WOSSSSS check: wind, obstacles, size and shape, surface and slope, shoots, sun, s(c)ivilization.
3. Soft-field landing.
4. Yes. Wind.
5. Ground speed will be higher. High airspeed. Reducing power.
6. Yes. Yes.

Review 38 Crosswind Operations

1. 10 knots.
2. 9 knots.
3. 7 knots.
4. 5 knots.
5. 14 knots.
6. 18 knots.
7. 10 knots.
8. 20 knots.
9. Section 1: Limitations. Section 4 : Normal Operations.
10. Smallest flap setting.
11. Into the wind.

12. Rudder.
13. Aileron.
14. More deflection.
15. Hold the airplane on the ground and lift off positively.
16. Yes. To avoid any sideloads on the landing gear on ground contact.
17. Yes.
18. Yes. The ball will centralize.
19. Yes.

Review 39
Crosswind Approach and Landing

1. A small flap setting. Reduced response to gusts.
2. Low flap setting. Reduced drag.
3. The crab method, the wing-down method and the combination method.
4. Wind correction angle. crab angle.
5. A stabilized approach.
6. Flare.
7. Yes.
8. Yes.
9. Upwind wing. By using rudder.
10. Right main wheel. Left main wheel.
11. Rudder. Aileron.
12. Directional control will be more direct.
13. The ailerons will become less effective.

Review 40
Short-Field Operations

1. Heavy weight, high density altitude, short runway or obstacles in the takeoff or landing paths.
2. Yes. Standing start. Steepest climb gradient.
3. The published obstacle-clearance speed for that flap setting. Required accuracy: +5/–0 knots.
4. Best angle-of-climb airspeed. +5/–0 knots. Minimum of 56 knots and a maximum of 61 knots.
5. Best rate-of-climb airspeed. Quickest climb to altitude. Lower. Faster. Accuracy is ±5 knots. 65 to 75 knots.
6. Adopt the gliding attitude to maintain flying speed and try to land approximately straight ahead.
7. Available runway distance is marginal and significant obstacles in the approach path.
8. Steep approach. Full flaps. Low airspeed.
9. No.
10. Low. Short. Yes.
11. ±5 knots. Airspeed and flight path are controlled with power, and attitude.
12. No. 200 feet for private pilots and 300 feet for commercial pilots.
13. Power-on.

Review 41
Soft-Field Operations

1. The wind direction, takeoff and landing surface, and obstructions or other hazards in the takeoff and approach paths.
2. There is a risk that the wheels might dig in.
3. Takeoff flaps.
4. Keep the weight off. By holding the control column back.
5. Keep rolling.
6. The liftoff is easier but greater at slower speed. Ground effect is used for acceleration.
7. Obstacle-clearance speed. V_X for clean takeoff. +5/– 0 knots.
8. V_Y. ±5 knots.
9. After-takeoff checklist.
10. Slowly as possible. By holding off.
11. Into wind and full flaps.
12. ±5 knots.
13. Avoid using brakes, keep rolling and taxi clear.
14. More power.
15. Hard surface.

Review 42
Steep Turns

1. 1,500 feet AGL. 3,700 feet MSL.
2. Increased lift. Increased drag. Additional power.
3. More load. Stall speed increases. The pilot feels load factor as increased weight.
4. Back pressure. High power.
5. Load factor increases.
6. Altitude within 100 feet, bank angle of 45° to within 5° for private pilots and 50° to within 5° for commercial pilots, airspeed within 10 knots, and roll-out heading within 10°.
7. Tighter.
8. Tighter.
9. Slight overbanking. The outer wing.
10. It will increase markedly.
11. Reduce bank angle. Raise the nose.
12. Tighten the turn. May increase g-loading beyond the aircraft limits.
13. High.

Review 43
Unusual Attitude Recoveries

1. Stall or spin.
2. Ease control column forward to reduce the angle of attack, apply sufficient rudder to prevent yaw, apply maximum power and roll level the wings with coordinated use of the rudder and ailerons.
3. Overspeed. Spiral dive.
4. Reduce power (close the throttle quickly and completely), roll the wings level with aileron and rudder but don't allow the nose to pitch up, ease out of the ensuing dive, and, as the airspeed reduces below V_{NO} and the nose passes through the horizon, reapply power and climb away.
5. Ease of the bank angle and raise the nose.
6. Elevator. Overstessing.

Review 44
Chandelle

1. Gain as much altitude as possible. 180°.
2. Higher than.
3. 1,500 feet.
4. 3,300 feet MSL. 1,500 feet AGL.
5. V_A or maneuvering speed.
6. Yes.
7. 30°. The airplane will hardly climb.
8. Yes.
9. Stay centered.
10. 180°. 5 knots above the stall speed. An increase.
11. Crosswind. Upwind.

Review 45
Lazy Eights

1. 180°.
2. Crosswind. Into the wind.
3. 45°. 15°. Increasing.
4. 30°. On the horizon. Lowest value. Highest value.
5. 135°. 15°. Decreasing.
6. Yes. Yes.
7. 100 feet. ±10 knots. 0°. ±10°.
8. Constant power set.
9. That for level flight. Wings level. Raise the nose, roll into turn in opposite direction.
10. Before the top of the turn.
11. 100 feet. 10 knots.
12. Reduce power.

Review 46
Low Flying and Wind Awareness

1. Airspeed.
2. Ground speed.
3. Be less than.
4. Higher speed. Airspeed indicator. You should avoid reducing airspeed.
5. Wind correction angle. Crab angle into wind.
6. Airspeed.
7. An illusion of a slip or a skid. By keeping the balance ball centered.
8. Tighter turn.
9. Wider turn.
10. Yes.
11. When flying directly downwind. Bank angle will have to be greatest.
12. When flying directly upwind. Bank angle will have to be least.
13. 500 feet AGL.
14. 600 to 1,000 feet AGL.
15. No.
16. Altitude ±100 feet, airspeed ±10 knots, bank angle ±45° and balance ball centered.
17. This indicates that VFR conditions of at least 3 miles visibility and/or a cloud ceiling of 1,000 feet above the airport elevation do not exist, and that a 1,000 feet AGL traffic pattern may not be possible.

Review 47
Eights-On-Pylons

1. Pivot the wing tip on a pylon.
2. No.
3. No.
4. With ailerons.
5. Pivotal altitude.
6. Above ground level. Mean sea level.
7. Speed only.
8. $\text{Pivotal altitude AGL} = \frac{\text{ground speed}^2}{11.3}\ \text{feet}$
9. 720 feet AGL.
10. 1,070 feet AGL or 1,870 feet MSL. 720 feet AGL or 1,520 feet MSL.
11. 30° to 40°.
12. Back pressure. An increase in altitude.
13. Forward pressure. A decrease in altitude.
14. Ground speed.
15. Higher pivotal altitude AGL.
16. Lower pivotal altitude AGL.

Review 48
First Solo Flight

1. The pilot in command.
2. The pilot in command may deviate from any rule of the part (Part 91) to the extent required to meet that emergency.
3. Upon request of the administrator.
4. Pilot in command.
5. True.
6. True.
7. Before takeoff and landing.
8. True.
9. Yes.
10. True.
11. An aircraft in distress.
12. A landing aircraft.
13. Lower.
14. False.
15. An altitude allowing, if a power unit fails, an emergency landing without undue hazard to persons or property on the surface.
16. 1,000 feet. 2,000 feet.
17. 500 feet AGL. 500 feet.
18. The current altimeter setting for that airport.
19. Set the airport elevation in the altimeter.
20. Yes.
21. For you to taxi, take-off and land.
22. Yes.
23. At all times, except in an emergency when you are, as pilot in command, think an alternative course of action is necessary.
24. As soon as possible, say, by radio.
25. Within 48 hours if requested by ATC.
26. Steady red means give way to other aircraft and continue to circle, flashing green means return for a landing, steady green means cleared to land, and flashing red means airport unsafe so do not land.
27. To the left.
28. Yes.
29. Basic VFR weather minimums: 3 statute miles flight visibility, 500 feet below clouds, 1,000 feet above clouds and 2,000 feet horizontally from clouds.
30. Yes.
31. The third-class medical certificate will expire the last day of the 60th month in which the medical was issued. A student pilot certificate is valid indefinitely unless suspended or revoked by the FAA.
32. Yes. Yes.
33. Yes.
34. 90 days.
35. No.
36. 3 statute miles.
37. No.
38. Yes.

Review 49
Cross-Country Flight

1. Yes.
2. 10 miles. Common traffic advisory frequency.
3. Pilotage.
4. Dead reckoning.
5. Yes.
6. Altitude ±200 feet, heading ±10°, airspeed ±10 knots, ETA ±5 minutes.
7. Yes.
8. 122.2 MHz.
9. Hazardous in-flight weather advisory service. Yes.
10. En route flight advisory service. Pilot report or PIREP.
11. Automated weather observing system (AWOS) and automated surface observing system (ASOS). ATIS: Automatic terminal information service.
12. Yes.
13. Yes
14. Yes.
15. 30 minutes. To prevent unnecessary search and rescue procedures from commencing.
16. No.
17. 30 minutes.

Review 50
Instrument Flight

1. False.
2. Instrument scan, instrument interpretation, and airplane control.
3. Instrument scan.
4. Attitude indicator and power indicator.
5. Altimeter and vertical speed indicator.
6. Heading indicator and turn coordinator.
7. Airspeed indicator.
8. Yes.
9. 1,000 feet, 4 nautical miles, 2,000 feet.
10. Airspeed ±10 knots, heading ±10°, altitude ±100 feet.
11. The balance ball.
12. Airspeed indicator.
13. Airspeed indicator.

14. Altimeter.
15. Turn coordinator.
16. Right rudder. Left rudder.
17. Up.
18. Nose-high with airspeed decreasing and nose-low with airspeed increasing.
19. 45° bank angle, 10° pitch up or down.

Review 51
Night Flight

1. Cones and rods.
2. Cone cells. Colors. Yes. Central vision.
3. Rod cells. Only black-and-white and gray. No. Peripheral vision.
4. Off-center.
5. Peripheral.
6. 30 minutes.
7. None—eyes affected immediately.
8. Smoking impairs night vision.
9. Yes.
10. Red.
11. You may not be able to.
12. Yes with fresh batteries.
13. When the aircraft is moving or about to be moved.
14. Refer to figure 51-2, page 526.
15. Red. Green. White.
16. Yes.
17. No.
18. Yes.
19. Green. Blue.
20. White. Green. Red.
21. Green-white-green-white. . .
22. Visual approach slope indicator. 3°.
23. Red.
24. Too low on slope.
25. Too high on slope.
26. Select the appropriate frequency on the VHF COM and then depress the mike key seven times within five seconds. They should stay on for 15 minutes.
27. Taxiing too fast.
28. Shift your attention to the flight instruments.
29. Flying too fast.
30. Yes.
31. Their use is greater.
32. No.
33. No.
34. No.
35. Underestimate. 20 nautical miles.
36. Lighter winds. Less vertical mixing of the layers of air.
37. Yes. Less vertical mixing of the layers of air.
38. Yes.

Review 52
Unmanned Aircraft Systems (UAS)

1. An unmanned aircraft (UA) is an aircraft operated without the possibility of direct human intervention from within or on the aircraft.
2. 14 CFR Part 107, Small Unmanned Aircraft Systems.
3. An autonomous operation is a flight during which an unmanned aircraft operates without pilot intervention in the management of the flight, and/or the UAS is preprogrammed for tasks apart from human-pilot control.
4. The remote pilot-in-command.
5. Recreational flyers are operating for fun or as a hobby. Commercial operators are operating for work or business.
6. False. While navigation lights can be beneficial to operations, Part 107 requires the drone to have only operational anti-collision lights—red or white, either flashing or strobe.
7. A UAS NOTAM is a notice filed by a remote pilot or crewmember advising of operations taking place. These are typically issued for operations within controlled airspace or within the lateral limits above and below controlled airspace. UAS NOTAMS are available at 1800WXBrief.com or by calling 1-800-WX-BRIEF.
8. True. However, both unmanned and manned aircraft pilots should play a vigilant role in scanning and see-and-avoid techniques.
9. The nearest NTSB field office should be notified immediately.
10. For unsafe unmanned aircraft operations, you can notify your local Flight Standards District Office. For illegal or criminal activity, you should immediately notify law enforcement or emergency personnel.
11. This enhanced identification capability will provide information about unmanned aircraft in flight, such as its identity, location, altitude, and control station or takeoff (launch) location.

INDEX

B

C

D

E

F

G

H

N

O

P

Q

R

S